Network Programmability with YANG

Network Programmability with YANG

The Structure of Network Automation with YANG, NETCONF, RESTCONF, and gNMI

Benoît Claise
Joe Clarke
Jan Lindblad

Addison-Wesley

Boston • Columbus • New York • San Francisco • Amsterdam • Cape Town • Dubai
London • Madrid • Milan • Munich • Paris • Montreal • Toronto • Delhi • Mexico City
São Paulo • Sydney • Hong Kong • Seoul • Singapore • Taipei • Tokyo

Network Programmability with YANG

For information about buying this title in bulk quantities, or for special sales opportunities (which may include electronic versions; custom cover designs; and content particular to your business, training goals, marketing focus, or branding interests), please contact our corporate sales department at corpsales@pearsoned.com or (800) 382-3419.

For government sales inquiries, please contact governmentsales@pearsoned.com.

For questions about sales outside the U.S., please contact intlcs@pearson.com.

Visit us on the Web: informit.com/aw

Library of Congress Control Number: 2019935319

ISBN-13: 978-0-13-518039-6
ISBN-10: 0-13-518039-2

ScoutAutomatedPrintCode

Warning and Disclaimer

This book is designed to provide information about YANG. Every effort has been made to make this book as complete and as accurate as possible, but no warranty or fitness is implied.

The information is provided on an "as is" basis. The authors and publisher shall have neither liability nor responsibility to any person or entity with respect to any loss or damages arising from the information contained in this book or from the use of the discs or programs that may accompany it.

Trademark Acknowledgments

All terms mentioned in this book that are known to be trademarks or service marks have been appropriately capitalized. Addison-Wesley cannot attest to the accuracy of this information. Use of a term in this book should not be regarded as affecting the validity of any trademark or service mark.

Many of the designations used by manufacturers and sellers to distinguish their products are claimed as trademarks. Where those designations appear in this book, and the publisher was aware of a trademark claim, the designations have been printed with initial capital letters or in all capitals.

The authors and publisher have taken care in the preparation of this book, but make no expressed or implied warranty of any kind and assume no responsibility for errors or omissions. No liability is assumed for incidental or consequential damages in connection with or arising out of the use of the information or programs contained herein.

Editor-in-Chief
Mark Taub

Director, IT Professional Product Management
Brett Bartow

Development Editor
Marianne Bartow

Managing Editor
Sandra Schroeder

Project Editor
Mandie Frank

Copy Editor
Bart Reed

Indexer
Ken Johnson

Proofreader
Abigail Manheim

Technical Reviewers
Peter Van Horne
Warren Kumari
Harjinder Singh

Designer
Chuti Prasertsith

Compositor
codeMantra

Credits

Table 1-1	ITU-T M.3400, SERIES M: TMN AND NETWORK MAINTENANCE: INTERNATIONAL TRANSMISSION SYSTEMS, TELEPHONE CIRCUITS, TELEGRAPHY, FACSIMILE AND LEASED CIRCUITS and ISO / IEC 7498-4 (Information processing systems -Open Systems Interconnection – Basic Reference Model, Part4: Management Framework).
	SDN: Software Defined Networks: An Authoritative Review of Network Programmability Technologies, Thomas D. Nadeau, Ken Gray, 2013, O'Reilly Media, Inc
	Amazon Web Services
	Marc Andreessen
	IP Flow Information Export (IPFIX), IETF LLC
	Writable MIB Module IESG Statement, IETF
	On the Difference between Information Models and Data Models, RFC 3444, The Internet Society
Unboxed element 1-1	Interview conversation with Victor Kuarsing
Unboxed element 1-2	Interview conversation with Russ White
Figure 1-8	The Internet Society
	The "Overview of the 2002 IAB Network Management Workshop," IETF LLC
	An Architecture for Network Management Using NETCONF and YANG, IETF LLC
	RFC 6241, "Network Configuration Protocol" (NETCONF)
	RESTCONF Protocol, IETF
	The "Overview of the 2002 IAB Network Management Workshop," IETF LLC, RFC 3535, Requirement #1
	The "Overview of the 2002 IAB Network Management Workshop," IETF LLC, RFC 3535, Requirement #4
	The "Overview of the 2002 IAB Network Management Workshop," IETF LLC, RFC 3535, Requirement #13
	The "Overview of the 2002 IAB Network Management Workshop," IETF LLC, RFC 3535, Requirement #5
	The "Overview of the 2002 IAB Network Management Workshop," IETF LLC, RFC 3535, Requirement #7
	The "Overview of the 2002 IAB Network Management Workshop," IETF LLC, RFC 3535, Requirement #2
	The "Overview of the 2002 IAB Network Management Workshop," IETF LLC, RFC 3535, Requirement #27
	The "Overview of the 2002 IAB Network Management Workshop," IETF LLC, RFC 3535, Requirement #2
	The "Overview of the 2002 IAB Network Management Workshop," IETF LLC, RFC 3535, Requirement #2

Unboxed element 2-1	Interview conversation with Jürgen Schönwälder
Unboxed element 3-1	Interview conversation with Martin Björklund
Unboxed element 4-1	Interview conversation with Kent Watson NETCONF Event Notifications, IETF
Unboxed element 5-1	Interview conversation with Alex Clemm
Figure 5-1	Screenshot of Cisco © Cisco Systems, Inc.
Unboxed element 6-1	Interview conversation with Carl Moberg
Figure 6-4	Screenshot of YANG catalog
Figure 6-5	Screenshot of YANG catalog
Figure 6-6	Screenshot of YANG catalog
Figure 6-7	Screenshot of Cisco © Cisco Systems, Inc.
Figure 6-8	Screenshot of YANG catalog
Unboxed element 7-1	Interview conversation with Einnar Nilson-Nygaard
Figure 7-1	Screenshot of YANG catalog
Figure 7-2	Screenshot of YANG catalog
Figure 7-3	Screenshot of YANG catalog
Figure 7-4	Screenshot of YANG catalog
Figure 7-5	Screenshot of YANG catalog
Figure 7-6	Screenshot of YANG catalog
Figure 7-7	Screenshot of YANG catalog
Figure 7-8	Screenshot of Postman © 2018 Postdot Technologies, Inc.
Figure 7-9	Screenshot of Postman © 2018 Postdot Technologies, Inc.
Figure 7-10	Screenshot of Postman © 2018 Postdot Technologies, Inc.
Figure 7-11	Screenshot of Grafana Copyright 2019 © Grafana Labs
Figure 7-12	Screenshot of Grafana Copyright 2019 © Grafana Labs
Figure 7-13	Screenshot of Cisco © Cisco Systems, Inc.
Figure 7-14	Screenshot of Cisco © Cisco Systems, Inc.
Figure 7-15	Screenshot of Cisco © Cisco Systems, Inc.
Figure 7-16	Screenshot of Cisco © Cisco Systems, Inc.
Figure 7-17	Screenshot of Itential © 2019 Itential
Unboxed element 8-1	Interview conversation with William Lupton
Figure 8-1	Screenshot of YANG catalog
Figure 8-2	Screenshot of YANG catalog
Unboxed element 9-1	Interview conversation with Radek Krejčí
Unboxed element 10-1	Interview conversation with Kristian Larsson Warren Kumari
Unboxed element 11-1	Interview conversation with Andy Bierman
Cover	Liu zishan/Shutterstock

Benoît: First, and most importantly, this book is dedicated to my family for their ongoing support during the very long journey of writing this book. Expressed differently: Lore, Julien, and Jocelyne, please accept my apologies for the multiple evenings and weekends I should have spent with you.

I also want to express my gratitude to the numerous people who help with data model–driven management in the industry. Many became friends—they should recognize themselves!

Finally, for some local connotations: "Oufti, quá bê lîve! Oufti! Oufti…"

Joe: To my wife, Julia, who was very patient with me. Thanks to the Learning@Cisco team, which helped with dictation of some chapters of this book after I broke my wrist.

Jan: To my family, at home and at work. In the hopes of replacing some duct tape with computer science.

Table of Contents

Introduction xxii

1 The Network Management World Must Change: Why Should You Care? 2

Introduction 2

The Industry Has Changed: What Are the Trends? 6

Reduced Deployment Time 6

CLI Is No Longer the Norm (If a Feature Cannot Be Automated, It Does Not Exist) 7

Hardware Commoditization and Disaggregation 9

The DevOps Time 11

Software-Defined Networking 13

Network Function Virtualization 15

Elastic Cloud: Pay As You Grow 16

Data Model–Driven Management 18

(Data Model–Driven) Telemetry 20

Intent-Based Networking 22

Software Is Eating the World 23

Existing Network Management Practices and Related Limitations 24

CLI: Is This an API? 24

SNMP: For Monitoring But Not for Configuration 27

NetFlow and IPFIX: Mainly for Flow Records 33

Syslog: No Structured Data 37

Data Modeling Is Key for Automation 39

The Differences Between Information Models and Data Models 39

The Challenges of Managing Networks with Different Data Models 41

Interview with the Experts 48

Q&A with Victor Kuarsing 48

Q&A with Russ White 50

Summary 52

References in This Chapter 53

Endnotes 53

2 Data Model–Driven Management 56

The Beginning: A New Set of Requirements 56

Network Management Is Dead, Long Live Network Management 59

YANG: The Data Modeling Language 61

The Key to Automation? Data Models 63
YANG and the Operators Requirements 65
Properties of Good Data Models 66
The Different Types of YANG Modules 67
Mapping YANG Objects from MIB Modules 68
The Management Architecture 69
Data Model–Driven Management Components 70
The Encoding (Protocol Binding and Serialization) 74
XML 75
JSON 75
Google Protobufs 76
CBOR 76
The Server Architecture: Datastore 77
The Protocols 78
NETCONF 78
RESTCONF 82
gNMI (gRPC) 83
CoMI 84
The Programming Language 85
Telemetry 86
The Bigger Picture: Using NETCONF to Manage a Network 86
Interview with the Experts 91
Q&A with Jürgen Schönwälder 91
Summary 93
References in This Chapter 93
Endnotes 94

3 YANG Explained 96
Introduction 96
Describe Your World of Data 96
Describe Your Data with Precision 101
Separate Your Data into Categories 106
Describing Possible Events 113
Actions and RPCs 113
Notifications 116
Separating Configuration from Operational Data 117

Constraints Keep Things Meaningful 122
Mandatory and Default Data 126
Conditional Content 127
Properly Following Pointers 128
Schema Nodes Don't Count 131
Augmenting, Extending, and Possibly Deviating 142
Extending YANG 146
Deviations 148
Network Management Datastore Architecture (NMDA) 149
Interview with the Expert 154
Q&A with Martin Björklund 154
Summary 156
References in This Chapter 157

4 NETCONF, RESTCONF, and gNMI Explained 158
Introduction 158
NETCONF 158
Fundamentals 159
XML Tags, Attributes, and Namespaces 162
RPC Mechanism 166
Message Framing 169
Message Overview 171
Hello Message 171
Get-Config Message 174
Edit-Config Message 176
Get Message 181
RPCs and Actions 184
Notifications 185
More NETCONF Operations 189
The NMDA Operations get-data and edit-data 189
RESTCONF 190
REST Principles 191
RESTCONF Versus NETCONF 192
Finding the RESTCONF Server URL 193
Reading and Navigating the RESTCONF Resources 194
Creating and Updating Configuration Using RESTCONF 201
Actions 210
Notifications 212

OpenConfig and gNMI 214
gRPC 214
gNMI CapabilityRequest 215
gNMI GetRequest 216
gNMI SetRequest 219
gNMI SubscribeRequest and Telemetry 224
YANG RPC, Action and Notification 225
Interview with the Expert 225
Q&A with Kent Watsen 225
Summary 227
References in This Chapter 227

5 Telemetry Explained 230
Introduction 230
Data Model–Driven Telemetry 230
Moving Away from SNMP to Telemetry 232
Telemetry Use Cases 235
Telemetry Components 236
Architecture 236
Transport Discussion: Monitoring Versus Events 239
Subscription Type: On-Change Versus Periodic 239
Dial-In and Dial-Out Modes 241
Telemetry Standard Mechanisms 242
NETCONF Event Notifications 243
IETF YANG Subscriptions 244
IETF YANG Push Versus OpenConfig: Some History 247
OpenConfig Streaming Telemetry 248
Interview with the Experts 249
Q&A with Alex Clemm 249
Summary 252
References in This Chapter 253
Endnotes 253

6 YANG Data Modeling Developments in the Industry 256
Introduction 256
The Beginning: The IETF 256
Embracing YANG Throughout the Industry 263
The OpenConfig YANG Model 268
Industry Coordination Is Required 270

Interoperability Testing 272
Implementing More Than One YANG Model for a Specific Functionality 274
Interview with the Expert 275
Q&A with Carl Moberg 275
Summary 278
References in This Chapter 279
Endnotes 279

7 Automation Is as Good as the Data Models, Their Related Metadata, and the Tools: For the Network Architect and Operator 282
Introduction 282
Getting to Know the Structure of a YANG Module 283
Finding the Right Modules Using the YANG Catalog 287
YANG Search 288
The Module Tree 290
Module [Metadata] Details 291
Moving from Nodes to RPCs and Scripts with YANG Suite 294
Interacting with Devices 299
NETCONF Tools 299
RESTCONF Tools 319
Telemetry Tools 325
Commercial Products 330
Interview with the Experts 331
Q&A with Einar Nilsen-Nygaard 331
Summary 335
Endnotes 335

8 Automation Is as Good as the Data Models, Their Related Metadata, and the Tools: For the Module Author 336
Introduction 336
Designing Modules 336
Learning from Others 337
Compiling and Validating Modules 339
Testing Modules 340
Sharing the Module Metadata 347
Understanding Your Module's Impact 349
Interview with the Expert 350
Q&A with William Lupton 350
Summary 352
Endnotes 352

9 **Automation Is as Good as the Data Models, Their Related Metadata, and the Tools: For the Application Developer 354**

Introduction 354

Working with YANG Modules 355

Integrating Metadata from YANG Catalog 355

Embedding Pyang 359

Pyang Plug-Ins 361

YANG Parsing with Libyang 365

Interacting with the Network 366

NETCONF with Ncclient 366

NETCONF Clients and Servers with Libnetconf2 371

Interacting with RESTCONF Servers 372

Making YANG Language Native 373

YDK 373

Pyangbind 378

Interview with the Expert 380

Q&A with Radek Krejčí 380

Summary 381

Endnotes 382

10 **Using NETCONF and YANG 384**

Introduction 384

So the Story Goes 385

Top-Down Service Model 386

Bottom-Up Device Templates 392

Service Logic Connecting the Dots 394

Setting Up NETCONF on a Device 398

Discovering What's on a Device 400

Managing Services 405

Manager Synchronization with Devices 413

Network-Wide Transactions 417

Interview with the Experts 425

Q&A with Kristian Larsson 425

Summary 428

11 **YANG Model Design 430**

Introduction 430

Modeling Strategy 430

Getting Started 431

You, the Four-Star General 432

YANG Modeling Tips 433
Naming a Module 433
Publishing a Module 434
Choosing YANG Identifiers 435
Accepting a Blank Configuration 435
Using Leafrefs 436
Minding That XPath Feature 437
Enumerating and More 437
Choosing Keys 439
Types Empty and Boolean 440
Reusing Groupings 440
Deviating from a Standard YANG Module 441
Transient Configuration and Other Dependencies 442
Augmenting YANG Models 442
Types Anyxml and Anydata 442
Common YANG Mistakes 443
Unclear Optional Leafs 443
Missing Ranges 444
Overusing Strings 444
Bad String Patterns 445
Blank Configuration Made Invalid 447
Misunderstanding When a Constraint Applies 447
Missing the Simple Constraints 448
Getting the Path Wrong 449
Disconnected Multikey Leafrefs 451
Mixing Up For One, For Any, and For All 454
Performance of XPath Expressions 456
Backward Compatibility 457
The Rules Versus Staying Relevant 457
Tooling 459
Interview with the Experts 460
Q&A with Andy Bierman 460
Summary 462
References in This Chapter 463

Index 464

Feedback Information

At Addison-Wesley, our goal is to create in-depth technical books of the highest quality and value. Each book is crafted with care and precision, undergoing rigorous development that involves the unique expertise of members from the professional technical community.

Readers' feedback is a natural continuation of this process. If you have any comments regarding how we could improve the quality of this book, or otherwise alter it to better suit your needs, you can contact us through email at community@informit.com. Please make sure to include the book title and ISBN in your message.

We greatly appreciate your assistance.

Register your copy of *Network Programmability with YANG* at informit.com for convenient access to downloads, updates, and corrections as they become available. To start the registration process, go to informit/com/register and log in or create an account. Enter the product ISBN 9780135180396 and click Submit. Once the process is complete, you will find any available bonus content under "Registered Products."

Acknowledgments

Special thanks to our experts from the "Interview with the Experts" sections for taking the time and generously sharing their wisdom with us:

- Victor Kuarsing
- Russ White
- Jürgen Schönwälder
- Martin Björklund
- Kent Watsen
- Alex Clemm
- Carl Moberg
- Einar Nilsen-Nygaard
- William Lupton
- Radek Krejčí
- Kristian Larsson
- Andy Bierman

We are also grateful for the constructive feedback from all the subject matter experts who spent time reviewing all or part of this work:

- Warren Kumari
- Peter Van Horne
- Harjinder Singh
- Martin Björklund
- John Lawitzke
- Mattias Ljunggren
- Many friends and colleagues who validated the code that accompanies this book

Finally, we are very happy with the strong belief in this project from its inception, as well as the engagement and effort shown by the staff at Addison-Wesley Professional, our publisher. It's always great to work with true professionals. Although the publishing team is large, specialized, and works as a crew, we would like to mention the following individuals in particular:

- Brett Bartow
- Marianne Bartow
- Bart Reed
- Mandie Frank

Thank you all for making this journey not only possible, but also highly enjoyable.

About the Authors

Benoît Claise, CCIE No. 2686, is a Cisco Fellow, working as an architect for embedded management. Areas of passion and expertise include Internet traffic monitoring, accounting, performance, fault, and configuration management. Benoît's area of focus these days is network automation with YANG as the data modeling language, NETCONF/RESTCONF, and telemetry as a feedback loop to solve intent-based networking.

Benoît was IETF Operations and Management Area (OPS) co-director from 2012 to 2018, a period during which much of the data model–driven management protocols, encoding, and data models were specified. He blogs on these topics on his web site http://www.claise.be/ and spends time on the yangcatalog.org developments.

Benoît is a contributor to the IETF, with 35 RFCs in the area of NetFlow, IPFIX (IP Flow Information eXport), PSAMP (Packet Sampling), IPPM (IP Performance Metrics), YANG, MIB module, energy management, and network management in general. Benoît is the co-author of the Cisco Press book *Network Management: Accounting and Performance Strategies*.

As a Cisco Customer Experience Engineer, **Joe Clarke**, CCIE No. 5384, has contributed to the development and adoption of many of Cisco's network management and automation products and technologies. He helps to support, enhance, and promote the embedded automation and programmability features, such as the Embedded Event Manager, Tcl, Python, NETCONF/RESTCONF, and YANG.

Joe evangelizes these programmability and automation skills in order to build the next generation of network engineers. He is a Cisco Certified Internetworking Expert and certified Cisco Network Programmability Engineer. Joe has authored numerous technical documents on Cisco network management, automation, and programmability products and technologies, as well as a chapter as co-author of *Network-Embedded Management and Applications: Understanding Programmable Networking Infrastructure*. He also served as one of the technical editors for the Cisco Press books *Tcl Scripting for Cisco IOS* and *Programming and Automating Cisco Networks: A Guide to Network Programmability and Automation in the Data Center, Campus, and WAN*. He is an alumnus of the University of Miami and holds a Bachelor of Science degree in computer science.

Outside of Cisco, Joe is a member of the FreeBSD project and the co-chair of the Ops Area Working Group at the IETF. Joe is a certified commercial pilot for single-engine airplanes with an instrument rating. He lives with his beautiful wife in the RTP area of North Carolina.

Jan Lindblad soldered together his first computer at age 12, wrote his first compiler at 16, and reached the million lines of code mark by 30. In 2006, when NETCONF was first published by IETF, Jan was at the then newly founded start-up company Tail-f Systems. Tail-f built the first commercial implementation of NETCONF and was a driving force behind the introduction of YANG.

Jan is an IETF YANG Doctor and has also authored and reviewed many YANG modules in other organizations. Jan has trained several hundred people on the theory and practice of NETCONF and YANG. At the yearly NETCONF/YANG interop event organized by EANTC in Berlin, Germany, Jan plays a central role.

Outside Cisco, Jan is an avid climate activist and environmentalist. He lives outside Stockholm, Sweden, and commutes to work by bike every day.

About the Technical Reviewers

Peter Van Horne attended the University of Michigan, in Ann Arbor, Michigan, graduating in 1977 with a B.S in computer engineering. He joined Cisco in 2000 through the acquisition of startup CAIS Software, which provided software- and systems-enabling public Internet access in airports, hotels, and other public places. He is a Principal Engineer at Cisco, leading projects such as YANG model-based programmatic interface development for multiple Cisco product lines. Peter is a holder of multiple patents in communications and Internet-related applications.

Warren Kumari, CCIE No. 9190, is a Chief Retro-Phrenologist/Senior Network Security Engineer with Google, and has been with the company since 2005. As a senior engineer, Warren is responsible for all aspects of keeping the Google production network both secure and operational as well as for mentoring other members of his team. He also participates in Google's industry standards groups.

Warren has more than 20 years of experience in the Internet industry, ranging from tiny start-up ISPs to large enterprises. Prior to Google, he was a Senior Network Engineer at AOL, and before that he was Lead Network Engineer at Register.com.

With security concerns becoming more and more prevalent, Warren has chosen to be an active participant of the IETF, the ICANN Security and Stability Advisory Committee, and NANOG. Warren is currently serving as an Operations and Management Area Director in the IETF. He has formed and chaired multiple IETF working groups (including DPRIVE, CAPPORT, OPSAWG, and OPSEC), has authored 17 RFCS, is a CCIE Emeritus (#9190), and CISSP and CCSP.

Harjinder Singh is a Tech Lead Engineer at Cisco Systems. His main passions are network automation and self-driving networks. Harjinder has been working in various organizations, primarily on network management, distributed systems, configuration management, closed-loop telemetry, and data model–driven technologies, with a focus on YANG, NETCONF/RESTCONF, gRPC, open config, and telemetry.

Command Syntax Conventions

The conventions used to present command syntax in this book are as follows:

- **Boldface** indicates commands that are entered literally as shown, or highlight certain elements in an example that are being discussed.
- Monospace font in running text indicates keywords in YANG and the protocols discussed, and is also used in code snippets and when quoting constructs from the code examples in running text.
- *Italics* in the running text indicates arbitrary names used in the YANG models. Such names are not part of the YANG language itself. Italics is also used for XPath paths. In code listings, italics indicates a place holder that needs to be replaced.

Introduction

Goals and Methods

The entire networking industry is being pressured to automate in order to scale and move faster; this book explains how to unlock the power of network automation using YANG.

There are many barriers to automation. The strongest one is a need for a common understanding between network operators and software and hardware providers. To build this understanding, three things are sorely needed.

First, the participants need to have a common language. This book provides common terminology, models, and awareness of use cases and tools so that effective communication is possible.

Second, automation is not something that happens because you make a computer run in a loop. Network automation is a very hard problem. It is a distributed, parallel, real-time, highly available, performance-sensitive, security-sensitive control problem at the heart of society. This requires a system architecture.

This system architecture already exists but is not well known. Even many seasoned professionals are missing key pieces of the overall picture. This book paints the landscape so all parties understand where their pieces fit and how to achieve common goals.

Third, as you may have heard, "He who knows how will be hired, she who knows why will be his manager." Understanding the reasons for an architectural choice is a core aspect of knowing the architecture itself. This book provides this background.

By giving rich backgrounds, using examples, explaining "why," and providing ample opportunities for hands-on work, we hope this book will be useful to you as a networking professional, as well as for the advancement of the industry as a whole.

Who Should Read This Book?

This book is intended for network professionals of all breeds with an interest in network automation. Whether you call yourself a network operator, DevOps engineer, networking software developer, network orchestration engineer, NMS/OSS architect, service engineer, or manager of any of this is less important. If you are an engineer who wants to transition from command-line-interface-based management toward data model–driven management, if you are an engineer who needs to complement her networking skills with some programmability skills to remain relevant in this industry, there is material for you here.

People with some knowledge of network management will benefit the most from this book. On the other hand, software engineers who want to manage the network the same way they have been managing storage and compute will also benefit from reading this book.

Clearly, there are different paths to getting through the material in this book. Each chapter begins with a summary of the intended audience and what you can expect to learn. Look through these introductions and find the path that best suits you. As you grow and learn in your career, you may find that you keep coming back to take different paths.

How This Book Is Organized

Although this book could be read cover to cover, it is designed to be flexible and allow you to skip chapters and sections of chapters to cover just the material you need more work with.

Chapters 1 through 11 cover the following topics:

- **Chapter 1: The Network Management World Must Change: Why Should You Care?** provides a background to why NETCONF and YANG were invented in the first place.
- **Chapter 2: Data Model–Driven Management** gives a wide-angle perspective on the requirements for network management and automation, as well as the layers and components of the solution. This is highly recommended material for all roles.
- **Chapter 3: YANG Explained** develops a YANG model for a business use case in stages, and new constructs are introduced and explained as the solution grows. These stages are accompanied with a GitHub project so that it becomes hands-on material for those who want to take this in fully. This is core material for the rest of the book, but if you have already developed many YANG modules, you can skip ahead. On the other hand, seasoned YANGers might want to scan this chapter quickly to find some new and useful discussions.
- **Chapter 4: NETCONF, RESTCONF, and gNMI Explained** dives into the transport protocols, looking at the essential operations and encodings. NETCONF, RESTCONF, and gNMI are covered and contrasted in numerous examples. Each example can be replicated in the GitHub companion project for anyone with a desire to get their hands dirty.
- **Chapter 5: Telemetry Explained** covers telemetry, the automation feedback-loop mechanism. Feedback is an essential component of any control system, but telemetry is still an area under construction, and many solutions do not use it today.
- **Chapter 6: YANG Data Modeling Developments in the Industry** covers where to go looking for YANG models as well as which standards-defining organizations to work with, what tools to use, and what to do if there is more than one model for a given functionality. Chapters 7–9 all cover YANG model metadata and tools, but from three different perspectives.
- **Chapter 7: Automation Is as Good as the Data Models, Their Related Metadata, and the Tools: For the Network Architect and Operator** covers the essential tools and module information that all roles will need to use.
- **Chapter 8: Automation Is as Good as the Data Models, Their Related Metadata, and the Tools: For the Module Author** is intended for YANG module authors.
- **Chapter 9: Automation Is as Good as the Data Models, Their Related Metadata, and the Tools: For the Application Developer** is intended for automation application developers.
- **Chapter 10: Using NETCONF and YANG** contains a complete automation journey. It starts with a business case, creates a service YANG model for it, adds a service implementation, connects with a collection of devices over NETCONF, creates a service instance, and looks in detail at what happens with messages flying back and forth. Then it modifies and undoes the service-level change. If you understand everything in this chapter, you know you have fully understood the material in this book. Skimming this chapter should give you a good overview of all the aspects of model-driven network automation.
- **Chapter 11: YANG Model Design** contains a lot of advice about how to, and how not to, design YANG modules, based on many years of YANG modeling experience.

Chapter 1

The Network Management World Must Change: Why Should You Care?

This chapter covers

- The latest trends in network management
- Why you should care about these trends
- Why network engineers need new skills for the future
- Why existing technologies such as CLI, SNMP, NetFlow/IPFIX, syslog, and so on are not sufficient for network management and automation
- Why working with multiple protocols and data models is a pain. Why mapping data models is a source of troubles.
- Why automation, automation, automation?

By the end of this chapter, you will understand why the typical ways of managing networks are not sufficient in today's world, why all the trends in the networking industry these days converge into more programmability, and why the move toward more automation is a compulsory transformation. If you are a network engineer, you will recognize the limitations of existing practices, such as using the command-line interface (CLI), Simple Network Management Protocol (SNMP), NetFlow/IP Flow Information eXport (IPFIX), syslog, and so on. Also, as a network operator, you will understand the challenges of needing to adapt, both your knowledge and your way of working, to be more efficient in managing the services in a network.

Introduction

The Internet changed all aspects of life for virtually everyone. Most of it is taken it for granted these days. When you hear in your house, "Hey, there is no Internet!", you know you must treat this like a top-priority case in any respectable technical assistance center in the world—assuming you want to keep some level of peace in your household. Granted, the Internet is more important today than ever before, whether for business, education, social networking, banking, or simply leisure. Expressed differently, the Internet continues to get more and more vital.

Behind the Internet infrastructure, network operators work hard to design, deploy, maintain, and monitor networks. What are those network operators actually doing? Trying to categorize the network operator job into different tasks (starting from the old but still sometimes relevant FCAPS model, which stands for Fault, Configuration, Accounting, Performance, and Security Management), the FCAPS model is an international standard, defined by the International Telecommunications Union (ITU),[1] that describes the various network management areas.

Table 1-1, the ITU-T FCAPS Model Reference ITU-T M.3400 and ISO / IEC 7498-4 (Open Systems Interconnection—Basic Reference Model, Part 4: Management Framework), describes the main objectives of each functional area in the FCAPS model.

TABLE 1-1 ITU-T FCAPS Model

Management Functional Areas (MFAs)	Management Function Set Groups
Fault	Alarm Surveillance; Fault Localization & Correlation; Testing; Trouble Administration; Network Recovery
Configuration	Network Planning & Engineering, Installation; Service Planning & Negotiation; Discovery; Provisioning; Status & Control
Accounting	Usage Measurement, Collection, Aggregation, Mediation; Tariffing & Pricing
Performance	Performance Monitoring & Control; Performance Analysis & Trending; Quality Assurance
Security	Access Control & Policy; Customer Profiling; Attack Detection, Prevention, Containment and Recovery; Security Administration

NOTE

Every respectable network management book contains a reference to FCAPS, so we'll quickly cover this topic and move on.

This model offers the benefit of segmenting the administration work into more independent and understandable aspects. Fault management is compulsory to analyze the fault situations and manage networks in a proactive way. Configuration management is essential, not only to instantiate new services, but also to improve services and fix mistakes. Accounting management helps with the traffic use measurements, for billing or simply collection. Performance management deals with the on-demand or continuous monitoring of services, in order to proactively detect network faults or degradations.

The one entry in FCAPS that may be more independent is security: With the growing pressure to secure network devices (wireless access points, switches, and routers) and all network-attached devices (PCs, tablets, smartphones, and so on), security engineer became a job all its own.

Note that, a couple of years ago, a new term started to appear next to FCAPS: FCAPS + E (Energy Management). All these devices consume a lot of energy, including core routers from the Internet, data centers full of servers, and also the devices connected to the Internet. For example, an IP phone consumes as little as 2.3 W (when idle) but up to 14.9 W, depending on the Power over Ethernet (PoE, Standard 802.3AF) classification and the enabled functionality.

Today's and tomorrow's customers care about services. The only time they care about the network is when it is not working. Providers who deliver services need to deliver them on demand and provide a great end-user customer experience. When a service is not operating to customer expectations, the provider needs to fix the service as quickly as possible. Existing methods of configuring, monitoring, and troubleshooting service-impacting network issues do not meet customer needs for on-demand, high-quality, instant services. Automating all aspects of service delivery is required—from the application server through the network connection to the end consumer. Automated monitoring of service quality, issue detection, and automated recovery are required to deliver a high-quality service experience. Programmatic automation is the key to large-scale and high-quality service delivery.

Network engineers who embrace programmatic automation will be key to the next generation of service delivery. By extending their skills to implement model-driven programmatic automation, they will be valuable contributors, helping their customers deliver the next generation of services.

The five (or six if you count Energy) FCAPS management categories require more automation and more programmability. The time for disconnected network management systems based on these categories is over. The network needs to be managed as a single entity. Obviously, automation of a single category is a step in the right direction. However, automating network configuration without integrating fault management, without looking at the performance of the network and services, without thinking about the security aspects, and without collecting the accounting information, does not provide a full automation picture. In that sense, the FCAPS categories are being blurred these days. Engineers coming from different FCAPS backgrounds will need to integrate their domain-specific knowledge into a company-wide, FCAPS-wide, common automation framework, basically working toward a DevOps model, which is addressed later in this chapter.

Network operators can clearly envision the services model of the future: All network elements are part of a single, programmable fabric. Services can be assembled from a wide range of virtualized devices on the fly, each automatically advertising their programmability capabilities. They can be designed at a high level, independent of the complexities and device dependencies of the heterogeneous underlying infrastructure.

As an example, network service chaining, also known as service function chaining (SFC),[2] is a feature that uses software-defined networking (SDN) capabilities to create a service chain of connected network services (such as traffic shaper, intrusion prevention system, intrusion detection system, content filtering, WAN acceleration, firewall, and so on) and connect them in a virtual chain. Network operators can automate SFC end-to-end and provision in order to create or even re-order the services within minutes.

This model is now achievable through the power of SDN and network function virtualization (NFV). Implementing it, however, requires a fully programmable network, whose server resources can scale as the demand grows. Virtualized network functions (VNFs) must be remotely programmable by an SDN controller, and configurations and changes must be entirely automated, without requiring manual intervention by human network operators. To make this possible, equipment vendors, VNF vendors, and server vendors across the industry must evolve their virtualized devices to be programmable in SDN environments. To do it, a standard configuration management protocol is needed to provide secured, reliable transport and support network-wide transactions in the creation, modification, and deletion of configuration information in VNFs.

Going one step further in the services model of the future, the framework should include service assurance. When a service is degraded, an event automatically triggers the network to reconfigure itself. Opening the door for intent-based networking, network operators must specify the service's characteristics (connectivity, bandwidth, performance metrics such as max delay/loss/jitter, and so on) as opposed to the network configuration. From there, the network will optimize its configuration to support all the services.

The industry zeroed in on NETCONF as a configuration protocol, along with the YANG data modeling language. Originally designed as a management protocol, the NETCONF/YANG combination provides a simple, standardized way to enable a programmable interface to any device or service. Using YANG as the data modeling language in the networking industry initiates a transformational change in network operation: data model–driven management. Throughout the book, you will discover the NETCONF/YANG combination's clear benefits to programmability, including the following:

- Faster service deployment enabled by automation
- Fewer service deployment errors enabled by programmatic validation of configuration changes
- Improved serviceability (that is, faster time to diagnose and repair issues)
- Reduced operating costs by reducing legacy network engineering expenses

As network engineer, you should invest in yourself and become the network engineering of the future using programmatic automation to improve your productivity and the customer experience. This book is a key step in your transformation.

The following sections examine industry trends, some initiated years ago. Most if not all of these trends point to transformation change and network programmability with YANG.

The Industry Has Changed: What Are the Trends?

This section analyzes some trends in the last few years in the networking industry. Analyzing all these trends helps you understand why some operators are embracing more automation and, if you're not convinced yet, why all operators must adopt data model–driven management now.

Reduced Deployment Time

Operators test router images extensively before going into production. This is obviously a required procedure. In the not-too-distant past, it was not unusual to test new router software for three to six months before effectively deploying a new service in production. This included a mix of manual configuration and network management testing.

Personal Experience

At some point in time, more than 15 years ago, I had to support a network management system (NMS) product managing Layer 3 virtual private networks (L3VPNs) from a configuration, monitoring, and accounting point of view. Being a Cisco Certified Internetwork Expert (CCIE), I enjoyed playing with the router's CLI to configure an MPLS core of Provider Edge (PE) and Provider (P) routers, Virtual Routing and Forwarding (VRF) on the PE routers, with different routing options between customer edges (CEs) and PE routers, such as a default gateway, Routing Information Protocol (RIP), Open Shortest Path First (OSPF), or Border Gateway Protocol (BGP). Those configurations, mixed with route targets and route distinguishers, were fun to play with in the lab. I enjoyed demoing this solution to customers in pre-sale projects. Then, as a logical next step, the operators wanted to deploy those services in production networks. I recall one of the operator's constraints: "Now, we want to go from the L3VPN customer order to production in 20 minutes!" That 20-minute goal sounded like a stretch at the time, considering all the tasks involved—from the service order to the service validation. Next to the configuration of new L3VPN services, the product maintained a topology of the networks (which implies a network discovery), a mapping of L3VPN to specific customers, IP address mapping, VRF naming, location, customer flow record monitoring, and so on. The automation at that time used a template-based mechanism composed of multiple variables populated on the fly, and then a Telnet-based set of scripts to push the configuration to the routers and screen-scrape "show" commands. That project not only involved a greenfield environment, where all L3VPN services were new, but also a brownfield environment, where existing L3VPN services had to be discovered. —Benoit Claise

More automation in routers and switches was already a goal at that time, but the traditional development lifecycle for equipment vendors was historically (too) long. Let's take a typical example from an SNMP management system. In this example, the equipment is missing Management Information Base (MIB) modules or some objects within an MIB module (more on SNMP and MIB modules in the section "SNMP: For Monitoring But Not for Configuration"). The expected lifecycle for this missing automation piece is as follows: reporting this feature request to the equipment vendor product management, "battling" for the relative position in the roadmap compared to all other requests, waiting for the implementation, validating a test image, validating the official image once available, and, finally, upgrading the production routers. Needless to say, a long time passed between the feature request and the new production service.

Deploying new services is the only way for operators to grow their revenue, and time to market is key. Spending months to validate a new network element image and a new service is not viable any longer. The rate of deploying new services must improve all the time. Today, operators want to "smoke test" (the preliminary testing to reveal simple failures severe enough to reject a prospective software release) their images, services, or even entire points of presence (PoPs) on virtual devices—before the real deployment. In cloud environments, new services are expected to be up and running in seconds.

Automation can help reduce the deployment time. Thanks to programmability, new features are validated, new services are deployed, and routers are upgraded in no time. This requires consistent and complete instrumentation application programming interfaces (APIs) in network devices with the end goal that everything that can be automated in networking vendors is automated. As a consequence, operators reduce the service deployment time and offer differentiated services compared to the competition. Adapting the management software is typically faster than waiting for the traditional development lifecycle for equipment vendors.

CLI Is No Longer the Norm (If a Feature Cannot Be Automated, It Does Not Exist)

While it may be enjoyable the first couple of times to configure networks manually for learning and testing, the CLI is not a scalable way to introduce new features in production networks. There have been countless "network down" situations due to manual misconfiguration, sometimes called "fat-finger typing." A typical example is with access list management: Some, if not most, network engineers have inadvertently locked themselves out from the router configuration while updating an access list at least once in their career. It is so easy to mistype an IP address. (You are probably smiling right now, remembering some similar experience in the past.)

The CLI is an interface for configuring and monitoring network elements, designed for consumption by users who will think through an extra space or an added comma, or even a submenu. Although the CLI is not an API, you unfortunately had to treat it as one because that is all you had for so long. However, using the CLI for automation is neither reliable nor cost-effective.

First off, many service-related configuration changes involve more than one device, such as the point-to-point L3VPN example, which requires the configuration of four different devices, or a fully meshed L3VPN, which could involve many more devices. Indeed, every new addition to the fully meshed L3VPN network can entail updating all L3VPN endpoints, updating an access list, introducing an IP service level agreement (SLA) type of probe, and so on. In these examples, only networking devices are discussed. Many modern services these days encompass more than traditional physical networking devices; they include virtual machines, containers, virtual network functions, and so on. The fact is that *configuration changes are becoming more and more complex.*

NOTE

An IP SLA is an active method of monitoring and reliably reporting on network performance. "Active" (as opposed to "passive") monitoring refers to the fact that an IP SLA continuously generates its own traffic across the network and reports on it in real time. Typically, IP SLA probes monitor performance metrics such as delay, packet loss, and jitter.

Second, using highly trained network experts (for example, CCIEs) to insert new commands on network elements is not very cost-effective, unless the goal is obviously to troubleshoot a problem. As the frequency of changes is rapidly increasing, the idea here is to get the human out of the loop for service configuration and monitoring. As a matter of fact, due to the frequency of changes in the network, *it became humanly impossible deal with the CLI*, as mentioned by Sam Aldrin, Google architect, in his "Data-Driven Ops at Scale: Sensors, Telemetry and Analytics in Large Data Center Networks" talk at the MPLS+SDN+NFVVOLRD conference in 2016.

Third, and most important, *although the CLI is human-friendly, it is not suitable for automation.* Consider the following:

- The CLI is not standardized. While the networking device configuration CLI is similar, it is not consistent from a syntax and semantic point of view across vendors or across a specific vendor's set of operating systems.
- There are dependency issues when configuring devices via the CLI. In some cases, a CLI command for configuring an interface must be entered before configuring a VLAN. If those steps aren't executed in the proper order, the configuration fails—or worse, it's only partially completed.
- In addition to those dependencies, the CLI provides limited error reporting—at least not error reporting in a format easily consumable by scripts.
- The CLI does not produce any structured output. Therefore, the only way to extract information from a **show** command is via "screen scraping" (or extracting data from output using regular expression pattern matching). Finally, the "**show** commands" change frequently, to display more features, more counters, and so on. This issue is that even the smallest change to a **show** command, such adding a space to the output, might break an Expect script that extracts a specific value.

Can you at least use some CLI-based tools? Looking back at the example of deploying those L3VPNs in the previous section, the NMS involved at that time used Expect[3] scripts for device configuration and monitoring, with all the known limitations. Expect is an extension to the Tcl scripting language,[4] to automate interactions with text-based interfaces for protocols such as Telnet, Secure Shell (SSH), and so on. Typically, you open a terminal session to a network element, introduce a command, and analyze the answer. For example, when you're logging on to a router, the script codes that the next anticipated word is "login," and you insert the login username string; then the next anticipated word is "password," to which the script responds with the password, and so on. This language works fine until the device provides an unexpected answer. A typical example is a customized prompt, changed from "login:" to "Welcome, please enter your credentials:". At this point, the script, which expected "login:", receives an unexpected answer and it fails. Another typical example from the technical assistance center (TAC) is the Authentication, Authorization, and Accounting (AAA) configuration that changes the "login:" and "password:" prompts to "username:" and "password:". The Expect scripts must be adapted for those new prompts. The Expect script customizations, which rely on the CLI for all the different use cases, cost a lot of time, money, and unplanned outages.

It is not impossible to use the CLI for management, but it is expensive and difficult, as the industry has noted well over the last three decades. In fact, this was identified as one of the main reasons why networking did not evolve as fast as the rest of the IT industry by the Stanford Clean Slate project,[5] the foundation of the SDN movement (see "The Future of Networking, and the Past of Protocols,"[6] by Scott Shenker et al.). On the tooling front, there is an abundance of libraries and tools to interact with the CLI. Next to Expect, tools such as Paramiko[7] in Python, Ansible,[8] Puppet,[9] Chef,[10] and so on exist, but when it comes to the CLI, there is no machine-consumable abstraction to make the work easy and more scalable. This results in spending time chasing CLI changes rather than focusing on the goals of automation. On top of that, CLI management has some unforeseen operational consequences. For example, some operators are afraid of upgrading their devices, fearing that the automation scripts will break, up to the point where even required security patches are delayed or not applied. As a side note, this fear of upgrading also explains why the adoption of data model–driven automation was slow: Starting from a clean state is impossible for operators, who have to rely on existing CLI-based automation scripts for legacy devices. Considering the time between a new protocol specification and its deployment in networks, it is interesting to observe a clear difference between the lifecycle of network management protocols and other types of protocols. A routing protocol might take a couple of years from specification to deployment, whereas network management protocols usually take a decade. The reasons are practical: You need to upgrade the devices and controller/NMS to benefit from the new management protocol, while also updating the CLI-based scripts as backup plan, and at the same time still managing legacy devices that cannot be upgraded.

In conclusion, some operators rightly assert nowadays that *if a feature cannot be automated, it does not exist*. (This assertion actually comes from a Google engineer during a presentation for a new feature without programmability.) That leads to the development of APIs to monitor and configure the network elements directly...and the full automation story.

Hardware Commoditization and Disaggregation

Another trend in the industry is hardware commoditization, mainly Linux based, as opposed to more exotic purpose-built hardware, along with software disaggregation from the hardware.

In the data center, it is a well-accepted practice to order servers from one hardware company and to buy, independently, the operating system best suited for your specific needs: Windows, Linux, another Unix variant, and so on. These days, you can even easily support multiple operating systems with virtualization.

In the network world, equipment vendors have historically provided their own hardware with their own software, running on proprietary Application-Specific Integrated Circuits (ASICs), with the consequence that customers had to buy a "package" of a specific software tied to a hardware. Although this hardware equipment is optimized for performance in the core, at the edge, in the data center... you name it, the challenge of managing a complete network increases. Indeed, the costs of validating, managing, and maintaining features/services across the network explode when different device types have different operating systems, different feature sets, different CLIs, different management, and different licenses—even sometimes from the same vendors!

There is a growing tendency in the industry *to disaggregate the software from the hardware*, starting with the data center operation. Off-the-shelf components, with common chips, make up the hardware part of a solution. These are often referred to as white boxes. Historically, the massively scalable data centers, also known as hyperscalers, were the first ones that automated at large scale (for example, with top-of-rack switches). For this automation, they requested an SDK (software development kit) and a related set of APIs. Automation at scale when using the same switch type, from the same vendor, with the same software version is not *that* difficult. However, the hyperscalers were also the first ones that wanted to go one step further in the disaggregation, with the ability to order or develop their own networking software, mainly from open source projects.

The end goal is to be able to assemble white boxes as unified hardware, with Linux as the operating system, and specific applications for the different networking functions—potentially buying the BGP function from one vendor, the interior gateway protocol (IGP) from another one, and the RADIUS and management functions from a third one. The future is that vendors compete on an application basis: features, robustness, quality, support, upgrade, and so on.

For operators following this trend, the advantages are clear:

- *Thanks to Linux on networking devices, network and server engineers now speak the same language as their respective devices.* They use the same tools, thus blurring the boundary between server and network management, and reducing the support costs (see the next section, "The DevOps Time"). Not only "routers" and "switches" run on Linux, but the Linux environment offers a plethora of tools and applications, including management operations.
- *Using Linux implies a broader common knowledge: people are better trained, starting directly in school.* With this hardware commoditization, networking is perceived as not being that hard any longer because the vendor CLI is not unique. In other words, different equipment vendors are no longer competing on the CLI front. Instead of hiring people who know the Cisco or Juniper CLI, operators can hire candidates with Linux and scripting skills. So senior network engineers should focus less on vendor specifics and more on the broader network architecture and technology underpinnings. On the vendor front, certifications such as CCIE, (partly) based on the CLI knowledge, should be re-centered on programming the network independent of the CLI and on the operational aspects.
- *Having the same hardware all over in the network, as opposed to more exotic, purpose-built hardware, reduces the network complexity* (with the disadvantage that a hardware bug would

hit all platforms). Specific software and applications, on the same generic hardware, might optimize some devices. It is a fact that networks become more and more complex, with an increased operational cost, consequently, so any simplification is welcome. Disaggregation specifically means that vendors need a more open and modular platform. Note that disaggregation does not prevent traditional vendors from competing, using proprietary ASICs with their software to gain advantage. For example, Cisco is joining the trend of disaggregation in data center networks, saying it now allows data center customers to run its Nexus operating system (NX-OS) on third-party switches and to use any network operating system on its Nexus switches, thus meeting the demands of hyperscalers and large service providers. The network administrator has some freedom to select the best software either on generic hardware to reduce the cost or on the best hardware (for some extra performance optimization). Expressed this way, the disaggregation might be an opportunity for traditional equipment vendors to provide their software on generic platforms.

- *Decoupling the software and hardware implies the advantage of having two independent lifecycle managements, one for the software and one for the hardware.* While dealing with two lifecycle managements adds a little to the complexity (traditionally the vendor assembled the software), disaggregation gives the added flexibility to pick the best of breed. In certain cases, that flexibility outweighs the complexity. A software upgrade is as simple as upgrading a Linux package. Replacing the software from one vendor with another, or even a different OS train from the same vendor, is easy because the software is just another package. As a Cisco example, moving from an IOS-XE train to an IOS-XR one should not require any hardware change. In the end, the requirement is to enable hardware innovation and software innovation to grow independently.

- *Network and server engineers can now focus on more business-oriented tasks as opposed to just network operation and maintenance.* More and more, the network is becoming a business enabler, and the link between the business and the network is precisely the software. Quickly adapting the software to the business needs becomes key—for example, to add an application for performance probing, to supplement the network with virtual load balancers, to inject specific routes on top of an IGP for particular applications...you name it. With the time gained from automation (coming from disaggregation in this case, but not only from disaggregation), engineers will be the key enablers of networking innovations to serve the business needs.

In summary, hardware commoditization and disaggregation allow for and require more automation. Programmatic management based on YANG, discussed throughout the rest of the book, is a way to manage these new networks.

The DevOps Time

Networks engineers need to adapt. The only constant in this networking industry is change. So how does one adapt? In other words, how does one stay relevant in a couple of years? Interestingly, pretty much all network engineer job descriptions these days require some sort of scripting skills. Reflecting on this, you should learn scripting as a way to automate network management tasks, and not just server tasks with shell scripts. If you were to ask around which programming language to learn, the answer will consistently be "start with Python."

Python is a modern programming language that is easy to read and write and yet is powerful enough to be used as a convenient tool for daily parsing tasks, performance management, and configuration. Many SDKs are provided in Python, and there is a vast number of available libraries. Useful scripts can be created in no time. Interacting with the Python command line adds to the fun of learning Python. As an example, a course such as "An Introduction to Interactive Programming in Python"[11] from Coursera[12] provides the required basics with weekly videos, quizzes, and mini-projects that master Python. With a few professionals teaching something interesting, a community around the world wanting to learn and ready to share its knowledge, you easily get a final project that looks like this YouTube video[13] [Asteroids game in Python (coursera.org)].

Personal Experience

While attending the Python Coursera course, I participated in a 24-hour hackathon, developing a feature requested from the product management and engineering team for some time: the export of new, specific IP Flow Information eXport (IPFIX, RFC 7011) Information Elements,[14] extracted from the Cisco router supporting Python. What a refreshing feeling: If engineering cannot produce "my" feature fast enough, I will just script it! Now back to reality: Is this feature ready to ship? Not really, it would require more testing, performance analysis, code review, and a way to support it in the future—but this is beside the point. Three people, 24 hours, and some passion/stubbornness are all it takes to demonstrate a proof of concept. This is the beauty of scripting! —Benoit Claise

Will all network engineers have to become full-time programmers in the future? No. The trend toward automation, SDN, cloud, virtualization, everything-as-a-service, and so on does not imply that network engineers will disappear. When a (young) application designer complains that his call to the API "get-me-a-new-service-over-the-network (bandwidth = infinite, packetloss = 0, one-way-delay = 0, jitter = 0, cost = 0)" doesn't work as expected, you will still need a network engineer to troubleshoot. The best (that is, the most efficient) network engineers will be the ones with the ability to script their automated network-related tasks, whether for configuration or service assurance, and can modify their scripts on the fly. Instead of repeating a manual task, you must automate it!

So, what is DevOps? The combination of *Development* and *Operations*, DevOps is a software engineering practice that aims at unifying the software development and software operations.

Why? Because software engineers do not necessarily understand networking, and networking engineers do not necessarily understand software, so combining forces to get the best out of both worlds makes sense.

DevOps advocates automation and monitoring at all steps of software construction, from integration, testing, and releasing to deployment and infrastructure management. Expressed differently, DevOps is the intersection of development, operations, and quality assurance, as it emphasizes the interdependence of applications (or services), development, and IT operations, as shown in Figure 1-1.

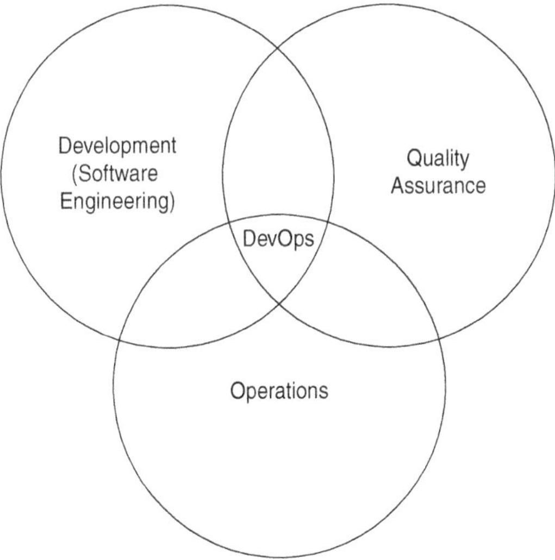

FIGURE 1-1 DevOps

This new DevOps mentality is about blending development and operations to provide quicker service deployment and iteration. As a practical example, it means that two historically distinct groups, the network support team and the application/server support team, now work as a single team, thus avoiding the ping-pong game of "this is a networking issue" versus "this is a server issue." The networking nirvana is being able to manage network elements the same way you manage servers.

NOTE

From now on, we'll stop making a distinction between network engineers and compute engineers (dealing with the servers), because in the future this distinction will completely disappear. Indeed, the networking and application worlds will come together. Unless we're making a specific point, we'll use the term "operation engineers" or "DevOps engineers" instead.

Software-Defined Networking

The new paradigm for many years now has been software-defined networking (SDN). Granted, although SDN is not a new term, it is an overloaded term—a buzzword that means many different things to many different people.

The first SDN discussions introduced the concept of the separation of the control and data plane entities, with a focus on OpenFlow (now part of the Open Networking Foundation[15]) as the open standard to configure the data plane—Forwarding Information Base (FIB), or Media Access Control (MAC) table.

Here are some of the use cases for configuring the control plane independent of an Interior Gateway Protocol (IGP) such as OSPF or IS-IS (Intermediate System to Intermediate System):

- Research in terms of programmable data planes: traffic engineering, service insertion, tunneling, and so on
- The ability to run control software on general-purpose hardware (commodity servers)
- A centralized controller taking care of all forwarding aspects for the entire network

Typically, an OpenFlow controller configures the data plane, via the API, the CLI, or a GUI, in an OpenFlow switch, as depicted in Figure 1-2. This OpenFlow controller manages the control plane, for which it requires the full topology view and the endpoints/flows.

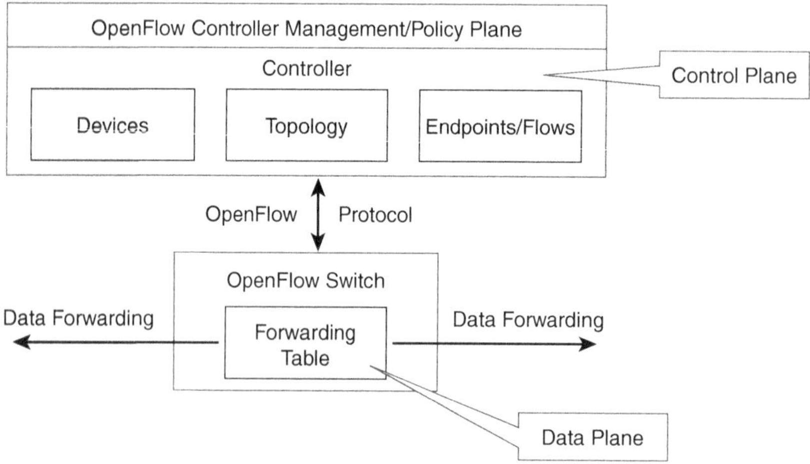

FIGURE 1-2 OpenFlow

Through the years, the notion of SDN has been evolving. OpenFlow, as a fundamental packet-forwarding paradigm, was actually an enabler—an enabler for more and easier network programmability. For example, the Open vSwitch Database Management Protocol (OVSDB, RFC 7047) is an open source effort to configure virtual switches in virtualized server environments. The OpenDaylight[16] project, an open source controller project, did a great job of adding multiple configuration protocols as southbound interfaces, next to OpenFlow:

- PCEP, the Path Computation Element communication Protocol (RFC 5440), is a communication protocol between a Path Computation Client (PCC) and a Path Computation Element (PCE), or between two PCEs, which includes path computation requests and path computation replies as well as notifications of specific states related to the use of a PCE in the context of Multiprotocol Label Switching (MPLS) and Generalized MPLS (GMPLS) traffic engineering.

- Forces, which stands for FORwarding and Control Element Separation (RFC 5810), aims to define a framework and associated protocol(s) to standardize information exchange between the control and forwarding plane.
- BGP-LS, which stands for BGP Link State Distribution (RFC 7752), is a mechanism by which link-state and traffic engineering information is collected from networks and shared with external components using the BGP routing protocol.
- NETCONF/YANG provides a simple, standardized way to enable a programmable interface to any device or service (covered extensively in this book).

Therefore, the term SDN evolved to mean a variety of things: network virtualization in the cloud, dynamic service chains for service provider subscribers, dynamic traffic engineering, dynamic network configuration, network function virtualization, open and programmable interfaces, and so on. What is for sure is that SDN is much more than OpenFlow and simply splitting the control and data planes.

A pragmatic definition of SDN comes from David Ward's foreword in the book *SDN: Software Defined Networks*,[17] by Ken Gray and Tom Nadeau: "SDN functionally enables the network to be accessed by operators programmatically, allowing for automated management and orchestration techniques; application of configuration policy across multiple routers, switches, and servers; and the decoupling of the application that performs these operations from the network device's operating system."

Some might say this is actually a definition of DevOps, not SDN. The bottom line is that SDN, as a control plane separation paradigm, enabled more network programmability requirements, optimized speed and flexibility, and made a move from configuration time to software time.

In the end, SDN as a control plane separation paradigm (configuring the Routing Information Base [RIB] or the FIB) and DevOps (which some call SDN) are complementary: They use the same concepts and the same tools. As a practical example, a network operator might be configuring an IGP for distributed forwarding with tools based on NETCONF and YANG and inject specific policies on top of the IGP, directly in the RIB.

Network Function Virtualization

Another trend in the industry, again explaining why some operators are embracing more automation these days, is network function virtualization (NFV). NFV offers more flexibility to customers in terms of service deployments and greatly reduces the complexity and time-to-market associated with new services. For example, virtual functions such as firewall, virtual intrusion detection system, deep packet inspection, and so on, are now added via the click of a button thanks to lifecycle service orchestration. Previously, those functions were integrated into dedicated hardware appliances, which added to the overall cost—not only of the installation, the connectivity, and the physical space, but also the ongoing maintenance.

As mentioned in the whitepaper "Trends in NFV Management,"[18] network operators have sound business reasons for embracing NFV. When network elements are virtualized instances rather than physical appliances, they can be provisioned and changed much more quickly. They scale dynamically with demand, allowing operators to spin up (or down) network resources for their customers as needed, in minutes or even seconds, rather than waiting weeks or months to deploy new hardware. They are automated and driven by machine logic rather than manual processes, thus driving down operational costs and complexity as well as reducing the risk of human error. And they radically shorten the time needed to move from receiving an order to generating revenue from a fully functional service. NFVs also allow operators more freedom to choose best-of-breed VNFs from a variety of vendors, and to easily move from one VNF to another due to superior pricing or features. The operator can take one VNF (say, a firewall) from one vendor and replace it with a similar VNF from another vendor—and accomplish this much more quickly and easily than replacing physical appliances.

Much of the discussion of VNF management among providers today focuses on onboarding—getting their VNFs booted and spun up in their initial configured state, placed in the right location, connected to the right physical and virtual networks, and ensuring that they have the appropriate resources and licenses. All of this "Day 1" and "Day 0" setup is important, and operators should be (and are) working to make it simpler. But often lost in the discussion is their responsibility for what happens "Day 1" and beyond, once VNFs are up and running. How do network operators link virtualized elements with service orchestration and other Operations Support System (OSS) and Business Support System (BSS) systems to allow for ongoing configuration changes? How do they automate the day-to-day management of multivendor VNFs in dynamic, large-scale networks?

Too many operators still view virtualization as a function of taking existing operating systems, booting them up in a virtual machine (VM), providing the same interfaces used when the product was a physical device, and that's it. Performing some runtime configuration management has been done for a long time for all devices, the thinking goes, and it has worked just fine, so there is no reason to do anything different. However, virtualized environments bring a new set of challenges that the tried-and-true mechanisms used for conventional physical appliances simply cannot account for.

Ultimately, it will be time to move away from the concept of "configuring" network appliances, as we begin to view virtualized functions as software to be programmed. This book discusses how to use NETCONF and YANG to introduce a more standardized API into network elements and unlock the value of full NFV automation.

Elastic Cloud: Pay As You Grow

Historically, new companies that wanted to enter a new business, relying on networking for that purpose, had to buy a series of networking equipment and operate it even before the first customer purchase order. CapEx (capital expenditure) is the money spent on buying, maintaining, and improving the fixed assets, while OpEx (operating expenditure) is the ongoing cost for operating the product or the business. For new companies, the CapEx is the cost of the network itself, while the OpEx is the IT employees' salaries (or the consulting fees) for operating the network. Not only does this CapEx require some nonnegligible amount of money to be invested by the young company, but ordering, installing, and operating this networking implies a delay before satisfying the first customer order. On top of that, sizing this network correctly might prove challenging for a new company: If it's sized too small, this might impact the future services and company growth, and if it's sized too big, this would be a waste of money.

These days, new businesses are not keen on investing such a huge amount of CapEx/OpEx on Day 1 for the networking aspects. Instead, having a linear cost as the business grows is the ideal solution: the more customers, the more revenue, and as a consequence the more investment in the infrastructure. This is the elastic concept, also known as "pay as you grow," with an ideal CapEx linear investment starting at an amount close to zero. When the elastic concept involves networking, it refers to the dynamic adaption of the network based on load. The cloud is the typical way to offer some compute, storage, and networking features, in an elastic way, thanks to virtualization—hence the name "elastic cloud."

Here is a typical example: A yangcatalog.org[19] website (a repository of YANG tools and the metadata around YANG models with the purpose of driving collaboration between authors and adoption by consumers) was staged by having a virtual computer on which to run the web service: an Amazon Web Service (AWS) EC2. The following is from the Amazon documentation: "Amazon Elastic Compute Cloud (Amazon EC2) is a web service that provides secure, resizable compute capacity in the cloud. It is designed to make web-scale cloud computing easier for developers. [...] Amazon EC2 reduces the time required to obtain and boot new server instances to minutes, allowing you to quickly scale capacity, both up and down, as your computing requirements change. Amazon EC2 changes the economics of computing by allowing you to pay only for capacity that you actually use."

Initially, a free AWS instance did the trick for the yangcatalog.org[19] website. However, as more services were added to the website, it required more capacity (memory, CPU, and storage). Based on the website's success, it was an investment in a real plan, paying for more resources and paying by the second for active servers (that is, "elastic cloud"). Although this example mentions AWS, you should note that multiple similar solutions exist in the industry, such as Microsoft Azure, Google Cloud Platform, and OVH Cloud, to name a few.

More complex examples than the YANG catalog include VNFs, such as virtual firewalls, virtual intrusion detection systems, load balancers, WAN accelerators, and so on, as mentioned in the previous section, but the elastic cloud principles remain.

In terms of cloud management, you need to distinguish two different types: on one side you have system-level management, and on the other side you have service management or NFV management inside the container or virtual machine.

System-level management consists of tasks such as the following:

- Preparing the environment with Linux packages installation
- Upgrading the OS and applying patches

- Setting up containers or virtual machines
- Scaling up, which means growing the infrastructure (compute, storage, and networking), to accommodate more/better services
- Scaling out, which means replicating the infrastructure

This system-level management, which is more of a procedural type of management (a workflow driven by action), might benefit from a Business Process Modeling Language (BPML) such as Topology or Orchestration Specification for Cloud Applications (TOSCA[20]), a template based mechanism that describes the topology of cloud-based services, their components, and their relationships.

The service management inside the container or virtual machine consists of tasks such as these:

- Starting up and stopping the service.
- More importantly, maintaining or upgrading the service. For example, in the case of updating an access list entry, you cannot stop the virtual firewall.

This management benefits more from a schema-like language such as YANG, which provides the API and semantic-based actions. This is the model-driven management paradigm, which is explored in the next section.

Data Model–Driven Management

Scripts are relatively easy to create and, to some extent, fun to write. The hard part is the maintainability. Try to look at one of your troubleshooting scripts one year after creation and, unless the script contains a well-known convention (such as PEP8,[21] a style guide for Python code), a clean structure, and some documentation, chances are it will look unfamiliar. Improving this script would require quite some time, and mostly likely the famous "If it ain't broke, don't fix it" principle would prevail.

Good scripts are based on good APIs (sets of functions and procedures that enable the creation of applications that access the features or data of an operating system, application, or other service), which fundamentally should provide the following benefits:

- **Abstraction**: A programmable API should abstract away the complexities of the underlying implementation. The DevOps engineers should not need to know unnecessary details, such as a specific order of configurations in a network element or specific steps to take if something fails. If this isn't intuitive for humans, the sequencing of commands becomes even more complex for configuration engines. Configurations should function more like filling in a high-level checklist (these are the settings you need; now the system can go figure out how to properly group and order them).

- **Data specification**: The key thing an API does—whether it is a software or network API—is provide a specification for the data. First, it answers the question of what the data is—an integer, string, or other type of value? Next, it specifies how that data is organized. In traditional programing, this is called the *data structure*, though in the world of network programmability and databases, the more common term is *schema*, also known as *data models*. Since the network is basically being treated as a (distributed) database, the term *(database) schema* is sometimes used.
- **Means of accessing the data**: Finally, the API provides a standardized framework for how to read and manipulate the device's data.

Data model-driven management builds on the idea of specifying in models the semantics, the syntax, the structure, and constraints of management objects. From there, scripts use APIs rendered from those models via tooling. The advantage is that, as long as the models are updated in a backward-compatible way, the previous set of APIs is still valid.

An important advantage of data model–driven management is the separation of the models from the protocols and encodings, which means that it is easier to add protocols and encodings. Data model–driven management was initially built on NETCONF and XML, but other protocols/encodings have since seen the light: RESTCONF with JavaScript Object Notation (JSON), gRPC Network Management Interface (gNMI) with protobuf, and so on. Note that XML and JSON are text-file formats used to store structured data for embedded and web applications. Chapter 2, "Data Model–Driven Management," covers the different protocols and encodings.

As you will see in Chapter 7, "Automation Is as Good as the Data Models, Their Related Metadata, and the Tools: For the Network Architect and Operator," once the models are well specified and the full toolchain is in place, then the automation is simplified and the OPEX reduced. While the data model–driven management concepts are not new, it is one viable type of management in today's networks. So data model–driven management is a special trend in this book, as this book is entirely dedicated to all aspects of this transition in the industry.

When applying an API to a complex environment, the key is that vendors implement it in a standards-based way. There should be a common way to define and access data across different devices and vendors—not separate, proprietary interfaces that operators must learn for every different device and function in their network.

Figure 1-3 illustrates how changing from management via static CLI scripts to a model-driven approach impacts the network operations. It shows a service provider in the Americas who was migrating its services from one set of older devices to a newer set. Notice that the transition was initially rather slow, and took some time to complete at the initial pace. Then a data model–driven automation tool was introduced in September 2016 (in this case, a Cisco product called NSO, Network Services Orchestrator) that fundamentally changed the way the network was transitioning.

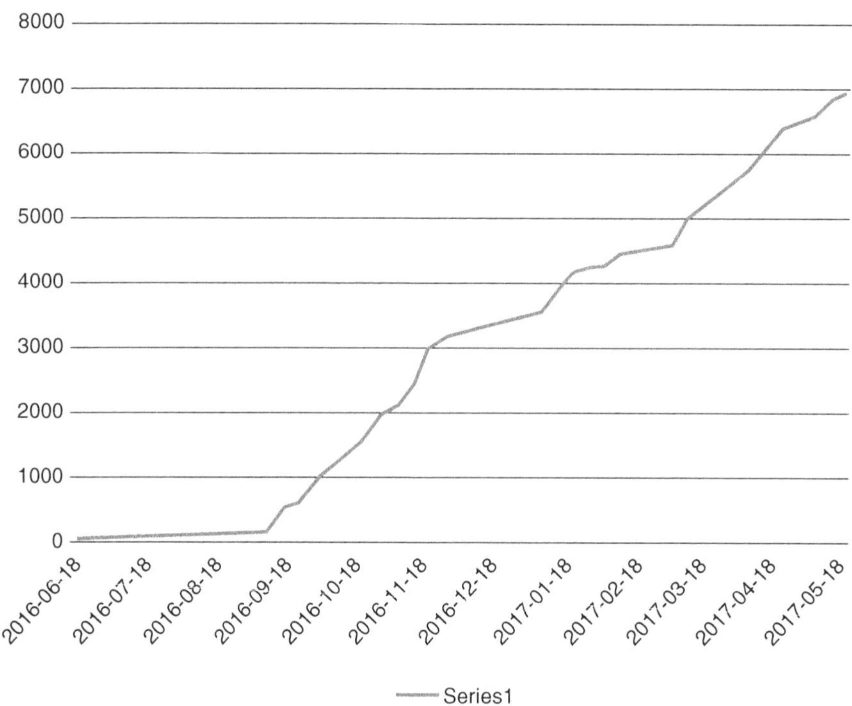

FIGURE 1-3 Number of Circuits Moved by Date, Initially Based on CLI Scripts, Then with Data–Model Driven Automation Software

(Data Model–Driven) Telemetry

Telemetry is a big buzzword in the networking industry these days. Like any buzzword, telemetry means different things to different people—exactly like SDN a few years ago. In different discussions with people from different backgrounds, telemetry meant the following:

- The science and technology of automatic measurement and transmission of measurement data.
- The mechanism to push any monitoring information to a collector (in that sense, NetFlow is a telemetry mechanism). Since it is about streaming data on regular basis, it is also known as "streaming telemetry."
- The data model–driven push of information, streaming YANG objects.
- The hardware-based telemetry, pushing packet-related information directly from ASICs.
- Device-level telemetry, such as the pushing of information about hardware and software inventory, configuration, the enabled/licensed features, and so on, with the intention to automate diagnostics, understand overall usage, and provide install base management.

In many discussions, the definition of telemetry had to be clarified:[22]

> "Telemetry is an automated communications process by which measurements and other data are collected at remote or inaccessible points and transmitted to receiving equipment for monitoring. Model-driven telemetry provides a mechanism to stream data from a model-driven telemetry-capable device to a destination.
>
> Telemetry uses a subscription model to identify information sources and destinations. Model-driven telemetry replaces the need for the periodic polling of network elements; instead, a continuous request for information to be delivered to a subscriber is established upon the network element. Then, either periodically, or as objects change, a subscribed set of YANG objects are streamed to that subscriber.
>
> The data to be streamed is driven through subscription. Subscriptions allow applications to subscribe to updates (automatic and continuous updates) from a YANG datastore, and this enables the publisher to push and in effect stream those updates."

In discussions, it is important to justify the reason why data model-driven telemetry is the most useful type of telemetry that requires automation. First off, why is telemetry necessary? You've heard all types of reasons: because SNMP is boring, because SNMP is slow, because SNMP is not precise in terms of polling time—you name it. You may have even heard "because SNMP is not secure." Well, SNMPv3 provides security with authentication and privacy! Anyway, there are bigger reasons to focus on data model–driven telemetry:

- SNMP does not work for configuration, although it is suitable for monitoring (see RFC 3535 for a justification).
- Network configuration is based on YANG data models, with protocol/encoding such as NETCONF/XML, RESTCONF/JSON, and gNMI/protobuf.
- Knowing that a configuration is applied does not imply that the service is running; you must monitor the service operational data on top.
- There is not much correlation between the MIB modules, typically used for network monitoring, and YANG modules used for configuration, except maybe a few indices such as the ifIndex in "The Interfaces Group MIB" (RFC 2863) or the interface key name in "A YANG Data Model for Interface Management" (RFC 7223, obsoleted by RFC 8343).
- Any intent-based mechanism requires a quality assurance feedback loop, which is nothing more than the telemetry mechanism, as explained in the next section.
- Therefore, since the configuration is "YANG data model driven," so must the telemetry.

The only exception to data model–driven telemetry *might* be one from hardware-based telemetry: pushing a lot of telemetry directly from ASICs (for a subset of the traffic, at line rate), which might not leave room on the network element for a YANG-related encoding without a penalty in terms of the telemetry export rate. However, it is still possible to describe the exported data with a YANG data model with most any encoding type.

Operations engineers need to manage the network as a whole, independently of the use cases or the management protocols. Here is the issue: with different protocols come different data models, and different ways to model the related type of information. In such a case, the network management must perform the difficult and time-consuming job of mapping data models: the one from configuration with the one from monitoring. Network management was a difficult task with the CLI, MIB modules, YANG models, IPFIX information elements, syslog plain text, TACACS+, RADIUS, and so on. Therefore, protocol design decisions that do not simplify this data model mapping issue are frowned upon. Ideally, the network should present data arriving over different protocols that use the same concepts, structures, and names so that the data can be merged into a single consistent view. In other words, a single data model is needed.

Intent-Based Networking

The services are becoming more and more complex, with a mix of networking functions at the edge, the core, and the data center, as well as the combination of networking, compute, and storage in the cloud. With this increased complexity today and, at the same time, an increased frequency of changes, it is important to know to get the humans out of the loop, to focus on automation. Data model–driven management simplifies the automation and specifies that the telemetry must be data model driven. Now, does the network behave as expected? Are the new services operational? Are the SLAs respected? You could check that the network device, the virtual machine, or the container is reachable and check that the services or the VNFs are correctly configured. However, validating the configuration and reachability of individual components does not imply that the services are running optimally or meet the SLAs.

The cost of service failure is going up significantly these days. Imagine the monetary implications of one hour of downtime for Facebook services, whose business model depends solely on advertisements. Imagine the monetary implications of one hour of downtime for AWS, whose business model depends on web service utilization.

This is where the notion of intent-based networking comes to play, with networks constantly learning and adapting. Historically, managing in a prescriptive mode by focusing on detailing the necessary network configuration steps was common. Contrary to the prescriptive approach, the intent-based approach focuses on the higher-level business policies and on what is expected from the network. In other words, the prescriptive approach focuses on *how*, while the intent-based approach focuses on *what*. For example, the prescriptive way of configuring an L3VPN service involves following a series of tasks, expressing the *how*. For example, you must configure a VRF called "customer1" on provider edge router1 under the interface "eth0," a default gateway pointing to router1 on the customer edge router, the MPLS-VPN connectivity between the provider edge router1 and router2, and so on.

Conversely, the intent-based way focuses on what is required from the network (for example, a VPN service between the London and Paris sites for your customer).

Where intent-based networking creates the most value is with constant learning, adapting, and optimizing, based on the feedback loop mechanism, as shown in the following steps:

STEP 1. Decomposition of the business intent (the *what*) to network configuration (the *how*). This is where the magic happens. For a single task such as "a VPN service between the London and Paris sites for customer C," you need to understand the corresponding devices in Paris and London, the mapping of the operator topology, the current configuration of the customer devices, the operator core network configuration, the type of topology (such as hub and spoke or fully meshed), the required Quality of Service (QoS), the type of IP traffic (IPv4 and/or IPv6), the IGP configuration between the customer and the operator, and so on. Examine all the possible parameters for an L3VPN service in the specifications of the YANG data model for L3VPN service delivery (RFC 8299).

STEP 2. The automation. This is the easy part, once the *what* is identified. Based on the data model–driven management and a good set of YANG models, a controller or orchestrator translates the YANG service model (RFC 8299) into a series of network device configurations. Thanks to NETCONF and two-phase commit (more on this later), you are now sure that all devices are correctly configured.

STEP 3. The monitoring with data model–driven telemetry provides a real-time view of the network state. Any fault, configuration change, or even behavior change is directly reported to the controller and orchestrator (refer to the previous section).

STEP 4. Data analytics correlate and analyze the impact of the new network state for service assurance purposes, isolating the root cause issue—sometimes, even before the degradation happens. From there, the next network optimization is deduced, almost in real time, before going back to step 1 to apply the new optimizations.

This constant feedback loop, described in four steps, is the foundation for networks that constantly learn and adapt. It allows moving away from reactive network management where a network fault (or worse, a customer call) triggers the troubleshooting to constant monitoring focused on the SLAs. The combination of predictive analytics and artificial intelligence, combined with continuous learning and adapting, is the main enabler here. From here, the next logical step is not too futuristic: self-healing networks.

Even if this book doesn't cover the "intent," per se, it covers steps 2 and 3 in order to realize intent-based networking.

Software Is Eating the World

As Marc Andreessen correctly predicted in the article "Why Software Is Eating The World"[23] in the *Wall Street Journal* in 2011, "software programming tools and Internet-based services make it easy to launch new global software-powered start-ups in many industries—without the need to invest in new infrastructure and train new employees."

This is a trend in the industry, where consumers are offered all the possibilities: online banking, hotel and flight booking, virtual lobby assistants, booking a taxi via an application, placing calls from their PCs, watching TV or reading a book on a tablet, listening to music on their mobile phones, and connected cars. While those offer more flexibility to the end users, the service provider wants to reduce its own OpEx by using software, thus reducing the human interaction and hence costs.

Coming back to the world of networking, in no time these days you can register a domain name, create multiple email addresses, and host a website. Almost instantaneously, with a few clicks, you can enable IPv6, add a database to your website, enable protection with a firewall, and create an SSL certificate. The on-demand cloud computing platforms, which offer some storage, compute resources, and some basic networking, can add a virtual network and include some virtual networking functions such as firewall, virtual intrusion detection system, or accounting.

The main point is that all these new services are available almost immediately, thanks to software. And this software in the background is composed of automation and sometimes data analytics for customization.

Existing Network Management Practices and Related Limitations

Managing networks is not new. This section looks at "traditional" network management practices. Traditionally, networks have used different management protocols for different FCAPS management aspects, with different management models and different practices—typically, CLI and "screen scraping," SNMP, NetFlow and IPFIX, and syslog. From there, you can observe the respective protocol limitations, which highlight the issue of the different data models in the next section.

These protocols describe the current practical normality of most of the network operation that happens in the world today. While each section can seem a little disparate and contain a multitude of little details, the picture comes together in the summary at the end of the chapter. The big picture will be clearer once you have seen a snapshot of how each of these environments work to get a glimpse into some of their gory details.

CLI: Is This an API?

Most devices have a built-in command-line interface (CLI) for configuration and troubleshooting purposes. Network access to the CLI has traditionally been through the Telnet protocol, with the addition of the SSH protocol to address security issues associated with Telnet. At some point in time, the CLI was the only way to access devices, for both configuration and troubleshooting. And the CLI grew with any new features to become a huge list of configuration and **show** commands.

CLI: Explained

CLIs are generally task-oriented, which makes them easier to use for human operators. As the goal is human consumption, the design principle is for the CLI to change to be more readable. As an example, an old IOS command was changed from **show mac-address-table** to **show mac address-table**, probably motivated by a developer thinking it was better from an interface point view or maybe to be consistent with a new "show mac" feature. For users, who most of the time use the command autocomplete function while interacting with the device, this change is not be an issue. Indeed, most command-line interfaces provide context-sensitive help that reduces the learning curve. However, a script that sends commands to the device would now fail as a consequence of this CLI change.

On the other side, a saved sequence of textual commands is easily replayed: Typically, the same access list, in the form of a CLI snippet, can be applied to multiple devices. With simple substitutions and arbitrary text-processing tools, operation engineers can apply similar CLI snippets to network elements. Typically, the access-list snippet contains a couple of arguments to be replaced, depending on the managed device characteristics.

CLI: Limitations

The "CLI is No Longer the Norm" section covered already most of the CLI limitations, and this section adds some practical configuration examples, such as the following snippet:

```
Conf t
  router ospf x
  vrf xxx
```

Here is another example:

```
Conf t
  vrf xxx
  router ospf x
```

In other words, it is very well possible that a command on different devices, even from the same vendor, behaves differently. What is the root cause behind those differences? CLIs typically lack a common data model.

These VRF examples lead to the second CLI limitation: The CLI is context-sensitive and order-specific. A question mark helps with the listing of all available options, but entering one command might offer a submenu of commands. While adding commands raises a problem, removing commands offers some challenges, too. Coming back to the VRF example, removing a VRF might remove the entire VRF-related set of commands, again depending on device implementation. Since CLIs are proprietary, in syntax and semantics they cannot be used efficiently to automate processes in an environment with a heterogenous set of devices.

The command-line interface is primarily targeted at human users, who can adapt to minor syntax and format changes easily. Using the CLIs as a programmatic interface is troublesome because of parsing complexities. For example, CLIs don't report consistent error code in case of failure—a necessary automation property. On top of that, there is no way to discover new CLI changes: CLIs often lack proper version control for the syntax and the semantics. It is therefore time-consuming and error-prone to maintain programs or scripts that interface with different versions of a command-line interface.

What's more, the CLIs keep evolving, as more features are introduced. Sure, those changes are documented in the release notes, at least for the configuration commands, but the automation cannot consume those release notes.

So, is the CLI an API? It was used like one, but it is fragile.

As a quiz, Example 1-1 shows four potential situations operations engineers might encounter dealing with a CLI. Can you find the errors? What is wrong with these outputs?

EXAMPLE 1-1 CLI Quizzes

```
Router1#show run
Command authorization failed
Router1#

Router2#show run
Unable to read configuration. Try again later
Router2#

Router3#show run
Router3#

Router4#show run
...
 description %Error with interface
...
Router4#
```

The show command on Router1 looks like an AAA (Authorization, Authentication, Accounting) issue, while it might point to an non volatile random-access memory (NVRAM) issue on Router2. The Router3 output doesn't look right, unless the configuration is empty. Finally, the Router4 output looks like an error, while actually it's not! In this particular case, the operations engineer configured the interface description with "%Error with interface" to flag an issue with this specific interface. Again, for a user, this description helps; however, for a CLI-based script, the consequences might be unexpected. In this particular case, this caused a bug in an Expect[3] script in automating configuration archival. When the script tried to upload the configuration, it stopped working once it encountered this particular description line, thinking that the script itself was in error. Indeed, the script was based on a regular expression (regex) based on "Error". This example perfectly illustrates the difficulties of using the CLI for automation. Let's face it—the CLI is not suited for automation. It is not machine-friendly and lacks a well-defined format. The CLI has been used for years, as it was the only way to configure and collect device information, but it's very fragile.

SNMP: For Monitoring But Not for Configuration

SNMP, the Simple Network Management Protocol, is a protocol specified by the IETF. Actually, there have been multiple protocol versions. Here is a brief history of the different SNMP versions:

- **SNMPv1 (historic)**: The first version of the protocol, specified by RFC 1157. This document replaces the earlier versions that were published as RFC 1067 and RFC 1098. The security is based on SNMP *community strings*.
- **SNMPsec (historic)**: This version of the protocol added strong security to the protocol operations of SNMPv1 and is specified by RFC 1351, RFC 1352, and RFC 1353. Security is based on *parties*. Few, if any, vendors implemented this version of the protocol, which is now largely forgotten.
- **SNMPv2p (historic)**: For this version, much work was done to update the SNMPv1 protocol and Structure of Management Information version 1, and not just security. The result was updated protocol operations, new protocol operations and data types, and party-based security from SNMPsec. This version of the protocol, now called party-based SNMPv2, is defined by RFC 1441, RFC 1445, RFC 1446, RFC 1448, and RFC 1449. (Note that this protocol has also been called *SNMPv2 classic*, but that name has been confused with community-based SNMPv2. Thus, the term SNMPv2p is preferred.)
- **SNMPv2c (experimental)**: This version of the protocol is called community string-based SNMPv2. Specified by RFC 1901, RFC 1905, and RFC 1906, it is an update of the protocol operations and data types of SNMPv2p and uses community-based security from SNMPv1.
- **SNMPv2u (experimental)**: This version of the protocol uses the protocol operations and data types of SNMPv2c and security based on *users*. It is specified by RFC 1905, RFC 1906, RFC 1909, and RFC 1910.
- **SNMPv3 (standard)**: This version of the protocol is a combination of user-based security and the protocol operations and data types from SNMPv2p and provides support for proxies. The security is based on that found in SNMPv2u and SNMPv2*, and updated after much review. The documents defining this protocol are multiple:
  - RFC 3410: Introduction and Applicability Statements for Internet-Standard Management Framework.
  - RFC 3411: An Architecture for Describing SNMP Management Frameworks. Now updated by RFC 5343: Simple Network Management Protocol (SNMP) Context EngineID Discovery, and by RFC 5590: Transport Subsystem for the Simple Network Management Protocol (SNMP).
  - RFC 3412: Message Processing and Dispatching for SNMP.
  - RFC 3413: SNMPv3 Applications.
  - RFC 3414: User-Based Security Model (USM) for version 3 of SNMPv3.

- RFC 3415: View-Based Access Control Model (VACM) for SNMP.
- RFC 3584: Coexistence between Version 1, Version 2, and Version 3 of the Internet-standard Network Management Framework.

The goal of this book is not to delve into the SNMP details. There are plenty of valuable references, books, and tutorials dedicated to the technical aspects of SNMP, Structure of Management Information (SMI), and Management Information Base (MIB), so there is no point in covering everything here, especially when one of the key messages from this book, as you will quickly realize, is to move away from SNMP. However, let's look at just a few concepts that are necessary within this book.

SNMP: Explained

As displayed in Figure 1-4, an SNMP Agent, embedded in a device to be managed (typically a router or a switch in the networking context), responds to requests for information and actions from the SNMP Manager, sitting in a Network Management System (NMS): typical information includes interface counters, system uptime, the routing table, and so on. These data sets are stored in the device memory and are retrieved from a network management application by SNMP polling. The MIB is the collection of those managed objects residing in a virtual information store in the SNMP Agent. A collection of related managed objects is defined in a specific MIB module. For example, interfaces-related objects are specified in the "Interfaces Group MIB" document, detailed by the IETF in the RFC 2863. The SMI defines the rules for describing management information, using the Abstract Syntax Notation One (ASN.1) as an interface description language. In other words, SMI is the data-modeling language used to describe objects to be managed via the SNMP protocol.

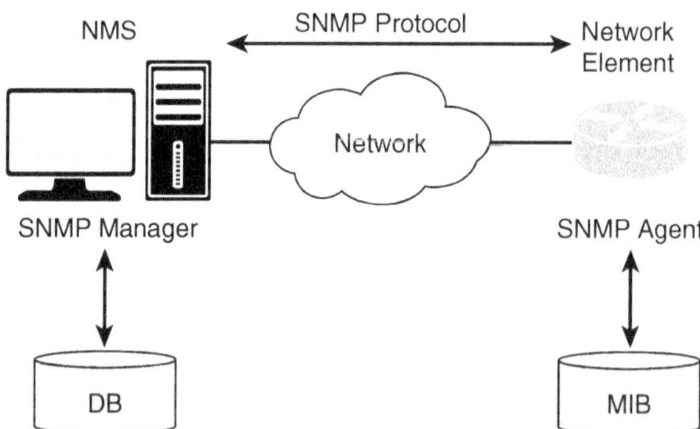

FIGURE 1-4 The SNMP Basic Model

The following types of interactions occur between the SNMP Manager and SNMP Agent:

- **Read**: The ability to read managed objects from the SNMP Agent, characterized by "read-only" objects in MIB modules. A typical example is the polling of interface counters' statistics, described by the ifInOctets and ifOutOctets managed objects (RFC 2863).

- **Write**: The ability to set managed objects in an SNMP Agent, if the managed objects are specified with a "read-write" status in the MIB module (for example, changing an interface administrative status with the ifAdminStatus managed objects [RFC 2863]).
- **Notification, also known as trap or inform**: This is a push-based mechanism (as opposed to pull, when the SNMP Manager polls information from the SNMP Agent) from the SNMP Agent to the SNMP Manager. A typical example is a linkUp or linkDown notification [RFC 2863], sent to the SNMP Manager when the interface operational status changes.

SNMP: Limitations

The idea behind the SNMP specifications was to develop a generic protocol used for the configuration and monitoring of devices and networks, effectively covering the FCAP aspects, with the S of Security being treated separately. The SNMP notifications covers the Fault aspects, the configuration of read-write MIB objects covers the Configuration aspects, while the myriad of read-only MIB objects could cover some aspects of Accounting and Performance.

SNMPv1 was published in 1990, and SNMPv3 was finished in 2002. So many years of experience went into the third version. While it took some time for SNMPv3, with its added security considerations, to be widely implemented, years later it drew an important conclusion: *SNMP has always done a good job in terms of monitoring devices. However, it fails at device configuration.*

In 2003, RFC 3535, "Overview of the 2002 IAB Network Management Workshop," documented the outcomes of a dialogue started between network operators and protocol developers to guide the IETFs' focus on future work regarding network management. This paper reported a list of strong (+), weak (-), and neutral (o) points related to the SNMP protocol.

SNMP Analysis

The SNMP management technology was created in the late 1980s and has since been widely implemented and deployed in the Internet. There are lots of implementational and operational experiences, and the characteristics of the technology are thus well understood.

+ SNMP works reasonably well for device monitoring. The stateless nature of SNMP is useful for statistical and status polling.
+ SNMP is widely deployed for basic monitoring. Some core MIB modules, such as the IF-MIB (RFC 2863), are implemented on most networking devices.
+ There are many well-defined proprietary MIB modules developed by network device vendors to support their management products.
+ SNMP is an important data source for systems that do event correlation, alarm detection, and root-cause analysis.

- o SNMP requires applications to be useful. SNMP was, from its early days, designed as a programmatic interface between management applications and devices. As such, using SNMP without management applications or smart tools appears to be more complicated.
- o Standardized MIB modules often lack writable MIB objects that can be used for configuration, and this leads to a situation where the interesting writable objects exist in proprietary MIB modules.
- There are scaling problems with regard to the number of objects in a device. While SNMP provides reasonable performance for the retrieval of a small amount of data from many devices, it becomes rather slow when retrieving large amounts of data (such as routing tables) from a few devices.
- There is too little deployment of writable MIB modules. While there are some notable exceptions in areas, such as cable modems, where writable MIB modules are essential, it appears that router equipment is usually not fully configurable via SNMP.
- The SNMP transactional model and the protocol constraints make it more complex to implement MIBs, as compared to the implementation of commands of a command-line interface interpreter. A logical operation on an MIB can turn into a sequence of SNMP interactions where the implementation has to maintain state until the operation is complete, or until a failure has been determined. In case of a failure, a robust implementation must be smart enough to roll the device back into a consistent state.
- SNMP does not support easy retrieval and playback of configurations. One part of the problem is that it is not easy to identify configuration objects. Another part of the problem is that the naming system is very specific, and physical device reconfigurations can thus break the capability to play back a previous configuration.
- There is often a semantic mismatch between the task-oriented view of the world usually preferred by operators and the data-centric view of the world provided by SNMP. Mapping from a task-oriented view to the data-centric view often requires some nontrivial code on the management application side.
- Several standardized MIB modules lack a description of high-level procedures. It is often not obvious from reading the MIB modules how certain high-level tasks are accomplished, which leads to several different ways to achieve the same goal, which increases costs and hinders interoperability.

Multiple factors prevented SNMP from replacing the device CLI as the primary configuration approach. Some points are briefly addressed in RFC 3535 and complemented with some experience here:

- First, a question of money: The SNMP Agent code costs too much to develop, test, and maintain, compared to the CLI code. SNMP seems to work reasonably well for small devices that have a limited number of managed objects and where end-user management applications are shipped by the vendor. For more complex devices, SNMP becomes too expensive and too hard to use [SNMP Set: Can it be saved?].[24]

- Poor performance for bulk data transfers, due to User Datagram Protocol (UDP) characteristics. The typical examples are routing tables, with the polling of the BGP table, which takes a considerable amount of time. SNMP has the same data transfer behavior as Trivial File Transfer Protocol (TFTP), which is UDP-based, so a lot of time is spent waiting. Especially if there is any latency in the network, this becomes problematic. However, the good thing about SNMP being UDP-based is that the traffic can get through in case of congestion. Note that one operator who went from SNMP polling to NETCONF saw a tenfold increase in performance in a real production network. A more typical value is two or three times faster with NETCONF (which is TCP-based, so it's an FTP-style transfer).

- Poor performance on query operations that were not anticipated during the MIB design. A typical example is the following query: Which outgoing interface is being used for a specific destination address?

- It is usually not possible to retrieve complete device configurations via SNMP so that they can be compared with previous configurations or checked for consistency across devices. There is usually only incomplete coverage of device features via the SNMP interface, and there is a lack of differentiation between configuration data and operational state data for many features. For example, while SNMP Manager set the interface state with the ifAdminStatus object, it must poll the ifOperStatus object to check the applied operational state. This example is an obvious one for any network operator, but this link between those two objects cannot be discovered in a programmatic way.

- MIB modules and their implementations are not available in a timely manner (sometimes MIB modules lag years behind), which forces users to use the CLI. Indeed, as already mentioned, it is a reality that device management has been an afterthought. Once operators are "forced" to use scripts to manage their CLI (for example with Expect scripts), there is not much incentive to use a different mechanism for not much added value.

- Lexicographic ordering is sometimes artificial with regard to internal data structures and causes either significant runtime overhead or increases implementation costs or implementation delay, or both. A typical example is the routing table, whose data needs to be rearranged before answering an SNMP request.

- Operators view current SNMP programming/scripting interfaces as being too low-level and thus too time-consuming and inconvenient for practical use. Also, device manufacturers find SNMP instrumentations inherently difficult to implement, especially with complex table indexing schemes and table interrelationships. As a practical example, RFC 5815 specifies an MIB module for the monitoring and configuration of IPFIX (IP Flow Information eXport), also known as NetFlow version 10. Created in a very flexible way, this MIB module allows all possible configuration options allowed by the Flexible NetFlow CLI options. Therefore, some table entries require up to four indices, increasing the complexity to a point where it is not recommended implementing this MIB module. For the record, the same exercise was performed with a YANG module and produced RFC 6728: Configuration Data Model for the IPFIX and Packet Sampling (PSAMP) Protocols.

- There is a semantic mismatch between the low-level data-oriented abstraction level of MIB modules and the task-oriented abstraction level desired by network operators. Bridging the gap with tools is in principle possible, but in general it is expensive because it requires some serious development and programming efforts.
- MIB modules often lack a description of how the various objects can be used to achieve certain management functions. MIB modules are often characterized as a list of ingredients without a recipe.
- SNMP lacks a way to find out the version of the SNMP MIB modules implemented on the device, let alone a mechanism to get a copy. Accessing the vendor website or calling customer support is a compulsory step.
- The SMI language is hard to deal with and not very practical.
- SNMP traps are used to track state changes, but often syslog messages are considered more useful since they usually contain more information to describe the problem. SNMP traps usually require subsequent SNMP GET operations to figure out what the trap really means.

Note that an IETF effort to fix SMI and SNMP, SMIng (SMI Next Generation),[25] concluded in 2003 without clear results.

Personal Experience

Around 2006, during a CiscoLive show, I enquired about the SNMP usage for configuration. After looking at the Cisco network management products, and after interrogating the network management partners and the customers during my presentations, the conclusions were (again) clear and completely in line with the industry: SNMP is used extensively for monitoring (polling and notifications) but is not used for configuration. The first exception is IP SLA, a protocol that monitors the service level agreement (SLA) parameters such as delay, packet loss, jitter, and so on for IP traffic. Three factors explained this specific IP SLA case:

As a management protocol, IP SLA is naturally configured by a management protocol (SNMP).

The MIB module was always kept in line with the CLI configuration, while in practice most MIB modules have been an afterthought.

Most important, the IP SLA operations are configured on a dedicated device called a shadow router, avoiding the management station to interact with a forwarding traffic device and potentially degrading its performance by enabling too many IP SLA operations.

The second exception was the CISCO-CONFIG-COPY-MIB, an MIB module that facilitates writing of configuration files of an SNMP Agent running Cisco's IOS in the following ways: to and from the network, copying running configurations to startup configurations and vice-versa, and copying a configuration (running or startup) to and from the local IOS file system. —Benoit Claise

In 2014, the Internet Engineering Steering Group (IESG),[26] the IETF group responsible for technical management of IETF activities and the Internet standards process, issued a statement on "Writable MIB modules."[27]

IESG Statement Regarding Writable MIB Modules

"The IESG is aware of discussions in the OPS area and in a number of working groups about the current practice for standards-based approaches to configuration. The OPS area has shown strong support for the use of NETCONF/YANG, while many working groups continue to specify MIB modules for this purpose. The IESG wishes to clarify this situation with this statement:

IETF working groups are therefore encouraged to use the NETCONF/YANG standards for configuration, especially in new charters.

SNMP MIB modules creating and modifying configuration state should only be produced by working groups in cases of clear utility and consensus to use SNMP write operations for configuration, and in consultation with the OPS ADs/MIB doctors."

If not already clear before from the state of the industry, this statement definitively discourages specifying MIB modules for configuration and sets the new direction by pointing to the NETCONF/YANG solution.

NetFlow and IPFIX: Mainly for Flow Records

The first flow-related BoF (Birds of a Feather) took place in London in Summer 2001 during IETF meeting 51. A few months later, the IP Flow Information eXport (IPFIX) working group (WG)[28] was created, with the following chartered goal: "This group will select a protocol by which IP flow information can be transferred in a timely fashion from an 'exporter' to a collection station or stations and define an architecture which employs it. The protocol must run over an IETF-approved congestion-aware transport protocol such as TCP or SCTP." The charter planned for three deliverables: the requirements, the architecture, and the data model. At that time, the intent was to standardize NetFlow, a Cisco proprietary implementation that was already deployed in operator networks. And so it started.

The WG debated for a long time on the requirements for the future IPFIX protocol selection and hence the IPFIX architecture. There were five candidate protocols, with different capabilities, to select from, and each of the candidate proponents were obviously pushing their own protocol. From there, the WG chairs decided that the WG should classify all requirements as "must," "should," "may," and "don't care." RFC 3917, "Requirements for IPFIX," documented this outcome. An independent team, in charge of evaluating the different protocols in light of documented requirements concluded that the goals of the IPFIX WG charter were best served by starting with NetFlow v9, documented in the mean time in the informational RFC 3954.

The next couple of years were dedicated to IPFIX protocol specifications. The WG spent a year or so on transport-related discussions: should you use TCP or Stream Control Transmission Protocol (SCTP) as the congestion-aware transport protocol? Or use UDP, as most operators only cared about UDP when the flow export collection is exclusively within their management domain? On top of that, the distributed function of forwarding ASICs complicate congestion-aware transport requirements such as TCP or SCTP. The final specifications compromised on the following:

"SCTP [RFC4960] using the PR-SCTP extension specified in [RFC3758] MUST be implemented by all compliant implementations. UDP MAY also be implemented by compliant implementations. TCP MAY also be implemented by compliant implementations."

The IPFIX protocol (RFC 5101) and the IPFIX information model (RFC 5102) were finally published in January 2008 as proposed standards. In the end, IPFIX is an improved NetFlow v9 protocol with extra features and requirements such as transport, string variable-length encoding, security, and template withdrawal messages.

The IPFIX WG closed in 2015, with the following results:

- The IPFIX protocol and information model, respectively RFC 7011 and RFC 7012, published as Internet standards
- A series of RFCs regarding IPFIX mediation functions
- Almost 30 IPFIX RFCs[29] in total (architecture, protocol extensions, implementation guidelines, applicability, MIB modules, YANG module, and so on)

From there, theIPFIX community worked on PSAMP (Packet SAMPling),[30] another WG, which selected IPFIX to export packet sampling information, and produced four RFCs.[31] Note: a series of sampled packets is nothing more than a flow record with some specific properties.

NetFlow and IPFIX: Explained

Like for SNMP, there are numerous books, videos, and references explaining NetFlow and IPFIX in details, so this short explanatory section only focuses on the aspects required in this book.

In a nutshell, an IPFIX exporter, which is typically a router, starts by exporting a template record containing the different key fields and non-key fields in the flow record definition. The metering process inside the IPFIX exporter observes some flow records with these key and non-key fields and, after some flow expiration, exports them according to the template record. A key field is a field that makes a flow unique: So if a packet is observed with a (set of) key field value(s) not yet available in the IPFIX cache, a new flow record is created in that cache, as shown in Figure 1-5.

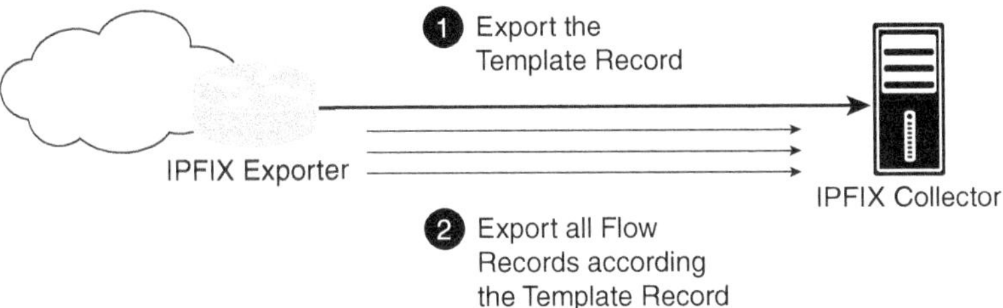

FIGURE 1-5 The IPFIX Basic Model

Figure 1-6 shows a typical flow record, composed of numerous IPFIX information elements, where the flow keys are displayed in grey and the non-key fields in light blue.

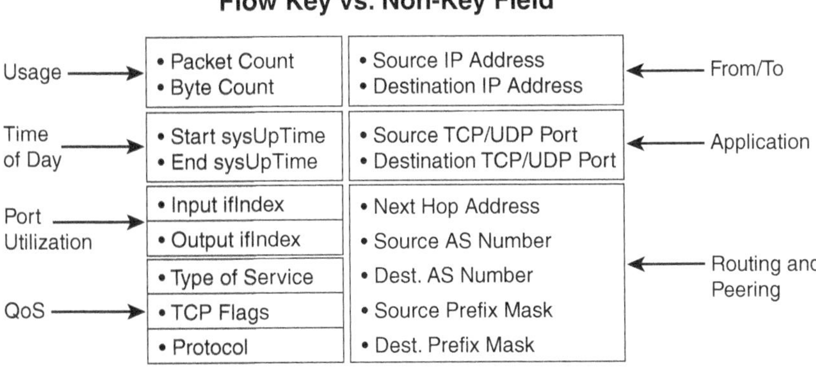

FIGURE 1-6 NetFlow Version 5 Flow Format

The IPFIX information elements are specified by the IETF in an IANA (Internet Assigned Number Authority) registry, or they can be vendor specific. From Figure 1-6, the Packet Count and Input ifIndex are specified, respectively, as shown in Example 1-2.

EXAMPLE 1-2 NetFlow Packet Count and Input IfIndex Specifications

```
packetTotalCount

  Description:
    The total number of incoming packets for this Flow at the
    Observation Point since the Metering Process (re-)initialization
    for this Observation Point.
  Abstract Data Type: unsigned64
  Data Type Semantics: totalCounter
  ElementId: 86
  Status: current
  Units: packets
```

```
ingressInterface

   Description:
      The index of the IP interface where packets of this Flow are
      being received.  The value matches the value of managed object
      'ifIndex' as defined in RFC 2863.  Note that ifIndex values are
      not assigned statically to an interface and that the interfaces
      may be renumbered every time the device's management system is
      re-initialized, as specified in RFC 2863.
   Abstract Data Type: unsigned32
   Data Type Semantics: identifier
   ElementId: 10
   Status: current
   Reference:
      See RFC 2863 for the definition of the ifIndex object.
```

Based on the distinction between data model and information models, covered later on in this chapter, it is debatable whether the IPFIX information model (RFC 7012) and IPFIX information elements should not be called, respectively, IPFIX data model and IPFIX data model elements, as they are directly linked to the implementation details.

NetFlow and IPFIX: Limitations

IPFIX is widely deployed in the world of flow monitoring, for capacity planning, security monitoring, application discovery, or simply for flow-based billing. The flexibility of the Flexible NetFlow metering process offers the ability to select any IPFIX information element as key field or non-key field, thus creating multiple use cases for deploying IPFIX.

The biggest IPFIX limitation is that it only reports flow-related information, even if, in practice, it became a generic export mechanism. Let's play with the IPFIX acronym.

I P F I X

IPFIX was created for IP, but is not limited to IP: It can export more than IP layer information, such as MAC address, MPLS, TCP/UDP ports, applications, and so on.

~~I P~~ F I X

That leaves us with FIX, but from a protocol point of view, nothing prevents us from forwarding non-flow-related information, such as the CPU, for example.

~~F~~ I X

That leaves with us with IX, for "Information eXport," as an acronym for this generic export mechanism.

I X

This proposal was discussed, more to make a point, during one of the IPFIX IETF WG meetings, but the name change was never, rightly, acted upon.

Two other proposals went into that direction of a generic export mechanism:

- RFC 6313 specifies an IPFIX protocol extension to support hierarchical structured data and lists (sequences) of information elements in data records. This extension allows for the definition of complex data structures such as variable-length lists and specification of hierarchical containment relationships between templates. One of initial ideas behind this specification was to export complete firewall rules, along with the blocked flow records.
- RFC 8038 specifies a way to complement IP Flow Information Export (IPFIX) data records with Management Information Base (MIB) objects, avoiding the need to define new IPFIX information elements for existing MIB objects that are already fully specified. One of the initial ideas behind this specification was to export next to the flow record and its QoS class map the class-based QoS counters available in the MIB module.

Those two proposals, created to extend the IPFIX protocol scope, arrived too late after the IPFIX specifications at the time when the interest for IPFIX remains focused on flow-related information. However, those two proposals, initially proposed in 2009 and 2010, were early signs that more automation and data model consolidation in the industry were under way.

Syslog: No Structured Data

Syslog was developed in the 1980s as a mechanism to produce logs of information enabling software subsystems to report and save important error messages either locally or to a remote logging server, as shown in Example 1-3.

EXAMPLE 1-3 Typical Syslog Messages

```
00:00:46: %LINK-3-UPDOWN: Interface Port-channel1, changed state to up
00:00:47: %LINK-3-UPDOWN: Interface GigabitEthernet0/1, changed state to up
00:00:47: %LINK-3-UPDOWN: Interface GigabitEthernet0/2, changed state to up
00:00:48: %LINEPROTO-5-UPDOWN: Line protocol on Interface Vlan1, changed state to
down
00:00:48: %LINEPROTO-5-UPDOWN: Line protocol on Interface GigabitEthernet0/1, changed
state to down 2
*Mar  1 18:46:11: %SYS-5-CONFIG_I: Configured from console by vty2 (10.34.195.36)
18:47:02: %SYS-5-CONFIG_I: Configured from console by vty2 (10.34.195.36)
*Mar  1 18:48:50.483 UTC: %SYS-5-CONFIG_I: Configured from console by vty2
(10.34.195.36)
```

With many implementations, starting with the Unix-like operating systems (with the documentation in the Unix manual pages), syslog became a de facto standard. Years later, the IETF[32] documented this common practice in informational RFC 3164, "The BSD Syslog Protocol."

RFC 5424, "The Syslog Protocol," was standardized in 2009, with the goal to separate message content from message transport while enabling easy extensibility for each layer, and to obsolete RFC 3164. It describes the standard format for syslog messages and outlines the concept of transport mappings. It also describes structured data elements, which are used to transmit easily parseable, structured information, and allows for vendor extensions. Unfortunately, the implementations did not follow the standard publication. As of today, the authors know of only one commercial implementation.

Syslog: Explained

Since RFC 5424 was not adopted by the industry, this section explains the RFC 3164 de facto standard characteristics.

Syslog is a very basic reporting mechanism, composed of plain English text: It does not contain information elements like in IPFIX or variable bindings like in SNMP. Syslog messages are transmitted from the syslog agent (the device under monitoring) to the syslog daemon over UDP, in an unacknowledged way. The syslog header format offers a filtering field, the "facility," and a "level" field that flags the urgency level, from 7 to 0 (debug: 7, information: 6, notification: 5, warning: 4, error: 3, critical: 2, alert: 1, emergency: 0), as perceived by the sender, as shown in Figure 1-7.

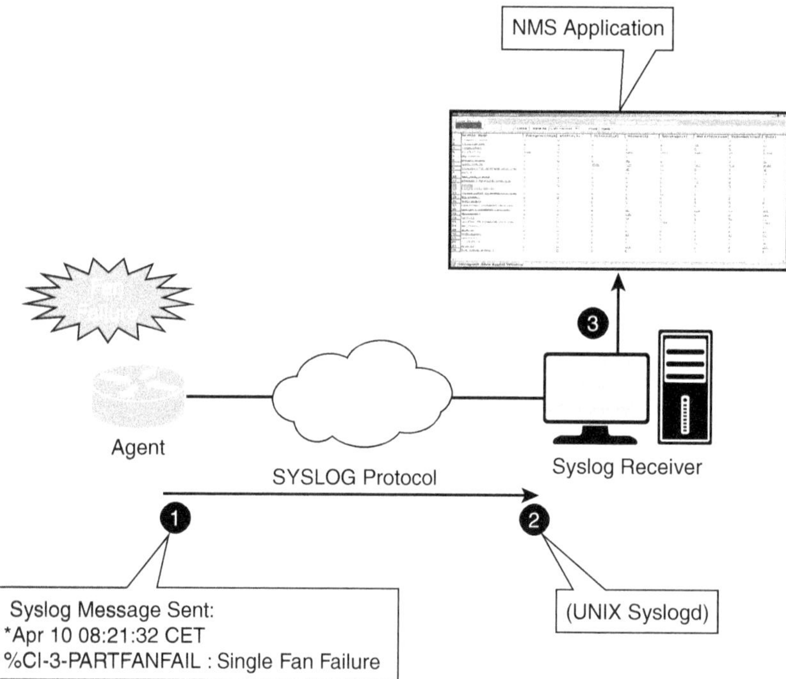

FIGURE 1-7 Syslog Basic Model

Syslog: Limitations

On one side, the syslog message content in plain English text is an advantage for developers, as creating a new syslog message is as easy as printing a US-ASCII string (such as the C language **printf** function). This is also an advantage for network operators who can quickly interpret the readable syslog message. On the other side, this English text freeform content is also the biggest drawback. Except for some basic syslog messages (such as linkUp or linkDown), there is little uniformity in the syslog message content, which prevents automatic processing. To some extent, this prevents human processing, too, if there are many messages. The typical use is to search for keywords, then to read a few entries around that point in time in hopes of understanding what's going on.

Example 1-4 shows the format of Network Address Translation (NAT) information logged for ICMP Ping via NAT Overload configurations.

EXAMPLE 1-4 Syslog Message for NAT for ICMP Ping via NAT Overload Configurations

```
Apr 25 11:51:29 [10.0.19.182.204.28] 1: 00:01:13: NAT:Created icmp
135.135.5.2:7 171 12.106.151.30:7171 54.45.54.45:7171
54.45.54.45:7171
Apr 25 11:52:31 [10.0.19.182.204.28] 8: 00:02:15: NAT:Deleted icmp
135.135.5.2:7 172 12.106.151.30:7172 54.45.54.45:7172
54.45.54.45:7172
```

With a list of four IP address/port pairs, how do you determine which pairs represent the pre- and post-NAT processing, or the inside and outside IP addresses? A syslog daemon cannot make any assumptions based on the syslog message content, and no message processing automation is possible without knowing or assuming the syslog message convention for that device type or at best the device vendor.

Data Modeling Is Key for Automation

This section explores the challenges to managing a network with different protocols and data models.

Before delving into data models, it is important you understand the differences between information models and data models.

The Differences Between Information Models and Data Models

The following is from RFC 3444:

"The main purpose of an information model is to model managed objects at a conceptual level, independent of any specific implementations or protocols used to transport the data. The degree of specificity (or detail) of the abstractions defined in the information model depends on the modeling needs of its designers. In order to make the overall design as clear as possible, an information model should hide all protocol and implementation details. Another important characteristic of an information model is that it defines relationships between managed objects.

Data models, conversely, are defined at a lower level of abstraction and include many details. They are intended for implementors and include protocol-specific constructs.

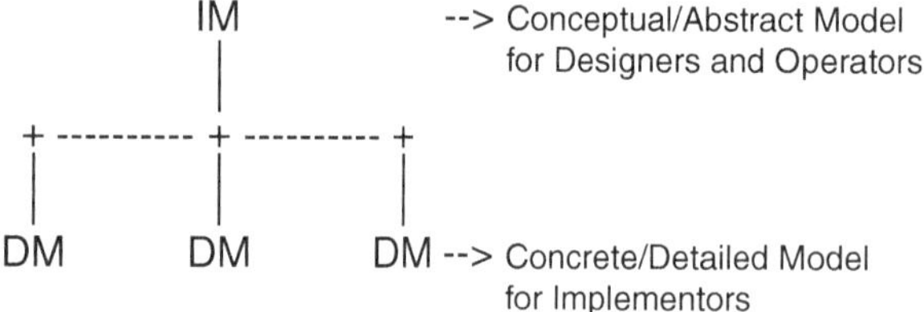

The relationship between an information model (IM) and data model (DM) is shown in the drawing above. Since conceptual models can be implemented in different ways, multiple data models can be derived from a single information model."

"… IMs are primarily useful for designers to describe the managed environment, for operators to understand the modeled objects, and for implementors as a guide to the functionality that must be described and coded in the DMs. The terms 'conceptual models' and 'abstract models,' which are often used in the literature, relate to IMs. IMs can be implemented in different ways and mapped on different protocols. They are protocol neutral.

An important characteristic of Information Models is that they can (and generally should) specify relationships between objects. Organizations may use the contents of an Information Model to delimit the functionality that can be included in a DM."

Information models can be defined in an informal way, using natural languages such as English. Alternatively, information models can be defined using a formal language or a semi-formal structured language. One of the possibilities to formally specify information models is to use class diagrams of the Unified Modeling Language (UML).[33] An important advantage of UML class diagrams is that they represent objects and the relationships between them in a standard graphical way. Because of this graphical representation, designers and operators may find it easier to get an overview of the underlying management model.

Compared to information models, data models define managed objects at a lower level of abstraction. They include implementation- and protocol-specific details (for example, rules that explain how to map managed objects onto lower-level protocol constructs).

Most of the management models standardized to date are data models. Some examples include the following:

- Management Information Base (MIB) modules, specified with SMI.
- Common Information Model (CIM) schemas, developed within the Distributed Management Task Force (DMTF). The DMTF publishes them in two forms: graphical and textual. The graphical forms use UML diagrams and are not normative (because not all details can be represented graphically).

- Taking into account the data model and information model definitions, the authors believe that the IPFIX information model (RFC 7102) should be called a "data model."

Operations engineers need to manage networks as a whole, independent of the use cases or the management protocols. And here is the issue: with different protocols come different data models, and different ways to model the same type of information.

The Challenges of Managing Networks with Different Data Models

As an example used throughout the rest of this section, let's look at the management of the simple "interface" concept, through the different protocols and data models as well as the challenges faced by an NMS.

ifIndex Definition from the The Interfaces Group MIB [RFC 2863]

"A unique value, greater than zero, for each interface. It is recommended that values are assigned contiguously starting from 1. The value for each interface sub-layer must remain constant at least from one re-initialization of the entity's network management system to the next re-initialization."

Figure 1-8 depicts the interfaceIndex in the Interfaces MIB module in RFC 2863, and from the same RFC, Figure 1-9 show the ifEntry, Figure 1-10 show the ifTable, Figure 1-11 shows the ifAdminStatus, and Figure 1-12 shows the ifOperStatus.

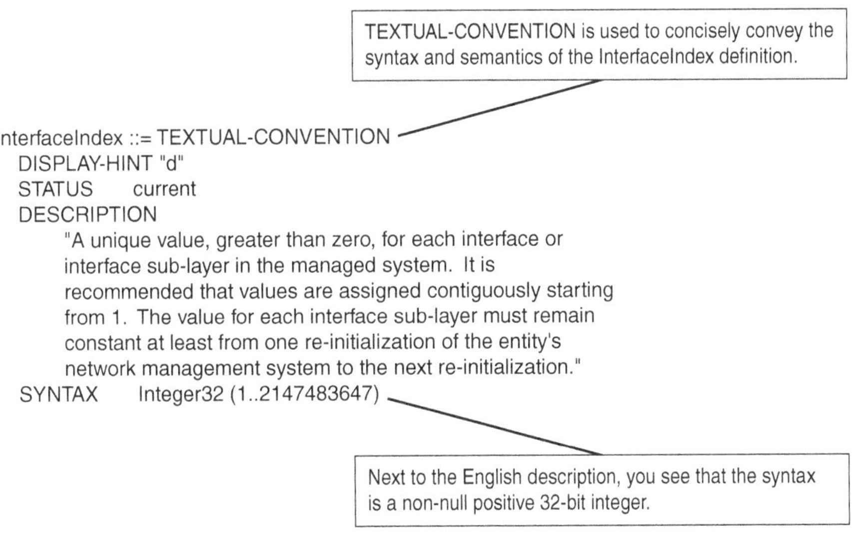
TEXTUAL-CONVENTION is used to concisely convey the syntax and semantics of the InterfaceIndex definition.
InterfaceIndex ::= TEXTUAL-CONVENTION
DISPLAY-HINT "d"
STATUS current
DESCRIPTION
"A unique value, greater than zero, for each interface or
interface sub-layer in the managed system. It is
recommended that values are assigned contiguously starting
from 1. The value for each interface sub-layer must remain
constant at least from one re-initialization of the entity's
network management system to the next re-initialization."
SYNTAX Integer32 (1..2147483647)
Next to the English description, you see that the syntax is a non-null positive 32-bit integer.

FIGURE 1-8 InterfaceIndex in the Interfaces Group MIB Module

```
IfEntry ::=
  SEQUENCE {
    ifIndex            InterfaceIndex,
    ifDescr            DisplayString,
    ifType             IANAifType,
    ifMtu              Integer32,
    ifSpeed            Gauge32,
    ifPhysAddress      PhysAddress,
    ifAdminStatus      INTEGER,
    ifOperStatus       INTEGER,
    ...
  }

ifIndex OBJECT-TYPE
  SYNTAX      InterfaceIndex
  MAX-ACCESS  read-only
  STATUS      current
  DESCRIPTION
      "A unique value, greater than zero, for each interface.  It
      is recommended that values are assigned contiguously
      starting from 1.  The value for each interface sub-layer
      must remain constant at least from one re-initialization of
      the entity's network management system to the next re-
      initialization."
  ::= { ifEntry 1 }
```

Here is the list of the first interface-related objects in the ifTable. Each object is indexed by the ifIndex value, uniquely representing an interface in the managed device.

See the RFC 2863 for the full objects list.

The ifIndex object syntax is specified according to the InterfaceIndex TEXTUAL-CONVENTION previously specified.

FIGURE 1-9 ifEntry in the Interfaces Group MIB Module

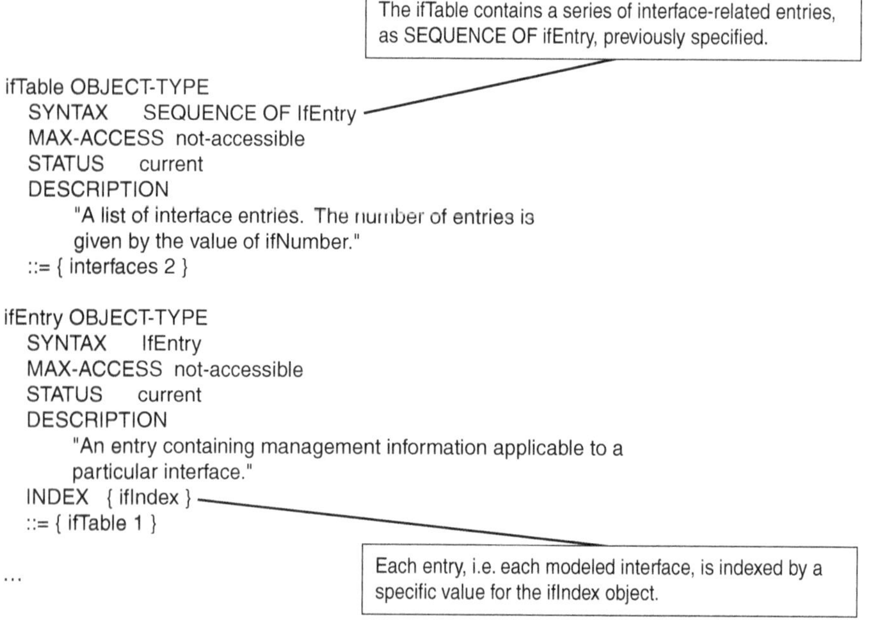

The ifTable contains a series of interface-related entries, as SEQUENCE OF ifEntry, previously specified.

```
ifTable OBJECT-TYPE
  SYNTAX      SEQUENCE OF IfEntry
  MAX-ACCESS  not-accessible
  STATUS      current
  DESCRIPTION
      "A list of interface entries.  The number of entries is
      given by the value of ifNumber."
  ::= { interfaces 2 }

ifEntry OBJECT-TYPE
  SYNTAX      IfEntry
  MAX-ACCESS  not-accessible
  STATUS      current
  DESCRIPTION
      "An entry containing management information applicable to a
      particular interface."
  INDEX   { ifIndex }
  ::= { ifTable 1 }

...
```

Each entry, i.e. each modeled interface, is indexed by a specific value for the ifIndex object.

FIGURE 1-10 ifTable in the Interfaces Group MIB Module

The interface administrative status is set with the ifAdminStatus object, while the corresponding operational status is read with the ifOperStatus object, with the same ifIndex value, as shown in Figure 1-10.

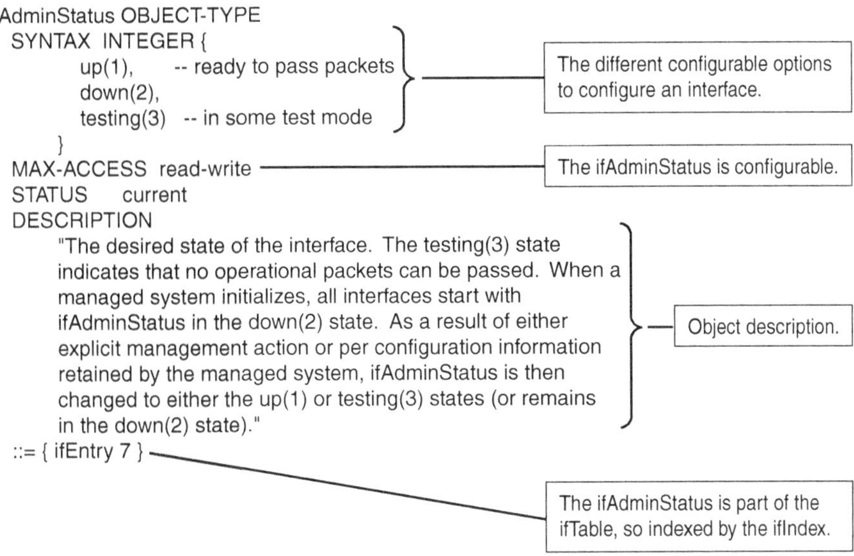

ifAdminStatus OBJECT-TYPE
SYNTAX INTEGER {
up(1), -- ready to pass packets
down(2),
testing(3) -- in some test mode
}
MAX-ACCESS read-write
STATUS current
DESCRIPTION
"The desired state of the interface. The testing(3) state indicates that no operational packets can be passed. When a managed system initializes, all interfaces start with ifAdminStatus in the down(2) state. As a result of either explicit management action or per configuration information retained by the managed system, ifAdminStatus is then changed to either the up(1) or testing(3) states (or remains in the down(2) state)."
::= { ifEntry 7 }
The different configurable options to configure an interface.
The ifAdminStatus is configurable.
Object description.
The ifAdminStatus is part of the ifTable, so indexed by the ifIndex.

FIGURE 1-11 ifAdminStatus in the Interfaces Group MIB Module

```
ifOperStatus OBJECT-TYPE
  SYNTAX  INTEGER {
          up(1),        -- ready to pass packets
          down(2),
          testing(3),   -- in some test mode
          unknown(4),   -- status can not be determined
                        -- for some reason.
          dormant(5),
          notPresent(6),    -- some component is missing
          lowerLayerDown(7) -- down due to state of
                            -- lower-layer interface(s)
      }
  MAX-ACCESS  read-only
  STATUS      current
  DESCRIPTION
      "The current operational state of the interface. The
      testing(3) state indicates that no operational packets can
      be passed. If ifAdminStatus is down(2) then ifOperStatus
      should be down(2). If ifAdminStatus is changed to up(1)
      then ifOperStatus should change to up(1) if the interface is
      ready to transmit and receive network traffic; it should
      change to dormant(5) if the interface is waiting for
      external actions (such as a serial line waiting for an
      incoming connection); it should remain in the down(2) state
      if and only if there is a fault that prevents it from going
      to the up(1) state; it should remain in the notPresent(6)
      state if the interface has missing (typically, hardware)
      components."
  ::= { ifEntry 8 }
```

The different configurable options to configure an interface.

The ifOperStatus is not configurable.

Object description, which mentions the connection between the ifOperStatus and IfAdminStatus.

The ifOperStatus is part of the ifTable, so is indexed by the ifIndex.

FIGURE 1-12 ifOperStatus in the Interfaces Group MIB Module

Notice that the ifOperStatus English description is the only place where there's a connection between the two important objects: the ifAdminStatus to configure the interface state and the ifOperStatus to monitor the effective interface status. That highlights yet another important SNMP drawback: The mapping between the intended and applied status is not deduced automatically by tooling. Careful inspection of the description clauses reveals the information, but this requires extensive knowledge of the MIB content. In turn, this mapping must be hardcoded in the SNMP-based NMS.

Not all interface counters on managed devices are available via MIB modules. As an example, the interface load is not available, as shown in Example 1-5.

EXAMPLE 1-5 Interface Load

```
router# show interfaces
Serial0/2 is up, line protocol is up
  Hardware is GT96K with 56k 4-wire CSU/DSU
  MTU 1500 bytes, BW 56 Kbit, DLY 20000 usec,
     reliability 255/255, txload 1/255, rxload 1/255
  Encapsulation FRAME-RELAY IETF, loopback not set
  Keepalive set (10 sec)
  LMI enq sent  2586870, LMI stat recvd 2586785, LMI upd recvd 0, DTE LMI up
  LMI enq recvd 24, LMI stat sent  0, LMI upd sent  0
  LMI DLCI 0  LMI type is ANSI Annex D  frame relay DTE
  Broadcast queue 0/64, broadcasts sent/dropped 0/0, interface broadcasts 0
  Last input 00:00:05, output 00:00:05, output hang never
  Last clearing of "show interface" counters 42w5d
  Input queue: 0/75/0/13 (size/max/drops/flushes); Total output drops: 0
  Queueing strategy: fifo
  Output queue: 0/40 (size/max)
  5 minute input rate 0 bits/sec, 0 packets/sec
  5 minute output rate 0 bits/sec, 0 packets/sec
     9574781 packets input, 398755727 bytes, 0 no buffer
     Received 0 broadcasts, 0 runts, 0 giants, 0 throttles
     2761 input errors, 2761 CRC, 1120 frame, 624 overrun, 0 ignored, 2250 abort
     9184611 packets output, 289103201 bytes, 0 underruns
     0 output errors, 0 collisions, 195 interface resets
     0 output buffer failures, 0 output buffers swapped out
     668 carrier transitions
     DCD=up  DSR=up  DTR=up  RTS=up  CTS=up
```

In this case, operations engineers must poll multiple objects to deduce the load, as shown in the following snippet:

```
utilization = (ifInOctets + ifOutOctets) * 800 / hour / ifSpeed
```

The alternative is to screen-scrape the value from the **show interfaces** command, with all the "screen scraping" difficulties.

In some other cases, "screen scraping" is the only solution. For example, a Cisco ASR1000 device offers some Cisco QuantumFlow Processor (QFP) counters at the ASIC level: Those counters are not available via MIB modules. So, on top of SNMP, the NMS requires "screen scraping."

Now, let's assume that the same NMS must correlate the SNMP information with the syslog messages—not an easy task! As shown in the "Syslog: Limitations" section earlier in the chapter, the syslog message content in plain English text is basically freeform text. For user consumption, the interface name, as opposed to the ifIndex, is used within interface-related syslog messages, as shown in Example 1-6.

EXAMPLE 1-6 Interface Down Syslog Message

```
*Apr  7 21:45:37.171: %LINK-5-CHANGED: Interface GigabitEthernet0/1, changed state to
administratively down
*Apr  7 21:45:38.171: %LINEPROTO-5-UPDOWN: Line protocol on Interface
GigabitEthernet0/1,
changed state to down
```

Therefore, an NMS must first extract the interface name from the syslog messages—again, not an easy task, as there are no conventions for naming interfaces in the industry. Syslog messages might contain "GigabitEthernet0/1" or "GigE0/1," "GigEth 0/1," or any other variation, which complicates the regular expression search. Once done, the NMS must correlate the interface name with yet another MIB object, the ifName, representing the interface name. This works fine if and only if the managed devices keep the same naming convention for both the ifName and the syslog messages, which is not a given. The NMS becomes complex when dealing with different protocols and data models, starting with MIB, CLI, and syslog messages.

Now, let's assume that the same NMS, to combine flow-related use cases, must integrate the NetFlow or IPFIX flow records information. That NMS application needs to map yet a different data model: the NetFlow/IPFIX one. While specifying the IPFIX information elements, the designers carefully aligned the IPFIX definition with the ifIndex MIB value. However, the Interfaces Group MIB module does not specify the notion of direction as an interface attribute. Instead, the octet counters in the ifTable aggregate octet counts for unicast and non-unicast packets into a single octet counter per direction (received/transmitted). IPFIX, on the other hand, needs the notion of an interface direction: Are the flow records observed on an ingress or egress interface? That slightly different semantic in interface definition has led to two distinct IPFIX information elements, as opposed to the unique ifIndex object in the SNMP world. The two IPFIX information elements, as specified in the IANA registry,[34] are the ingressInterface and the egressInterface, as shown in Example 1-7.

EXAMPLE 1-7 ingressInterface and egressInterface IPFIX Definitions

```
ingressInterface

  Description:
    The index of the IP interface where packets of this Flow are being
    received.  The value matches the value of managed object 'ifIndex'
```

```
      as defined in RFC 2863.  Note that ifIndex values are not assigned
      statically to an interface and that the interfaces may be
      renumbered every time the device's management system is
      re-initialized, as specified in RFC 2863.
   Abstract Data Type: unsigned32
   Data Type Semantics: identifier
   ElementId: 10
   Status: current
   Reference:
      See RFC 2863 for the definition of the ifIndex object.

egressInterface

   Description:
      The index of the IP interface where packets of this Flow are being
      sent.  The value matches the value of managed object 'ifIndex' as
      defined in RFC 2863.  Note that ifIndex values are not assigned
      statically to an interface and that the interfaces may be
      renumbered every time the device's management system is
      re-initialized, as specified in RFC 2863.
   Abstract Data Type: unsigned32
   Data Type Semantics: identifier
   ElementId: 14
   Status: current
   Reference:
      See RFC 2863 for the definition of the ifIndex object.
```

An NMS mapping IPFIX flow records with MIB objects must hardcode this MIB-object-versus-IPFIX-information-elements mapping.

Now, in the AAA (Authorization, Authentication, and Accounting) world, the interface is again modeled differently. In the AAA world, the port represents the interface on which a user tries to authenticate. In the RADIUS (Remote Authentication Dial In User Service) protocol (RFC 2865), the interface notion is specified as the "NAS-Port,"[35] as shown in Example 1-8.

EXAMPLE 1-8 RADIUS NAS-Port Interface Definition

```
NAS-Port

   Description

      This Attribute indicates the physical port number of the NAS which
      is authenticating the user.  It is only used in Access-Request
      packets.  Note that this is using "port" in its sense of a
      physical connection on the NAS, not in the sense of a TCP or UDP
```

```
   port number.  Either NAS-Port or NAS-Port-Type (61) or both SHOULD
   be present in an Access-Request packet, if the NAS differentiates
   among its ports.


A summary of the NAS-Port Attribute format is shown below.  The
fields are transmitted from left to right.

 0                   1                   2                   3
 0 1 2 3 4 5 6 7 8 9 0 1 2 3 4 5 6 7 8 9 0 1 2 3 4 5 6 7 8 9 0 1
+-+-+-+-+-+-+-+-+-+-+-+-+-+-+-+-+-+-+-+-+-+-+-+-+-+-+-+-+-+-+-+-+
|     Type      |    Length     |             Value
+-+-+-+-+-+-+-+-+-+-+-+-+-+-+-+-+-+-+-+-+-+-+-+-+-+-+-+-+-+-+-+-+
          Value (cont)          |
+-+-+-+-+-+-+-+-+-+-+-+-+-+-+-+-+

Type

   5 for NAS-Port.

Length

   6

Value

   The Value field is four octets.
```

In TACACS+ (Terminal Access Controller Access-Control System Plus),[36] the interface is again modeled differently, as shown in Example 1-9.

EXAMPLE 1-9 TACACS+ port and port_len Interface Definition

```
port, port_len

The US-ASCII name of the client port on which the authentication is
taking place, and its length in bytes.  The value of this field is
client specific.  (For example, Cisco uses "tty10" to denote the
tenth tty line and "Async10" to denote the tenth async interface).
The port_len indicates the length of the port field, in bytes.
```

The NMS wanting to integrate the authentication, authorization, and accounting with the MIB and IPFIX world must hardcode the data model mapping and the semantic mapping.

This example of an NMS that must integrate information from MIB modules, CLI, syslog messages, NetFlow and IPFIX, and AAA protocols such as RADIUS and TACACS+ shows the basic difficulties of dealing with different data models, which obviously don't use the same syntax and semantics. Even for a basic "interface" concept, which is well know from an information model point of view, this leads to much implementation complexity for the NMS. Figure 1-13 is a summary of the interface definition for the different data models used in this example, minus the CLI, which might not have a data model.

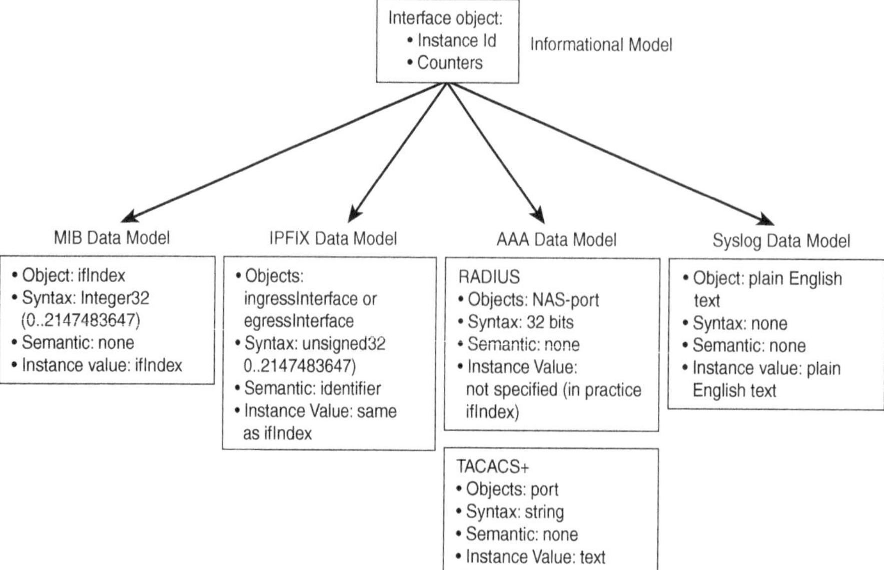

FIGURE 1-13 Interface Object Information Model and Related Data Models

In these different trends, you have seen that the CLI is no longer the norm. Software-defined networking and DevOps need clear APIs with well-known semantics and consistent syntax. This leads to the era of data model–driven management. In fact, intent-based networking is extremely difficult, if not impractical and impossible, without a consistent data model to work from. To go one step further, machine learning, yet another important trend in the coming years, will simply be impossible without the right foundation—data models that can present consistent information, both from a syntax and semantic point of view, as input to machine learning.

Interview with the Experts

Q&A with Victor Kuarsing

Victor Kuarsing is co-chair of the IETF's Link State Vector Routing working group and a longstanding contributor focused on operational input into the standards development process. He is a technical and organizational leader at Oracle Cloud, where he contributes to the architecture and deployment of next-generation networks and systems. Throughout his career, Victor has been focused on building large-scale and specialized networks and platforms. His current focus is on the cloud networking space, ensuring that systems are modernized and meet the ever-changing demands of rapidly evolving services and customer expectations.

Question:

Victor, as a director of networking engineering and data center operations at Oracle and as an active participant in the IETF, which trends do you see in the industry (both in networking and the data center) and how do they affect your business?

Answer:

When we look at how networks were built years ago, there has been a fundamental shift in how we approach modern network designs and deployments. Historically, networks were built in a manner indicative of an operational model, where the network administrator interacted with the system to a high degree. Whether the administrator was deploying systems, modifying systems, or managing systems, it was typically via a command-line interface. The historical model we used served us quite well given the relative size and complexity of the network systems we had built. The early model, either directly or indirectly, resulted in a configuration pattern that lent itself and was optimized for human interaction. For example, if a designer or administrator was attempting to build complex policies, such as one would do with a peering router using BGP toward peers, it was crafted in a manner that minimized the amount of configuration syntax to aid in readability.

Early networks not only were optimized for user interaction, they were also, in general, simpler and smaller compared to some of the networks we build today. Earlier networks were often deployed on a per-service basis (less service aggregation) and did not require as much integration of services. When we look at today's networks, the level of complexity in many environments has increased. In other networks, even if simplicity can be achieved, such as pushing complexity to a network or service overlay, the scale of newer networks drastically exceeds what we built years ago. Data centers are getting larger, backbone networks aggregate more functions and services, and access networks grow more vast and complex.

To meet the demands brought on by larger and often more complex environments, we have shifted how we approach network design. Networks can no longer, in most cases, be designed with a fully interactive model expected for deployment and management. Designs now are focused on having software interact with the underlying infrastructure. This change in focus shifts how we then structure configuration. Compression of configuration stanzas doesn't supply inherit benefits in a mode of operation where software is used to deploy systems, detect anomalies, and make changes. Configuration structures that lend themselves to logic patterns that can interact with systems play an increasingly critical role in modern designs.

Scale and complexity are not the only reasons for the shift in how we build and manage networks and supporting systems. Modern expectations on service delivery now demand that new functions be deployed into the network at an accelerated rate. We need to deploy, fix, and alter the network at rates that just cannot be achieved by a user manually interacting with a system. Software is used to achieve fast and efficient interaction with the network. An additional byproduct of this newer model, and one of the early drivers of automation, is deployment quality. Manual user interaction lends itself to errors and variation in how networks are configured. The focus on templates and configuration structures during the design phase allows for consistent configuration deployment and empirically has shown vast improvements in build quality (fewer errors).

The shift in how we build networks has also changed hiring needs and practices in many places. The shift to these modern build and management patterns is not consistent everywhere, and each industry segment will see the change at a different rate. However, the basic needs of a modern network designer and operator are not focused on jockeying a router but rather building and working with software that interacts with the system as a whole. As a hiring manager, it's becoming increasingly hard to find multidomain expertise in network engineers who are also competent in software design and use. The software skills are becoming increasingly more important, and how far the pendulum shifts towards a pure developer is not yet known.

In terms of how to build for automation, there are many historical, and now modern, options. Years ago, we built scripts that would screen-scrape the CLI and apply configuration as needed. Although this worked well, it was limiting in how it could be used, and it varied by vendor, making reuse of any automation difficult and onerous. Today, we have a strong movement toward more standardized ways to apply configuration to devices, and we have models we can use to represent intended configuration. NETCONF and YANG represent a pair of options to help achieve consistent and standard ways to build and apply configuration for network elements. Whether one chooses to use these methods and tools or chooses other options, they are needed, not for technological purity, but to achieve the business goal of automated network configuration and management. We need automation tools and protocols like this to help us achieve the goals of making networks bigger, changing them faster, and improving the consistency of how we deploy and change them.

Q&A with Russ White

Russ White began working with computers in the mid-1980s and computer networks in 1990. He has experience in designing, deploying, breaking, and troubleshooting large-scale networks, and he's a strong communicator from the white board to the board room. Across that time, he has co-authored more than 40 software patents, participated in the development of several Internet standards, helped develop the CCDE and the CCAr, and has worked in Internet governance with the Internet Society. Russ has a background covering a broad spectrum of topics, including radio frequency engineering and graphic design, and is an active student of philosophy and culture.

Russ is a co-host at the Network Collective, serves on the Routing Area Directorate at the IETF, co-chairs the BABEL working group, serves on the Technical Services Council as a maintainer on the open source FR Routing project, and serves on the Linux Foundation (Networking) board. His most recent works are *Computer Networking Problems and Solutions*, *The Art of Network Architecture*, *Navigating Network Complexity*, and *Intermediate System to Intermediate System LiveLesson*.

Question:

Russ, you have been a renowned network architect for many years now. How have network architecture and network management been evolving? What are your biggest issues and how do you solve them?

Answer:

When I started in network engineering, the big problems were around managing multiprotocol networks and choosing the best set of protocols to cope with constrained resources. The networking world has changed in many ways, but interestingly enough, it hasn't changed in many others. The multiprotocol problem has crept up the stack and become a virtualization problem, and the constrained resources problem has crept up the stack to become a virtualization problem (intentionally constraining resources, rather than managing constrained resources). Architecturally, the "holy grail" of networking has always been "the network that runs itself," while the "holy grail" of network engineers has always been to be able to solve every problem with a bit of duct tape and a nerd knob, and never say "no" to a request, no matter how outlandish.

The solution is often to "throw network management at the problem," in an attempt to make a very complex network very easy to run—often in the form of automation of simple and routine tasks. Network management, and network automation in particular, is at the intersection of various competing interests.

In the last few years, the seeds of a new way of looking at networks have been sown: rethinking the structure of networks, control planes, and the relationship between hardware and software. These seeds have led to an explosion of new ideas and concepts, including software-defined networks (SDNs), cloud-based systems, and even serverless systems. The most obvious result has been the decline of the command-line interface (CLI) as the normal way to interact with network devices, and a movement toward "native automation" forms of network management and control.

How will these things change network architecture, and with it, network automation?

To begin, the networking world will ultimately split into a larger part and a smaller one. The larger part will be composed of organizations that consider the network a cost center, or like the plumbing in their buildings. The network, and information technology in general, is necessary, but it is not treated as a source of advantage. This set of organizations will want simple-to-manage networks. These networks will be "rip and replace" affairs, purchased at some cost, but then replaced when they are no longer effective. The network itself will be seen as a "unit," a "single thing," or even a hidden component of a larger system. This is the world of both on- and off-premises cloud computing, for instance, or serverless. Here, the role of network automation is obvious—from reducing the time spent in day-to-day management, to standing up new networks as quickly as possible. The network needs to be automated to become essentially invisible.

The smaller part will consist of companies that find enough value in information—as information—to put at least some focus into the realm of managing that information in a way that provides some form of business advantage. These organizations will disaggregate their networks in many different ways, exploring different options for driving value and increasing their ROI. The network will be part of a larger system that is seen as a source of value, rather than as a source of costs. Rather than minimizing costs, the idea will be to maximize value. In these organizations, the point of network automation will be to make the network transparent in making the network visible, for the only way to drive value out of information is by handling information quickly and correctly, and the only way to handle information quickly and correctly is to measure how information is being handled in detail.

Whatever path an organization takes, network automation is going to interact with network architecture in more important and interesting ways than it has in the past. And in both cases, management and architecture interact in this way: Things that are simpler are easier to manage, and networks should be built as simple as possible, and not one bit simpler.

Summary

This chapter analyzed some of trends in the networking industry. The most relevant trend in this book is that everything that can be automated in networking *must* be automated, with the end goal of reducing the service deployment time and offering differentiated services compared to the competition. As a matter of fact, due to the ever-increasing frequency and the complexity of changes in networks, it has become humanly impossible deal with the CLI. Therefore, some operators rightly assert nowadays that if a feature cannot be automated, it does not exist. That has led to the development of APIs to monitor and configure the network elements directly—and thus the full automation story. One way to execute on this automation story points to DevOps, a software engineering practice that aims to unify the software development and software operations.

The SDN discussions introduced the concept of the separation of the control and data plane entities, with a focus on OpenFlow as the open standard for configuring the data plane. Throughout the years, the notion of SDN has been evolving. OpenFlow, as a fundamental packet-forwarding paradigm, was actually an enabler, one that reinforced the need for more and easier network programmability.

On top of this automation and programmability shift, there is a growing tendency in the industry to disaggregate the software from the hardware, starting with the data center operation. The end goal is to be able to assemble white boxes as unified hardware, with Linux as the operating system and specific applications for the different networking functions. With this trend, network and server engineers can now focus on more business-oriented tasks as opposed to simply network operation and maintenance. For example, they can now focus on the network function virtualization definitions and deployments, most likely in a cloud environment, following the elastic cloud "pay as you grow" principle.

This chapter stressed the need for data model–driven management several times, which builds on the idea of specifying the semantics, the syntax, the structure, and the constraints of management objects in models, regardless of whether the models are used for configuration, for monitoring operational data, or for telemetry, APIs are generated from those models via tooling. The limitations of the existing management practices were also reviewed in this chapter. First off, the CLI, which is not an API, then SNMP, which is not used for configuring, followed by NetFlow, which only focuses on flow records, and finally, syslog, which doesn't have any consistent syntax and semantics.

The final part of the chapter illustrated the challenges of managing networks with different data models with a hypothetical NMS dealing with the basic "interface" concept. Those challenges reinforced the requirement that the worlds of software-defined networking and DevOps need clear APIs with well-known semantics and consistent syntax. In the end, automation via APIs is the only way to provide holistic, intent-based networking, where networks constantly learn and adapt, and is the proper foundation for machine learning.

References in This Chapter

This chapter is by no means a complete analysis of the trends in the industry, as the industry keeps evolving (faster and faster). Table 1-2 lists some documents you may find interesting to read.

TABLE 1-2 YANG-Related Documents for Further Reading

Topic	Content
RFC 3535	http://tools.ietf.org/html/rfc3535 Operator requirements in terms of network management; still valid today
RFC 3444	http://tools.ietf.org/html/rfc3444 The difference between information models and data models
SNMP Set: Can it be saved?	https://www.simple-times.org/pub/simple-times/issues/9-1.html#introduction Andy Bierman, *The Simple Times*, Volume 9.

Endnotes

1. https://www.itu.int/en/Pages/default.aspx
2. https://datatracker.ietf.org/wg/sfc/about/
3. http://expect.sourceforge.net/
4. https://sourceforge.net/projects/tcl/
5. https://www.sdxcentral.com/listings/stanford-clean-slate-program/
6. https://www.slideshare.net/martin_casado/sdn-abstractions
7. https://pypi.org/project/paramiko/
8. https://www.ansible.com/
9. https://puppet.com/
10. https://www.chef.io/
11. https://www.coursera.org/learn/interactive-python-1
12. https://www.coursera.org/

13. https://www.youtube.com/watch?v=Xl3gAvCKN44

14. https://www.iana.org/assignments/ipfix/ipfix.xhtml

15. https://www.opennetworking.org/

16. https://en.wikipedia.org/wiki/OpenDaylight_Project

17. https://www.safaribooksonline.com/library/view/sdn-software-defined/9781449342425/

18. http://info.tail-f.com/hubfs/Whitepapers/Whitepaper_Tail-f%20VNF%20Management.pdf?submissionGuid=7ac7486e-124f-484c-8526-9b34dbdcbeb1

19. https://www.yangcatalog.org/

20. https://docs.oasis-open.org/tosca/TOSCA-Simple-Profile-YAML/v1.1/TOSCA-Simple-Profile-YAML-v1.1.html

21. https://www.python.org/dev/peps/pep-0008/

22. https://www.cisco.com/c/en/us/td/docs/ios-xml/ios/prog/configuration/166/b_166_programmability_cg/model_driven_telemetry.html

23. https://www.wsj.com/articles/SB10001424053111903480904576512250915629460?ns=prod/accounts-wsj

24. https://ris.utwente.nl/ws/portalfiles/portal/6962053/Editorial-vol9-num1.pdf

25. https://datatracker.ietf.org/wg/sming/about/

26. https://www.ietf.org/about/groups/iesg/

27. https://www.ietf.org/iesg/statement/writable-mib-module.html

28. https://datatracker.ietf.org/wg/ipfix/charter/

29. http://datatracker.ietf.org/wg/ipfix/documents/

30. http://datatracker.ietf.org/wg/psamp/charter/

31. http://datatracker.ietf.org/wg/psamp/documents/

32. https://www.ietf.org/

33. https://www.omg.org/spec/UML/

34. https://www.iana.org/assignments/ipfix/ipfix.xhtml

35. https://tools.ietf.org/html/rfc2865#section-5.5

36. https://datatracker.ietf.org/doc/draft-ietf-opsawg-tacacs/

Chapter 2

Data Model–Driven Management

This chapter covers

- The operator requirements, leading to the NETCONF and YANG specifications
- YANG as a data modeling language
- The data model properties and types
- The different encodings (XML, JSON, and so on) and protocols (NETCONF, RESTCONF, and so on)
- The server and client architecture
- The datastore concept
- Code rendering from data model–driven management
- A real-life service scenario, putting all the pieces together

This chapter describes the architecture behind data model–driven management and covers high-level concepts with a minimum of technical detail. Occasionally, specific points are made or examples are given that contain concepts that have not yet been explained. Don't fret. Chapter 3, "YANG Explained," and Chapter 4, "NETCONF, RESTCONF, and gNMI Explained," clarify it all. At the end of the chapter, you will understand the data model–driven management reference model and how all the different building blocks fit together.

The Beginning: A New Set of Requirements

During a workshop organized in 2002 between network operators and protocol developers, the operators voiced their opinion that the developments in IETF did not really address the requirements for network management. The "Overview of the 2002 IAB Network Management Workshop" (RFC 3535) documented the outcomes of this dialog to guide the IETF focus on future work regarding network management.

The workshop identified a list of relevant technologies (available or under active development) with their strengths and weaknesses. Among others, Simple Network Management Protocol (SNMP) and the command-line interface (CLI) were covered. As mentioned in Chapter 1, "The Network Management World Must Change: Why Should You Care?", the SNMP protocol is not well adapted to be used for configuration but is well suited for monitoring, whereas the CLI is a very fragile application programming interface (API). Since no published material at the time clearly documented the collective requirements of the operators, they were asked to identify their needs not sufficiently addressed in standards. The results produced during the breakout session resulted in the following list of operator requirements (quoted from RFC 3535):

Operator Requirements, quoted from the "Overview of the 2002 IAB Network Management Workshop" [RFC3535]

1. Ease of use is a key requirement for any network management technology from the operators' point of view.
2. It is necessary to make a clear distinction between configuration data, data that describes operational state, and statistics. Some devices make it very hard to determine which parameters were administratively configured and which were obtained via other mechanisms such as routing protocols.
3. It is required to be able to fetch separately configuration data, operational state data, and statistics from devices, and to be able to compare these between devices.
4. It is necessary to enable operators to concentrate on the configuration of the network as a whole rather than individual devices.
5. Support for configuration transactions across a number of devices would significantly simplify network configuration management.
6. Given configuration A and configuration B, it should be possible to generate the operations necessary to get from A to B with minimal state changes and effects on network and systems. It is important to minimize the impact caused by configuration changes.
7. A mechanism to dump and restore configurations is a primitive operation needed by operators. Standards for pulling and pushing configurations from/to devices are desirable.
8. It must be easy to do consistency checks of configurations over time and between the ends of a link in order to determine the changes between two configurations and whether those configurations are consistent.
9. Network-wide configurations are typically stored in central master databases and transformed into formats that can be pushed to devices, either by generating sequences of CLI commands or complete configuration files that are pushed to devices. There is no common database schema for network configuration, although the models used by various operators are probably very similar. It is desirable to extract, document, and standardize the common parts of these network-wide configuration database schemas.

10. It is highly desirable that text processing tools such as diff, and version management tools such as RCS or CVS, can be used to process configurations, which implies that devices should not arbitrarily reorder data such as access control lists.
11. The granularity of access control needed on management interfaces needs to match operational needs. Typical requirements are a role-based access control model and the principle of least privilege, where a user can be given only the minimum access necessary to perform a required task.
12. It must be possible to do consistency checks of access control lists across devices.
13. It is important to distinguish between the distribution of configurations and the activation of a certain configuration. Devices should be able to hold multiple configurations.
14. SNMP access control is data oriented, while CLI access control is usually command (task) oriented. Depending on the management function, sometimes data-oriented or task-oriented access control makes more sense. As such, it is a requirement to support both data-oriented and task-oriented access control.

The output of this workshop focused on current problems. The observations were reasonable and straightforward, including the need for transactions, rollback, low implementation costs, and the ability to save and restore the device's configuration data. Many of the observations give insight into the problems operators were having with existing network management solutions, such as the lack of full coverage of device capabilities and the ability to distinguish between configuration data and other types of data.

Some of the requirements outlined by the operators include ease of use for any new management system. This ease of use includes the ability to manage a network as a whole and not just a device in the network. In addition, there should be a clear distinction between a device's configuration state, operational state, and statistics information. The configuration state is everything explicitly configured (for example, IP addresses assigned manually to network interfaces), the operational state is the state learned from interaction with other devices (for example, an IP address obtained from a Dynamic Host Configuration Protocol [DHCP] server), and the statistics are the usage and error counters obtained by the device. Furthermore, the requirements mention that it should also be possible to stage a configuration, to validate it before committing, and to roll back the previous configuration in case of failure.

It is important to note that, even though this document dates from 2003, its requirements and recommendations are still very valid. Every protocol designer involved in automation should read this document—and even re-read it on a regular basis. This is the primary reason for including the preceding 14 requirements in this book.

Based on those operator requirements, the NETCONF working group[1] was formed the same year and the NETwork CONFiguration (NETCONF) protocol was created. This protocol defines a simple mechanism where network management applications, acting as clients, can invoke operations on the devices, which act as servers. The NETCONF specification (RFC 4741) defines a small set of operations but goes out of its way to avoid making any requirements on the data carried in those operations, preferring to allow the protocol to carry any data. This "data model agnostic" approach allows data models to be defined independently.

Lacking a means of defining data models, the NETCONF protocol was not usable for standards-based work. Existing data modeling languages such as the XML Schema Definition (XSD) [https://tools.ietf.org/html/rfc6244#ref-W3CXSD][2] and the Document Schema Definition Languages (DSDL; ISODSDL)[3] were considered but were rejected because of the problem of domains having little natural overlap. Defining a data model or protocol that is encoded in XML is a distinct problem from defining an XML document. The use of NETCONF operations places requirements on the data content that are not shared with the static document problem domain addressed by schema languages like XSD and RELAX NG.

In 2007 and 2008, the issue of a data modeling language for NETCONF was discussed in the IETF Operations and Management area as well as in the Application area. Consequently, the NETMOD working group[4] was formed. Initially named after "NETCONF modeling," since NETCONF was the initial protocol to operate YANG-based devices, a recent charter update modified it to "Network modeling" to stress the fact that multiple protocols can make use of YANG modules these days.

Considering that the operators' requirements are now 15 years old, it might seem like a long time for the data model–driven management paradigm to take off. This is a fair point, but it is important to observe that new management protocols take longer to adopt and deploy compared to nonmanagement protocols. As an example, specifying a new routing protocol (segment routing comes to mind)[5] and deploying it in production may take a couple of years, but for management protocols (IPFIX[6] or NETCONF comes to mind), the lifecycle is longer—up to 10 years. The reason is simple: The new management protocols must ideally be supported on all devices, old and new, as a prerequisite before the new network management systems start transitioning to the new management paradigm. However, these days, data model–driven management based on YANG/NETCONF is a well-established trend in the industry.

Network Management Is Dead, Long Live Network Management

Personal Experience

During my full-day interviews for a position with Cisco (a long time ago), the situation looked promising: Around noon, the Cisco representatives told me, "Good profile. Good protocol knowledge. We envision for you a position as TAC Customer Support Engineer in the Wide Area Network team." Then they were puzzled by my polite but firm answer: "Thanks, but no thanks: I would prefer to spend my career in network management." They were perplexed! I could see it in their eyes: "We found a crazy one!" They changed the interview schedules for the afternoon to meet up with some other crazy ones in the network management team. At the end of day, I signed my contract.

Let's face it: Network management was always treated as… special. On one side, network management was always a necessary activity. Sure, the operation team must manage the network.

On the other side, network management was an afterthought (that is, a post-sales activity). Years ago, who would have contacted the operations team to understand their needs at the time of buying networking equipment anyway? Fifteen years ago, network management was not considered "leading edge" and was not really glorious. In an industry where routing was the key technology, my routing guru (in the IT world, guru is a term often associated with routing, and rarely with network management, reflecting the relative job importance of networking) friends were teasing me: "What are you doing in network management?" What they were actually saying was, "Don't you want to work on something more interesting and fun?" The recurrent existential question, "Should network management be profitable or should it be a sales enabler? (we sell networking and provide the NMS products for free)," added to the "special" character of the beast.

Enough said about the past, let's focus on the present! —Benoit Claise

A fundamental shift started in the industry some years ago: A transition from network operators managing the network to operations engineers automating the network. This transition resulted from the combination of multiple trends, as discussed in Chapter 1. These included the multiplication of the number of devices in the network, the increased number of network management configuration transactions per second (with the strong desire to lower the operational expenditure [OpEx]), the shift to virtualization, faster and faster services deployments, a new licensing model on a pay-per-usage basis—and maybe simply the realization that network management is essential to conduct business.

This transition brought the world of operations and development closer together. New buzzwords appeared: controller, DevOps, network programmability, management plane, network APIs, and so on. And new initiatives blossomed:

- Some in the open source world, such as OpenFlow,[7] OpenStack,[8] OpenDaylight,[9] Open Vswitch,[10] and OpenConfig[11]
- Some in the research community, such as mapping the Unified Modeling Language (UML)[12] to YANG
- Some in standards organizations, such as the NETCONF and NETMOD working groups at the IETF, where some of the core building blocks for data model–driven management are specified

Interestingly, this new sandbox attracted many nontraditional, so-called network management people. Some came with a development background, some came from different technology areas, and some just surfed the wave. In the end, this was a good thing! For quite some time we were thinking of telling those people that their jobs were actually network management related. Although this was certainly the case, we didn't want scare them away by labeling their new job with old-school terminology: network management. However, having an automation-related job is certainly cool these days. Therefore, to respect people's sensibilities, a slightly less provocative section title would be "Network Management Is Dead, Long Live Automation," or even "Network Management Is Dead, Long Live DevOps."

Humor aside, the point is that the industry changed. It is common sense today to include security in all aspects of networking: from simply paying attention to the web server file permissions, to moving a web server to the secure Hypertext Transfer Protocol (HTTPS), to the full authentication and authorization mechanisms, and finally to the "let's encrypt everything" paradigm. The industry slowly but surely will reach this point for automation. As mentioned already, some operators rightly assert nowadays, "If a feature cannot be automated, it does not exist." Therefore, let's assert that the coming years will be the years of automation.

YANG: The Data Modeling Language

YANG has been mentioned numerous times so far, but what is it exactly? YANG is an API contract language. This means that you can use YANG to write a specification for what the interface between a client and server should be on a particular topic, as shown in Figure 2-1. A specification written in YANG is referred to as a "YANG module," and a set of YANG modules are collectively often called a "YANG model." A YANG model typically focuses on the data that a client manipulates and observes using standardized operations, with a few actions and notifications sprinkled in. Note that, in the NETCONF and RESTCONF terms, the controller is the *client* and the network elements are the *server*, as the controller initiates the configuration session. It's interesting to note that YANG is not an acronym—at least, it's never expanded or referenced as an acronym in any documentation. However, there is a special meaning behind the term, as a kind of joke. Indeed, it stems from Yet Another Next Gen (data modeling language).

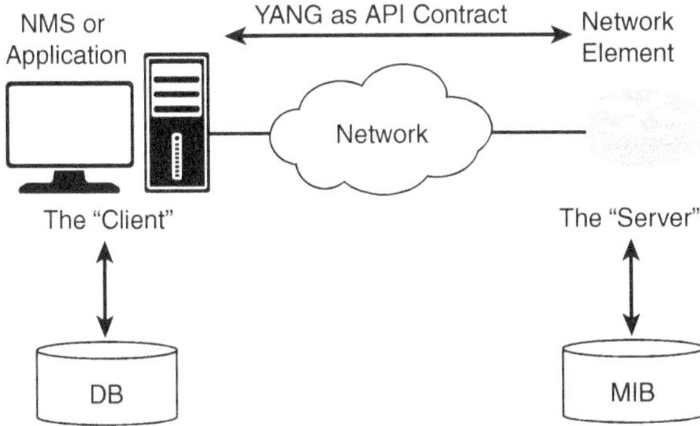

FIGURE 2-1 The Basic Model

Say you are designing the next cool server application. This application may or may not have some sort of interface for ordinary users, but it will almost certainly have a management interface, which the owner of the application can use to administrate and monitor the application. Obviously, this administrative interface needs to have a clear and concise API.

A YANG-based server publishes a set of YANG modules, which taken together form the system's YANG model. These YANG modules declare what a client can do. The four areas listed next are the same for all applications, but the specific data and operations will vary. For the sake of clarity, let's say that the application is a router. Other applications might have wildly different kinds of data and operations—it all comes down to what the YANG model contains.

- **Configure**: For example, decide where the log files are stored, state which speed a network interface uses, and declare whether a particular routing protocol is disabled or enabled, and if so, which peers it will have.
- **Monitor status**: For example, read how many lost packets there are on each network interface, check what the fan speeds are, and list which peers are actually alive in the network.
- **Receive notifications**: For example, hear that a virtual machine is now ready for work, be warned of the temperature crossing a configured threshold, or be alerted of repeated login failures.
- **Invoke actions**: For example, reset the lost packet counters, run a traceroute from the system to some address, or execute a system reboot.

As the author of the next cool application, it is up to you to decide what goes in the YANG module for your application. In the context of YANG, the application is an abstract service, such as a Layer 3 virtual private network (L3VPN) or access control service. Those applications often use networking devices, such as a router, load balancer, and base station controller. They could equally well be devices from other domains, such as a power distribution grid controller, a warehouse robot control system, and an office building control system. What else goes in your YANG module? In collaboration with the application operations engineer, you are perhaps able to select which authentication mechanism the application will use and where the authentication server sits. You may also want to provide the operations engineer with an operational status field indicating how many users are currently served by your application. Maybe the application will have a notification to report users abusing the application in some way? How about an action to produce a debug dump of the database contents for troubleshooting? In the end, your application would probably have a lot more that goes in the management interface.

The YANG model of a device is often called its "schema," as in database schema or blueprint. A schema is basically the structure and content of messages exchanged between the application and the device. This is very different from the instance data—the actual configuration and monitoring data in the system. The instance data describes the current configuration and the current monitoring values. The schema describes the potential configuration, potential monitoring data, potential notifications, and potential actions a manager decides to execute.

The YANG language also incorporates a level of extensibility and flexibility not present in other model languages. New modules can augment the data hierarchies defined in other modules, seamlessly adding data at appropriate places in the existing data organization. YANG also permits new statements to be defined, allowing the language itself to be expanded in a consistent way. Note that the YANG model (keep in mind the API contract) does not change unless there is a software upgrade of the server, or perhaps if a license for a new feature is installed. The instance data changes as soon as a manager decides to change the configuration or if the system state changes due to internal or external events.

A small YANG model may declare just a dozen different elements, or even a single one (for example, a model that just defines the reboot operation). Some YANG models are very large, however, with thousands of elements. In a car or factory, each element would correspond to a button, control dial, indicator gauge, meter, or light. A modern car might have over a hundred elements on the dashboard and around the vehicle. A nuclear power plant might have over a thousand. Core routers are vastly more complicated, however, with well over 100,000 control interface elements.

Since the schema defines elements that can have many instances (for example, interfaces or access control rules), the instance data can be very much larger than the schema, with many millions of instances.

The YANG language itself is defined by the Internet Engineering Task Force (IETF).[13] The latest version is YANG 1.1, defined in RFC 7950, and YANG 1.0 is an older version defined in RFC 6020. As of this writing, both YANG 1.0 and YANG 1.1 are in popular use. This new YANG 1.1 (RFC 7950) does *not* obsolete YANG 1.0 (RFC 6020). YANG 1.1 is a maintenance release of the YANG language, addressing ambiguities and defects in the original specification. As a reference, YANG concepts are explained in Chapter 3. The extra YANG 1.1 capabilities are documented in Section 1.1 of RFC 7950. These days, YANG 1.1 should be the default when you're writing YANG modules.

The Key to Automation? Data Models

In the world of data model–driven management, as the name implies, the essential part is the set of data models. From the data models, you deduce APIs. Figure 2-2 displays a YANG data model (granted, an incomplete one, but sufficient at this point in time) on the left and RESTCONF RPCs (GET, POST, PUT, and DELETE) to manage the respective resources on the right. Paying attention to the color scheme, notice how the RESTCONF operations are built from the YANG module keywords, showing how the APIs are generated from a YANG model.

```
module my-interfaces {
 namespace "urn:example";

  container interfaces {
       list interface {
         key name;
         leaf name { type string; }
         leaf admin-status { type enumeration; }
       }
  }

  rpc flap-interface {
       input {
         leaf name { type string; }
       }
       output {
         leaf result { type boolean; }
       }
  }
}
```

```
GET : Gets a resource
GET /restconf/data/my-interfaces:interfaces
GET /restconf/data/my-interfaces:interfaces/

POST : Creates a resource or invoke operation
POST my-interfaces:flap-interface

PUT : Replaces a resource
PUT /restconf/data/ :interfaces/
    + JSON/XML Form Data (name, admin-status)

DELETE : Removes a resource
DELETE /restconf/data/my-
interfaces:interfaces/ /<some name>
```

FIGURE 2-2 Data Model–Driven Management Example with RESTCONF

Discussing how data models generate APIs is a good segue to stress one more time the differences between information models and data models. As specified in "On the Difference Between Information Models and Data Models" (RFC 3444), covered in Chapter 1, the main purpose of an information model is to model managed objects at a conceptual level, independent of any specific implementations or protocols used to transport the data. An extra distinction, in light of this YANG module figure, is that data models generate APIs. This is a key message: Automation is driven by APIs (not models that are a means to an end). However, an information model, typically expressed in Unified Modeling Language (UML) do not generate the full APIs, as they lack some of the implementation- and protocol-specific details (for example, rules that explain how to map managed objects onto lower-level protocol constructs). Generating APIs from UML is, however, a field of research and experimentation. In the authors' view, if the information model would contain all the information to generate complete APIs, then that information model is really a data model.

To get a bit more concrete on the difference between an information model and data model, let's consider an example. A UML information model might declare that a book object should have title, author, ISBN, language, and price attributes. It might say that the title should be a string, the author should be a reference to an author object, and the price should be a numeric type.

To turn that UML information model into a data model, you would need to add additional information—for example, that ISBNs need to adhere to a very particular format in order to be valid, that the author relation is mandatory while language is not, or that a book isn't eligible for sale if its price is zero. You would also need to state that there will be a list of books called the catalog and that this list is to be indexed by title. It is only when you add this sort of detailed information that the model becomes usable as an API—that is, as a contract between the client and server where both peers know what to expect and implement for.

YANG and the Operators Requirements

The YANG language addressed many of the issues raised during the "Overview of the 2002 IAB Network Management Workshop" (RFC 3535), as expressed in "An Architecture for Network Management Using NETCONF and YANG" (RFC 6244). Indeed, per RFC 6244, the YANG language was created to address the following requirements:

- **Ease of use**: YANG is designed to be human friendly, simple, and readable. Many tricky issues remain due to the complexity of the problem domain, but YANG strives to make them more visible and easier to deal with.
- **Configuration and state data**: YANG clearly divides configuration data from other types of data.
- **Generation of deltas**: A YANG module gives enough information to generate the delta needed to change between two configuration data sets.
- **Text friendly**: YANG modules are very text friendly, as is the data they define.
- **Task oriented**: A YANG module can define specific tasks as RPC operations. A client can choose to invoke the RPC operation or to access any underlying data directly.
- **Full coverage**: YANG modules can be defined that give full coverage to all the native capabilities of the device. Giving this access avoids the need to resort to the command-line interface (CLI) using tools such as Expect [EXPECT].[14]
- **Timeliness**: YANG modules can be tied to CLI operations, so all native operations and data are immediately available.
- **Implementation difficulty**: YANG's flexibility enables modules that can be more easily implemented. Adding "features" and replacing "third normal form" with a natural data hierarchy should reduce complexity. YANG moves the implementation burden from the client to the server, where SNMP was simple for the server. Transactions are key for client-side simplicity.
- **Simple data modeling language**: YANG has sufficient power to be usable in other situations. In particular, on-box APIs and a native CLI can be integrated to simplify the infrastructure.
- **Human-friendly syntax**: YANG's syntax is optimized for the reader, specifically the reviewer, on the basis that this is the most common human interaction.
- **Semantic mismatch**: Richer, more descriptive data models will reduce the possibility of semantic mismatch. With the ability to define new primitives, YANG modules will be more specific in content, allowing more enforcement of rules and constraints.
- **Internationalization**: YANG uses UTF-8 (RFC 3629) encoded Unicode characters.

NOTE

While the authors have tried to detail the high-level concepts and advantages in this chapter, understandably if you are not yet familiar with YANG, some points will make more sense after you read Chapter 3.

Properties of Good Data Models

Although there are many ways to design good management interfaces (or API contracts), there are even more ways to design bad ones. Just like there are certain properties to look for when writing good contracts, there are certain things to look for when designing an interface. In fact, the list of good properties for these two activities is essentially the same, as displayed in the bullet list that follows. To make this point, the following bullet points are taken from the legal website www.ohiobar.org. It's like designing a domain-specific language (DSL), with verbs, nouns, adjectives, and so on, plus (grammar) rules for how these elements may be combined. The most expressive, and therefore useful, languages generally have relatively few words, but focus on how the words can be combined into a near infinite number of different messages.

- **Accuracy**: The most important aspect of a contract is that it is accurate and therefore makes the reaction of the other party predictable. If there are many exceptions (ifs, whens, and buts) beyond what is mentioned in the contract, the contract loses its value. The contract needs to use relevant terminology correctly, be precise, and cover all cases.
- **Clarity**: Unless all parties come to the same understanding when reading the contract, interoperability is not going to happen. The language needs to be unambiguous, internally consistent, and use familiar terms. The document must be structured in a way that is easy to consume. Defaults enhance the clarity on what happens when a short message does not mention everything. Consistency constraints clarify how meaningful messages can be constructed.
- **Efficiency**: A classic way to make sure a contract is not read is to make it very long. An even more sure way is to start repeating yourself. When the same lengthy wording appears in section after section, the readability and maintainability are lost. Repeating patterns are great, but only if referenced and reused, rather than repeated each time.
- **Simplicity**: While it is tempting to use complicated in-group terms and language, it is usually better to write for a wider audience that may not understand the topic the contract is about at the same depth as the authors. Another important simplicity aspect is to write with the principle of least surprise (a.k.a. the principle of least astonishment) in mind. If something breaks an established pattern, either redesign or make it stand out as different.
- **Resonance**: Make sure the contract stays on topic. If the topic is wide, several modular contracts in a suite may make it easier to consume. The contract should spell out sensible defaults to allow the parties to be lazy. The contract needs to consider the needs and terminology of both parties (or all if more than two).

Although YANG adheres to these properties, at this point you might be wondering, why YANG and not another schema language—for example, the Common Information Model (CIM), specified in the Distributed Management Task Force (DMTF)? A pragmatic answer is, YANG was defined as the modeling language for the NETCONF protocol, and although it has pros and cons compared to other modeling languages, the designers within the IETF community chose YANG.

The Different Types of YANG Modules

With the success of YANG as a modeling language, the industry is creating many YANG models to ease automation. YANG modules come from three different sources these days:

- Standards development organizations (SDOs)
- Consortiums, forums, and open source projects
- Native/proprietary YANG models

While Chapter 6, "YANG Data Modeling Developments in the Industry," covers the YANG data modeling developments in the industry in more much detail, in this chapter we just cover and compare the preceding three categories. The goal of this section is to highlight a couple of differences from the YANG models' point of view.

As the SDO that specified the YANG language, the IETF was the initial SDO specifying the YANG modules—first in the NETMOD working group and then in different working groups with specific expertise. Different SDOs followed the trend, including the IEEE and ITU-T.[15]

Also, some consortiums, forums, and open source projects contributed to the YANG models development. To name a few, in no particular order, OpenConfig,[11] MEF Forum,[16] OpenDaylight,[11] Broadband Forum,[17] and Open ROADM[18] all contributed.

The SDO-produced YANG modules receive the most attention (at least for the IETF, in which the book's authors participate) as they are reviewed by many people. This review process comes at the cost of taking a long time to finalize the specifications. When developing applications around those YANG modules, it is important to understand that they contain a kind of common denominator, as opposed to the full coverage of the different experimental or proprietary features proposed by the different networking vendors. Extensions for those experimental and proprietary features must be developed on top of the standard YANG models.

On the other end, YANG models produced by consortiums, forums, and open source projects are most of the time targeted toward specific use cases, thus proposing complete solutions. When centered on use cases, a few committers maintain the coherence of the different YANG models, thus guaranteeing the consistency of the entire solution. Quick iterations of the YANG modules certainly improve the speed of delivery, based on the experience gained, but can be perceived as a burden for implementers who have to always keep their developments up to date with the latest version. Note that, in the case of open source projects, code is proposed next to the YANG models. Among all the open source projects, OpenConfig is worth mentioning, as it is getting some traction in the industry (more on this in Chapter 4).

The final category is "native YANG models," also called "proprietary YANG models." In order to offer some automation right now, with full coverage (for the entire set of supported features), some networking vendors propose YANG models, based on their proprietary implementations. Most of the time those YANG models are generated from internal databases or CLI representations, which implies that automation across vendors proved difficult. In case of generated YANG models, another potential issue is that new software versions can generate non-backward-compatible YANG modules, mapping the internal backward incompatibility. According to the YANG specifications, changes to published modules are not allowed if they have any potential to cause interoperability problems between a client using an original specification and a server using an updated specification. Expressed differently, a new module name is necessary if there are non-backward-compatible changes. However, in practice, that rule is not always followed. Therefore, there are discussions at the IETF to revise the YANG module update procedures (that is, to relax the rules concerning the condition of documenting the non-backward-compatible changes).

The industry has started to centralize all important YANG modules in GitHub [https://github.com/YangModels/yang], with the YANG Catalog [https://yangcatalog.org/][19] as the graphical interface. Those are two excellent starting points if you are not sure where to begin.

Mapping YANG Objects from MIB Modules

Before we begin this section about generating YANG modules as a translation from Management Information Based (MIB) modules, you should note that it refers to a couple of technical concepts introduced in later in this chapter and in the next two chapters. Since there is no other natural place to discuss mapping YANG objects from MIB modules later in the book, you are advised to re-read this section once you have mastered YANG and NETCONF.

When the IETF started its modeling work, there were no YANG modules (although there were plenty of MIB modules) to be used with the SNMP protocol. As already mentioned, many MIB modules were actively used for monitoring in network management. Therefore, it was only natural to invent a method to leverage what was good from SNMP and convert the MIB modules into YANG modules.

"Translation of Structure of Management Information Version 2 (SMIv2) MIB Modules to YANG Modules" (RFC 6643) describes a translation of SMIv2 (RFC 2578, RFC2579, and RFC 2580) MIB modules into YANG modules, enabling read-only access to SMIv2 objects defined in SMIv2 MIB modules via NETCONF. While this translation is of great help to access MIB objects via NETCONF, there is no magic bullet.

First off, the result of the translation of SMIv2 MIB modules into YANG modules, even if SMIv2 objects are read-write or read-create, consists of read-only YANG objects. One reason is that the persistency models of the underlying protocols, SNMP and NETCONF, are quite different. With SNMP, the persistence of a writable object depends either on the object definition itself (that is, the text in the DESCRIPTION clause) or the persistency properties of the conceptual row it is part of, sometimes controlled via a columnar object using the StorageType textual convention. With NETCONF, the persistence of configuration objects is determined by the properties of the underlying datastore. Furthermore, NETCONF, as defined in RFC 6241, does not provide a standard operation to modify operational state. The **<edit-config>** and **<copy-config>** operations only manipulate configuration data. You might say that the mapping of read-write or read-create objects is a moot point as there are not many of them in MIB modules. This is correct. Keep in mind that MIB modules do a good job of monitoring but have failed to emerge as a standard for configuring networks.

Second, using the MIB-translated YANG models along with the YANG-defined models still raises a basic problem of data model mapping because the MIB and YANG worlds specify conceptual objects differently. "Translation of Structure of Management Information Version 2 (SMIv2) MIB Modules to YANG Modules" (RFC 6643) might be of some help in creating the YANG module. In practice, new data structures are often created instead of using a mix of hand-edited (in case of MIB data naming misalignment with the YANG data structures or in case of writable objects) and auto-generated YANG modules. As an example, the YANG Interface Management (RFC 7223) followed this approach.

The Management Architecture

From an architecture point of view, there are multiple API locations, all deduced from YANG modules. A controller typically configures network elements (routers and switches in the networking world) based on the network element YANG modules—typically network interfaces, routing, quality of service, and so on—as shown in Figure 2-3.

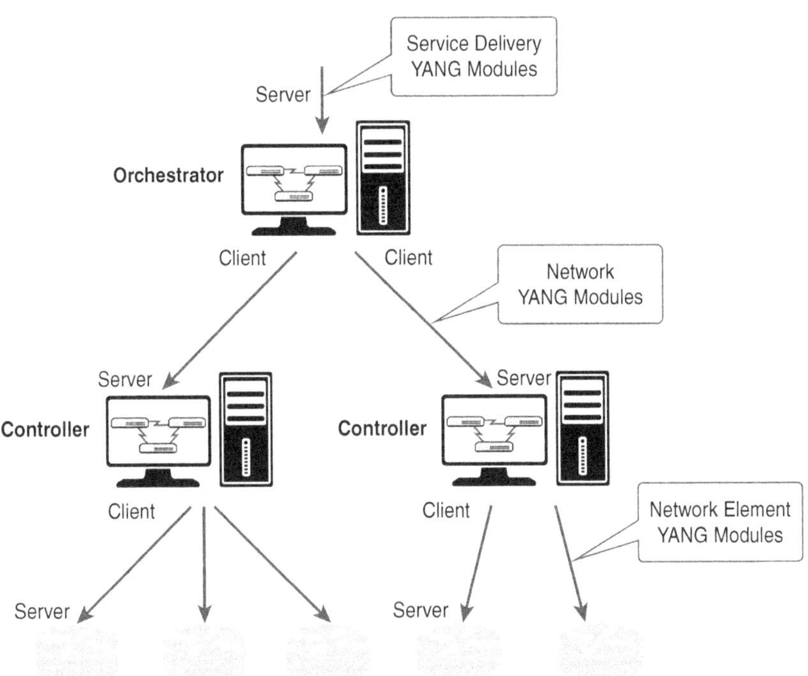

FIGURE 2-3 The Management Architecture

Controllers focus on one specific network domain or a specific technology. On top of the controllers, the orchestrator configures one or more controllers based on the network YANG modules' APIs. With the architecture in Figure 2-3 in mind, let's introduce the notion of northbound and southbound interfaces. From a controller point of view (as an example), the northbound interface is the interface toward the orchestrator, whereas the southbound interface is the one toward the server. Operators can also automate the orchestrator northbound interface to create/modify/delete their services, based on the service delivery YANG modules. A service YANG model is the management interface toward a software application, whereas a device YANG model is generally attached to a physical or virtual device. The classical service example is a Layer 3 virtual private network, or L3VPN, which touches the configuration on multiple devices in the network, configuring network element YANG modules on each point. Then this service is decomposed in the controller, where the required servers are configured.

Note that separating the controller and orchestrator in two different systems is not a requirement: An orchestrator might also handle the tasks of the controller system or connect directly to network elements without any controller function. Examples of systems that can take on various roles in this space are OpenDaylight,[11] Network Services Orchestrator (NSO), Contrail, and CloudOpera.

Coming back to the different types of YANG modules, having network element YANG modules standardized for the industry offers some easier automation in case of cross-vendor development. The service delivery YANG modules, on the other hand, are mainly proprietary, as operators tend to differentiate themselves from the competition. There are two notable exceptions with the standardization of the L3VPN service delivery (RFC 8299) and L2VPN service delivery (soon an RFC). More details on the different YANG module types can be found in "YANG Module Classification" (RFC 8199) and "Service Modules Explained" (RFC 8309).

There is a need for standard mechanisms to allow system owners to control read, write, and execute access for particular parts of the YANG tree to different kinds of users. The Network configuration Access Control Model (NACM; RFC 8341) specifies the access control mechanisms for the operations and content layers of NETCONF and RESTCONF, thanks to the ietf-netconf-acm YANG module. This is the role-based access control (RBAC) mechanism most commonly used in the YANG model–driven world.

Data Model–Driven Management Components

Data model–driven management is built on the idea of applying modeling languages to formally describe data sources and APIs. This includes the ability to generate behavior and code from the models. YANG is *the* data model language of choice; it allows a modeler to create a data model, to define the organization of the data in that model, and to define constraints on that data. Once published, the YANG module acts as a contract between the client and server, with each party understanding how its peer expects it to behave. A client knows how to create valid data for the server and knows what data will be sent from the server. A server knows the rules that govern the data and how it should behave.

As displayed in Figure 2-4, which covers the data model–driven management components, once the YANG models are specified and implemented, a network management system (NMS) can select a particular encoding (XML, JSON, protobuf, thrift, you name it) and a particular protocol (NETCONF,

RESTCONF, or gNMI/gRPC) for transport. Yes, there are differences in capabilities between the different protocols and, yes, there are some limitations in the combination of the encodings and protocols (marked by the arrows in the figure), and those are reviewed later in this chapter.

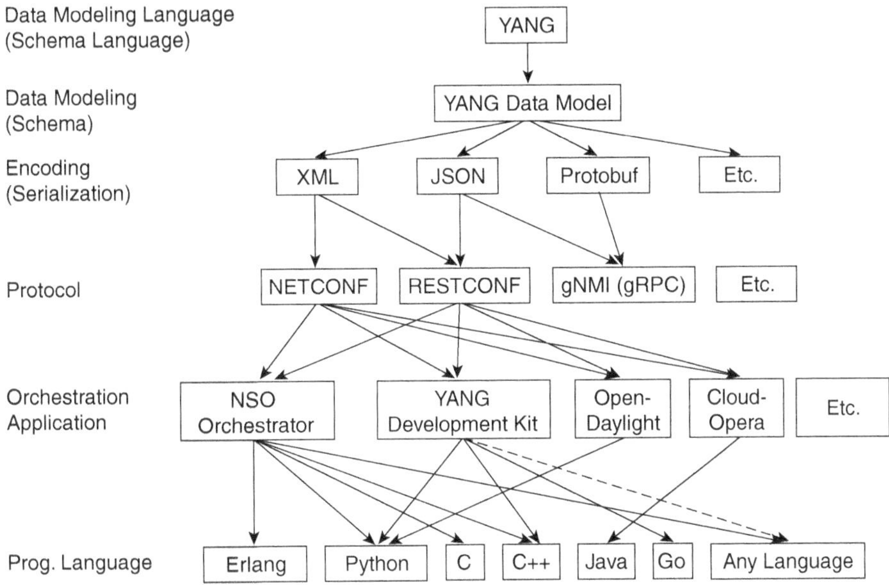

FIGURE 2-4 The Data Model–Driven Management Components

Typically, an orchestrator delivers service automation through multiple protocols/encodings. Based on the encoding and protocol selections, you can generate behavior or code to access the YANG objects on managed devices (for example, in Python, C++, Go, or basically any programming language). Note that as time passed, more and more arrows were added to this figure. In the end, all combinations become possible.

Orchestrators use code generation in their automation. A good showcase to demonstrate data model–driven management concepts and how the related code is rendered might be an open source tool such as the YANG Development Kit (YDK), which provides APIs directly based on YANG models and ready to use in scripts. The main goal of YDK is to reduce the learning curve involved with YANG data models by expressing the model semantics in an API and abstracting the protocol/encoding details. Example 2-1 shows a sample Python program illustrating the use of a generated API, oc-interfaces.py, which in turn is derived from the open-config-interfaces YANG module.

EXAMPLE 2-1 Python YDK Example of Configuring a BGP Session

```
from __future__ import print_function
from ydk.types import Empty, DELETE, Decimal64
from ydk.services import CRUDService
import logging
```

```
from session_mgr import establish_session, init_logging
from ydk.models.openconfig.openconfig_interfaces import Interfaces
from ydk.errors import YError


def print_interface(interface):
    print('*' * 28)
    print('Interface %s'%interface.name)

    if interface.config is not None:
        print('  config')
        print('     name:-%s'% interface.config.name)
        if interface.config.type is not None:
            print('     type:-%s'%interface.config.type.__class__)
        print('    enabled:-%s'%interface.config.enabled)

    if interface.state is not None:
        print('  state')
        print('     name:-%s'% interface.state.name)
        if interface.state.type is not None:
            print('     type:-%s'%interface.state.type.__class__)
        print('     enabled:-%s'%interface.state.enabled)
        if interface.state.admin_status is not None:
            enum_str = 'DOWN'
            if interface.state.admin_status == interface.state.AdminStatusEnum.UP:
                enum_str = 'UP'
            print('     admin_status:-%s'%enum_str)
        if interface.state.oper_status is not None:
            oper_status_map = { interface.state.OperStatusEnum.UP : 'UP',
                                interface.state.OperStatusEnum.DOWN : 'DOWN',
                                interface.state.OperStatusEnum.TESTING : 'TESTING',
                                interface.state.OperStatusEnum.UNKNOWN: 'UNKNOWN',
                                interface.state.OperStatusEnum.DORMANT : 'DORMANT',
                                interface.state.OperStatusEnum.NOT_PRESENT :
                                'NOT_PRESENT',
                                }
            print('     oper_status:-%s'%oper_status_map[interface.state.oper_status])

        if interface.state.mtu is not None:
            print('      mtu:-%s'%interface.state.mtu)
        if interface.state.last_change is not None:
            print('      last_change:-%s'%interface.state.last_change)
```

```
        if interface.state.counters is not None:
            print('     counters')
            print('        in_unicast_pkts:-%s'%interface.state.counters
                           .in_unicast_pkts)
            print('        in_octets:-%s'%interface.state.counters.in_octets)
            print('        out_unicast_pkts:-%s'%interface.state.counters
                           .out_unicast_pkts)
            print('        out_octets:-%s'%interface.state.counters.out_octets)
            print('        in_multicast_pkts:-%s'%interface.state.counters
                           .in_multicast_pkts)
            print('        in_broadcast_pkts:-%s'%interface.state.counters
                           .in_broadcast_pkts)
            print('        out_multicast_pkts:-%s'%interface.state.counters
                           .out_multicast_pkts)
            print('        out_broadcast_pkts:-%s'%interface.state.counters
                           .out_broadcast_pkts)
            print('        out_discards:-%s'%interface.state.counters.out_discards)
            print('        in_discards:-%s'%interface.state.counters.in_discards)
            print('        in_unknown_protos:-%s'%interface.state.counters
                           .in_unknown_protos)
            print('        in_errors:-%s'%interface.state.counters.in_errors)
            print('        out_errors:-%s'%interface.state.counters.out_errors)
            print('        last_clear:-%s'%interface.state.counters.last_clear)

        if interface.state.ifindex is not None:
            print('     ifindex:-%s'%interface.state.ifindex)

    print('*' * 28)

def read_interfaces(crud_service, provider):

    interfaces_filter = Interfaces()

    try:
        interfaces = crud_service.read(provider, interfaces_filter)
        for interface in interfaces.interface:
            print_interface(interface)
    except YError:
        print('An error occurred reading interfaces.')


def create_interfaces_config(crud_service, provider):

    interface = Interfaces.Interface()
    interface.config.name = 'LoopbackYDK'
    interface.name = interface.config.name
```

```
    try:
        crud_service.create(provider, interface)
    except YError:
        print('An error occurred creating the interface.')


if __name__ == "__main__":
    init_logging()
    provider = establish_session()
    crud_service = CRUDService()
    read_interfaces(crud_service, provider)


    provider.close()
exit()
```

Obviously, other tools for code generation exist; for example, in the world of OpenConfig, see http://www.openconfig.net/software/.[20]

Notice that the primary source of information to generate code is the set of YANG modules. This is the reason why the IETF and the industry in general are spending so much energy specifying these YANG modules as precisely as possible.

The Encoding (Protocol Binding and Serialization)

If YANG plus a YANG model can be compared to a language such as English, defined by a dictionary of known words and a grammar describing how the words can be combined, you still need to work out an encoding for your language before you can communicate. English has two very commonly used encodings: text and voice. The text encoding can be further divided into computer encodings like ASCII, Windows-1252, and UTF-8. Text can also be encoded as pixels of different colors in a photo file, as ink on paper, microfiche, or grooves on a stone or a copper plate.

Similarly, there are several different encodings of messages (also known as protocol bindings or serialization) relating to YANG-based models, each more or less suitable depending on the context. The most commonly mentioned (and used) YANG-related encodings are XML, JavaScript Object Notation (JSON; in two variants), and protobuf. As time has passed, new encodings have emerged. For example, this section also covers Concise Binary Object Representation (CBOR).

Figure 2-4, shown earlier in this chapter, displays the different possible encodings for a specific protocol. Keep in mind that more encodings are available all the time: It makes sense as, in the end, an encoding is just… an encoding.

XML

Ask most IT professionals if they know XML, and the reply is invariably "yes." As most IT folks know, XML stands for Extensible Markup Language. If you ask the same IT professionals to outline the extensibility mechanism in XML, however, only a tiny fraction will give you a reasonable reply. This is why there is a brief recap of the most important XML features, including the extensibility mechanism, in Chapter 3.

Most people think of XML as those HTML-like text documents full of angle brackets (**<some>xml </some>**), which may seem as a rather small and simple concept. It is not, however. XML and its family of related standards is a complicated and far-reaching dragon. It has a well-designed extensibility mechanism that allows XML-based content to evolve nicely over time, it has a query language called XPath, it has a schema language called XML Schema, and it has a transformation language called XSLT—just to mention a few features. Keep in mind that a schema is the definition of the structure and content of data (names, types, ranges, and defaults).

Because of these qualities and the abundant availability of tools, the NETCONF working group decided to base its protocol on XML for the message encoding. In the beginning, before YANG was invented, a lot of people assumed that NETCONF would be modeled using XML Schema Description (XSD). It was even used, together with a set of additional mapping conventions, as the official modeling language for about half a year. This was when the group was attempting to craft the first standard models for NETCONF. Then a serious flaw was found in one of the early models made by the NETCONF gurus. This led to a rather heated debate around how such a major flaw could be introduced and not be found in review by even the inner circle of NETCONF pundits. The root cause for the situation was eventually declared to be the hard-to-read nature of XML Schema. This situation triggered tiny teams from separate organizations across the industry to get together to define a new schema language, with the fundamental requirement that models must be easy to read and write. Those team members' names are found in RFC 6020. Today, this language is known as YANG.

This explains why the ties between NETCONF and XML were (and remain) very strong, and even why YANG 1.0 depends on XML mechanisms quite a bit. With different encodings these days, YANG 1.1 is designed as much more neutral to the protocol encodings.

JSON

As the demand for a REST-based approach similar to the functionality standardized in NETCONF was rising, the NETCONF WG started developing RESTCONF.[21] REST-based transports use a fairly wide variety of message encodings, but there is no question that the most popular one is JavaScript Object Notation (JSON). It has its roots in the way objects are represented in JavaScript: It was a very simple collection of encoding rules that fit on a single page. This simplicity was a major driver for JSON's popularity. Today there is a clear, precise, and language-independent definition of JSON in RFC 7159, and further updated in RFC 8259.

While simplicity is always welcome, the downside is that JSON in its simple form handled many use cases quite poorly. For example, there were no mechanisms for evolution and extension, no counterpart of the YANG namespace mechanism. Another example is that JSON has a single number type with an integer precision of about 53 bits in typical implementations. The 64-bit integers in YANG therefore must be encoded as something other than as numbers (strings). To handle these and many other similar-but-not-so-obvious mapping cases, a set of encoding conventions were needed on top of JSON itself (just like with XSD for XML, as mentioned earlier). For the YANG-to-RESTCONF mapping, these conventions are found in "JSON Encoding of Data Modeled with YANG" (RFC 7951; do not confuse this with RFC 7159, mentioned earlier, despite their similar numbers). The general JSON community is also working with standardization around additional use cases for JSON, and today JSON is approaching XML in versatility and complexity.

Besides JSON, the RESTCONF specification (RFC 8040) also defines how to encode the data as XML. Some RESTCONF servers support JSON, some XML, and many support both. When the encoding is JSON, it really means JSON as specified in RFC 7159, plus all the conventions in RFC 7951.

Google Protobufs

Protocol buffers, or protobufs, are another supported encoding in gNMI. Protobufs were originally invented by Google and are widely used in much of Google's products and services, where communication over the wire or data storage is required.

You specify how you want the information you are serializing to be structured by defining protocol buffer message types in .proto files. Once you define your messages, you run the protocol buffer compiler for your application's language on your .proto file to generate data access classes. Protobufs have built-in support for versioning and extensibility, which many see as an edge over JSON. The messaging mechanism is openly available with bindings for a long list of languages, which has led to very broad usage.

Protobufs come in two formats: self-describing and compact. The self-describing mode is three times larger in terms of bits on the wire. The compact mode is a tight binary form, which has the advantage of saving space on the wire and in memory. As a consequence, this mode is two times faster. This encoding is therefore well suited for telemetry, where a lot a data is pushed at high frequency toward a collector. On the other hand, the compact format is hard to debug or trace—without the .proto files, you cannot tell the names, meaning, or full data types of fields.

CBOR

Concise Binary Object Representation (CBOR) is another encoding being discussed, and is particularly useful for small, embedded systems, typically from the Internet of Things (IoT). CBOR is super-efficient, as it compresses even the identifiers. CBOR is used in connection with the CoAP Management Interface (CoMI) protocol on the client side.

As of this writing, CBOR (RFC 7049) is not in wide use with YANG-based servers, but discussions are ongoing in the IETF CORE (Constrained RESTful Environments) working group, where a document called "CBOR Encoding of Data Modeled with YANG" is being crafted.

The Server Architecture: Datastore

In the typical YANG-based solution, the client and server are driven by the content of YANG modules. The server includes the definitions of the modules as metadata that is available to the NETCONF/RESTCONF engine. This engine processes incoming requests, uses the metadata to parse and verify the request, performs the requested operation, and returns the results to the client, as shown in Figure 2-5.

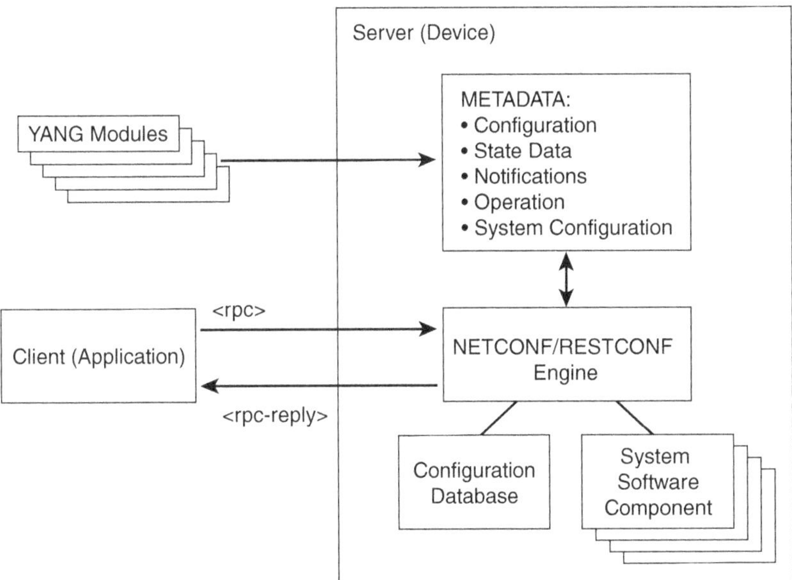

FIGURE 2-5 The Server Architecture (RFC 6244)

The YANG modules, which model a specific problem domain, are loaded, compiled, or coded into the server.

The sequence of events for the typical NETCONF client/server interaction occur as follows:

1. A client application opens a NETCONF session to the server (device).
2. The client and server exchange **<hello>** messages containing the list of capabilities supported by each side. This hello exchange includes the list of YANG 1.0 modules supported by the server.
3. The client builds and sends an operation defined in the YANG module, encoded in XML, within NETCONF's **<rpc>** element.
4. The server receives and parses the **<rpc>** element.
5. The server verifies the contents of the request against the data model defined in the YANG module.

6. The server performs the requested operation, possibly changing the configuration datastore.
7. The server builds the response message, containing the response itself, any requested data, and any errors.
8. The server sends the response, encoded in XML, within NETCONF's **<rpc-reply>** element.
9. The client receives and parses the **<rpc-reply>** element.
10. The client inspects the response and processes it as needed.

The Protocols

As a quick introduction before we dive into the different protocols, Table 2-1 provides a comparison of the most common protocols used in data model–driven management: NETCONF, RESTCONF, and gNMI.

TABLE 2-1 Quick NETCONF/RESTCONF/gNMI Protocol Comparison

	NETCONF	RESTCONF	gNMI
Message and Payload Encoding	XML.	JSON or XML.	gNMI notifications with JSON (two variants) or protobuf payload.
Operation Semantics	NETCONF specific; network-wide transactions.	RESTCONF specific, based on HTTP verbs. Single-target, single-shot transactions.	gNMI specific. Single-target, single-shot, sequenced transactions.
RPC Mechanism	NETCONF specific; XML based.	REST style.	gRPC.
Transport Stack	SSH/TCP/IP.	HTTP/TLS/TCP/IP.	HTTP2/TLS/TCP/IP.

NETCONF

The NETCONF protocol addressed many of the issues raised during the "Overview of the 2002 IAB Network Management Workshop" (RFC 3535). Here are just a few of them:

- **Transactions**: NETCONF provides a transaction mechanism that guarantees the configuration is correctly and entirely applied.
- **Dump and restore**: NETCONF provides the ability to save and restore configuration data. This can also be performed for a specific YANG module.
- **Configuration handling**: NETCONF addresses the ability to distinguish between distributing configuration data and activating it.

NETCONF provides a transaction mechanism, which is a major advantage compared to a protocol such as SNMP. A transaction is characterized by the "ACID test" (which comes from the database world):

- **Atomicity**: All-or-nothing. Either the entire change is applied or it is discarded. This constitutes a major advantage for error handling.
- **Consistency**: All-at-once. The data needs to be valid with respect to YANG rules. There is no concept of time inside the transaction, no "before" and "after." No "first this, then that." This is great for simplicity.
- **Independence**: No cross-talk. Multiple clients can make configuration changes simultaneously without the transactions interfering with each other.
- **Durability**: Once executed, the transaction is guaranteed to stick, even if there is a power outage or a software crash. In other words, "when it's done, it's done."

Here is how RFC 6241, "Network Configuration Protocol (NETCONF)," defines the NETCONF protocol:

RFC 6244 NETCONF Definition

"NETCONF defines an XML-based remote procedure call (RPC) mechanism that leverages the simplicity and availability of high-quality XML parsers. XML gives a rich, flexible, hierarchical, standard representation of data that matches the needs of networking devices. NETCONF carries configuration data and operations as requests and replies using RPCs encoded in XML over a connection-oriented transport."

XML's hierarchical data representation allows complex networking data to be rendered in a natural way. Example 2-2 places network interfaces in the OSPF routing protocol areas. The **<ospf>** element contains a list of **<area>** elements, each of which contains a list of **<interface>** elements. The **<name>** element identifies the specific area or interface. Additional configuration for each area or interface appears directly inside the appropriate element.

EXAMPLE 2-2 OSPF Areas NETCONF Configuration

```
<ospf xmlns="http://example.org/netconf/ospf">

  <area>
    <name>0.0.0.0</name>

    <interface>
      <name>ge-0/0/0.0</name>
```

```
      <!-- The priority for this interface -->
      <priority>30</priority>
      <metric>100</metric>
      <dead-interval>120</dead-interval>
    </interface>

    <interface>
      <name>ge-0/0/1.0</name>
      <metric>140</metric>
    </interface>
  </area>

  <area>
    <name>10.1.2.0</name>

    <interface>
      <name>ge-0/0/2.0</name>
      <metric>100</metric>
    </interface>

    <interface>
      <name>ge-0/0/3.0</name>
      <metric>140</metric>
      <dead-interval>120</dead-interval>
    </interface>
  </area>
</ospf>
```

NETCONF includes mechanisms for controlling configuration datastores. Each datastore is a specific collection of configuration data to be used as source or target of the configuration-related operations. The device indicates whether it has a distinct "startup" configuration datastore, whether the current or "running" datastore is directly writable, and whether there is a "candidate" configuration datastore where configuration changes can be made that will not affect the device operations until a "commit-configuration" operation is invoked.

The NETCONF protocol provides a small set of low-level operations, invoked as RPCs from the client (the application) to the server (running on the device), to manage device configurations and retrieve device state information. The base protocol provides operations to retrieve, configure, copy, and delete configuration datastores. The Table 2-2 lists these operations.

TABLE 2-2 NETCONF Operations

Operation	Description
get-config	Retrieve all or part of a configuration datastore.
edit-config	Change the contents of a configuration datastore.
copy-config	Copy one configuration datastore to another.
delete-config	Delete the contents of a configuration datastore.
lock	Prevent changes to a datastore from another party.
unlock	Release a lock on a datastore.
get	Retrieve the running configuration and device state information.
close-session	Request a graceful termination of the NETCONF session.
kill-session	Force the termination of another NETCONF session.
get-data	More flexible way to retrieve configuration and device state information. Only available on some newer systems (requires the Network Management Datastore Architecture (NMDA, [RFC8342]) support, which you will learn about in chapter 3)
edit-data	More flexible way to change the contents of a configuration datastore. Only available on some newer systems (requires NMDA support).

NETCONF's "capability" mechanism allows the device to announce the set of capabilities that the device supports, including protocol operations, datastores, data models, and other capabilities, as shown in Table 2-3. These are announced during session establishment as part of the **<hello>** message. A client can inspect the hello message to determine what the device is capable of and how to interact with the device to perform the desired tasks. This alone is a real advantage compared to a protocol such as SNMP. In addition, NETCONF fetches state data, receives notifications, and invokes additional RPC methods defined as part of a capability.

TABLE 2-3 Optional NETCONF Capabilities

Capability	Description
:writable-running	Allow writing directly to the running configuration datastore so that changes take effect immediately.
:candidate	Support a separate candidate configuration datastore so that changes are validated first and activated later.
:confirmed-commit	Allow activating the candidate configuration during a trial period. If anything goes wrong during the trial period, or if the manager does not approve it, the transaction rolls back automatically. Required for network-wide transactions.
:rollback-on-error	Rollback in case of error. This is the core capability for transaction support. Without this capability, NETCONF becomes less useful than SNMP.
:validate	Support validating a configuration without activating it. Required for network-wide transactions.

This collection of capabilities effectively offers a robust network-wide configuration, via the **:rollback-on-error**, **:candidate**, **:confirmed-commit**, and **:validate** capabilities. With this ACID concept in place, you can view the network as a distributed database. When a change is attempted that affects multiple devices, these capabilities hugely simplify the management of failure scenarios, resulting in the ability to have transactions that dependably succeed or fail atomically. This network-wide transaction mechanism is known as a three-phase transaction (PREPARE, COMMIT, and CONFIRM) in the database world.

NETCONF also defines a means of sending asynchronous notifications from the server to the client, described in RFC 5277.

In terms of security, NETCONF runs over transport protocols secured by Secure Shell (SSH), or optionally HTTP/TLS (Transport Layer Security), allowing secure communications and authentication using well-trusted technology.

RESTCONF

Just as NETCONF defines configuration datastores and a set of Create, Read, Update, Delete, Execute (CRUDX) operations to be used to access these datastores, RESTCONF specifies HTTP methods to provide the same operations. Exactly like NETCONF, RESTCONF is a programmatic interface for accessing data defined in YANG.

So why did the IETF specify yet another protocol, similar to NETCONF? In Chapter 1, you learned that automation is only as good as your toolchain. Furthermore, at this point in this book, you understand a key message: In the world of data model–driven management, what is important is the set of YANG data modules from which APIs are deduced. Therefore, because some operations engineers were developing HTTP-based tools, it was natural to specify a data model–driven management protocol using the same HTTP-based toolchain.

RFC 8040 RESTCONF: a New Protocol, as a Subset of the NETCONF Functionality

"RESTCONF does not need to mirror the full functionality of the NETCONF protocol, but it does need to be compatible with NETCONF. RESTCONF achieves this by implementing a subset of the interaction capabilities provided by the NETCONF protocol—for instance, by eliminating datastores and explicit locking.

RESTCONF uses HTTP methods to implement the equivalent of NETCONF operations, enabling basic CRUD operations on a hierarchy of conceptual resources.

The HTTP POST, PUT, PATCH, and DELETE methods are used to edit data resources represented by YANG data models. These basic edit operations allow the running configuration to be altered by a RESTCONF client.

RESTCONF is not intended to replace NETCONF, but rather to provide an HTTP interface that follows Representational State Transfer (REST) principles [REST-Dissertation][22] and is compatible with the NETCONF datastore model."

The following is from the RESTCONF specifications (RFC 8040) so that you will understand the relationship between NETCONF and RESTCONF.

Note that Chapter 4 provides a more technical comparison of NETCONF and RESTCONF. RESTCONF adds a new possible encoding, as compared to NETCONF, because it supports XML or JSON. With RESTCONF, the server reports each YANG module, any deviations, and features it supports using the ietf-yang-library YANG module, defined in the YANG Module Library (RFC 7895) and the brand new YANG library [RFC8525] that obsoletes the previous version.

The RESTCONF protocol has no concept of multiple calls making up a transaction. Each RESTCONF call is a transaction by itself, as it uses the HTTP POST, PUT, PATCH, and DELETE methods to edit data resources represented by YANG data models. RESTCONF lacks any way of validating without also activating a configuration. However, the validation is implicit, part of the RESTCONF calls, which succeed or fail transactionally.

With the capabilities of NETCONF in mind, the natural service automation flow is the NETCONF **<lock>** operation (on the running and candidate datastores), editing the configuration in the candidate configuration datastore, validating the configuration, committing to apply the configuration in the candidate datastore to the running datastore, and finally the unlock operations. These operations are done on multiple devices in parallel from an orchestrator, to achieve network-wide transactions. RESTCONF doesn't provide the notion of locking, candidate configuration, or commit operations; the configuration changes are applied immediately. RESTCONF does not support transactions that happen in three phases (PREPARE, COMMIT, and CONFIRM). However, it supports transactions that happen in two phases (PREPARE and COMMIT), but only for data given in a single REST call.

Therefore, RESTCONF does not support network-wide transactions, but only device-by-device configuration. RESTCONF is therefore suitable between a portal and an orchestrator (because there is only one), but not from an orchestrator toward a network with many devices.

It is a little bit over-simplistic to think that, if you are a web developer, you "just" select RESTCONF as the protocol, as opposed to NETCONF. However, remember the importance of tooling. Automation in general, and specifically network configuration, implies the integration of an entire toolchain. And, if the existing toolchain (for example, storage and compute) is centered around HTTP, the RESTCONF option might be the best one. In the end, it is all about seamless integration and reduced costs.

It's important to understand the disadvantages of using RESTCONF for device configuration so that you know the consequences of choosing RESTCONF simply because it uses HTML. As a piece of advice, when you have the choice (that is, you are not constrained by the toolchain), use NETCONF for network elements configuration. RESTCONF might be fine as the northbound interface of the orchestrator or/and controller.

gNMI (gRPC)

The gRPC Network Management Interface (gNMI) protocol comes from the OpenConfig consortium,[20] a group of network operators led by Google, with the following mission: "OpenConfig is an informal working group of network operators sharing the goal of moving our networks toward a more dynamic, programmable infrastructure by adopting software-defined networking principles such as declarative configuration and model-driven management and operations."

The initial focus of OpenConfig was on compiling a consistent set of vendor-neutral data models written in YANG, based on actual operational needs from use cases and requirements from multiple network operators. While OpenConfig continues to evolve the set of YANG modules, Google developed gNMI as a unified management protocol for streaming telemetry and configuration management that leverages the open source gRPC[23] framework.

There is sometimes a confusion between gNMI and gRPC—hence the two names in this section. To clarify, gNMI is the management protocol and gRPC is the underlying RPC framework.

One of the gNMI encodings is protobuf, discussed earlier. Protobufs have the advantage of being more compact on the wire, but they also provide an operationally more complex deployment. With NETCONF and RESTCONF, only the YANG schema is required to understand the payload. With gNMI over gRPC with protobuf transport, distribution of .proto files is also required. This adds complexity, especially when some devices are upgraded and so on.

CoMI

The CoAP Management Interface (CoMI) protocol extends the set of YANG-based protocols (NETCONF/RESTCONF/gNMI) with the capability to manage constrained devices and networks.

The Constrained Application Protocol (CoAP; RFC 7252) is designed for machine-to-machine (M2M) applications such as smart energy, smart city, and building control, for use with constrained nodes and constrained (for example, low-power, lossy) networks. The IoT nodes often have 8-bit microcontrollers with small amounts of ROM and RAM, while constrained networks such as IPv6 over low-power wireless personal area networks (6LoWPANs) often have high packet error rates and a typical throughput of tens of kilobits per second.

Those constrained devices must be managed in an automatic fashion to handle the large quantities of devices that are expected in future installations. Messages between devices need to be as small and infrequent as possible. The implementation complexity and runtime resources also need to be as small as possible.

CoMI specifies a network management interface for those constrained devices and networks, where CoAP is used to access datastore and data node resources specified in YANG. CoMI uses the YANG-to-CBOR mapping[24] and converts YANG identifier strings to numeric identifiers for payload size reduction. In terms of protocol stack comparison, CoMI runs on top of CoAP, which in turn runs on top of User Datagram Protocol (UDP), while NETCONF/RESTCONF/gNMI all run on top of Transmission Control Protocol (TCP).

At the time of writing, CoMI is in its last stage of standardization at the IETF.

The Programming Language

Good scripts are based on good application programming interfaces (APIs). An API is a set of functions and procedures that allow the creation of applications that access the features or data of an operating system, application, or other service. Fundamentally, an API should provide the following features:

- **Abstraction**: The programmable API should abstract away the complexities of the underlying implementation. The network programmer should not need to know unnecessary details, such as a specific order of configurations or specific steps to take if something fails. Configurations should function more like filling in a high-level checklist (these are the settings you need; now the system can go figure out how to properly group and order them).
- **Data specification**: The key thing an API does—whether it is a software or network API—is provide a specification for the data. First, it answers the question of what the data is—integer, string, or other type of value. Next, it specifies how that data is organized. In traditional programming, that would be called the data structure—though in the world of network programmability, the more common term is "schema," also known as "data models."
- **Means of accessing the data**: Finally, the API provides a standardized framework for how to read and manipulate the device's data.

You saw a YANG Development Kit (YDK)[25] example earlier (refer to Example 2-1). The main goal of YDK is to reduce the learning curve of YANG data models by expressing the model semantics in an API and abstracting protocol/encoding details. YDK is composed of a core package that defines services and providers, plus one or more module bundles[26] that are based on YANG models. Each module bundle is generated using a bundle profile and the ydk-gen tool. YDK-Py[27] provides Python APIs for several model bundles. Similarly, YDK-Cpp[28] includes C++ and Go APIs for the same bundles. A similar bundle exists for the C language.

Taking some more examples from the OpenConfig world this time, here are some more tools currently available:

- Ygot[29] (YANG Go Tools): For generating Go structures or protobufs from YANG modules.
- Goyang:[30] A YANG parser and compiler in the Go language.
- Pyangbind:[31] A plug-in for pyang that converts YANG data models into a Python class hierarchy.

These examples prove one more time the importance of the toolchain, of which the programming language (C, C++, Python, Go, you name it) is just one component. Assuming that the operations engineers were developing and supporting scripts based on a specific language, it makes perfect sense to continue developing the YANG-based automation scripts in the same programming language.

Telemetry

The inefficiencies associated with a polling mechanism like SNMP needed to be removed. Network operators poll periodically because they want the data at regular intervals. So why not just send them the data they want when they want it and skip the overhead of polling? Thus the idea of "streaming" was born. Instead of pulling data off the network, you can sit back and let the network push it for you to a collector.

From Chapter 1, you already know that telemetry is a trend in the industry. Telemetry is a new approach for network monitoring in which data is streamed from network devices continuously using a push model and provides near real-time access to operational statistics. You can precisely define what data you want to subscribe to using standard YANG models, with no CLI required. It allows network devices to continuously stream real-time configuration and operating state information to subscribers. Structured data is published at a defined cadence or on-change, based on the subscription criteria and data type. Telemetry data must be structured in a sensible way to make it easy for monitoring tools to ingest. In other words, good telemetry data must be model based—hence the term *data model–driven telemetry*, even if everyone uses the term *telemetry*. The networking industry has converged on YANG as a data modeling language for networking data, making it the natural choice for telemetry. Whether you prefer your data in native, OpenConfig, or IETF YANG models, data model–driven telemetry delivers it to you.

Of course, you want all this data to be easy to use because you know that sooner or later someone will come to your desk and ask for data analytics. Telemetry data needs to be normalized for efficient consumption by Big Data tools. In the software world, encodings such as JSON, protobuf, and XML are widely used to transfer data between software applications. These encodings have an abundance of open source software APIs that make it easy to manipulate and analyze the data.

In terms of protocols, two are possible: the OpenConfig streaming telemetry and the IETF push mechanism. The OpenConfig streaming telemetry uses protobuf as the encoding: The protobuf compact mode is perfectly suited for this, as an efficient encoding (at the cost of managing the .proto files). In the IETF push mechanism, subscriptions are created over existing NETCONF sessions and are developed using XML RPCs. The establish-subscription RPC is sent from a client or collector to the network device.

Model-driven telemetry is your first step in a journey that will transform how you monitor and operate networks. With the power of telemetry, you will discover things you never imagined and will begin to ask more and better questions. More on telemetry can be found in Chapter 6.

The Bigger Picture: Using NETCONF to Manage a Network

It happens so easily when talking about management protocols that the conversation ends up being about its components—the client, server, and protocol details. The most important topic is somehow lost. The core of the issue is really the use cases you want to implement and how they can be realized. The overarching goal is to simplify the life of the network operator. *"Ease of use is a key requirement for any network management technology from the operators point of view"* (RFC 3535, Requirement #1).

Network operators say they would want to *"concentrate on the configuration of the network as a whole rather than individual devices"* (RFC 3535, Requirement #4). Since the building blocks of networks are devices and cabling, there is really no way to avoid managing devices. The point the operators are trying to make, however, is that a raised abstraction level is convenient when managing networks. They would like to do their management using network-level concepts rather than device-level commands.

This is seen as a good case for network management system (NMS) vendors, but in order for the NMS systems to be reasonably small, simple, and inexpensive, great responsibility falls on the management protocol. Thirty years of industry NMS experience has taught us time after time that with poorly designed management protocols, NMS vendors routinely fail on all three accounts.

What does NETCONF do to support the NMS development? Let's have a look at the typical use case in network management: how to provision an additional leg on an L3VPN.

At the very least, a typical L3VPN consists of the following:

- Consumer Edge (CE) devices located near the endpoints of the VPN, such as a store location, branch office, or someone's home
- Provider Edge (PE) devices located on the outer rim of the provider organization's core network
- A core network connecting all the hub locations and binding to all PE devices
- A monitoring solution to ensure the L3VPN is performing according to expectations and promises
- A security solution to ensure privacy and security

In order to add an L3VPN leg to the network, the L3VPN application running in the NMS must touch at least the CE device on the new site, the PE device to which the CE device is connected, the monitoring system, and probably a few devices related to security. It could happen that the CE is a virtual device, in which case the NMS may have to speak to some container manager or virtual infrastructure manager (VIM) to spin up the virtual machine (VM). Sometimes 20 devices or so must be touched in order to spin up a single L3VPN leg. All of them are required for the leg to be functional. All firewalls and routers with access control lists (ACLs) need to get their updates, or traffic does not flow. Encryption needs to be set up properly at both ends, or traffic is not safe. Monitoring needs to be set up, or loss of service is not detected.

To implement the new leg in the network using NETCONF, the manager runs a network-wide transaction toward the relevant devices, updating the candidate datastore on them and validating it; if everything is okay, the manager then commits that change to the **:running** datastore. *"It is important to distinguish between the distribution of configurations and the activation of a certain configuration.*

Devices should be able to hold multiple configurations." (RFC 3535, Requirement #13). Here are the steps the manager takes in more detail:

STEP 1. Figure out which devices need to be involved to implement the new leg, according to topology and requested endpoints.

STEP 2. Connect to all relevant devices over NETCONF and then lock (**<lock>**) the NETCONF datastores **:running** and **:candidate** on those devices.

STEP 3. Clear (**<discard-changes>**) the **:candidate** datastore on the devices.

STEP 4. Compute the required configuration change for each device.

STEP 5. Edit (**<edit-config>**) each device's **:candidate** datastore with the computed change.

STEP 6. Validate (**<validate>**) the **:candidate** datastore.

In transaction theory, transactions have two (or three) phases when successful. All the actions up until this point were in the transaction's PREPARE phase. At the end of the PREPARE phase, all devices must report either **<ok>** or **<rpc-error>**. This is a critical decision point. Transaction theorists often call this the "point of no return."

If any participating device reports **<rpc-error>** up to this point, the transaction has failed and goes to the ABORT phase. Nothing happens to the network. The NMS safely drops the connection to all devices. This means the changes were never activated and the locks now released.

In case all devices report **<ok>** here, the NMS proceeds to the COMMIT phase.

Next, commit (**<commit>**) each device's **:candidate** datastore. This activates the change.

Splitting the work to activate a change into a two-phase commit with validation in between may sound easy and obvious when described this way. At the same time, you must acknowledge that this is quite revolutionary in the network management context—not because it's hard to do, but because of what it enables.

Unless you have programmed NMS solutions, it's hard to imagine the amount of code required in the NMS to detect and resolve any errors if the devices do not support transactions individually. In the example, you even had network-wide transactions. In a mature NMS, about half the code is devoted to error detection and recovery from a great number of situations. This recovery code is also the most expensive part to develop since it is all about corner cases and situations that are supposed not to happen. Such situations are complicated to re-create for testing, and even to think up.

The cost of a software project is largely proportional to the amount of code written, so this means more than half of the cost of the traditional NMS is removed when the devices support network-wide transactions.

The two-phase, network-wide transaction just described is widely used with NETCONF devices today. This saves a lot of code but is not failsafe. The **<commit>** operation could fail, the connection to a device could be lost, or a device might crash or not respond while sending out the **<commit>** to all devices. This would lead to some devices activating the change, while others do not. In order to tighten this up even more, NETCONF also specifies a three-phase network-wide transaction that managers may want to use.

By supplying the flag **<confirmed>** in the preceding **<commit>** stage, the transaction enters the third CONFIRM phase (going from PREPARE to COMMIT followed by CONFIRM). If the NMS sends this flag, the NMS must come back within a given time limit to reconfirm the change.

If no confirmation is received at the end of the time limit, or if the connection to the NMS is lost, each device rolls back to the previous configuration state. While the transaction timer is running, the NMS indulges in all sorts of testing and measurement operations, to verify that the L3VPN leg it just created functions as intended. And if not, simply close the connections to all the devices involved in the transaction to make it all go away. If all looks good, commit and unlock, as follows:

STEP 1. Give another <**commit**>, this time without the <**confirmed**> flag.

STEP 2. Unlock (<**unlock**>) the **:running** and **:candidate** datastores.

There are a lot more options and details on NETCONF network-wide transactions that could be discussed here, but the important points were made, so let's tie this off. With this sort of underlying technology, the NMS developers can become real slackers. Well, not really, but they do get twice as many use cases completed compared to life without transactions. Those use cases also work a lot more reliably. This discussion highlights the value of network-wide transactions. *"Support for configuration transactions across a number of devices would significantly simplify network configuration management"* (RFC 3535, Requirement #5).

Let's zoom out one level more and see how the network-wide transactions fit into the bigger picture. Look at network management from a control-theory perspective. As any electrical or mechanical engineer knows, the proper way to build a control system that works well in a complex environment is to get a feedback loop into the design. The traditional control-theory picture is shown in Figure 2-6.

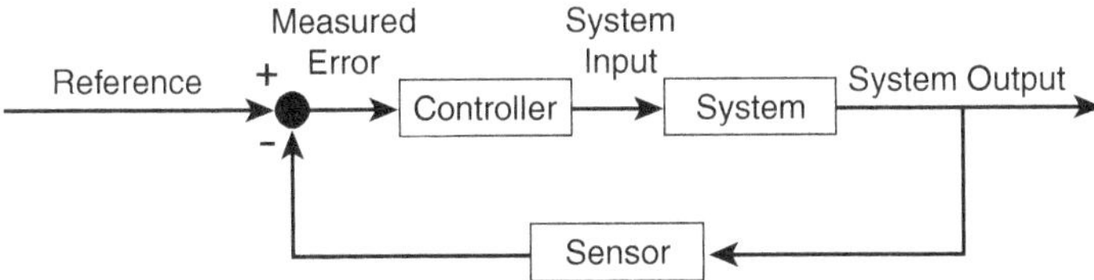

FIGURE 2-6 Feedback Loop

Translating that into your network management context, the picture becomes what is shown in Figure 2-7.

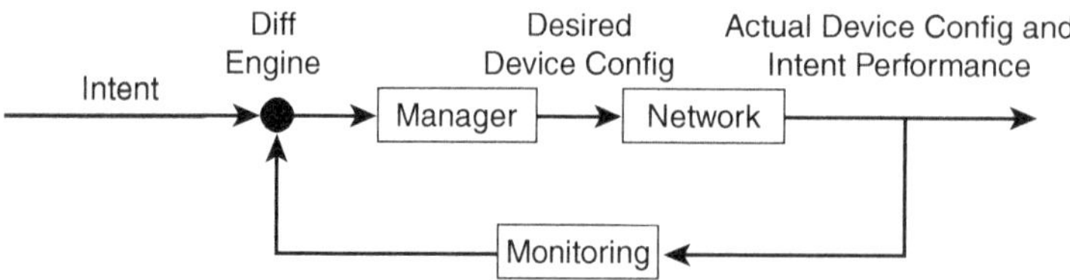

FIGURE 2-7 Feedback Loop in Network Management

As you can see in this figure, a mechanism to push and pull configurations to and from the network is obviously required. *"A mechanism to dump and restore configurations is a primitive operation needed by operators. Standards for pulling and pushing configurations from/to devices are desirable"* (RFC 3535, Requirement #7).

The network-wide transaction is an important mechanism for the manager to control the network. Without it, the manager would become both very much more complex and less efficient (in other words, the network would be consistent with the intent a lesser portion of the time). In order to close the loop, each of the other steps is just as important, however. When the monitoring reads the state of the network, it leverages the NETCONF capability to separate configuration from other data. *"It is necessary to make a clear distinction between configuration data, data that describes operational state, and statistics. Some devices make it very hard to determine which parameters were administratively configured and which were obtained via other mechanisms such as routing protocols"* (RFC 3535, Requirement #2).

With NETCONF, this data is delivered using standardized operations (**<get>** and **<get-config>**) with semantics consistent across devices. *"It is required to be able to fetch separately configuration data, operational state data, and statistics from devices, and to be able to compare these between devices"* (RFC 3535, Requirement #3). The data structure is consistent, too, through the use of standardized YANG models on the devices.

The diff engine then compares the intent performance to the original intent to see how well the current strategy to implement the intent works (remember the intent-based networking trend in Chapter 1), and it compares the actual network configuration with the desired one. If a change in strategy is required or desired (for example, because a peer went down, or the price of computing is lower in a different data center now), the manager computes a new desired configuration and sends it to the network. *"Given configuration A and configuration B, it should be possible to generate the operations necessary to get from A to B with minimal state changes and effects on network and systems. It is important to minimize the impact caused by configuration changes"* (RFC 3535, Requirement #6).

Clearly, for this to work, the definition of a transaction needs to be pretty strong. The diff engine computes an arbitrary bag of changes in no particular order. The complexity of the manager increases steeply if it has to sequence all of the diffs in some particular way. And unless that particular way is described in machine-readable form for every device in the network, that NMS remains a dream.

Therefore, it follows that the transaction definition used with NETCONF must describe a set of changes, that taken together and when applied to the current configuration must be consistent and make sense. It's about *consistent configurations*, not about *atomic sequences of changes. "It must be easy to do consistency checks of configurations over time and between the ends of a link in order to determine the changes between two configurations and whether those configurations are consistent"* (RFC 3535, Requirement #8).

This is not the same as a sequence of operations that are carried out in the order they are given, and where each intermediate step must be a valid configuration in itself. The server (device) side is clearly easier to implement if the proper sequencing comes from the manager, like the tradition in the SNMP world, which is why many implementers are tempted to go with this interpretation. Let's state clearly then that NETCONF transactional consistency is at the end of the transaction. Otherwise, the feedback controller use case dies, and you would be back to simple scripts shooting configurations at a network in the dark.

The same feedback capability is essential in those networks where human operators are allowed or required to meddle with the network at the same time as the manager. This is a common operational reality today and invariably leads to unforeseen situations. Unless there is a mechanism with a feedback loop that can compute new configurations and adjust to the ever-changing landscape, the more sophisticated use cases will never emerge.

Interview with the Experts

Q&A with Jürgen Schönwälder

Jürgen Schönwälder is professor of computer science at Jacobs University Bremen. His research interests include network management and measurement, network security, embedded systems, and distributed systems. He has co-authored more than 40 network management–related specifications and standards in the IETF, with major contributions to network management protocols (SNMP and NETCONF) and associated data modeling languages (SMIv2, SMIng, and YANG). He supervised the work on YANG 1.1 while serving as co-chair of the NETMOD working group.

Question:

Jürgen, you have been a key designer for many protocols and data models at the IETF, starting with SNMP, MIB, NETCONF, RESTCONF, and YANG. What is so special about data model–driven management based on YANG?

Answer:

Network management was always about automation. I got involved in network management technologies in the early 1990s, when SNMP became widely implemented and deployed. The design of SNMP was relatively simple (let's ignore the ASN.1/BER details, which clearly were not that simple), but due to the way data was organized and communicated, SNMP was relatively difficult to use to automate configuration tasks. Even basic operations like retrieving a snapshot of the configuration of a device for backup and restore purposes was difficult to implement via SNMP. (Some devices allowed you to trigger configuration snapshots via SNMP, but the configuration data was then typically delivered via FTP in a proprietary format.)

Given the assembly language nature of SNMP, operators often found it more convenient to configure devices via proprietary command-line interfaces. Since command-line interfaces were not designed to be used as programmatic APIs, automation via scripted command-line interfaces turned out to be somewhat brittle since the data representation was often optimized for human readers but not for programmatic access.

While there were attempts to evolve the SNMP technology and its data modeling language at the beginning of this millennium, they failed to reach sufficient momentum, and the IETF finally started an effort to create a new management protocol to solve the configuration management problem. The goal was to provide a robust API to manage the configuration of a device. Once the initial protocol work was done, a group of people gathered in 2007 to design a data modeling language supporting the new configuration protocol, which was the origin of YANG. All this took place at a time where XML and XML Schema were hot topics in the industry, but the designers of YANG felt that a domain-specific language was needed that's easier to read and write than XML Schema and is designed to assemble rather complex data models in an incremental fashion.

At the same time, configurations of devices became increasingly dynamic, amplifying the need for robust configuration transactions running almost constantly and affecting many devices. The YANG language started to fill a niche, as it was readily available, including basic tool support. While YANG originally used XML to encode instance data, it was relatively straightforward to support other data representations. In addition, the YANG language was designed to be extensible. As a consequence, vendors and operators were able to replace proprietary APIs with APIs that were driven by YANG data models, even though in several cases nonstandard data encodings and protocols were used. The fact that YANG allowed this to happen was a benefit for its adoption. Another driving force was the movement toward software-defined networks, where certain control functions are moved from devices to external controllers. YANG started to play a role here as well, both as an interface to the devices managed by a controller (the southbound interface) but also as a higher-level interface toward other controller and service management systems (the northbound interface).

While YANG was a success story, there is ongoing work to further improve the technology. Just recently, an architecture for network management datastores was published, which develops the architectural concept of datastores, on which YANG rests, further. Once implemented, applications managing devices or controllers will be able to access configuration data at different stages in the internal configuration processing workflows of devices and controllers and key metadata becomes available, explaining how a specific setting became effective, which enables new applications that can reason about why the actual behavior of a device differs from its intended behavior.

Data-driven management via programmatic APIs derived from YANG data models started to evolve network management toward service management. In the future, one can expect that there will be less focus on the individual devices and their APIs. Novel network and service programming concepts will appear, allowing network operators to build and extend service management systems orchestrating complex services at a much higher pace than ever before.

Summary

This chapter is by no means a complete account of everything you can do in YANG, but it aims at providing you a good grasp of all the most important concepts, what problems YANG solves, and how to go about making new YANG models.

In particular, you learned about the data model–driven management architecture and components. YANG is an API-contract language that creates a specification for the interface between a client and server (configure, monitor status, receive notifications, and invoke actions). The most common protocols used are NETCONF, RESTCONF, and gNMI, for which you understand the pros and cons in light of the tooling environment. Those protocols support different encodings: XML, JSON, protobuf, and so on. In the end, those data models generate APIs to be used directly in programming, thus hiding the low-level details of a YANG model or an encoding.

Even though "Overview of the 2002 IAB Network Management Workshop" (RFC 3535) is 15 years old, the requirements in this document are still applicable and relevant today. Therefore, this document is a good read for anyone wanting to understand the issues faced by operators.

References in This Chapter

To further extend your knowledge, you should look at the RFCs as a next step. They are actually quite readable and a good source of detailed information, and many have usage examples. In particular, have a look at the items referenced in Table 2-4.

TABLE 2-4 YANG-Related Documents for Further Reading

Topic	Content
RFC 3535	https://tools.ietf.org/html/rfc3535 Operator requirements in terms of network management. Still valid today.
Architecture	http://tools.ietf.org/html/rf6244 "An Architecture for Network Management Using NETCONF and YANG" (RFC 6244)
NETCONF WG	https://datatracker.ietf.org/wg/netconf/documents/ The IETF Network Configuration Working Group. This is the group that defines NETCONF and RESTCONF. Look here for the latest drafts and RFCs.
NETMOD WG	https://datatracker.ietf.org/wg/netmod/documents/ The IETF Network Modeling Working Group. This is the group that defines YANG and many of the YANG modules. Look here for the latest drafts and RFCs.
yangcatalog.org	https://www.yangcatalog.org/ Catalog of YANG modules, searchable on keywords and metadata. Also has YANG tools for validation, browsing, dependency graphs, and REGEX validation. At the time of writing, there are about 3,500 YANG modules in the catalog.
RFCs 8199 and RFC 8309	http://tools.ietf.org/html/rfc8199 and http://tools.ietf.org/html/rfc8309 The different YANG module types.

Endnotes

1. https://datatracker.ietf.org/wg/netconf/charter
2. https://tools.ietf.org/html/rfc6244#ref-W3CXSD
3. https://tools.ietf.org/html/rfc6244#ref-ISODSDL
4. https://datatracker.ietf.org/wg/netmod/charter/
5. https://datatracker.ietf.org/doc/rfc8402/
6. https://datatracker.ietf.org/doc/rfc7011/
7. https://www.sdncentral.com/what-is-openflow/
8. http://www.openstack.org/
9. http://www.opendaylight.org/
10. http://openvswitch.org/
11. http://openconfig.net/
12. http://uml.org/
13. https://www.ietf.org/
14. https://core.tcl.tk/expect/index
15. https://www.itu.int/en/ITU-T/Pages/default.aspx
16. https://www.mef.net/
17. https://www.broadband-forum.org/
18. http://www.openroadm.org/home.html
19. https://yangcatalog.org/
20. http://www.openconfig.net/software/
21. https://datatracker.ietf.org/doc/rfc8040/
22. https://tools.ietf.org/html/rfc8040#ref-REST-Dissertation
23. http://www.grpc.io/
24. https://datatracker.ietf.org/doc/draft-ietf-core-yang-cbor/
25. https://developer.cisco.com/site/ydk/

26. https://github.com/CiscoDevNet/ydk-gen/blob/master/profiles/bundles

27. https://github.com/CiscoDevNet/ydk-py

28. https://github.com/CiscoDevNet/ydk-cpp

29. https://github.com/openconfig/ygot

30. https://github.com/openconfig/goyang

31. https://github.com/robshakir/pyangbind

Chapter 3

YANG Explained

This chapter covers

- What a YANG module looks like and what it contains
- Building a simple YANG module, then extending it
- How to describe tabular data in YANG
- Defining actions, RPCs, and notifications
- The fundamental difference between configuration and operational data
- Why and how to ensure data is valid using constraints of many different types
- Modeling data that is only relevant sometimes
- Properly navigating with YANG pointers, using XPath
- Augmenting YANG modules, evolving them over time
- Network Management Datastore Architecture

Introduction

This chapter takes you on a journey to build a real, usable YANG model. This is done in stages with different themes, building up a more and more comprehensive model. Each stage is available as a hands-on project you can clone from GitHub, and then build, run, and play with as you please. Instructions for how to obtain the necessary free tools are found within the project README file at https://github.com/janlindblad/bookzone.

Describe Your World of Data

Consider the following situation: A fictitious bookstore chain called *BookZone* decided to define a proper, consistent interface for each store so that client applications can browse the inventory of each store and the central management applications can add new titles and authors to the affiliate stores.

Table 3-1 shows a data structure with the sort of information BookZone wants to keep track of, i.e. the title, ISBN, author and price of each book. ISBN stands for International Standard Book Number. It is used by publishers and book stores to uniquely identify a particular book title, including its edition and variation (for example, hardcover or paperback). The table has some sample data filled in. Such data is called *instance data*. In order to get organized, you need to create a *schema* for this data so you can describe it to your peers with precision rather than by example. Examples are great for general understanding, but they are never precise.

A description of the YANG structure of this table is provided shortly. As time goes by, the instance data (that is, the particular entries in this table) may come and go, but the YANG structure with these four columns remains.

TABLE 3-1 Tabular Representation of the Book Catalog Using Example Data

title	isbn	author	price
The Neverending Story	9780140386332	Michael Ende	8.50
What We Think About When We Try Not To Think About Global Warming: Toward a New Psychology of Climate Action	9781603585835	Per Espen Stoknes	16.00
The Hitchhiker's Guide to the Galaxy	0330258648	Douglas Adams	22.00
The Art of War	160459893X	Sun Tzu	12.75
I Am Malala: The Girl Who Stood Up for Education and Was Shot by the Taliban	9780297870913	Malala Yousafzai	19.50

To define a basic book catalog schema in YANG, refer to Example 3-1.

EXAMPLE 3-1 YANG Schema Representation of the Book Catalog

```
container books {
  list book {
    key title;

    leaf title {
      type string;
    }
    leaf isbn {
      type string;
      mandatory true;
    }
    leaf author {
      type string;
    }
```

```
      leaf price {
        type decimal64 {
          fraction-digits 2;
        }
        units sim-dollar;
      }
    }
  }
```

Notice that each line in YANG consists of a keyword (`container`, `list`, `key`, `leaf`, `type`, `mandatory`) followed by a name (*books*, *book*, *title*, *isbn*, or *author*) or a value with predefined meaning (`string`, `true`). Each line is followed either by a semicolon (`;`) or by a block surrounded by curly braces (`{...}`).

A YANG `container` is suitable when you have a collection of information elements that belong together. By placing the container *books* at the top level like this, it is easy for the user to find everything related to books. Authors are added later, and they go in a different container, obviously.

A YANG `list` works like a container, placing related things together—except that with a list, you can have many instances of what is inside the list. Inside the list *book*, there will be many *titles*. Think of a YANG list as a table with columns.

By placing a YANG `leaf` inside the list four times, you get a table with four columns. Each leaf has a `type` statement inside that defines what kind of data this particular leaf can hold. In this case, three leafs are strings, and one is a number with two digits after the decimal point. The leaf *isbn* has been marked `mandatory true`. This means that it must have a value. By default, all leafs are optional, unless they are marked as keys or as mandatory. In Example 3-1, both *isbn* and *title* are mandatory, while *author* and *price* are optional.

Think of the whole structure as a tree, with the container *books* as the trunk, the list *book* as the branching point of four branches, and then the four leaves: *title*, *isbn*, *author*, and *price*.

The `key` *title* statement in Example 3-1 means the title column is the key column of this list. The key column is what identifies which entry is which in the list. For example, if you wanted to update the *author* value ("Sun Tzu") of the book *The Art of War*, so that it also includes his name written with Chinese characters, you would have to use the key column to specify which of the books in the list you wanted to update. If you are familiar with relational databases, the `key` concept in YANG corresponds with the primary set of keys in a relational table.

You could say the following: Update */books/book[title='The Art of War']/author* to be "Sun Tzu (孫子)". This notation with slashes and brackets is called XPath; it is the language used to navigate the instance data in a database that uses the YANG model as its schema. XPath is explained in some more detail later in this chapter, but just to step through the reference at the beginning of this paragraph, you read the XPath expression like this:

> The slash (/) at the beginning means go to the root of the YANG model. Next, *books/book* means go into the container *books*, then into the list *book*. The square brackets imply filtering among the instances. There are five instances in this example. The filter matches only the one that has the *title* value equal to the given string. When it's found, navigate to the leaf *author*. This way, the XPath expression points out a single element. That element gets a new value, which includes some Chinese characters.

Let's discuss the selection of the key for the list for a moment. In this list, the leaf *title* was selected to be the key. Another viable candidate could have been *isbn*, since that, too, could be used to uniquely identify a book. Alternatively, inventing and adding a completely meaningless random value, such as a universally unique identifier (UUID) or a plain number, would work. There's no right or wrong choice, but the choice decides how a user would interact with the system.

By choosing *title* to be the key, you have a meaningful identifier to use when thinking about the data. Had you chosen *isbn* as the key, the update to the author name would look like this: Update */books/book[isbn='160459893X']/author* to be "Sun Tzu (孫子)". Clearly, this less meaningful key increases the chance of mistakes going through undetected. This is a general philosophy in YANG modeling: use meaningful keys, when possible, and allow the user to use any string as an identifier rather than, for example, only numbers. If there was a strong requirement to support multiple books with identical titles, obviously *title* would not work as a key. In this case, maybe *isbn* would be the best remaining option. It has at least some real-world identification value.

Before the YANG in Example 3-1 is put to actual use, it needs a boilerplate header. The header uniquely identifies the module and states what revision date it has. The complete, first version of the module is shown in Example 3-2.

EXAMPLE 3-2 The Complete bookzone-example.yang Module for a Basic Catalog of Books

```
module bookzone-example {
  yang-version 1.1;
  namespace 'http://example.com/ns/bookzone';
  prefix bz;

  revision 2018-01-01 {
    description "Initial revision. A catalog of books.";
  }

  container books {
    list book {
      key title;

      leaf title {
        type string;
```

```
        }
        leaf isbn {
          type string;
          mandatory true;
        }
        leaf author {
          type string;
        }
        leaf price {
          type decimal64 {
            fraction-digits 2;
          }
          units sim-dollar;
        }
      }
    }
}
```

Each YANG module must start with the keyword `module`, followed by the module name. The filename of the module must match this name, plus an extension of `.yang`. The next line declares that the module is written in YANG 1.1, as opposed to YANG 1.0, or any other future version. In this little example, everything would still work fine if you specified yang-version 1.0, but in later updates to this module there are a few things that use YANG 1.1 features. Let's use yang-version 1.1. That should also be the default when you are writing new modules at this time; there is no particular benefit to use YANG 1.0.

NOTE

More information about the differences between YANG 1.1 and YANG 1.0 is available in RFC 7950 Section 1.1.

Each YANG module must have a world-unique namespace name, defined by the `namespace` statement. No two YANG modules in the world should have the same namespace string. It's up to you, as a YANG author, to ensure that. The key thing with the namespace is that it should be world unique, so the recommendation is that you take your organization's URL and then add something to ensure it will be unique within your organization. That's why, in Example 3-2, the namespace string looks like a URL. If you paste that into your browser, however, you'll get a 404 (page not found) error.

Sometimes you see namespaces beginning with `urn:`. Such namespaces are used by IETF, for example. Namespaces starting with `urn:` are supposed to be registered with the Internet Assigned Numbers Authority (IANA). Many organizations mistakenly pick such namespace strings without registering them, however. Do not do that, or you risk pointless trouble.

Since namespace strings must be world unique, they also tend to be rather long, so there is something called a *prefix*, which is essentially an abbreviation of the module name. In theory, prefixes do not need to be unique. In practice, however, users (operators, programmers, and DevOps engineers) as well as many tools tend to be rather confused when the same prefix is used by several YANG modules. Be sure to pick prefixes that are likely to be unique, especially within the set of modules you author. Example 3-2 uses "bz" as an abbreviation for bookzone. Ideally, a little longer prefix would be good to improve the chances of uniqueness. If you are designing a YANG module, don't pick an obvious prefix name like *if*, *snmp*, *bgp*, or *aaa*, because many other module authors have already used them. YANG module readers and users easily get confused when there are several different modules with the same prefix from different vendors.

Next, there is a `revision` statement with a date. These statements are not strictly required, but it is certainly a good idea to add one every time a new version of the YANG module is "published." A YANG module is typically considered published when it becomes accessible to people or systems outside the team responsible for it. Anyone will agree who has had to sort out a situation with different versions of programming interfaces with no easy way to determine whether they are the same and, if not, which one is the newer one.

Describe Your Data with Precision

Keeping track of book inventory is certainly key for a bookstore. Before you start doing business, however, you need to keep track of users (who will pay you) and authors (whom you have to pay).

Example 3-3 adds a few lines of YANG for basic user management. Each user has a system-unique user ID (*user-id*) and a screen name that may occasionally be the same for multiple users. The type `string` in YANG allows the full UTF-8 character set, so nothing special is required to allow German or Japanese users on the system.

EXAMPLE 3-3 Simple List of Users with user-id as the Key and a Screen Name

```
container users {
  list user {
    key user-id;

    leaf user-id {
      type string;
    }
    leaf name {
      type string;
    }
  }
}
```

Then there are the authors. In Example 3-4 it was decided that all authors be addressed by their full name, and not use any sort of user IDs or numbers, since that has caused confusion in the past. Model creators should decide how to address the items in a list, and this time the full name was chosen. As a consequence, you have to ensure that the full name used for authors contains middle names and suffixes like "Jr." and "III" so that all authors are uniquely identified by name. Additionally, each author must have a payment account number with the finance department. A single unsigned integer works. Since you know the finance department numbers its accounts starting at 1001, it is reasonable to say so in the model and catch potential errors. The keyword `max` in the range simply means the highest possible number the type can represent.

EXAMPLE 3-4 List of Authors with name as the Key and an account-id

```
container authors {
  list author {
    key name;

    leaf name {
      type string;
    }
    leaf account-id {
      type uint32 {
        range 1001..max;
      }
    }
  }
}
```

Since containers *users* and *authors* with their lists go outside the *books/book* container and list, you're forming a small forest in the YANG module, with three tree-like structures. In order to get an overview, you can use the so-called *tree representation* to display the YANG module in a compact way, as shown in Example 3-5.

EXAMPLE 3-5 YANG Tree Representation of the Book Catalog

```
module: bookzone-example
    +--rw authors
    |  +--rw author* [name]
    |     +--rw name           string
    |     +--rw account-id?    uint32
    +--rw books
    |  +--rw book* [title]
    |     +--rw title        string
    |     +--rw isbn         string
    |     +--rw author?      string
    |     +--rw price?       decimal64
    +--rw users
       +--rw user* [user-id]
          +--rw user-id    string
          +--rw name?      string
```

The tools and specification (RFC 8340) behind these tree diagrams are discussed further in Chapter 7, "Automation Is as Good as the Data Models, Their Related Metadata, and the Tools: For the Network Architecture and Operator." You have a list of authors now. There is a leaf in the *book* list that names the author. Remember? The following snippet depicts the leaf *author* as a plain string:

```
leaf author {
  type string;
}
```

This string should, of course, match the name of one of the authors in the list *author*; otherwise, how would you know which author to pay? The construct in the previous snippet allows mistakes. In YANG, it is easy to close that loophole; just make this a leaf reference instead, or `leafref`, as it's called in YANG.

A `leafref` is a pointer to a column in some YANG list somewhere, and any value that happens to exist in that key column is a valid value for the pointing leaf. In this case, the `leafref` version of the leaf *author* is shown in Example 3-6.

EXAMPLE 3-6 Leaf author from Example 3-2 as a leafref

```
leaf author {
  type leafref {
    path /authors/author/name;
  }
}
```

Notice that the leafref contains a path pointing out which YANG list and which key column in that list contains the valid values for the author value. The expression in the `path` statement is simplified XPath, meaning not all XPath magic can be used here. The path starts at the root of the YANG tree (/), then goes into container *authors* and list *author*. Finally, the path points to the *name* leaf in the list.

Any */authors/author/name* leaf (a string) is a valid value for the */books/book/author* leafref, which is therefore also a string.

If the */books/book/author* leaf changes to something that does not exist in any */authors/author/name*, validation of the transaction containing the change fails, since the reference no longer points to a valid instance. It isn't an error to change the */books/book/author* leaf to a value that is not listed in */authors/author/name* at the time you are typing this in, as long as you ensure the name is added to */authors/author/name* before the transaction is committed.

Another thing you want to add to *books* is information about which language they are written in, so that client applications can search and display books that may be more relevant to users.

It would be easy to simply add a leaf called *language* with a string value for the language. However, in YANG, you normally want to be specific about the allowed values when possible. Here, an enumeration of possible language options is fitting. You could enumerate all the languages right inside the leaf, but since this language choice may be relevant in other places in the model, you should define a reusable type for languages. The leaf *language* with the user-defined type *language-type* is shown in the following snippet and looks like this in the */books/book* list:

```
leaf language {
  type language-type;
}
```

And somewhere in the YANG module you need to define the language type, as shown in Example 3-7.

EXAMPLE 3-7 Type Definition of the language-type

```
typedef language-type {
  type enumeration {
    enum arabic;
    enum chinese;
    enum english;
    enum french;
    enum moroccan-arabic;
    enum swahili;
    enum swedish;
    // List not exhaustive in order to save space
  }
  description
    "Primary language the book consumer needs to master "+
    "in order to appreciate the book's content";
}
```

The convention in YANG is to have all identifiers in all lowercase (with dashes when necessary) for anything an operator might type. Note that this convention applies to enumerations as well. This makes it easy for operators to type the names, if need be. YANG is case-sensitive, so `enum ARABIC` and `enum arabic` are two distinct values.

Similarly, the ISBN for the book is currently a string, but as you know, ISBNs have a certain format. Actually, there are (essentially) two variants of ISBNs: one is 10 digits and the other, more modern one is 13 digits, which is adapted to the barcode system. Because you need to handle some older literature, the YANG module must support both formats. The following snippet shows how to sharpen the leaf *isbn* type to allow precisely the format needed. Leaf *isbn* is lowercase; remember the YANG convention to use all lowercase identifiers.

First, change the type from type `string` to a type you define yourself:

```
leaf isbn {
  type ISBN-10-or-13;
}
```

From here, you need to define this type. By convention, type definitions are placed near the top of the module, as shown in Example 3-8. It's fine if type names contain uppercase letters, as type names are not typed by operators anyway.

EXAMPLE 3-8 Type Definition of the User-Defined Type ISBN-10-or-13

```
typedef ISBN-10-or-13 {
  type union {
    type string {
      length 10;
      pattern '[0-9]{9}[0-9X]';
    }
    type string {
      length 13;
      pattern '97[89][0-9]{10}';
    }
  }
  description
    "The International Standard Book Number (ISBN) is a unique
     numeric commercial book identifier.

     An ISBN is assigned to each edition and variation (except
     reprintings) of a book. [source: wikipedia]";
  reference
    "https://en.wikipedia.org/wiki/International_Standard_Book_Number";
}
```

The `union` YANG construct allows multiple types—any type listed within the construct. In this case, you have two member types: two strings, each of a specific length (10 and 13 characters, respectively). On top of this requirement, the 10-character variant must consist of the digits 0–9 repeated nine times, and then a last check digit (either 0–9 or the letter X). This is simply how 10-digit ISBNs are defined. The 13-character variant always starts with a 9 followed by a 7. The third digit is either 8 or 9. Then follows 10 digits (0–9). This reflects how the ISBN was fit into the barcode system, as if all books were produced in a single country (called *bookland*). The first few digits in barcodes normally indicate the country of origin.

Since ISBNs are defined by a standard and a standards body, it's nice to give this type a suitable description. The YANG keyword `reference` is used to help the reader to find more information on the topic—usually the name of some specification, or as in this case, a link to the Web.

By using specific type definitions (for example, `pattern`, `union`, and `range`), you make the YANG contract clear, and systems can validate the input and output automatically.

Separate Your Data into Categories

Another aspect to consider when it comes to ISBNs is that there is not one ISBN per title; instead, there is one ISBN per title and delivery format. If a given title comes in paperback, hardcover, and EPUB, each one has a different ISBN. With the current model, you need to have separate entries for every book, depending on which format it is in. For your purposes, this is not ideal. Instead, make a list of formats and ISBNs inside the list of books, as shown in Table 3-2.

TABLE 3-2 Tabular Representation of the List Format with ISBN Information Inserted into List See Example 3-9

title	author	formats		
The Neverending Story	Michael Ende	isbn	format	price
		9780140386332	paperback	8.50
		9781452656304	mp3	29.95
What We Think About When We Try Not To Think About Global Warming: Toward a New Psychology of Climate Action	Per Espen Stoknes	isbn	format	price
		9781603585835	paperback	16.00
The Hitchhiker's Guide to the Galaxy	Douglas Adams	isbn	format	price
		0330258648	paperback	22.00
		9781400052929	hardcover	31.50
The Art of War	Sun Tzu	isbn	format	price
		160459893X	paperback	12.75
I Am Malala: The Girl Who Stood Up for Education and Was Shot by the Taliban	Malala Yousafzai	isbn	format	price
		9780297870913	hardcover	19.50

Having lists inside lists is perfectly normal in YANG. Some people who spent a lot of time with relational databases and modeling find their heads spinning at this point. Actually, there is nothing particularly strange about having lists inside lists. Your computer's file system has directories inside directories, and nobody finds that strange at all.

This reflects how typical network elements have their command-line interfaces (CLIs) organized. YANG was designed to be able to reflect this natural way of modeling device management data. In fact, one of the reasons Simple Network Management Protocol (SNMP) was considered so hard to use was just this: Living in the relational world, where tables inside tables are not possible, made the SNMP model look very different from how most people looked at and worked with the data in the network elements. There was always a high cost of translation between users' minds (living in the CLI world) and the relational SNMP tables.

The structure of the model with a list inside a list is shown in Example 3-9.

EXAMPLE 3-9 List Format Added Inside the List book

```
  container books {
    list book {
      key title;

      leaf title {
        type string;
      }
...
      list format {
        key isbn;
        leaf isbn {
          type ISBN-10-or-13;
        }
        leaf format-id {
...
        }
      }
```

What about the leaf *format-id*? You could make that a string. This allows for all possible formats, current and future. However, it will inevitably lead to some misspelled or ambiguous entries. An enumeration is clearly better than a string here, since that restricts the user to a predetermined set of well-defined values. The downside with enumerations is that they are hard to expand over time, and they do not cope well with variants.

In the *language* enumeration there is both Arabic and Moroccan-Arabic. The latter is a variant of the former, but in the enumeration the values are distinct. If you have some YANG expressions that depend on whether a language is Arabic or not, it would have to test against both *arabic* and *moroccan-arabic*. And, if you add another Arabic variant, the expression would need to be updated to take each new variant into account.

This concept of some enumeration values belonging together is common in networking, and in the world at large. Just think of how many interface types there are, and how many variants of Ethernet there are now, all the way from 10-Base-T to 1000GE. In YANG, these enumerations with kind-of relations are modeled using the YANG keyword `identity`. If you are familiar with object-oriented design principles, this is referred to as *subclassing* in that context.

Here are the book formats that BookZone chose to use identities to describe. See how each identity has a `base`. Identity *paperback* has a base of *paper*, which means it is a "kind-of" paper book. Identity *paper*, in turn, has a base of *format-idty*, which means *paper* is a "kind-of" book delivery format. The suffix *-idty* is just an abbreviation added here to the each of the root identities to make it easier to remember it is an `identity`, as shown in Example 3-10.

EXAMPLE 3-10 YANG Identities Forming a Tree of Is-a-Kind-Of Relations

```
identity format-idty {
  description "Root identity for all book formats";
}
identity paper {
  base format-idty;
  description "Physical book printed on paper";
}
identity audio-cd {
  base format-idty;
  description "Audiobook delivered as Compact Disc";
}
identity file-idty {
  base format-idty;
  description "Book delivered as a file";
}
identity paperback {
  base paper;
  description "Physical book with soft covers";
}
identity hardcover {
  base paper;
  description "Physical book with hard covers";
}
identity mp3 {
  base file-idty;
  description "Audiobook delivered as MP3 file";
}
identity pdf {
  base file-idty;
  description "Digital book delivered as PDF file";
}
identity epub {
  base file-idty;
  description "Digital book delivered as EPUB file";
}
```

The point with recording these relations becomes apparent in later sections in this chapter.

Now that you have a number of formats defined, return to leaf *format-id*. By you specifying type `identityref` and a root identity, this leaf can take the value of any identity that directly or indirectly is based on this root identity. As shown in later sections, additional identities may also be defined in other modules. When they are, they immediately become valid values for the *format-id* leaf. Example 3-11 shows how leaf *format-id* is typed as a (mandatory) `identityref` with a `base` *format-idty*.

EXAMPLE 3-11 Leaf format-id with Type identityref

```
leaf format-id {
  mandatory true;
  type identityref {
    base format-idty;
  }
}
```

By you specifying type identityref base *format-idty*, all the book formats previously listed immediately become valid values for this leaf, because they are based, directly or indirectly, on *format-idty*. Leaf *format-id* was made mandatory since each ISBN is for a given format. You do not want to allow listing a book with an ISBN without saying which format you are talking about.

Before you go ahead and publish all of these additions, take a moment to write a new `revision` statement. The `revision` statement should describe what is new since the last revision, and each new revision should be placed before earlier `revision` statements.

With that addition, the entire module looks like Example 3-12.

EXAMPLE 3-12 Complete YANG Module at Revision 2018-01-02

```
module bookzone-example {
  yang-version 1.1;
  namespace 'http://example.com/ns/bookzone';
  prefix bz;

  import ietf-yang-types {
    prefix yang;
  }

  revision 2018-01-02 {
    description
      "Added book formats, authors and users, see
       /books/book/format
       /authors
       /users";
  }
  revision 2018-01-01 {
    description "Initial revision. A catalog of books.";
  }

  typedef language-type {
    type enumeration {
      enum arabic;
      enum chinese;
      enum english;
```

```
      enum french;
      enum moroccan-arabic;
      enum swahili;
      enum swedish;
      // List not exhaustive in order to save space
    }
    description
      "Primary language the book consumer needs to master "+
      "in order to appreciate the book's content";
  }

  identity format-idty {
    description "Root identity for all book formats";
  }
  identity paper {
    base format-idty;
    description "Physical book printed on paper";
  }
  identity audio-cd {
    base format-idty;
    description "Audiobook delivered as Compact Disc";
  }
  identity file-idty {
    base format-idty;
    description "Book delivered as a file";
  }
  identity paperback {
    base paper;
    description "Physical book with soft covers";
  }
  identity hardcover {
    base paper;
    description "Physical book with hard covers";
  }
  identity mp3 {
    base file-idty;
    description "Audiobook delivered as MP3 file";
  }
  identity pdf {
    base file-idty;
    description "Digital book delivered as PDF file";
  }
  identity epub {
    base file-idty;
    description "Digital book delivered as EPUB file";
  }
```

```
typedef ISBN-10-or-13 {
  type union {
    type string {
      length 10;
      pattern '[0-9]{9}[0-9X]';
    }
    type string {
      length 13;
      pattern '97[89][0-9]{10}';
    }
  }
  description
    "The International Standard Book Number (ISBN) is a unique
     numeric commercial book identifier.

     An ISBN is assigned to each edition and variation (except
     reprintings) of a book. [source: wikipedia]";
  reference
    "https://en.wikipedia.org/wiki/International_Standard_Book_Number";
}

container authors {
  list author {
    key name;

    leaf name {
      type string;
    }
    leaf account-id {
      type uint32 {
        range 1001..max;
      }
    }
  }
}

container books {
  list book {
    key title;

    leaf title {
      type string;
    }
```

```
      leaf author {
        type leafref {
          path /authors/author/name;
        }
      }
      leaf language {
        type language-type;
      }
      list format {
        key isbn;
        leaf isbn {
          type ISBN-10-or-13;
        }
        leaf format-id {
          mandatory true;
          type identityref {
            base format-idty;
          }
        }
        leaf price {
          type decimal64 {
            fraction-digits 2;
          }
          units sim-dollar;
        }
      }
    }
  }

  container users {
    list user {
      key user-id;

      leaf user-id {
        type string;
      }
      leaf name {
        type string;
      }
    }
  }
}
```

Describing Possible Events

Beyond configuration changes that flow from the client to the server, events may occur on either side, and the other party may need to react to them. Information about such events also needs to be part of the YANG contract. When a client informs a server, it's called an `action` or `rpc`. Events taking place on a server are sent to the client as a `notification`.

Actions and RPCs

The model you have may serve you well as a book catalog and to store information about users (buyers) and authors, but it still lacks something quite fundamental. There is still no way for a client application to request a purchase to take place. For this, you need a YANG action or rpc. RPC stands for *remote procedure call*, a computer science term for a client asking a server to perform a specified operation.

In YANG, the only difference between an `rpc` and an `action` is that an rpc can only be declared at the top level of the YANG model (that is, outside all containers, lists, and so on). An action, on the other hand, cannot be used at the top level, but only inside containers, lists, and so on. Otherwise, they mean exactly the same thing. There are really only historic reasons for separating the two. The `action` keyword is new in YANG 1.1 and does not exist in YANG 1.0, so many YANG models in the field use only `rpc`.

When writing new YANG models, use `action` when the operation you are defining acts on a specific node (object) in the YANG tree and use `rpc` if the operation cannot be associated with some specific node.

When defining an action (or rpc) in a YANG model, you can specify an `input` and `output` parameter section inside the YANG action.

If you elected to make an `rpc`, which must live outside all containers and lists, the input section for your *purchase* action might contain a leafref to the buying *user*, a leafref to which *title* and *format* you want to buy, and the *number-of-copies* to order.

Invoke rpc */purchase* with the following input:

- *user*: "janl"
- *title*: "The Neverending Story"
- *format*: "bz:paperback"
- *number-of-copies*: 1

If instead you elect to make an `action`, you could define the action inside the *user* list. This way, the user that purchases the book is specified in the path to the action. Perhaps this could be called a bit more object oriented?

Invoke action */users/user[name="janl"]/purchase*:

- *title*: "The Neverending Story"
- *format*: "bz:paperback"
- *number-of-copies*: 1

Notice that there is no major difference between the two forms. You can always turn an action into an rpc by adding a leafref to the object the action operates on. The reverse is not always true, since there are rpcs that don't operate on any object in the YANG model. A prime example is adding an rpc *reboot*. There may be no natural place for that rpc within the YANG structure. In this case, it would not fit naturally within */users*, certainly not */books*, and not */authors*.

The action `output` parameter section lists the data that will come out of the action.

Example 3-13 shows what a complete *purchase* action might look like. As defined here, this action definition lives inside list *user*. It could equally have been an rpc (add leafref to *user*) or defined inside *book* (remove the leafref to *title* and *format* and add a leafref to *user*). Object orientation pundits may still prefer this model layout since the user can be thought of as the "active part" that invokes the action.

EXAMPLE 3-13 Action Purchase with Input and Output Data

```
action purchase {
  input {
    leaf title {
      type leafref {
        path /books/book/title;
      }
    }
    leaf format {
      type leafref {
        path /books/book/format/format-id;
        // Reviewer note: This should be improved
      }
    }
    leaf number-of-copies {
      type uint32 {
        range 1..999;
      }
    }
  }
  output {
    choice outcome {
      case success {
        leaf success {
          type empty;
```

```
            description
              "Order received and will be sent to specified user.
               File orders are downloadable at the URL given below.";
          }
          leaf delivery-url {
            type string;
            description
              "Download URL for file deliveries.";
          }
        }
        leaf out-of-stock {
          type empty;
          description
            "Order received, but cannot be delivered at this time.
             A notification will be sent when the item ships.";
        }
        leaf failure {
          type string;
          description
            "Order cancelled, for reason stated here.";
        }
      }
    }
  }
```

In this case, the output is modeled as a `choice`. A YANG choice lists a number of alternatives, of which (at most) one can be present. Each of the alternatives can be listed as a `case` inside the choice. The `case` keyword can be skipped if the case contains only a single YANG element, like a single leaf, container, or list.

With the `choice` statement in Example 3-13, there are three different cases that the action can return:

1. `leaf` *success* and/or *delivery-url*.
2. `leaf` *out-of-stock*
3. `leaf` *failure*

There is actually a fourth case as well. With this YANG model, it would also be valid to return nothing. The `choice` was not marked `mandatory true`, so it is not necessarily present at all.

The choice and case nodes are YANG schema nodes. This means that they are invisible in the data tree. When the action returns, it simply returns the contents of one of the case statements, and never mentions anything about `choice` *outcome* or `case` *success*. When specifying paths to nodes (for example, in a leafref), always omit schema nodes.

Another first encounter in Example 3-13 is the type `empty`. In YANG, leafs of type `empty` have no value (hence the name), but they can exist or not exist. A type `empty` leaf can thus be created and deleted, but not assigned. Type `empty` leafs are often used to indicate flag conditions, such as *success* or *enabled*. The *delivery-url* and *failure* are modeled as strings, as opposed to `empty`, because they return the URL and failure reason, respectively.

Notifications

Notice in the *purchase* action the possibility that the store is out of stock at the moment. In this scenario, the order is still recorded and will be delivered at a later time. In this case, a notification is sent out to the buyer when the delivery is about to actually happen. This notification *shipping* includes a reference to the buying *user*, the *title* and delivery *format* of the book, as well as the number of copies.

Notifications are always defined at the top level, outside any containers, lists, and so on, like rpcs, as they're independent of any YANG objects. In this case, most of the data is pointers into the configuration data model, as seen in Example 3-14.

EXAMPLE 3-14 Notification Shipping with Output Data

```
notification shipping {
  leaf user {
    type leafref {
      path /users/user/name;
    }
  }
  leaf title {
    type leafref {
      path /books/book/title;
    }
  }
  leaf format {
    type leafref {
      path /books/book/format/format-id;
      // Reviewer note: This should be improved
    }
  }
  leaf number-of-copies {
    type uint32;
  }
}
```

The way the leafref in leaf *format* is constructed is not perfect (more on that in the next section).

Before you publish the improved model, add a `revision` statement, as shown in Example 3-15.

EXAMPLE 3-15 YANG Module Revision Statement 2018-01-03

```
revision 2018-01-03 {
  description
    "Added action purchase and notification shipping.";
}
```

Separating Configuration from Operational Data

The management at BookZone is quite happy with the progress on standardizing the book catalog. One thing they still miss, however, is some business intelligence and statistics to improve the relevance of titles to book buyers. In particular, a popularity metric would be nice to have for each title.

The popularity metric is not something that a manager could configure; instead, this is operational data—data generated by the system as a reflection of events taking place. This is typically information that a manager would want to monitor or use in troubleshooting activities. In YANG, such data is marked as `config false` to highlight the operational nature, as opposed to configuration data, which is flagged with `config true`.

Leafs, containers, lists, and so on that are marked `config false` can be placed anywhere in a YANG model—at the top level or deep inside some structure. Once `config false` is applied to a YANG container, list, and so on, everything inside that structure is `config false`. It is not possible to add a `config true` leaf somewhere in a `config false` list, for example. This is quite natural if you think about it. It wouldn't work to have configuration come and go based on some operational state in the system.

Example 3-16 illustrates leaf *popularity* added in */books/book*. It is marked `config false` to indicate that it is a status value, not something a manager can set/configure/order.

EXAMPLE 3-16 Operational Leaf Popularity Added Inside List book

```
container books {
  list book {
...
    leaf popularity {
      config false;
      type uint32;
      units copies-sold/year;
      description
        "Number of copies sold in the last 12-month period";
    }
```

Naturally, the system that implements this YANG model needs to have some sort of code that provides the current value whenever a client asks to see it. Alternatively, the system must tie this to a database that delivers the value on request, but needs to be updated whenever things change.

Another metric the BookZone management is asking for is inventory data per book: the total number of items in stock, the number reserved by a potential buyer, and the number immediately available for delivery.

Example 3-17 provides a model for this.

EXAMPLE 3-17 Operational Container number-of-copies Added Inside List format

```
container books {
    list book {
...
      list format {
...
        container number-of-copies {
          config false;
          leaf in-stock {
            type uint32;
          }
          leaf reserved {
            type uint32;
          }
          leaf available {
            type uint32;
          }
        }
```

If a container, list, leaf or other YANG element is not marked with either `config true` or `config false`, it inherits its "config-ness" from its parent. In Example 3-17, leafs *in-stock*, *reserved*, and *available* are `config false` because the container *number-of-copies* is `config false`. The top-level `module` statement of every YANG module is considered `config true`, so unless there are any `config false` statements in a YANG module, everything in it is `config true`.

The next feature to incorporate in your YANG module is a purchase history for each user. A natural way to organize this is to place a list of purchased items under the */users/user* list. Each purchase list item would have a reference to the title and format of the purchased item, the number of copies purchased, and a date.

Example 3-18 is a suggested list *purchase-history* placed inside the existing list *user*.

EXAMPLE 3-18 Operational List purchase-history Added Inside List user

```
  container users {
    list user {
...
      list purchase-history {
        config false;
        key "title format";
```

```
        uses title-format-ref;
        leaf transaction-date-time {
          type yang:date-and-time;
        }
        leaf copies {
          type uint32;
        }
      }
    }
  }
```

This list happens to have two keys: the *title* and *format*. Both are needed to specify a particular row in this list. When you have YANG lists with multiple keys, you specify the key names by separating them by a space inside quotes in the YANG `key` statement.

For `config false` data, YANG allows keyless lists, which are simply lists without any key. Since a keyless list has no key, there is no way to navigate in this data or ask for parts of it. From a client perspective, the list needs to be read in its entirety or not at all. There is no way to read just the first 20 entries or to continue to the second page if the operator hits the Page Down key. This can lead to hugely inefficient management protocol exchanges. Do not use keyless lists if there is any way to avoid it.

The `uses` statement is another keyword you need to be acquainted with. Quite often when YANG modeling, you will notice some collection of leafs or a deeper structure with multiple lists that appears in more than one place in the model. In this case, it may be convenient to define this reusable collection in a YANG `grouping`. You can then recall this grouping wherever needed without repeating everything inside multiple times. The `uses` keyword is used to instantiate a copy of such a grouping. You can think of a grouping as a kind of macro. Actually, groupings are more than just macros, but we won't digress into those details.

Following the `uses` keyword is the name of the grouping to recall (*title-format-ref* in this case). Obviously, you need to point to a *title* and book *format-id* in the purchase history. As you might recall, you already wrote some YANG for this in the *shipping* notification. Cut the YANG lines from there and replace them with the `uses` statement shown in Example 3-19.

EXAMPLE 3-19 The Notification shipping with Output Data

```
notification shipping {
  leaf user {
    type leafref {
      path /users/user/name;
    }
  }
  uses title-format-ref;
  leaf number-of-copies {
    type uint32;
  }
}
```

Then paste the cut lines into a grouping, as shown in Example 3-20.

EXAMPLE 3-20 Grouping title-format-ref with Commonly Occurring Reference Leafs

```
grouping title-format-ref {
  leaf title {
    type leafref {
      path /books/book/title;
    }
  }
  leaf format {
    type leafref {
      path /books/book/format/format-id;
      // Reviewer note: This should be improved
    }
  }
}
```

One of the merits of using groupings like this is that the number of lines in the YANG module gets smaller, so you have less model text to maintain. Another benefit is that if you improve the grouping, the improvement immediately applies everywhere. Just make sure that is what you want! A downside with using too many groupings is that it sometimes gets hard to follow multiple levels of `uses` statements crisscrossing the model. In other words, do not go overboard with groupings.

Actually, the same references to *title* and *format* are also found in the *purchase* action. Update it to use your new grouping to be consistent (and save a few lines), as shown in Example 3-21.

EXAMPLE 3-21 Action purchase That Uses the Grouping title-format-ref

```
container users {
  list user {
    key user-id;
...
    action purchase {
      input {
        uses title-format-ref;
        leaf number-of-copies {
          type uint32 {
            range 1..999;
          }
        }
      }
```

By now, you are using the grouping in three places: in the `config false` list *purchase-history*, the notification *shipping*, and the action *purchase*. This is reuse in practice! Example 3-22 illustrates the latest tree diagram of your model. In tree diagrams, all groupings are expanded so that you can see the full tree.

EXAMPLE 3-22 YANG Tree Representation of the Module with Revision 2018-01-04

```
module: bookzone-example
  +--rw authors
  |  +--rw author* [name]
  |     +--rw name          string
  |     +--rw account-id?   uint32
  +--rw books
  |  +--rw book* [title]
  |     +--rw title         string
  |     +--rw author?       -> /authors/author/name
  |     +--rw language?     language-type
  |     +--ro popularity?   uint32
  |     +--rw format* [isbn]
  |        +--rw isbn               ISBN-10-or-13
  |        +--rw format-id          identityref
  |        +--rw price?             decimal64
  |        +--ro number-of-copies
  |           +--ro in-stock?    uint32
  |           +--ro reserved?    uint32
  |           +--ro available?   uint32
  +--rw users
     +--rw user* [user-id]
        +--rw user-id               string
        +--rw name?                 string
        +---x purchase
        |  +---w input
        |  |  +---w title?              -> /books/book/title
        |  |  +---w format?             -> /books/book/format/format-id
        |  |  +---w number-of-copies?   uint32
        |  +--ro output
        |     +--ro (outcome)?
        |        +--:(success)
        |        |  +--ro success?        empty
        |        |  +--ro delivery-url?   string
        |        +--:(out-of-stock)
        |        |  +--ro out-of-stock?   empty
        |        +--:(failure)
        |           +--ro failure?        string
        +--ro purchase-history* [title format]
           +--ro title                     -> /books/book/title
           +--ro format                    -> /books/book/format/format-id
           +--ro transaction-date-time?    yang:date-and-time
           +--ro copies?                   uint32
```

```
notifications:
  +---n shipping
     +--ro user?              -> /users/user/name
     +--ro title?             -> /books/book/title
     +--ro format?            -> /books/book/format/format-id
     +--ro number-of-copies?  uint32
```

Before you publish the new version, add a `revision` statement, as shown in Example 3-23.

EXAMPLE 3-23 Revision Statement 2018-01-04

```
revision 2018-01-04 {
  description
    "Added status information about books and purchases, see
     /books/book/popularity
     /books/book/formats/number-of-copies
     /users/user/purchase-history
     Turned reference to book title & format
     into a grouping, updated references in
     /users/user/purchase
     /shipping";
}
```

Constraints Keep Things Meaningful

More than anything else, it is essential that a contract is clear and precise. Both sides should know what to expect, and few surprises should be discovered down the line. This builds confidence and utility. YANG is a contract, so for clear interoperability, it is essential that both sides understand the terms and that the contract is precise in its details.

A common beginner's mistake is to bring a YANG model where all leafs are declared as strings or integers with no constraints or precision. That model is seldom useful, since there are pretty much always a lot of formats, ranges, and dependencies that must be respected. How would a client know what to do, and what is the chance that two server implementers would use the same way of encoding the information in this case?

Sometimes really complex business logic is required to determine what is valid and what is not. Just as you do not want to encode your entire business process within a contract, there are plenty of details not to model in YANG. Find a balance. A really long and super-detailed contract may be useful at times, whereas a more open and sloppier one is easier to write. Generally, the highest global utility is when you find a balance where the contract is fairly precise, but not too long or dense.

You have already used `mandatory true`, which is one kind of constraint on valid data. Since YANG model leafs are optional by default, another common beginner's mistake is to not describe what it means if the leaf is not present. Marking the leaf `mandatory true` is one way out. Another one is to add a `default` statement to the leaf; then it is clear how to interpret the leaf if nobody has touched it. At the very least, the modeler ought to specify in the leaf `description` the system behavior when the leaf has no value.

Coming back to the bookzone-example, in the *purchase* action, you need to know the number of book copies to deliver. If not specified, assume the buyer means one copy. In order to make this clear, add a `default 1` statement to leaf *number-of-copies*, as shown in Example 3-24.

EXAMPLE 3-24 Action purchase with default 1 for Leaf number-of-copies

```
action purchase {
  input {
    uses title-format-ref;
    leaf number-of-copies {
      type uint32 {
        range 1..999;
      }
      default 1;
    }
```

In your book catalog, the *price* leaf is optional. You could go ahead and make it mandatory so that whenever a book is being added, a price must be specified. This is not how BookZone likes to work, though. BookZone wants to sometimes add entries before the item in question is orderable and details like price were worked out. Therefore, keep *price* optional, just make sure the item isn't orderable until it has a price. This is easy to do by adding a `must` statement. A `must` statement in YANG prescribes a constraint that must hold true at all times. In this case, since you are placing it inside an `action`, the constraint must hold true at the time the action is invoked.

The *purchase* action contains a reference to the *title* and *format* through the `uses title-format-ref` construct, which brings in the grouping *title-format-ref*. The *format* leafref points to the */books/book/format/format-id* of the book you are looking at. If you follow this pointer, you can navigate to the price of the book in this particular book format by backing up a level and going into the *price* leaf. Then you can check that it is greater than zero.

A common beginner's mistake is to make a `must` statement that just points directly to the leaf that is to be tested (in this case, *price*), as shown in this snippet:

```
must "/books/book/format/price>0"
```

Even if this expression seems simple enough, its simplicity is deceiving. What this means is that the *purchase* action can only be invoked if there is any book (at least one) that has a price greater than zero. Here, you only really care if the particular book you are ordering has a price, so you must look up the price of this particular book. Therefore, the `must` statement you want to add is shown in Example 3-25.

EXAMPLE 3-25 A **must** Statement with a Proper **deref()**

```
action purchase {
  input {
    must "deref(format)/../price>0" {
      error-message "Item not orderable at this time";
    }
    uses title-format-ref;
    leaf number-of-copies {
      type uint32 {
        range 1..999;
      }
      default 1;
    }
```

Let's look at what the `must` statement really means, step by step. First, the value that follows the keyword `must` is an expression in the XPath language. XPath is a language that comes from the family of languages around the XML standard. In YANG, XPath is used to point at other parts of the model, and here it is used as a true/false Boolean expression for something that needs to be true for the action to be valid and executable.

The expression needs to be within quotes because it contains special characters. The first part is an XPath function call to an XPath function called `deref()`. This function follows a leafref pointer, which is specified as input to the function within the parentheses (in this case, leaf *format*). Leaf *format* is not immediately visible in the preceding YANG because it's inside the grouping called with `uses title-format-ref`. Calling `deref(format)` takes you to where *format* points: a particular book of a particular format, pointing to its *format-id*. The full path is */books/book/format/format-id* in XPath speak. This appears at #1 in Example 3-26.

EXAMPLE 3-26 YANG Tree Diagram with XPath Navigation from format-id to price

```
module: bookzone-example
...
    +--rw books
    |  +--rw book* [title]
    |     +--rw title          string
    |     +--rw author?        -> /authors/author/name
    |     +--rw language?      language-type
    |     +--ro popularity?    uint32
    |     +--rw format* [isbn]
    |        #2
    |        +--rw isbn                  ISBN-10-or-13
    |        +--rw format-id #1          identityref
    |        +--rw price?    #3          decimal64
```

From there you want to go up one level into the leaf *price*. "Go up one level" is expressed with two dots (..), taking your to the position marked #2. Then you want to go down into *price* with the slash *price* at the end, shown as position #3. Look at the tree diagram of the */books/book* part of the model to see how the expression takes you closer and closer to your target node.

Once you finally reach the *price* leaf, compare it to see if it is greater than zero. If *price* does not exist or if it is not greater than zero, the `must` statement is not true, and all parties can agree that the *purchase* action cannot be executed according to the contract (a.k.a. the YANG model). This is what clarity and precision in the YANG model means.

Another detail to consider is the *purchase* action's reference to the *format-id*. The *format-id* is the name of the format of the book, such as *paperback*, *hardcover*, or *mp3*. This is not the key to list *format*, so in principle, there could exist several ISBNs for a given book title with the same format. This could happen, for example, if a given title is published by more than one publisher. ISBN 9780140386332 and 9780140317930 are both paperback editions in English of *The Neverending Story*, just to give one example.

You could have (some might argue *should* have) made the *purchase* action point out an ISBN instead of a title and format, but you remember that someone in the BookZone marketing department made the following comment: "People buy books by title and format, and care little about ISBNs. As much as those numbers are loved internally for their clarity, users order by title and format." This is indeed how the *purchase* action was modeled earlier in this chapter.

As a consequence, BookZone customers do not have any reliable way of knowing what ISBN they receive if they order *The Neverending Story* in case there are several ISBNs for the same format (such as for paperback).

Since this is not ideal, BookZone decided that in their book catalog, this should never be allowed to happen. Therefore, BookZone only carries one ISBN for each *title* and *format* combination (in this case, only one paperback variant of *The Neverending Story*).

To enforce this, add a `unique` statement to the YANG module, as shown in Example 3-27.

EXAMPLE 3-27 Uniqueness Constraint in a YANG List

```
  container books {
    list book {
...
      list format {
        key isbn;
        unique format-id;
        leaf isbn {
          type ISBN-10-or-13;
        }
```

```
        leaf format-id {
          mandatory true;
          type identityref {
            base format-idty;
          }
        }
```

This enforces that within any given list *book* entry, no two list entries in list *format* have the same value for leaf *format-id*. New list *format* entries that violate this rule can be added within a transaction, but when the transaction is committed, each entry must have a unique *format-id* value.

Mandatory and Default Data

Another similar case is leaf *author* under *book*. No book should ever be listed without an author, so this leaf should be mandatory. Therefore, you need to add that in. Beyond that, BookZone does not allow books to be orderable unless the author of the book has an account set up with the finance department.

You could of course make leaf *account-id* under list *author* be mandatory as well so that no author can ever be added until the account setup is completed. The BookZone finance department does not like that idea, as it does not match their internal process. Instead, you must ensure that whenever a book is added to list *book*, at that point the book's *author* must have an *account-id* with finance. This is done with another `must` statement, as shown in Example 3-28.

EXAMPLE 3-28 Leaf author with a **must** Statement Checking If the Author's account-id Is Set

```
  container books {
    list book {
...
      leaf author {
        type leafref {
          path /authors/author/name;
        }
        must 'deref(current())/../account-id' {
          error-message
            "This author does not yet have an account-id defined.
             Books cannot be added for authors lacking one.
             The Finance Department is responsible for assigning
             account-id's to authors.";
        }
        mandatory true;
      }
```

Let's decode the `must` statement in Example 3-28. You already know the `deref()` XPath function follows a leafref pointer. This time, however, the argument to `deref` is another XPath function call.

The `current()` XPath function returns the YANG element that the `must` statement is sitting on (leaf *author* in this case). The leafref points to */authors/author/name*. From there, you need to move up one level to get into the list *author*, then onward into *account-id*.

In XPath, just pointing to a leaf without comparing it to anything turns into an existence test, so the `must` expression basically says "the current author must have an account-id." The `error-message` statement is simply a message displayed to the operator in case the `must` statement condition is not fulfilled.

Conditional Content

XPath expressions also come in handy for the YANG `when` statement. These statements determine when a particular YANG construct is relevant and make it disappear when it is not relevant.

An example of this is the container *number-of-copies*, which contains three leafs with information about how many books are in stock, how many are reserved by a potential customer, and how many are available for sale. These parameters obviously only apply to the books with a physical form factor. For those books based on file delivery, this container is simply not relevant.

What you want here is for this container to be disregarded when the book format is derived from the *bz:file-idty* identity, as shown in Example 3-29. Here is where the YANG identities get to shine, because using them you can now make a rule that applies to a whole range of different book formats. This range can even grow in the future while the rule still works.

EXAMPLE 3-29 Container That Is Not Relevant for Any File-Based Delivery Formats

```
  container books {
    list book {
...
      list format {
...
        container number-of-copies {
          when 'not(derived-from(../format-id, "bz:file-idty"))';
          config false;
          leaf in-stock {
            type uint32;
          }
          leaf reserved {
            type uint32;
          }
          leaf available {
            type uint32;
          }
        }
```

In the `when` expression, notice two new XPath functions being used. The first is `not()`, which does exactly what it sounds like: It negates the logical value of the argument. The second is `derived-from()`, which checks whether some leaf of type identityref has a value that is derived from the given identity. In this case, the *../format-id* leaf (which is an identityref) can have the value *bz:mp3*, *bz:pdf*, or *bz:epub*—or any other identity value added in the future and based directly on *bz:file-idty* or indirectly on any other identity derived from it in turn.

Properly Following Pointers

As you may have noticed, there was a "reviewer note" that the *format* leafref should be improved somehow. Before revealing the fix, let's have a look at the problem.

If you look at leaf *title*, it can point to the title of any book. That's exactly what you want: The user should be able to purchase any title. So far so good. Then you have leaf *format*. With a simple `leafref` statement, it can point to any book format. This may sound right at first, but this is actually too liberal—you could end up with nonexistent combinations of the titles and formats.

Valid values for *format* should only be formats available for the particular book pointed to by *title*. Table 3-3 includes sample data, reflecting the inventory of a particular BookZone store.

TABLE 3-3 List Format Inside list book in a Tabular Representation

title	format
The Hitchhiker's Guide to the Galaxy	bz:paperback
	bz:hardcover
The Neverending Story	bz:mp3

Now let's consider leaf *title*. It's a leafref to */books/book/title*, which means any value that exists in that list column is a valid value for this leaf. With this sample data, that could be either "The Hitchhiker's Guide to the Galaxy" or "The Neverending Story".

If the leaf *format* is modeled as a simple leafref pointing to */books/book/formats/format-id*, any book format value that exists in the *format-id* column is allowed. With this sample data, that is "bz:paperback", "bz:hardcover", or "bz:mp3".

The problem with this simple YANG model is that it allows *title* to be "The Hitchhiker's Guide to the Galaxy" while *format* is "bz:mp3". Or *title* is "The Neverending Story" and *format* is "bz:paperback" or "bz:hardcover". These are combinations that are not available in the BookZone store inventory!

The YANG model is too lax here, allowing combinations of values that are not meaningful. YANG is not expressive enough to describe all possible business logic constraints on data that you could ever encounter. You may need to implement business logic beyond what you can describe in YANG. When you use constraints described in YANG, however, it brings clarity to the contract between the client and server. Common requirements like in the case at hand can certainly be properly described in YANG.

Clearly, the user should be able to select any *title* in list *book*, so *title* being a leafref to any *book* is fine. The problem with the current model is that leaf *format* can point to any *format-id* under list *book/format*, not just the formats actually available for the current *title*.

The way to fix this is to change the leafref in leaf *format* so that it dereferences *title*. Leaf *title* points to a specific *book*, and if the *format* leafref followed that pointer to the specific book, and only allowed selecting a *format-id* present under that specific *book*, you would be home free.

By using an XPath predicate, i.e. an XPath filter inside square brackets, the *format* leafref can follow leaf *title* to the *book* in question and limit the valid values to an existing *format-id* under that *book*. Examples 3-25 and 3-28 showed XPath expressions with similar purpose using the XPath deref() function. Unfortunately the YANG specification does not formally allow the use of deref() in leafref paths, so the traditional XPath predicate approach must be used here, arriving at the exact same functionality in a more verbose way. There is no reason why the YANG specification doesn't allow deref() in leafref paths, but the fact is that it doesn't. Still, many tools do allow it.

Because dereferencing and XPath navigation are not easy topics to grasp, let's review this in detail. Example 3-30 shows what the grouping that provides a pointer to a particular *title* and *format-id* combination becomes.

EXAMPLE 3-30 XPath Navigation from format to title

```
grouping title-format-ref {
  #2
  leaf title { #3
    type leafref {
      path /books/book/title;
    }
  }
  leaf format { #1
    type leafref {
      path /books/book[title=current()/../title]/format/format-id;
      // The path above expressed using deref():
      // path deref(../title)/../format/format-id;
    }
  }
}
```

The point with leaf *format* is to allow the operator to pick one *format-id* value from the list of available values in */books/book/format/format-id*. Just pointing to that path gives the operator the possibility to choose from all valid values for any book, so in order to limit the choices to the formats available for the current book, a filter expression is required. This way the leafref can only point to *format-id* values relevant for the current *title*.

The leafref path in leaf *format* is decoded as follows. First, look at all */books/book* entries. The expression in the square brackets is the predicate (filter), and selects only books that have a *title* leaf that equals the value to the right of the equals sign. That will be a single book. The value to the right of the equals sign navigates from the current node (#1: leaf *format*), up one level (#2: wherever this grouping is used), and then into leaf *title* (#3). There might be many such *title* nodes in the data tree, since */books/book/format* is a list. Essentially, this expression allows any *format-id* value from the list *format* within the current */books/book*.

In a comment, Example 3-30 also shows the exact same path and filter function expressed using `deref()`: The first piece is `deref()`, an XPath function that follows a leafref. In this case, the leafref to follow is the one in leaf *title*. A path pointing out leaf *title* is provided as an argument (that is, inside the parentheses) to the `deref()` function. The two dots mean "go up one level" from #1 to #2, just like in a directory tree path. This moves you out of leaf *format*. The slash and word *title* moves us into leaf *title*, at #3. The `deref(../title)` part of the expression takes you to wherever *title* points. This will be a particular *title* in list */books/book* (see #4 in Example 3-31).

EXAMPLE 3-31 YANG Tree Instance Data Diagram with XPath Navigation from title to format-id

```
Instance data diagram:
   +--rw books
   |  +--rw book [0]
   |  |  +--rw title              "The Hitchhiker's Guide to the Galaxy"
   |  |  +--rw author?            "Douglas Adams"
   |  |  +--rw language?          english
   |  |  +--rw format [0]
   |  |  |  +--rw isbn            "0330258648"
   |  |  |  +--rw format-id       bz:paperback
   |  |  |  +--rw price?          22.00
   |  |  +--rw format [1]
   |  |     +--rw isbn            "9781400052929"
   |  |     +--rw format-id       bz:hardcover
   |  |     +--rw price?          31.50
   |  +--rw book [1]
   |     #5
   |     +--rw title #4           "The Neverending Story"
   |     +--rw author?            "Michael Ende"
   |     +--rw language?          english
   |     +--rw format [0]
   |        #6
   |        +--rw isbn            "9781452656304"
   |        +--rw format-id #7    bz:mp3
   |        +--rw price?          29.95
```

Use the instance data diagram in Example 3-31 to follow the navigation in Example 3-30. An instance data diagram is a cross between the YANG tree diagram shown earlier and a database dump. Here you see some sample database data in the YANG tree structure.

If, for example, the user specified "The Neverending Story" for *title*, the leafref expression so far would point to */books/book[title="The Neverending Story"]/title* (see #4).

However, you want it to point to */books/book[title="The Neverending Story"]/format/format-id*, so you go up one level (#5), then into list *format* (#6), and finally into leaf *format-id* (#7).

Now the YANG model is safe and sound. Since you updated the grouping, the fix immediately gets to all three places where you reference a *title* and *format*. This is the beauty of the grouping concept.

It is a very common YANG modeling mistake to think that a relative path and an absolute path pointing to the same leaf are equivalent. As demonstrated in Example 3-31, in YANG, they often are not. A relative path such as *deref(../title)/../format/format-id* does not evaluate to the same set of values as */books/book/title/format/format-id*, even though they point to the same *format-id* leaf, unless some XPath predicates (filters) are added.

Schema Nodes Don't Count

Another one of the most common errors when constructing or walking XPath expressions is to mistakenly pay attention to schema nodes that are not data nodes. When you're constructing the path in an XPath expression, only data nodes should be counted and referenced. Basically, there are a bunch of keywords in a YANG schema that must be disregarded in paths since they work on a "meta level." Think of them as macros, if that helps. These include `input`, `output`, `choice`, `case`, `grouping`, and `uses`.

To illustrate this point, add some payment methods to */users/user* and a way to specify which payment method to use in the *purchase* action, as shown in Example 3-32.

EXAMPLE 3-32 Leafref path Crossing a Schema Node

```
container users {
  list user {
    key user-id;

    leaf user-id {
      type string;
    }
    leaf name {
      type string;
    }
    container payment-methods {
      list payment-method {
        key "method id";
```

```
        leaf method {
          type enumeration {
            enum bookzone-account;
            enum credit-card;
            enum paypal;
            enum klarna;
          }
        }
        leaf id {
          type string;
        }
      }
    }
    action purchase {
      input {
        must "deref(format)/../price>0" {
          error-message "Item not orderable at this time";
        }
        uses title-format-ref;
        leaf number-of-copies {
          type uint32 {
            range 1..999;
          }
          default 1;
        }
        container payment {
          leaf method {
            type leafref {
              path ../../../payment-methods/payment-method/method;
            }
          }
          leaf id {
            type leafref {
              path "../../../payment-methods/"+
                   "payment-method[method=current()/../method]/id";
              // The path above expressed using deref():
              // path deref(../method)/../id;
            }
          }
        }
      }
```

How to construct that leafref path in leaf *method*? The first .. is used to get out of leaf *method*. The second .. is used to get out of container *payment*. Then you have the keyword `input`, which does not count for the path, as it is not a data node. The third .. is thus used to get out of action *purchase*.

From there, you dive into container *purchase-methods*, into list *purchase-method*, and finally into leaf *method*.

In order to verify that the XPath expressions are correct, it is strongly advised that you use proper tools. Sadly, many YANG tools (compilers) historically have never checked the XPath expressions for correctness. Some still don't. This has resulted in many YANG modelers believing that their modules were good since the compiler was happy, when in fact they still contained a good deal of broken XPath.

The final, complete model is shown in Example 3-33.

EXAMPLE 3-33 Complete bookzone-example YANG Module with Revision 2018-01-05

```
module bookzone-example {
  yang-version 1.1;
  namespace 'http://example.com/ns/bookzone';
  prefix bz;

  import ietf-yang-types {
    prefix yang;
  }

  organization
    "BookZone, a fictive book store chain";

  contact
    "YANG book project:   https://github.com/janlindblad/bookzone

     Editor:   Jan Lindblad
               <mailto:janl@tail-f.com>";

  description
    "BookZone defines this model to provide a standard interface for
     inventory browser and management applications.

     Copyright (c) 2018 the YANG book project and the persons
     identified as authors of the code.  All rights reserved.

     Redistribution and use in source and binary forms, with or
     without modification, is permitted pursuant to, and subject
     to the license terms contained in, the Simplified BSD License
     set forth in Section 4.c of the IETF Trust's Legal Provisions
     Relating to IETF Documents
     (http://trustee.ietf.org/license-info).";

  revision 2018-01-05 {
    description
```

```
    "Added constraints that
     - author needs to have an account set before listing a book
     - number of copies in stock only shows for physical items
     - makes a book not orderable unless it has a price
     - book leafrefs are chained correctly
     Added /users/user/payment-methods and a way to choose which
     one to use in action purchase.";
}
revision 2018-01-04 {
  description
    "Added status information about books and purchases, see
     /books/book/popularity
     /books/book/formats/number-of-copies
     /users/user/purchase-history
     Turned reference to book title & format
     into a grouping, updated references in
     /users/user/purchase
     /shipping";
}
revision 2018-01-03 {
  description
    "Added action purchase and notification shipping.";
}
revision 2018-01-02 {
  description
    "Added book formats, authors and users, see
     /books/book/format
     /authors
     /users";
}
revision 2018-01-01 {
  description "Initial revision. A catalog of books.";
}

typedef language-type {
  type enumeration {
    enum arabic;
    enum chinese;
    enum english;
    enum french;
    enum moroccan-arabic;
    enum swahili;
    enum swedish;
    // List not exhaustive in order to save space
  }
```

```
  description
    "Primary language the book consumer needs to master "+
    "in order to appreciate the book's content";
}

identity format-idty {
  description "Root identity for all book formats";
}
identity paper {
  base format-idty;
  description "Physical book printed on paper";
}
identity audio-cd {
  base format-idty;
  description "Audiobook delivered as Compact Disc";
}
identity file-idty {
  base format-idty;
  description "Book delivered as a file";
}
identity paperback {
  base paper;
  description "Physical book with soft covers";
}
identity hardcover {
  base paper;
  description "Physical book with hard covers";
}
identity mp3 {
  base file-idty;
  description "Audiobook delivered as MP3 file";
}
identity pdf {
  base file-idty;
  description "Digital book delivered as PDF file";
}
identity epub {
  base file-idty;
  description "Digital book delivered as EPUB file";
}

typedef ISBN-10-or-13 {
  type union {
    type string {
      length 10;
```

```
        pattern '[0-9]{9}[0-9X]';
      }
      type string {
        length 13;
        pattern '97[89][0-9]{10}';
      }
    }
    description
      "The International Standard Book Number (ISBN) is a unique
       numeric commercial book identifier.

       An ISBN is assigned to each edition and variation (except
       reprintings) of a book. [source: wikipedia]";
    reference
      "https://en.wikipedia.org/wiki/International_Standard_Book_Number";
  }

  grouping title-format-ref {
    leaf title {
      type leafref {
        path /books/book/title;
      }
    }
    leaf format {
      type leafref {
        path /books/book[title=current()/../title]/format/format-id;
        // The path above expressed using deref():
        // path deref(../title)/../format/format-id;
      }
    }
  }

  container authors {
    list author {
      key name;

      leaf name {
        type string;
      }
      leaf account-id {
        type uint32 {
          range 1001..max;
        }
      }
    }
  }
```

```
container books {
  list book {
    key title;

    leaf title {
      type string;
    }
    leaf author {
      type leafref {
        path /authors/author/name;
      }
      must 'deref(current())/../account-id' {
        error-message
          "This author does not yet have an account-id defined.
           Books cannot be added for authors lacking one.
           The Finance Department is responsible for assigning
           account-id's to authors.";
      }
      mandatory true;
    }
    leaf language {
      type language-type;
    }
    leaf popularity {
      config false;
      type uint32;
      units copies-sold/year;
      description
        "Number of copies sold in the last 12-month period";
    }
    list format {
      key isbn;
      unique format-id;
      leaf isbn {
        type ISBN-10-or-13;
      }
      leaf format-id {
        mandatory true;
        type identityref {
          base format-idty;
        }
      }
      leaf price {
        type decimal64 {
          fraction-digits 2;
        }
```

```
          units sim-dollar;
        }
        container number-of-copies {
          when 'not(derived-from(../format-id, "bz:file-idty"))';
          config false;
          leaf in-stock {
            type uint32;
          }
          leaf reserved {
            type uint32;
          }
          leaf available {
            type uint32;
          }
        }
      }
    }
  }

  container users {
    list user {
      key user-id;

      leaf user-id {
        type string;
      }
      leaf name {
        type string;
      }
      container payment-methods {
        list payment-method {
          key "method id";
          leaf method {
            type enumeration {
              enum bookzone-account;
              enum credit-card;
              enum paypal;
              enum klarna;
            }
          }
          leaf id {
            type string;
          }
        }
      }
```

```
action purchase {
  input {
    must "deref(format)/../price>0" {
      error-message "Item not orderable at this time";
    }
    uses title-format-ref;
    leaf number-of-copies {
      type uint32 {
        range 1..999;
      }
      default 1;
    }
    container payment {
      leaf method {
        type leafref {
          path ../../../payment-methods/payment-method/method;
        }
      }
      leaf id {
        type leafref {
          path "../../../payment-methods/"+
               "payment-method[method=current()/../method]/id";
          // The path above expressed using deref():
          // path deref(../method)/../id;
        }
      }
    }
  }
  output {
    choice outcome {
      case success {
        leaf success {
          type empty;
          description
            "Order received and will be sent to specified user.
             File orders are downloadable at the URL given below.";
        }
        leaf delivery-url {
          type string;
          description
            "Download URL for file deliveries.";
        }
      }
```

```
          leaf out-of-stock {
            type empty;
            description
              "Order received, but cannot be delivered at this time.
               A notification will be sent when the item ships.";
          }
          leaf failure {
            type string;
            description
              "Order cancelled, for reason stated here.";
          }
        }
      }
    }
    list purchase-history {
      config false;
      key "title format";
      uses title-format-ref;
      leaf transaction-date-time {
        type yang:date-and-time;
      }
      leaf copies {
        type uint32;
      }
    }
  }
}

notification shipping {
  leaf user {
    type leafref {
      path /users/user/name;
    }
  }
  uses title-format-ref;
  leaf number-of-copies {
    type uint32;
  }
}
}
```

Example 3-34 shows a tree representation of the model.

EXAMPLE 3-34 Complete bookzone-example YANG Tree with Revision 2018-01-05

```
module: bookzone-example
  +--rw authors
  |  +--rw author* [name]
  |     +--rw name          string
  |     +--rw account-id?   uint32
  +--rw books
  |  +--rw book* [title]
  |     +--rw title         string
  |     +--rw author        -> /authors/author/name
  |     +--rw language?     language-type
  |     +--ro popularity?   uint32
  |     +--rw format* [isbn]
  |        +--rw isbn                 ISBN-10-or-13
  |        +--rw format-id            identityref
  |        +--rw price?               decimal64
  |        +--ro number-of-copies
  |           +--ro in-stock?    uint32
  |           +--ro reserved?    uint32
  |           +--ro available?   uint32
  +--rw users
     +--rw user* [user-id]
        +--rw user-id               string
        +--rw name?                 string
        +--rw payment-methods
        |  +--rw payment-method* [method id]
        |     +--rw method    enumeration
        |     +--rw id        string
        +---x purchase
        |  +---w input
        |  |  +---w title?                -> /books/book/title
        |  |  +---w format?               -> /books/book[title=current()/../title]/
                                             format/format-id
        |  |  +---w number-of-copies?      uint32
        |  |  +---w payment
        |  |     +---w method?   -> ../../../payment-methods/payment-method/method
        |  |     +---w id?       -> ../../../payment-methods/payment-method[method=
                                  current()/../method]/id
        |  +--ro output
        |     +--ro (outcome)?
        |        +--:(success)
        |        |  +--ro success?        empty
        |        |  +--ro delivery-url?   string
```

```
  |        +--:(out-of-stock)
  |        |  +--ro out-of-stock?   empty
  |        +--:(failure)
  |           +--ro failure?        string
  +--ro purchase-history* [title format]
     +--ro title                    -> /books/book/title
     +--ro format                   -> /books/book[title=current()/../title]/
                                       format/format-id
     +--ro transaction-date-time?   yang:date-and-time
     +--ro copies?                  uint32

notifications:
  +---n shipping
     +--ro user?              -> /users/user/name
     +--ro title?             -> /books/book/title
     +--ro format?            -> /books/book[title=current()/../title]/format/
                                 format-id
     +--ro number-of-copies?  uint32
```

Augmenting, Extending, and Possibly Deviating

The company is grateful for all the work you have done in building up the BookZone YANG model. BookZone is now thriving thanks to the well-defined interface to all subsidiary stores.

One day, one of the BookZone employees had an idea for a new business venture. She presented the idea to the management team, and soon enough they decided to spin off a side venture to go after this new market. They formed AudioZone, for selling online subscriptions to a library of audio books.

Obviously, having a catalog like the BookZone catalog system is key for this new line of business. Clearly, some tweaks are necessary, though, such as allowing users to rate and review audio books they have listened to, and tracking users' friends in order to give the app some social aspects.

You could certainly go and edit the BookZone YANG files to add in what is needed for AudioZone, but as the module evolves on both sides, that would soon become a mess. YANG offers a better option. Using the YANG `augment` statement, you can graft new content in one YANG module onto the context of another module. Thanks to the extensible nature of XML (which stands for Extensible Markup Language, after all), these augmentations can be mapped to XML-based protocols like NETCONF in way that's really easy to deal with, even for managers who have no prior knowledge about the augmented content.

The first thing you need to do is to create a new AudioZone YANG module. The header is shown in Example 3-35.

EXAMPLE 3-35 YANG Module audiozone-example

```
module audiozone-example {
  yang-version 1.1;
  namespace 'http://example.com/ns/audiozone';
  prefix az;

  import bookzone-example {
    prefix bz;
  }
  import ietf-yang-types {
    prefix yang;
  }

  organization
    "AudioZone, a subsidiary of the fictive book store chain BookZone";

  contact
    "YANG book project:   https://github.com/janlindblad/bookzone

     Editor:   Jan Lindblad
               <mailto:janl@tail-f.com>";

  description
    "AudioZone defines this model to provide a standard interface for
     inventory browser and management applications. This module extends
     the bookzone-example.yang module.

     Copyright (c) 2018 the YANG book project and the persons
     identified as authors of the code.  All rights reserved.

     Redistribution and use in source and binary forms, with or
     without modification, is permitted pursuant to, and subject
     to the license terms contained in, the Simplified BSD License
     set forth in Section 4.c of the IETF Trust's Legal Provisions
     Relating to IETF Documents
     (http://trustee.ietf.org/license-info).";

  revision 2018-01-09 {
    description "Initial revision.";
  }
```

Note how the module uses an `import bookzone-example` statement to make all the types and definitions in that module available in the current module. The `import` statement will not copy the contents of that module into this one, unlike `#include` and such in other languages. It simply makes this module aware of the other module's existence and makes it legal to refer to content in that module from here.

References to content in the imported module use the prefix given in the `import` statement (*bz* in this case), as specified in `prefix bz`, under the `import bookzone-example` statement. The prefix given in an `import` statement is usually the same as the prefix in the header of that module, but that is not a requirement.

Now, you need to add a new book format, *streaming*, for the content streamed to all clients, as shown in Example 3-36.

EXAMPLE 3-36 Additional Delivery Format Identity

```
identity streaming {
  base bz:file-idty;
  description
    "Audiobook streaming.";
}
```

This declares a new identity in your module. By adding *bz:* in front of *file-idty*, it's clear that you mean an identity found in the *bookzone-example* module. By simply declaring a new identity and basing it on an identity that directly or indirectly is referenced by some identityrefs in any module, you cause the new value immediately to become a valid option in all those places. Talk about easy to extend!

If you look back at the *bookzone-example* module, */books/book/format/format-idty* is an identityref that allows the leaf *format-id* to have as a value the name of any identity derived from *format-idty*. Your new identity, *streaming*, is based on *file-idty*, which is based on *format-idty*. In any system that supports the *audiozone-example* module, *streaming* is now a valid value for *format-id*. In effect, the *bookzone-example* YANG module is unmodified, yet it has been extended with a new valid value. This happens because the server implements and advertises the *audiozone-example* YANG module, not because of any YANG `import` statements. Example 3-37 is a reminder excerpt from *bookzone-example* showing the *format-id* identityref leaf.

EXAMPLE 3-37 Leaf format-id from Example 3-33

```
leaf format-id {
  mandatory true;
  type identityref {
    base format-idty;
  }
}
```

Now, the next step is to augment the *bookzone-example* module with some *recommendations* for each */books/book*, as shown in Example 3-38.

EXAMPLE 3-38 List Recommendations Augmenting List book from Example 3-33

```
augment /bz:books/bz:book {
  list recommendations {
    key review-date;
    leaf review-date {
      type yang:date-and-time;
    }
    leaf score {
      type uint32 {
        range 1..5;
      }
    }
    leaf review-comment {
      type string;
    }
  }
}
```

The `augment` keyword simply adds the content inside the statement to the location given after the keyword. The target location is usually in a different module, perhaps one created by a standards body. In this case, the target is the *bookzone-example* module, which you can see since the path uses the *bz:* prefix.

Augments may also extend the same module they are defined in. This could be useful at times, such as when you want to build up a nice and concise list of something (say, interfaces) and then add details for all the different kinds of interfaces further down in your module.

The final addition needed for the AudioZone venture is a list of friends for each user, as shown in Example 3-39. You can just augment it here by using a simple kind of list called a `leaf-list`. Leaf-lists are good when you want a list of a single thing. This is a special case for single-column lists that eliminates some typing.

EXAMPLE 3-39 Leaf-list friends Augmenting List user from Example 3-33

```
augment /bz:users/bz:user {
  leaf-list friends {
    type leafref {
      path /bz:users/bz:user/bz:name;
    }
  }
}
```

With this, you have a complete *audiozone-example* module that you can load up in your NETCONF server—of course, together with the imported *bookzone-example* module.

A topic that often comes up is how to think about YANG model modularity. Should all the functionality be defined in one grand module, or is it better with a hundred smaller ones?

You just saw one reason for having separate modules—you are adding to a module developed by a different organization. The most common reason for splitting functionality into different modules is versioning.

If a system with a given YANG interface is upgraded with additional functionality, it is nice if the consumers of the interface can see roughly where it changed and where it is the same. By stepping the version on four of, say, 14 YANG modules provided, you allow the users to quickly determine what areas, if any, they care about being changed (or not). If there are hundreds of modules, understanding this gets harder again.

Extending YANG

The YANG language itself is extensible; you can define your own keywords that describe some aspects of your model that the base YANG language does not capture. For example, people have added code-generation statements, user-documentation-generation directives, additional validation logic, and test-case data to their models. You can read more about the `extension` keyword in RFC 7950.

Declaring your own keyword is easy. Simply use the YANG `extension` keyword, followed by the name of your new keyword.

Let's say BookZone wants to build a function to export some of their YANG lists to an SQL database. You could declare an `extension` keyword of your own that the BookZone system applications can use to figure out what SQL tables should be used. You could then apply that extension to the relevant lists. This way, the export function would be guided by the YANG modules alone, and not rely on additional files or hardcoding.

In Example 3-40, three new keywords are declared in a new YANG module. Two of them take one argument, and the last one takes none.

EXAMPLE 3-40 YANG Module Declaring Three **extension** Keywords

```
module bookzone-example-extensions {
  yang-version 1.1;
  namespace 'http://example.com/ns/bookzone-extensions';
  prefix bzex;

  extension sql-export-to-table {
    argument table-name;
  }
  extension sql-export-to-column {
    argument column-name;
  }
  extension sql-export-as-key;
}
```

In order to use these new keywords now, all you need to do is import the module in which they are declared (you can skip this if they are declared in the same module as where they are being used) and then refer to the prefixed name of the new keywords, as shown in Example 3-41.

EXAMPLE 3-41 Import and Usage of **extension** Keywords from Previous Example

```
module bookzone-example {
...
  import bookzone-example-extensions {
    prefix bzex;
  }
...
  container users {
    list user {
      bzex:sql-export-to-table users;
      key user-id;

      leaf user-id {
        bzex:sql-export-to-column id;
        bzex:sql-export-as-key;
        type string;
      }
      leaf name {
        bzex:sql-export-to-column login_name;
        type string;
      }
      container payment-methods {
```

Many YANG parsers would have no idea what your new keyword means. Since you declared them correctly, well-written YANG parsers will still be able to correctly compile the entire module, ignoring the extension.

In many other languages, similar effects are accomplished by adding comments with particular (odd) formats, or by using pragma statements and such. The downside with this approach is that any misspelled comment or pragma wouldn't be detected by the compiler, and the whole construct may not be clear to people who don't recognize the special meaning of the comment.

Note also that it must remain optional for YANG parsers to understand the new keyword and that the module must still be valid while ignoring it. Extensions can therefore not break YANG rules. It is valid, however, to require an understanding of and respect for certain extension keywords as part of implementing a YANG feature. The feature description could very well say that in order to announce this feature, a conforming device must do this or that as indicated by some extensions in the module.

Extension keywords can have zero or one argument to fit in with the general YANG syntax rules. If more information is needed, either multiple extensions could be used or the format of the argument could be something complex, as shown in Example 3-42.

EXAMPLE 3-42 Two Different Alternatives for Mapping Multiple Pieces of Information Using the YANG **extension** Keyword

```
leaf name {
  object-relational-map:key "Name";
  object-relational-map:type "UnicodeStringType";
  type name-type;
}

// -- or like this --

leaf name {
  object-relational-map:key-of-type "Name:UnicodeStringType";
  type name-type;
}
```

Deviations

As standards-defining organizations (SDOs) release YANG modules, they have usually thought through the use cases for their modules in good detail. In order to reach consensus, the models tend to include everybody's favorite use case—and sometimes legacy ways of doing things.

Organizations that implement these standard models may need to release a first version of their code before all the use cases allowed by the YANG model are covered. It may even be decided that certain use cases will never be implemented. The implementation cannot be said to fully implement the model in these cases, but it may still provide great customer value. If an implementation isn't complete, it's prudent to make clear what parts aren't covered using the YANG `deviation` keyword.

Let's say an implementor has developed support for ietf-interfaces.yang, but is not (currently) able to support the leaf *last-change* in the model. Skipping the implementation and then letting people find out by themselves may cause a lot of extra work and irritation for everybody, so that's not a good option. Writing about it in a release notes document is better, but any tools would still have no clue. A better and more precise option then is to declare this lack of support with a `deviation` statement in a new YANG module, as shown in Example 3-43.

EXAMPLE 3-43 Deviation Module for ietf-interfaces.yang

```
module ietf-interfaces-deviations {
  yang-version 1.1;
  namespace "https://example.org/ns/ietf-interfaces-deviations";
  prefix ietf-interfaces-deviations;
```

```
  import ietf-interfaces {
    prefix if;
    revision-date 2018-02-20; // The NMDA version of ietf-interfaces
  }

  deviation /if:interfaces/if:interface/if:last-change {
    deviate not-supported;
  }
}
```

Note, however, that simply declaring a deviation does not make client applications understand your deviated model. Most likely, many client applications will fail to correctly interface with your system if you introduce deviations, so declaring a deviation is no good substitute for a correct and full implementation.

A server that implements a standard YANG module with deviations is not implementing that standard module, even if deviations were properly declared.

On rare occasions, engineers have been found to edit standard modules, rather than use deviation statements, in order to remove or change some content. That is a really bad idea. In most jurisdictions, that would be a copyright infringement and punishable by law. To misrepresent the contents of a module without changing the namespace is also likely to cause a lot of headaches for clients.

The `deviation` statement allows for other changes than just `not-supported`. It is possible to declare that a certain leaf uses a different type, for example, or uses a different default. Such deviations are much harder for clients to support, and therefore have limited value. If the purpose of declaring a deviation is to enhance the chance of interoperability with clients, those chances are pretty bleak if you go beyond `not-supported`, and not great even if you limit yourself to using only that.

Network Management Datastore Architecture (NMDA)

Most of the time when the operations engineer makes a configuration change and commits, the change takes effect immediately. Well, within few seconds maybe, depending on the change and the type of device. Some changes may not take effect immediately, however, because they depend on some required hardware that is not currently installed, for example.

Some NETCONF servers outright reject configurations that cannot be implemented immediately, but many accept configurations that are inherently valid, just not implementable at this time because of some missing dependency. They allow this because it is a very useful feature, often referred to as *pre-provisioning* or *preconfiguration*. The operator can preconfigure a feature, and the minute the right hardware is installed, the feature kicks into action.

With this background, it is easy to see that some configuration objects will not be found in the operational view of the system, at least not immediately and possibly never. Who knows what the future has in store? Similarly, some operational objects may exist despite not being configured yet. This is true in general, but let's take a closer look at network interface management as an example, as shown in Table 3-4.

TABLE 3-4 Interfaces with Different Configuration and Operational States

Interface	Configuration View (config true)	Operational View (config false)
GigEth1/1	Configured	Absent due to missing hardware
GigEth2/2	Configured	Running as configured
Loopback0	Absent	Running with factory default settings

Some device might have a network interface called GigEth1/1 in the configuration, but this interface does not exist in the operational state because there is no line card in slot 1 right now. There might be another interface called GigEth2/2 in the configuration. The hardware for this interface is present and the interface is running at full speed. Then there might be an interface called Loopback0. It was never configured, so it is absent in the configuration, but exists operationally, operating under some default settings.

Remembering the operators' strong emphasis on the importance of separating configuration data from operational data in the requirements list in RFC 3535, the IETF working group invented the `config true` and `config false` concepts in the YANG language. Since a YANG list has to be either `config true` or `config false`, it's not possible to have a single interface list that contains the sum of all the interfaces. In Table 3-4, the configuration view contains only two of three interfaces, and so does the operational view.

To accommodate the need for both types of information, the working group made sure all the standard YANG modules have a two lists—one for the configuration objects (for example, *interfaces*) and the other for the operational objects (for example, *interfaces-state*). The old standard ietf-interfaces.yang module (RFC 7223) is shown in Example 3-44.

EXAMPLE 3-44 A Tree Representation of ietf-interfaces.yang in Its Original Form (Abridged)

```
module: ietf-interfaces
  +--rw interfaces
  |  +--rw interface* [name]
  |     +--rw name                      string
  |     +--rw description?              string
  |     +--rw type                      identityref
  |     +--rw enabled?                  boolean
  +--ro interfaces-state
     +--ro interface* [name]
        +--ro name               string
        +--ro type               identityref
        +--ro oper-status        enumeration
```

```
+--ro last-change?          yang:date-and-time
+--ro phys-address?         yang:phys-address
+--ro higher-layer-if*      interface-state-ref
+--ro lower-layer-if*       interface-state-ref
+--ro speed?                yang:gauge64
```

This approach worked fine and was used for many years. Over time, however, more and more people started to realize there is a problem with this style of modeling.

As you might expect, most interfaces are present in both lists. They are both configured and have an operational state. The missing piece is how to navigate between the two. If you configured */interfaces/interface[name='GigEth2/2']*, how would you know where the operational data for this interface lives? At this point, you might glance at Example 3-44 and sneer that it's obviously *interfaces-state/interface[name='GigEth2/2']*. And you'd be right.

The question is how you teach a computer to do what you just did. You do not want to hardcode a lot of information into your NMS systems about */interfaces/interface* being linked to *interfaces-state/interface*. This knowledge must be built in directly in the protocol (for example, NETCONF), language (YANG), and modules (for example, ietf-interfaces.yang), in order to be automatically discoverable.

NOTE

Similarly, taking an example from the SNMP world, hardcoding in the NMS that the ifAdminStatus and ifOperstatus Management Information Base (MIB) objects from RFC 2863 represent the read-write (the desired state of the interface) and read-only (the current operational state of the interface) views of the same object is costly—and most importantly, hardcoding every such piece of information does not scale.

Someone might suggest (and someone did) that the NMS simply rely on the naming convention that any configuration list called *xyz* would have an operational list called *xyz-state* next to it. While elegant in its simplicity, at least in this simple case, this idea was dismissed. Talk to your favorite software architect, and you'll hear that reliance on naming conventions tends to go downhill in the long run. Every single YANG module would have to follow this rule, which would be difficult to enforce. And what seemed a simple rule turned out quite strange in certain cases.

Another disadvantage with the previously mentioned approach to modeling configuration and operational state separately is that there is a fair amount of duplication. There are two containers and lists for interfaces, and the keys (the interface name) are modeled twice. In this case, the interface type is also duplicated.

Combined with some new ideas for how to represent new forms of information that advanced servers might want to expose (for example, to support macros, system defaults, and sources of configuration other than operators and managers), the idea of extending the NETCONF datastore concept won strong support.

Instead of modeling the configuration and operational data separately, with a few small adjustments to a few RFCs, they could use a single, unified model. The client would just specify which datastore it is looking at as well as the running configuration or the operational one. Thus, the Network Management Datastore Architecture (NMDA, RFC 8342) was born.

With the revised NMDA model, the data objects are defined only once in the YANG schema, but independent instantiations can appear in different datastores (for example, one for a configured value and another for an operationally used value). This provides a more elegant and simpler solution to the problem. The downside is that many existing models would have to be redesigned. This is clearly a major drawback, even if the redesign is fairly natural and mechanical. This work is currently in progress at IETF. The reworked ietf-interfaces.yang module (RFC 8343), following NMDA, is shown in Example 3-45.

EXAMPLE 3-45 A Tree Representation of the NMDA-Compliant ietf-interfaces.yang (Abridged)

```
module: ietf-interfaces
  +--rw interfaces
  |  +--rw interface* [name]
  |     +--rw name                        string
  |     +--rw description?                string
  |     +--rw type                        identityref
  |     +--rw enabled?                    boolean
  |     +--ro oper-status                 enumeration
  |     +--ro last-change?                yang:date-and-time
  |     +--ro phys-address?               yang:phys-address
  |     +--ro higher-layer-if*            interface-ref
  |     +--ro lower-layer-if*             interface-ref
  |     +--ro speed?                      yang:gauge64
```

Notice that the complexity and length of the model decreased significantly. Since there is only one list for all data pertaining to all interfaces, there is no longer any need for naming conventions or other crutches for finding all the pieces of information pertaining to a given interface.

What about the new datastores then? NETCONF initially specified three datastores, as shown in Figure 3-1.

- `:startup` (optional)
- `:candidate` (optional)
- `:running` (always present)

Those three datastores map a typical router architecture, which contains some combination of a startup configuration, a running configuration, and candidate configuration.

NOTE

Capabilities in NETCONF have very long and unwieldy formal names, with lots of colons. The datastores are capabilities and therefore are afflicted by this as well. It isn't surprising, then, that people started abbreviating the names, keeping only a colon (to indicate it's an abbreviation) and the last word when referring to them. The `:startup` datastore's formal name is `urn:ietf:params:netconf:capability:startup:1.0`.

With the NMDA architecture, additional datastores with described semantics may be defined for systems that support more advanced processing chains converting configuration to operational state. For example, some systems support configuration that is not currently used (so-called "inactive configuration") or they support configuration templates that are used to expand configuration data via a common template. Such specifications may come from IETF or any other party. The NMDA specification itself took the opportunity to define two:

- `:intended`
- `:operational`

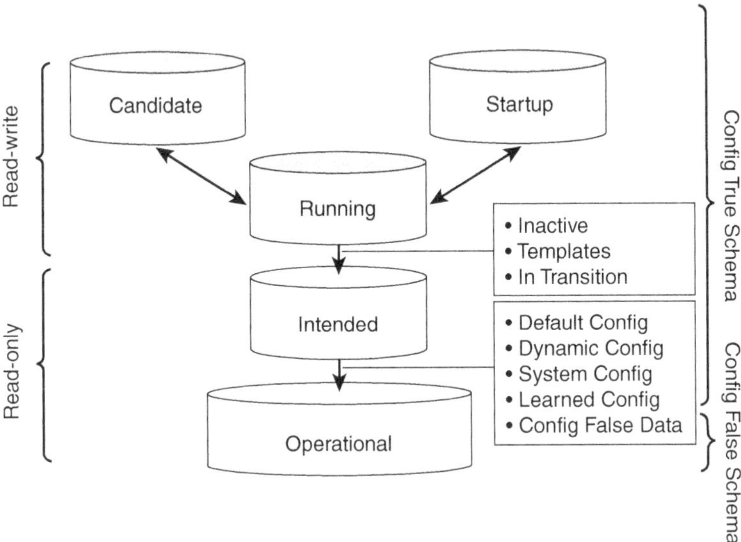

FIGURE 3-1 The Most Common Datastores in the NMDA Architecture

Let's examine the NMDA specification (RFC 8342) for the details regarding the content of each datastore.

The `:operational` datastore is a kind of old concept from the NETCONF world, now dressed up as a datastore; it holds all `config false` data and a read-only copy of all the `config true` data. It was just never officially named a datastore before. Then there is the brand-new `:intended` datastore. In simple servers, this one contains the same information as `:running`. In more advanced servers that might support a service concept, templates, and inactive (commented-out) configuration, the `:running` datastore contains the input data to services, templates, and inactive configuration, while `:intended` contains the result when those services and template constructs are expanded to concrete configuration elements, with inactive configuration removed. The `:intended` datastore is a read-only datastore, but it may still be useful to see what all those services, templates, and inactive elements expanded to.

The `:operational` datastore then contains all the configuration elements actually in use right now. No preconfigured elements. It also contains all the operationally active elements—even those that were not configured.

Interview with the Expert

Q&A with Martin Björklund

Martin Björklund is the editor (main contact) of the IETF YANG specifications RFC 6020, and later RFC 7950, and is also deeply involved in many other related documents. Martin co-founded Tail-f Systems in 2005, which was acquired by Cisco just under ten years later. Martin still works with the Tail-f products inside Cisco as architect, programmer, and distinguished engineer. Martin has a past as a serial entrepreneur, with a number of projects that were acquired or resulted in well-known companies.

Question:

What gave you and the original participants the audacity to design a yet another data modeling language and think you could change the world this way?

Answer:

(Laughter) We really hadn't thought that it would receive the uptake we're seeing now. We were completely focused on solving the NETCONF modeling problem. Well, actually, not only NETCONF. We already had our own proprietary language that applied to all management interfaces. That was always how we wanted to do this. Then there were political reasons for saying that this language was only for NETCONF. There had been several failed attempts at making modeling languages, not least at IETF. So trying to make a language that was good for everything was not popular. Don't boil the ocean. Therefore, we kept limiting ourselves to NETCONF. That really worked well as a tactic to get it done, but later we have occasionally had to pay the price when obvious shortcomings for the more general case have showed up.

Question:

How did the cross-industry team behind this form in the first place?

Answer:

It started with general talk around mid 2006. The talk was that maybe something ought to be done, but that it would be hard. Everybody had different ideas. Some wanted to use XSD, some RelaxNG. Some thought there was no need for a language at all—why would it make sense to standardize the modeling language? At that time everybody had their own modeling language. We had ours, Ericsson had theirs, Juniper had their own. At IETF in Prague I spoke with Ericsson about this, then I shared a cab back to the airport with Phil Shafer at Juniper. That's when we decided to give it a go. So it was that Phil Shafer, David Partain, Balász Lengyel, Jürgen Schönwälder and myself started this work. Later Andy Bierman joined the design team.

Question:

What were the main sources of influence for YANG?

Answer:

The point was that everybody had their own proprietary language. We had ours. Juniper had something. Ericsson had theirs. Jürgen was part of the SMIng design team at IETF, which never got around to be used. YANG started out with the concepts from those. Mostly ours and Juniper's, with some SMIng factored in. The whole type system comes from SMIng, more or less. We took the best parts of each language and melded them together.

Question:

Did that help to make it acceptable among all the participants, since everybody contributed something?

Answer:

Yes, that definitely helped. That everybody would be writing YANG specs was hard to imagine back then. For a long time, nothing seemed to happen in the industry, while we kept building our tools. We got a head start of several years. Finally, people saw what it could do.

Question:

Ten years later, are you satisfied with the result?

Answer:

Yes, I have to say yes. Even if there are things that could have been done better. Technical details that should have been different. Definitely. Still, one has to be content with the end result. I think it's good.

Question:

What's so good with YANG compared to earlier languages?

Answer:

One cornerstone is readability. Most people that get a YANG document in front of them understand. People intuitively understand. Many other languages are much harder to grasp. It's a pretty natural way to model hierarchical structures. Of course there are some constructs that aren't easy, but overall, it's easy to read. Fairly compact. The other very important thing is the extensibility. The way augment works, which allows amalgamating models from different sources and times. Augment allows you to extend existing models without changing the original, or even having to plan for extension, all the while keeping good backwards compatibility. There really aren't any other languages that do this.

Question:

Is YANG finished now, or what happens?

Answer:

Yes, I hope it's done now. The more popular the language gets, the more people are drawn in to contribute with their use cases and ideas. Wouldn't it be nice if we could add … for example, making YANG more object oriented. Many of these ideas don't really fit into the YANG concept, and with every big change or addition, you always jeopardize the language. A version 2 or 3 of a language often kills it. Stability is a key feature of a language.

I hope the community will add things with some caution. No dramatic changes. We're at YANG 1.1 now. YANG 1.2 with some fixes would probably be a good thing. Unfortunately, the most problematic issues with YANG right now aren't small. The most annoying thing, in my mind, is that we have context-dependent values. Values that are instance identifiers, identities and XPath expressions are encoded differently for different YANG-based protocols. It's not good when the values are coded using XML namespaces in XML, when you use JSON, which doesn't have that. To update YANG to fix this in a good way won't be easy, however.

Summary

This chapter started off with showing you how to take some real-world data and turn that into a formal YANG contract describing the type and structure of that data. This allows clients to know what to expect, and servers to implement industry standards. Model-driven APIs are essential in a software-defined world.

Then the modeling turned to more complex features in order to mirror real-world data organization. For example, tables in tables, keys, and references—as well as how to model data where the set of acceptable values grows over time. Extensibility is a key feature of YANG, both with respect to the values, the elements, and the YANG language itself.

Traditionally, part of the management interface that was the hardest to get right was configuration. Much attention was therefore given to the strong consistency mechanisms in YANG, such as `must` and `when` expressions. Tight and specific YANG contracts make the models dependable and useful. The strong separation between configuration and operational data must also be counted as a consistency feature.

After the configuration discussion, `action`, `rpc`, and `notification` constructs were used to define client/server communication beyond the configuration transactions and operational status collection.

The section towards the end on pointers and XPath explained (and hopefully prevents) some of the most common mistakes that crop up repeatedly in YANG Doctor reviews in recent years.

At the end of the chapter was a discussion around the background and implications of the now ongoing redesign of essentially all the standard IETF YANG models, to adhere to the principles of the Network Management Datastore Architecture (NMDA). This shift allows simpler and more compact models, while also giving greater flexibility for clients to work more closely with servers that implement advanced features like macro expansion, data learned from the network, and pre-provisioning.

References in This Chapter

This chapter is by no means a complete account of everything you can do in YANG, but it aims at providing you a good grasp over all the most important concepts, what problems YANG solves, and how to go about making new YANG models.

To go deeper, the next step is the RFCs. They are actually quite readable and a good source of detailed information, and many have usage examples. In particular, have a look at the references in Table 3-5.

TABLE 3-5 YANG-Related Documents for Further Reading

Topic	Content
YANG 1.1 YANG 1.0	https://tools.ietf.org/html/rfc7950 https://tools.ietf.org/html/rfc6020 YANG Data Modeling Language is defined in RFC 7950 (YANG 1.1) and RFC 6020 (YANG 1.0). Defines all YANG keywords and the mapping to NETCONF. Provides some examples.
XPath	https://www.w3.org/TR/1999/REC-xpath-19991116/ XML Path Language (XPath) Version 1.0 is the XPath version used in YANG. It is defined by the World Wide Web Consortium (W3C). Defines the XPath language used inside YANG `path`, `must` and `when` statements.
REGEX	https://www.w3.org/TR/2004/REC-xmlschema-2-20041028/ XML Schema Part 2: Datatypes Second Edition defines the flavor of regular expressions used in YANG `pattern` statements. YANG `pattern` statements use WWW (a.k.a. XML) regular expressions, which is not exactly the same as in Perl, Python, and so on.
NMDA	https://tools.ietf.org/html/rfc8342 Network Management Datastore Architecture is defined in RFC 8342. This is the new recommended way of structuring YANG modules.
YANG Guidelines	https://tools.ietf.org/html/rfc8407 Guidelines for Authors and Reviewers of YANG Data Model Documents are defined in RFC 8407. This is highly recommended reading before reviewing or writing YANG modules. Contains conventions and checklists.
NETMOD WG	https://datatracker.ietf.org/wg/netmod/documents/ IETF Network Modeling Working Group. This is the group that defines YANG and many of the YANG modules. Look here for the latest drafts and RFCs.
IETF YANG GitHub	https://github.com/YangModels/yang IETF's repository of IETF, other SDOs, open source, and vendor-specific YANG models. Good place to take inventory, but necessarily incomplete and often outdated. About 10,000 YANG modules are checked in at the time of writing.
yangcatalog.org	https://yangcatalog.org/ Catalog of YANG modules, searchable on keywords and metadata. Also has YANG tools for validation, browsing, dependency graphs, and REGEX validation. At the time of writing there are about 3500 YANG modules in the catalog.

Chapter 4

NETCONF, RESTCONF, and gNMI Explained

This chapter covers

- The transport layer of NETCONF, RESTCONF and gNMI
- What tools you could use to play with these protocols
- Connection, hello, and capability negotiation in each protocol
- Extensible Markup Language (XML) tags and namespaces (optional section)
- Reading and writing configuration and operational data
- The transactionality mechanism in each protocol
- Invoking YANG actions and RPCs
- Subscriptions for operational notifications and telemetry updates

Introduction

This chapter exercises the *BookZone* YANG model developed in Chapter 3, "YANG Explained," using three YANG model-driven management protocols: NETCONF, RESTCONF, and gNMI. You are welcome to simply read about each example provided in this chapter, but if you prefer a more hands-on approach, you can also clone the GitHub project from Chapter 3 and run each example presented here on your own laptop. Instructions for how to obtain the necessary free tools can be found within the project README file at https://github.com/janlindblad/bookzone.

NETCONF

As discussed in Chapter 2, "Data Model–Driven Management," the Internet Engineering Task Force (IETF) developed NETCONF because network operators complained that they were struggling with their network management using the standards and tools available at the time—primarily Simple Network Management Protocol (SNMP). The "Simple" in SNMP refers to the simplicity with which device vendors can implement it. However, SNMP was definitely not simple to use for the network operators in some use cases. Configuration tasks especially turned out to be difficult.

With NETCONF, the equation was reversed, with a focus on making network management simple to use, but not necessarily simple to implement in devices. NETCONF, therefore, has a different focus and set of operation that it offers, to meet the network operators' requirements. This background and the requirements are well summarized in RFC 3535.

Fundamentals

NETCONF 1.1 (RFCs 6241 and 6242) is a network management protocol specified by the IETF. It defines an extensible set of operations that a NETCONF client can send to a NETCONF server. A NETCONF client typically has the role of network manager, and the NETCONF server has a role of managed network device. In many cases, there are also intermediate systems that control a particular aspect or domain. They are often referred to as "controllers." A controller acts as a server to its managers and as a client to its devices. A manager that manages controllers or large numbers of devices is often called an "orchestrator," but there is no fundamental difference between an orchestrator and controller. In the NETCONF specification, really the only terms used are "client" and "server." A small scale setup is shown in Figure 4-1.

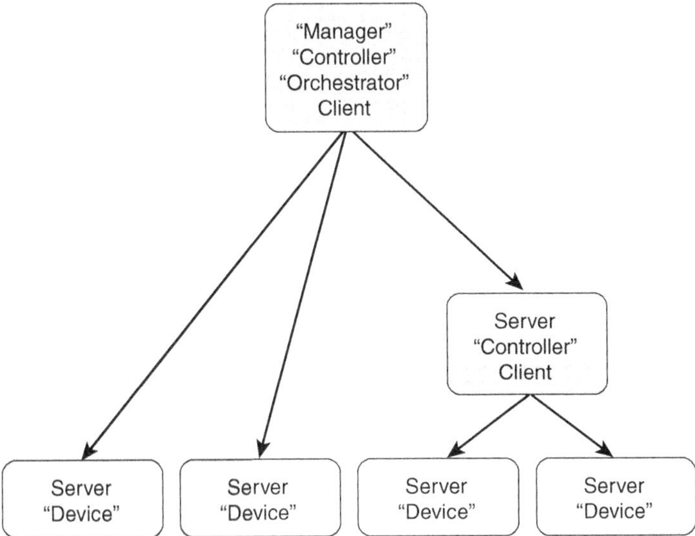

FIGURE 4-1 A NETCONF Client (Manager) Manages a Collection of NETCONF Servers (Devices) and a Controller, Which in Turn Is Both a Server and a Client

To allow the network manager to manage the devices, NETCONF defines the following operations:

- Monitoring the operational status of the device
- Updating the device configuration (the orders the manager has for the device)

In addition, NETCONF defines a mechanism for NETCONF server implementers to define additional operations, "actions," and notifications. Using this mechanism, network managers typically also perform the following:

- Invoke management actions
- Subscribe to notifications from the managed device

Normally, all the data to be retrieved or updated when monitoring or configuring the device, as well as the management actions and device notifications, are described by YANG modules. This is the contract the device offers and the way the manager can know what objects can be manipulated, notifications subscribed to, and so on.

Note that NETCONF was defined before YANG and has no fundamental dependency on YANG. Other languages were used to describe valid NETCONF operations. For all practical purposes, however, YANG is the only schema language widely used for NETCONF today.

Each NETCONF session established from a NETCONF client to a NETCONF server consists of a sequence of messages. Apart from the hello message, which both parties send immediately when they are connected, all message exchanges are initiated by the client (manager). The hello message is a declaration where both sides state which NETCONF protocol version(s) they can speak and the server states which optional capabilities it supports.

Each NETCONF message is either a remote procedure call (RPC) or an rpc-reply. Each RPC is a request from the client that the server execute a given operation. The rpc-reply is sent by the server when it has completed or failed to complete the request. Some rpc-replies are short answers to a simple query, or just an OK that the order was executed. Some are long and may contain the entire device configuration or status. Rpc-replies to subscriptions consist of a message that technically never ends. As the subscribed-to event occurs, additional pieces of the rpc-reply are produced by the server. An rpc-reply may also be an rpc-error, indicating that the requested operation was not carried out.

Each NETCONF message is encoded in an XML-based structure defined by the NETCONF specification. The communication flows over Secure Shell (SSH), which in turn runs on top of Transmission Control Protocol/Internet Protocol (TCP/IP). Internet Assigned Numbers Authority (IANA) has assigned port 830 as the default port for NETCONF management, and this assignment is usually reflected in real implementations. Some systems allow connecting to the NETCONF server on port 22 (nonstandard for NETCONF) as well as on port 830.

SSH supports a subsystem concept. The default subsystem typically gives a shell prompt on the remote system, but a widely known subsystem is `sftp` (Secure File Transfer Protocol). Connecting to the standard SSH port 22 on a device while specifying the `sftp` subsystem typically connects to the SFTP server instead.

Similarly, NETCONF has its own subsystem: `netconf`. To connect to the NETCONF server on a typical NETCONF capable system, run the following:

```
ssh user@system -p 830 -s netconf
```

This normally gives you the NETCONF hello message. It might look something like Example 4-1.

EXAMPLE 4-1 NETCONF **hello** Message

```
<hello xmlns="urn:ietf:params:xml:ns:netconf:base:1.0">
 <capabilities>
  <capability>urn:ietf:params:netconf:base:1.1</capability>
...
 </capabilities>
 <session-id>4281045817</session-id>
</hello>
]]>]]>
```

If you get a message like this, you know you reached the device's NETCONF server. The hello message may be very long, as some NETCONF servers support hundreds of capabilities.

When you first connect to an SSH server, the connection has only one channel. It is possible for the client to open additional channels within the same SSH connection, without a new SSH authentication procedure. Each channel is transported across independently of other channels.

This is useful when a manager (NETCONF client) wants to perform several things in parallel toward a particular device. It may use one SSH channel to configure the device, another to read the operational status, and a third to subscribe for changes in some particularly interesting operational status—say, the health of BGP peers, if the device is a router. All channels run within the same, single SSH connection.

Figure 4-2 shows a client and server communicating over three SSH channels, over the SSH connection subsystem `netconf`, over TCP port 830, and over IP address 10.20.30.40. The three channels have a NETCONF payload for three different purposes and function independently and asynchronously.

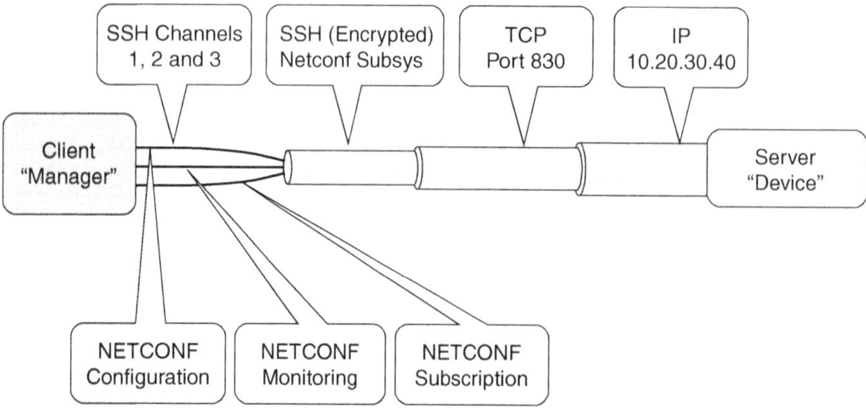

FIGURE 4-2 Exploded View of a Sample Three-Channel NETCONF Client-Server Connection

XML Tags, Attributes, and Namespaces

Since NETCONF is encoded in XML, let's briefly recap of some basic XML terminology.

XML Tag

An XML document contains structured data. The structure is provided by tags. A tag consists of a start tag, end tag, and usually, some data between the tags. Tags declare what each piece of data contained within the document really means. A start tag is created by surrounding a name with angle brackets. For example, `<rpc>` might be a start tag for some remote procedure call parameters. An end tag looks like its start tag with a slash in front of the name. For example, `</rpc>` means that the RPC parameters you started to define earlier ends here.

Tags that have no data inside are called empty tags. They can be written as a start tag immediately followed by an end tag (for example, `<quick></quick>`). Or they can be written sort of like a start tag merged with an end tag, so that there is a slash at the end instead (for example, `<quick/>`). This means exactly the same thing as a start tag immediately followed by an end tag. Both forms can be used interchangeably. Example 4-2 shows an outer `rpc` tag with three tags inside. Two of the inner tags carry some data, while the last is an empty tag.

EXAMPLE 4-2 Sample XML Structure with a Top-Level Tag Containing Two Tags with Values and an Empty Tag

```
<rpc>
  <what>ping</what>
  <who>10.20.30.40</who>
  <quick/>
</rpc>
```

XML Attribute

Tags may also have attributes. In NETCONF context, XML attributes convey meta-level information about the message, as shown in Example 4-3 (for example, the `message-id` or that a certain configuration item deep down in some structure should be deleted, while another one should be created). Attributes are added after the start tag name, still inside the angle brackets. Each attribute has a name, an equals sign, and a value. In strict XML, the value needs to appear within single or double quotes, but in reality it is not uncommon to skip the quotes around the value.

EXAMPLE 4-3 Sample XML Structure with an Attribute

```
<rpc message-id="17">
  <what>ping</what>
  <who>10.20.30.40</where>
  <quick/>
</rpc>
```

XML Namespaces

XML stands for Extensible Markup Language. What makes XML extensible is the namespace mechanism. Each tag and attribute in an XML document belongs to a particular namespace. It is the namespace it belongs to that defines what it means and which specification the tag or attribute comes from.

A special attribute is used to declare which namespace tags and attributes are defined in. It is called `xmlns`. The following snippet shows an XML representation of a NETCONF `get` request. You can tell it's a NETCONF `get` because the `xmlns` value matches the one from the NETCONF specification exactly.

```
<rpc xmlns="urn:ietf:params:xml:ns:netconf:base:1.0" message-id="17">
 <get></get>
</rpc>
```

There are probably many other specifications in the world that also define a tag "get" for their XML documents with wildly different meanings. This is fine. They use a different namespace value for their definition. The one used by the IETF NETCONF working group was registered with IANA, so no one else should use this namespace value. It's a pretty long and complicated string, too, with infinitesimal probability that anyone would chance upon it.

Namespaces are not necessarily registered with IANA, however. Any company that needs a world-unique namespace string is encouraged to take their company URL, which tends to be unique, and then append something that makes it unique within the company. In Chapter 3, the *BookZone* example uses the following namespace:

```
http://example.com/ns/bookzone
```

This looks like a URL, but it's really just a world-unique string. Pasting this into your web browser won't make you any wiser.

An `xmlns` attribute applies to the tag it sits on, any other unqualified attributes on this tag, and everything inside until the corresponding end tag, as shown in Example 4-4. Even if the `xmlns` namespace normally applies to everything within the tag it is added to, child tags and attributes can explicitly refer to a different namespace by specifying their own `xmlns` attribute.

EXAMPLE 4-4 Sample Real-World XML Structure with Multiple Namespaces, Attributes, and Deeply Structured Tags

```
<rpc message-id="1" xmlns="urn:ietf:params:xml:ns:netconf:base:1.0">
  <get-config>
    <source>
      <running/>
    </source>
    <filter type="subtree">
      <authors xmlns="http://example.com/ns/bookzone"/>
      <books xmlns="http://example.com/ns/bookzone"/>
    </filter>
  </get-config>
</rpc>
```

Never mind what all these tags actually mean—that's covered later in this chapter. Just look at the tags. Here the tags `rpc`, `get-config`, `source`, `running`, and `filter` are defined in the NETCONF base specification, while `authors` and `books` are defined in the BookZone YANG module (specification).

In cases where you need to switch between several namespaces, use a prefix to qualify which namespace a particular tag or attribute belongs to. To define a prefix, a special form of the `xmlns` attribute is used. Say you want to define the prefix nc (short for NETCONF) to easily refer to things in the NETCONF specification; it would look like this:

```
xmlns:nc='urn:ietf:params:xml:ns:netconf:base:1.0'
```

Within the tag that has this `xmlns:nc` attribute, you can refer to anything from the NETCONF specification by simply adding `nc:` in front of the tag or attribute in question.

For example, the same message just shown could be written like Example 4-5. Note how the default namespace is now that of *bookzone* instead. All references to NETCONF specification objects are now prefixed with `nc:`.

EXAMPLE 4-5 Exactly the Same XML Message as in Example 4-4, But Coded with a Different Default Namespace

```
<nc:rpc nc:message-id="1"
        xmlns:nc="urn:ietf:params:xml:ns:netconf:base:1.0"
        xmlns="http://example.com/ns/bookzone">
```

```
  <nc:get-config>
    <nc:source>
      <nc:running/>
    </nc:source>
    <nc:filter nc:type="subtree">
      <authors/>
      <books/>
    </nc:filter>
  </nc:get-config>
</nc:rpc>
```

The real value of this mixing and matching namespaces is to be able to point to objects in all sorts of specification documents (YANG modules in this context), but still being able to chip in with a NETCONF attribute here and there, if needed. Here's an example: Note how the `edit-config` tag declares the `nc:` prefix to refer to the NETCONF specification. Then inside the `config` tag, each tag is coming from a new specification (YANG module), until you get to the one you're looking to delete. To delete the book tag, you need to reference the NETCONF operation attribute, defined in the NETCONF specification, so simply say `nc:operation`.

Example 4-6 deletes a book called *The Art of War* from the book catalog, but the NETCONF operations weren't introduced yet, so don't worry about the finer points here. All you're interested in at the moment is the use of namespaces in this NETCONF message.

EXAMPLE 4-6 Sample XML Structure That Declares a Namespace, nc, and Refers to It Deeper Inside the Structure. This XML Structure Also Happens to be a Real-World NETCONF Message to Delete an Item from a List.

```
<rpc message-id="1" xmlns="urn:ietf:params:xml:ns:netconf:base:1.0">
  <edit-config xmlns:nc="urn:ietf:params:xml:ns:netconf:base:1.0">
    <target>
      <running/>
    </target>
    <error-option>rollback-on-error</error-option>
    <config>
      <books xmlns="http://example.com/ns/bookzone">
        <book nc:operation="delete">
          <title>The Art of War</title>
        </book>
      </books>
    </config>
  </edit-config>
</rpc>
```

XML Processing Instructions

There's really only one processing instruction in common use with typical NETCONF servers today:

```
<?xml version="1.0" encoding="UTF-8"?>
```

This simply means that the document is plain-old XML and that the text inside is encoded in the UTF-8 character set. Basically, it means that everything is normal and proper. You can safely ignore this line.

RPC Mechanism

Like most other management protocols, NETCONF has a remote procedure call (RPC) layer. There's nothing particularly exciting or special about how RPCs are done in NETCONF, but in order to understand the protocol, let's have a brief look anyway.

Apart from the initial hello message, every NETCONF message is an RPC request from client to server, or an rpc-reply from server to client. The rpc-reply can be a simple OK message, a reply with some data, or an rpc-error. All of these are encoded in XML. Each RPC request has a `message-id` XML attribute with a value chosen by the client. The corresponding rpc-reply or rpc-error message has the exact same `message-id` so that the client (manager) can match up which reply is for which request. This is very useful if the client shoots several requests to the server in rapid succession.

A typical RPC message from a client to a server might look like Example 4-7.

EXAMPLE 4-7 NETCONF **get-config** Request with a Source and Filter, Sent by a NETCONF Client to a Server

```
<?xml version="1.0" encoding="UTF-8"?>
<rpc message-id="1" xmlns="urn:ietf:params:xml:ns:netconf:base:1.0">
  <get-config>
    <source>
      <running/>
    </source>
    <filter type="subtree">
      <authors xmlns="http://example.com/ns/bookzone"/>
      <books xmlns="http://example.com/ns/bookzone"/>
    </filter>
  </get-config>
</rpc>
```

The first line is an XML processing instruction that asserts that this is plain, ordinary XML and the character encoding is Unicode UTF-8. The second line says that this is a NETCONF RPC. The `xmlns` value exactly matches the string given in the NETCONF specification; that's how you know it is NETCONF. The `message-id` is 1, so when the server replies to this operation, the reply should be marked the same way.

The actual RPC operation is `<get-config>`, as defined in the NETCONF specifications. The `get-config` operation accepts a payload that describes exactly what to get (more on that later in the chapter). The `<filter>` tag, according to the section on the `get-config` operation in the NETCONF specification (RFC 6241, Section 7.1), means that the server should fetch only data that corresponds to the YANG elements inside the `<filter>` tag.

If the server supports the *bookzone* YANG module (which has the namespace string `"http://example.com/ns/bookzone"` to be precise), then the `get-config` operation should return the list of authors, books, and all information you have on them. The data is to be fetched from the datastore `running`, meaning the currently active data in the database. More on NETCONF datastores later.

Example 4-8 illustrates a possible reply from the server system.

EXAMPLE 4-8 NETCONF Reply to the Request in Example 4-7, Sent by the Server Back to the Client


```
<?xml version="1.0" encoding="UTF-8"?>
<rpc-reply xmlns="urn:ietf:params:xml:ns:netconf:base:1.0" message-id="1">
  <data>
    <authors xmlns="http://example.com/ns/bookzone">
      <author>
        <name>Douglas Adams</name>
        <account-id>1010</account-id>
      </author>
      <author>
        <name>Malala Yousafzai</name>
        <account-id>1011</account-id>
      </author>
      <author>
        <name>Michael Ende</name>
        <account-id>1001</account-id>
      </author>
      <author>
        <name>Per Espen Stoknes</name>
        <account-id>1111</account-id>
      </author>
      <author>
        <name>Sun Tzu</name>
        <account-id>1100</account-id>
      </author>
    </authors>
    <books xmlns="http://example.com/ns/bookzone">
      <book>
        <title>I Am Malala: The Girl Who Stood Up for Education and Was Shot by the
Taliban</title>
```

```
      <author>Malala Yousafzai</author>
      <format>
        <isbn>9780297870913</isbn>
        <format-id>hardcover</format-id>
      </format>
    </book>
    <book>
      <title>The Art of War</title>
...
```

The first line is an XML processing instruction, which is optional and may or may not be there. The second line is the rpc-reply. Apparently the operation went well. The rpc-reply has a `message-id` attribute that matches the one from the request. The `<data>` tag contains the answer to the request query, which was a `<get-config>` operation in this case.

The response `data` body contains the `authors` and `books` tags defined in the *bookzone-example* YANG module, with some `author` and a couple of `book` instances, with each book in at least one `format`.

Some RPCs might not return any actual data. The request could look like Example 4-9.

EXAMPLE 4-9 NETCONF Request to Lock the Candidate Datastore

```
<?xml version="1.0" encoding="UTF-8"?>
<rpc xmlns="urn:ietf:params:xml:ns:netconf:base:1.0" message-id="4">
 <lock><target><candidate/></target></lock>
</rpc>
```

This RPC requests the NETCONF server to lock the `candidate` datastore so that nobody else can change it while this client is doing something. The response is a simple `<ok/>`, as shown in Example 4-10.

EXAMPLE 4-10 NETCONF Reply with Success

```
<?xml version="1.0" encoding="UTF-8"?>
<rpc-reply xmlns="urn:ietf:params:xml:ns:netconf:base:1.0" message-id="4">
 <ok/>
</rpc-reply>
```

In the case of success, that is. If the lock is already taken by another session, the reply could look like Example 4-11.

EXAMPLE 4-11 NETCONF Reply with Failure

```
<?xml version="1.0" encoding="UTF-8"?>
<rpc-reply xmlns="urn:ietf:params:xml:ns:netconf:base:1.0" message-id="4">
```

```
 <rpc-error>
  <error-type>protocol</error-type>
  <error-tag>lock-denied</error-tag>
  <error-severity>error</error-severity>
  <error-message>Lock failed, lock held by other session</error-message>
  <error-info>
   <session-id>8</session-id>
  </error-info>
 </rpc-error>
</rpc-reply>
```

There could potentially be more than one rpc-error returned in an rpc-reply.

Message Framing

To clearly separate messages from each other, NETCONF uses a framing mechanism. The framing mechanism is responsible for turning the stream of characters into separate XML messages.

There are two ways this is happening in NETCONF, because it is different in NETCONF 1.0 and NETCONF 1.1 (the two NETCONF versions that exist today). Actually, this difference in framing mechanism is the main difference between the two protocol versions.

In NETCONF 1.0, the messages are separated by a six-character string that is unlikely to ever appear inside a message:

```
]]>]]>
```

When a NETCONF client connects to a NETCONF 1.0 server, it inserts that string in between every rpc-request, in order to ensure both sides are in sync at the start of every message, and to be able to resync in case a message has some XML issue, such as unbalanced or misspelled tags.

Even if this character sequence is highly unlikely to appear spontaneously in the data, after NETCONF 1.0 was released, someone considered this mechanism a security problem. If a client didn't properly sanitize all input data everywhere, it's conceivable that an attacker could inject some data that contained this string into a field on a portal (say, in an input field labeled *Name*). And the unsuspecting portal might then feed this user-entered string into the NETCONF payload it sends off.

If the attacker entered this string followed by a NETCONF message he crafted, he could obtain great black-hat power—a classic case of injection attack. The true remedy is proper sanitation, but the NETCONF working group decided to make this kind of attack harder.

In NETCONF 1.1, the framing mechanism is different. Instead of having a character sequence that could appear anywhere in the payload, the sender sends a # character, a byte count in ASCII, followed by a block of that many bytes. Each message may consist of many blocks. Finally, the sender sends a special marker, ##, which signifies there are no more blocks in this message. A simple message with NETCONF 1.1 framing might look like Example 4-12.

EXAMPLE 4-12 NETCONF Message with NETCONF 1.1 Framing

```
#137
<?xml version="1.0" encoding="UTF-8"?>
<rpc-reply xmlns="urn:ietf:params:xml:ns:netconf:base:1.0" message-id="2">
    <ok/>
</rpc-reply>

##
```

The blocks can be large (for example, megabytes) or many (for example, thousands). The XML text may be interrupted at any place within the block framing, as shown in Example 4-13.

EXAMPLE 4-13 Large NETCONF Message with NETCONF 1.1 Framing

```
#16376
<?xml version="1.0" encoding="UTF-8"?>
<rpc-reply xmlns="urn:ietf:params:xml:ns:netconf:base:1.0" message-id="1"><data><aaa
xmlns="http://cisco.com/ns/ciscosb/aaa-trans"><authentication><users><user>
<name>cisco</name>
        … a few kilobytes later …
</description></category><category><id>29</id><parent>2</parent>
<name>Reference and Research</name><description>Personal, pro

#16376
fessional, or educational reference material, including online dictionaries, maps,
census, almanacs,
library catalogs, genealogy, and scientific information.</description>

        Here the server was apparently sending the payload in blocks of 16376 bytes.
        After sending many such blocks, the last block comes here:

#1234
v6-enabled><v4-enabled>false</v4-enabled><ripng><interfaces><interface>
        … a kilobyte later …
</system></data></rpc-reply>

##
```

With this new framing, it is considerably harder for an attacker to gain access to the NETCONF stream. Even if he was able to guess the number of bytes that remain in the block where he is targeting his injection attack and then pad that many bytes before entering the block end marker *##*, client portals would still have to compute the length of the payload and simply add the attacker's extra characters into the length of the payload. All he'd get is unusually weird-looking content in that *Name* field.

The rest of this chapter does not show any of the framing or the opening XML version processing instruction, which is optional and may or may not be there. Also, the XML content will be pretty-printed to make it human readable. It's acceptable to send pretty-printed XML content, as shown in Example 4-14, over the wire.

EXAMPLE 4-14 Pretty-Printed NETCONF Message Displayed Without Framing

```
<rpc xmlns="urn:ietf:params:xml:ns:netconf:base:1.0" message-id="1">
 <get-config>
  <source>
   <running/>
  </source>
 </get-config>
</rpc>
```

Most of the time, however, a payload like the one shown in Example 4-14 is actually sent without whitespace, as shown in Example 4-15.

EXAMPLE 4-15 The Characters Actually Sent in the Message from Example 4-14.

```
#168
<?xml version="1.0" encoding="UTF-8"?><rpc xmlns="urn:ietf:params:xml:ns:netconf:base
:1.0" message-id="1"><get-config><source><running/></source></get-config></rpc>

##
```

Message Overview

As shown, NETCONF has an RPC mechanism and an XML message encoding that allow clients to invoke functionality on servers and for servers to respond in a well-formed way. There is nothing special about these mechanisms in NETCONF. There are plenty of other RPC mechanisms and message encodings out there already—many just as good as the one used in NETCONF.

The real essence, innovation, and value of NETCONF lie in a few predefined management operations—or more specifically, in the definitions of how these operations work.

The most important ones are `hello`, `get`, `get-config`, `edit-config`, `rpc`, and `create-subscription`. Each of these fundamental operations are discussed in the following sections. For modern systems with Network Management Datastore Architecture (NMDA) support (see Chapter 3), there are a couple of additional operations—`get-data` and `edit-data`—that are covered as well.

Hello Message

As mentioned earlier, the hello message is the first message sent by both parties immediately as a new NETCONF session is established. This message contains a declaration of the capabilities of each party—for example, which NETCONF version each party supports (1.0, 1.1 or both). A server announcing support for 1.0 and 1.1 (and a few other things) might send something like what's shown in Example 4-16.

EXAMPLE 4-16 NETCONF **hello** Message with a Collection of Supported Capabilities

```
<hello xmlns:nc="urn:ietf:params:xml:ns:netconf:base:1.0"
 xmlns="urn:ietf:params:xml:ns:netconf:base:1.0">
 <capabilities>
  <capability>urn:ietf:params:netconf:base:1.0</capability>
  <capability>urn:ietf:params:netconf:base:1.1</capability>
  <capability>urn:ietf:params:netconf:capability:writable-running:1.0</capability>
  <capability>urn:ietf:params:netconf:capability:rollback-on-error:1.0</capability>
...
 </capabilities>
 <session-id>5</session-id>
</hello>]]>]]>
```

At the end of the hello message, the server sends a `session-id` number. This ID can be used to identify this particular session. No other session will get the same number.

The root NETCONF specification (RFC 6241 for NETCONF 1.1) defines a number of mandatory operations that any NETCONF server must support (for example, `get`, `get-config`, and `edit-config`). It also defines some optional capabilities, such as the `writable-running` capability, as shown. Most operations and capabilities, however, are defined in separate, additional specifications (often RFCs) and are optional to support (for example, `create-subscription` and `with-defaults`). Each such additional specification defines one or more optional capabilities, and it's the names of these capabilities that are announced in the hello message so that the client knows the server understands and can use them.

For example, a server that supports NETCONF notifications as defined in RFC 5277 includes a line in the hello message like this:

```
<capability>urn:ietf:params:netconf:capability:notification:1.0</capability>
```

This capability string is defined in that RFC and registered with IANA.

Since these capability names tend to be rather long, the convention is to informally refer to them in presentation material, mail, and literature in an abbreviated form. The capabilities used in this section are typically informally called `:notification`, `:writable-running`, and `:rollback-on-error`.

In systems with YANG 1.0 modules, the hello message also lists all the YANG modules the server supports, where the namespace string for each module is listed as a capability. Remember that YANG module namespaces that are not from a standards body like IETF usually are constructed to look like a company URL. Each namespace name may be decorated with the `module` name and `revision`, in URL-encoded form, as shown in Example 4-17.

EXAMPLE 4-17 NETCONF Server Announcing a Set of YANG 1.0 Modules It Supports, Taken from a NETCONF Hello Message

```
<capability>urn:ietf:params:xml:ns:yang:ietf-inet-types?module=ietf-inet-types&amp;
revision=2013-07-15</capability>
<capability>urn:ietf:params:xml:ns:yang:ietf-netconf-acm?module=ietf-netconf-acm&amp;
revision=2012-02-22</capability>
<capability>urn:ietf:params:xml:ns:yang:ietf-netconf-monitoring?module=ietf-netconf-
monitoring&amp;revision=2010-10-04</capability>
```

This way, the client (manager) knows which YANG modules are supported by a particular server.

In YANG 1.1, this mechanism was abandoned and replaced by the YANG Module Library. The problem with the hello way of declaring capabilities at connect time is that as the number of YANG modules supported by a server grows, the hello formalities take more and more time. Some of the modern routers now approach a thousand YANG modules, which makes the YANG 1.0 mechanism a kind of long-winded way of saying hello.

Therefore, a YANG 1.1 server must support and announce the following capability:

```
<capability>urn:ietf:params:netconf:capability:yang-library:1.0?
       revision=     &module-set-id=    <capability>
```

All the YANG 1.0 modules are still announced in hello, but all YANG 1.1 modules are retrieved with a `get` (or `get-data`) operation from */modules-state/module* instead, as shown in Example 4-18. To relieve the clients from having to read through that list just the same, the `module-set-id` attribute in the capability is guaranteed to have a different value every time the set of YANG 1.1 modules on the server changes. This way, the server can determine quickly if anything changed since last connection.

EXAMPLE 4-18 Server Replies with the List of Supported YANG 1.1 Modules (Incomplete)

```
<rpc-reply xmlns="urn:ietf:params:xml:ns:netconf:base:1.0" message-id="1">
  <data>
    <modules-state xmlns="urn:ietf:params:xml:ns:yang:ietf-yang-library">
      <module-set-id>7aec0b1b1d4e5783ff4d305475e6e92c</module-set-id>
      <module>
        <name>audiozone-example</name>
        <revision>2018-01-09</revision>
        <schema>https://localhost:8888/restconf/tailf/modules/audiozone-example
/2018-01-09</schema>
        <namespace>http://example.com/ns/audiozone</namespace>
        <conformance-type>implement</conformance-type>
      </module>
```

```
    <module>
      <name>bookzone-example</name>
      <revision>2018-01-05</revision>
      <schema>https://localhost:8888/restconf/tailf/modules/bookzone-example
/2018-01-05</schema>
      <namespace>http://example.com/ns/bookzone</namespace>
      <conformance-type>implement</conformance-type>
    </module>
    <module>
      <name>iana-crypt-hash</name>
      <revision>2014-08-06</revision>
```

Get-Config Message

The NETCONF `get-config` operation retrieves all or some of the configuration from a server.

In NETCONF, there is a very clear separation between what is configuration and what is not. A NETCONF client (manager) should be able to retrieve the configuration, store it, and later send it back to the server to make it do the same thing as last time around.

This may sound as very obvious and basic functionality. And it is, if you ask network operations people. But the fact is that most other network management protocols in wider use present obstacles to this use case. In SNMP, for example, not everything that is writable is part of the configuration, so someone needs to know what not to include. In other protocols, there is often no way to retrieve a representation of the full configuration without using a massive number of operations.

Having an operation that retrieves all, or specific subsets, of the configuration and nothing but the configuration is actually critical for the efficient common understanding between client and server.

A basic `get-config` request might look like what is shown in Example 4-19.

EXAMPLE 4-19 Basic NETCONF **get-config** Request

```
<rpc xmlns="urn:ietf:params:xml:ns:netconf:base:1.0" message-id="1">
 <get-config>
  <source>
   <running/>
  </source>
 </get-config>
</rpc>
```

As a response, the server is expected to return the full running configuration, as Example 4-20 illustrates.

EXAMPLE 4-20 Basic NETCONF **get-config** Reply

```
<rpc-reply xmlns="urn:ietf:params:xml:ns:netconf:base:1.0" message-id="1">
  <data>
    <authors xmlns="http://example.com/ns/bookzone">
      <author>
        <name>Douglas Adams</name>
        <account-id>1010</account-id>
      </author>
      <author>
        <name>Malala Yousafzai</name>
...
    </authors>
    <books xmlns="http://example.com/ns/bookzone">
      <book>
        <title>I Am Malala: The Girl Who Stood Up for Education and Was Shot by the
Taliban</title>
        <author>Malala Yousafzai</author>
        <format>
          <isbn>9780297870913</isbn>
          <format-id>hardcover</format-id>
        </format>
      </book>
      <book>
        <title>The Art of War</title>
        <author>Sun Tzu</author>
...
    <aaa xmlns="http://tail-f.com/ns/aaa/1.1">
      <authentication>
        <users>
          <user>
            <name>admin</name>
            <uid>9000</uid>
...
  </data>
</rpc-reply>
```

The `get-config` operation also supports two different kinds of filters. Filters are used to retrieve only select parts of the configuration. Example 4-21 shows a `get-config` request that only fetches the contents for *authors* and *books*.

EXAMPLE 4-21 Filtered NETCONF **get-config** Request

```
<rpc xmlns="urn:ietf:params:xml:ns:netconf:base:1.0" message-id="1">
 <get-config>
  <source>
   <running/>
  </source>
  <filter>
   <authors xmlns="http://example.com/ns/bookzone"/>
   <books xmlns="http://example.com/ns/bookzone"/>
  </filter>
 </get-config>
</rpc>
```

This is called a subtree filter and is a mandatory part of the NETCONF protocol. Subtree is the default style, but could be spelled out like this:

```
<filter type="subtree">
```

The subtree filter can be quite a bit more specific than this. You could ask for only a specific book, for example, or all books but only their titles and prices. If you need to make a complex, SQL-like search, use an XPath filter instead with your `get-config` operation. XPath filtering is an optional capability, so some NETCONF servers/devices do not support it.

Using a `get-config` operation with an XPath filter, you could, for example, request the list of *authors* with more than five titles in the catalog, or all books with a *price* less than 10 sim-dollars. You can see a few examples on XPath filters in the "Get Message" section later in this chapter.

Edit-Config Message

The NETCONF `edit-config` operation changes some or all of the configuration on a server.

NETCONF has a number of necessary but nonunique features (for example, the RPC and security mechanisms). Then there are a few things that bring new value to the network management arena, which is where NETCONF really stands out. The most important among these jewels is the `edit-config` operation.

The key features that make the `edit-config` operation really useful in network management is that it is transactional. It also allows you to change the configuration any way you like using a single call, and it's entirely based on the (YANG) data model. Well, in theory a system could support NETCONF without being transactional, because the transactional behavior is an optional capability called `:rollback-on-error`. If the NETCONF server/device doesn't advertise this capability, the `edit-config` operation is suddenly no better than corresponding operations in SNMP or any other legacy protocol. Fortunately, NETCONF servers that lack `:rollback-on-error` tend to be extremely rare.

Everybody must be realizing that investing in NETCONF infrastructure without also implementing this core feature is pointless.

What the `:rollback-on-error` capability says is that the `edit-config` content is treated as a transaction. This means that all the changes in the `edit-config` request are implemented by the server/device. In the case the configuration is invalid in some way, or is valid but the server fails to process it (for example, runs out of memory), none of the changes are implemented. This capability guarantees the outcome will be one or the other—either completely implemented or not implemented at all.

This is good news for managers. A traditional network management system (NMS) easily has half of the code devoted to detecting failure and rolling back changes to a consistent state if something goes wrong. This recovery code is no easy code to write, and it's even harder to test. In other words, it's code that's very expensive to develop. A server may fail to accept the new configuration in a gazillion ways, and ensuring that you can recover from every one of them it not trivial—so if the server says it will take care of this itself, that's truly good news.

Apart from transactions being "all or nothing," they are normally also "all at once." This means there is no concept of time inside a transaction. From a logical standpoint, the change happens all at once. This means that the manager doesn't need to sequence the configuration data so that, say, access control (ACL) rules are created before interfaces are modified, which might be the case if the server was managed from the command-line interface (CLI). If a server needs to process the information in a configuration change in a particular order, that's fine. But it's not something that the manager should be relied upon to know. This, too, makes life for the manager tremendously easier, not having to sort and rearrange the configuration payload according to (often poorly documented) implementation details from each and every server (device) vendor.

With many non-NETCONF-based management APIs (many REST APIs come to mind), there is often a catalog of different API calls a manager can make to create something, update this, or delete that. This API-catalog-based approach is classic and may feel very natural. For example, to create an interface in a traditional API might mean calling `CreateInterface` with the following parameters: location= "1/1/2", type="vlan", tag="10", name="v10", and description="Volvo vlan 10".

Later, let's say the type needs to be changed to vxlan instead, so the manager needs to make an `UpdateInterface` call. Most likely this call takes a similar list of parameters, except a few that "cannot be changed." All the parameters that could possibly be changed need to be passed in, even though only one actually changed. This sort of mechanism makes it complicated for a manager to update an existing configuration efficiently. First, it has to retrieve the existing values, update what was supposed to change, and then push the whole thing back again.

How does this work in NETCONF? The `edit-config` operation is transactional, and there is only a single `edit-config` operation to call no matter what combination of elements needs to be created, merged, replaced, deleted, and so on. Example 4-22 shows what an `edit-config` might look like.

EXAMPLE 4-22 NETCONF **edit-config** Request to Create, Update, and Delete Various Book Data

```
<edit-config xmlns:nc='urn:ietf:params:xml:ns:netconf:base:1.0'>
  <target>
   <running/>
  </target>
  <test-option>test-then-set</test-option>
  <error-option>rollback-on-error</error-option>
  <config>
   <authors xmlns="http://example.com/ns/bookzone"
            xmlns:nc="urn:ietf:params:xml:ns:netconf:base:1.0">
    <author>
     <name>Michael Ende</name>
     <account-id nc:operation="replace">1001</account-id>
    </author>
    <author nc:operation="delete">
     <name>Sun Tzu</name>
    </author>
   </authors>
   <books xmlns="http://example.com/ns/bookzone"
          xmlns:nc="urn:ietf:params:xml:ns:netconf:base:1.0">
    <book>
     <title>The Buried Giant</title>
     <author>Kazuo Ishiguro</author>
     <language>english</language>
     <format>
      <isbn>9781467600217</isbn>
      <format-id>mp3</format-id>
      <price>55</price>
     </format>
    </book>
    <book>
     <title>The Neverending Story</title>
     <format>
      <isbn>9780140386332</isbn>
      <price nc:operation="merge">16.5</price>
     </format>
    </book>
    <book nc:operation="remove">
     <title>The Art of War</title>
    </book>
   </books>
   <authors xmlns="http://example.com/ns/bookzone"
            xmlns:nc="urn:ietf:params:xml:ns:netconf:base:1.0">
```

```
    <author nc:operation="create">
      <name>Kazuo Ishiguro</name>
      <account-id>2017</account-id>
    </author>
   </authors>
  </config>
</edit-config>
```

It changes the *account-id* for the author *Michael Ende* and deletes the author *Sun Tzu*. It adds a new book, *The Buried Giant*, by a new author, *Kazuo Ishiguro*; adjusts the price for the paperback variant of *The Neverending Story* (ISBN 9780140386332); and removes the book *The Art of War*. Finally, it adds the author *Kazuo Ishiguro*, without whom the book entry for *The Buried Giant* would be invalid, since it names him as the author.

The NETCONF operation attribute declares how a particular leaf or subtree needs to be changed. Here are the possible values:

- `create`: The leaf or subtree is created. If any part of this already exists in the server configuration, the transaction fails.
- `merge`: The leaf or subtree is created if it does not exist, or updated to the given values where values already exist.
- `replace`: The leaf or subtree below the current point on the server is removed and then replaced with the given values.
- `delete`: The leaf or subtree is deleted. If it does not exist in the server, the transaction fails.
- `remove`: The leaf or subtree is deleted if it exists. Nothing happens if it does not exist already.
- If no operation tag is specified, as in the case of the book *The Buried Giant*, the default operation is `merge`. A different default operation may be specified in the `edit-config` header, but wasn't specified here.

The server response to the preceding `edit-config` might be the data listed in Example 4-23.

EXAMPLE 4-23 NETCONF **edit-config** Response with Success

```
<rpc-reply message-id="3"
  xmlns="urn:ietf:params:xml:ns:netconf:base:1.0">
 <ok/>
</rpc-reply>
```

Since these operations can be mixed and matched on different parts of the transaction content, there is no need for more than a single `edit-config` operation to go from any configuration on the server to any other desired configuration. This is not only a very convenient and efficient property of a network management protocol; it is actually a cornerstone of the value NETCONF provides.

To understand why this is so fundamentally important, consider what would happen if this wasn't the case. In many non-transactional systems, you'd need one operation for updating the author name and account number and one more for deleting an author. Yet another operation for adding a new book, plus another one for updating the price on a book. Then another to remove a book, and finally one more to add a new author. Six operations. A little chatty, perhaps, but if that was the only problem, you might be able to live with it.

The real issue comes if any operation fails for any reason. Imagine the first two changes were accepted, but the third one failed (that is, the addition of the new book *The Buried Giant* failed). What does the client need to do to recover from this inconsistent state?

The current state is halfway in between the desired state and the previous state. Right now, the author account has been updated, but not the price of his books. This might be a breach of contract with the author. Since the client cannot get to the desired state, the next best thing is to go back to the previous state. That state was consistent, at least.

First, the client needs to figure out how to undo the first two changes that have already taken effect. In many application programming interfaces (APIs), this in itself is not trivial—there isn't always a precise inverse function to call for every possible API call. The client needs to retrieve the previous price information first and store that in order to be able to potentially undo the price update operation.

Then the client needs to send these undo operations to the server. If everything goes smoothly, the server returns to the previous state, and the only damage done is that the system was in an inconsistent state for a little while. For example, since the account number changed momentarily, if someone placed an order for the book right at that moment, the author would get paid based on the unchanged price on the new account. This is obviously not ideal, and it creates confusion and churn.

Then there is the possibility that the client's attempt at recovery doesn't go smoothly. The undo of the price change may be rejected by the server. What's the server supposed to do in this case? It's halfway through a change, and now it's stuck so that it can't proceed to completion, nor can it revert back to the previous state.

As if that wasn't bad enough, what if the client software crashes or loses power during these recovery actions? The consistency of the data in the system now depends on the client not failing. To ensure consistency, the client would need to implement high-availability mechanisms so that a standby client is ready to take over at any moment in the middle of this operation, should the primary fail, and save the progress of the operation persistently to disk so that it can recover later in case of a power loss.

The closer you look at the situation, the clearer it gets: It's really hard to be the well-behaved client everyone likes under these circumstances. This is the fundamental realization that the IETF had back in 2002, when the decision was made to start a working group to provide a solution to this decades' long problem. The result is known today as NETCONF, and transactional behavior is at the heart of what NETCONF is.

Another important observation in this exchange is the sequence of events in all the changes—or more precisely, the lack of sequencing. Transactions, as defined in the NETCONF/YANG world, are atomic and instantaneous. Obviously, the set of changes is communicated as a string of edit operations, and this string has a beginning, middle, and end. The point here is that the validity of the change is taken as one atomic unit. If all the edits, taken together, lead to a valid datastore, the change is valid.

It is therefore perfectly valid to name the deletion of *Sun Tzu* as author "before" (a concept that doesn't exist within a transaction) deleting his book *The Art of War*—as long as both changes happen within the same transaction. Similarly, it's perfectly valid to add the author *Kazuo Ishiguro* "after" (a concept that doesn't exist within a transaction) the addition of his book *The Buried Giant*.

This, too, is fundamentally important, because without transactions being instantaneous, it falls on the client to figure out which sequences are valid. This isn't a trivial matter, and in many cases it's undocumented. A programmer making a script might be able to find a solution by trial and error, but an automation engine would not. In order to reach high levels of automation, it is essential that software applications are able to compute configuration changes without also sorting all operations according to YANG leafref dependency graphs and unwritten implementation-specific dependency rules.

Get Message

The NETCONF `<get>` operation retrieves all or some of the operational state and configuration from a server.

The amount of operational state that exists on many servers (devices) is massive, so it's seldom a good idea to ask a server to get everything without a filter. With some servers, a `get` request without a filter would pump data for hours or days.

As with `get-config`, the filter may be of the `subtree` type or `xpath`. As the name suggests, the subtree filter selects one or more subtrees with information. The XPath filter can do fairly advanced searches, like returning all interfaces where the word "Volvo" is found in the description, or all books in English with *popularity* over a given threshold. See the "Edit-Config Message" section earlier in this chapter for an example of a subtree filter. An XPath example follows.

Regardless of filter type, if the filter doesn't match any data, the server responds with a message with an empty `<data/>` tag. In other words, it's not an error to ask for things that don't exist on this system. Empty responses are often seen when people misspell tags or make a mistake regarding the namespace.

There is no NETCONF standard operation to return only the operational state without the configuration. This is because many YANG data models have some operational state modeled under configuration items, so it does not make sense to return only the operational elements. For example, the *interface* list of a server is typically configuration data. The packet counters associated with an interface might be modeled inside the *interface* list. If this is so, the packet counters can't be returned without also returning the interface name, which is a piece of the configuration. Returning a bunch of packet counters without knowing which interface each counter belongs to is pointless.

To get finer control over the query, if the server supports it, use an XPath expression to select the data to get. In the context of the *BookZone* example, say you want to know the name of the *author* of *The Hitchhiker's Guide to the Galaxy*. You could use a simple command-line tool like `netconf-console` to send your query, like this:

```
netconf-console --get --xpath '/books/book[title="The Hitchhiker&apos;s Guide to the
Galaxy"]/author'
```

Note how you have to encode characters with special meaning in XML (&) for this to work. A smarter tool might have done this for you, but here it serves as a reminder of the XML world you are in. The tool translates this into a NETCONF query, as shown in Example 4-24.

EXAMPLE 4-24 NETCONF **get** Request about a Book Author

```
<rpc message-id="1" xmlns="urn:ietf:params:xml:ns:netconf:base:1.0">
  <get>
    <filter select='/books/book[title="The Hitchhiker&apos;s Guide to the Galaxy"]/
author' type="xpath"/>
  </get>
</rpc>
```

As Example 4-25 illustrates, the server replies with the name of the *author* and the minimal context for the leaf you asked about.

EXAMPLE 4-25 NETCONF **get** Reply with a Single Leaf about a Book Author

```
<rpc-reply message-id="1" xmlns="urn:ietf:params:xml:ns:netconf:base:1.0">
  <data>
    <books xmlns="http://example.com/ns/bookzone">
      <book>
        <title>The Hitchhiker's Guide to the Galaxy</title>
        <author>Douglas Adams</author>
      </book>
    </books>
  </data>
</rpc-reply>
```

Actually, the apostrophe in the reply from the server is properly XML encoded as `'`, but the `netconf-console` tool translates the reply back into pretty-printed plaintext with XML entities replaced by readable characters, unless you ask it not to. The pretty-printing makes the reply nice to look at, but this isn't valid XML anymore, so don't cut and paste this text into your tools.

Here is a slightly more complex query, just to show what is possible, and what such a query would look like. This one gets the number of *books* in stock for those books that are sold in more than one *format* and have a *popularity* of less than one copy sold per day. Before you ask: *The Neverending Story* ends up among the results because it is sold in a digital *mp3* format as well as in *paperback* format. Only the paperback edition has any stock, so only a single entry comes up in the result. As is usual in computing, you get the reply you deserve:

```
netconf-console --get --xpath '/books/book[count(format) &gt; 1]
[popularity &lt; 365]/format/number-of-copies/in-stock'
```

This causes the `netconf-console` tool to send the query shown in Example 4-26.

EXAMPLE 4-26 NETCONF XPath **get** Request about Books in Stock

```
<rpc message-id="1" xmlns="urn:ietf:params:xml:ns:netconf:base:1.0">
  <get>
    <filter select=" /books/book[count(format) &gt; 1][popularity &lt; 365]/format/
number-of-copies/in-stock" type="xpath"/>
  </get>
</rpc>
```

The server's response is found in Example 4-27.

EXAMPLE 4-27: NETCONF **get** Reply about Books in Stock

```
<rpc-reply xmlns="urn:ietf:params:xml:ns:netconf:base:1.0" message-id="1">
  <data>
    <books xmlns="http://example.com/ns/bookzone">
      <book>
        <title>The Hitchhiker's Guide to the Galaxy</title>
        <format>
          <isbn>0330258648</isbn>
          <number-of-copies>
            <in-stock>32</in-stock>
          </number-of-copies>
        </format>
        <format>
          <isbn>9781400052929</isbn>
          <number-of-copies>
            <in-stock>3</in-stock>
          </number-of-copies>
        </format>
      </book>
```

```
      <book>
        <title>The Neverending Story</title>
        <format>
          <isbn>9780140386332</isbn>
          <number-of-copies>
            <in-stock>4</in-stock>
          </number-of-copies>
        </format>
      </book>
    </books>
  </data>
</rpc-reply>
```

RPCs and Actions

From a functional perspective, an RPC and an action are almost identical. They can do pretty much anything. The only real difference between an RPC and an action is where they can sit in a YANG module, as explained in Chapter 3, and because actions are not at the top level in YANG, they need a slightly different encoding over the wire (for example, in NETCONF) to convey which object they are acting on.

The most common use cases are to provide a command that changes the operational state of the server and to perform a short-lived task. The RPC (or action) could very well change the configuration of the server, if this is made clear in the RPC description. To clarify, here are a couple of different kinds of RPCs:

- *Ping*: A server (device) might have a ping operation that takes an IP address and optionally interface name as parameters. The server sends out four ICMP ping messages toward the given IP address and reports back the ping response latency. This operation does not really change the operational state and definitely not the configuration.
- *Setup-interface*: A server might have a setup-interface operation. It takes the location name of the interface as argument. The operation runs a sequence of probing scripts and eventually configures the interface with some appropriate type, speed, encapsulation, maximum transfer unit (MTU), and other settings. This operation might change both the operational state (the interface is now up) and the configuration (probed configuration values were entered into the configuration).
- *Purchase a book*: An e-commerce system might have a purchase operation for the products in the catalog. It is invoked on the buyer and takes four mandatory arguments: the book title and format, the method of payment, and the account ID to use on that payment platform. The number of items to buy is left at the default, which is one. This operation changes the operational state (the stock of books and the order history), but not the configuration (the catalog of books).

To invoke this purchase action, a client might send what's shown in Example 4-28. Have a look at the bookzone-example.yang in Chapter 3 to compare with the YANG model.

EXAMPLE 4-28 Invocation of NETCONF Action to Purchase a Book

```
<rpc message-id="1" xmlns="urn:ietf:params:xml:ns:netconf:base:1.0">
  <action xmlns="urn:ietf:params:xml:ns:yang:1">
    <users xmlns="http://example.com/ns/bookzone">
      <user>
        <user-id>janl</user-id>
        <purchase>
          <title>What We Think About When We Try Not To Think About Global Warming:
Toward a New Psychology of Climate Action</title>
          <format>paperback</format>
          <payment>
            <method>paypal</method>
            <id>4711.1234.0000.1234</id>
          </payment>
        </purchase>
      </user>
    </users>
  </action>
</rpc>
```

See how the YANG action is encoded with an `action` tag inside the `rpc` envelope. Then, inside the `action` tag follows the tags and keys needed to point to a specific object, the *book* in the specific *format* desired, and finally the name of the action, *purchase*. Inside the `purchase` tag follows the input data of the action. If the purchase action was an RPC instead, the *purchase* tag would have appeared directly inside the `rpc` envelope, properly prefixed with a namespace.

The server might give this response to the action invocation in Example 4-28. Again, compare the result with the YANG declaration of the *purchase* action in Chapter 3.

```
<rpc-reply xmlns="urn:ietf:params:xml:ns:netconf:base:1.0" message-id="1">
  <out-of-stock xmlns="http://example.com/ns/bookzone"/>
</rpc-reply>
```

Uh, oh. Too bad for your order. In the context of the *BookZone* example, this reply is supposed to mean that the purchase order was recorded, but there will be no immediate delivery. A notification will be sent later, when the shipping procedure starts.

Notifications

NETCONF notifications are a mechanism where a server informs the client of events happening. Events are sent to indicate problematic situations on a server (device), to be treated as alarms. They could be completion notifications, indicating some previously ordered action is now complete. They could be informational events, such as informing about users logging in and out, or periodically sent measurement data, such as temperature or system load.

When the specification for NETCONF notifications was written, the notification reference of the day was SNMP. Notifications in the SNMP world mean User Datagram Protocol (UDP) broadcasts of messages of three different kinds: traps, notifications, and informs. UDP is great when networks are congested. Broadcasts are very simple to set up on the server side, as it does not require any information about the receiving side.

This scheme is not a very efficient way to transfer information, however, and reliability is somewhat questionable. So is security. Even when encryption is used in SNMPv3, there is little control over where packets end up, and a spy can easily factor out which traffic is notifications, as it is broadcast this way.

The NETCONF working group (WG) decided to make NETCONF notifications very different—efficient, reliable, and secure, but also a bit more complicated to set up, and not great in a congested network. NETCONF notifications always travel over SSH (which runs over TCP). This means even substantial amounts of data are transferred efficiently. To receive a notification, the client needs to be connected. In order to listen to notifications from a thousand servers at the same time, a thousand SSH connections are required. Because of this, the WG added a replay feature so that a client that wasn't connected to a server for a while can ask for any news since a given point in time, and the server then replays the events from that point on.

Since there is always an established SSH session, it's difficult for an outside observer to guess what kind of data the parties are exchanging, and the connection is very reliable. Since the server knows which clients are listening for which kinds of events, it sends just the right messages to the right destination—and only sends a notification at all if someone is actually listening.

All NETCONF notifications are sent to one or more NETCONF notification streams. A stream is a bit like a radio station. Some radio stations are good sources of international news, while others have a lot of information for consumers (known as ads) or provide local news. Every NETCONF server that supports the `:notification` capability has a default stream called `NETCONF`. It's up to the server implementer to decide what notifications are sent on this stream. Each server can have any number of additional streams on whatever topics they see fit. A server implementer could decide to have a notification stream for each customer or interface, if she wanted.

To see which streams are available on a given server, a NETCONF `<get>` query on the `netconf-state` gives the answer. Here the simple `netconf-console` tool is used to encode and send the query:

```
netconf-console --get --xpath /netconf-state/streams
```

This sends the message shown in Example 4-29 to the server.

EXAMPLE 4-29 NETCONF **get** Request to List Server's Notification Streams

```
<rpc message-id="1" xmlns="urn:ietf:params:xml:ns:netconf:base:1.0">
  <get>
    <filter select=" /netconf-state/streams" type="xpath"/>
  </get>
</rpc>
```

The server replies with the name of two streams, as shown in Example 4-30.

EXAMPLE 4-30 Server's Response with List of Supported Notification Streams

```
<rpc-reply xmlns="urn:ietf:params:xml:ns:netconf:base:1.0" message-id="1">
  <data>
    <netconf-state xmlns="urn:ietf:params:xml:ns:yang:ietf-netconf-monitoring">
      <streams xmlns="http://tail-f.com/yang/netconf-monitoring">
        <stream>
          <name>NETCONF</name>
          <description>default NETCONF event stream</description>
          <replay-support>false</replay-support>
        </stream>
        <stream>
          <name>Trader</name>
          <description>BookZone trading and delivery events</description>
          <replay-support>true</replay-support>
        </stream>
      </streams>
    </netconf-state>
  </data>
</rpc-reply>
```

In this case, the server implements a Tail-f proprietary namespace for the content, but the IETF standard namespace looks just the same.

In this *BookZone* example, a notification is sent out every time shipping is initiated after an order that got an *out-of-stock* situation. These are sent on the NETCONF notification stream *Trader*.

In order for a client to receive the notifications, it needs to connect to the server and issue a subscription request. Using the simple `netconf-console` tool, this might look like the following:

```
netconf-console --create-subscription=Trader
```

The NETCONF request actually sent to the server is shown in Example 4-31.

EXAMPLE 4-31 NETCONF **create-subscription** Request to the Trader Notification Stream

```
<rpc message-id="1" xmlns="urn:ietf:params:xml:ns:netconf:base:1.0">
  <create-subscription xmlns="urn:ietf:params:xml:ns:netconf:notification:1.0">
    <stream>Trader</stream>
  </create-subscription>
</rpc>
```

If the server supports the *Trader* stream, it take notes of the client waiting for updates and responds with "ok":

```
<rpc-reply message-id="1" xmlns="urn:ietf:params:xml:ns:netconf:base:1.0">
  <ok/>
</rpc-reply>
```

Now the session remains open, but no messages are arriving.

At some point, when the stars align, the server decides to send out a notification. It is simply sent after the rpc-reply just mentioned, on the same session. This could be two milliseconds, two days, or two years later. Have a look at the bookzone-example.yang to compare this output with the YANG declaration of the shipping notification shown in Example 4-32.

EXAMPLE 4-32 Server Sending Shipping Notification on the Trader Notification Stream

```
<notification xmlns="urn:ietf:params:xml:ns:netconf:notification:1.0">
  <eventTime>2018-07-31T10:51:37+00:00</eventTime>
  <shipping xmlns="http://example.com/ns/bookzone">
    <user>janl</user>
    <title>What We Think About When We Try Not To Think About Global Warming:
Toward a New Psychology of Climate Action</title>
    <format xmlns:bz="http://example.com/ns/bookzone">bz:paperback</format>
    <copies>1</copies>
  </shipping>
</notification>
```

Should the client lose connection with the server, for any reason (for example, due to a network error or because the client disconnected voluntarily), it just reconnects when possible and issues the subscription again. If the stream supports replay, it could then ask for a replay of everything that happened since the point they were last in contact.

At the time of this writing, a lot of work is going on inside IETF to define *YANG Push*. This is the next level of notifications. It allows more precision over what information is sent, and when. There will also be several different ways for transporting these push notifications.

More NETCONF Operations

The main NETCONF operations are the ones mentioned earlier (`hello`, `get`, `get-config`, `edit-config`, `create-subscription`, and the RPC/action invocation mechanism), but there are a few more mandatory operations, and many more optional ones (note that just a few are mentioned briefly here to give an idea of what's available):

- `commit` and `validate` are the most important optional operations. They are essential for network-wide transactions, but optional because not all servers support this feature. See Chapter 2 for a high-level example of how it is used. Chapter 10, "Using NETCONF and YANG," contains a detailed example with a network-wide transaction.
- `copy-config` copies an entire datastore. This is used to copy `:running` to `:candidate`, or a URL to `:candidate`, for example.
- `delete-config` deletes an entire datastore. It's good to get a clean starting point, but an empty datastore isn't useful in itself.
- `lock` prevents other clients from changing a named datastore until this client either unlocks or closes the connection to the server. `unlock` opens up the named datastore for other clients again.
- `close-session` is a polite way for a client to say goodbye, but simply closing the connection has the same effect.
- `kill-session` is a not-so-polite way for a client to kill some other management session (subject to permission, of course). This is useful to remove a hanging session, or perhaps as a last resort for removing a rogue session. The ietf-netconf-monitoring YANG module provides a way to list the existing sessions, if supported by the server.
- `partial-lock` is used to lock a certain element or subtree in the configuration from changes by other clients, and not the entire datastore. This could be used to lock a particular interface, service, customer, or subsystem for changes, if the server supports it.
- `get-schema` allows a client to download the actual YANG text for the YANG modules hosted by a particular server. This is very useful for data-driven clients that can connect to a server and find out which YANG modules and versions are hosted by this server. If any of them are new to the client, it can ask for the modules in real time and then compile and load them. Suddenly, managing a new type of server became a lot easier. No more scouting the Internet or calling the vendor only to get almost the right version.

The NMDA Operations get-data and edit-data

As noted earlier, the NMDA architecture changes the way data is retrieved and edited a bit. In effect, two new operations, `get-data` and `edit-data`, replace three old operations: `get`, `get-config` and `edit-config`. It also expands the set of valid datastores for a few of the other NETCONF operations: `lock`, `unlock`, `validate`.

The new `get-data` operation works much like the old `get-config` operation, with a few differences:

- The datastore it operates on can be any datastore available in NMDA, including the new operational datastore.
- A query parameter decides whether to include only `config true` nodes or all nodes.
- Apart from traditional subtree and XPath filtering, there is also a possibility to filter on the origin of an element.
- A query parameter decides whether to return information about the origin for every element in the reply.

The `origin` concept lets every data node in the operational datastore be annotated with an origin value, which tells where the element came from (basically why the element exists there). Here are some examples of possible origins:

- `intended`: The element is configured directly by a client, or the element was created through expansion from a template, service, or some similar mechanism.
- `system`: The element represents the configuration created by the system itself. This might be related to installed hardware, objects that always exist, or the system factory default.
- `default`: The element represents a default value from the YANG module.
- `learned`: The element value was learned through some protocol, such as Dynamic Host Configuration Protocol (DHCP).
- `unknown`: The server doesn't know.

The new `edit-data` operation works much like the old `edit-config` operation. The main difference is that it may target any of the writable NMDA datastores. Note that `:intended` and `:operational` are not directly writable, so for many systems the set of available writable datastores will remain the same as without NMDA—possibly just `:running`, or `:running` and `:candidate` and/or `:startup`.

RESTCONF

In recent years, REST has become a hugely popular RPC mechanism. Transported over Hypertext Transfer Protocol (HTTP) and HTTPS, traffic traverses firewalls with typical configurations with ease. REST is quite simple (for good and bad) and has a wide array of tools and bindings for all the popular programming languages. No wonder then that demand rose for "NETCONF, but over REST."

At IETF, the NETCONF WG eventually decided to satisfy the demand and started designing a REST-based variant of NETCONF. The result was published as RESTCONF in RFC 8040 in January 2017. RESTCONF follows the REST principles, but this does not mean that all kinds of REST-based APIs are now compatible or even comparable to RESTCONF. Far from it.

Before taking a closer look at RESTCONF, let's have a brief reminder about what REST really is first.

REST Principles

REST is not a protocol, and it has no specification. REST is a design pattern. The closest counterpart to a specification is the doctoral dissertation by Roy Fielding in 2000, who coined the term REST. There's also an often cited Wikipedia article "Representational state transfer" that outlines the main principles.

REST in itself uses the basic HTTP verbs—basically `GET`, `PUT`, `POST`, `PATCH`, and `DELETE`. REST defines some but not much of the semantics around what it means to `GET`, `PUT`, or `POST` something. It does define a number of core principles, however:

- **Client-server**: Messages are initiated by a client and sent to a server. The server responds back to the client.
- **Statelessness**: After the server responds to a client, it retains no memory of the client. It is stateless. A client typically sends a sequence of messages, but the server has no memory of the client in between the messages of such a sequence (except, potentially, authentication information).
- **Cacheability**: The data received by a client, often in the form of links (URLs), should be constructed such that it is cacheable (that is, it's likely to stay valid for a reasonably long time).
- **Layered system**: The client's relationship to the server is a relationship to a logical endpoint, or address if you will. The server may actually consist of a cluster of servers with many internal layers. Beyond the authentication and security to the server's address, the client has no knowledge of the server's internal implementation.
- **Uniform interface**: The interface is built around a small number of standardized requests (`GET`, `PUT`, `POST`, `PATCH`, and `DELETE`).
  - Each request takes a resource-id parameter indicating which "resource" it operates on. Resources are all equal from a REST perspective; the operations work the same way on all resources.
  - All resources can be "represented" in the REST messages; all information required for resources to be created, updated, and deleted are part of the REST requests.
  - All resources are self-described; sufficient information about the resource is contained in the request that the server knows how to process it without other prior knowledge. For example, REST requests specify their Multipurpose Internet Mail-Extensions Media Type (MIME type) of the payload resources.
  - Hypermedia as the Engine of Application State (HATEOAS) responses to REST requests typically contain links to further requests. These links capture the state that the client needs to provide to the server in future requests.

In the REST world, resources are generally divided into elements and collections. This is similar to a file system directory that contains many files, or a playlist with many songs. The directories and playlists are collections, while the files and songs are elements. The REST operations generally work differently, depending on if the given resource-id (usually meaning the URL) points to a collection or element.

RESTCONF Versus NETCONF

Many of the REST principles are very similar to how NETCONF works. The client-server model, the layered system principle, and the first two uniform interface principles are exactly the same. A key differentiator is the stateless server principle. NETCONF is based on clients establishing a session to the server, and that is certainly not stateless. In NETCONF, clients often connect and then manipulate the candidate datastore with a number of `edit-config` operations. At a certain time, the client may issue a validation call. If that succeeds on all servers, a commit operation may follow.

This sort of behavior is not possible in RESTCONF or any system that strictly follows the REST principles. It requires the server to keep some client state. If that was added to RESTCONF, the protocol no longer fulfills the design principles of REST. Neither could this be added in a future version of RESTCONF, for the same reason. Strictly speaking, it wouldn't be "REST" anymore.

NOTE

There are serious discussions in IETF about doing this anyway. That would imply being a bit less strict about the REST principles in future versions of RESTCONF.

This has deep implications. It means that in RESTCONF, any request the client wants to send needs to be sent in its entirety and acted upon by the server immediately. No transactions that span multiple messages are possible.

This means that some of the key features of NETCONF, especially network-wide transactions, are not possible in RESTCONF. If that is an important feature for your use case, RESTCONF is not the protocol for you. You need NETCONF.

In practical terms, this means that RESTCONF is useful when the client needs to manage a single system. This is often the case for web portals or applications running on top of a controller or orchestrator. The abundance of REST tools in the web programming environment makes RESTCONF a self-evident choice for many in that situation.

NETCONF is much better suited when the client needs to manage multiple systems. This is often the case for the controller/orchestrator itself. Servers that participate in scenarios where they are managed by a controller/orchestrator need to support NETCONF.

In Figure 4-3, all devices need to support NETCONF in order to support network-wide transactions. Without network-wide transactions, the clients have to deal with all the different failure scenarios, and the attractive simplicity that people are looking for in NETCONF is lost.

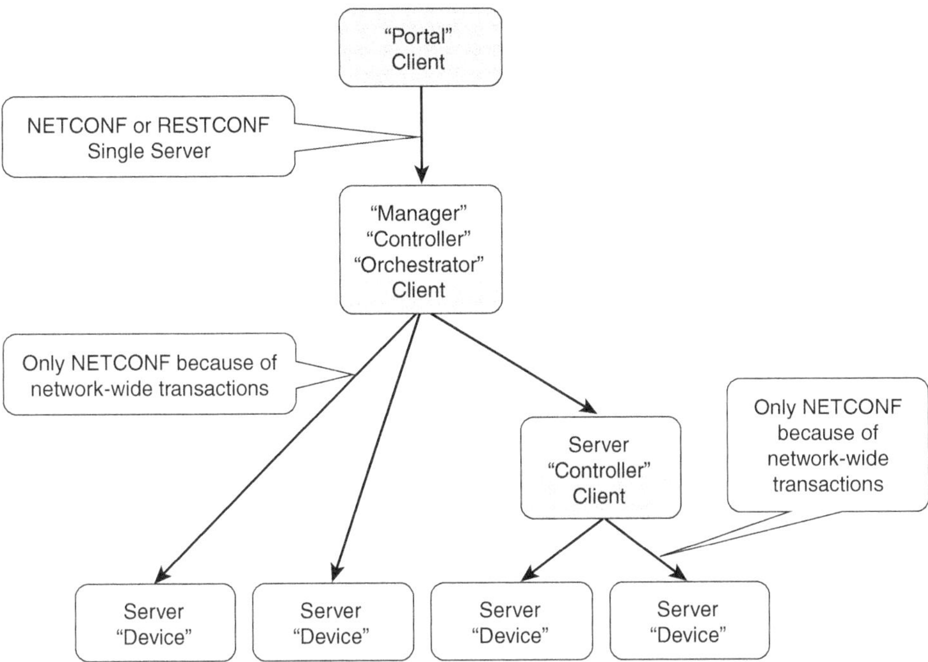

FIGURE 4-3 Different Use Cases Where NETCONF and RESTCONF Are Suitable

Since RESTCONF can't cover all the functionality of NETCONF, the NETCONF WG decided to drop a few additional NETCONF features from the RESTCONF design in order to remove some complexity for client programmers.

Apart from dropping the session concept, the most prominent simplification in RESTCONF is dropping the NETCONF datastore concept. In NETCONF, there are the candidate, running, and startup datastores. In RESTCONF, there is a single "unified" datastore that behaves mostly like the running datastore in NETCONF.

There are also no locks or even a concept of locking in RESTCONF. If a datastore, or parts of one, is locked (through NETCONF or other mechanisms), RESTCONF operations fail with a suitable error code. There are no RESTCONF operations to acquire or otherwise see any locks.

Finding the RESTCONF Server URL

To find your RESTCONF server, you obviously need to know its address and port. The address and port only lead you to a HTTP server, though, which may serve many purposes. In order to find out what the root URL is for the RESTCONF subsystem, a client should use the Web Host Metadata mechanism defined in RFC 6415.

Essentially, the client runs a GET toward the /.well-known/host-meta URL. This should return a list of links to various services available on this HTTP server. If indeed this is a RESTCONF server, one of the links will have an attribute rel='restconf' and another attribute, href=, that points out the root URL to use to speak to the RESTCONF server.

If you know you have a RESTCONF server running on localhost port 8080 that accepts a user called "admin" with the password "admin", use the curl tool like this:

```
curl -i -X GET http://localhost:8080/.well-known/host-meta
--header "Accept: application/xrd+xml" -u admin:admin
```

The curl command actually sends the message shown in Example 4-33.

EXAMPLE 4-33 GET Request for the Well-Known host-meta Information

```
GET /.well-known/host-meta HTTP/1.1
Host: localhost:8080
Authorization: Basic YWRtaW46YWRtaW4=
User-Agent: curl/7.54.0
Accept: application/xrd+xml
```

To which the server might respond as shown in Example 4-34.

EXAMPLE 4-34 GET Reply for Well-Known host-meta Information

```
Server:
Date: Thu, 04 Jan 2018 13:19:29 GMT
Content-Length: 107
Content-Type: application/xrd+xml
Vary: Accept-Encoding

<XRD xmlns='http://docs.oasis-open.org/ns/xri/xrd-1.0'>
    <Link rel='restconf' href='/restconf'/>
</XRD>
```

By concatenating the server address [http://localhost:8080] with the href parameter response (/restconf), you now know that the root URL for this particular server is http://localhost:8080/restconf.

Reading and Navigating the RESTCONF Resources

The REST design pattern names the HTTP/HTTPS operations as the operations to be used in REST. It further defines certain semantics around the URLs and what the operations are supposed to do beyond what is mentioned in the HTTP and HTTPS specifications.

Rather than simply listing all the operations top to bottom, let's look at one of the key REST principles: Hypermedia as the Engine of Application State, or HATEOAS. What this really means is that REST interfaces are meant to be navigated by exploration and discovery.

The previous section gave the root URL for a RESTCONF server, `http://localhost:8080/restconf`. What next? Well, let's run a GET on it and explore:

```
curl -i -X GET http://localhost:8080/restconf -u admin:admin
```

This sends the information shown in Example 4-35.

EXAMPLE 4-35 GET Request for the restconf Root

```
GET /restconf HTTP/1.1
Host: localhost:8080
Authorization: Basic YWRtaW46YWRtaW4=
User-Agent: curl/7.54.0
Accept: */*
```

Example 4-36 shows the server's response.

EXAMPLE 4-36 GET Reply for the restconf Root

```
HTTP/1.1 200 OK
Server:
Date: Thu, 04 Jan 2018 13:22:18 GMT
Cache-Control: private, no-cache, must-revalidate, proxy-revalidate
Content-Length: 157
Content-Type: application/yang-data+xml
Vary: Accept-Encoding
Pragma: no-cache

<restconf xmlns="urn:ietf:params:xml:ns:yang:ietf-restconf">
  <data/>
  <operations/>
  <yang-library-version>2016-06-21</yang-library-version>
</restconf>
```

Okay, so you discovered that from the root URL */restconf* there are three resources: `data`, `operations`, and `yang-library-version`. Are there any other operations than `GET` that would work here? Let's find out with the `OPTIONS` operation. `OPTIONS` is allowed for any RESTCONF URL:

```
curl -i -X OPTIONS http://localhost:8080/restconf -u admin:admin
```

This sends the information shown in Example 4-37.

EXAMPLE 4-37 OPTIONS Request for the restconf Root

```
OPTIONS /restconf HTTP/1.1
Host: localhost:8080
Authorization: Basic YWRtaW46YWRtaW4=
User-Agent: curl/7.54.0
Accept: */*
```

Example 4-38 shows how the server responded.

EXAMPLE 4-38 OPTIONS Reply for the restconf Root

```
HTTP/1.1 200 OK
Server:
Allow: GET, HEAD
Cache-Control: private, no-cache, must-revalidate, proxy-revalidate
Content-Length: 0
Content-Type: text/html
Pragma: no-cache
```

`Allow: GET, HEAD` in Example 4-38 means only `GET` and `HEAD` are supported on the root node. Okay, that doesn't sound very interesting, so let's move on. You found that `data` resource earlier. Let's "GET" it and see:

```
curl -i -X GET http://localhost:8080/restconf/data -u admin:admin --verbose
```

This sends the message in Example 4-39.

EXAMPLE 4-39 GET Request for restconf/data

```
GET /restconf/data HTTP/1.1
Host: localhost:8080
Authorization: Basic YWRtaW46YWRtaW4=
User-Agent: curl/7.54.0
Accept: */*
```

Example 4-40 shows how the server responded.

EXAMPLE 4-40 GET Reply for restconf/data

```
HTTP/1.1 200 OK
Server:
Date: Thu, 04 Jan 2018 13:30:20 GMT
Last-Modified: Tue, 21 Nov 2017 15:02:00 GMT
Cache-Control: private, no-cache, must-revalidate, proxy-revalidate
Etag: 1511-276521-37084
```

```
Content-Type: application/yang-data+xml
Transfer-Encoding: chunked
Pragma: no-cache

<data xmlns="urn:ietf:params:xml:ns:yang:ietf-restconf">
  <authors xmlns="http://example.com/ns/bookzone">
    <author>
      <name>Douglas Adams</name>
      <account-id>1010</account-id>
    </author>
    <author>
      <name>Malala Yousafzai</name>
      <account-id>1011</account-id>
    </author>
    <author>
...
</data>
```

Wow, that gave you a lot of data—over 30kB. This data is the server's complete configuration and operational state.

Before continuing this exploration, let's discuss the `Etag` header. The value there is a string that is guaranteed to change every time the configuration changes, and not otherwise. This makes it easy for a client to detect if any change has happened since a previous `GET` operation.

If exploration is about collecting as much data as possible, you just hit bingo. But shouldn't exploration be more about insight? This was a bit too much detail to make much sense. How could you get an overview of the data available on this system? Let's look at only the top-level resources inside `data`.

This is achieved by adding a query parameter to the URL. Add `?depth=1` at the end of the URL and try again:

```
curl -i -X GET http://localhost:8080/restconf/data?depth=1 -u admin:admin
```

Let's omit the details of what is being sent and the headers received from now on, unless there's something really interesting there. If you are interested to see exactly what `curl` sends in your own experiments, just add the `--verbose` flag.

Example 4-41 shows the payload content of what the server responded with.

EXAMPLE 4-41 GET Reply to restconf/data with Depth One

```
<data xmlns="urn:ietf:params:xml:ns:yang:ietf-restconf">
  <authors xmlns="http://example.com/ns/bookzone"/>
  <books xmlns="http://example.com/ns/bookzone"/>
  <users xmlns="http://example.com/ns/bookzone"/>
  <nacm xmlns="urn:ietf:params:xml:ns:yang:ietf-netconf-acm"/>
```

```
  <netconf-state xmlns="urn:ietf:params:xml:ns:yang:ietf-netconf-monitoring"/>
  <restconf-state xmlns="urn:ietf:params:xml:ns:yang:ietf-restconf-monitoring"/>
  <modules-state xmlns="urn:ietf:params:xml:ns:yang:ietf-yang-library"/>
  <aaa xmlns="http://tail-f.com/ns/aaa/1.1"/>
  <confd-state xmlns="http://tail-f.com/yang/confd-monitoring"/>
</data>
```

Now that's better. Now you have something that looks like a table of contents, and you can navigate where you want. Take a look at the *books* resource, and keep that `?depth=1` query parameter so you don't drown:

```
curl -i -X GET http://localhost:8080/restconf/data/books?depth=1 -u admin:admin
```

Example 4-42 shows the server's response.

EXAMPLE 4-42 GET Reply to restconf/data/books with Depth One

```
<books xmlns="http://example.com/ns/bookzone"
    xmlns:bz="http://example.com/ns/bookzone">
  <book/>
  <book/>
  <book/>
  <book/>
  <book/>
</books>
```

Okay, you see there are five books, but you can't navigate into any specific one because you don't even know their names. You may change the `depth` query parameter to 2 and use the same URL again:

```
curl -i -X GET http://localhost:8080/restconf/data/books?depth=2 -u admin:admin
```

Example 4-43 shows the server's response.

EXAMPLE 4-43 GET Reply to restconf/data/books with Depth Two

```
<books xmlns="http://example.com/ns/bookzone"  xmlns:bz="http://example.com/ns/
bookzone">
  <book>
    <title>I Am Malala: The Girl Who Stood Up for Education and Was Shot by the
Taliban</title>
    <author>Malala Yousafzai</author>
    <popularity>89</popularity>
    <format/>
  </book>
  <book>
```

```
    <title>The Art of War</title>
    <author>Sun Tzu</author>
    <language>english</language>
    <format/>
  </book>
  <book>
    <title>The Hitchhiker's Guide to the Galaxy</title>
    <author>Douglas Adams</author>
    <language>english</language>
    <popularity>289</popularity>
    <format/>
    <format/>
  </book>
  <book>
    <title>The Neverending Story</title>
...
</books>
```

Okay, good. You got the information about the books and all their top-level attributes. But in your efforts to explore, would it not be much better to see just the names and descriptions of these books? By extracting exactly the information need, you could plug it into other information streams, or, say, paste the reply in an email.

You can use several query parameters in the same query. Just separate them with & (an ampersand). As previously shown, a RESTCONF GET request returns both `config true` and `config false` elements. The *title* and *author* leafs are `config true`, for example, while *popularity* is `config false`. Using the query parameter `content=`, you can control what is returned. Requesting `content=all` (default) returns everything, while `content=config` only returns the configuration. The query flag `content=nonconfig` is supposed to return all the operational data, plus a minimum of the configuration to make it possible to identify the operational data. It doesn't make much sense to return *popularity 89* if that number isn't tied to the book title, even if the title happens to be `config true`. Several server implementations have trouble here, however, so check this before you depend on it.

The `fields` query parameter allows you to select one or more fields you are interested in. Let's say you want the *title* and *author* of each book. Since the *title* and *author* resources are both inside *book*, which in turn is inside *books*, which is the resource you are sending the query about, you need to prepend with *book/* in the filter. The query thus becomes the following:

```
curl -i -X GET "http://localhost:8080/restconf/data/books?depth=2&content=config&
fields=book/title;book/author" -u admin:admin
```

Example 4-44 shows the server's response.

EXAMPLE 4-44 GET Reply with Certain Fields from restconf/data/books

```
<books xmlns="http://example.com/ns/bookzone"
xmlns:bz="http://example.com/ns/bookzone">
  <book>
    <title>I Am Malala: The Girl Who Stood Up for Education and Was Shot by the
Taliban</title>
    <author>Malala Yousafzai</author>
  </book>
  <book>
    <title>The Art of War</title>
    <author>Sun Tzu</author>
  </book>
  <book>
    <title>The Hitchhiker's Guide to the Galaxy</title>
    <author>Douglas Adams</author>
  </book>
  <book>
    <title>The Neverending Story</title>
    <author>Michael Ende</author>
  </book>
  <book>
    <title>What We Think About When We Try Not To Think About Global Warming: Toward
a New Psychology of Climate Action</title>
    <author>Per Espen Stoknes</author>
  </book>
</books>
```

That was better!

Notice that the responses received are encoded in XML. As the client, you have not specified what sort of responses to accept, so you got whatever the server felt like sending by default. If you wanted this information in JSON format instead, you could ask for it. To do that, use an `Accept:` header, like so:

```
curl -i -X GET "http://localhost:8080/restconf/data/books?depth=2&fields=book/title;
book/author" --header "Accept: application/yang-data+json" -u admin:admin
```

Example 4-45 shows the server's response.

EXAMPLE 4-45 GET Certain Fields from restconf/data/books in JSON

```
{
  "bookzone-example:books": {
    "book": [
      {
        "title": "I Am Malala: The Girl Who Stood Up for Education and Was Shot by the
Taliban",
```

```
        "author": "Malala Yousafzai"
      },
      {
        "title": "The Art of War",
        "author": "Sun Tzu"
      },
      {
        "title": "The Hitchhiker's Guide to the Galaxy",
        "author": "Douglas Adams"
      },
      {
        "title": "The Neverending Story",
        "author": "Michael Ende"
      },
      {
        "title": "What We Think About When We Try Not To Think About Global Warming:
Toward a New Psychology of Climate Action",
        "author": "Per Espen Stoknes"
      }
    ]
  }
}
```


It's up to each RESTCONF server to support XML or JSON encoding—or, as in this case, both, with XML as the default. Clients that need to communicate with all RESTCONF servers in the world need to support content encoded in both XML and JSON.

Creating and Updating Configuration Using RESTCONF

Let's say now you want to add a new *book* to the list of books. Is that supported? This is checked using the OPTIONS request. You can issue an OPTIONS request to any RESTCONF URL to find out what you can do with it:

```
curl -i -X OPTIONS "http://localhost:8080/restconf/data/books/book" -u admin:admin
```

Example 4-46 shows the server's response

EXAMPLE 4-46 OPTIONS Response for restconf/data/books/book

```
HTTP/1.1 200 OK
Server:
Allow: DELETE, GET, HEAD, PATCH, POST, PUT, OPTIONS
Cache-Control: private, no-cache, must-revalidate, proxy-revalidate
Content-Length: 0
Content-Type: text/html
Accept-Patch: application/yang-data+xml, application/yang-data+json
Pragma: no-cache
```

All right, so there are three operations you could use to update this content: PATCH, POST, and PUT. Also note that there's a header called `Accept-Patch:`, which is discussed later in the "PATCH" section.

The *book* element is a YANG list. This is represented as a collection in REST terminology. You have five books, so obviously it's something there can be many of. It would be a collection even if there was only one, however, because you could have five of these even if you only had one at the moment. To find out in plain REST, you'd have to look at the OPTIONS to see that POST is supported, which means it's a collection.

POST

If you ask a REST expert how to add an entry to a collection, you will most likely be told POST is the operation to use. This is true in RESTCONF as well: POST creates a new element in a collection, as shown in Example 4-47. If an element by that name already exists, POST fails with an error. POST cannot be used to update something that already exists.

EXAMPLE 4-47 Curl Command to POST a New Author

```
curl -i -X POST "http://localhost:8080/restconf/data/authors"
--header "Content-Type: application/yang-data+json"
--header "Accept: application/yang-data+json"
--data @rc/add-kazuo-ishiguro.rc.json -u admin:admin
```

The file add-kazuo-ishiguro.rc.json contains what's shown in Example 4-48.

EXAMPLE 4-48 Contents of the add-kazuo-ishiguro.rc.json POST Payload

```
{
  "author": [
    {
      "name": "Kazuo Ishiguro",
      "account-id": 2017
    }
  ]
}
```

The server returns with the request shown in Example 4-49.

EXAMPLE 4-49 POST Reply for a New Author

```
HTTP/1.1 201 Created
Server:
Location: http://localhost:8080/restconf/data/bookzone-example:authors/
author=Kazuo%20Ishiguro
Date: Wed, 11 Jul 2018 11:34:19 GMT
```

```
Last-Modified: Wed, 11 Jul 2018 11:34:19 GMT
Cache-Control: private, no-cache, must-revalidate, proxy-revalidate
Etag: 1531-260735-677653
Content-Length: 0
Content-Type: text/html
Pragma: no-cache
```

Venturing to run the same command one more time, the server returns a different reply, as shown in Example 4-50.

EXAMPLE 4-50 Second POST Reply for a New Author

```
HTTP/1.1 409 Conflict
Server:
Date: Wed, 11 Jul 2018 11:38:44 GMT
Cache-Control: private, no-cache, must-revalidate, proxy-revalidate
Content-Length: 281
Content-Type: application/yang-data+json
Vary: Accept-Encoding
Pragma: no-cache

{
  "errors": {
    "error": [
      {
        "error-message": "object already exists: /bz:authors/bz:author[bz:name='Kazuo
Ishiguro']",
        "error-path": "/bookzone-example:authors",
        "error-tag": "data-exists",
        "error-type": "application"
      }
    ]
  }
}
```

Notice that POST is no good for updating existing information. To update, there are three different ways in RESTCONF, with some different properties: PUT, plain PATCH, and YANG-PATCH. Technically, DELETE is a kind of update as well, so let's have a look at all four here.

PUT

The PUT method is very simple, for good and bad. It is useful if you have a small and focused change, such as a single leaf, or one specific, complete list instance. With PUT, you point to a resource and provide a complete replacement for that resource—anything from a single leaf to a single list instance, a single list, or the entire datastore, but only one "thing."

Say you want to update the price for the hardcover version of Douglas Adam's *The Hitchhiker's Guide to the Galaxy*. The `curl` command is shown in Example 4-51 using PUT in JSON.

EXAMPLE 4-51 Curl Command to PUT a New Book Price

```
curl -i -X PUT "http://localhost:8080/restconf/data/bookzone-example:books/
book=The%20Hitchhiker%27s%20Guide%20to%20the%20Galaxy/format=9781400052929/price"
--header "Accept: application/yang-data+json"
--header "Content-Type: application/yang-data+json"
--data '{ "price" : "38.0" }'
-u admin:admin
```

The server responds with the body-less positive reply shown in Example 4-52.

EXAMPLE 4-52 PUT Reply for a New Book Price

```
HTTP/1.1 204 No Content
Server:
Date: Wed, 11 Jul 2018 13:21:17 GMT
Last-Modified: Wed, 11 Jul 2018 13:21:17 GMT
Cache-Control: private, no-cache, must-revalidate, proxy-revalidate
Etag: 1531-267216-364977
Content-Length: 0
Content-Type: text/html
Pragma: no-cache
```

This is great if you just want to make a single quick change. But what if you wanted to change several prices in a single transaction? Then you could not point to one specific price in the URL; instead, you would have to point to the deepest common element in the model and replace everything below this point.

In the case of multiple prices, you have to point to the list *book* and replace not only all the particular books that you want to update the price on, but all the books. Clearly this is not very practical. What if you did this anyway? Could you GET the contents of the entire list *book*, edit the result in a text editor, and then PUT it back again? Technically this would work fine. It assumes that no other changes are happening during this operation, however. There is no lock to keep anyone else out. If anyone else makes any change, those changes are immediately overwritten when you run your PUT operation.

In scenarios where a single person is in control, this may work. With more people involved, or when automation is running, PUT is rarely what you need. PUT is a very basic and rather crude method. It replaces a single resource with a new one.

PATCH

Due to the limitations with PUT, the web community invented the PATCH operation. It allows you to overwrite anything in the resource you point to with new values, rather than replace it with a new document. This is very handy for multiple updates. The downside with PATCH is that it can never delete anything; it only overwrites and adds. The `curl` command is shown in Example 4-53.

EXAMPLE 4-53 Curl Command to PATCH Several Book Prices

```
curl -i -X PATCH "http://localhost:8080/restconf/data/bookzone-example:books/book"
--header "Accept: application/yang-data+json"
--header "Content-Type: application/yang-data+json"
--data @rc/update-prices.rc.json -u admin:admin
```

Example 4-54 shows the contents of update-prices.rc.json.

EXAMPLE 4-54 Contents of update-prices.rc.json PATCH Payload


```
{
  "book": [
    {
      "title": "The Hitchhiker's Guide to the Galaxy",
      "format": [
        {
          "isbn": "9781400052929",
          "price": 36.0
        }
      ]
    },
    {
      "title": "I Am Malala: The Girl Who Stood Up for Education and Was Shot by the
Taliban",
      "format": [
        {
          "isbn": "9780297870913",
          "price": 26.0
        }
      ]
    }
  ]
}
```


The server responds with the body-less positive reply shown in Example 4-55.

EXAMPLE 4-55 PATCH Reply for Updates to Several Book Prices

```
HTTP/1.1 204 No Content
Server:
Date: Wed, 11 Jul 2018 15:06:55 GMT
Last-Modified: Wed, 11 Jul 2018 15:06:55 GMT
Cache-Control: private, no-cache, must-revalidate, proxy-revalidate
Etag: 1531-273615-851931
Content-Length: 0
Content-Type: text/html
Pragma: no-cache
```

This updated the price for *Hitchhiker's Guide* and added a price for Malala's book. It did not remove all the other preexisting formats or books.

DELETE

DELETE does exactly what you think: It deletes a resource. As shown, a resource can be a single leaf, a list instance, an entire list or container, or the entire datastore.

To delete the book *The Art of War*, including the children *format* and *price*, you could issue the DELETE call shown in Example 4-56.

EXAMPLE 4-56 Curl Command to DELETE a Book

```
curl -i -X DELETE "http://localhost:8080/restconf/data/bookzone-example:
books/book=The%20Art%20of%20War"
--header "Accept: application/yang-data+json"
--header "Content-Type: application/yang-data+json" -u admin:admin
```

The server responds with the body-less positive reply shown in Example 4-57.

EXAMPLE 4-57 DELETE Reply for Removing a Book

```
HTTP/1.1 204 No Content
Server:
Date: Wed, 11 Jul 2018 15:26:00 GMT
Last-Modified: Wed, 11 Jul 2018 15:26:00 GMT
Cache-Control: private, no-cache, must-revalidate, proxy-revalidate
Etag: 1531-274772-193783
Content-Length: 0
Content-Type: text/html
Pragma: no-cache
```

YANG-PATCH

So now you've seen POST, which creates but does not update or delete, and you've seen PUT, which replaces resources and thereby implicitly creates, updates, and deletes, but in most cases in an inefficient and problematic way. You've also seen PATCH, which is good at updating but can't delete, and DELETE, which only deletes.

All of these can of course be combined to do any arbitrary update—except that each operation becomes a separate transaction, and if you paid attention to previous chapters in this book, you know that a sequence of transactions isn't half as good as a single transaction.

So how about an operation that can mix all Create-Read-Update-Delete (CRUD) operations into a single RESTCONF request, in a single transaction? There was no such operation in common use within the REST community, so the RESTCONF working group decided to define one. The result is called YANG-PATCH. It's actually a good-old PATCH operation, where the data sent or provided isn't a traditional resource, like you have seen so far. Instead, the input to the PATCH operation is a sequence of edit operations specified in a particular format detailed in RFC 8072. In REST parlance, this is a new Media type. Actually, there are two new Media types, called `application/yang-patch+xml` and `application/yang-patch+json`. Pick the one you want, depending on whether you prefer XML or JSON encodings.

With this Media type, the input data to the PATCH operation is a laundry list of all the CRUD operations to apply at different locations, all within the same transaction. This is the king of the RESTCONF update methods—the one to rule them all. You could very well decide to never use any of the other edit operations—assuming that the RESTCONF server you're talking to supports this Media type. It's optional for servers to implement. This time, let's encode the request in XML rather than JSON, just to show that XML could be used too.

To demonstrate how YANG-PATCH works, let's construct a single transaction that performs the following tasks:

1. Merges a book (*The Buried Giant*, by Kazuo Ishiguro).
2. Creates a new book (*The Girl with the Dragon Tattoo*, by Stieg Larsson).
3. Creates a new author (Stieg Larsson).
4. Sets the price of the hardcover edition of *The Hitchhiker's Guide to the Galaxy* to 44.
5. Deletes the paperback edition of *The Neverending Story*.
6. Sets the price of the MP3 edition of *The Neverending Story* to 40.

The `curl` command to execute this looks just like the earlier PATCH command, except that the `Content-type` is set to `application/yang-patch+xml`. The command is shown in Example 4-58.

EXAMPLE 4-58 Curl Command to YANG-PATCH Six Changes

```
curl -i -X PATCH "http://localhost:8080/restconf/data"
--header "Accept: application/yang-data+xml"
--header "Content-Type: application/yang-patch+xml"
--data @rc/many-changes.rc.yangpatch.xml -u admin:admin
```

Example 4-59 displays the many-changes.yangpatch.xml, which contains the detailed instructions for how to edit the datastore.

EXAMPLE 4-59 Contents of many-changes.yangpatch.xml YANG-PATCH Payload


```
<yang-patch xmlns="urn:ietf:params:xml:ns:yang:ietf-yang-patch">
  <patch-id>many-changes</patch-id>
  <edit>
    <edit-id>#1</edit-id>
    <operation>merge</operation>
    <target>/books/book=The%20Buried%20Giant</target>
    <value>
      <book xmlns="http://example.com/ns/bookzone">
        <title>The Buried Giant</title>
        <author>Kazuo Ishiguro</author>
        <language>english</language>
        <format>
          <isbn>9781467600217</isbn>
          <format-id>mp3</format-id>
          <price>55</price>
        </format>
      </book>
    </value>
  </edit>
  <edit>
    <edit-id>#2</edit-id>
    <operation>create</operation>
    <target>/books/book=The%20Girl%20with%20the%20Dragon%20Tattoo</target>
    <value>
      <book xmlns="http://example.com/ns/bookzone">
        <title>The Girl with the Dragon Tattoo</title>
        <author>Stieg Larsson</author>
        <language>english</language>
        <format>
          <isbn>9781616574819</isbn>
          <format-id>mp3</format-id>
          <price>45</price>
        </format>
```

```
      </book>
    </value>
  </edit>
  <edit>
    <edit-id>#3</edit-id>
    <operation>create</operation>
    <target>/authors/author=Stieg%20Larsson</target>
    <value>
      <author xmlns="http://example.com/ns/bookzone">
        <name>Stieg Larsson</name>
        <account-id>2004</account-id>
      </author>
    </value>
  </edit>
  <edit>
    <edit-id>#4</edit-id>
    <operation>merge</operation>
    <target>/books/book=The%20Hitchhiker%27s%20Guide%20to%20the%20Galaxy/format=
9781400052929/price</target>
    <value>
      <price xmlns="http://example.com/ns/bookzone">44</price>
    </value>
  </edit>
  <edit>
    <edit-id>#5</edit-id>
    <operation>delete</operation>
    <target>/books/book=The%20Neverending%20Story/format=9780140386332</target>
  </edit>
  <edit>
    <edit-id>#6</edit-id>
    <operation>merge</operation>
    <target>/books/book=The%20Neverending%20Story/format=9781452656304/price</target>
    <value>
      <price xmlns="http://example.com/ns/bookzone">40</price>
    </value>
  </edit>
</yang-patch>
```

Example 4-60 shows the server's response.

EXAMPLE 4-60 YANG-PATCH Reply to Six Changes

```
HTTP/1.1 100 Continue
Server:
Allow: GET, POST, OPTIONS, HEAD
Content-Length: 0
```

```
HTTP/1.1 200 OK
Server:
Date: Thu, 12 Jul 2018 13:20:34 GMT
Allow: GET, POST, OPTIONS, HEAD
Last-Modified: Thu, 12 Jul 2018 13:20:34 GMT
Cache-Control: private, no-cache, must-revalidate, proxy-revalidate
Etag: 1531-349919-767171
Content-Length: 141
Content-Type: application/yang-data+xml
Vary: Accept-Encoding
Pragma: no-cache


 <yang-patch-status xmlns="urn:ietf:params:xml:ns:yang:ietf-yang-patch">
   <patch-id>many-changes</patch-id>
   <ok/>
 </yang-patch-status>
```

See how this YANG-PATCH media type is a laundry list of operations to be executed, rather than just a lump of replacement data, as with POST, PUT, and PATCH. These operations are guaranteed to be executed in order, top to bottom. This is important so that complex operations like move, insert before, or insert after (not shown in this book) have a well-defined, exact meaning.

Make no mistake: This is still a transaction with the atomicity and consistency properties intact. The client can still generate these edits in any order it likes, and the validation only happens at the end of the transaction. In the data set just mentioned, for example, edit #2 created the book *The Girl with the Dragon Tattoo*, by the author Stieg Larsson. If the transaction ended there, the transaction would fail since there was no author by that name under *authors* yet. That was added in edit #3. Since it was added before the end of the transaction, the change set, taken as a whole, is still valid.

A client that wanted to implement all the changes in this YANG-PATCH operation using traditional POST, PUT, and DELETE operations would end up with several transactions and have to carefully consider the sequence in which they are sent, so that the author is created before it is referenced. This is not required with YANG-PATCH, since there is proper transaction support.

Actions

With many REST servers, the POST operation is used for both creating new items in a collection and invoking actions. This is reflected in RESTCONF as well. When the URL points to a collection (for example, a YANG list), POST means the creation of a new instance. When it points to a YANG action, it means invoking that action. To invoke an RPC, the URL is */operations/rpc-name* from the server root.

The POST payload is used as the input parameters to the action or RPC. In order to purchase a copy of *What We Think About When We Try Not to Think About Global Warming: Toward a New Psychology of Climate Action*, you could issue the `curl` command shown in Example 4-61.

EXAMPLE 4-61 Curl Command to Invoke the **purchase** Action

```
curl -i -X POST "http://localhost:8080/restconf/data/users/user=janl/purchase"
--header "Content-Type: application/yang-data+json"
--header "Accept: application/yang-data+json"
--data @rc/purchase-book.rc.json -u admin:admin
```

The purchase-book.rc.json file contains the payload to the action invocation, as shown in Example 4-62.

EXAMPLE 4-62 Contents of purchase.rc POST Payload


```
{
  "bookzone-example:input" : {
    "title" : "What We Think About When We Try Not To Think About Global Warming:
Toward a New Psychology of Climate Action",
    "format": "paperback",
    "payment": {
      "method": "paypal",
      "id": "4711.1234.0000.1234"
    }
  }
}
```


The server replies *out-of-stock*, as shown in Example 4-63, but this time we were prepared. The same thing happened in the NETCONF case earlier.

EXAMPLE 4-63 POST Reply to **purchase** Action Invocation

```
HTTP/1.1 200 OK
Server:
Date: Wed, 01 Aug 2018 13:37:47 GMT
Cache-Control: private, no-cache, must-revalidate, proxy-revalidate
Content-Length: 66
Content-Type: application/yang-data+json
Vary: Accept-Encoding
Pragma: no-cache

{
  "bookzone-example:output": {
    "out-of-stock": [null]
  }
}
```

Notifications

RESTCONF clients set up notification subscriptions by directing a GET to a stream-specific URL. This GET operation will in principle never end, in the sense that the server will never signal end-of-file on the request. The server will simply deliver more data whenever there is a notification to be delivered.

The first task is to find out what the stream-specific URLs are. This is done in traditional REST fashion (that is, by running a GET, which returns a bunch of links). The list of RESTCONF notification stream URLs is retrieved like this:

```
curl -i -X GET "http://localhost:8080/restconf/data/ietf-restconf-monitoring:
restconf-state/streams" -u admin:admin
```

A possible server response is shown in Example 4-64.

EXAMPLE 4-64 GET Reply with RESTCONF Notification Stream Information

```
<streams xmlns="urn:ietf:params:xml:ns:yang:ietf-restconf-monitoring"
xmlns:rcmon="urn:ietf:params:xml:ns:yang:ietf-restconf-monitoring">
  <stream>
    <name>NETCONF</name>
    <description>default NETCONF event stream</description>
    <replay-support>false</replay-support>
    <access>
      <encoding>xml</encoding>
      <location>https://localhost:8888/restconf/streams/NETCONF/xml</location>
    </access>
    <access>
      <encoding>json</encoding>
      <location>https://localhost:8888/restconf/streams/NETCONF/json</location>
    </access>
  </stream>
  <stream>
    <name>Trader</name>
    <description>BookZone trading and delivery events</description>
    <replay-support>true</replay-support>
    <access>
      <encoding>xml</encoding>
      <location>https://localhost:8888/restconf/streams/Trader/xml</location>
    </access>
    <access>
      <encoding>json</encoding>
      <location>https://localhost:8888/restconf/streams/Trader/json</location>
    </access>
  </stream>
</streams>
```

There are two streams with two encodings each, totaling four links. The rest of this section does not use any of them, however, since they are HTTPS addresses. HTTPS is of course great for this, but in order to avoid spending valuable time in this book on certificate setup, let's stay with HTTP for now. The same information is available with both root URLs.

The following `curl` command subscribes to BookZone *Trader* notifications in JSON encoding. The command keeps running indefinitely, as there could always be yet another notification coming soon.

```
curl -i -X GET http://localhost:8080/restconf/streams/Trader/json -u admin:admin
```

As the server processes this request, it know which streams have active listeners. The server immediately responds with an HTTP header block, but no actual payload, as shown in Example 4-65.

EXAMPLE 4-65 Subscription Acknowledgment for Trader Notifications

```
HTTP/1.1 200 OK
Server:
Date: Wed, 01 Aug 2018 13:45:13 GMT
Cache-Control: private, no-cache, must-revalidate, proxy-revalidate
Content-Type: text/event-stream
Transfer-Encoding: chunked
Pragma: no-cache
```

At some point, the server might feel like sending a notification to the connected listeners. This then appears as data arriving to the hanging `curl` command, shown in Example 4-66.

EXAMPLE 4-66 Subscription Trader Notification Arriving

```
data: {
data:   "ietf-restconf:notification": {
data:     "eventTime": 2018-08-01T13:46:38+00:00,
data:     "bookzone-example:shipping": {
data:       "user": "janl",
data:       "title": "What We Think About When We Try Not To Think About
Global Warming: Toward a New Psychology of Climate Action",
data:       "format": "bz:paperback",
data:       "copies": 1
data:     }
data:   }
data: }
```

Additional events may arrive at any time, so the `curl` session just hangs, waiting for more.

In case you're wondering about that `data:` prefix on every line, it's actually supposed to be there. It comes from a W3C Recommendation on Server-Sent Events by the W3C Web Applications WG.

OpenConfig and gNMI

As you know, the NETCONF and RESTCONF network management protocols are specified by IETF. While IETF is a giant in the Internet specification world, it's far from the only standards-defining organization (SDO) with a history of setting standards in networking. A fairly recent addition to the network management scene comes from Google and the OpenConfig consortium. OpenConfig (OC) proposes to use the gNMI framework. gNMI stands for gRPC Network Management Interface; in turn, gRPC stands for gRPC Remote Procedure Call. This recursive acronym never really tells where the letter *g* comes from. Google has always been at the forefront of bringing some fun into the industry, so maybe this is a little quiz.

The gNMI specification is openly available at OpenConfig's GitHub account. The consortium also submitted a version of this document to IETF in the form of an informational RFC (draft-openconfig-rtgwg-gnmi-spec-01). In other words, it's a document that describes a de facto standard, not engaging in IETF's rather slow and tedious standardization process of rough consensus and working code.

At a high level, the gNMI protocol resembles NETCONF and RESTCONF in many ways, and is a possible alternative to these. Most of the gNMI use seems to be together with YANG models, but the gNMI authors expressly point out that YANG is one of several possible interface description languages (IDLs).

The OpenConfig consortium has also defined a fair number of standard YANG models to go with the protocols. These YANG models describe many essential networking features, all the way from interfaces to Quality of Service (QoS), Wi-Fi, Border Gateway Protocol (BGP), and many more. While everyone refers to these modules as YANG modules, it is worth noting that it is a slightly deviated kind of YANG that is being used in the modules from OpenConfig. This has led to some interoperability issues, heated debates, and the YANG-centric world being split into two camps: the IETF and OC schools of thought.

One could always debate which side has the greater right to the definition of YANG, who has the technically better solutions, for which use cases that question should be evaluated, which organization is taking interoperability more seriously, and so on. This book is not the place for that discussion, however. Anyone interested can find plenty available in the mailing list archives. Actually, today it is possible to see some signs of this age-old schism slowly closing. Perhaps it's finally the end users' interest in properly working systems that will bring all the parties together and the industry forward in the end.

gRPC

A Remote Procedure Call (RPC) mechanism generally allows a client to invoke operations (in earlier days, often called "procedures"; you can tell "RPC" is a very old computer science term) on a server. A typical RPC mechanism has the following components:

- An interface description language (IDL) used to specify what procedures the server offers, as well as the input and output data from them

- A client library that makes it easy for client applications to call upon those procedures, possibly for several different programming languages
- A serialization, marshalling, and transport mechanism for the messages (generally called a protocol)

Google's RPC mechanism gRPC obviously has all of this. You can find the details at https://grpc.io/docs/. The traditional use of gRPC would be with Google's protobufs, which provide an IDL where any operation can be specified, with any kind of input and output data.

This is where gNMI connects up with gRPC. gNMI defines a particular set of gRPC operations—namely, `CapabilityRequest`, `GetRequest`, `SetRequest`, and `SubscribeRequest`. These operations correspond more or less to the NETCONF/RESTCONF messages for `hello`, `get`/`get-config`, `edit-config` and a subscription mechanism that has many more capabilities than the IETF base specification for NETCONF notifications. Each request message obviously has a response message as well, each defined in gRPC.

gNMI CapabilityRequest

The `CapabilityRequest` operation conveys much the same information as the `hello` message in NETCONF, but only in the direction from server to client. It is up to the server to decide which protocol version to use, and the server declares which YANG modules and encodings it supports. A number of encodings are supported in gNMI. Two variants of JSON, called `JSON` and `JSON_IETF`, dominate.

What is called JSON_IETF in the gNMI context is the same encoding as what's called JSON in the RESTCONF case (that is, RFC 7159 plus the RFC 7951 conventions). When the gNMI encoding is JSON, the RFC 7951 conventions do not apply. In this case, it is up to the server implementer to decide how YANG namespaces, large integers, empty lists, and so on are encoded.

A gNMI CapabilityRequest has no content, so is not shown here. The CapabilityResponse message that comes back might look like what is shown in Example 4-67.

EXAMPLE 4-67 gNMI CapabilityResponse Message

```
== capabilitiesResponse:
supported_models: <
  name: "bookzone-example"
  organization: ""
  version: "2.0.0"
>
supported_models: <
  name: "openconfig-interfaces"
  organization: "OpenConfig working group"
  version: "2.0.0"
>
```

```
supported_models: <
  name: "openconfig-openflow"
  organization: "OpenConfig working group"
  version: "0.1.0"
>
supported_models: <
  name: "openconfig-platform"
  organization: "OpenConfig working group"
  version: "0.5.0"
>
supported_models: <
  name: "openconfig-system"
  organization: "OpenConfig working group"
  version: "0.2.0"
>
supported_encodings: JSON
supported_encodings: JSON_IETF
gNMI_version: "0.7.0"
```

gNMI GetRequest

When fetching information from a gNMI server, you have two options. The `GetRequest` is most useful when retrieving a small amount of data. The data returned is a snapshot, which means it's internally consistent and therefore may need to be kept in the server's (device's) temporary memory for a while. The `SubscribeRequest`, on the other hand, is better suited for larger queries, such as the entire routing table or BGP peer list. Despite its name, it is the operation of choice when the amount of data is large, even when the result is desired immediately and one time only.

In order to add some flavor to this section, you can install a set of gNMI tools yourself and play around, just as with the NETCONF and RESTCONF sections. The Google tools used here are in the gNXI toolset. This is based on the Go language. See the BookZone repository for detailed instructions. Note that the instructions on GitHub may deviate slightly from what you see here, since these tools are updated frequently.

At the time of writing, the gNXI tools do not yet support YANG 1.1, so you must back down to bookzone-example.yang revision 2018-01-02 (that is, the second version published). It doesn't use any YANG 1.1 features.

The gNXI tools contain a simple gNMI server, `gnmi_target`, in order for you to have something to play with. Before starting it, you need to compile the YANG files to be supported by the server using the tool `ygot` (YANG Go Tool), for generating Go data structures. You also have to create a Transport Layer Security (TLS) certificate and key as well as a database initialization file so the server doesn't start blank. Here it's called bookzone.json and contains the same data as shown in the earlier chapters. With this done, the server is started, as shown in Example 4-68.

EXAMPLE 4-68 gNXI Command to Start a Sample gNMI Server

```
go run gnmi_target.go \
  -bind_address :10161 \
  -config bookzone.json \
  -key MyKey.key \
  -cert MyCertificate.crt \
  -ca MyCertificate.crt \
  -username foo \
  -password bar \
  -alsologtostderr
```

Once the server is running, it waits for gNMI requests on port 10161 (an homage to SNMP, perhaps?). To test the setup, issue a gNMI GetRequest. For example, request the list of all authors plus the name of the author of *The Neverending Story*. Using the gNXI tools, the GetRequest is sent, as shown in Example 4-69.

EXAMPLE 4-69 gNXI Command to Run a GetRequest for Two Paths

```
go run gnmi_get.go \
  -xpath "/authors" \
  -xpath "/books/book[title=The Neverending Story]/author" \
  -target_addr localhost:10161 \
  -target_name gnmi \
  -key MyKey.key \
  -cert MyCertificate.crt \
  -ca MyCertificate.crt \
  -username foo \
  -password bar \
  -alsologtostderr
```

Running the `gnmi_get.go` script generates a gNMI GetRequest with two queries, as shown in Example 4-70.

EXAMPLE 4-70 gNMI GetRequest for Two Paths

```
== getRequest:
path: <
  elem: <
    name: "authors"
  >
>
path: <
  elem: <
    name: "books"
  >
```

```
  elem: <
    name: "book"
    key: <
      key: "title"
      value: "The Neverending Story"
    >
  >
  elem: <
    name: "author"
  >
>
encoding: JSON_IETF
```

To these queries, the server gives the response shown in Example 4-71.

EXAMPLE 4-71 GetResponse for Two Paths

```
== getResponse:
notification: <
  timestamp: 1531927528820201450
  update: <
    path: <
      elem: <
        name: "authors"
      >
    >
    val: <
      json_ietf_val: "{\"bookzone-example:author\":[{\"account-id\":1010,\"name\":
\"Douglas Adams\"},{\"account-id\":2017,\"name\":\"Kazuo Ishiguro\"},{\"account-id\":
1011,\"name\":\"Malala Yousafzai\"},{\"account-id\":1001,\"name\":
\"Michael Ende\"}]}"
    >
  >
>
notification: <
  timestamp: 1531927528820354611
  update: <
    path: <
      elem: <
        name: "books"
      >
      elem: <
        name: "book"
        key: <
          key: "title"
```

```
            value: "The Neverending Story"
          >
        >
        elem: <
          name: "author"
        >
      >
      val: <
        string_val: "Michael Ende"
      >
    >
  >
```

Since the client specifically requested `JSON_IETF` encoding, the server responds with a value labeled `json_ietf_val`. With the GetRequest, there is no way to specify specific attributes or a maximum depth of the information to return. Once the path specified in the request is reached, all information below that point is returned.

gNMI SetRequest

The way to create, update, replace, or delete a configuration in a gNMI server is to use a SetRequest. The SetRequest contains an ordered sequence of edit operations. The whole request is atomic, so if there are any issues, with validation or otherwise, none of the operations are applied.

The SetRequest Specification

> The server MUST process deleted paths (within the delete field of the SetRequest), followed by paths to be replaced (within the replace field), and finally updated paths (within the update field). The order of the replace and update fields MUST be treated as significant within a single SetRequest message.
>
> SetResponse message MUST be populated with an error message indicating the success or failure of the set of operations within the SetRequest message
>
> All changes to the state of the target that are included in an individual SetRequest message are considered part of a transaction. That is, either all modifications within the request are applied, or the target MUST rollback the state changes to reflect its state before any changes were applied. The state of the target MUST NOT appear to be changed until such time as all changes have been accepted successfully. Hence, telemetry update messages MUST NOT reflect a change in state until such time as the intended modifications have been accepted.

To demonstrate how this works, Example 4-72 provides a SetRequest to end the relation with Michael Ende, removing both him from the author list and his title *The Neverending Story* from the book catalog. Finally, there is also an adjustment to the price of the title *The Art of War*.

EXAMPLE 4-72 gNXI Command to Send a SetRequest for Two Books and an Author

```
go run gnmi_set.go \
  -delete "/authors/author[name=Michael Ende]" \
  -delete "/books/book[title=Neverending Story]" \
  -update "/books/book[title=The Art of War]/format[isbn=160459893X]/
price:\"16.50\"" \
  -target_addr localhost:10161 \
  -target_name gnmi \
  -key MyKey.key \
  -cert MyCertificate.crt \
  -ca MyCertificate.crt \
  -username foo \
  -password bar \
  -alsologtostderr
```

When you run this script, the request generated toward the `gnmi_target` server is shown in Example 4-73.

EXAMPLE 4-73 SetRequest for Two Books and an Author

```
== setRequest:
delete: <
  elem: <
    name: "authors"
  >
  elem: <
    name: "author"
    key: <
      key: "name"
      value: "Michael Ende"
    >
  >
>
delete: <
  elem: <
    name: "books"
  >
  elem: <
    name: "book"
```

```
      key: <
        key: "title"
        value: "Neverending Story"
      >
    >
  >
  update: <
    path: <
      elem: <
        name: "books"
      >
      elem: <
        name: "book"
        key: <
          key: "title"
          value: "The Art of War"
        >
      >
      elem: <
        name: "format"
        key: <
          key: "isbn"
          value: "160459893X"
        >
      >
      elem: <
        name: "price"
      >
    >
    val: <
      string_val: "16.50"
    >
  >
```

This request reveals an important finding, either with the gNMI specification or with the `gnmi_target` implementation, as shown in Example 4-74.

EXAMPLE 4-74 SetReply for Two Books and an Author

```
F0718 18:26:26.156011   61136 gnmi_set.go:160] Set failed: rpc error: code = Internal
desc = error in creating config struct from IETF JSON data: field name Author value
Michael Ende (string ptr) schema path /device/books/book/author has leafref path
/authors/author/name not equal to any target nodes
exit status 1
```

The meaning of this error is that the server refuses to delete *Michael Ende* from the list of authors because there is still a book referring to his name. That book is also deleted within the same transaction, but listed "after" the deletion of the author. Essentially, each individual edit operation within the transaction must be sequenced by the client such that the datastore is in a consistent state after each operation. This differs from NETCONF and RESTCONF.

If you reverse the sequence of the delete operations (that is, delete the book first, then the author), the validation succeeds. The problem with reversing them is that if operations only work if the client is trained to know or is smart enough to deduce the "right" sequence for every pair of elements across all server (device) types and versions, the cost of the client skyrockets. It's a killer. With some YANG models, there may not even exist any sequence where two objects can be deleted separately from each other. This sort-ordering issue is listed in RFC 3535 as one of the fundamental problems with SNMP and the reason for its failure as a configuration protocol.

With NETCONF and RESTCONF, the validity of the datastore is checked only after all the edits are taken into account. This allows the client (manager) to remain ignorant of the details of dependency, allowing the employment of untrained engineers or half-witted automation engines that compute what needs to be done to move from configuration A to configuration B on the fly.

Although the gNMI specification talks about transactions, this transaction definition is of a weaker kind than the one used with NETCONF and RESTCONF.

Back to the SetRequest: If you drop the deletion of the author, the request looks like what's shown in Example 4-75.

EXAMPLE 4-75 SetRequest for Two Books but No Author

```
== setRequest:
delete: <
  elem: <
    name: "books"
  >
  elem: <
    name: "book"
    key: <
      key: "title"
      value: "Neverending Story"
    >
  >
>
update: <
  path: <
    elem: <
      name: "books"
    >
```

```
    elem: <
      name: "book"
      key: <
        key: "title"
        value: "The Art of War"
      >
    >
    elem: <
      name: "format"
      key: <
        key: "isbn"
        value: "160459893X"
      >
    >
    elem: <
      name: "price"
    >
  >
  val: <
    string_val: "16.50"
  >
>
```

To this uncontroversial request, the response is success, as seen in Example 4-76.

EXAMPLE 4-76 SetResponse for Two Books but No Author

```
== getResponse:
response: <
  path: <
    elem: <
      name: "books"
    >
    elem: <
      name: "book"
      key: <
        key: "title"
        value: "Neverending Story"
      >
    >
  >
  op: DELETE
>
```

```
response: <
  path: <
    elem: <
      name: "books"
    >
    elem: <
      name: "book"
      key: <
        key: "title"
        value: "The Art of War"
      >
    >
    elem: <
      name: "format"
      key: <
        key: "isbn"
        value: "160459893X"
      >
    >
    elem: <
      name: "price"
    >
  >
  op: UPDATE
>
```

gNMI SubscribeRequest and Telemetry

The OpenConfig consortium invested heavily into thought and code around telemetry (that is, the process of recording and transmitting the readings of an instrument). A substantial portion of all the specifications, code examples, and discussions revolve around this theme.

And no wonder, since telemetry is useful and essential to a wide variety of different use cases in the network management area:

- Metering and billing
- Network problem resolution and optimization
- Network monitoring
- Flow analysis and capacity planning

- Lawful intercept
- Big data plus AI/deep learning

Each gNMI SubscribeRequest may contain several paths in the YANG model to subscribe to. All data under each path is returned. The data returned is not a snapshot, which means it need not be internally consistent if changes happened during the delivery of the update. This is the preferred delivery method for any queries that generate larger amounts of data, since storing a consistent snapshot of a large query demands a lot of memory and CPU time from the server.

The subscriber specifies a frequency of delivery, where the following are possible values:

- `ONCE`: The data is returned as soon as possible, and only once.
- `POLL`: The data is returned every so often, as requested by the client.
- `STREAM`: The data is returned when the data has changed.

There are several options in each of these modes that can make them behave as hybrids of each other.

The gNXI tools do not support subscriptions at the time of writing. The SubscribeRequest and SubscribeReply messages have a lot in common with those of GetRequest and GetReply.

YANG RPC, Action and Notification

At this time there are no protocol operations in gNMI corresponding to the YANG rpc, action, and notification constructs. There is a project and repository called gNOI where support for this sort of functionality is under development. Check the repository for the latest additions.

Interview with the Expert

Q&A with Kent Watsen

Kent Watsen started programming computers in 1982 on a Timex Sinclair 1000, purchased with money saved from lawnmowing. Never losing sight of his passion with computers, Kent spent a decade doing low-level graphics for virtual reality, and almost two decades doing network management and security. Within the network management space, Kent architected four successful commercial network management systems, authored eight Internet standards, and was awarded eight software patents. Currently, Kent is a Principal Engineer at Juniper Networks within the Cloud Services Platform team, co-chair of the IETF NETCONF working group, co-chair of the IETF NETMOD working group, as well an active contributor in both the NETCONF and NETMOD working groups.

Question:

Kent, you were active at the IETF as NETCONF co-chair, NETMOD co-chair, and a key participant. You participated in the NETCONF and RESTCONF specifications and witnessed the gNMI development. What are the strengths and weaknesses of the different protocols?

Answer:

It is firstly my opinion that the three protocols share more in common than not. At the most basic level, they all are data model–driven RPC and notification-based protocols, and, furthermore, they all predominantly use YANG to define the data models. However, to answer the question, these protocols are compared here based on the following criteria: features, runtime performance, and ease of use.

Feature differences are mostly only meaningful when raised to the level of being visible to operators. NETCONF uniquely delivers support for commits that will auto roll back unless confirmed, which can make the difference between a truck roll or not. NETCONF also uniquely delivers support for network-wide transactions, which can reduce service interruptions for certain configuration update operations. Both NETCONF and RESTCONF support call-home connections, which enable some deployment scenarios otherwise not possible (for example, devices deployed behind a NAT/FW). gNMI uniquely supports the streaming of telemetry data, which is a critical underpinning for a usable SDN.

Runtime performance is, again, mostly only meaningful when raised to the level of being visible to operators. Performance matters for workflows requiring low latency (for example, SDN) or high throughput (for example, streaming telemetry data). gNMI, with its gRPC/protobuf-based (that is, binary-based) protocol, excels in this regard. In all fairness, it should be noted that NETCONF and RESTCONF will soon also support the streaming of telemetry data, and, for configured subscriptions, it is the intention to support a high-throughput binary encoding.

Ease of use is mostly only meaningful to developers. If programming language bindings are important, gNMI comes with built-in support for a number of popular programming languages, while bindings for NETCONF and RESTCONF are available only as third-party add-ons. This is perhaps the most striking distinction between these protocols as, truly, NETCONF and RESTCONF are defined as protocols, whereas gNMI is an API interface and an accompanying tool chain. Of course, RESTCONF, being an HTTP-based protocol, has tremendous tooling support and is the most familiar. On the flip side, if portability is paramount, both NETCONF and RESTCONF provide ultimate flexibility, as anyone can develop the code (and many have) to implement these rather simple protocols, whereas extending gNMI may be a chore for some.

Question:

How do you see the operator world adopting automation?

Answer:

Adopting automation is, of course, the only sensible path forward, in order to support future scalability and elasticity demands. The expectation is that neural networks will enable adaptive and self-healing networks. To this end, we are making progress, but there is still a long way to go.

Summary

This chapter introduced practical examples of how to use the three most commonly used wire protocols (namely, NETCONF, RESTCONF and gNMI) that are used together with YANG models. Each section is full of hands-on commands using free tools to try out the functionality provided in each protocol, which you could experiment with in your own environment if you like. The YANG model used for all examples was the BookZone model from Chapter 3.

The NETCONF section started with a refresher on how XML works, since that is essential for understanding NETCONF. Contrary to common belief, there are many hidden dragons in XML. Then the NETCONF connection, hello, and framing mechanisms, which come in NETCONF 1.0 and 1.1 flavors, are also affected by whether modules are using YANG 1.0 or 1.1. A rather long discussion followed around transaction semantics and how `edit-config` content may be served out-of-order content, even split into separate messages, as long as everything is consistent at each transaction boundary. Examples of reading using the `get` operation, invoking RPCs, and receiving notifications were also given, as well as a brief discussion of less prominent functionality like locking and datastore manipulations. At the end of the section was a discussion of what the new NMDA-defined operations `get-data` and `edit-data` bring.

Generally speaking, RESTCONF can be described as a lightweight version of NETCONF based on web technology. The content is JSON or XML encoded. REST principles apply. The NETCONF transaction concept is still here, but features like datastores and network-wide transactions were removed. The section described the difference between the different HTTP verbs for write operations: POST, PUT, PATCH, DELETE, and YANG-PATCH. At the end, actions and notifications were also covered.

The last protocol discussed was gNMI, which is particularly popular among the OpenConfig consortium players and developed by Google. The YANG model-driven approach and set of operations make it rather similar to RESTCONF. An important difference is in the transaction definition, which requires clients to sequence the transaction content according to device-specific rules that are not part of the YANG contract. Telemetry data collection is an area that is receiving generous coverage in the gNMI specifications.

References in This Chapter

This chapter does not aim to explain everything there is to say about NETCONF, RESTCONF or gNMI, but seeks to highlight the fundamentally important mechanisms required for a deep understanding. Details beyond that are best found in the original specifications.

From here, you can expand your knowledge by trying out these protocols and tools on your own. The BookZone project on GitHub explains how to get started and replicate the examples from this book. To go deeper on the theory side, the next step is to look at the RFCs and specifications. In particular, have a look at the references in Table 4-1.

TABLE 4-1 NETCONF, RESTCONF and gNMI-Related Documents for Further Reading

Topic	Content
Network management requirements	https://tools.ietf.org/html/rfc3535 RFC 3535 provides an overview of a workshop held by the IETF Internet Architecture Board (IAB) on network management in 2002. The goal of the workshop was to guide the future work regarding network management.
NETCONF	https://tools.ietf.org/html/rfc6241 RFC 6241 and RFC 6242 define the NETCONF 1.1 protocol, while RFC 4741 and RFC 4742 define NETCONF 1.0.
NETCONF WG	https://datatracker.ietf.org/wg/netconf/about/ IETF's NETCONF Work Group is the team behind NETCONF and RESTCONF.
REST Overview	(search on Wikipedia) Wikipedia article on Representational State Transfer (REST).
REST root URL	https://tools.ietf.org/html/rfc6415 RFC 6415 defines the mechanism to obtain the root URL for a REST-based service.
RESTCONF	https://tools.ietf.org/html/rfc8040 RFC 8040 defines the RESTCONF protocol.
YANG-PATCH	https://tools.ietf.org/html/rfc8072 RFC 8072 defines the YANG-PATCH media type used when making more than one change in a single transaction using RESTCONF.
OpenConfig	http://www.openconfig.net/ The OpenConfig work group is the team behind gNMI and the OpenConfig YANG model.
OpenConfig's GitHub	https://github.com/openconfig The go-to location for OpenConfig tools and YANG modules.
gRPC	https://grpc.io/docs/ gRPC is the underlying transport protocol for gNMI.

Topic	Content
gNMI	https://github.com/openconfig/reference/blob/master/rpc/gnmi/gnmi-specification.md The gRPC Network Management Interface (gNMI) specification.
gNXI	http://github.com/google/gnxi Google's GitHub repository for the gNXI tools.
gNOI	https://github.com/openconfig/gnoi OpenConfig's GitHub repository for the gNOI tools.
Go language	https://golang.org/doc/install The Go language download site. The Go language is used with many open source tools provided/curated by Google.
BookZone repository	https://github.com/janlindblad/bookzone The BookZone repository contains the examples used in Chapters 3, 4, and 10 of this book.

Chapter 5

Telemetry Explained

This chapter covers

- The different telemetry-related terms
- The need to move away from Simple Network Management Protocol (SNMP)
- The telemetry components and how all the different building blocks fit together
- An overview of IETF's YANG Push and the OpenConfig streaming telemetry
- Some help on selecting your telemetry mechanism

Introduction

This chapter describes the concepts and architecture behind data model–driven telemetry. Reading through this chapter, you might perceive an unmistakable air of "under construction" to this topic—and you would be right, as telemetry keeps evolving in the industry. This chapter covers the state of the art of telemetry and provides some pointers.

Data Model–Driven Telemetry

Telemetry, as a generic term, is the science or process of telemetering data, where *telemetering* is the act of measuring a quantity (such as pressure, speed, or temperature) and transmitting the result, especially by radio, to a distant station. In the networking world, telemetry is an automated communications process by which measurements and other data are collected at remote or inaccessible points and transmitted to receiving equipment for monitoring. Typical networking examples are SNMP notifications, NetFlow (RFC 3954) and IP Flow Information eXport (RFC 7011) records, and syslog messages. Telemetry is not new in this industry, although data model–driven telemetry certainly is. SNMP notifications, NetFlow, and even syslog messages have existed for decades.

At times when networks grow bigger and more complex, and therefore generate more and more monitoring data from physical and virtual entities, network management requires telemetry. Telemetry helps stream data out of the network faster, enabling the streaming of large amounts of data in real time or close to real time.

Chapter 1, "The Network Management World Must Change: Why Should You Care?", justified why data model–driven telemetry is the most useful type of telemetry in this world that required automation. Note that this book focuses on the following telemetry definition.

Telemetry

An automated communications process by which measurements and other data are collected at remote or inaccessible points and transmitted to receiving equipment for monitoring. Model-driven telemetry provides a mechanism to stream data from a model-driven telemetry-capable device to a destination.

Telemetry uses a subscription model to identify information sources and destinations. Model-driven telemetry replaces the need for the periodic polling of network elements; instead, a continuous request for information to be delivered to a subscriber is established upon the network element. Then, either periodically, or as objects change, a subscribed set of YANG objects are streamed to that subscriber.

While the exact term is data model–driven telemetry, this book uses the term "telemetry," also known as "model-driven telemetry" for short, and "streaming telemetry." Indeed, Chapter 2, "Data Model–Driven Management," made the case that efficient automation is based on data models.

For most operations engineers, telemetry refers to the streaming of monitoring data, helping network monitoring and troubleshooting. Note that telemetry might also contain the information about the applied configuration, especially when used with non-fully transactional protocols, such as RESTCONF and gRPC. Combining the two pieces of information (monitoring and configuration) is the basis for automation and for intent-based networking (that is, creating the feedback that enables constant learning and adapting; refer to the "Intent-Based Networking" section in Chapter 1). This type of telemetry could be called "operational telemetry" (even if nobody uses that term in the industry) as opposed to business telemetry.

Business telemetry, a clarifying term, is the use of telemetry to stream information to help business developments. For example, how is the network inventory in terms of hardware, software, and licenses related to each customer? Knowing this inventory certainly helps the vendor sales teams, on top of knowing how customers use your specific functionality and service (what is enabled and how?). There is also a great advantage for the support teams, who could proactively warn of potential defects, thus reducing in parallel the support costs. Business developers, (senior) vice presidents, and top execs speak of telemetry, but they actually mean business telemetry. Some could argue that any telemetry fulfills a business purpose in the end; hence the "business" prefix in "business telemetry" is not necessary and even confusing. However, the term business telemetry helps to make a clear distinction of the audience in telemetry discussions.

For sure, (operational) telemetry and business telemetry meet somewhere, as some of the streamed data might be overlapping or even identical—similar data, but different usage. For example, streaming telemetry to troubleshoot a network issue requires a data manifest to understand where the information comes from and how to interpret it. Typically, the data manifest consists of device or network inventory, software version, enabled features, licensing information, and so on. Exactly like a Technical Assistance Center (TAC) engineer consistently requires the output of "show technical support" to start investigating a case, telemetry requires the data manifest to interpret the data. Getting some counters information without context is not terribly useful. What is interesting is that a different audience (in this case, business developers) would benefit from almost the exact same information to ensure that customers have the right set of products for their business outcome—jumping at the opportunity to sell some more, obviously.

Moving Away from SNMP to Telemetry

Forgetting for a moment the fundamental argument that a single data model for both configuration and monitoring is required, which alone justifies the move away from SNMP notifications to (YANG-based) telemetry, let's cover a couple of extra reasons why SNMP (notifications) is not efficient.

As Shelly Cadora mentioned in her blog [https://blogs.cisco.com/sp/the-limits-of-snmp],[1] to retrieve large amounts of data, SNMP polling relies on the GetBulk operation. Introduced in SNMPv2, GetBulk performs a continuous GetNext operation that retrieves all the columns of a given table (for example, statistics for all interfaces). When polled, a router returns as many columns as can fit into a packet. After the first GetBulk packet is filled up, the SNMP agent on the router continues its lexicographical walk and fills up another packet. When the poller detects that the router "walked off the table" (by sending Object Identifiers [OIDs] that belong to the next table), it stops sending GetBulk operations. For very large tables, this could take a lot of requests, and the router must process each one as it arrives.

This situation is bad enough if you have a single network management system (NMS) polling, but what if you have multiple NMS's polling? Obviously, since polling is not synchronized between the different NMS's, the router must process each request independently, finding the requested place in the lexical tree and doing the walk, even if both SNMP pollers requested the same Management Information Base (MIB) objects at more or less the same time. Many network operators know this empirically: The more SNMP pollers you have, the slower the SNMP response. One operator mentioned to me up to 200 NMS's were polling his network, most of them polling similar information from the interface table: a terrible situation that stems from a mix of different NMS's focusing on different technologies, different departments having their own NMS, a mix of mergers and acquisitions, or simply the fear of breaking something by touching a legacy NMS. Telemetry gains efficiency over SNMP by eliminating the polling process altogether. Instead of sending requests with specific instructions that the router must process each and every time, telemetry uses a configured policy to know what data to collect, how often, and to whom to send it. Telemetry using the compact Google Protocol Buffer (GPB) encoding is way more efficient from an encoding viewpoint compared to SNMP: All the interface statistics fit into a single GPB telemetry packet, whereas multiple SNMP packets are required to export the same information. Bandwidth reduction is great, but the real benefit is actually somewhere else: The router does a single dip into the internal data structures to acquire the data, as opposed to multiple times when answering a polling request. If there are multiple interested receivers, the router can just duplicate the packet for different destinations—a very trivial task for a router. Therefore, sending telemetry to one receiver has the same latency and overhead as sending it to five.

Polling is not the only a computational burden that SNMP imposes on a router. An equally significant performance factor is how data is ordered and exported. SNMP imposes a very tight model when it comes to indexing and exporting. Take the example of the SNMP interface table (ifTable, RFC 2863), as displayed in Table 5-1. Each column of the table represents a different parameter for a given interface, indexed by the ifIndex, the unique identifier for the interface.

TABLE 5-1 Some Entries in the SNMP Interface Table

ifIndex	ifDescr	ifType	ifMTU	ifSpeed
3	GigabitEthernet0	6	1514	1000000000
4	GigabitEthernet1	6	1514	1000000000
5	Loopback0	24	1500	0

The strict semantics of the GetNext/GetBulk operations force the router to traverse the table, column by column (returning the list of ifIndex, followed by a list of ifDescr, ifType, and so on), from lowest index value to highest. From a router's perspective, this doesn't fit the internal data representation. Therefore, the router must reorder the data into a table and walk the columns to fulfill the GetBulk request. Obviously, both SNMP polling and SNMP notifications suffer from the same drawback.

Polling the interface table entails this "reordering" extra load on the router, obviously multiplied by the number of pollers, if multiple pollers require the same information. A different example, suffering from the same reordering issue, well known to operators is polling the routing table. It brings a router to its knees or at least takes a very long time (depending on the relative priority of the SNMP process). Polling the entire Border Gateway Protocol (BGP) table 15 years ago, when it contained about 1,000 entries, took about 30 minutes. These days, the BGP routing table contains almost 800,000 routes [https://bgp.potaroo.net/].[2] Do the math!

How much better it would be if we could just free the router to present its data in the natural order! Well, that's exactly what telemetry does. Telemetry collects data using the internal bulk data collection mechanisms, does some minimal processing to filter and translate the internal structure to a Google Protocol Buffer, and then pushes the whole thing to the collector at the configured intervals. The goal is to minimize processing overhead at every step, so you get the fastest, freshest data possible with the least amount of work.

Finally, telemetry offers yet another advantage compared to SNMP polling: a consistent observation time. Typically, NMS's poll devices on a regular basis, called the SNMP polling interval. Operators usually poll the interface counters every 5 or 30 minutes, to graph the usage evolution for capacity planning. Fine, but SNMP polling for troubleshooting purposes requires precise observation time. For example, let's try to correlate counters from multiple MIB tables (for example, interface, quality of service, and flow). When SNMP pollers request those three tables via SNMP, the requests are processed at different times on the router due to transmission delays, potential retransmissions, reordering extra processing, or simply different NMS's not synchronizing their polling times. Therefore, the counters are observed at different times, thus impeding correlation. On top of that, SNMP is based on User Datagram Protocol (UDP) and polling cycles may be missed, so packets may get lost, often when the network is under stress and the need for the data is the greatest. With telemetry, operators subscribe to the three tables directly on the agent, and the polling is internal to the agent, thus minimizing this negative timing effect.

Note that SNMP pollers always keep on polling. In the meantime, data might become irrelevant. So, combining two telemetry aspects—the periodic subscriptions with some event-driven telemetry, where telemetry is triggered by a specific change—eliminates or reduces this problem drastically. See the notion of two types of subscriptions—periodic and on-change—later on in this chapter.

So, you are now convinced that you need to move away from SNMP. How do you upgrade to model-driven telemetry? The first step is to convert your SNMP notifications to telemetry. The YANG Catalog search engine [https://www.yangcatalog.org/yang-search/][3] helps you find the right YANG objects. For example, the interface configuration and operation information is available in the ietf-interfaces [https://www.yangcatalog.org/yang-search/module_details/?module=ietf-interfaces][4] and openconfig-interfaces [https://www.yangcatalog.org/yang-search/module_details/?module=openconfig-interfaces][5] YANG modules. A couple of us are working on a Telemetry Data Mapper tool that directly maps MIB module OIDs to YANG objects. For example, for ifIndex, ifAdminStatus, and ifOperStatus and the MIB variables in the linkDown and linkUp SNMP notifications (RFC 2863), the tool returns what is illustrated in Figure 5-1.

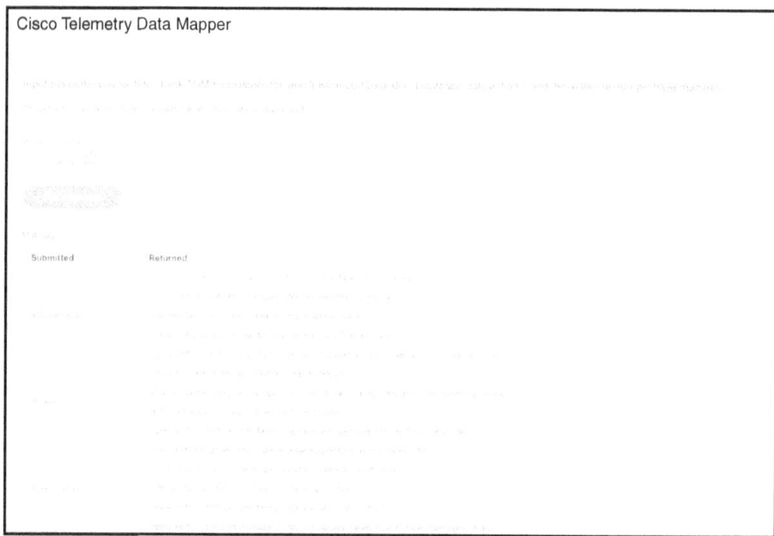

FIGURE 5-1 ifIndex, ifAdminStatus, and ifOperStatus MIB Objects Mapping to Operational YANG Objects

The goal behind this tool is to map MIB OIDs to *operational* YANG objects, for telemetry.

The mappings for the configuration objects might be slightly different. For example, the ifAdminStatus *configuration* objects are as follows:

- openconfig-interfaces:interfaces/interface/config/enable
- openconfig-interfaces:interfaces/interface/subinterfaces/subinterface/config/enable
- ietf-interfaces:interfaces/interface/enabled
- Cisco-IOS-XR-ifmgr-cfg:interface-configuration/interface-configuration/shutdown

For systems that don't yet support the Network Management Datastore Architecture (NMDA; see Chapter 3, "YANG Explained"), the ietf-interfaces (RFC 7223) ifAdminStatus configuration maps to ietf-interfaces:interfaces/interface/enabled.

For modern systems supporting NMDA with the ietf-interfaces (RFC 8343, which updates RFC 7223 with NMDA support), the ifAdminStatus configuration maps to the same object for the **:startup**, **:candidate**, **:running**, and **:intended** datastores.

The plan is to integrate the Telemetry Data Mapper with the YANG Catalog set of tools. In the meantime, the GitHub repository with the code is located at https://github.com/cisco-ie/tdm.[6]

Telemetry Use Cases

Streaming telemetry provides a mechanism to select data of interest from publishers and to transmit it in a structured format to remote management stations for monitoring. This mechanism enables automatic tuning of the network based on real-time data, which is crucial for its seamless operation. The finer granularity and higher frequency of data available through telemetry enables better performance monitoring and, therefore, better troubleshooting. It helps with more service-efficient bandwidth utilization, link utilization, risk assessment and control, remote monitoring, and scalability. Streaming telemetry thus converts the monitoring process into a data analytic proposition that enables the rapid extraction and analysis of massive data sets to improve decision-making.

Telemetry lets users direct data to a configured receiver/collector. This is achieved by leveraging the capabilities of machine-to-machine communication. The data is used by development and operations (DevOps) personnel who plan to optimize networks by collecting network analytics in real time, locate where problems occur, and investigate issues in a collaborative manner.

There are many use cases around telemetry, some of which are listed here:

- Network state indicators, network statistics, and critical infrastructure information are exposed to the application layer, where they are used to enhance operational performance and to reduce troubleshooting time (for example, streaming all information about the health of devices).

- Real-time reports on a portion of the operational state (and sometimes applied configuration) are desired. Multiple operations groups care about the status of overlapping objects in a device. One operations group owning a device does not want to give full access to the device—just a read-only feed to an NMS with read-only type credentials. Another example is any relevant operations/config updates directly pushed to a tenant, or a service provider providing a separate network function virtualization for an enterprise.
- Quickly replicating the network current, for post-processing (for example, streaming the network topology, routing information, configuration, interface stats, core traffic matrix, and so on for network simulation and optimization).
- Telemetry as a feedback loop mechanism, such as directing a flow down an alternate path based on changing network conditions received via telemetry (for example, changes in operational performance data driving network rebalancing for optimized facilities usage).
- Conditional telemetry, where you establish a push connection and forward targeted telemetry data to a targeted recipient when certain criteria are met. As an example, only send packet drop counters info when a different interface is down. This might require on-change telemetry (discussed later in the chapter).
- Peer misconfiguration, where you monitor the configuration of adjacent network elements to see if common parameters are set the same on either side.

When describing telemetry use cases, it's important to understand that, in the end, telemetry is a protocol (that is, it's a means to an end for applications that benefit from the deep knowledge that telemetry delivers). In other words, the value is not in the telemetry protocol itself or even in data models, but in the information streamed and in the data analytics based on this information.

Telemetry Components

The section covers the telemetry architecture, the notion of events in telemetry, as well as the two dial telemetry modes.

Architecture

From a multilayer point of view, the telemetry architecture is similar to the management architecture (refer to Figure 2-3 in Chapter 2), as displayed in Figure 5-2.

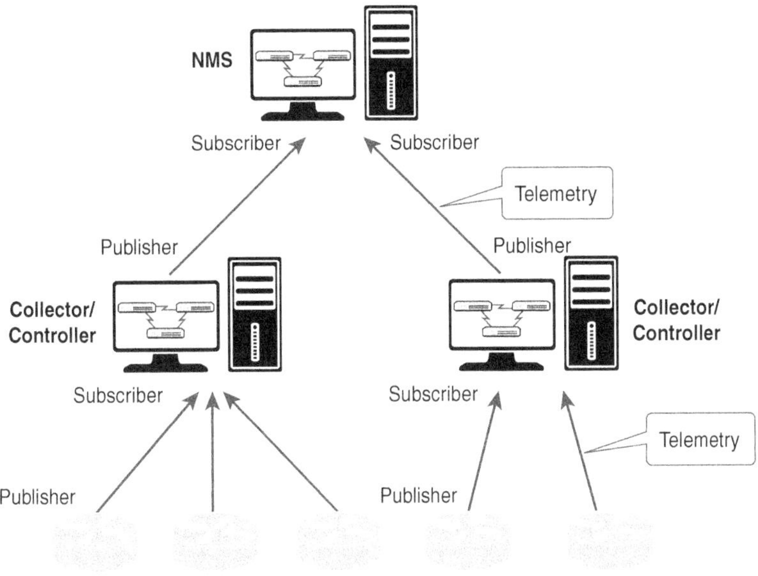

FIGURE 5-2 Telemetry Architecture

Network elements (whether physical or virtual) stream telemetry information from the publishers to the collector, sometimes called the telemetry receiver. This information is integrated in the collector (sometimes co-located with a controller), which summarizes it, correlates it, and aggregates it. The aggregation can occur in time (that is, in time series) or in a space (that is, from multiple publishers in different locations in the network). Finally, the collector forwards the collected/correlated/aggregated telemetry to the NMS. Considering the huge of amount telemetry pushed, at potentially high frequency, from multiple publishers, this is a key process in the collector/controller.

Obviously with model-driven telemetry, the source of information is the series of YANG objects. Having the same data language as the source of information facilitates the correlation, aggregation, and data analytics, as mentioned in Chapter 1's "The Challenges of Managing Networks with Different Data Models" section (where you were introduced to the challenges of managing a simple concept such as the interface using different data model languages). However, the reality in the industry is that not all sources of information are "YANGified" at this point in time. In some situations, YANGifying all information in devices is not even worthwhile—YANG doesn't require re-engineering everything in the world! As an example, one of the telemetry use cases mentions the core traffic matrix, which is typically computed out of NetFlow (or IPFIX) flow records. Practically speaking, in this case, the collector would receive NetFlow/IPFIX flow records from multiple key locations in the network and generate the core traffic matrix, potentially complemented with telemetry data. From there, creating a YANG module modeled after the core traffic matrix is a relatively easy job, and the collector could advertise it before pushing its content via telemetry. If YANG objects, along with non-YANG objects, must be streamed (for example, to complement the YANG-based telemetry) from a single telemetry protocol, this is done with one of the current telemetry mechanisms: NETCONF, RESTCONF, or gNMI. gNMI clearly mentions in its documentation that it can be used for any data (that is, non-YANG data), with the following characteristics:

- A structure that can be represented by a tree, where nodes are uniquely identified by a path consisting of node names, or node names coupled with attributes
- Values can be serialized into a scalar object

And even with YANG itself, there is no problem at all describing information not specified by a schema, with the **anyxml** or **anydata** construct, or by modeling as strings and binaries. Of course, how to interpret that data requires a data model, and whatever data you want to stream, you need to have a way to refer to it in your telemetry subscription. If you want to enable subscriptions with filtering at the node level and such, then of course you should have a common schema or data model; it is hard for subscription filters to refer to arbitrary data in a structured way.

The analogy with the Network YANG modules specifically designed for the interface between the orchestrator and the controller is obvious (again, see Figure 2-3 in Chapter 2). Therefore, the multilayer architecture helps data aggregation, correlation, and data analytics from potentially diverse sources of information, even if the ideal goal is to receive model-driven telemetry at every layer.

From a publisher configuration point of view, here are the typical elements:

- **Sensor path**: Describes the data you want to stream to a collector that is the YANG path or a subset of data definitions in a YANG model with a tree. In a YANG model, the sensor path can be specified to end at any level in the container hierarchy.
- **Subscription request for one or more YANG subtrees (including single leafs)**: This is made by the subscriber of a publisher and is targeted to a collector. A subscription may include constraints that dictate how often or under what conditions YANG information updates might be sent. A subscription is a contract that stipulates the data to be pushed and the associated terms. In other terms, it binds everything together for the router to start streaming data at the configured intervals.
- **Initialization of streaming session**: Describes who initiates the streaming of data from the router toward the collector. Two possible options are dial-in mode (the collector initiates a session to the router and subscribes to data to be streamed out) and dial-out mode (the router initiates a session to the destinations based on the subscription).
- **Transport protocol**: Describes the protocol you want to use to deliver to your collector/controller the information you selected with sensor paths—for example, NETCONF, RESTCONF, or some new protocol based on gRPC, Transmission Control Protocol (TCP), or even UDP.
- **Encoding**: Describes the format of the data on the wire—for example, Extensible Markup Language (XML), JavaScript Object Notation (JSON), or GPB.

Transport Discussion: Monitoring Versus Events

What is the right transport protocol (UDP- or TCP-based) to be used with telemetry? It's interesting to observe that the telemetry discussions in the industry today are identical to the IPFIX (IP Flow Information Export) standardization discussions from about 10 years ago (noticeably, because IPFIX is also a telemetry protocol). Indeed, telemetry is potentially a new buzzword for some, but it is certainly not a new concept: IPFIX is already a telemetry protocol.

In the end, transport discussions boil down to operational issues. With the unreliable UDP transport, if no streaming information is received on the collector, what does it mean? The publisher is down, not reachable, or simply has no streaming information to send? Obviously, you could include a message identifier, indicating whether some records were lost (like in NetFlow and IPFIX), but is this enough? It depends on the telemetry content. In case of telemetry for monitoring, such as interface statistics, missing a few telemetry packets in the time series is not a big deal. However, in the extreme case of using telemetry data for accounting, you can't miss any telemetry information. Ten years ago, the IPFIX solution mandated Stream Control Transmission Protocol (SCTP) Partial Reliability Extension (RFC 3748) as the mandatory-to-implement protocol. However, SCTP did not take off as an important transport protocol in the industry. So, the industry is left with this binary choice: TCP-based or UDP-based transport protocols. Expecting a publisher to keep a buffer full of telemetry records, for potential re-export, is not practical when the publishers are routers streaming a lot of telemetry data at high frequency. The key point is that if you can't work from samples or if you rely on telemetry to take an action, then telemetry must be considered as an event-based mechanism, and then the transport must be connection-oriented. In both IETF YANG Push and OpenConfig streaming telemetry, the transport is the connection-oriented protocol TCP, encrypted. Refer to Table 2-1 in Chapter 2, which focuses on the different transport stacks. Finally, note that TCP offers yet another advantage compared to UDP—nonrepudiation, which is especially important in case of events.

There are IETF discussions around a UDP-based publication channel for streaming telemetry used to collect data from devices [https://tools.ietf.org/html/draft-ietf-netconf-udp-pub-channel].[7] The future will tell to which operational use cases this specification is applicable.

Subscription Type: On-Change Versus Periodic

There are two types of subscriptions: periodic and on-change. With a periodic subscription, data is streamed out to the destination at the configured interval. It continuously sends data for the lifetime of that subscription. With an on-change subscription, data is published only when a change in the data occurs. On-change is also called event-driven telemetry. On-change is mainly applicable to state-like types of objects, typically an interface going down or a neighbor appearing. Note that using on-change for monitoring counters should not be discarded as being irrelevant. For example, a BGP peer reset counter is a perfect candidate for event-driven telemetry, as opposed to periodic. However, some system might have an implied load penalty (for example, if not implemented in shared memory) on top of changing the software behavior for every counter.

So how do you discover which YANG objects support on-change telemetry? Here is an example for Cisco IOS-XR-based devices. Extracted from the Cisco-IOS-XR-types.yang YANG module [https://github.com/YangModels/yang/blob/master/vendor/cisco/xr/651/Cisco-IOS-XR-types.yang],[8] Example 5-1 displays an extension called *event-telemetry*, used to flag on-change-capable objects. Example 5-2 shows such two objects: the *address* leaf and the *information-source* leaf, part of the *ipv4-rib-edm-path* list, for which the on-change subscription type is implemented.

EXAMPLE 5-1 The Cisco IOS-XR event-telemetry Extension

```
extension event-telemetry {
  argument description;
  description
    "Node eligible for telemetry event subscription";
}
```

Example 5-1 illustrates the YANG language extensibility, with the **extension** keyword, briefly mentioned in Chapter 3. As a reminder, the **extension** statement allows for the definition of new statements within the YANG language. From there, this new statement definition can be imported and used by other modules—in this case, by the Cisco-IOS-XR-ip-rib-ipv4-oper-sub1.yang displayed in Example 5-2.

EXAMPLE 5-2 Event-driven Telemetry Example from Cisco-IOS-XR-ip-rib-ipv4-oper-sub1.yang

```
...
import Cisco-IOS-XR-types {
  prefix xr;
}
...
grouping IPV4-RIB-EDM-PATH {
  description
    "Information of a rib path";
  list ipv4-rib-edm-path {
    description
      "ipv4 rib edm path";
    leaf address {
      type Ipv4-rib-edm-addr;
      description
        "Nexthop";
      xr:event-telemetry "Subscribe Telemetry Event";
    }
    leaf information-source {
      type Ipv4-rib-edm-addr;
      description
        "Infosource";
      xr:event-telemetry "Subscribe Telemetry Event";
    }
```

While waiting for yangcatalog.org to report the very useful on-change capability metadata for each YANG object, Example 5-3 uses the Unix **grep** function to highlight all on-change implementations among all YANG modules from the IOS XR 6.5.1 posted in GitHub [https://github.com/YangModels/yang/tree/master/vendor/cisco/xr/651].[9]

EXAMPLE 5-3 All YANG Modules Supporting Event-Driven Telemetry

```
VM:~/yanggithub/yang/vendor/cisco/xr/651$ grep "xr:event-telemetry" *
Cisco-IOS-XR-bundlemgr-oper-sub2.yang:      xr:event-telemetry "Subscribe Telemetry
Event";
Cisco-IOS-XR-controller-optics-oper-sub1.yang:      xr:event-telemetry "Subscribe
Telemetry Event";
Cisco-IOS-XR-ip-rib-ipv4-oper-sub1.yang:        xr:event-telemetry "Subscribe
Telemetry Event";
Cisco-IOS-XR-ip-rib-ipv6-oper-sub1.yang:        xr:event-telemetry "Subscribe
Telemetry Event";
Cisco-IOS-XR-ipv6-ma-oper-sub1.yang:      xr:event-telemetry "Subscribe Telemetry
Event";
Cisco-IOS-XR-pfi-im-cmd-oper-sub1.yang:      xr:event-telemetry "Subscribe Telemetry
Event";
Cisco-IOS-XR-pmengine-oper-sub1.yang:      xr:event-telemetry "Subscribe Telemetry
Event";
...
```

Dial-In and Dial-Out Modes

A telemetry session is initiated using one of two modes: the dial-in mode or the dial-out mode.

In dial-out mode, the publisher dials out to the collector. In this mode, sensor paths and destinations are configured (typically with a telemetry configuration YANG module) and bound together into one or more subscriptions. The device continually attempts to establish a session with each destination in the subscription and stream data to the receiver. The dial-out mode of subscriptions is persistent. When a session terminates, the device continually attempts to reestablish a new session with the receiver every 30 seconds. There are three steps to configuring the router for telemetry with dial-out:

STEP 1. **Create a destination group**. The destination group specifies the destination address, port, encoding, and transport that the router should use to send out telemetry data.

STEP 2. **Create a sensor group**. The sensor group specifies a list of YANG paths to be streamed.

STEP 3. **Create a subscription**. The subscription associates a destination group with a sensor group and sets the streaming interval.

In dial-in mode, the collector dials in to the device and subscribes dynamically to one or more sensor paths or subscriptions. The device (publisher) acts as the server, and the receiver is the client. The device streams telemetry data through the same session. The dial-in mode of subscriptions is dynamic.

This dynamic subscription terminates when the receiver cancels the subscription or when the session terminates. The dial-in mode is suitable when the collector knows exactly its telemetry requirements or when there is a single collector. The dial-in mode is supported only over gRPC Network Management Interface (gNMI; that is, the collector initiates a gRPC session to the router and specifies a subscription). The router sends whatever data is specified by the sensor group in the subscription requested by the collector.

Telemetry Standard Mechanisms

Figures 5-3 and 5-4 help you find your way in the nascent and still-evolving telemetry world. They offer a quick way to navigate through the different telemetry options. Detailed mechanism discussions follow in subsequent sections.

Mode	Dial-In						
Encoding (Serialization)	Protobuf				JSON (IETF or OpenConfig)		XML
	Self-Describing		Compact				
Telemetry Protocol	gNMI	TCP (Vendor)	gNMI	TCP (Vendor)	gNMI	TCP (Vendor)	NETCONF

FIGURE 5-3 Dial-in Telemetry Options

Mode	Dial-Out						
Encoding (Serialization)	Protobuf						JSON (IETF)
	Self-Describing			Compact			
Telemetry Protocol	gRPC	gNMI	TCP (Vendor)	gRPC	gNMI	TCP (Vendor)	RESTCONF

FIGURE 5-4 Dial-out Telemetry Options

One way to discover the most well-suited telemetry mechanism is to start with this question: dial-out or dial-in mode? Figure 5-3 shows the dial-in telemetry options, whereas Figure 5-4 shows the dial-out telemetry options. The dial-out mode offers RESTCONF, gRPC, gNMI, and a proprietary TCP implementation as protocols, along with the respective encodings JSON and Protocol buffers (protobuf). On the other side, the dial-in mode works with NETCONF, gNMI, or a proprietary TCP implementation. Once gNMI is selected, the encoding selection (JSON according to the IETF specifications, JSON according to the openconfig specifications, or protobuf) is a mix of two considerations:

- The first consideration is the encoding efficiency. Protobuf compact mode (as opposed to the protobuf self-describing mode, XML, and JSON) is a tight binary form that saves space on the wire and in memory. This encoding is therefore well-suited for telemetry, when a lot a data is pushed at high frequency toward a collector (typically long and high-frequency time series, the entire Forwarding Information Base (FIB), the BGP Routing Information Base (RIB), quality of service (QoS) statistics, and so on). Compared to the most verbose XML encoding, protobuf provides significant efficiency advantages with a 3-to-10 times reduction in data volume.

- The second consideration is the tooling type and expertise in place in the network operations center. For example, an existing JSON toolset along with JSON expertise in the network operation center might determine JSON as the encoding of choice.

NETCONF Event Notifications

RFC 5277, "NETCONF Event Notifications," from 2008, defines a mechanism as an optional capability, built on top of the base NETCONF definition, whereby the NETCONF client indicates interest in receiving event notifications from a NETCONF server by creating a subscription to receive event notifications. The NETCONF server replies to indicate whether the subscription request was successful and, if so, begins sending the event notifications to the NETCONF client as the events occur within the system. These event notifications are sent until either the NETCONF session is terminated or the subscription terminates for some other reason. The event notification subscription allows a number of options, specified when the subscription is created, to enable the NETCONF client to specify which events are of interest. Once created, a subscription cannot be modified. To change the subscription, you must create a new subscription and drop the old one. This mechanism reduces the risk of race conditions.

The "NETCONF Event Notifications" specification described a few key terms that are reused in today's telemetry: subscription, event, and stream.

Subscription

An agreement and method to receive event notifications over a NETCONF session. A concept related to the delivery of notifications (if there are any to send) involving destination and selection of notifications. It is bound to the lifetime of a session.

Event

An event is something that happens that may be of interest—a configuration change, a fault, a change in status, crossing a threshold, or an external input to the system, for example. Often, this results in an asynchronous message, sometimes referred to as a notification or event notification, being sent to interested parties to notify them that this event occurred.

Stream

An event stream is a set of event notifications matching some forwarding criteria and available to NETCONF clients for subscription.

The specification specifies the **<create-subscription>** operation, which initiates an event notification subscription that sends asynchronous event notifications to the initiator of the command until the subscription terminates. An optional filter indicates which subset of all possible events is of interest. The **<notification>** operation is sent to the client who initiated a **<create-subscription>** command asynchronously when an event of interest (that is, meeting the specified filtering criteria) occurred. An event notification is a complete and well-formed XML document. Note that **<notification>** is not a remote procedure call (RPC) method but rather the top-level element identifying the one-way message as a notification.

RFC 5277 NETCONF event notifications implementations exist, but this old specification suffered from one drawback. Initially, YANG models focused on configuration information only, and there is limited interest to push configuration objects via telemetry only. Indeed, the operational states, sometimes combined with the configuration, are much more valuable. In the meantime, new requirements emerged and the new telemetry work started.

IETF YANG Subscriptions

In 2014, work on "Requirements for Subscription to YANG Datastores" started, eventually finalized as RFC 7923. This document provides the telemetry foundational set of requirements for a service that can be summarized as a "pub/sub" service for YANG datastore updates. Based on criteria negotiated as part of a subscription, updates are pushed to targeted recipients, which eliminates the need for periodic polling of YANG datastores by applications. The document also includes some refinements: the periodicity of object updates, the filtering out of objects underneath a requested a subtree, and delivery QoS guarantees. RFC 7923 is a quick and easy read, providing the right terminology, offering the business drivers for a push solution, comparing (quickly) the pub/sub mechanism to SNMP, describing some use cases, and providing a series of requirements. Reading this document and specifically those requirements can help you understand the goals behind YANG subscription, which is the basis for model-driven telemetry.

At the time of writing, there are four different IETF specifications for what is called "YANG Push and Friends," as displayed in Table 5-2. Those documents are in the final phase of standardization and, by the time this book is published, you should see the RFCs published.

TABLE 5-2 The Four IETF Specifications Related to "YANG Push and Friends"

IETF Specification Documents	Website
Subscription to YANG Event Notifications	https://datatracker.ietf.org/doc/draft-ietf-netconf-subscribed-notifications/[10]
Subscription to YANG Datastores	https://datatracker.ietf.org/doc/draft-ietf-netconf-yang-push/[11]
Dynamic Subscription to YANG Events and Datastores over NETCONF	https://datatracker.ietf.org/doc/draft-ietf-netconf-netconf-event-notifications/[12]
Dynamic Subscription to YANG Events and Datastores over RESTCONF	https://datatracker.ietf.org/doc/draft-ietf-netconf-restconf-notif/[13]

There are more companion documents, but they require some more work before finalization. Among those documents, you already learned in this chapter about the UDP-based publication channel for streaming telemetry [https://tools.ietf.org/html/draft-ietf-netconf-udp-pub-channel].[7]

In Table 5-2, the main building block is the "Subscription to YANG Event Notifications" document. This document provides a superset of the subscription capabilities initially defined within "NETCONF Event Notifications" (RFC 5277), taking into account its limitations, as described in "Requirements for Subscription to YANG Datastores" (RFC 7923). It also specifies a transport-independent capability (remember, RFC 5277 is specific to NETCONF), a new data model, and a remote procedure call (RPC) operation to replace the operation "create-subscription," and it enables a single transport session to intermix notification messages and RPCs for different subscriptions. What is identical between the old and new specifications is the **<notification>** message and the contents of the "NETCONF" event stream. Note that a publisher may implement both specifications concurrently. Instead of going into the details of the specifications (for this, it would be best for the final RFC to be published), let's list the key capabilities, as taken from the "Subscription to YANG Event Notifications" document.

Subscription to YANG Event Notifications

"Various limitations in RFC 5277 are discussed in RFC 7923. Resolving these issues is the primary motivation for this work. Key capabilities supported by this document include:

- Multiple subscriptions on a single transport session
- Support for dynamic and configured subscriptions
- Modification of an existing subscription in progress
- Per-subscription operational counters
- Negotiation of subscription parameters (through the use of hints returned as part of declined subscription requests)
- Subscription state change notifications (e.g., publisher driven)
- Suspension, parameter modification
- Independence from transport"

At the minimum, from the same document, you must understand the following concepts.

Subscription to YANG Event Notifications

"Two types of subscriptions are supported:

1. Dynamic subscriptions, where a subscriber initiates a subscription negotiation with a publisher via an RPC. If the publisher is able to serve this request, it accepts it, and then starts pushing notification messages back to the subscriber. If the publisher is not able to serve it as requested, then an error response is returned. This response "MAY" include hints at subscription parameters that, had they been present, may have enabled the dynamic subscription request to be accepted.
2. Configured subscriptions, which allow the management of subscriptions via a configuration so that a publisher can send notification messages to a receiver. Support for configured subscriptions is optional, with its availability advertised via a YANG feature.

Additional characteristics differentiating configured from dynamic subscriptions include:

- The lifetime of a dynamic subscription is bound by the transport session used to establish it. For connection-oriented stateful transports like NETCONF, the loss of the transport session will result in the immediate termination of any associated dynamic subscriptions. For connectionless or stateless transports like HTTP, a lack of receipt acknowledgment of a sequential set of notification messages and/or keep-alives can be used to trigger a termination of a dynamic subscription. Contrast this to the lifetime of a configured subscription. This lifetime is driven by relevant configuration being present within the publisher's applied configuration. Being tied to configuration operations implies configured subscriptions can be configured to persist across reboots, and implies a configured subscription can persist even when its publisher is fully disconnected from any network.
- Configured subscriptions can be modified by any configuration client with write permission on the configuration of the subscription. Dynamic subscriptions can only be modified via an RPC request made by the original subscriber, or a change to configuration data referenced by the subscription."

Note that dynamic subscription was already discussed in the context of dial-in and dial-out mode, earlier in this chapter. In the IETF, even the dynamic subscriptions use the YANG model for configuration. This is a key difference with the OpenConfig dial-in feature, which doesn't require the openconfig-telemetry YANG model for configuration.

The second document in Table 5-2, "Subscription to YANG Datastores," specifies how subscriber applications may request a continuous, customized stream of updates from a YANG datastore (that is, a solution that provides a subscription service for updates from a datastore). Basically, this solution supports dynamic as well as configured subscriptions to updates of datastore nodes. It enhances the subscription model with selection filters that identify targeted YANG datastore nodes and/or datastore subtrees for which updates are to be pushed, with periodic and on-change update policies. It also specifies the encoding and a YANG model for the management of datastore push notifications.

The third document, "Dynamic subscription to YANG Events and Datastores over NETCONF," provides a NETCONF binding to the dynamic subscription capability of both subscribed notifications and YANG Push. Similarly, the fourth document, "Dynamic Subscription to YANG Events and Datastores over RESTCONF," provides the RESTCONF binding (that is, how to establish and maintain dynamic subscriptions over RESTCONF).

IETF YANG Push Versus OpenConfig: Some History

As displayed in Figure 5-5, it's interesting to observe how the industry subscription specification has progressed.

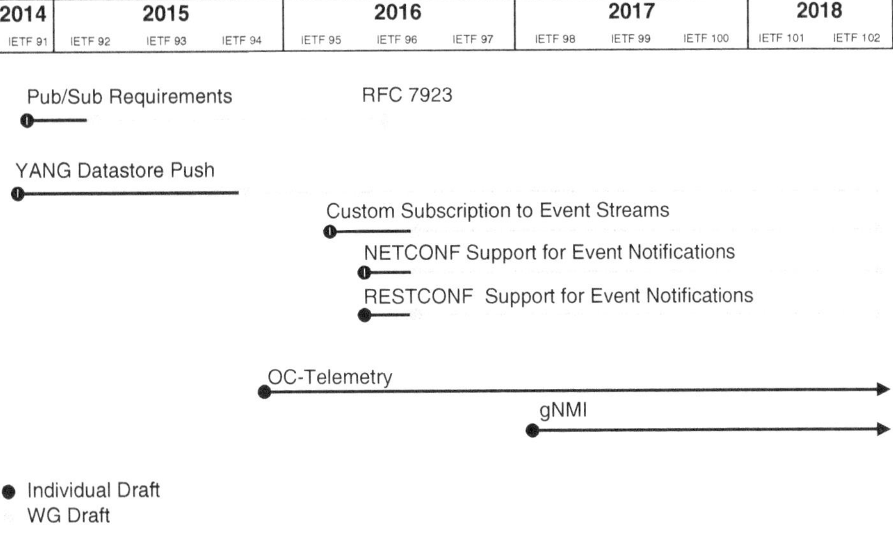

FIGURE 5-5 Industry Subscription Specification Progress

Not considering RFC 5277, "NETCONF Event Notifications" (from 2008), which was an early attempt at telemetry, focusing solely on NETCONF, the first observation from the figure is the IETF started to work on the new set of requirements and on the YANG Datastore Push in 2014, while at the same time, the OpenConfig consortium did not even mention telemetry. The OpenConfig Telemetry work started at the end of 2015, at the time when IETF was finalizing the pub/sub requirements and when the YANG Datastore Push became a working group document. Note that the OpenConfig telemetry YANG model [https://github.com/openconfig/public/blob/master/release/models/telemetry/openconfig-telemetry.yang][14] went through five revisions since its inception, integrating more and more of the features initially foreseen by the IETF specifications. Finally, gNMI, with its dial-in feature, was first specified in early 2017.

This OpenConfig step-by-step evolution, based on running code (while the IETF specifications are not yet finalized at the time of writing—but should be soon), might explain OpenConfig's success in terms of implementation by the different router vendors versus the IETF "YANG Push and Friends" telemetry. Undoubtedly, taking more than four years of work for IETF to standardize the requirements and YANG Push mechanisms is way too long, up to the point where the industry started to move away from the IETF regarding telemetry. The IETF solution thought about many concepts Day One: dynamic configuration with parameter negotiation, stop time configuration, replay, virtual routing and forwarding (VRF) support, multiple receivers, suspend and resume operations, filtering based on subtree/substring/range, quality of service, admission control, on-change and periodic, and so on. In the end, it doesn't matter that OpenConfig selected the most useful concepts from the IETF solution, up to the point where both the IETF and OpenConfig telemetries have some commonalities, as displayed by the Figure 5-6.

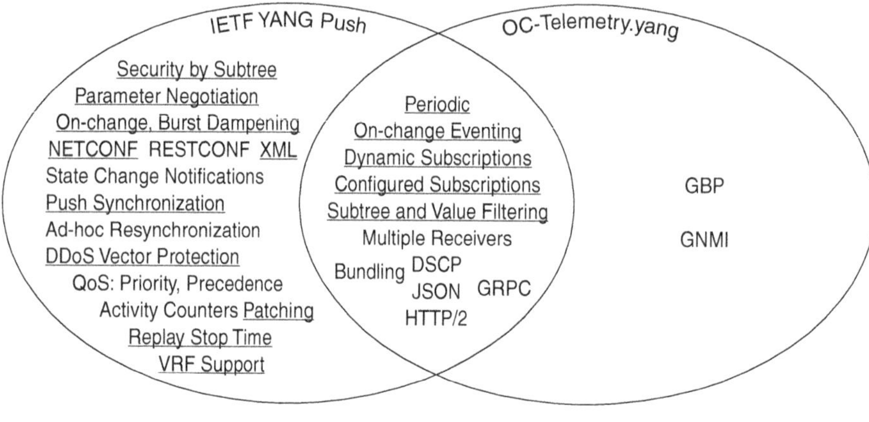

FIGURE 5-6 Requirement Coverage Between IETF YANG Push and OpenConfig Telemetry

OpenConfig Streaming Telemetry

As seen in Figure 5-4, the OpenConfig version comes in two flavors, or mainly in two evolutions: the OC telemetry and gNMI. The first one is the OpenConfig telemetry YANG module for telemetry configuration and monitoring on the publisher and the second one is gNMI [https://github.com/openconfig/gnmi][15] with the dial-in mode. As detailed in Chapter 4, gNMI is a protocol for configuration manipulation and state retrieval.

gNMI telemetry makes use of the SubscribeRequest (see Chapter 4's section titled "gNMI Subscribe-Request and Telemetry" or go directly the OpenConfig "Subscribing to Telemetry Updates" docu-mentation at https://github.com/openconfig/reference/blob/master/rpc/gnmi/gnmi-specification.md#35-subscribing-to-telemetry-updates).[16] Note that the OpenConfig telemetry YANG model is not required for dial-in mode: From the "user" perspective, the collector just dials in to the publisher and specifies the sensor path it wants to monitor.

Notice in Figure 5-3 the subtle difference between two encodings: JSON (IETF) and JSON (OpenConfig). gNMI supports the JSON encoding, as defined by the IETF in "JSON Encoding of Data Modeled with YANG" (RFC 7951). However, using that specification means the telemetry variables that are 64-bit integers become strings. A value of the "int64", "uint64", or "decimal64" type is represented as a JSON string whose content is the lexical representation of the corresponding YANG type, which is not ideal in collectors. The argument is that the encoding of values is best done using native types. OpenConfig adopted native protobuf encodings, with a mapping from the schema types if required, as indicated by "JSON (OpenConfig)" in Figure 5-3.

Interview with the Experts

Q&A with Alex Clemm

Alex Clemm is a distinguished engineer at Huawei's Future Networks and Innovation group in Santa Clara, California. He has been involved in networking software, distributed systems, and management technology throughout his career. He has provided technical leadership for many products, from conception to customer delivery, most recently in the areas of high-precision networks and future networking services as well as network analytics, intent, and telemetry. He has served on the Organizing and Technical Program Committees of many management and network softwarization conferences, most recently as technical program chair of IEEE NetSoft 2017 and IFIP/IEEE IM 2019. He has around 50 publications and 50 issued patents. He has also authored several books (including *Network Management Fundamentals*) and RFCs. Alex holds an MS degree in computer science from Stanford University and a Ph.D. from the University of Munich, Germany.

Question:

Can you stress the importance of telemetry in automation?

Answer:

Telemetry provides users and applications with visibility into the network. It allows users to analyze what is going on in the network, to assess the network's health, to see if there is anything unusual going on that would demand attention. For example, telemetry data allows you to detect when things are trending in certain ways, perhaps pointing to deteriorating conditions of some sort or to conditions that are somehow out of the ordinary, which might point to other problems such as an attack on the network. The actual analysis is generally up to an experienced end user or, more commonly these days, a smart analytics application. However, the fuel for this analysis is telemetry. It provides the underlying data to act on.

Telemetry is important for automation in several ways. For one, it lets you automate actions in response to certain conditions—for example, when it appears that a problem is building up and some configuration adjustments or tuning of parameters is needed. In that sense, telemetry data in effect provides the trigger for automated actions. Second, telemetry data lets you assess whether actions are having the desired effect. Smart automation typically involves control loops, in which some condition that may be rooted in the observation of telemetry data triggers an action, whose effects are then monitored for conditions that may subsequently trigger further actions. Whenever you have smart automation that involves control loops, telemetry becomes an important part of the equation.

Question:

What is the connection between telemetry and configuration?

Answer:

Telemetry first and foremost concerns operational data that is discovered from the network—things like health information, utilization data, interface statistics, and queue states, those sort of things. In general, it does not concern configuration data, as that data is controlled by the user and does not need to be "found out." However, there is still a connection with configuration at several levels.

For one, users may be interested in assessing whether configuration actions are having the desired effect on the network. Telemetry is an important key to answering those questions. For example, a configuration action might affect the location of a performance bottleneck; it might change the balance of interface utilization; it might change how certain flows are routed and what packets are dropped. All of these effects can be analyzed by inspecting telemetry data.

Second, under certain circumstances it can be of interest to also include configuration data as part of telemetry. This is the case in scenarios where configuration data can change unexpectedly and dynamically—for example, in the case of virtualized resources and multiple orchestrators. It can also help to consolidate configuration and operational data for certain machine-learning scenarios, particularly when analysis of data in the context of specific configurations is involved.

Finally, it should be pointed out that telemetry itself needs to be configured—not just the collection of telemetry data from the device but the generation of telemetry data by the device. Telemetry imposes significant load on the device; therefore, what telemetry data to generate and how much of it becomes an important configuration decision. While telemetry itself is streamed to the outside client, internal registers and state may need to be polled. Telemetry data also needs to be encoded and exported, which can become an important factor as the volume of the data can easily get very large. It is one thing to export selected interface statistics once a minute or so, but trying to take a complete dump of device state every millisecond may not be feasible. Therefore, users and applications need to carefully weigh what telemetry data is actually required and determine the point where the benefit of obtaining more fine-grained telemetry outweighs the cost of generating it and collecting it. In addition, the relevance of data may vary. For example, some data may be of interest only under certain conditions, such as when a "hot spot" needs to be analyzed. All this requires the ability to dynamically configure, and reconfigure, the generation of telemetry.

Question:

Can you describe your telemetry work at the IETF? How does it compare to the OpenConfig streaming telemetry?

Answer:

In the IETF, I am working on the YANG Push suite of Internet drafts. This work actually involves many people, including Eric Voit, Balazs Lengyel, Reshad Rahman, Henk Birkholz, Andy Bierman, Alberto Gonzalez Prieto, Walker Zheng, Tianran Zhou, to name just a few. YANG Push started out as a single draft that specified a means to let NETCONF clients subscribe to YANG datastore updates without needing to poll, supporting two subscription models: periodic and on-change. At this point, the work has proliferated into several drafts in order to generalize the mechanism provided and make them reusable. Specifically, the mechanism for subscriptions to notifications has been separated out from the more specific mechanism to subscribe to datastore updates. Also, the mechanism to deliver updates has been separated from the subscription mechanism itself. NETCONF and RESTCONF can both be used, and the architectural model allows you to plug in other transports as well.

Prior to the work on YANG Push, NETCONF, RESTCONF, and YANG had focused mostly on the needs of applications related to fulfillment. It basically centered around the problem of automating device configuration and obviating the need for CLI-based configuration files. While YANG did allow for the definition of non-configuration data, applications related to service assurance were clearly an afterthought. With YANG Push, we set out to change that and address the need of applications related to service assurance. Those applications heavily rely on telemetry data, which using plain NETCONF or RESTCONF would basically have required polling. The need to poll has led to many problems with other technologies in the past, most notably SNMP. This includes the fact that polling introduces a lot of avoidable load that impacts scalability, as well as problems with regard to reliability and precise synchronization of polling intervals required to make data more comparable and useful. It was clear that something better would be needed for the next generation of management technology. Given the proliferation of YANG, it was also important to choose an approach that would integrate with, build on, and extend the existing NETCONF/RESTCONF/YANG architecture.

YANG Push actually predates OpenConfig streaming telemetry. The fact that it has taken a long time to standardize is a testament to the fact that the IETF standardization process unfortunately does not always move as quickly as we would like. That said, there are various detail differences. Most obviously, YANG Push focuses on operating with IETF's NETCONF/RESTCONF/YANG framework, offering support for NETCONF and RESTCONF both for control of subscriptions and for delivery of updates, whereas OpenConfig leverages non-IETF, Google-owned technologies such as Google Protocol Buffers and Google RPC. In addition, as it is not primarily focused on data center management, YANG Push is more feature rich and offers additional capabilities, such as the ability to negotiate subscription parameters, the prioritization of subscriptions, push synchronization, and VRF support.

Question:

Telemetry is still evolving in the industry. What do we still need to accomplish?

Answer:

It is only the first phase of telemetry that is coming to a conclusion as we are wrapping up standardization.

Of the things that come next, perhaps the most relevant involves making telemetry "smarter" and more actionable. Instead of simply generating huge volumes of telemetry data and exporting it for external analysis, some of that analysis can occur right at the source. As a result, the volume of data that needs to be exported, collected, and analyzed can get greatly reduced. This lowers cost, simplifies operations, and reduces reaction time.

For example, one next step involves the ability to define smart filters. Instead of simply exporting any and all data, a simple smart filter would allow exporting data only when its value crosses a threshold. Similarly, another smart filter would allow exporting data only when a high-water mark has been breached (such as maximum utilization within the past 10 minutes per a rolling window), or when the data represents a local maximum within the devices (such as the currently most utilized interface). Further down the road it's conceivable to add the ability to aggregate raw data, for example, to provide medians, percentiles, and distributions of parameter ranges, or to plug in anomaly detection modules that notify clients when telemetry data is outside "normal" operating ranges. Many of those capabilities may not be standardized but become competitive differentiators. However, it is important that telemetry frameworks can be extended in ways to accommodate such functionality. Ultimately, all this will allow for smarter embedded automation, control loops, and intelligence at the network edge.

Summary

Two important telemetry terms are used in this chapter:

- *Telemetry* (also known as data model–driven telemetry, model-driven telemetry, and streaming telemetry). By default, telemetry deals with operational information. Therefore, it could be called operational telemetry, even if nobody uses that term in the industry. Network and operations engineers speak of just telemetry.
- *Business telemetry* refers the use of telemetry to stream information useful for business developments. When business developers, (senior) vice presidents, and top execs speak of telemetry, they actually mean business telemetry.

In this chapter, you learned about the telemetry concepts and the different telemetry mechanisms. As (model-driven) telemetry is still an evolving field in the industry, Figure 5-3 offers a quick way to navigate through the different telemetry options by taking a couple of questions/points into consideration.

References in This Chapter

To further extend your knowledge, here are a few of references in Table 5-3.

TABLE 5-3 Telemetry-Related Pointers

Topic	Content
Model-Driven Telemetry	https://www.cisco.com/c/en/us/solutions/service-provider/cloud-scale-networking-solutions/model-driven-telemetry.html
	Beginner, intermediate, and expert content related to model-driven telemetry on Cisco's website.
The Limits of SNMP	https://blogs.cisco.com/sp/thelimits-of-snmp]
	Shelly Cadora, in her blog, explains why SNMP is not suitable for telemetry.
gNMI	https://github.com/openconfig/gnmi
	gRPC Network Management Interface
gNMI Telemetry	https://github.com/openconfig/reference/blob/master/rpc/gnmi/gnmi-specification.md#35-subscribing-totelemetry-updates
	gNMI Telemetry Specifications
RFC 7923	http://tools.ietf.org/html/rfc7923
	"Requirements for Subscription to YANG Datastores."
Four IETF soon-to-be-published RFCs	See Table 5-2.

Endnotes

1. https://blogs.cisco.com/sp/the-limits-of-snmp
2. https://bgp.potaroo.net/
3. https://www.yangcatalog.org/yang-search/
4. https://www.yangcatalog.org/yang-search/module_details/?module=ietf-interfaces
5. https://www.yangcatalog.org/yang-search/module_details/?module=openconfig-interfaces
6. https://github.com/cisco-ie/tdm
7. https://tools.ietf.org/html/draft-ietf-netconf-udp-pub-channel
8. https://github.com/YangModels/yang/blob/master/vendor/cisco/xr/651/Cisco-IOS-XR-types.yang
9. https://github.com/YangModels/yang/tree/master/vendor/cisco/xr/651

10. https://datatracker.ietf.org/doc/draft-ietf-netconf-subscribed-notifications/
11. https://datatracker.ietf.org/doc/draft-ietf-netconf-yang-push/
12. https://datatracker.ietf.org/doc/draft-ietf-netconf-netconf-event-notifications/
13. https://datatracker.ietf.org/doc/draft-ietf-netconf-restconf-notif/
14. https://github.com/openconfig/public/blob/master/release/models/telemetry/openconfig-telemetry.yang
15. https://github.com/openconfig/gnmi
16. https://github.com/openconfig/reference/blob/master/rpc/gnmi/gnmi-specification.md#35-subscribing-to-telemetry-updates

Chapter 6

YANG Data Modeling Developments in the Industry

This chapter covers

- The industry "groups" that develop the different data model–driven management components
- The "groups" that specify the YANG data models
- How the industry collaborates… or overlaps
- Where to find the YANG models: GitHub repositories and the YANG Catalog
- Interoperability testing

Introduction

This chapter analyzes the current state of affairs of YANG in the industry, how the industry organizes itself, and who the key players involved are.

Because automation based on data model–driven management is a priority in the industry today, and because multiple "groups" are involved, the landscape keeps evolving. Those "groups" consist of standards-development organizations (SDOs), consortiums, forums, open source projects, and even networking equipment vendors with their native/proprietary models. We have attempted to keep a chronological order, whenever possible, to help you understand how the industry has evolved.

The Beginning: The IETF

As you know from the previous chapters, the Internet Engineering Task Force (IETF) specified the Network Configuration Protocol (NETCONF), then the RESTCONF protocol. Starting with the NETMOD IETF working group, the IETF started to specify some standard models. To provide you a look back in history, Figure 6-1 presents the key data model–driven RFCs.

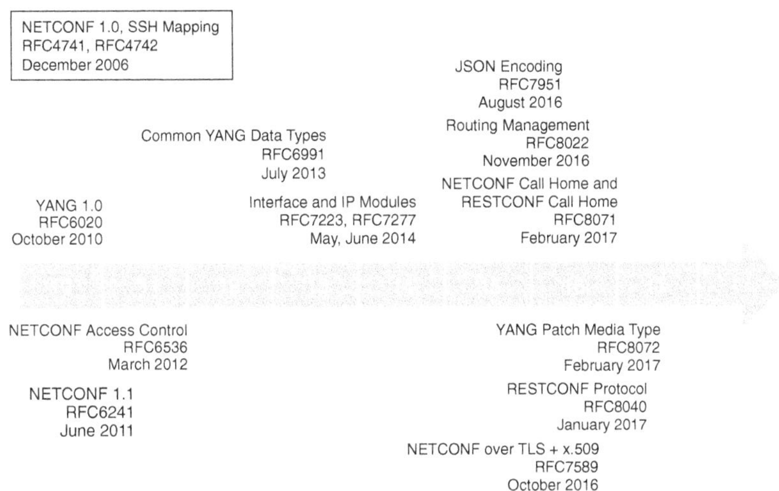

FIGURE 6-1 Timeline for Key Data Model–Driven RFCs

Once YANG knowledge spread out throughout the IETF, each working group became responsible for the specifications of the YANG module for their specific technologies, which certainly makes sense. As an example, the segment routing experts in the IETF Source Packet Routing in Networking (SPRING) working group[1] are the right persons to describe how to manage a segment routing network. With the help of the YANG Doctors[2]—a group of YANG experts at the IETF in charge of reviewing every YANG module before ratification for correctness, ease of use, and consistency—the IETF produced many YANG module specifications. At the time of writing, more than 85 YANG modules are standardized, as displayed in Figure 6-2 (source: http://www.claise.be/IETFYANGOutOfRFC.png).[3] Note that many, if not all, reports, graphs, and figures initially created on http://www.claise.be[4] are being migrated to the yangcatalog.org[5] website.

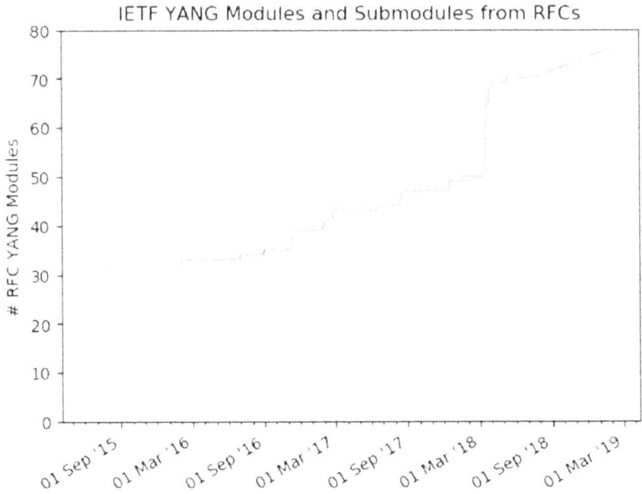

FIGURE 6-2 IETF YANG Modules and Submodules from RFCs

Table 6-1 (source: http://www.claise.be/IETFYANGOutOfRFC.html)[6] contains all the YANG modules produced in RFCs. From the YANG module names themselves, you can already guess the content. Note also that some YANG modules have multiple versions, meaning that they were updated (for example, ietf-interfaces@2015-05-08.yang and ietf-interfaces@2018-02-20.yang). In this particular case, the latter version offers Network Management Datastore Architecture (NMDA) compliance.

TABLE 6-1 IETF YANG Modules and Submodules from RFCs

YANG Module (and Submodule)	RFC	YANG Module (and Submodule)	RFC
iana-crypt-hash@2014-08-06.yang[7]	RFC 7317	ietf-netconf-partial-lock@2009-10-19.yang	RFC 5717
iana-hardware@2018-03-13.yang[8]	RFC 8348	ietf-netconf-time@2016-01-26.yang	RFC 7758
iana-if-type@2014-05-08.yang	RFC 7224	ietf-netconf-with-defaults@2011-06-01.yang	RFC 6243
iana-routing-types@2017-12-04.yang	RFC 8294	ietf-netconf@2011-06-01.yang	RFC 6241
ietf-complex-types@2011-03-15.yang	RFC 6095	ietf-network-state@2018-02-26.yang	RFC 8345
ietf-datastores@2018-02-14.yang	RFC 8342	ietf-network-topology-state@2018-02-26.yang	RFC 8345
ietf-dslite@2019-01-10.yang	RFC 8313	ietf-network-topology@2018-02-26.yang	RFC 8345
ietf-foo@2016-03-20.yang	RFC 8407	ietf-network@2018-02-26.yang	RFC 8345
ietf-hardware-state@2018-03-13.yang	RFC 8348	ietf-origin@2018-02-14.yang	RFC 8342
ietf-hardware@2018-03-13.yang	RFC 8348	ietf-restconf-monitoring@2017-01-26.yang	RFC 8040
ietf-i2rs-rib@2018-09-13.yang	RFC 8431	ietf-restconf@2017-01-26.yang	RFC 8040
ietf-inet-types@2010-09-24.yang	RFC 6021	ietf-routing-types@2017-12-04.yang	RFC 8294
ietf-inet-types@2013-07-15.yang	RFC 6991	ietf-routing@2016-11-04.yang	RFC 8022
ietf-interfaces@2014-05-08.yang	RFC 7223	ietf-routing@2018-03-13.yang	RFC 8349
ietf-interfaces@2018-02-20.yang	RFC 8343	ietf-snmp-common@2014-12-10.yang	RFC 7407
ietf-ip@2014-06-16.yang	RFC 7277	ietf-snmp-community@2014-12-10.yang	RFC 7407
ietf-ip@2018-02-22.yang	RFC 8344	ietf-snmp-engine@2014-12-10.yang	RFC 7407
ietf-ipfix-psamp@2012-09-05.yang	RFC 6728	ietf-snmp-notification@2014-12-10.yang	RFC 7407
ietf-ipv4-unicast-routing@2016-11-04.yang	RFC 8022	ietf-snmp-proxy@2014-12-10.yang	RFC 7407
ietf-ipv4-unicast-routing@2018-03-13.yang	RFC 8349	ietf-snmp-ssh@2014-12-10.yang	RFC 7407

YANG Module (and Submodule)	RFC	YANG Module (and Submodule)	RFC
ietf-ipv6-router-advertisements@2016-11-04.yang	RFC 8022	ietf-snmp-target@2014-12-10.yang	RFC 7407
ietf-ipv6-router-advertisements@2018-03-13.yang	RFC 8349	ietf-snmp-tls@2014-12-10.yang	RFC 7407
ietf-ipv6-unicast-routing@2016-11-04.yang	RFC 8022	ietf-snmp-tsm@2014-12-10.yang	RFC 7407
ietf-ipv6-unicast-routing@2018-03-13.yang	RFC 8349	ietf-snmp-usm@2014-12-10.yang	RFC 7407
ietf-key-chain@2017-06-15.yang	RFC 8177	ietf-snmp-vacm@2014-12-10.yang	RFC 7407
ietf-l2vpn-svc@2018-10-09.yang	RFC 8466	ietf-snmp@2014-12-10.yang	RFC 7407
ietf-l3-unicast-topology-state@2018-02-26.yang	RFC 8346	ietf-system@2014-08-06.yang	RFC 7317
ietf-l3-unicast-topology@2018-02-26.yang	RFC 8346	ietf-template@2010-05-18.yang	RFC 6087
ietf-l3vpn-svc@2017-01-27.yang	RFC 8049	ietf-template@2016-03-20.yang	RFC 8407
ietf-l3vpn-svc@2018-01-19.yang	RFC 8299	ietf-voucher@2018-05-09.yang	RFC 8366
ietf-lmap-common@2017-08-08.yang	RFC 8194	ietf-vrrp@2018-03-13.yang	RFC 8347
ietf-lmap-control@2017-08-08.yang	RFC 8194	ietf-x509-cert-to-name@2014-12-10.yang	RFC 7407
ietf-lmap-report@2017-08-08.yang	RFC 8194	ietf-yang-library@2016-06-21.yang	RFC 7895
ietf-nat@2019-01-10.yang	RFC 8512	ietf-yang-metadata@2016-08-05.yang	RFC 7952
ietf-netconf-acm@2012-02-22.yang	RFC 6536	ietf-yang-patch@2017-02-22.yang	RFC 8072
ietf-netconf-acm@2018-02-14.yang	RFC 8341	ietf-yang-smiv2@2012-06-22.yang	RFC 6643
ietf-netconf-monitoring@2010-10-04.yang	RFC 6022	ietf-yang-types@2010-09-24.yang	RFC 6021
ietf-netconf-notifications@2012-02-06.yang	RFC 6470	ietf-yang-types@2013-07-15.yang	RFC 6991

In order to help with the YANG module development, and in particular with the validation, all YANG modules are extracted from IETF drafts thanks to xym,[9] (eXtract Yang Module), a tool initially developed by Jan Medved and then improved by Einar Nilsen-Nygaard. From there, the modules are run through four validators (pyang, yanglint, confdc, and yangdump-pro). All validation errors and warnings are analyzed and provided to the authors, via web reports on the same website.

The top line in Figure 6-3 (source: http://claise.be/IETFYANGPageCompilation.png)[10] shows the constant increase of YANG modules in IETF drafts, even if some are now published in RFCs, at which point the related IETF drafts disappear. The middle line in Figure 6-3 shows the increase in YANG modules passing validation, implying that the YANG knowledge spread throughout the industry, while the bottom line shows the number of YANG modules facing a validator warning and no errors. xym and the YANG validators are discussed in more detail in Chapter 7, "Automation Is as Good as the Data Models, Their Related Metadata, and the Tools: For the Network Architect and Operator."

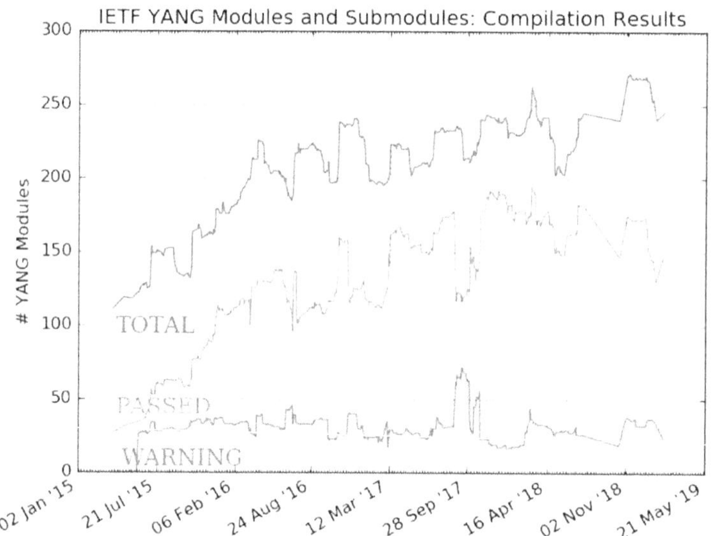

FIGURE 6-3 IETF YANG Modules and Submodules Extracted from IETF Drafts: Validation Results

The spikes in the graph are due to a combination of draft publication deadlines, draft expirations, validator improvements (as you learned about YANG, the validators improved along the way), or simply drafts becoming RFCs.

Probably the biggest issue in developing those technology-specific YANG modules is the interconnection between all these modules. Indeed, in order to create services based on those technologies, the YANG modules must work together. This explains the dependencies between them as well as the ripple effect of modifying one of the core modules.

During one of the early IETF hackathons, Jan Medved developed the symd.py[11] tool, which generates a variety of YANG module dependency graphs and output suitable for visualization with D3.js[12] tools. A typical example is shown in Figure 6-4 (source: http://www.claise.be/ietf-routing.png).[13] This example illustrates the importance of the ietf-routing YANG module, as it is imported by many other YANG modules. This ietf-routing YANG module is represented as squares, as it is now published as RFC 8022, as opposed to circles, which indicate IETF drafts. The symd.py tool was later improved by Einar Nilsen-Nygaard and then by Hari Ananthakrishnan. Hari added an extra option to contact all authors of dependent YANG models, with the message, "new imported YANG model updated, please update yours." This feature is especially important for the import-by-revision YANG feature because when the imported module is updated, all dependent YANG modules must be updated.

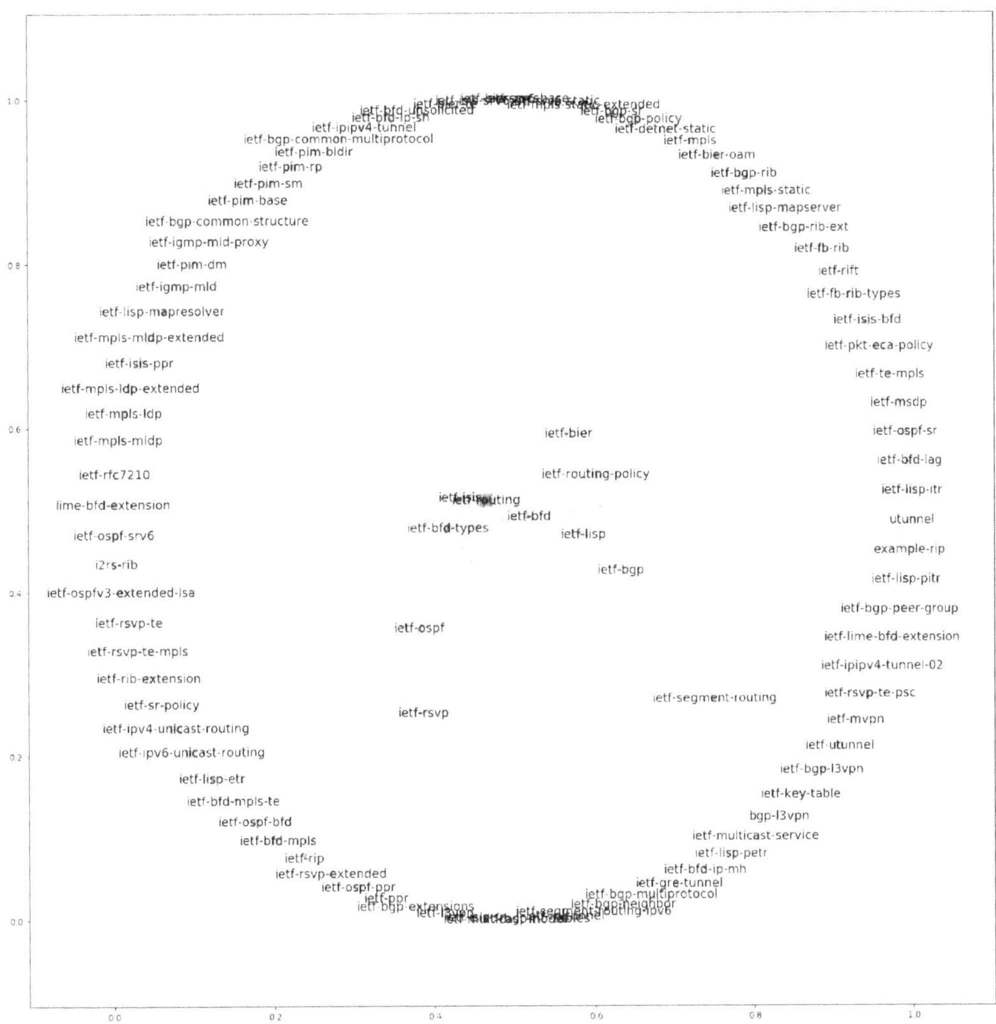

FIGURE 6-4 ietf-routing Dependency Graph

During the IETF 97 Hackathon, Joe Clarke created an interesting visual dependency tool[14] based on the output of symd. Whereas the symd output was either purely textual or static pictures, this tool has more functionalities:

- The ability to display the IETF draft or RFC from which the YANG module is extracted by moving the mouse over the YANG module
- The ability to move the YANG modules around (for example, to group the YANG modules stemming from the same document)
- The ability to discover the next YANG module the community should focus on (the bottleneck is highlighted with a black circle)

For completeness, the same ietf-routing YANG module with the visual dependency tool is displayed in Figure 6-5 (source https://www.yangcatalog.org/yang-search/impact_analysis/?modtags=ietf-routing&orgtags=&recursion=0&show_rfcs=1&show_subm=1&show_dir=both).

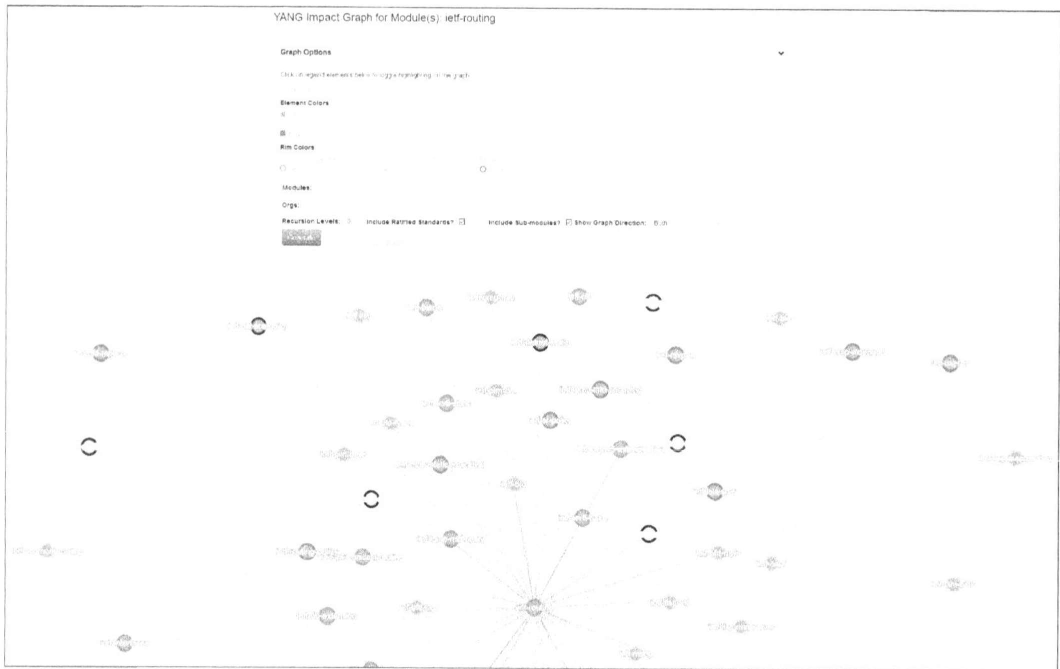

FIGURE 6-5 ietf-routing Dependency Graph in the Visual Dependency Tool

Years ago, by looking at the IETF dependency graph (which shows how all YANG modules extracted from RFCs and drafts depend on each other), the community realized the complexity of producing all those YANG modules. All modules are required at the same time, and they must all work with each other. The goal is certainly not to be able to read all entries in Figure 6-6, but to illustrate the problem of complexity from a high level.

Finally, for the IETF, there are blogs focusing on the current state of affairs of YANG data models in the industry (for example, "YANG Data Models in the Industry: Current State of Affairs,"[15] on the claise.be website).

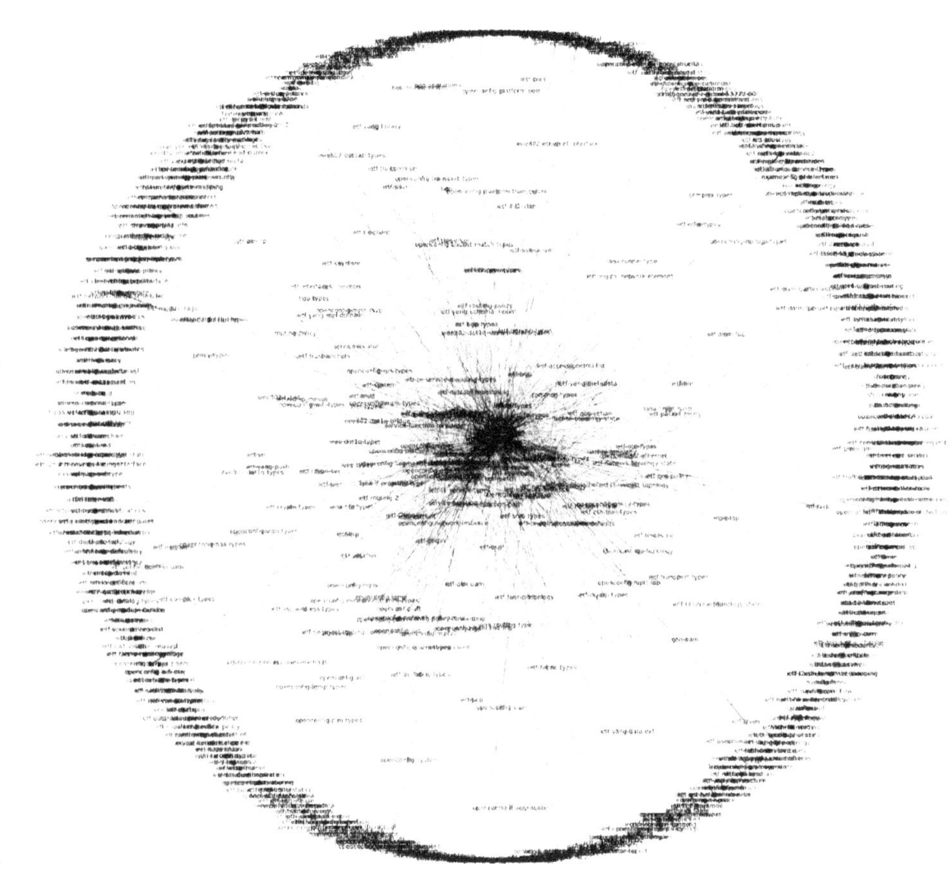

FIGURE 6-6 All IETF YANG Modules Dependency Graph

Embracing YANG Throughout the Industry

This section covers the history, in a more or less chronological order, behind an entire industry embracing YANG. Doing so, it explains how the different "groups" have been developing their YANG models for the respective technologies. The intention is to stress that the YANG data modeling language starts to cover many different areas in the industry, by listing the different technologies and use cases. However, there is no intention to start explaining all the references. The authors intentionally confined the scope of this chapter to provide pointers. We understand that reading all those references might be disconcerting, if this is not your field of interest.

The OpenDaylight[16] controller project was one of the early YANG adopters. It's an open source project formed under the Linux Foundation with the goal of furthering the adoption and innovation of software-defined networking (SDN) through the creation of a common vendor-supported framework. Its architecture is based on Model-Driven Service Adaptation Layer (MD-SAL), a set of infrastructure services aimed at providing common and generic support to application and plug-in developers. The MD-SAL approach, entirely based on YANG models, provides service abstraction to unify the northbound and southbound APIs of the SDN controller, but also provides the data structures used in various services and components of an SDN controller itself.

The OpenDaylight MD-SAL documentation, https://wiki.opendaylight.org/view/OpenDaylight_Controller:MD-SAL:Explained, mentions:

OpenDaylight MD-SAL Documentation

In our previous attempts at programmable systems, we have seen an attempt to abstract the entire system out. While this works when the technology set is known beforehand, failure to account for a technology typically incurs either a major slowdown while the technology is retrofitted into the existing APIs, or a fork of those APIs with the need to reintegrate. In both cases the progress becomes limited by the throughput of a single team which maintains the abstraction APIs, as that team needs to have a domain expert in the technology being integrated to ensure the abstractions and interactions are cohesive and do the right thing from both the technology and the API style perspective.

MD-SAL grew out of the realization that this extensibility problem should not exist, as anyone should be able to at least prototype their APIs and the "SAL" layer should just work, even if the prototype code will remain an island within the larger system.

During early evaluation we came across YANG as an emerging standard in the area of network element management and it proved to be a very sound base for the use cases we were able to throw at it. Some of the key features considered important were:

- Decentralized extension mechanism ("augment")
- Data vs. document structure validation ("when")
- Extensible language ("extension")
- Pre-composed objects ("grouping")
- Extensible data type hierarchy
- Inclusion of basic interactions (RPC and notification)
- Existing tools and community (yang-central, NETCONF/NETMOD IETF WGs, etc.)

As proof of early YANG adoption, the OpenDaylight Lithium release in June 2015 already included more than 480 YANG modules—and that number kept growing with the most recent releases. The next two releases, Beryllium (Feb 2016) and Boron (Nov 2016), included 703 and 857 YANG modules, respectively.

Then the Broadband Forum (BBF),[17] a nonprofit consortium focusing on the development of broadband specifications, adopted YANG as the data modeling language for the access network (not, for example, for the home, which is covered by TR-069 and its successor User Services Platform [USP]). At the time of writing, more than 200 BBF YANG (sub)modules cover technologies such as Ethernet, fiber, Digital Subscriber Line (DSL), Very-high-bit-rate DSL (VDSL), Fiber to the Distribution Point (FTTdP), PPPoE, Passive Optical Networking (PON), and more, as well as common YANG modules for interfaces, subinterfaces, subscribers, types, and quality of service (QoS).

BBF realized very early that it did not make sense to reinvent the wheel. Wherever possible and practicable, the BBF modules leveraged and extend modules from other SDOs; for example, some BBF modules import the IETF interface's YANG module. Therefore, even though the "work in progress" in BBF is only available to BBF members, an exception was made for the YANG modules, which were posted in GitHub (https://github.com/YangModels/yang,[18] under "draft"). This way, the toolchain in place for the IETF also benefits BBF.

MEF Forum[19] also started to develop YANG modules. Formerly known as Metro Ethernet Forum, MEF is no longer focusing only on Carrier Ethernet; its mission is to enable the development and worldwide adoption of agile, assured, and orchestrated network services.

Its scope is all connectivity services, but primarily focusing on the product and service layers (as opposed to network devices). As such, MEF Forum focuses on the service's YANG modules. Very early in the process, MEF Forum created MEF 38, "Service Operations, Administration, and Maintenance (OAM) Fault Monitoring," and MEF 39 is "Service OAM Performance Measurement" (G.8013/Y.1731 PM). Then it focused on the following:

- Carrier Ethernet services, i.e. API from business apps to service orchestrator ("legato"), for EVC-based services as defined in "MEF 10.3" [https://www.mef.net/Assets/Technical_Specifications/PDF/MEF_10.3.pdf][20] and OVC-based services as defined in "MEF 26.2" [https://www.mef.net/Assets/Technical_Specifications/PDF/MEF_26.2.pdf][21]
- Network Resource Provisioning, i.e. API from Service Orchestrator to Domain Controller ("presto")
- YANG for IP Services expected to eventually augment the IETF L3SM model
- YANG models for SD-WAN services, based on the SD-WAN services definition specification, targeted for completion in early 2019.

NOTE

More YANG models are expected for legato and presto APIs for other technologies (IP and optical) and other operations (service assurance, performance reporting, and so on). YANG for inter-provider APIs is also expected.

Another SDO, the Institute of Electrical and Electronics Engineers (IEEE),[22] which historically has specified MIB modules, even for configuration, started to develop YANG for its set of technologies. The IEEE 802.1 working group, dealing with local area networks (LANs) and metropolitan area networks (MANs), published its first YANG-based standard in June of 2018: A YANG model for 802.1Q bridging (802.1Qcp), i.e. Customer VLAN bridges, Provider bridges, and Two-Port MAC relays. There is also some work in progress in 802.1, related to 802.1Xck, Port-Based Network Access Control YANG model, close to being published as a standard:

- 802.1Qcx. CFM (Continuity Fault Management OAM protocol).
- 802.1Qcw. YANG data models related to TSN (Time sensitive networking).
- 802.1CBcv FRER (Frame Replication and Elimination for Reliability). Project just started, related to TSN.
- 802.1AX. Link aggregation. Some discussion about producing a related YANG model.

The 802.3 working group, which focuses on the physical layer and data link layer's Media Access Control (MAC) of wired Ethernet, is busy working on an Ethernet YANG covering Ethernet interfaces, Link OAM, Ethernet PON and Power over Ethernet (in 802.3cf). For years now, there was a close collaboration between the IEEE and IETF, focusing on the transition from MIB to YANG in the IEEE. Stemming from this effort, the IEEE created the YANGsters, the IEEE 802 YANG editors' coordination group. This group is responsible for discussing common practice for YANG models supporting IEEE 802 protocols. This common practice includes, but is not limited to, Universal Resource Name (URN) root, a common approach to style and layout for consistency in 802, tooling, and process. While the primary attendees are expected to be editors of existing IEEE 802 YANG projects, other experts interested in YANG are welcome.

Exactly like the IETF and BBF, both the MEF Forum and the IEEE posted their YANG modules in GitHub (https://github.com/YangModels/yang).[18] This GitHub repository has evolved into a place where most YANG modules throughout the industry are posted: for specifications (ratified standards), for work in progress (drafts), and even for vendor-specific modules. As those modules depend on each other, having a single location with one set of toolchains makes a lot of sense. Reports containing the validation results and the statistics of all public industry efforts are reported at http://www.claise.be/2018/06/ietf-yang-modules-statistiques/.[4]

Some other "groups" that joined the YANG community include the following:

- The Distributed Management (DMTF) task force considered YANG in their Redfish project,[23] a RESTful interface utilizing JavaScript Object Notation (JSON) and OData, with the goal of addressing all the components in a data center with a consistent API. Basically, the Redfish project wants to use the networking YANG models developed by the IETF, convert them to Common Schema Definition Language (CSDL, a JSON encoding of OData, which is an OASIS standard) in order to have JSON schemas and provide access to the switches with a Redfish interface.

- The Open Source Sysrepo project, a YANG-based[24] configuration and operational datastore for Unix/Linux applications, typically home gateways. Applications can use sysrepo to store their YANG-modeled configuration instead of using flat configuration files. Sysrepo ensures data consistency of the data stored in the datastore and enforces data constraints defined by the YANG model. With the help of the Netopeer 2 NETCONF server, the applications also automatically become remotely manageable via NETCONF.
- The ITU Telecommunication Standardization Sector (ITU-T)[25] started developing their first YANG model for Ethernet ring protection.
- The Open ROADM Multi-Source Agreement (MSA)[26] defines interoperability specifications for Reconfigurable Optical Add/Drop Multiplexers (ROADM). Included are the ROADM switch as well as transponders and pluggable optics. Specifications consist of both optical interoperability as well as YANG data models. The GitHub location for the YANG module is https://github.com/OpenROADM/OpenROADM_MSA_Public.
- FD.io, a vector packet processing technology. The "Honeycomb" agent exposes YANG models for VPP functionality via NETCONF and RESTCONF. A controller that supports NETCONF/YANG, such as OpenDaylight, can "mount" the Honeycomb management agent.
- xRAN was formed to develop, standardize, and promote a multivendor, extensible "lower-layer split" Radio Access Network (xRAN) architecture. It has standardized the interfaces between critical elements of the xRAN architecture, specifically between the remote "radio unit" and the centralized "lower-layer-split central unit." From a management plane perspective, xRAN has defined the use of IETF's NETCONF/YANG standard for programmatically configuring and managing its lower-layer split RAN architecture.
- The 3rd Generation Partnership Project (3GPP) produces the reports and specifications that define 3GPP technologies. Lately, it also focuses on producing YANG modules: 3GPP has active work items to define YANG models for the Network Resource Model (NRM), Network Slicing, and NR RAN (Radio Access Network). A "3GPP YANG solution set style guide" is also in the works.
- European Telecommunication Standards Institute (ETSI) Network Functions Virtualization (NFV) is the home for the Industry Specification Group for NFV. Its publications provide detailed specifications (Release 2 and Release 3) and early proof of concepts (PoCs). As part of those specifications, ETSI has published a set of information models that define the Virtual Network Function Descriptor (VNFD) in ETSI NFV IFA 011[27] and Network Services Descriptor (NSD) in ETSI NFV-IFA 014.[28] The solutions Working Group within ETSI took up the task of defining data models for these information models. One of those tasks is defining a YANG model for the two information models. An early draft is available today, with the final standard being available by 2019.

Figure 6-7 shows some of the different open source projects and SDOs involved in YANG, mapping them based on the hierarchy of infrastructure, management and control, and services (svcs).

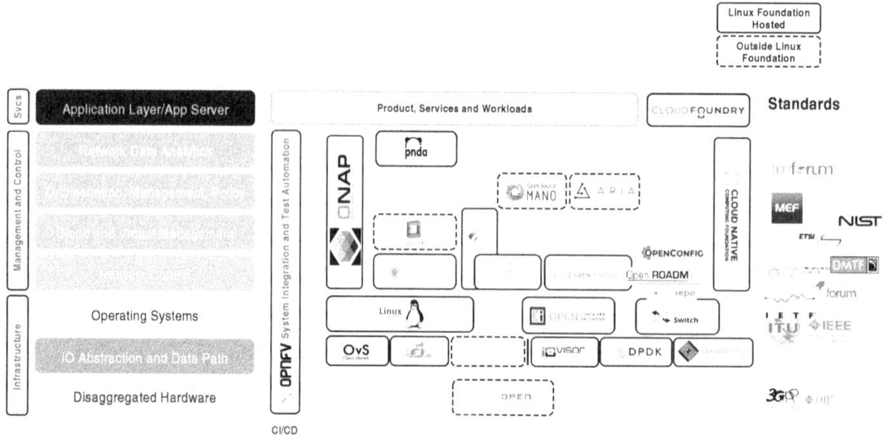

FIGURE 6-7 Open Source and SDOs Landscape

The OpenConfig YANG Model

From the previous section, there is clearly one key "group" missing from the list: OpenConfig. In regard to its importance today, OpenConfig deserves its own section in this chapter, even though Chapter 2, "Data Model–Driven Management," covers it briefly.

OpenConfig is an informal working group of network operators, let by Google, sharing the goal of moving networks toward a more dynamic, programmable infrastructure by adopting software-defined networking principles such as declarative configuration and model-driven management and operations.

Although the IETF started to specify some YANG modules earlier, the OpenConfig effort stemmed from a certain frustration that those YANG modules were not being produced fast enough. This was certainly reinforced by the strict IETF adherence to the YANG specifications, which dictate that a new YANG module version can only introduce backward-compatible changes. The OpenConfig consortium is hard at work defining standard YANG models for a variety of technologies. Since the OpenConfig consortium members are not equipment manufacturers, the models will contain the features the network operators are actually interested in, modeled in a way that is a little removed from the actual implementation. This is a great starting point. OpenConfig works with its own GitHub repository. Since there is a handful of committers for that repository, this guarantees some compatibility with a new set of YANG modules (called a bundle). OpenConfig allows non-backward-compatible changes, which are tagged with the semantic versioning (semver.org).

So far, OpenConfig has produced about 60,000 lines of code for YANG modules. This is on par with what IETF was able to produce, even though the IETF model saw many more participants and was developed over a much longer time period. Example 6-1 shows how many lines of YANG text there is in each directory of the OpenConfig repository. Each dot represents 100 lines.

EXAMPLE 6-1 Amount of YANG Code in Different OpenConfig Subdirectories

```
Acl                 1.5k ...............
Aft                 1.2k ............
Bfd                  .7k .......
Bgp                 5.1k ...................................................
Catalog             1.0k .........
Interfaces          3.6k ....................................
Isis                7.2k .................................................
Lacp                 .5k .....
Lldp                 .9k .........
local-routing        .4k ....
mpls                5.5k ......................................................
multicast            .9k .........
network-instance    2.0k ....................
openflow             .4k ....
optical-transport   4.3k ...........................................
ospf                4.7k ...............................................
platform            2.1k .....................
policy              1.3k .............
policy-forwarding   1.0k ..........
probes               .6k ......
qos                 2.2k ......................
relay-agent          .8k ........
rib                 2.7k ...........................
segment-routing     1.2k ............
stp                 1.0k ..........
system              3.6k ....................................
telemetry            .9k .........
types               1.0k ..........
vlan                 .6k ......
wifi                2.6k ..........................
```

The OpenConfig YANG modules use a slightly different dialect of YANG than what is specified in YANG 1.0 (RFC 6020) or YANG 1.1 (RFC 7950). For example, the regular expressions used in pattern statements are so-called perl-regex rather than W3C-regex. For some reason, many XPath expressions have been and remain incorrect today, even in the published standard YANG files. The problems are certainly fixable by YANG-savvy engineers who can patch up the modules before compiling them, but this has led to a good amount of interoperability issues with other tools and vendors.

The OpenConfig model uses a different convention for structuring the content than the original IETF modules. It is also different from the new IETF NMDA style. Instead of having two separate lists for configuration and state data (original IETF), the OpenConfig model has a single list with a config branch and a state branch underneath, as shown in Example 6-2.

EXAMPLE 6-2 A Tree Representation of openconfig-interfaces.yang (Abridged)

```
module: openconfig-interfaces
  +--rw interfaces
     +--rw interface* [name]
        +--rw name                 -> ../config/name
        +--rw config
        |  +--rw name?             string
        |  +--rw type              identityref
        |  +--rw mtu?              uint16
        |  +--rw description?      string
        |  +--rw enabled?          boolean
        +--ro state
        |  +--ro name?              string
        |  +--ro type               identityref
        |  +--ro mtu?               uint16
        |  +--ro description?       string
        |  +--ro enabled?           boolean
        |  +--ro ifindex?           uint32
        |  +--ro admin-status       enumeration
        |  +--ro oper-status        enumeration
        |  +--ro last-change?       oc-types:timeticks64
```

This solves the problem of teaching computers how to navigate between the configuration and state data sides for a given interface (or other objects in other modules). A downside with this approach is that it does not lend itself well to situations with preconfiguration or operational objects that have no configuration. Only configured elements may exist here.

A minor quirk that anyone looking to be hands-on with OpenConfig modules needs to get acquainted with is that the name of every configuration item must be provided twice. Let's say you're configuring a new interface called "GigEth3/3." You have to fill in this name under **/interfaces/interface/name**, then again under **/interfaces/interface/config/name**. The names have to match, or else the configuration is invalid.

As a reminder, Google also developed (under the OpenConfig umbrella) the gRPC Network Management Interface (gNMI) as a unified management protocol for streaming telemetry and configuration management that leverages the Open Source gRPC framework.

Industry Coordination Is Required

The rapid growth of YANG models has not come without its challenges. Primary among the challenges is the coordination of all these models. While all models are doing a great job of defining how a particular feature can be configured or monitored, service composition–based data model–driven management requires the modeling of all aspects of the configuration and monitoring. Therefore, all YANG should not only be published at the same time, but they need to interact with others. This interaction does not limit itself to the IETF, as other SDOs are also involved. A couple of years ago, as part of an investigation of the dependencies, the image shown in Figure 6-8 was created. This figure contains a few thousand YANG modules known to public GitHub repositories and displays the relationships among them.

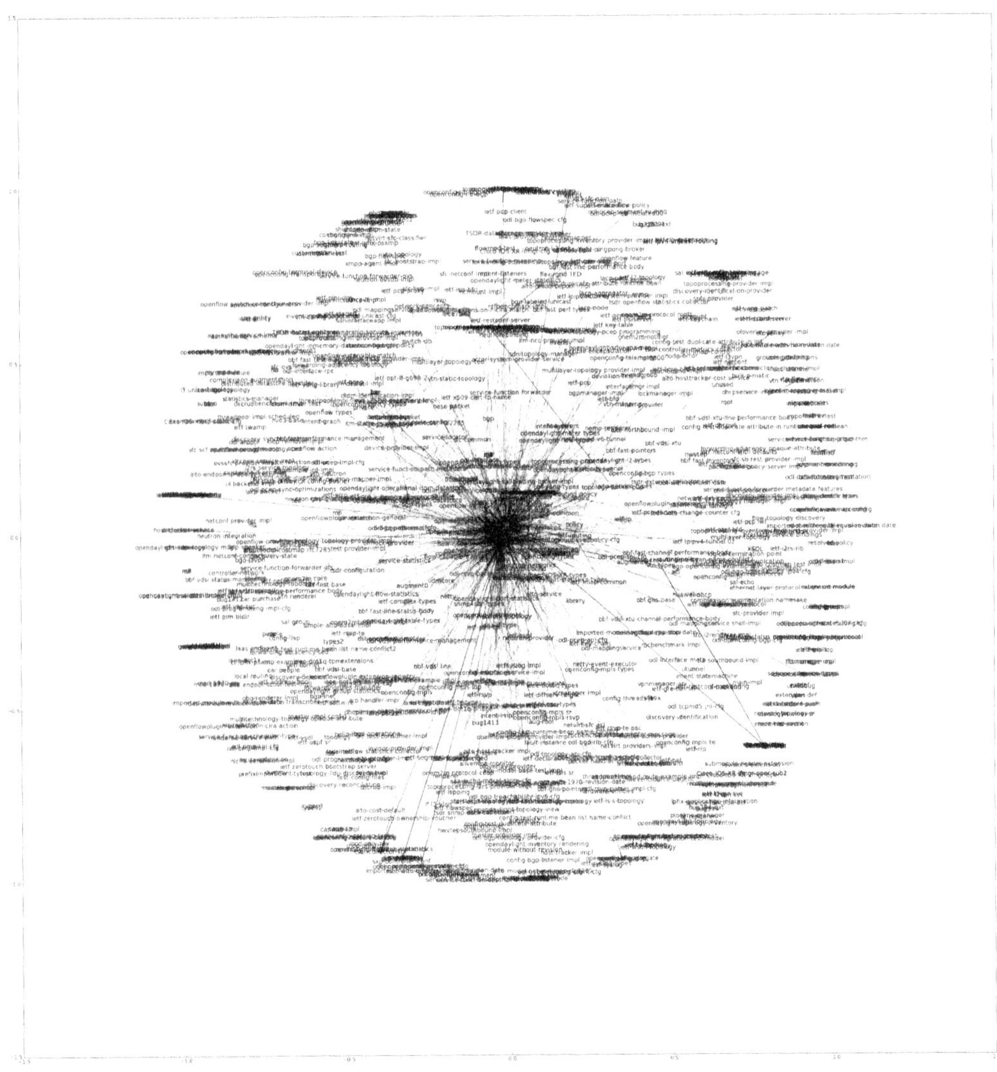

FIGURE 6-8 All YANG Modules Dependency Graph, YANG Catalog Symbol

Clearly the development of all these YANG modules required cross-industry coordination, which the IETF tried to lead. In 2014, the IESG redistributed the area directors' workload in order to allow for resources to be focused on YANG model coordination. Primary oversight responsibility and coordination of this work across areas (AD document ownership) become the responsibility of Benoit Claise. A YANG model coordination group was created to assist and complement the work of the YANG doctors and area director. The IETF's goal was not to standardize all the YANG modules in the world, but to focus on the couple hundred YANG modules at the center of the picture (that is, the core set of models from which all others depend, such as the interfaces, the access lists, the routing, and so on).

The second reason why coordination across the industry is required concerns the versioning. Even if great care was taken when creating those initial YANG models, it is wholly unrealistic to believe that they are complete, perfect, and will remain so forever. This adds another dimension to the complexity of this picture: YANG module versioning. New YANG module versions incorporate two types of changes: backward-compatible changes for completeness and non-backward-compatible changes. How to document the latter and minimize its automation cost (for both the client and the server) is at the heart of many discussions these days.

To facilitate the coordination and versioning issues in the industry, the YANG Catalog (https://www.yangcatalog.org)[5] was created, with the goal of becoming a one-stop site for YANG modules information and related tooling. The benefit, compared to a normal GitHub repository, resides in the following:

- The ability to validate YANG modules (including IETF drafts) with multiple validators
- The related metadata regarding implementation, maturity level, model type, and so on
- The ability to visualize the dependencies between YANG modules, including the bottleneck in case of standardization at the IETF
- The search capabilities on any field, YANG keyword, and metadata: a useful feature for YANG module consumers but also for YANG module designers (facilitating re-use)
- The REST APIs to query and post any content
- Demonstration of the connection to data model–driven management with open source tools such as YANG explorer and YANG Development Kit

The YANG Catalog adopted the image in Figure 6-8 as its primary logo on the website.

Interoperability Testing

Specifying standards is a compulsory first step, but testing that the different implementations interoperate is another important one. Interoperability tests help implementers identify any bugs in the code and any ambiguities in the IETF RFC specifications. In short, these tests help fix implementations and specifications. Also, note that the interoperability between genetically different implementations is one of the requirements in IETF in order to advance a protocol on the standards track (based on the conditions from RFC 6410).

A single-situation scenario does not impose software interoperability, which is the case of a single open source implementation that's used by everybody. While this *might* be true for a ubiquitous tool, this is clearly not the case for the NETCONF/RESTCONF/gRPC/etc. protocols and YANG modules to be implemented by multiple vendors.

Tooling development and interoperability testing typically happen in hackathons, with the IETF hackathon[29] being precursory in the world of data model–driven management. From there, different industry public (or even individual) efforts contribute to the toolbox, as you will see in Chapter 7.

The IETF also organized some protocols interoperability testing. For example, during the IETF 85, participants from CESNET, Jacobs University, Juniper, MG-Soft, SegueSoft, Tail-f, and YumaWorks tested the interoperability of their NETCONF client, NETCONF server, NETCONF browser, and test suite. As a consequence of those robust set of interoperable implementations (see the interop high-level report in the IETF 85 NETCONF proceedings,[30] https://www.ietf.org/proceedings/85/slides/slides-85-netconf-3.pdf), NETCONF was deemed mature and the set of NETCONF-related RFCs ready for advancement on the standards track. For example, the NETCONF Configuration Protocol RFC 4741 was obsoleted by the Network Configuration Protocol (NETCONF) RFC 6241.

Independent of the IETF, the European Advanced Networking Test Center (EANTC) arranged a series of NETCONF, RESTCONF, and YANG interoperability test events. EANTC is an institute spun off from the Technical University in Berlin in 1991. Since then, the institute helped many organizations test their networking solutions, and frequently takes on the role of independent certification body.

One of the EANTC initiatives most appreciated in the industry is the yearly interop event held for two weeks on-site in Berlin in the early spring. This is neutral ground where vendors from all over the world meet and test out their implementations of new standards with each other. EANTC defines the test cases to build every year. When vendors manage to prove that a test case is working exactly the way prescribed in the EANTC test specification, the combination is recorded. All recorded interop combinations are then presented at the MPLS+SDN+NFV World Congress in Paris some weeks later and also described in a detailed, downloadable report.

All the interop work happens under a strict nondisclosure agreement (NDA), which means any failed combinations, of which there are many, are not spoken about publicly. This has the great advantage of allowing engineers to be bold and try out interesting combinations that are on the bleeding edge. This is truly a great place to be for learning. There aren't many other occasions when interop testing happens, except at actual customer sites, where boldness is generally seen rather sparingly.

NETCONF/YANG interop testing has been part of the EANTC interop program since 2015. Both controllers/orchestrators and devices of diverse kinds show up there to participate in the prescribed test cases. The 2018 edition of the interop event had about 50 test cases described in the catalog, of which three were specifically targeting NETCONF/YANG. The test cases at the event involved an L3VPN, an L2VPN, and an NFV setup. Additional use cases involved NETCONF/YANG interfaces with a focus on other technologies. The official test report is found at http://www.eantc.de/fileadmin/eantc/downloads/events/2017-2020/MPLS2018/EANTC-MPLSSDNNFV2018-PostReport_online.pdf.[31]

Implementing More Than One YANG Model for a Specific Functionality

As you know from Chapter 2, there are different types of YANG modules: some stem from SDOs; some from consortiums, forums, and open source projects; and some from the native/proprietary models that directly map the networking vendor internal database or command-line interface (CLI) representations. The industry today still pursues all three tracks, sometimes with competing solutions.

Therefore, some devices implement more than one YANG model to manage the same functionality—for example, one proprietary ("native") YANG module for interface management, plus the IETF standard module for the same functionality, and the OpenConfig interface module as well. Any one of these could be used to create an interface, change the interface description, or look at the number of lost packets. This is nice since it allows the network operator to choose the style of management interface they prefer and may have management applications adapted for already.

The complexity for the server-side implementer of supporting multiple models simultaneously can be very high, however. Often supporting one model or the other for a given functionality is straightforward, while supporting both (or more than two) at the same time conjures up dragons. It may not even be logically possible to do it right. This is not unlike the bad interactions sometimes seen when taking several medications together.

As a client, it is generally a good idea to choose one style of model and stick with that. At least, it is certainly advisable to not touch multiple YANG modules controlling the same underlying functionality within a single transaction. To explain why, let's try breaking this recommendation in an example.

Say the user has an NMS application that creates an interface on a device using the OpenConfig YANG model. Then a need arises to update this application so that it also sets the interface *frobozz* flag to **true**. Unfortunately, the *frobozz* flag is proprietary and only exists in the native YANG model of the device. So the user updates the network management system (NMS) application so that after he creates the interface "vpn-${custno}" using the OpenConfig interface module, it uses the native module to set the *frobozz* flag on the same interface. However, in the native view, no such interface exists yet. Therefore, the NMS application has to create the interface in the native YANG module as well.

Will the device correctly handle the same interface being created twice in the same transaction? As it happens, the *frobozz* flag only makes sense for tunnel interfaces, so it has a YANG **must** statement to verify the type of interface. Will the device validate this correctly against the interface type set in the OpenConfig interface YANG model? On this device, when tunnel interfaces are created, they are usually mapped to the native L2TP YANG model in the device. When *frobozz* mode is enabled, however, many of the parameters should be mapped to functionality in the native Multiprotocol Label Switching (MPLS) YANG instead.

Will the device handle the *frobozz* mode correctly when the interface details come in through the OpenConfig model? *Perhaps*. The point is that the complexity of the model-to-model mapping starts to shine through when more than one model is being used. The convenient illusion of coherence the vendor built up with smoke and mirrors starts to come apart when you observe the system from several angles concurrently.

If "perhaps" is not the answer for you, then heed this advice: Choose one YANG module type for configuration and stick with it. There are no YANG rules or NETCONF principles on your side, should you ever get into trouble with a vendor that does not implement what you think is the logical combination of several different YANG modules. In fact, this place may be as far from "interoperable" as it is possible to get.

To top it off, remember that if you collect the configuration from a device using three different YANG models (that is, three different encodings of the same information), it's bound to take proportionally longer and eat up more of your bandwidth.

On top of that, once you have selected a specific YANG module type for configuration (say, OpenConfig or IETF), stick to that YANG module type for monitoring as well. It is obviously important to be able to automatically map the YANG path used in configuration and in monitoring (for instance, in the case of telemetry), which is possible with the same YANG module type. However, the YANG module structures might be different among the various YANG module types: The IETF modules follow the NMDA structure, while the OpenConfig modules follow a different structure. If service configuration and monitoring use both types of YANG modules, the mapping of the information will require some extra tooling and intelligence, thus adding to the complexity of the service creation and monitoring. Note that the YANG Catalog now contains a new tool for automatic YANG modules mapping between IETF non-NMDA, IETF NMDA, and OpenConfig. This tool proposes a good starting point in mapping the structure of the different module types.

Interview with the Expert

Q&A with Carl Moberg

Carl Moberg is a technology director at Cisco in the Cloud Platform and Solutions Group (CPSG) and leads the engineering product management team for the Network Service Orchestrator (NSO) product. He has spent many years trying to solve network management issues, with special focus on automation and orchestration.

His current focus is on building solutions that make networks more programmable through better abstractions. This effort is largely based on work done in the IETF around the YANG language and the NETCONF and RESTCONF protocols. He is a contributor to the development of the YANG language and has authored or contributed several YANG modules across a number of standards organizations, including the first performance and fault management modules in the MEF, the OF-CONFIG modules for managing OpenFlow switches, and the first-generation YANG modules for CableLabs, and he is co-author of RFC 8199, "YANG Module Classification." He is an active member of the YANG Doctors in the IETF, reviewing YANG modules as part of the IETF document lifecycle.

Question:

Carl, how do you see software mindsets, practices, and experiences influencing the way forward for networking in general? And why now?

Answer:

Clearly, the benefits of network transformation are quite real. My experience from working with many teams in charge of managing networks at scale is that getting there can be pretty challenging.

We all understand that we are simply not able rely on lengthy, error-prone manual processes and custom-coding efforts every time we need to set up, change, or tear down network services. But when we go after more advanced topics like network programmability and network functions virtualization—not to mention new operation models like DevOps—we quickly find that they are profoundly different from the way network service delivery has been handled in the past.

I believe that the concept of abstractions is fundamental to solving these challenges. In the networking domain, this means taking on the challenge of providing robust and effective abstractions for managing the configuration and state of physical and virtual networks for people with software tools. These abstractions are aimed at connecting the networking domain with the software development domain by mapping the concepts of networking through known and well-understood technologies into the tools used by software practitioners.

Delivery of network services obviously requires more than just automation and orchestration. In order to reliably deliver realistic services, full-stack solutions include at least the following other aspects:

- Tracking physical resources still matters to a great degree in networking. Inventory systems track available resources and expose them to allow for appropriate placement decisions in the physical world. For example, which is the next available physical port for us to use?
- Many fundamental networking constructs rely on configuring resources out of a pool. This ranges from picking appropriate (and non-overlapping) IP addresses or VLAN tags, to understanding which Border Gateway Protocol (BGP) community tags to use for which purposes. In these cases, automation systems need to be integrated with logical resource management systems (for example, IP Address Management [IPAM]) to request or hand back resources used by services in flight.

- Assuring the services by reliably collecting, correlating, and reporting on appropriate measurable aspects of the services delivered in the network. The right approach here is to allow service and assurance automation systems to cooperate on what services are in flight, and how to measure for them.

The end goal is to tie together many sources of information and enrich the required data to be able to satisfy the needs of the end-state configuration and state of the network—and perhaps more importantly, being able to do this in a rapid and cheap way as adjacent systems shift and are being developed and employing tools and technologies that are comfortable to use.

All of this opens up for two disruptive processes. The first is to allow network engineers to venture into software to more efficiently manage their network without losing control over the network. The second is to lower the barrier of entry for software practitioners to become useful in the networking domain. This combined movement can also be said to be at the heart of applying DevOps-style culture and processes across the application and networking domain.

Question:

How did you witness the industry organizing, and how have you been contributing to the change? How did the way of working change?

Answer:

Introducing a new modeling language into an existing industry with its entrenched ways of working and tooling is no small undertaking. My observation is that the arrival of the YANG language was very timely. Mostly in the sense that the urgency in the problem space (programmatic networking) was rapidly growing and that the legacy approaches (for example, ASN.1 for MIBs in SNMP, OMG IDL for CORBA) were either running out of steam or did not meet the basic expectations of the market. YANG had, if you will, a first-mover advantage at the time as the problem space became better understood. It also nicely matched the influx of software engineers into the networking industry as the concept of software-defined networking took hold. This allowed us to build on some very well-understood concepts from computer science around schema languages, type systems, and some fundamental database concepts (for example, locks, rollbacks, and transactions).

This was also the time where Linux became the default operating system choice for new network equipment. This move quickly commoditized the user-land application layer in routers and switches and opened for much wider reuse of commercial and open source software in networking stacks including the management plane. This, combined with increasing pressure from the market (service providers and large enterprises) to focus on lowering the cost of managing networks, resulted in vendors adding more people to their management feature engineering teams, and we saw a sharp rise in people who designed and built products supporting YANG and NETCONF. Practically speaking, this resulted in an increased number of people authoring, reading, and writing YANG modules.

Another interesting effect of this transition was that as YANG became a requirement, we naturally saw many more vendors integrating YANG into their toolchain. This, in turn, contributed to a rise in the availability of open source and commercial tools for authoring and integrating YANG modules in products. We saw a formidable explosion of an ecosystem around this technology, including interoperability testing, standards work, and operator groups (for example, OpenConfig), and YANG became the subject matter of many talks and workshops across industry events.

As a result, we now have a well-understood and robust language, a growing set of standard modules, and vibrant ecosystem with both open source and commercial tooling and runtime software readily available. The cost has been lowered, and the time to market for manageable networking equipment has been significantly reduced. Vendors can focus on the value-providing aspects of their offerings and deliver software-defined manageability.

Question:

What is missing from the technology stack at this point?

Answer:

Going back to the three bullets mentioned in the first question, I think we still have some work to do around service assurance. Most of the fundamental building blocks are in place, but we need to come together for a fully integrated architecture around model-driven telemetry and correlation of the collected data with instances of services. This is, in fact, the next step of the industry. When we have that, we will have a fully understood and well-defined device-to-service software stack using robust standards based on the common experience of the industry.

The next step up in the stack is the OSS/BSS and ITSM systems, so watch this space.

Summary

As YANG became the defacto language for data model–driven management in the networking industry, the landscape of SDOs, consortiums, forums, and open source projects has been quickly evolving. Obviously, the situation still keeps evolving, with new segments of the industry adopting YANG on regular basis. Some of the latest examples, as discussed in this chapter, are the 3GPP and xRAN for the radio access networks (Note that xRAN merged to create the O-RAN alliance [https://www.o-ran.org/]). This chapter covered history, in a more or less chronological order, and explained how the different "groups" have been developing and how all these YANG models came together or actually diverged (with the OpenConfig example). Finally, it touched on the interoperability testing in the industry, with EANTC.

References in This Chapter

Instead of listing all possible links of all different projects, we'll limit ourselves to just a few references—the primary starting points, if you will—as listed in Table 6-2.

TABLE 6-2 YANG-Related Documents for Further Reading

Topic	Content
yangcatalog.org	https://yangcatalog.org
	Catalog of YANG modules, searchable on keywords and metadata
OpenConfig	http://www.openconfig.net
	OpenConfig reference, including a link to the GitHub for YANG modules
YANG GitHub	https://github.com/YangModels/yang
	Contains many of the YANG modules in the industry, including some native ones

Endnotes

1. https://datatracker.ietf.org/wg/spring/about/
2. https://datatracker.ietf.org/group/yangdoctors/about/
3. http://www.claise.be/IETFYANGOutOfRFC.png
4. http://www.claise.be/2018/06/ietf-yang-modules-statistiques/
5. https://www.yangcatalog.org
6. http://www.claise.be/IETFYANGOutOfRFC.html
7. https://www.yangcatalog.org/yang-search/module_details/?module=iana-crypt-hash@2014-08-06
8. https://www.yangcatalog.org/yang-search/module_details/?module=iana-hardware@2018-03-13
9. https://github.com/xym-tool/xym
10. http://claise.be/IETFYANGPageCompilation.png
11. https://github.com/xym-tool/symd/tree/7f757df8e901c040a4a74db9a4e7e4656d24ddee
12. https://d3js.org
13. http://www.claise.be/ietf-routing.png

14. https://www.yangcatalog.org/yang-search/impact_analysis/
15. http://www.claise.be/2018/03/yang-data-models-in-the-industry-current-state-of-affairs-march-2018/
16. http://www.opendaylight.org
17. https://www.broadband-forum.org
18. https://github.com/YangModels/yang
19. http://www.mef.net
20. https://www.mef.net/Assets/Technical_Specifications/PDF/MEF_10.3.pdf
21. https://www.mef.net/Assets/Technical_Specifications/PDF/MEF_26.2.pdf
22. https://www.ieee.org
23. http://redfish.dmtf.org
24. http://tools.ietf.org/html/rfc6020
25. https://www.itu.int/en/ITU-T/Pages/default.aspx
26. http://www.openroadm.org/home.html
27. https://www.etsi.org/deliver/etsi_gs/NFV-IFA/001_099/011/02.01.01_60/gs_NFV-IFA011v020101p.pdf
28. https://www.etsi.org/deliver/etsi_gs/NFV-IFA/001_099/014/02.01.01_60/gs_NFV-IFA014v020101p.pdf
29. https://ietf.org/how/runningcode/hackathons/
30. https://www.ietf.org/proceedings/85/slides/slides-85-netconf-3.pdf
31. http://www.eantc.de/fileadmin/eantc/downloads/events/2017-2020/MPLS2018/EANTC-MPLSSDNNFV2018-PostReport_online.pdf

Chapter 7

Automation Is as Good as the Data Models, Their Related Metadata, and the Tools: For the Network Architect and Operator

This chapter covers

- How to make sense of a YANG module's structure
- Which YANG module to use to perform configuration changes and gather network data
- What metadata is available for a YANG module and how it helps with network management and automation decisions
- What tools to use to test YANG-modeled protocols such as NETCONF and RESTCONF
- How to learn from others when creating your own YANG modules
- How to test your own YANG modules

Introduction

Thus far you've taken a hard look at the thinking leading up to the creation of data model–driven management, as well as the structure and syntax of YANG modules. This chapter shifts focus to how to use these paradigms and modules practically in support of network management and automation. In order to do that, you need to look at the tools and module metadata to help you understand how to turn the modeled data into useful actions. There is a growing number of both commercial and open source tools for model-based management and automation. Some commercial tools are mentioned, but the primary focus of this chapter is on the open source offerings.

This chapter begins by taking a practical look at the YANG module structure, the rich metadata around those modules, and the tools needed to understand modules and use them to automate configuration changes to and gather data from the network.

By the end of this chapter, you will have a good understanding of how to identify pertinent YANG modules in order to perform management and automation tasks within their network. You'll know what metadata and tools to use both as a module consumer and as a module designer to make their tasks easier and less error-prone. Finally, as either a network administrator or operator, you will be familiar the commonly available tools that can help get you started down the path of model-driven network automation.

Getting to Know the Structure of a YANG Module

The first thing you must do is *find* the modules you want to use. If you have access to the device(s) you will be automating (and they are running the right version of code, of course), the modules they support may be fetched directly from the devices. This approach is explored later in this chapter. Here, you will look at finding modules independent from devices. While different vendors and standards-definition organizations (SDOs) post modules in various locations, many are centralizing around GitHub and linking to the https://github.com/YangModels/yang repository specifically. Generally speaking, there are two main directories in this repository where modules are found: vendor and standard. The vendor directory contains either links to other GitHub repositories or directories that contain actual modules themselves. The standard directory contains the same, but for various SDOs.

Clone this repository and then start to walk through the various available modules. Since this repository contains links to other repositories, be sure to clone it recursively, pulling in all git submodules, like so:

```
$ git clone --recurse-submodules https://github.com/YangModels/yang.git
```

Next, choose a common, standards-based module and take a look at it. Say that you want to automate the collection of routes from a device. Under the standard/ietf/RFC subdirectory, you find ietf-routing@2018-03-13.yang. This module, as its description states, defines essential components for managing a routing subsystem. Example 7-1 shows an excerpt of text from this module.

EXAMPLE 7-1 Excerpt of ietf-routing@2018-03-13.yang

```
/* Type Definitions */

typedef route-preference {
  type uint32;
  description
    "This type is used for route preferences.";
}
```

```
/* Groupings */

grouping address-family {
  description
    "This grouping provides a leaf identifying an address
     family.";
  leaf address-family {
    type identityref {
      base address-family;
    }
    mandatory true;
    description
      "Address family.";
  }
}

grouping router-id {
  description
    "This grouping provides a router ID.";
  leaf router-id {
    type yang:dotted-quad;
    description
      "A 32-bit number in the form of a dotted quad that is used by
       some routing protocols identifying a router.";
    reference
      "RFC 2328: OSPF Version 2";
  }
}
```

So where do you begin? As you saw in Chapter 3, "YANG Explained," YANG modules can get complex quickly. When you just read through a YANG module, it is difficult to get a good overview of its structure. As you see in Example 7-1, there are identities, typedefs, and groupings. While these are useful for module authors to create extensible and reusable constructs, they make it more difficult to understand the exact path to a data element you may want to extract from or configure on a device.

Fortunately, there are tools to help with this. One such tool—and this will likely be a go-to utility in your tool belt for many things—is pyang. Pyang is an open source, Python-based application and set of libraries that make working with YANG modules much easier by allowing you to transform modules into different formats. Additionally, pyang provides ways to validate module syntax and check for backward incompatibilities between two modules.

Pyang is available in GitHub from https://github.com/mbj4668/pyang, and it is also in the PyPI package index, which means it can be installed with the Python **pip** command:

```
$ pip install pyang
```

Pyang has the **-f** argument, which prints a module in a variety of output formats. In order to better understand the structure of the ietf-routing module, use the "tree" format:

```
$ pyang -f tree ietf-routing\@2018-03-13.yang
```

This command produces the tree output shown in Example 7-2.

EXAMPLE 7-2 Tree Structure of the ietf-routing Module

```
module: ietf-routing
   +--rw routing
   |  +--rw router-id?                 yang:dotted-quad
   |  +--ro interfaces
   |  |  +--ro interface*   if:interface-ref
   |  +--rw control-plane-protocols
   |  |  +--rw control-plane-protocol* [type name]
   |  |     +--rw type             identityref
   |  |     +--rw name             string
   |  |     +--rw description?     string
   |  |     +--rw static-routes
   |  +--rw ribs
   |     +--rw rib* [name]
   |        +--rw name              string
   |        +--rw address-family    identityref
   |        +--ro default-rib?      boolean {multiple-ribs}?
   |        +--ro routes
   |        |  +--ro route*
   |        |     +--ro route-preference?   route-preference
   |        |     +--ro next-hop
   |        |     |  +--ro (next-hop-options)
   |        |     |     +--:(simple-next-hop)
   |        |     |     |  +--ro outgoing-interface?   if:interface-ref
   |        |     |     +--:(special-next-hop)
   |        |     |     |  +--ro special-next-hop?     enumeration
   |        |     |     +--:(next-hop-list)
   |        |     |        +--ro next-hop-list
   |        |     |           +--ro next-hop*
   |        |     |              +--ro outgoing-interface?   if:interface-ref
   |        |     +--ro source-protocol      identityref
   |        |     +--ro active?              empty
   |        |     +--ro last-updated?        yang:date-and-time
   |        +---x active-route
   |        |  +--ro output
   |        |     +--ro route
   |        |        +--ro next-hop
```

```
     |        |        | +--ro (next-hop-options)
     |        |        |    +--:(simple-next-hop)
     |        |        |    | +--ro outgoing-interface?   if:interface-ref
     |        |        |    +--:(special-next-hop)
     |        |        |    | +--ro special-next-hop?     enumeration
     |        |        |    +--:(next-hop-list)
     |        |        |       +--ro next-hop-list
     |        |        |          +--ro next-hop*
     |        |        |             +--ro outgoing-interface?   if:interface-ref
     |        |        +--ro source-protocol    identityref
     |        |        +--ro active?            empty
     |        |        +--ro last-updated?      yang:date-and-time
     |        +--rw description?      string
     o--ro routing-state
        +--ro router-id?                   yang:dotted-quad
        o--ro interfaces
        | o--ro interface*   if:interface-state-ref
        o--ro control-plane-protocols
        | o--ro control-plane-protocol* [type name]
        |    o--ro type    identityref
        |    o--ro name    string
        o--ro ribs
           o--ro rib* [name]
              o--ro name                string
              +--ro address-family      identityref
              o--ro default-rib?        boolean {multiple-ribs}?
              o--ro routes
              | o--ro route*
              |    o--ro route-preference?   route-preference
              |    o--ro next-hop
...
```

This output makes understanding the module's structure much easier. Looking at a module this way for the first time gives you a good, "in a nutshell" view of the module's content. It strips away the identities and typedefs and presents the groupings exactly where they get referenced within the module's containers. Therefore, it's clearer as to what the path will be to a given element.

However, there are a number of new symbols here that require some explanation so you can fully understand the tree. These symbols and the tree structure itself are explained in detail in RFC 8340. Let's look at a breakdown of the various relevant symbols used in the tree view in Example 7-2.

The leading "+" indicates a current node in the tree. The "o" instead of a "+" indicates that the node is obsolete and should not be used. The "rw," "ro," and "x" indicates the type of access you have for a given node. The "rw" indicates that this is configuration data, and thus it is writable (as well as readable). The "ro" indicates state or operational data, and that it can only be read. The "x" is short for "executable," and in the context of YANG, this points to either a remote procedure call (RPC) or an action (in the case of **active-route**, this is an action).

A "?" at the end of a node name indicates that the node is optional. An "*" next to a node name indicates that the node is either a list or a leaf-list. Whereas a leaf-list does not have any child nodes, a list has child nodes and typically has key elements. A list's key elements, which must be present if the list contains keys, is shown in "[ ]" at the end of the list's node name (for example, the rib list has a key of name of **rib* [name]**).

The node name within "( )" signifies a choice, with the ":(...)" notation indicating a specific case for the choice. For example, in the tree just mentioned, **next-hop-options** is a choice and **simple-next-hop** is one of its cases.

Let's get back to the case of wanting to enumerate the routes on a device. Using the preceding tree structure, you know that the path to do so, for all Routing Information Bases (RIBs), is **routing** → **ribs** → **rib** → **routes**.

Pyang and its tree output are discussed again later in this chapter when you start to construct queries and configuration requests.

Finding the Right Modules Using the YANG Catalog

What if you did not know that ietf-routing was the right module for what you wanted to do? There are many modules in the "YangModules" GitHub repository, and many more in the industry in general. Even if you know the specific platform for which you will be automating, finding the right module can be a challenge. Fortunately, there is help. An open source project called the YANG Catalog was created to be a central point to search for YANG modules across multiple vendors, SDOs, and open source projects. The YANG Catalog is a collection of tools that allow you to search for modules and nodes based on keyword, visualize the modules' relationships, inspect metadata, and determine which modules are supported in a given platform from a given vendor. It is not a repository from which you can download YANG modules. However, it does provide links to the canonical locations from where modules can be downloaded. The YANG Catalog project is found at https://yangcatalog.org.

The YANG Catalog project began at the Internet Engineering Task Force (IETF) at the hackathons that started ahead of regular meetings. Its mission is to help the *industry*, *network operators*, and *equipment vendors*. For the industry, the YANG Catalog provides a record of what was created to help share best practices. For the network operator, it helps with finding the right YANG module to use for a given task. For the equipment vendors, it eases end-user adoption of the YANG modules.

At first, it was completely developed by a small group of volunteers with a passion for YANG and giving back to the community at large (Benoit Claise, Carl Moberg, and Joe Clarke); later, it received some private funding but was still developed with the broader community in mind. Over time, more tools (such as a regular expression validator as well as the YANG Suite tool discussed next) were added. YANG Catalog is still evolving, and the interfaces shown are likely to change as the suite of tools matures.

YANG Search

The YANG Search feature of YANG Catalog allows you to find modules and nodes based on keywords in the node name, module name, or module description. This is useful if you do not know exactly what module to use for your purposes. Even if you readily have access to devices, it is difficult to search the YANG modules on those devices to find exactly what you want. While the Unix **grep** command is your friend for searching text, it is not always the most efficient tool when dealing with structured data like YANG modules. Additionally, YANG Catalog's search feature exposes *metadata* that shows you what devices (and their versions of code) support specific YANG modules. This metadata is composed of elements that provide more context as to the module and its nodes' usability and applicability to help you identify the right solution. More details on the types of metadata are provided next.

Therefore, YANG Search is a good place to start if you are drafting a request for proposal, building a composite YANG service module, or are simply interested in what might be the best model for configuring or gathering data from a feature.

The search form offers a number of options; however, the default functionality searches for module names, node names, and node descriptions that match a given keyword, and this is usually sufficient to get started. As before, you want to print the routes on a given device. If you search for "routes," you get a large number of results. So how can you pare down these results to identify the most relevant nodes and modules?

The search returns the following columns:

- The name of the node that was matched
- The revision of the YANG module that contains that node
- The matching node's schema type
- The XPath notation for the node (useful when wanting to query a device)
- The name of the YANG module that contains the matched node
- Links to additional YANG Catalog tools
- Whether or not the module that contains the matched node is vendor specific or industry defined

- The organization that produced the related YANG module
- The maturity of the YANG module (more on this later)
- The number of times the module has been imported by other modules
- The module's compilation status
- The description of the node that was matched

Some of these metadata fields are described in more detail later in this chapter when you look at metadata with a designer's eye. From a user's perspective, the origin and maturity indicate how supported and stable the module is. For example, a module that originates from an SDO and ratified was reviewed extensively and could potentially be supported by multiple vendors' devices.

The default result set, sorted by matching node name, may seem unwieldy, especially with such a generic term like "routes." However, there are some features of the search that can help you identify good candidates for further exploration. For example, if you are looking to get routes from a specific vendor's device (and you cannot query the device in question directly), further filter the results based on that vendor's organization. If you are looking to gather routes across multiple vendors' devices, using a standards-based module is preferable. Using the search filter field, the modules can be pared down to just those whose origin is "Industry Standard." You can also uncheck the search option "Node Description" so that only node names and module names are searched. However, even that may leave a lot of results. How can the set be winnowed down even further?

While you could scan through the descriptions of each node, it would first be desirable to identify the most "trustworthy" sources of modules. This is where YANG Catalog's store of metadata comes into play. While having a module along with its nodes and their descriptions is valuable, there are numerous other properties of that module that factor into its usability. Some of these properties (like revision, references, organization, and author) can be extracted directly from the contents of the module itself. Others (like a module's maturity, how many times it has been imported by other modules, whether or not it has expired, and its compilation status) cannot be directly ascertained. Fortunately, YANG Catalog collects all of these *extractable* and *non-extractable* metadata values.

Some of the metadata fields are shown in the search results. Specifically, once you've narrowed the results down to Industry Standard modules, sort on Maturity to prioritize those modules that were ratified—or fully standardized—by their authoring body. The IETF is a well-known organization where vendors collaborate to define Internet standards (including YANG modules), so any modules—especially those about routing—authored by that organization that were ratified have had a number of very well-trained eyes look at them. Now you're looking at a much shorter list. If you also consider those modules that were imported by other modules a greater number of times, you have a set that is much easier to scan to find interesting modules. This prioritized short list is shown in Figure 7-1.

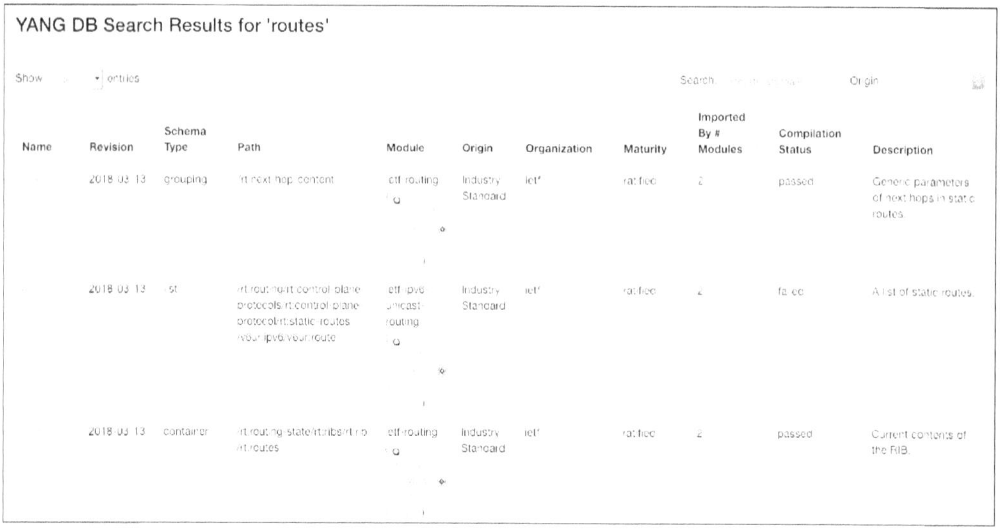

YANG DB Search Results for 'routes'

Show [ ] entries Search: Origin

Name	Revision	Schema Type	Path	Module	Origin	Organization	Maturity	Imported By # Modules	Compilation Status	Description
	2018-03-13	grouping	/rt:next-hop-content	ietf-routing	Industry Standard	ietf	ratified	2	passed	Generic parameters of next hops in static routes.
	2018-03-13	list	/rt:routing/rt:control-plane-protocols/rt:control-plane-protocol/rt:static-routes/v6ur:ipv6/v6ur:route	ietf-ipv6-unicast-routing	Industry Standard	ietf	ratified	2	failed	A list of static routes.
	2018-03-13	container	/rt:routing-state/rt:ribs/rt:rib/rt:routes	ietf-routing	Industry Standard	ietf	ratified	2	passed	Current contents of the RIB.

FIGURE 7-1 Filtered and Sorted YANG Catalog Search Results

Note that the "routes" container (the bottom node in Figure 7-1) is what you looked at in the previous section. So, you've arrived at the ietf-routing module that you looked at before. You also have an XPath notation for this same element that you can use in other tools. Under the Module column, take a deeper look at the ietf-routing module by using other tools within the YANG Catalog. These include *Tree View*, which provides a graphical tree view of the module; *Impact Analysis*, which shows how this module is affected by other modules, as well as how this module affects other modules (discussed later in this chapter); and *Module Details*, which allows you to browse all of the module's metadata.

The Module Tree

The tree view, shown in Figure 7-2, is perhaps a prettier—and definitely more detailed—version of pyang's "tree" output plug-in, with another important feature missing in pyang: XPaths for each node. Once you find a node or module in which you are interested, the node's XPath notation is a handy way to query a device for the data at that node, as well as critical for subscribing to telemetry streams.

YANG Tree for Module: 'ietf-routing'

Module: ietf-routing@2018-03-13, **Namespace:** urn:ietf:params:xml:ns:yang:ietf-routing, **Prefix:** rt

for ietf-routing@2018-03-13

Element	Schema	Type	Flags	Opts	Status	Path
ietf-routing	module	module				
routing	container	container	config		current	/rt:routing
routing-state	container	container	no config		obsolete	/rt:routing-state
router-id	leaf	yang:dotted-quad	no config	?	current	/rt:routing-state/rt:router-id
interfaces	container	container	no config		obsolete	/rt:routing-state/rt:interfaces
control-plane-protocols	container	container	no config		obsolete	/rt:routing-state/rt:control-plane-protocols
ribs	container	container	no config		obsolete	/rt:routing-state/rt:ribs
rib	list	list	no config		obsolete	/rt:routing-state/rt:ribs/rt:rib
name	leaf	string	no config		obsolete	/rt:routing-state/rt:ribs/rt:rib/rt:name
address-family	leaf	identityref	no config		current	/rt:routing-state/rt:ribs/rt:rib/rt:address-family
default-rib	leaf	boolean	no config	?	obsolete	/rt:routing-state/rt:ribs/rt:rib/rt:default-rib
routes	container	container	no config		obsolete	/rt:routing-state/rt:ribs/rt:rib/rt:routes
active-route	action		no config		obsolete	/rt:routing-state/rt:ribs/rt:rib/rt:active-route

FIGURE 7-2 YANG Catalog Tree Output of the ietf-routing Module

Module [Metadata] Details

Following the *Module Details* link from the search results page shows the metadata details for a given module seen in Figure 7-3. These metadata fields are themselves defined in a YANG module that was created as a backing store for the YANG Catalog.

FIGURE 7-3 Module Details Page for ietf-routing

The full set of metadata available is defined in the yang-catalog.yang module, which is described at https://tools.ietf.org/html/draft-clacla-netmod-model-catalog-03 and enumerated in the following list (note that some of these fields are discussed in more detail in the next section):

- Module name
- Module revision
- Organization that produced the module (if this is "ietf," the IETF workgroup that developed the module is also provided)
- Module namespace
- Link to download the module
- From where the module was generated (if a native module)
- Module maturity level
- Document name that further describes or defines the module
- Module author's email
- Link to the module's related document
- Module classification (for example, a network device model or a network service model)
- Module's compilation status
- Link to the module's compilation output (if a failure occurred)
- Module prefix
- YANG version used by the module
- Description of the module
- Contacts for the module
- Type of module (for example, submodule or main module)
- Parent module (if current module is a submodule)
- Tree type (for example, nmda-compatible, openconfig, split tree, and so on)
- Link to the **pyang -f tree** output for the module
- When the module expires (if it expires)
- List of any applicable submodules
- List of module dependencies

- List of dependent modules
- The module's embedded semantic version (if it exists)
- The module's derived semantic version
- List of known implementations of the module

On the metadata details page, within the "Specify Module" box, there are links to the same Tree View and Impact Analysis tools shown in the search results. The YANG Suite link is new. This tool is covered from a module exploration perspective in a subsequent section.

Quite a few fields here are of value to a module consumer. First and foremost, the "schema" field offers a canonical link from which you can download the module itself. Extracting modules directly from devices is described later on in this chapter, but if you need an alternate source, the YANG Catalog provides an excellent resource for this. The module's dependencies (if any) are also found here. Therefore, the YANG Catalog allows you to get all the module components needed to load into a network management system.

The next piece of interesting metadata is the supporting reference document. This is generally only available for modules that were created by a standards body. This reference provides additional details to help clarify certain nodes, explain the reasoning behind design choices, and so on. Combine this with the contact field, and you have both a document that explains the module as well as a group to which you can reach out for more help or information about the module.

The implementations, semantic-version, and derived-semantic-version fields provide important details as to where the module is implemented in various vendors' devices, as well as how this module compares from a backward-compatibility standpoint. If you were working with a specific module previously, and you find that a new revision is implemented in your platform, how do you know if that revision is backward compatible with previous revisions? This is where semantic-version and derived-semantic-version come into play. Essentially, the semantic version fields are a dotted set of three numbers: MAJOR.MINOR.PATCH. If the MAJOR number changes between different revisions of the same module, then there are non-backward-compatible changes between those two revisions. This means you should inspect the differences between the two module revisions to determine if there are changes needed to your automation scripts and applications. If the MINOR version changes, then new features were added, but the later revision is still backward compatible with the earlier revision. Likewise, if the PATCH version changes, the later revision of the module is backward compatible with the earlier revision, but the later version has additional bug fixes. More details on the structure of semantic versions can be found at semver.org. With respect to the YANG Catalog, the semantic-version field reflects the version taken directly from the YANG module. Not all YANG modules provide this (as of this writing, only Openconfig modules have it). The derived-semantic-version is computed automatically by the YANG Catalog when new revisions of a module are added. In this example, the ietf-routing module at revision 2018-03-13 has a derived-semantic-version of 11.0.0. This means that since the first revision of ietf-routing, there were two additional major, non-backward-compatible changes.

Notice that the *automation is as good as the data models, their related metadata, and the tools*. Understanding that, metadata enables better use and integration of the module into network management and automation systems. YANG Catalog is revisited later on both from a module author perspective as well as from a developer perspective.

Moving from Nodes to RPCs and Scripts with YANG Suite

Following the YANG Suite link from the Module Details page launches the YANG Suite tool hosted on yangcatalog.org. While this tool can be launched directly from the yangcatalog.org home page by clicking the "YANG exploration" link, invoking it from within Module Details automatically imports the current module (and its dependencies) into YANG Suite. In this example, ietf-routing is preloaded into YANG Suite, allowing you to explore and interact with its various nodes. Figure 7-4 shows the YANG Suite user interface (UI) with the ietf-routing module preloaded. In this section, YANG Suite is used to explore a YANG module or set of YANG modules.

NOTE

At the time of writing, YANG Suite is part of the industry-centric yangcatalog.org. It may move to a Cisco-specific instance of the Catalog at https://yangcatalog.cisco.com, however.

In the next section, YANG Suite is used to interact directly with devices.

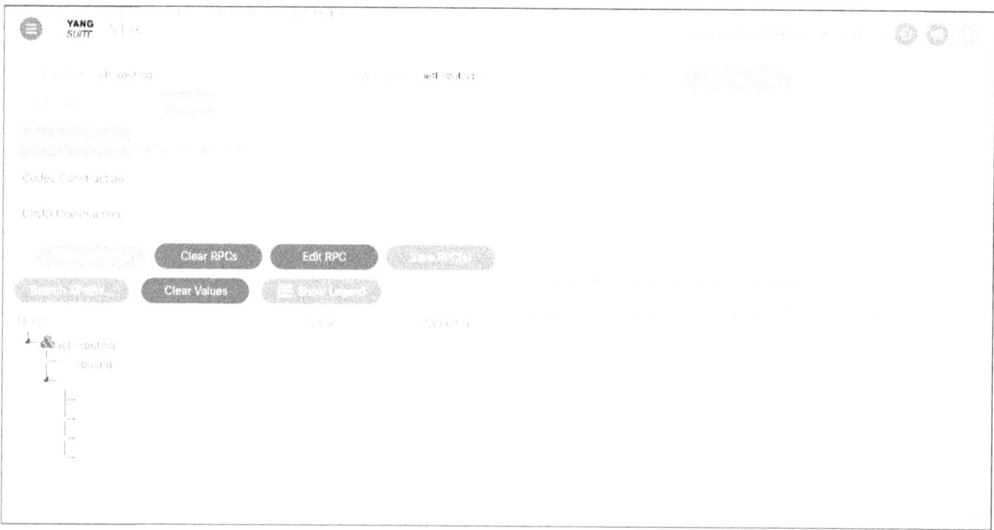

FIGURE 7-4 YANG Suite with the ietf-routing Module Loaded

The tree diagram looks very similar to the one that is directly linked from the module search results. However, in addition to being able to expand and collapse nodes, this tree allows you to interact with individual module nodes, set values, and then generate RPCs and scripts.

By default, the YANG Suite interface starts by showing the selected module tree (ietf-routing in this example) in the YANG exploration mode. In the version of YANG Suite on yangcatalog.org at the time of writing, this mode allows you to generate Python scripts that use the YANG Development Kit (YDK)[1] and ncclient to perform **get**, **get-config**, and **edit-config** NETCONF operations. YDK is covered in much more detail in Chapter 9, "Automation Is as Good as the Data Models, Their Related Metadata, and the Tools: For the Application Developer," along with other development tools. For now, click Protocols > NETCONF from the YANG Suite menu on the left and select the "ietf-routing" YANG Set and load the "ietf-routing" module. The same tree hierarchy is drawn, and from this interface, raw NETCONF RPCs can be created. Figure 7-5 shows YANG Suite's NETCONF interface.

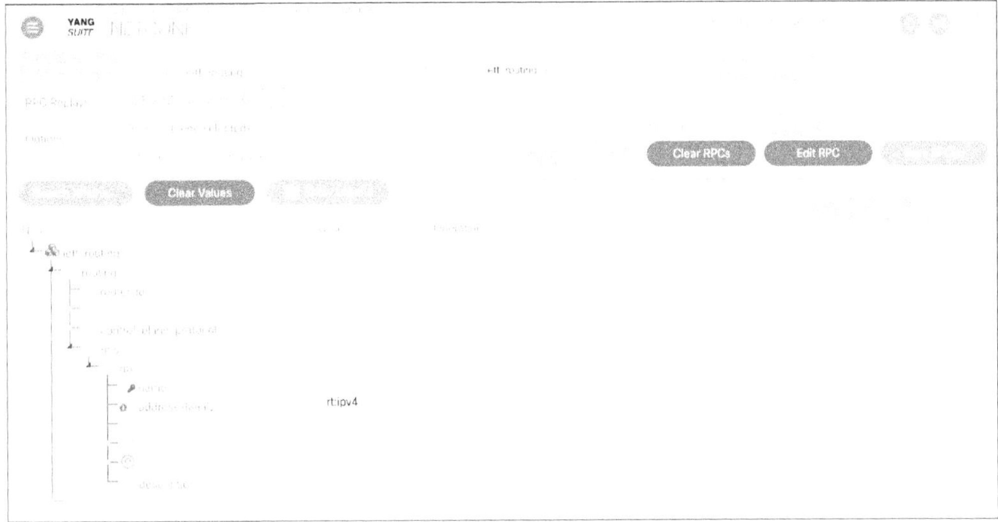

FIGURE 7-5 YANG Suite's NETCONF Protocol Screen with ietf-routing Loaded

In this view, the default operation is **edit-config**; notice that some of the ietf-routing tree is disabled. For example, the entire routing-state subtree is grayed out. This is because all of these nodes are marked **config false** and thus do not apply to **edit-config** and **get-config** operations.

To see what you can do with an **edit-config** operation, expand the /ietf-routing/routing subtree, click the Value cell next to the *router-id* leaf, and enter **192.168.1.1**. In the Operation cell next to the value, select "merge" from the pull-down list. What you are telling YANG Suite is that you want to merge in a new router ID of 192.168.1.1. On the top left of the screen, there is an Options tab below the selected RPC Construction tab. Click this to reveal additional parameters to control the RPC generation. Once you perform one task, it should become a bit clearer as to what the different options do. For now, leave the parameters with their default values. Click back to RPC Construction and then click the Build RPC button.

The text area below the buttons now has XML in it corresponding to the operation you defined in the tree to the left. That code is shown in Example 7-3.

EXAMPLE 7-3 RPC Body to Change the router-id Leaf

```
1. <rpc xmlns="urn:ietf:params:xml:ns:netconf:base:1.0" message-id="101">
2.  <edit-config>
3.    <target>
4.      <running/>
5.    </target>
6.    <config>
7.      <routing xmlns="urn:ietf:params:xml:ns:yang:ietf-routing">
8.        <router-id xmlns:nc="urn:ietf:params:xml:ns:netconf:base:1.0"
nc:operation="merge">192.168.1.1</router-id>
9.      </routing>
10.    </config>
11.  </edit-config>
12. </rpc>
```

The numbers next to each line are added here to break down the RPC to see how the different options in YANG Suite affect the results.

This XML is exactly what would be sent from a client to a NETCONF server to perform the desired **edit-config** operation. Since you clicked the Add RPC button, it makes sense that line 1 define an RPC. Line 2 indicates that this is an **edit-config** operation. Lines 3 through 5 specify that the target for this operation is the candidate datastore. This makes sense given that you left the Datastore pull-down at the default, "candidate," and why you were prompted to add a **commit** operation. Lines 6 through 10 define the meat of the operation. In this case, you are using the ietf-routing module (as shown on line 7) to merge a new router ID of 192.168.1.1 (shown on line 8). If you change the value of some of the options in YANG Suite (for example, if you change "merge" to be "remove"), clear, and add a new RPC, you will note how the RPC changes.

YANG Suite also makes it easy to craft RPCs and scripts for getting data from a device. Change the "NETCONF operation" from **edit-config** to **get**, and the whole tree becomes active. As you know, the NETCONF **get** operation allows you to retrieve configuration and operational data from a NETCONF server. To build a **get** RPC, you need to select the elements from the module that you want to see in the resulting output. For example, if you want to retrieve all of the routing state from a device, click the Value box next to the /ietf-routing/routing-state subtree. A check appears in the box. Now click the Build RPC button on the right. The resulting raw RPC is shown in Example 7-4.

EXAMPLE 7-4 Get RPC Body Filtering on routing-state

```
<rpc xmlns="urn:ietf:params:xml:ns:netconf:base:1.0" message-id="101">
  <get>
    <filter>
      <routing-state xmlns="urn:ietf:params:xml:ns:yang:ietf-routing"/>
    </filter>
  </get>
</rpc>
```

While these raw RPCs illustrate what a NETCONF server sees and help to crystalize some of the different options surrounding YANG-based management, they are not ideal for automating actual configuration or monitoring tasks. Use the script generation capabilities of YANG Suite to help move from learning a YANG module to automating operations for it. As was mentioned before, the default YANG Suite view on yangcatalog.org allows you to create YDK scripts. This view allows you to create scripts that use the Python ncclient package. More of ncclient is explained in Chapter 9. Back under the Options tab, select Display RPC(s) as "Python ncclient script" from the pull-down, return to the RPC Construction tab, and click the Build RPC button again. The RPC text area displays the Python code shown in Example 7-5.

EXAMPLE 7-5 Python Script Generated from YANG Suite

```
#! /usr/bin/env python
import lxml.etree as et
from argparse import ArgumentParser
from ncclient import manager
from ncclient.operations import RPCError

payload = [
'''
<get xmlns="urn:ietf:params:xml:ns:netconf:base:1.0">
  <filter>
    <routing-state xmlns="urn:ietf:params:xml:ns:yang:ietf-routing"/>
  </filter>
</get>
''',
]

if __name__ == '__main__':

    parser = ArgumentParser(description='Usage:')

    # script arguments
    parser.add_argument('-a', '--host', type=str, required=True,
                        help="Device IP address or Hostname")
    parser.add_argument('-u', '--username', type=str, required=True,
                        help="Device Username (netconf agent username)")
    parser.add_argument('-p', '--password', type=str, required=True,
                        help="Device Password (netconf agent password)")
    parser.add_argument('--port', type=int, default=830,
                        help="Netconf agent port")
    args = parser.parse_args()

    # connect to netconf agent
    with manager.connect(host=args.host,
```

```
                         port=args.port,
                         username=args.username,
                         password=args.password,
                         timeout=90,
                         hostkey_verify=False,
                         device_params={'name': 'csr'}) as m:

        # execute netconf operation
        for rpc in payload:
            try:
                response = m.dispatch(et.fromstring(rpc))
                data = response.data_ele
            except RPCError as e:
                data = e._raw

            # beautify output
            print(et.tostring(data, encoding='unicode', pretty_print=True))
```

Note that the payload variable is set to the same value as the raw RPC you saw in your **get** operation. This script is designed to be executed by specifying a few command-line parameters, and it performs the requested NETCONF operation. For example, if you save the script as get-routing.py and you have a device with IP address 10.1.1.1 with a user account called "admin" with a password of "admin," you can run the script in the following way:

```
$ ./get-routing.py -a 10.1.1.1 -u admin -p admin
```

NOTE

These scripts demonstrate how to make use of these modules at the network element level. They serve as simple examples of code based on YANG modules, providing a nice educational, testing, and troubleshooting set of tools. The YANG Catalog toolchain, including YANG Suite, provides excellent documentation over the API that is the zoo of YANG modules so that you can focus more on the YANG API and less on the YANG language. However, more than just a few scripts are required for robust network automation.

YANG Suite, because of the interactivity it provides, offers a great way to get to know specific YANG modules. By generating RPCs and scripts, you can understand how various configuration and monitoring operations will look on the wire and begin to think through potential use cases. More of YANG Suite is included in the next section as you transition from YANG module exploration to interacting with devices using YANG.

Interacting with Devices

Thus far, you focused on tooling to explore and dissect YANG modules. The reason these modules exist, though, is so you can manage your devices in well-defined, machine-consumable ways. Additionally, you will want to further abstract things so that you can manage the network holistically and enable end-to-end automation.

This section highlights some tools used to interact with devices using model-driven protocols such as NETCONF and RESTCONF, as well as tools to consume telemetry streams from devices. These tools provide a good introduction to how these protocols work and how the YANG-modeled data is turned into practical device-level operations. They are good additions to your model-driven toolbelt. Some of these tools are command line-based while others present a graphical user interface (GUI). The tools you use will depend on your use cases. Command-line tools work well within scripts, while GUI tools offer a human ease-of-use angle, especially useful for wrapping your head around YANG, NETCONF, RESTCONF, and telemetry concepts. Some basic functionality is explained here, and more in-depth, real-world examples of device interactions are covered in Chapter 10, "Using NETCONF and YANG."

NETCONF Tools

The tools described in these next sections allow you to interact with devices through NETCONF. This includes typical operations such as fetching configurations and operational data and modifying configurations, as well as some "meta" operations such as determining what modules a network element supports and obtaining local copies of those modules directly from the network elements themselves.

YANG Suite

Previously in this chapter you looked at YANG Suite as a tool offered in the YANG Catalog, which enables you to explore YANG modules and generate sample RPCs and scripts. In addition to offering a graphical interface to device interactions, it has a number of features aimed at easing the exploration of device capabilities and creating useful subsets of YANG modules to accomplish specific tasks. YANG Suite is also available as a Python package that can be installed on Linux, macOS, and Windows so that you can use it as a way to directly interact with devices using a web-based interface.

NOTE

At the time of writing, the distribution plans for YANG Suite are still being determined. The latest information is that YANG Suite is expected to be released as a downloadable product in calendar year 2019. Some of the screen images and instructions may change between now and then, but the underlying capabilities and intent behind YANG Suite will remain the same.

Install YANG Suite using the instructions found in its included README file. YANG Suite runs a web server on port 8480 by default. Use a browser to connect to http://localhost:8480, log in using the username and password you created during installation, and then begin to use the YANG Suite features locally.

With YANG Suite on the YANG Catalog site, the module you wanted was automatically added to YANG Suite with all of its dependencies from the other YANG Catalog tools. Since you are now running it locally, you are responsible for finding the modules and adding their dependencies. Fortunately, YANG Suite has a feature to retrieve modules directly from devices using the NETCONF protocol.

YANG Suite uses "device profiles" to understand the basic communication and credential aspects of devices. You must set up a device profile for each device with which you want to work. Currently, YANG Suite supports NETCONF as the YANG-based transport; however, RESTCONF support is under development. Figure 7-6 shows the New Device Profile setup screen when creating a profile for the 192.168.10.48 test device.

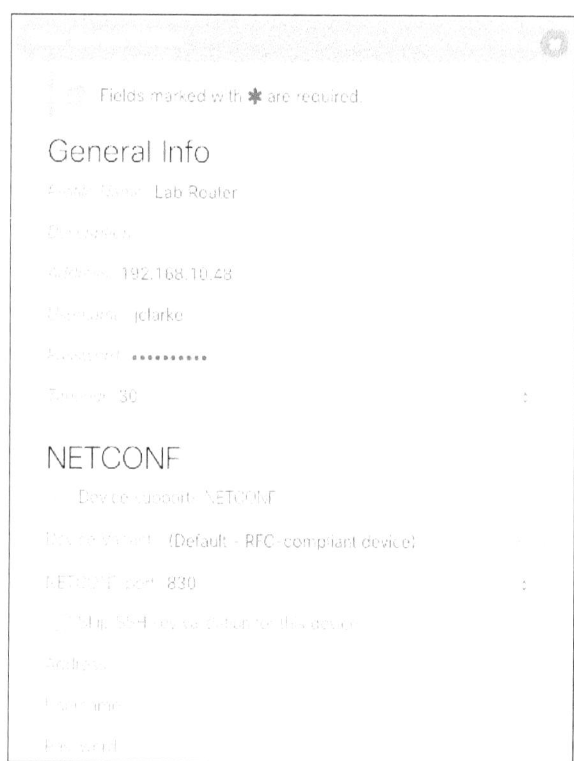

FIGURE 7-6 YANG Suite Device Profile Settings

Once you have a device profile, you need to create a YANG Suite repository. Set up a new empty repository, and you are prompted for two options to add modules to it. One is to load them manually from the file system. The other is to download them using one of your device profiles. Select the device profile you just created and get the schema list. For this step to work, the device must support the ietf-netconf-monitoring module.

NOTE

The device Timeout value shown in the device profile may need to be increased from its default value of 30 seconds in order to support downloading the entire schema successfully.

Once YANG Suite retrieves the list, choose which modules to import into your repository. While you might think to just add the module (or modules) you are explicitly going to use, know that doing so requires you to resolve all of the dependencies for that module yourself. Instead, import *all* of the modules from the device. Pare those down later using YANG module sets.

With the repository created, you move to defining a YANG module set (or multiple YANG sets). YANG module sets (or just YANG sets) group modules from a given repository for purposes of exploration or for interacting with devices for specific tasks. While you can certainly create a YANG set with all of the modules in a repository, it helps to focus the module list in a set to reduce the tree size and complexity as well as reduce load time in the user interface. A nice feature of YANG Suite is that the YANG set interface helps you identify modules that fit into a set as you add other modules. For example, since you are looking at the ietf-routing module, you might decide to create a YANG set that contains only that module. However, that module has dependencies. There are also modules that augment ietf-routing and introduce derived identities (such as ietf-ipv4-unicast-routing). Because you added all of the modules from your device to your repository, YANG Suite knows about these interrelations. As you add modules to your set, YANG Suite suggests additional modules that are either required because they are dependencies or nice to have because they add more context.

Figure 7-7 shows a YANG set defined with the ietf-routing module, its dependencies, and the ietf-ipv4-unicast-routing module all added. If there are additional modules in the repository that would add more definitions and flesh out the tree context, they are displayed in the center selection field.

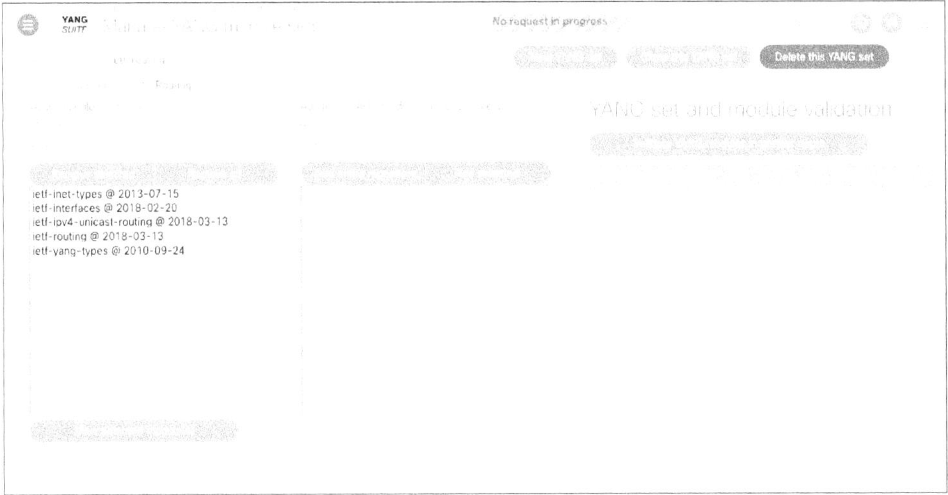

FIGURE 7-7 YANG Set in YANG Suite

Now move to the Operations > NETCONF screen. This will look familiar from the version on YANG Catalog. However, now that you have a local instance, you can test the generated RPCs against your device. First thing to do is select the YANG set that you previously created. This then allows you to choose a module for drawing the tree. In the routing example, select ietf-routing and click the "Load module(s)" button. Notice that even though you didn't choose the ietf-interfaces module, the subtree for it is displayed. This is because YANG Suite automatically resolves dependencies and additional augmentations based on the modules found within the YANG set. This also means that the ietf-routing subtree contains the ietf-ipv4-unicast-routing additions.

At the top, select the Get-config NETCONF operation, expand the ietf-routing subtree, and click in the Value column next to *routing* to "check" that column for inclusion. Click the Add RPC button on the right. With the YANG Catalog version, you can simply review the RPC. With your local instance, select your device profile from the Device pull-down and choose an appropriate datastore. Then click the Run RPC button, and the results of the executed RPC display in a pop-up window frame.

YANG Suite helps simple **edit-config** operations by providing a visual, tree representation of the nodes to be configured. This tree interface also shows which leafs are keys so you can be sure you've filled in the correct elements. For example, if you want to create a new IPv4 static route in the default routing-instance that points to prefix 10.20.30.0/24 to 192.168.20.1, first fill in the values next to all leafs that have a lock icon next to them (these are mandatory keys). Finally, fill in the respective values for v4ur:destination-prefix and v4ur:next-hop-address. Add the RPC and run it. If your device supports a candidate datastore, perform the **edit-config** there, and YANG Suite prompts you if you want to add a **commit** after making the configuration change.

The RPC text area in YANG Suite is additive, meaning you can continue to add operations to perform within a single NETCONF transaction. There may also be sets of RPCs that you want to reuse multiple times either for a single device or across multiple devices. You can create saved tasks within YANG Suite for this purpose. Once the RPC text area contains the specific recipe you'd like to save, click the Save as Task button and give your task a name and description. The task is then listed in the Task List pull-down on the right of the window. Like YANG repositories and sets, tasks are persistent for the current user.

If the device supports NETCONF notifications (as defined in RFC 5277), then clicking Notifications next to the device pull-down displays a window listing the available streams on the device. Subscribe to one or more of them, and YANG Suite displays the notifications it receives in real time in a new pop-up window.

In addition to these device interactions tasks, your local instance of YANG Suite can do everything the YANG Catalog version can do. With its multiuser capability, it's a great tool to spin up in your network to give engineers a way to consistently explore YANG modules and test device interactions.

Netconf-console

Netconf-console is a handy Python-based command-line utility for interacting with devices using the NETCONF protocol. Like pyang, it is available in the PyPI Python package index, and thus is installable with the pip utility. Netconf-console not only allows you to make configuration changes and gather operational data, but you can use it to discover device capabilities and retrieve YANG module schema directly from the devices themselves. Thus, if you've determined the module you want to use, you can confirm that the device supports it directly by querying the device, or you can get the modules the device supports and explore them to understand the device's management capabilities.

To get started with netconf-console, install it using pip:

```
$ pip install netconf-console
```

This command installs, among other Python libraries, a netconf-console executable. By default, netconf-console wants to establish a NETCONF session to localhost on port 2022. However, it supports a number of command-line options to get it to interact with remote devices. Run **netconf-console** with the **--help** argument to get its command-line options.

The next step is to find out what your device supports. If you have a device with IP address 192.168.10.48 that is configured with NETCONF on the standard port of 830, you can request its capabilities (that is, the NETCONF features and YANG modules it supports) using the **--hello** argument to netconf-console, as shown next. The abridged output is shown in Example 7-6.

```
$ netconf-console --host 192.168.10.48 --port 830 -u username \ -p password --hello
```

EXAMPLE 7-6 Output of **<hello>** from netconf-console

```
<nc:hello xmlns:nc="urn:ietf:params:xml:ns:netconf:base:1.0">
  <nc:capabilities>
    <nc:capability>urn:ietf:params:netconf:capability:rollback-on-error:1.0
  </nc:capability>
    <nc:capability>urn:ietf:params:xml:ns:netconf:base:1.0?module=ietf-netconf&amp;
revision=2011-06-01</nc:capability>
    <nc:capability>urn:ietf:params:xml:ns:yang:ietf-routing?module=ietf-routing&amp;
revision=2015-05-25&amp;features=router-id,multiple-ribs&amp;deviations=cisco-xe-
ietf-routing-deviation</nc:capability>
    <nc:capability>urn:ietf:params:xml:ns:yang:ietf-interfaces?module=ietf-
interfaces&amp;revision=2014-05-08&amp;features=pre-provisioning,if-mib,
arbitrary-names</nc:capability>
    <nc:capability>urn:ietf:params:xml:ns:yang:ietf-ipv4-unicast-routing?module=
ietf-ipv4-unicast-routing&amp;revision=2015-05-25&amp;deviations=cisco-xe-ietf-
ipv4-unicast-routing-deviation</nc:capability>
    <nc:capability>http://cisco.com/ns/cisco-xe-ietf-ipv4-unicast-routing-deviation?
module=cisco-xe-ietf-ipv4-unicast-routing-deviation&amp;revision=2015-09-11
</nc:capability>
    ...
  </nc:capabilities>
</nc:hello>
```

So far, you've explored the ietf-routing YANG module at revision 2018-03-13. The 2018-03-13 revision represents the latest ratified standard version as of this writing. The 192.168.10.48 device supports the ietf-routing module, but an older revision. Use the netconf-console utility to pull this module directly off of the device much like you did with YANG Suite. Instead of the **--hello** argument, run netconf-console with **--schema ietf-routing** to get the full contents of ietf-routing@2015-05-25 (that is, the exact revision of the module supported by the device), as shown next. The abridged output is shown in Example 7-7.

```
$ netconf-console --host 192.168.10.48 --port 830 -u username \
                  -p password --schema ietf-routing
```

EXAMPLE 7-7 Excerpt of the ietf-routing Schema Extracted from a Device

```
<data xmlns="urn:ietf:params:xml:ns:yang:ietf-netconf-monitoring"
xmlns:nc="urn:ietf:params:xml:ns:netconf:base:1.0">   module ietf-routing {

     namespace "urn:ietf:params:xml:ns:yang:ietf-routing";

     prefix "rt";

     import ietf-yang-types {
       prefix "yang";
     }

     import ietf-interfaces {
       prefix "if";
     }
...
```

While this provides the entire ietf-routing@2015-05-25 module, like other NETCONF data, it is returned encoded in XML. In order to use this module with tools like pyang, the content of the **<data>** element must be extracted and decoded. This is done in a number of ways, but an easy and reliable way to do it is to install the XML-Twig utilities from http://www.xmltwig.org/xmltwig/. One of the utilities, xml_grep, allows you to specify an XPath and pull out that node's data. Using xml_grep along with netconf-console, you can extract the device's ietf-routing YANG module into a file to be used with other YANG exploration and network automation tools, as shown in Example 7-8.

EXAMPLE 7-8 Use xml_grep to Extract the ietf-routing Module into a Local File

```
$ netconf-console --host 192.168.10.48 --port 830 -u username \
                  -p password --get-schema ietf-routing \
        | xml_grep 'data' --text_only \
        > ietf-routing@2015-05-25.yang
```

Using pyang, you get this module's tree structure, as shown in Example 7-9.

EXAMPLE 7-9 Tree Structure of Extracted ietf-routing Module

```
module: ietf-routing
  +--ro routing-state
  |  +--ro routing-instance* [name]
  |     +--ro name                 string
  |     +--ro type?                identityref
  |     +--ro router-id?           yang:dotted-quad
  |     +--ro interfaces
  |     |  +--ro interface*   if:interface-state-ref
  |     +--ro routing-protocols
  |     |  +--ro routing-protocol* [type name]
  |     |     +--ro type    identityref
  |     |     +--ro name    string
  |     +--ro ribs
  |        +--ro rib* [name]
  |           +--ro name              string
  |           +--ro address-family    identityref
  |           +--ro default-rib?      boolean {multiple-ribs}?
  |           +--ro routes
  |              +--ro route* [destination-prefix]
  |                 +--ro route-preference?     route-preference
  |                 +--ro destination-prefix    string
  |                 +--ro metric?               uint32
  |                 +--ro next-hop
  |                 |  +--ro (next-hop-options)
  |                 |     +--:(simple-next-hop)
  |                 |     |  +--ro outgoing-interface?   string
  |                 |     |  +--ro next-hop-address?     string
  |                 |     +--:(special-next-hop)
  |                 |        +--ro special-next-hop?     enumeration
  |                 +--ro source-protocol       identityref
  |                 +--ro active?               empty
  |                 +--ro last-updated?         yang:date-and-time
  |                 +--ro update-source?        string
  +--rw routing
     +--rw routing-instance* [name]
        +--rw name                 string
        +--rw type?                identityref
        +--rw enabled?             boolean
        +--rw router-id?           yang:dotted-quad
        +--rw description?         string
        +--rw interfaces
        |  +--rw interface*   if:interface-ref
```

```
      +--rw routing-protocols
      |  +--rw routing-protocol* [type name]
      |     +--rw type             identityref
      |     +--rw name             string
      |     +--rw description?     string
      |     +--rw static-routes
      +--rw ribs
         +--rw rib* [name]
            +--rw name              string
            +--rw address-family?   identityref
            +--rw description?      string

augment /if:interfaces-state/if:interface:
  +--ro routing-instance?   string

rpcs:
  +---x fib-route
     +---w input
     |  +---w routing-instance-name    string
     |  +---w destination-address
     |     +---w address-family    identityref
     +--ro output
        +--ro route
           +--ro address-family     identityref
           +--ro next-hop
           |  +--ro (next-hop-options)
           |     +--:(simple-next-hop)
           |     |  +--ro outgoing-interface?   string
           |     |  +--ro next-hop-address?     string
           |     +--:(special-next-hop)
           |        +--ro special-next-hop?     enumeration
           +--ro source-protocol    identityref
           +--ro active?            empty
           +--ro last-updated?      yang:date-and-time
```

There are a number of differences between the ietf-routing module supported by this device and the latest standard. For example, the *routing-state* subtree was not obsoleted, and the *fib-route* node is an RPC as opposed to an action.

Going back to the capabilities list, note that this device's implementation of the ietf-routing module has a set of deviations. Those are described in the "cisco-xe-ietf-routing-deviation" module. Just as with the ietf-routing module itself, use netconf-console to download the deviation module, as shown in Example 7-10.

EXAMPLE 7-10 Use xml_grep to Extract the cisco-xe-ietf-routing-deviation Module into a Local File

```
$ netconf-console --host 192.168.10.48 --port 830 -u username \ -p password
--get-schema \
        cisco-xe-ietf-routing-deviation | xml_grep 'data' \
        --text_only > cisco-xe-ietf-routing-deviation.yang
```

Example 7-11 shows the deviations extracted from this module.

EXAMPLE 7-11 Deviations for the ietf-routing Module

```
  deviation /rt:routing/rt:routing-instance/rt:type {
    deviate not-supported;
    description  "Not supported in IOS-XE 3.17 release.";
  }

  deviation /rt:routing/rt:routing-instance/rt:enabled {
    deviate not-supported;
    description  "Not supported in IOS-XE 3.17 release.";
  }

  deviation "/rt:routing/rt:routing-instance/rt:routing-protocols" +
            "/rt:routing-protocol/rt:description" {
    deviate not-supported;
    description  "Not supported in IOS-XE 3.17 release.";
  }

  deviation "/rt:routing-state/rt:routing-instance/rt:ribs/rt:rib/rt:routes/rt:route/
rt:last-updated" {
        description
            "Modifies the usage of yang:date-and-time in itef-routing
             temporarily to string so that Router's time notation is
             passed as it is without conversion to yang:date-and-time format.";

        deviate replace {
            type string;
        }

    }
```

The four deviations indicate that this particular device does not support the **/rt:routing/rt:routing-instance/rt:type, /rt:routing/rt:routing-instance/rt:enabled**, or the **/rt:routing/rt:routing-instance/rt:routing-protocols/rt:routing-protocol/rt:description** nodes; and the **/rt:routing-state/rt:routing-instance/rt:ribs/rt:rib/rt:routes/rt:route/rt:last-updated** node returns a string and not a **yang:date-and-time**. This is valuable information to build out an automation solution: You must design for the capabilities the network presents to you.

Pyang makes it easy to visualize these deviations within the tree structure. With both the downloaded ietf-routing.yang and cisco-xe-ietf-routing-deviation.yang modules in the same directory, run the following command to obtain the tree shown in Example 7-12. Note that this tree omits the nodes that are not supported and adjusts the type on the *last-updated* leaf. Annotations were added to the tree here to make it easier to spot the differences.

```
$ pyang -f tree \
     --deviation-module=cisco-xe-ietf-routing-deviation.yang \
     ietf-routing.yang
```

EXAMPLE 7-12 Combined ietf-routing Tree Taking Deviations into Account

```
module: ietf-routing
  +--ro routing-state
  |  +--ro routing-instance* [name]
  |     +--ro name                   string
  |     +--ro type?                  identityref
  |     +--ro router-id?             yang:dotted-quad
  |     +--ro interfaces
  |     |  +--ro interface*   if:interface-state-ref
  |     +--ro routing-protocols
  |     |  +--ro routing-protocol* [type name]
  |     |     +--ro type    identityref
  |     |     +--ro name    string
  |     +--ro ribs
  |        +--ro rib* [name]
  |           +--ro name                string
  |           +--ro address-family    identityref
  |           +--ro default-rib?      boolean {multiple-ribs}?
  |           +--ro routes
  |              +--ro route* [destination-prefix]
  |                 +--ro route-preference?     route-preference
  |                 +--ro destination-prefix    string
  |                 +--ro metric?               uint32
  |                 +--ro next-hop
  |                 |  +--ro (next-hop-options)
  |                 |     +--:(simple-next-hop)
  |                 |     |  +--ro outgoing-interface?   string
  |                 |     |  +--ro next-hop-address?     string
  |                 |     +--:(special-next-hop)
  |                 |        +--ro special-next-hop?     enumeration
```

```
|                 +--ro source-protocol       identityref
|                 +--ro active?               empty
|                 +--ro last-updated?         string ← Note: type UPDATED
|                 +--ro update-source?        string
+--rw routing
   +--rw routing-instance* [name]
      +--rw name                     string
      +--rw router-id?               yang:dotted-quad

                     → Note: MISSING type and enabled nodes here

      +--rw description?             string
      +--rw interfaces
      |  +--rw interface*   if:interface-ref
      +--rw routing-protocols
      |  +--rw routing-protocol* [type name]
      |     +--rw type                 identityref
      |     +--rw name                 string

                     → Note: MISSING description node here

      |     +--rw static-routes
      +--rw ribs
         +--rw rib* [name]
            +--rw name                 string
            +--rw address-family?   identityref
            +--rw description?      string

augment /if:interfaces-state/if:interface:
  +--ro routing-instance?   string

rpcs:
  +---x fib-route
     +---w input
     |  +---w routing-instance-name    string
     |  +---w destination-address
     |     +---w address-family    identityref
     +--ro output
        +--ro route
           +--ro address-family     identityref
           +--ro next-hop
           |  +--ro (next-hop-options)
           |     +--:(simple-next-hop)
           |     |  +--ro outgoing-interface?   string
```

```
|     | +--ro next-hop-address?     string
|     +--:(special-next-hop)
|        +--ro special-next-hop?     enumeration
+--ro source-protocol     identityref
+--ro active?             empty
+--ro last-updated?       yang:date-and-time
```

Now that you know what the device supports, and you've pulled down the modules, perform a **<get-config>** operation to gather the configured routing data. The **--get-config** argument to netconf-console takes two optional arguments: **--db** to specify a datastore, and **-x** to specify an XPath filter. If neither is specified, the full configuration is returned from the "running" datastore. In order to focus only on the routing configuration, provide an XPath filter to limit the output. When you were looking at the ietf-routing module within the YANG Catalog tools, all of the XPaths began with **/rt:routing**. You see in your tree here that routing is a top-level node with the "rw" notation next to it (recall that means it's a **config true** node). You can use this **/rt:routing** XPath filter with netconf-console, but you first need to tell it what the full namespace is for the prefix *rt*. To do that, specify the **--ns** argument with "prefix=namespace" notation (in this case, "rt=urn:ietf:params:xml:ns:yang:ietf-routing"). The full command is found in Example 7-13 and followed by its output in Example 7-14.

EXAMPLE 7-13 Obtain the Configuration Filtered on the /rt:routing Path

```
$ netconf-console --host 192.168.10.48 --port 830 -u username \
   -p password \
   --ns rt= urn:ietf:params:xml:ns:yang:ietf-routing \
   --get-config -x /rt:routing
```

EXAMPLE 7-14 Configuration Filtered to Show Only the /rt:routing Path

```
<data xmlns="urn:ietf:params:xml:ns:netconf:base:1.0"
xmlns:nc="urn:ietf:params:xml:ns:netconf:base:1.0">
  <routing xmlns="urn:ietf:params:xml:ns:yang:ietf-routing">
    <routing-instance>
      <name>VRF4</name>
      <interfaces/>
      <routing-protocols>
        <routing-protocol>
          <type>static</type>
          <name>1</name>
        </routing-protocol>
      </routing-protocols>
    </routing-instance>
    <routing-instance>
      <name>default</name>
      <description>default-vrf [read-only]</description>
      <interfaces/>
```

```
      <routing-protocols>
        <routing-protocol>
          <type xmlns:ospf="urn:ietf:params:xml:ns:yang:ietf-ospf">ospf:ospfv2</type>
          <name>1</name>
          <ospf xmlns="urn:ietf:params:xml:ns:yang:ietf-ospf">
            <instance>
              <af xmlns:rt="urn:ietf:params:xml:ns:yang:ietf-routing">rt:ipv4</af>
              <nsr>
                <enable>false</enable>
              </nsr>
              <auto-cost>
                <enable>false</enable>
              </auto-cost>
              <redistribution xmlns="urn:ietf:params:xml:ns:yang:cisco-ospf">
                <rip/>
              </redistribution>
            </instance>
          </ospf>
        </routing-protocol>
        <routing-protocol>
          <type>static</type>
          <name>1</name>
          <static-routes>
            <ipv4 xmlns="urn:ietf:params:xml:ns:yang:ietf-ipv4-unicast-routing">
              <route>
                <destination-prefix>10.10.10.10/32</destination-prefix>
                <next-hop>
                  <next-hop-address>192.168.20.236</next-hop-address>
                </next-hop>
              </route>
            </ipv4>
            <ipv6 xmlns="urn:ietf:params:xml:ns:yang:ietf-ipv6-unicast-routing">
              <route>
                <destination-prefix>::/0</destination-prefix>
                <next-hop>
                  <next-hop-address>2001:db8::7:1</next-hop-address>
                </next-hop>
              </route>
            </ipv6>
          </static-routes>
        </routing-protocol>
      </routing-protocols>
    </routing-instance>
  </routing>
</data>
```

Note that a number of namespaces other than ietf-routing's "urn:ietf:params:xml:ns:yang:ietf-routing" are referenced in this output. These are defined in other modules that augment the ietf-routing configuration structure. Pull these down using the same method just described by getting the module name from the capabilities output.

Pull down the ietf-ipv4-unicast-routing module and use it to build the configuration needed to add a static IPv4 route using **<edit-config>**, as shown in Example 7-15.

EXAMPLE 7-15 Use xml_grep to Extract the ietf-ipv4-unicast-routing Module into a Local File

```
e$ netconf-consol --host 192.168.10.48 --port 830 -u username \ -p password
--get-schema \
        ietf-ipv4-unicast-routing \
        | xml_grep 'data' --text_only \
        > ietf-ipv4-unicast-routing@2015-05-25.yang
```

Example 7-16 also shows that the ietf-ipv4-unicast-routing module has its own deviations for this device, so pull down that module as well.

EXAMPLE 7-16 Use xml_grep to Extract the cisco-xe-ietf-ipv4-unicast-routing-deviation Module into a Local File

```
$ netconf-console --host 192.168.10.48 --port 830 -u username \ -p password
--get-schema \
        cisco-xe-ietf-ipv4-unicast-routing-deviation \
        | xml_grep 'data' --text_only \
        > cisco-xe-ietf-ipv4-unicast-routing-deviation.yang
```

Pass all of the modules you downloaded thus far to pyang using the command shown in Example 7-17 to get the combined tree shown in Example 7-18.

EXAMPLE 7-17 Display a Composite Tree with All Related Routing Modules

```
$ pyang -f tree \
  --deviation-module=cisco-xe-ietf-routing-deviation.yang \
  --deviation-module=cisco-xe-ietf-ipv4-unicast-routing-deviation.yang \
  ietf-routing@2015-05-25.yang \
  ietf-ipv4-unicast-routing@2015.05-25.yang
```

EXAMPLE 7-18 Composite Routing Tree with All Deviations and Augmentations Added

```
module: ietf-routing
  +--ro routing-state
  |  +--ro routing-instance* [name]
  |     +--ro name                  string
```

```
|     +--ro type?                 identityref
|     +--ro router-id?            yang:dotted-quad
|     +--ro interfaces
|     |  +--ro interface*   if:interface-state-ref
|     +--ro routing-protocols
|     |  +--ro routing-protocol* [type name]
|     |     +--ro type    identityref
|     |     +--ro name    string
|     +--ro ribs
|        +--ro rib* [name]
|           +--ro name              string
|           +--ro address-family    identityref
|           +--ro default-rib?      boolean {multiple-ribs}?
|           +--ro routes
|              +--ro route* [destination-prefix]
|                 +--ro route-preference?     route-preference
|                 +--ro destination-prefix    string
|                 +--ro metric?               uint32
|                 +--ro next-hop
|                 |  +--ro (next-hop-options)
|                 |     +--:(simple-next-hop)
|                 |     |  +--ro outgoing-interface?   string
|                 |     |  +--ro next-hop-address?     string
|                 |     +--:(special-next-hop)
|                 |        +--ro special-next-hop?     enumeration
|                 +--ro source-protocol       identityref
|                 +--ro active?               empty
|                 +--ro last-updated?         string
|                 +--ro update-source?        string
+--rw routing
   +--rw routing-instance* [name]
      +--rw name                  string
      +--rw router-id?            yang:dotted-quad
      +--rw description?          string
      +--rw interfaces
      |  +--rw interface*   if:interface-ref
      +--rw routing-protocols
      |  +--rw routing-protocol* [type name]
      |     +--rw type              identityref
      |     +--rw name              string
      |     +--rw static-routes
      |        +--rw v4ur:ipv4
      |           +--rw v4ur:route* [destination-prefix]
      |              +--rw v4ur:destination-prefix    inet:ipv4-prefix
      |              +--rw v4ur:next-hop
      |                 +--rw (v4ur:next-hop-options)
```

```
        |                      +--:(v4ur:simple-next-hop)
        |                      |  +--rw v4ur:outgoing-interface?   string
        |                      +--:(v4ur:special-next-hop)
        |                      |  +--rw v4ur:special-next-hop?     enumeration
        |                      +--:(v4ur:next-hop-address)
        |                         +--rw v4ur:next-hop-address?     inet:ipv4-address
        +--rw ribs
           +--rw rib* [name]
              +--rw name              string
              +--rw address-family?   identityref
              +--rw description?      string

  augment /if:interfaces-state/if:interface:
    +--ro routing-instance?   string

...
```

The part of the tree you want to use is shown in bold font in Example 7-18. The ietf-ipv4-unicast-routing module augments the base ietf-routing module to add IPv4 unicast-specific routing elements. One of the augmentations it provides is support for IPv4 static routes. Such a route has an IPv4 destination prefix and a choice of IPv4 next-hop address. Looking at the **<get-config>** output from your device, you see it already has a number of IPv4 static routes that correspond to the schema shown in Example 7-18.

To add a new static route for prefix 172.16.1.0/24 with a next hop of 192.168.20.1, create a file called new-route.xml with the contents shown in Example 7-19. (Hint: You can also use YANG Suite to create this RPC, as shown earlier.) These contents resemble the results of the **<get-config>** operation.

EXAMPLE 7-19 Body of the **<edit-config>** Configuration Structure to Add a Static Route

```
<routing xmlns="urn:ietf:params:xml:ns:yang:ietf-routing">
    <routing-instance>
      <name>default</name>
      <routing-protocols>
        <routing-protocol>
          <type>static</type>
          <name>1</name>
          <static-routes>
            <ipv4 xmlns="urn:ietf:params:xml:ns:yang:ietf-ipv4-unicast-routing"
xmlns:nc="urn:ietf:params:xml:ns:netconf:base:1.0" nc:operation="merge">
              <route>
                  <destination-prefix>172.16.1.0/24</destination-prefix>
                <next-hop>
```

```
                <next-hop-address>192.168.20.1</next-hop-address>
              </next-hop>
            </route>
          </ipv4>
        </static-routes>
      </routing-protocol>
    </routing-protocols>
  </routing-instance>
</routing>
```

The addition of **nc:operation="merge"** here instructs the device to merge this configuration into the current configuration. If you were to use an operation such as **replace**, the static routes are overwritten with the contents of this new **<edit-config>**.

Perform the **<edit-config>** operation to the device with the following command:

```
$ netconf-console --host 192.168.10.48 --port 830 -u username \
                  -p password --edit-config new-route.xml
```

NOTE

Just as with **--get-config**, netconf-console accepts an optional **--db** argument to specify a datastore other than "running." This example inserts this route directly into the default running datastore.

Netconf-console displays an **<ok>** result if the device accepted the **<edit-config>** operation. If any error occurred, the resulting error tag and details are displayed.

In addition to showing configuration data, netconf-console can perform **<get>** operations to display operational data. The ietf-routing module supported by this device supports a routing-state subtree that has nodes marked with "ro" in the tree (indicating **config false** or operational state nodes). Using the **--get** argument with the same **--ns** argument and an XPath filter of **/rt:routing-state**, you can display the operational state of routing on this device, as shown next. The output of this command is shown in Example 7-20.

```
$ netconf-console --host 192.168.10.48 --port 830 -u username -p password \
        --ns rt=urn:ietf:params:xml:ns:yang:ietf-routing \
        --get -x /rt:routing-state
```

EXAMPLE 7-20 The Operational State of the Device Filtered to Only Show the routing-state Path

```
<routing-state xmlns="urn:ietf:params:xml:ns:yang:ietf-routing">
    <routing-instance>
      <name>default</name>
      <ribs>
        <rib>
          <name>ipv4-default</name>
          <address-family>ipv4</address-family>
          <default-rib>false</default-rib>
          <routes>
            <route>
              <destination-prefix>0.0.0.0</destination-prefix>
              <route-preference>1</route-preference>
              <metric>1</metric>
              <next-hop>
                <outgoing-interface/>
                <next-hop-address>192.168.10.1</next-hop-address>
              </next-hop>
              <source-protocol>static</source-protocol>
              <active/>
            </route>
            <route>
              <destination-prefix>172.16.1.0</destination-prefix>
              <route-preference>0</route-preference>
              <metric>0</metric>
              <next-hop>
                <outgoing-interface/>
                <next-hop-address>192.168.20.1</next-hop-address>
              </next-hop>
              <source-protocol>direct</source-protocol>
              <active/>
            </route>
          </routes>
        </rib>
        <rib>
          <name>ipv6-default</name>
          <address-family>ipv6</address-family>
          <default-rib>false</default-rib>
          <routes>
            <route>
              <destination-prefix>::</destination-prefix>
              <route-preference>1</route-preference>
              <metric>1</metric>
              <next-hop>
```

```
            <outgoing-interface/>
            <next-hop-address>2001:db8::7:1</next-hop-address>
          </next-hop>
          <source-protocol>static</source-protocol>
          <active/>
        </route>
      </routes>
    </rib>
  </ribs>
</routing-instance>
</routing-state>
```

This result shows the contents of the active routing state on the device and also indicates that the route for 172.16.1.0/24 that you configured with **<edit-config>** was properly installed into the Routing Information Base (RIB).

Looking back through the usage help for netconf-console, you can see that it offers a number of other operations, such as saving the running datastore to the startup datastore, validating the configuration to be deployed, performing custom RPCs, and locking devices for multistep transactions. It also features an interactive mode (with the **-i** argument) that drops you to a **netconf>** prompt, which allows you to perform the same set of commands, but in more of a Unix-like shell environment.

Ansible

Ansible[2] is a popular automation framework used in many different areas of IT. It started out as a way to automate the deployment of new compute services and grew plug-ins to automate the deployment and configuration of network devices, applications, and services.

At its core, Ansible uses the concepts of "playbooks," "roles," and "tasks" to string together atomic operations in order to build complex automations. Ansible does not require an agent or a piece of client software to be installed on the remote elements in order to interact with them. Instead, it uses Secure Shell (SSH) (and Windows Remote Management [WinRM] in the case of Windows) to execute its automations. Depending on the type of element to be automated, Ansible may copy Python or PowerShell code over to it temporarily, or it may execute the Python code locally. This makes getting started with Ansible relatively easy.

When the first Ansible modules were written for the networking space, they essentially provided a means to execute command-line interface (CLI) commands on network devices from within the Ansible playbooks. These modules evolved to embrace more programmatic interfaces that some devices possessed. Starting in Ansible 2.2, those interfaces included NETCONF with the introduction of the netconf_config module.

The netconf_config module provides a way to execute **edit-config** RPCs given an XML payload. It supports options for specifying a datastore to modify as well as an option to save to the startup configuration (if it exists). The **edit-config** operation to add a new static route that you performed using netconf-console can be done as an Ansible task, as shown in Example 7-21.

EXAMPLE 7-21 Ansible Task to Add a New Static Route Using netconf_config

```
- name: Configure static route to service network
  netconf_config:
    host: "{{ item }}"
    datastore: running
    xml: |
      <config>
        <routing xmlns="urn:ietf:params:xml:ns:yang:ietf-routing">
          <routing-instance>
            <name>default</name>
            <routing-protocols>
              <routing-protocol>
                <type>static</type>
                <name>1</name>
                <static-routes>
                  <ipv4 xmlns="urn:ietf:params:xml:ns:yang:ietf-ipv4-unicast-routing"
xmlns:nc="urn:ietf:params:xml:ns:netconf:base:1.0" nc:operation="merge">
                    <route>
                        <destination-prefix>{{ service_network }}</destination-prefix>
                      <next-hop>
                        <next-hop-address>{{ service_gateway }}</next-hop-address>
                      </next-hop>
                    </route>
                  </ipv4>
                </static-routes>
              </routing-protocol>
            </routing-protocols>
          </routing-instance>
        </routing>
      </config>
  with_items: "{{ groups['devices'] }}"
```

NETCONF support in Ansible has evolved since 2.2. Ansible 2.3 and higher offer a way to create persistent NETCONF sessions with its netconf connection plug-in. Ansible 2.6 introduced the netconf_rpc plug-in, which provides a way to execute RPCs other than **edit-config**. Version 2.6 also introduced the netconf_get plug-in specifically for retrieving operational data. Both the netconf_rpc and netconf_get plug-ins have a "display" parameter that enables the XML data the device returns to be rendered as either XML or JSON. This makes it easy to extract relevant details from a device and then push back the right configuration changes.

The NETCONF capabilities within Ansible offer a marked improvement of straight CLI for automating configuration changes and operational data retrievals. However, you still need to know the XML structure of the modules, and you still need to work device-by-device. In Chapter 11, "YANG Model Design," Ansible integration with Cisco's Network Services Orchestrator (NSO) is discussed, which provides a layer of network and service abstraction, making your Ansible automation even more powerful.

RESTCONF Tools

In addition to YANG-based tools that use the NETCONF protocol for interacting with devices, there are a number of tools you can use to explore a device's RESTCONF interface. Because RESTCONF uses a Hypertext Transfer Protocol (HTTP), Representational State Transfer (REST)–like flow, many tools you would use to interact with REST APIs are used with devices that support RESTCONF.

cURL

One example is the cURL[3] utility that has been mentioned a few times in previous chapters. cURL is a veritable Swiss army knife of HTTP and File Transfer Protocol (FTP) operations. While not specifically built for interacting with REST application programming interfaces (APIs), it is fairly ubiquitous (at least on Unix-like platforms) and works well for testing REST functionality. Say, like with netconf-console, you wanted to get the capabilities from a device that supports RESTCONF. Remember that unlike NETCONF, RESTCONF doesn't have a session in which a capabilities exchange is done. That is, there is no **<hello>** message. For a RESTCONF client to ascertain which modules are supported by a RESTCONF server, that server must support the ietf-yang-library (RFC 7895). Fetch the instance data from this module using the following cURL command with some sample output shown in Example 7-22:

```
$ curl -H 'Accept: application/yang-data+json' -u 'user:password'
https://192.168.10.48/restconf/data/ietf-yang-library:modules-state
```

EXAMPLE 7-22 Excerpt of the ietf-yang-library Output Fetched Using cURL


```
{
  "ietf-yang-library:modules-state": {
    "module-set-id": "5d8861a42ef514753381d55ca1a32aae",
    "module": [
      {
        "name": "ATM-FORUM-TC-MIB",
        "revision": "",
        "schema": "https://192.168.10.48:443/restconf/tailf/modules/ATM-FORUM-TC-MIB",
        "namespace": "urn:ietf:params:xml:ns:yang:smiv2:ATM-FORUM-TC-MIB",
        "conformance-type": "import"
      },
```

```
      {
        "name": "ATM-MIB",
        "revision": "1998-10-19",
        "schema": "https://192.168.10.48:443/restconf/tailf/modules/ATM-MIB/1998-10-19",
        "namespace": "urn:ietf:params:xml:ns:yang:smiv2:ATM-MIB",
        "conformance-type": "implement"
      },
      {
...
```


By default, cURL does an HTTP GET operation to the target URL, so no additional action verb needs to be specified in order for you to fetch the ietf-yang-library's module-states container. The **-H** argument tells cURL to add a custom header. In this case, you set the "Accept" header to be "application/yang-data+json" so that the RESTCONF server returns JSON output. The **-u** argument passes your username and password to the device. Finally, the URL points to the modules-state container defined in the module ietf-yang-library.

cURL allows you to test configuration changes through RESTCONF as well. For example, if you want to patch in a new interface description for GigabitEthernet2, create a file called intf.json with the structure shown in Example 7-23.

EXAMPLE 7-23 Payload for Setting an Interface Description Using RESTCONF and cURL


```
{
  "ietf-interfaces:interfaces": {
    "interface": [
      {
        "name": "GigabitEthernet2",
        "description": "Set by cURL"
      }
    ]
  }
}
```


Then reference this file with the **-d @intf.json** notation on the cURL command line, as shown next:

```
$ curl -X PATCH -H 'Content-type: application/yang-data+json' -H 'Accept:
application/yang-data+json' -u 'user:password'
https://192.168.10.48/restconf/data/ietf-interfaces:interfaces -d @intf.json
```

The **-X** argument changes the HTTP verb from GET to PATCH, and the **-d** argument with @ tells cURL to load the contents of the PATCH body from the file named intf.json. The Content-type header is also added to let the server know that the content being provided for the patch is JSON-encoded YANG data.

While cURL is a very handy tool for testing RESTCONF, it is not a RESTCONF (or even a REST) tool by design. Note in the output of Example 7-24 that the JSON looks well-formatted. However, cURL simply returns the data how the server presents it. There is no inherent understanding of the content type. In fact, many people use cURL as a command-line way to download binary files because it preserves the source data. Therefore, when working with some RESTCONF servers, the cURL output may have to be post-processed in order to view the data in an easy-to-read way.

HTTPie

A command-line alternative to the cURL utility is HTTPie.[4] Like cURL, HTTPie interacts with HTTP servers, but offers rich capabilities specifically geared toward RESTful services and APIs. For example, it understands JSON output, formats it in a sane manner, and color-codes the output for easier reading. Its command-line syntax is also a bit simpler when it comes to interacting with services like RESTCONF.

Considering the ietf-routing module once again, Example 7-24 shows the commands to pull a list of configured static routes using both cURL and HTTPie.

EXAMPLE 7-24 Commands to Obtain Static Routes Using RESTCONF

```
$ curl -H 'Accept: application/yang-data+json' -u 'user:password'
https://192.168.10.48/restconf/data/ietf-routing:routing/routing-
instance=default/routing-protocols/routing-protocol=static,1

$ http -a 'user:password' https://192.168.10.48/restconf/data/ietf-
routing:routing/routing-instance=default/routing-protocols/routing-protocol=static,1
'Accept: application/yang-data+json'
```

The HTTPie command, though similar to the cURL command, more closely resembles how the HTTP request is structured on the wire, thus making it a bit more intuitive. Additionally, the output has color-coding enabled by default and "pretty-prints" JSON with easy-to-read indentation regardless of the format the server presents it in.

HTTPie follows the same HTTP-like request structure for performing other operations such as PATCH. To patch in a new interface description with HTTPie, use the following command:

```
$ http -a 'user:password' PATCH \ https://192.168.10.48/restconf/data/
ietf-interfaces:interfaces \
'Content-type: application/yang-data+json' \ 'Accept: application/yang-data+json' \
< intf.json
```

While command-line tools like cURL and HTTPie are useful for testing RESTCONF concepts and visually inspecting data, as well as pushing simple configuration snippets manually or from shell scripts, what about extracting data from JSON structures that are returned? There are numerous text-processing tools like sed, awk, and grep that regular expression wizards can use to grab a single piece of data out of a large JSON blob, but that can be complex and error-prone. The jq[5] utility presents a solution to this by natively understanding JSON structure. cURL and HTTPie output can be piped to jq to pinpoint specific elements in a JSON structure, perform transformations, construct custom objects, and so on.

For example, to extract only the next-hop-address value for the IPv4 default route in the static-route configuration output, pipe the data to jq and specify the path to the desired element. The command output is simply the next-hop address, or 192.168.10.1 in this case, as shown in Example 7-25.

EXAMPLE 7-25 Filtering the RESTCONF JSON Results with jq

```
$ http -a 'user:password' https://192.168.10.48/restconf/data/ietf-
routing:routing/routing-instance=default/routing-protocols/routing-protocol=static,1
'Accept: application/yang-data+json' | jq '."ietf-routing:routing-protocol"."static-
routes"."ietf-ipv4-unicast-routing:ipv4"."route"[]
 | select(."destination-prefix" == "0.0.0.0/0")."next-hop"."next-hop-address"'
```

The jq command walks the JSON structure down into the static-routes list and selects the static-route object that has the destination-prefix value of 0.0.0.0/0. Then it extracts only the next-hop-address element value. More examples and a tutorial for jq are found at https://stedolan.github.io/jq/tutorial/.

Postman

Command-line tools are not the only way to interact and test out RESTCONF servers. A popular GUI tool for working with RESTful services and APIs is Postman[6] (see Figure 7-8). Postman started out as a Google Chrome extension and is now a standalone application for macOS, Windows, and Linux.

FIGURE 7-8 The Postman Main Screen

Under the covers, Postman interoperates with RESTCONF servers in much the same way as the command-line tools discussed previously. However, it also offers a number of nice features, not only to test out RESTCONF operations, but also to move from simple testing to more formal application-based automations.

NOTE

Since RESTCONF relies on Secure Hypertext Transfer Protocol (HTTPS), network elements need Secure Socket Layer (SSL) / Transport Layer Security (TLS) certificates. Unless you use a trusted Certificate Authority (CA) to sign these certificates, they will be self-signed and untrusted by default. In order for Postman to accept them, you need to go to Preferences and disable "SSL certificate verification."

First, it includes a *collections* system whereby you can group a number of requests (for example, to demonstrate the API for an application) and bundle them together so that they are easily shared with other users. As you use it to explore different aspects of RESTCONF, begin to save your requests into collections. Even if you have no intention of sharing them, they are useful to review later on or test against new devices.

To create a collection, click on the Collections tab and then click the "New collection" widget. Fill in a name and an optional description and then move to the Authorization tab.

Another advantage of using collections is that you can specify common attributes to be used across the entire collection. Since there will be multiple requests, each needing to be authenticated to the device, you can create a collection-wide template for authentication here. However, since you likely do not want to store *your* username and password here—especially if you want to share this collection—consider using a variable. Postman variables are in the form of {{*var_name*}}—that is, the variable name is enclosed within double curly braces. Set the Type to Basic Auth and fill in {{restconf_username}} and {{restconf_password}} for Username and Password, respectively.

Before finalizing the new collection, go to the Variables tab. Here, you can add other common collection-wide variables. For example, remembering the MIME types for RESTCONF's JSON and XML encoding can be tough. Therefore, adding variables for content_json and content_xml that point to application/yang-data+json and application/yang-data+xml, respectively, can prove useful.

Once the new collection is created, requests can be added to it. Before adding to a collection, it's useful to create an *environment* to be used to expand some of the variables (such as {{restconf_username}}) for *your* Postman session. That is, the environment is unique to you and is not shared unless you choose to share the collection. Create a new environment by clicking the gear widget in the top-right corner of the Postman window (that is, the Manage Environments button). From here, add a new environment. Add variable definitions for "restconf_username" and "restconf_password" that point your RESTCONF server's username and password, respectively. Also add definitions for "ip_addr" and "port" that point to your RESTCONF server's IP address (or hostname) and port, respectively. Finally, adding a variable such as "restconf_accept" that points to one of the previously defined MIME type variables allows you to easily switch between JSON and XML encoding.

Add a new request to this collection that gets the list of static routes configured on the device. If this is your first request for the collection, click the "Add requests" link. Otherwise, duplicate an existing request. By default, the HTTP action used by Postman is GET, and that's what you want here.

For the URL, fill in **https://{{ip_addr}}:{{port}}/restconf/data/ietf-routing:routing/routing-instance=default/routing-protocols/routing-protocol=static,1**. Note the use of the {{ip_addr}} and {{port}} variables previously defined in the Postman environment.

Next, go to the Headers tab and add a new header for Accept with the value {{restconf_accept}}. Once you start typing the braces to reference a variable, Postman attempts to auto-complete the variable name, which is nice if you forget exactly what you called the variable.

Finally, provide a name for this request within the collection, such as "Get Static Routes."

Before the request is executed, you must select the environment to use such that all of the variables listed are properly dereferenced. The pull-down at the top right lists all of the configured environments within Postman. Select the environment you created previously for RESTCONF and then click the Send button to perform the request. As you need to test different devices, use different credentials, and so on, the environment variables can be changed without you needing to change the underlying request parameters, as shown in Figure 7-9.

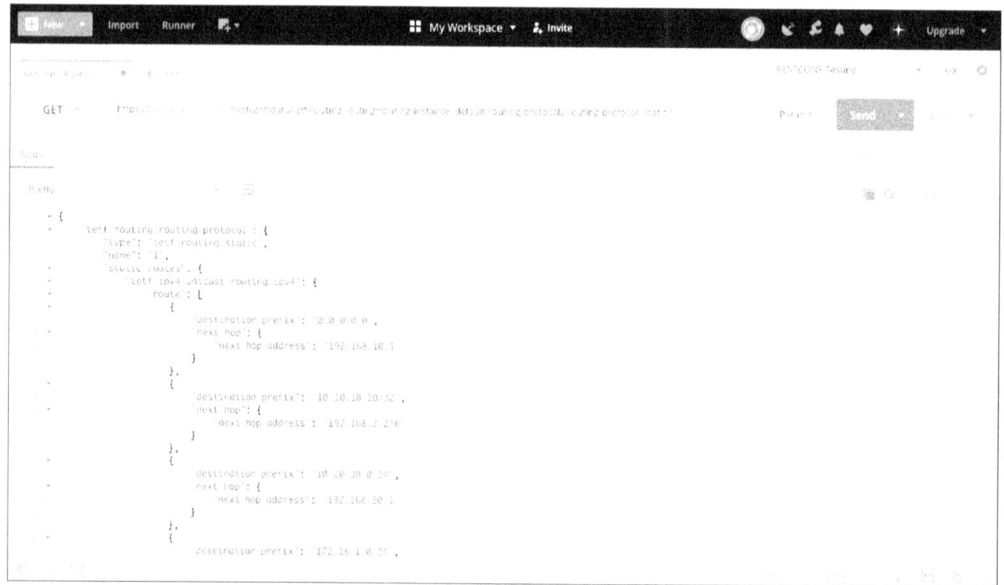

FIGURE 7-9 Postman Request for Static Routes via RESTCONF

Another very useful feature of Postman as you move from simply testing network elements with RESTCONF to beginning to develop scripts and applications is its code generation feature. Below the Send button is a Code link. This link opens a new window that shows the current request embedded into a number of different programming languages, as shown in Figure 7-10. For example, if you're looking to move from testing requests in Postman to a Python-based script, generate a starter script by selecting the desired Python library from the pull-down. While there is much more work to do (for example, you have to handle Postman variable expansions yourself, add error checking, and so on), this approach may be easier than developing a new script from a blank page.

FIGURE 7-10 Postman's Python Code Generation

Libraries that are useful for programming network elements using YANG-based protocols are explored in more detail in Chapter 8, "Automation Is as Good as the Data Models, Their Related Metadata and the Tools: For the Module Author."

Telemetry Tools

The NETCONF and RESTCONF tools shown thus far work well for pushing configuration and querying devices for operational data, but what about consuming model-driven, streaming telemetry from devices? Model-driven telemetry provides tremendous value, as it allows devices to push data to your management servers in order to assure network and service functionality. While you could continue to poll for this type of operational data, telemetry producers publish data only when it changes. Not only does this reduce network traffic, it allows a network administrator to be aware of the operational state of the network in real time, thus assuring network changes are always properly applied. As such, being able to consume and visualize telemetry data is extremely useful. The tooling for model-driven telemetry is still nascent, partially because the work to define and standardize how data is streamed and encoded is still underway. That said, some open source tools for telemetry consumption are starting to emerge.

Pipeline

Cisco contributed a tool called Pipeline[7] (or Big Muddy Pipeline) to the open source community. Currently, Pipeline is geared toward consuming model-driven telemetry streams from Cisco IOS-XR and NX-OS devices. Pipeline takes these streams and sends then to other tools, such as a time-series database like InfluxDB[8] or Prometheus[9] and a data analytics tool like PNDA.[10] This means Pipeline acts as a broker, allowing you to configure one set of telemetry exports and then plug in additional consumers on top of Pipeline.

Assuming you identified a set of key next-hop interfaces on your router that you want to monitor, you can build a telemetry graphing solution for router interface statistics (including bytes and packets transmitted and received, errors, and so on) using Pipeline, InfluxDB, and Grafana. First, clone Pipeline's GitHub repository, like so:

```
$ git clone https://github.com/cisco/bigmuddy-network-telemetry-pipeline.git
```

Pipeline stores its consumption and output sink configuration in the pipeline.conf file. By default, Pipeline consumes streaming telemetry sent over TCP to port 5432. This is defined in the base "testbed" configuration section shown in Example 7-26.

EXAMPLE 7-26 The pipeline.conf Contents for Handling a Telemetry Stream

```
[testbed]
stage = xport_input
type = tcp
encap = st
listen = :5432
```

Download and install InfluxDB from https://portal.influxdata.com/downloads. The pre-built packages make it much easier to get started. Additionally, the documentation at https://github.com/influxdata/influxdb provides a quick way to create a test database and generate some sample queries.

Create an InfluxDB called "mdtdb" to hold your model-driven telemetry streams that Pipeline sends, as shown next:

```
$ curl -XPOST "http://localhost:8086/query" --data-urlencode "q=CREATE DATABASE mdtdb"
```

Now that InfluxDB is running, configure Pipeline to send the data it receives from your router to your Influx instance. Edit pipeline.conf and add the section shown in Example 7-27.

EXAMPLE 7-27 The pipeline.conf Contents for Pushing Data to InfluxDB

```
[influxdb]
stage = xport_output
type = metrics
file = metrics.json
```

```
output = influx
influx = http://localhost:8086
database = mdtdb
```

Pipeline take the data it receives from xport_input (the input streams) and pushes it to the InfluxDB listening on TCP 8086. The metrics.json file included with Pipeline specifies the structure of the data so that it is properly inserted into external consumers like InfluxDB.

Install Grafana on your desired platform using the documentation at http://docs.grafana.org/installation/. Once Grafana is installed, add a new data source for InfluxDB. Next, create a new Grafana dashboard that contains the graphs for things like interface throughput. A set of sample queries for bytes sent is shown in Figure 7-11.

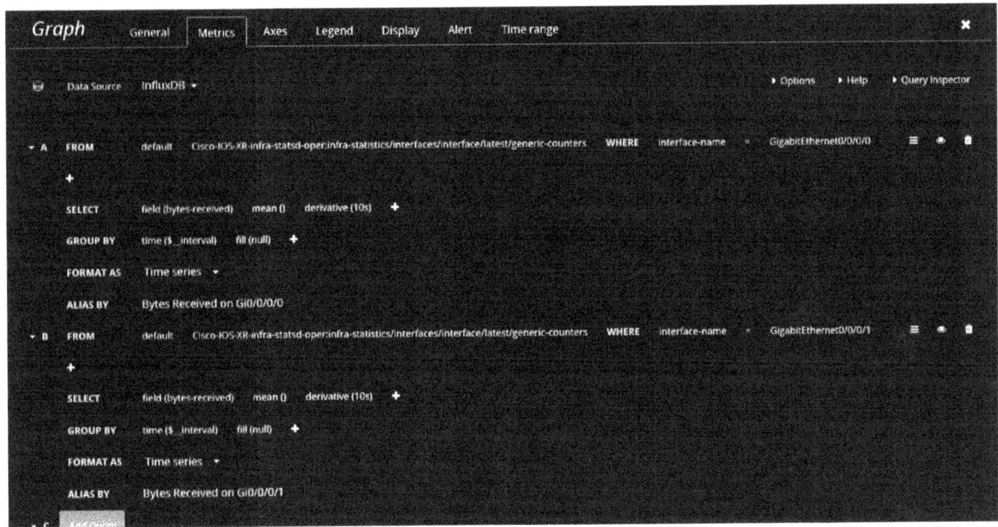

FIGURE 7-11 Grafana Queries to Extract Telemetry Data Stored in InfluxDB

Sample graphs showing the results of the telemetry "pipeline" are shown in Figure 7-12.

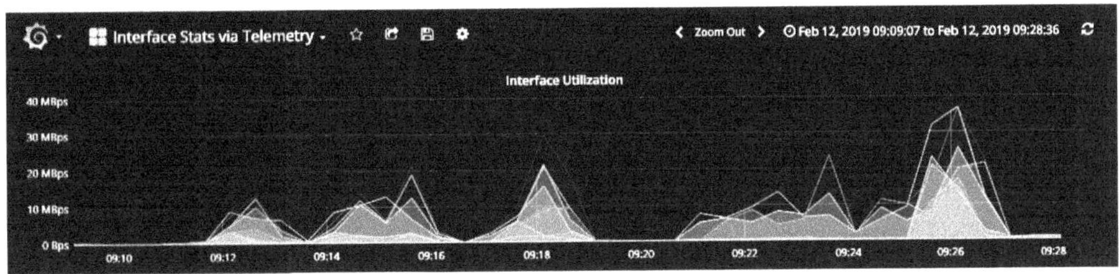

FIGURE 7-12 Grafana Graphs of Telemetry Data Streams

Advanced NETCONF Explorer

Another useful open source tool for getting to know streaming telemetry is Advanced NETCONF Explorer (ANX).[11] ANX, like YANG Suite, connects to network devices, pulls down the YANG modules that the devices support, and allows you to configure telemetry subscriptions and receive the resulting streams, as shown in Figure 7-13. ANX is containerized using Docker and Docker-compose. The instructions for starting it are found on its GitHub project page. Once installed and running, ANX presents a web-based interface, allowing you to enter a device IP or name and its credentials. Then it collects all of the modules from the device and constructs a YANG tree specific to that device.

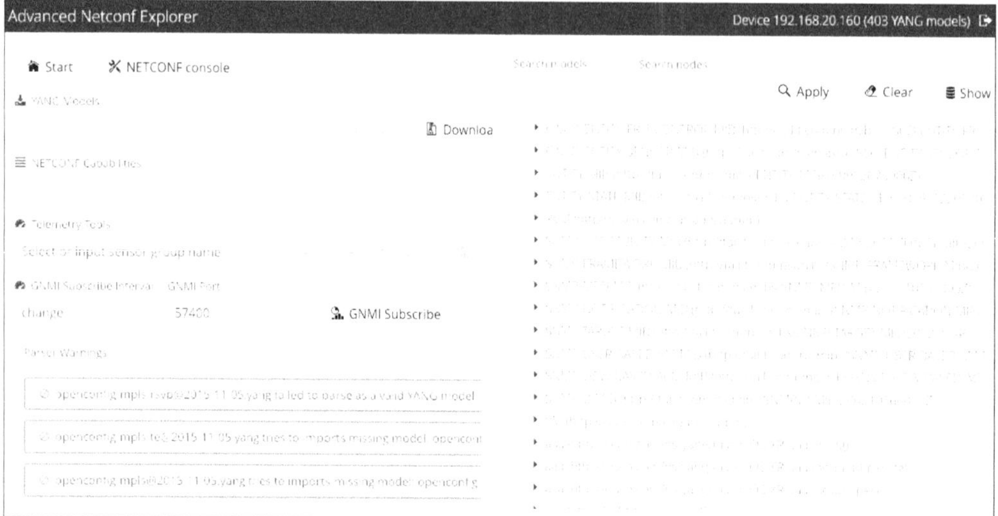

FIGURE 7-13 Advanced NETCONF Explorer

From the right-hand side, you can browse and search the module tree for the given device. When you click a node in the tree, the pane on the left-hand side updates to provide various parameters about the node and the module that contains it. One such parameter is Telemetry Path. This path is used to subscribe to telemetry streams from the device.

With routing configuration and state on the mind, create a telemetry feed within ANX that shows live routing changes. In the Telemetry Tools field in ANX, give your telemetry sensor group a name and then click the "Edit group" button. Add some routing node telemetry paths to the group. If your device supports the openconfig-network-instance module, this module provides a set of operational data nodes that deliver insight into the device's routing state. Figure 7-14 shows the sensor group editor window after a sensor path was added.

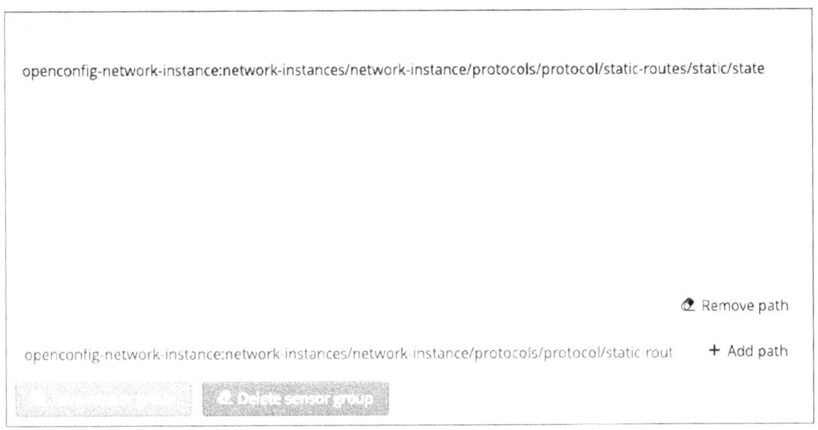

FIGURE 7-14 ANX Telemetry Group Configuration

Back at the main ANX screen, click the "Live data" button to begin receiving telemetry streams for your telemetry group. Depending on the types of streams the device supports, ANX may receive periodic pushes of data or data only when something changes (for example, a new route is added). Figure 7-15 shows ANX receiving and displaying telemetry updates after it programmed the network element.

Measurement

[19:20:14] openconfig-network-instance:network-instances/network-instance/protocols/protocol/static-routes/static/state

Telemetry Data (JSON format)


```
{
  "timestamp": "1549999214295",
  "keys": [
   {
    "name": "default"
   },
   {
    "identifier": "STATIC"
   },
   {
    "name": "DEFAULT"
   },
   {
    "prefix": "10.1.0.4/30"
   }
  ],
  "content": {
   "prefix": "10.1.0.4/30",
   "set-tag": 0
  }
}
```


FIGURE 7-15 ANX Telemetry Stream Messages

Pipeline and ANX provide a good way to begin to receive, process, and understand the value of streaming model-driven telemetry. As the telemetry standards mature and more platforms start to export telemetry streams, expect the tooling around telemetry to continue to evolve and improve as well.

Commercial Products

The tools explored for interacting with network elements are only some of the ones available. These are freely available as open source tools. There are other commercially available tools that integrate into a more end-to-end automation architecture.

Cisco offers one such tool called Network Services Orchestrator (NSO).[12] NSO allows you to build templates to automate the provisioning of single-device and entire network-level services. These templates are rendered as YANG models, and NSO acts as a NETCONF such that once a service is defined (in terms of its YANG schema) it is provisioned either through a single web interface or programmatically via NETCONF or RESTCONF. NSO then handles interacting directly with the network elements that make up the service. This means that it controls locking, backing out a configuration if errors are encountered, and maintaining the service-wide configuration across the entire network. While it use NETCONF to communicate with the underlying network elements if they support it, it can also fall back to legacy protocols like CLI over SSH. NSO, therefore, provides a service-level abstraction over the network to simplify service delivery.

Cisco distributes a free evaluation of NSO for non-production purposes from its DevNet site.[13] The evaluation is available for Linux and macOS, and it's the full NSO distribution with the exception that the number and functionality of network element drivers (NEDs) are limited. Additionally, the NSO evaluation does not support streaming telemetry. Figure 7-16 shows NSO displaying a service topology based on what was discovered from the configuration of the network elements within its inventory.

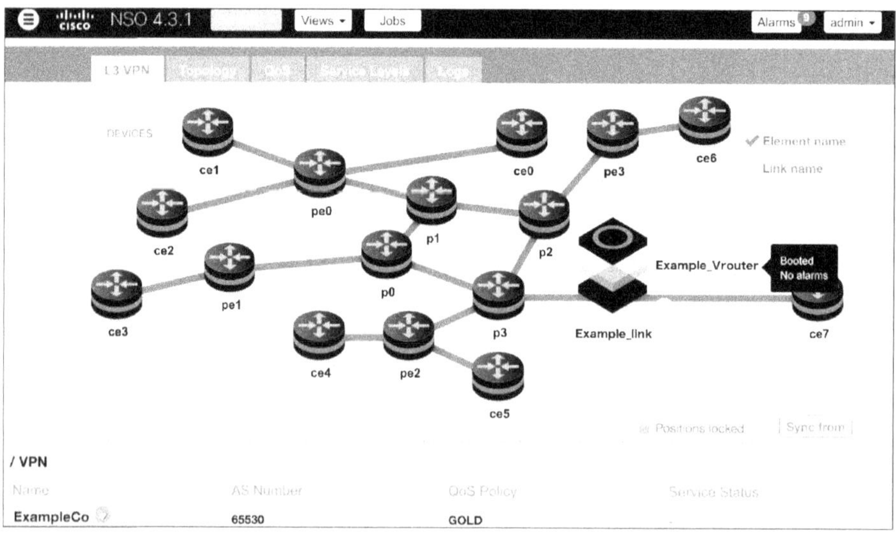

FIGURE 7-16 Cisco NSO's Web Interface

Building on the YANG model–based capabilities of NSO is Itential Automation Platform[14] from Itential. Itential Automation Platform provides a number of functions for service, policy, and configuration management. Itential Automation Platform provides another layer of service composition on top of the YANG models NSO exposes. In this manner, you can graphically draw out the service components, their interactions, and the overall user workflows, and then use NSO to provision the service. Once services and workflows are designed, they are grouped together as part of a service catalog, thus making it easier for IT administrators to choose the service they want and the type of workflow (such as provision or modify) and then execute the tasks across the entire network. Just as NSO offers a programmatic NETCONF and RESTCONF interface, Itential Automation Platform provides REST APIs to its underlying business logic components for northbound application integration. Figure 7-17 shows Itential Automation Platform workflow design center canvas.

FIGURE 7-17 Itential Automation Platform Workflow Builder

Interview with the Experts

Q&A with Einar Nilsen-Nygaard

Einar Nilsen-Nygaard is a principal engineer working in Cisco's Enterprise Networking group as the software architect for model-driven programmability and management across Cisco's core operating systems. In that role he works with an extended team of engineers across the various operating systems and platforms to deliver Cisco's device layer data models and APIs. He previously worked on element and network management software, policy-driven edge access, and deep packet inspection and flow-based data plane programming. Einar is involved in promoting the visibility of YANG across the industry by maintaining the multivendor, multi-SDO repository at https://github.com/YangModels/yang; working with Cisco platform teams to publish their models publicly; and developing tools such as ncc (based on the ncclient library), xym, and extensions to pyang. He provides feedback and guidance to working groups at the IETF on model development, and works extensively with software developers and network engineers to educate them on the benefits that model-based interfaces can bring to their day-to-day operations and to their software.

Question:

Einar, from your perspective as a YANG tool developer and data model contributor and advocate, what have you seen in terms of tool evolution, what have you learned from this, and where are we headed with respect to YANG tooling?

Answer:

What I've seen the most is that our industry at the moment still has an awful lot of inertia behind CLI-oriented ways of interacting with devices. One of the hardest things is moving people away from that focus and embracing a way of thinking that's first about data models versus anything else so that they're thinking about automation at the device level as a primary task rather than something that's nice to have. In the past, there was a struggle within the whole industry in the network management space to get Simple Network Management Protocol (SNMP) Management Information Bases (MIBs) in order to monitor or manage network elements and features. With YANG-based models, however, it will be easier for vendors to support rather than SNMP. End users, as well, will see YANG-based interfaces easier to adopt than SNMP-based interfaces.

That said, the current maturity of tooling for YANG is not particularly good across the industry in ways that make the benefits easily accessible to people who are not experts or developers. If you go back and read RFC 3535, which sets out the goals behind NETCONF and YANG, you can see a lot of stuff in there where we talk about making things easier for the end user, making it easier to develop, and making it more human readable. Some of these goals have stood the test of time, but you have to question things like making it appropriate for a human user. Is that still a goal with YANG models? We're kind of skipping beyond trying to make these interfaces appropriate for humans and focusing on making them appropriate for machine consumption. Therefore, the same requirements for readability and things of that nature don't really apply if your primary consumer is going to be a machine.

To put a counterpoint to that, why do we spend so much time developing tools like YANG Suite, Advanced NETCONF Explorer, and pyang with the "-f tree" argument? Why do we do that? We do that because there is still this gap between where our users are today and where the software that needs to consume these YANG models actually is—and that gap still needs to be bridged by humans. So, there is still a necessity to present YANG models in a way that humans can understand. That leads to the rise of these tools that let users visually get to grips with the model and visualize the structure and hierarchy within the models. This is why a lot of people are putting a lot of effort into tooling. Without this effort, we will have a hard time making use of the models that vendors release.

Question:

Why do you think that YANG and YANG-based protocols will be easier to adopt than SNMP?

Answer:

I think that the tooling we're developing around YANG models makes it easier to visualize what a YANG model is about. And the way we name things, the way we index things; we look at things more from a natural perspective that users are used to. For example, compare the IF-MIB to the ietf-interfaces YANG module. You have exactly the same information in both when it comes to semantics. However, when you look at the IF-MIB, you're presented with this thing called the "ifIndex," which is effectively a random number generated by the underlying platform. When you get back a set of data—say, from an SNMP GET-BULK request—you and the machine cannot make immediate sense of what the data is in relation to a specific interface without doing a measure of post-processing on that data. With SNMP, you get back these long strings of numbers in an object identifier (and maybe back in the day, I could decode these just by looking at packets), which adds burden to administrators and tooling to make sense of the data. This made sense at the time it was developed given the technology and the constraints. But today we're looking to transition the network engineer—who has been used to constructs that have logical names like "Ethernet1/0"—to think in more automation-centric terms. And this is the naming typically found across YANG models. While it is certainly more efficient to encode data as an integer than a string, the trade-off is the added complexity incurred in performing the mapping. As network speeds and feeds have increased, the balance has tilted to favoring the more natural naming to make it easier for developers to build software and users to consume the data. Sometimes, performance benefits at the software level are not worth the lack of understanding they create at the human level.

Question:

Where do you see the biggest gap in terms of tooling that can help promote more of this data model adoption?

Answer:

Unfortunately, that's a really easy one to answer *(a slight laugh)*. It's easy to answer in terms of what the problem is, but more difficult to answer in terms of the solution. Right now, we have a community of software developers and network engineers that are familiar with CLI and SNMP. This community needs to have a way to move forward from where they are today to a place where they can consume some of the newer YANG-based interfaces—be it with NETCONF, RESTCONF, model-based telemetry, you name it. The question we continue to get back from many, many internal and external sources is, "Okay, I'm polling this SNMP MIB today. I want to use telemetry tomorrow. What telemetry paths do I use to get the same data?" Then there's an uncomfortable silence as we try to figure out how in the heck *do* we actually do this? How do we move people forward? There isn't always a direct correlation between CLI output and SNMP MIBs to YANG model paths. While standards-based modules exist, they are not always complete when it comes to specific vendor features and platforms. Therefore, some vendors have gone to creating their own modules, specifically around operational data, that mirror how the data is stored within the platform. These are sometimes called "native models." They do not always have a one-to-one correspondence with SNMP MIBs or CLI command output fields. However, they are more aligned to the natural structure of the data any engineer familiar with the platform's implementation would expect. As such, they tend to perform better than using SNMP or executing CLI commands to gather the data. They may perform better than using standards-based YANG models, as no internal mapping is required. However, being faster or even easier to consume does not make up for the fact that you cannot map from what you're using today to these new models.

There isn't a magic answer to this. Some vendors are tackling this with CLI hooks on their platforms to provide mapping where it is known. Others are looking to develop external tooling to attempt to document and even crowd-source this knowledge. But this is the biggest challenge in tooling we face today in terms of adoption.

Question:

Today we hear a lot about software-defined, intent-based, controller-driven (and so on) networks. The common theme seems to be a layer of abstraction above the network device. This layer of abstraction can front-end programmatic instructions, and then use whatever device-level interface is available. How much are these model-driven paradigms going to matter if there is an abstraction between the network and the applications automating the network?

Answer:

This question gets asked a lot, and unfortunately there's not one good answer. As an industry, the devices we provide are consumed by a lot of different people with different levels of expertise and a lot of different abilities and willingness to engage at the device layer versus the controller layer versus "I just want a pre-packaged application I can use that does some stuff for me." Clearly, the vast majority of users are in the "pre-packaged application" camp. But how is the software they use going to be developed? Who is going to maintain what I'll call the "legacy" ways of interacting with devices? Who is going to invest in the infrastructure required to allow those pre-packaged applications to be developed? Speaking as a vendor who develops both pre-packaged applications as well as device-layer interfaces, the cost of maintaining software that uses those legacy interfaces is huge. What we're introducing with model-based interfaces lets devices become more self-describing, and they can tell a software developer, "This is the data I provide. This is the format I provide it in. Here are the things I don't actually do. Here are the RPCs you can invoke against me to do useful things." The value of that to vendors developing controllers—or pre-packaged applications on top of controllers—is huge.

There is also a large number of end users who roll their own operational support system (OSS) or controller layer. For those users who are building their own layer, they view dealing with legacy interfaces as a tax—as a vendor tax. They want the vendors to provide a good, well-structured management plane that is easy to integrate into their systems. No matter where you push the abstraction to deal with the legacy interfaces (be it a controller, a micro-service that does the mediation, or whatever), that tax will always be present. What we have seen, especially with larger, web-scale customers, is that they push back when we offer features without a model interface. To them, the stance is, if your feature doesn't have a model-based interface, then that feature doesn't exist for us—no model, no feature. The customers are driving model-based interfaces and interfaces to be first class. Even the coolest vendor doohickey will be ignored if it cannot be automated.

Summary

This chapter explored a number of YANG-centric tools for module exploration and understanding, interacting with devices to discover their capabilities and test simple automations, and testing and validating your new YANG modules. As important as the tools and the modules themselves are, the metadata associated with each module is vital for understanding how and where to use a module, how that module evolved, and how the module is supported in your devices.

YANG module tooling and the ability to consume module metadata do not stop with what was covered in this chapter. As discussed, there are other, commercially available tools that unlock the power of network device and service automation. Additionally, there are tools that aid with module writing and testing, and there are rich APIs and software development kits (SDKs) that enable you to create your own applications that can take advantage of model-based management, as well as consume module metadata as part of the application flow. Tools for module authors are discussed next in Chapter 8, and some of the programmatic aspects for application developers are covered in Chapter 9.

Endnotes

1. http://ydk.io
2. https://www.ansible.com/
3. https://curl.haxx.se/
4. https://httpie.org/
5. https://stedolan.github.io/jq/
6. https://www.getpostman.com/
7. https://github.com/cisco/bigmuddy-network-telemetry-pipeline
8. https://portal.influxdata.com/
9. https://prometheus.io/
10. http://pnda.io/
11. https://github.com/cisco-ie/anx
12. https://www.cisco.com/c/en/us/solutions/service-provider/solutions-cloud-providers/network-services-orchestrator-solutions.html
13. https://developer.cisco.com
14. https://www.itential.com/oss/

Chapter 8

Automation Is as Good as the Data Models, Their Related Metadata, and the Tools: For the Module Author

This chapter covers

- How to learn from others when creating your own YANG modules
- How to test your own YANG modules
- How to test your module's instance data
- How to share your module's metadata

Introduction

This chapter continues looking at YANG tools but from a module author angle. In addition to those tools that help with module writing, there are tricks and specific metadata that make this process easier. By the end of this chapter, you will have shortcuts to help you while writing a YANG module, as well as tools to help you test your module structure and validate instance data based on your module. You will understand how your module is affected by other modules as well as how your module impacts the community. Finally, you will learn how to provide your module's metadata back to the community.

Designing Modules

The tools (and their uses) you've seen thus far are geared toward network operators who are trying to use YANG modules to manage and automate their networks. This section shifts focus to tools that are useful for those in the industry and for network equipment vendors. These tools are also valuable to network operators who are developing their own service-level modules. This chapter has a tool-centric focus, whereas Chapter 11, "YANG Model Design," dives deeper into the art of module design.

Learning from Others

It can be daunting to take a blank sheet of paper (or text editor, as it were) and create a YANG module from scratch. However, even if you are inclined to jump right in and start writing, if you do not take a moment and explore what was done previously, you run the risk of making avoidable mistakes or, at the very least, reinventing constructs that were already tested and vetted by the industry.

This is where the YANG Catalog can help you in your module designer role. In Chapter 7 "Automation Is as Good as the Data Models, Their Related Metadata, and the Tools: For the Network Architect and Operator," you used the YANG Catalog search tool to find modules that could be used to configure and monitor routing attributes of network devices. This same search can also be used to locate YANG constructs to use when designing your modules.

For example, if you are designing a YANG service module that requires the use of a route distinguisher in order to create an L3VPN, how would you define that in your module? You could read through RFC 4364 and attempt to build a regular expression to match proper route distinguisher values, but why do all of that work if it has already been done? To find out if a canonical definition for a type like a route distinguisher already exists in YANG, search the YANG Catalog with a pattern that matches "route distinguisher" and use the advanced search options to filter only on "typedef" nodes.

The initial result set of such a search may be rather large. How can you find accurate and trustworthy candidates to use within your module? Sorting and filtering on the Origin, Maturity, and Imported By # Modules columns can pinpoint the most likely nodes to use. For example, enter **Industry** in the search field and select Origin from the pull-down menu. This greatly reduces the result set. Drilling into the resulting modules' details pages shows you the implementations of the modules, further indicating the modules you can borrow from. In the two shown in Figure 8-1 and Example 8-1, note that the *route-distinguisher* node defined in the ietf-routing-types module was ratified by the IETF, and this module was imported by 46 other YANG modules. Given those attributes, it stands a fairly good chance that this definition of route-distinguisher can be trusted. To further verify this, click the "route-distinguisher" link and confirm that the definition text matches what you expect.

NOTE

Standards bodies such as the IETF, IEEE, MEF, and BBF, as well as groups such as OpenConfig, provide modules that were peer reviewed and tested. These modules can generally be leveraged for subsequent work and extension. That said, there are many variations between modules from bodies like the IETF and OpenConfig, so choose base modules that not only meet your project's goals but are also supported by your network elements and services and adhere to any existing management standards your organization has established.

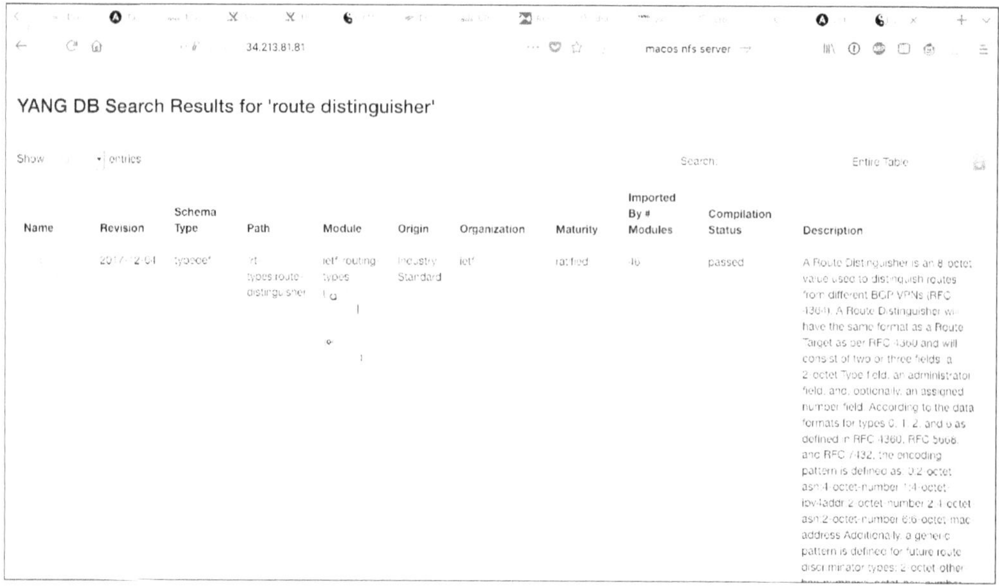

FIGURE 8-1 YANG Catalog Search Results for “route distinguisher” Typedefs

EXAMPLE 8-1 Definition of route-distinguisher

```
// From : ietf-routing-types@2017-12-04

typedef route-distinguisher {
.   type string {
.       pattern '(0:(6553[0-5]|655[0-2][0-9]|65[0-4][0-9]{2}|6[0-4][0-9]{3}|[1-5]
[0-9]{4}|[1-9][0-9]{0,3}|0):(429496729[0-5]|42949672[0-8][0-9]|4294967[01][0-9]
{2}|429496[0-6][0-9]{3}|42949[0-5][0-9]{4}|4294[0-8][0-9]{5}|429[0-3][0-9]{6}|
42[0-8][0-9]{7}|4[01][0-9]{8}|[1-3][0-9]{9}|[1-9][0-9]{0,8}|0))|(1:((([0-9]|[1-9]
[0-9]|1[0-9]{2}|2[0-4][0-9]|25[0-5])\.){3}([0-9]|[1-9][0-9]|1[0-9]{2}|2[0-4]
[0-9]|25[0-5])):(6553[0-5]|655[0-2][0-9]|65[0-4][0-9]{2}|6[0-4][0-9]{3}|[1-5][0-9]
{4}|[1-9][0-9]{0,3}|0))|(2:(429496729[0-5]|42949672[0-8][0-9]|4294967[01][0-9]
{2}|429496[0-6][0-9]{3}|42949[0-5][0-9]{4}|4294[0-8][0-9]{5}|429[0-3][0-9]{6}|42[0-8]
[0-9]{7}|4[01][0-9]{8}|[1-3][0-9]{9}|[1-9][0-9]{0,8}|0):(6553[0-5]|655[0-2][0-9]|
65[0-4][0-9]{2}|6[0-4][0-9]{3}|[1-5][0-9]{4}|[1-9][0-9]{0,3}|0))|(6(:[a-fA-F0-9]{2})
{6})|(([3-57-9a-fA-F]|[1-9a-fA-F][0-9a-fA-F]{1,3}):[0-9a-fA-F]{1,12})';

.   }
.   description "A Route Distinguisher is an 8-octet value used to
                distinguish routes from different BGP VPNs (RFC 4364).
                A Route Distinguisher will have the same format as a
                Route Target as per RFC 4360 and will consist of
                two or three fields: a 2-octet Type field, an administrator
                field, and, optionally, an assigned number field.
```

```
                According to the data formats for types 0, 1, 2, and 6 as
                defined in RFC 4360, RFC 5668, and RFC 7432, the encoding
                pattern is defined as:

                0:2-octet-asn:4-octet-number
                1:4-octet-ipv4addr:2-octet-number
                2:4-octet-asn:2-octet-number
                6:6-octet-mac-address

                Additionally, a generic pattern is defined for future
                route discriminator types:

                2-octet-other-hex-number:6-octet-hex-number

                Some valid examples are 0:100:100, 1:1.1.1.1:100,
                2:1234567890:203, and 6:26:00:08:92:78:00.";
    reference "RFC 4360: BGP Extended Communities Attribute.
                RFC 4364: BGP/MPLS IP Virtual Private Networks (VPNs).
                RFC 5668: 4-Octet AS Specific BGP Extended Community.
                RFC 7432: BGP MPLS-Based Ethernet VPN.";
}
```

This same approach can be done for other reusable node types, such as groupings, features, and identities.

NOTE

The bookzone module from Chapter 2, "Data Model–Driven Management," is used for the remainder of the module authoring sections.

Compiling and Validating Modules

When writing a module, you want to continually test as you go to ensure it compiles (that is, it's syntactically correct) and that the resulting data model is consistent and logical. For complex structures such as regular expressions, you want to ensure that they not only match the data you want, but that they are valid when it comes to YANG's specific syntax rules. Fortunately, there are tools to help you achieve all of these goals.

When it comes to checking modules for syntax, pyang provides a **--strict** flag as well as organization-specific additional validations (such as **--ietf** to validate against IETF-specific rules). However, pyang is not the only tool out there. At yangvalidator.org you can upload your module and check it against a suite of YANG validation tools. Currently, the YANG Validator site uses pyang,[1] confdc,[2] and yanglint.[3] It also uses the xym[4] tool, which extracts YANG modules from other files (for example, from IETF Internet drafts). By using the YANG Validator site, you get the benefit of having multiple compilation checks for different tools while not having to install and maintain those tools yourself. If your module passes all the validation tools, you can feel confident that it works with a given configuration management solution. If you are working on a set of modules—for example, as part of a service bundle—the YANG Validator site accepts a zipped archive of all modules for convenience. You can also upload documents that contain YANG modules, and the YANG Validator site will attempt to pull out all of the YANG modules contained within them and then validate them. The YANG Validator site also provides an API, and the code that drives it is open source.

Regular expressions in YANG must adhere to World Wide Web Consortium (W3C) XSD-schema syntax guidelines[5] in order to validate in the compilers just listed. While there are a number of tools to test other formats of regular expressions (POSIX, Perl-compliant, and so on), testing for W3C compliance can be challenging. Fortunately, there is a validator linked on the YANG Catalog home page, YANGRE.[6] This tool not only validates a regular expression is in valid W3C syntax, it also creates a small YANG schema, validates it, and tests any supplied test string to ensure it matches as well. In addition to validating regular expressions, YANGRE can help you decide on the right quoting scheme for your regular expression. For example, the **'\d'** (shorthand for matching a digit) cannot be put within double quotes in a YANG module. It must be bare or within single quotes. If you enter this with double quotes, YANGRE throws an error.

Testing Modules

After validating that your modules are syntactically correct, test the function of the modules using *ConfD*, which is a YANG-based engine for enabling NETCONF and RESTCONF support within network elements (be they devices or servers). It comes in a freely available basic distribution as well as an enterprise distribution. ConfD provides the ability to automatically render NETCONF interfaces based on any valid YANG module. Cisco makes the basic version of ConfD freely available from its DevNet site at https://developer.cisco.com/site/confD/ for Linux and macOS (Darwin) platforms. The basic version only supports rendering of modules into NETCONF interfaces. It is that rendering that enables you to test your modules, not just for syntax (as is done on the YANG Validator site), but also for basic model functionality. For example, you can instantiate your modules within ConfD and then send **edit-config** and **get-config** operations to it to ensure that data types and ranges are consistent with the values you wish to use. Additionally, you can build code hooks (for example, in Python) to invoke actions and handle various data element changes. ConfD includes a command-line interface (CLI) tool as well that emulates Cisco's IOS syntax. This is another way to see how users might interact with your modules. The ConfD distribution includes a number of examples that are found within the examples.confd directory. Some of the tools and operations covered by the examples are explored next.

The bookzone module introduced and developed in Chapter 2 can be found on GitHub at https://github.com/janlindblad/bookzone. Within this repository is the bootstrapping code necessary to load the module into ConfD. This is a great way to get started with ConfD, especially if you've taken to extending the bookzone module to get some more YANG practice. Install ConfD using the instructions found on the aforementioned DevNet site and then clone the bookzone repository from GitHub.

There is a Makefile within the bookzone repository that includes a number of targets to prepare the modules, as well as the associated hooks and applications, and to start the ConfD daemon. These targets wrap a number of tools from ConfD.

NOTE

Make sure to source the confdrc or confdrc.tcsh file into your current command shell before using the ConfD tools. The confdrc file is used for Bourne shell alternatives (such as bash), whereas the confdrc.tcsh file is used for C shell alternatives (such as tcsh).

Before a module is loaded into ConfD, it must first be compiled from the text .yang file into a binary .fxs file. This is achieved using the confdc (or ConfD compiler) tool included within the ConfD distribution. The simplest way to compile a module is with the following command:

```
$ confdc -c -o module.fxs module.yang
```

This compiles the module and generates an .fxs file. The bookzone Makefile uses additional options, **--fail-on-warnings** and **-a**, to support a more pedantic compilation and to merge annotations into a format defined by the company that created ConfD, Tail-F.

In addition to preparing your modules, you may also want to pre-seed ConfD with operational data. To do this, create an XML file that follows your module's schema. A sample snippet of pre-seeded operational data for the bookzone module is found in Example 8-2.

EXAMPLE 8-2 Bookzone Operational Data

```
<!-- Load using: confd_load -lCO operational-data.xml -->
<books xmlns="http://example.com/ns/bookzone">
  <book>
    <title>I Am Malala: The Girl Who Stood Up for Education and Was Shot by the
    Taliban</title>
    <popularity>89</popularity>
    <format>
      <isbn>9780297870913</isbn>
      <number-of-copies>
        <in-stock>12</in-stock>
        <reserved>2</reserved>
        <available>10</available>
      </number-of-copies>
    </format>
  </book>
...
</books>
```

The bookzone git repository includes a configuration file for ConfD (that is, confd.conf). You can use this as a model for other modules you develop. This file is in XML format, and, in general, little needs to be done to it for testing modules. One thing you may want to tweak is the NETCONF-over-SSH port. The repository version has the port set to 2022; however, the standard port is 830. This is modified in the block of code shown in Example 8-3.

EXAMPLE 8-3 confd.conf NETCONF Port Configuration

```
<netconf>
  <enabled>true</enabled>
  <transport>
    <ssh>
      <enabled>true</enabled>
      <ip>0.0.0.0</ip>
      <port>2022</port>  <!-- Change this to 830 -->
    </ssh>
```

Once you are satisfied with the configuration file, start the ConfD daemon from within the directory where the module .fxs files and the confd.conf file are located. The ConfD daemon is started with the following command:

```
$ confd -c confd.conf --addloadpath ${CONFD_DIR}/etc/confd
```

The **${CONFD_DIR}** variable is set when you source the confdrc file into the current environment. The additional module load path is specified so that the ConfD daemon can find some base modules (such as ietf-yang-types) that are included with the ConfD distribution.

The ConfD daemon starts in the background and immediately returns you to your command prompt. If you have created additional operational data to pre-seed the ConfD daemon, load that with the following command:

```
$ confd_load -lCO operational-data.xml
```

At this point, the daemon accepts NETCONF operations. The ConfD distribution also includes a confd_cli executable that creates a Cisco IOS-XR-like command-line environment for interacting with the ConfD daemon. This CLI environment allows you to view the configuration and operational data, as well as make changes to the ConfD configuration data stores. Example 8-4 shows a sample CLI session where a book's price is changed, the new configuration is committed, and then the running configuration is displayed.

EXAMPLE 8-4 Example ConfD CLI Session

```
$ confd_cli
confd#
confd# config terminal
Entering configuration mode terminal
```

```
confd(config)# books book "The Art of War"
confd(config-book-The Art of War)# format 160459893X
jamconfdahal(config-format-160459893X)# price ?
Possible completions:
  <decimal number>[12.75]
confd(config-format-160459893X)# price 13.75
confd(config-format-160459893X)# commit
Commit complete.
confd(config-format-160459893X)# end
confd# show running-config
authors author "Douglas Adams"
 account-id 1010
!
authors author "Malala Yousafzai"
 account-id 1011
!
authors author "Michael Ende"
 account-id 1001
!
authors author "Per Espen Stoknes"
 account-id 1111
!
authors author "Sun Tzu"
 account-id 1100
!
books book "I Am Malala: The Girl Who Stood Up for Education and Was Shot
by the Taliban"
 author "Malala Yousafzai"
 format 9780297870913
  format-id hardcover
 !
!
books book "The Art of War"
 author   "Sun Tzu"
 language english
 format 160459893X
  format-id paperback
  price     13.75
...
```

While the CLI is nice and could be quite comfortable to those who have experience in the networking world, you should test your module using a more automation-friendly approach. ConfD's NETCONF interface supports all the tools mentioned in this chapter. For example, you can use netconf-console to connect to the ConfD daemon and obtain the configuration, as shown in Example 8-5.

EXAMPLE 8-5 **<get-config>** from ConfD

```
$ netconf-console --get-config
<?xml version="1.0" encoding="UTF-8"?>
<rpc-reply xmlns="urn:ietf:params:xml:ns:netconf:base:1.0" message-id="1">
  <data>
    <authors xmlns="http://example.com/ns/bookzone">
      <author>
        <name>Douglas Adams</name>
        <account-id>1010</account-id>
      </author>
      <author>
        <name>Malala Yousafzai</name>
        <account-id>1011</account-id>
      </author>
      <author>
        <name>Michael Ende</name>
        <account-id>1001</account-id>
      </author>
      <author>
        <name>Per Espen Stoknes</name>
        <account-id>1111</account-id>
      </author>
      <author>
        <name>Sun Tzu</name>
        <account-id>1100</account-id>
      </author>
    </authors>
    <books xmlns="http://example.com/ns/bookzone">
      <book>
        <title>I Am Malala: The Girl Who Stood Up for Education and Was Shot
        by the Taliban</title>
        <author>Malala Yousafzai</author>
        <format>
          <isbn>9780297870913</isbn>
          <format-id>hardcover</format-id>
        </format>
      </book>
      <book>
        <title>The Art of War</title>
        <author>Sun Tzu</author>
        <language>english</language>
        <format>
          <isbn>160459893X</isbn>
          <format-id>paperback</format-id>
          <price>13.75</price>
...
```

NOTE

By default, netconf-console assumes localhost and port 2022 for NETCONF operations. If you changed the ConfD NETCONF port to 830, use the command-line argument **--port 830** with netconf-console.

NOTE

The configuration obtained with netconf-console includes the price change to *The Art of War*. The confd_cli tool is simply a frontend to the same NETCONF interface.

Netconf-console is also used to add and modify configuration within ConfD. Therefore, you can pass data sets to netconf-console to test whether or not your data adheres to the model defined (or perhaps the model needs to change given the data types and ranges required). If you specify something outside of the model's definition (that is, an illegal value), ConfD responds with an error, and this is caught within netconf-console. Example 8-6 shows what happens when an illegal ISBN value is specified when updating a book.

EXAMPLE 8-6 Testing Errors with ConfD and netconf-console

```
$ cat book-change.xml
<edit-config xmlns:nc='urn:ietf:params:xml:ns:netconf:base:1.0'>
  <target>
   <running/>
  </target>
  <test-option>test-then-set</test-option>
  <error-option>rollback-on-error</error-option>
  <config>
    <books xmlns="http://example.com/ns/bookzone"
          xmlns:nc="urn:ietf:params:xml:ns:netconf:base:1.0">
    <book>
     <title>The Neverending Story</title>
     <format>
      <isbn nc:operation="merge">978014038633</isbn>
     </format>
    </book>
   </books>
  </config>
 </edit-config>

$ netconf-console --rpc=book-change.xml
<?xml version="1.0" encoding="UTF-8"?>
<rpc-reply xmlns="urn:ietf:params:xml:ns:netconf:base:1.0" message-id="1">
```

```
  <rpc-error>
    <error-type>application</error-type>
    <error-tag>invalid-value</error-tag>
    <error-severity>error</error-severity>
    <error-path xmlns:bz="http://example.com/ns/bookzone"
    xmlns:nc="urn:ietf:params:xml:ns:netconf:base:1.0">
    /nc:rpc/nc:edit-config/nc:config/bz:books/bz:book[bz:title='The Neverending
    Story']/bz:format/bz:isbn
  </error-path>
    <error-message xml:lang="en">"978014038633" is not a valid value.</error-message>
    <error-info>
      <bad-element>isbn</bad-element>
    </error-info>
  </rpc-error>
</rpc-reply>
```

Upon encountering an error, ConfD supports the ability to roll back all other configuration applied in the same session.

The bookzone Makefile includes a number of targets that help to prepare the bookzone module, start up the ConfD daemon, and perform some basic NETCONF-based tests of the daemon. To quickly prepare the modules and get the ConfD daemon up and running, run the **make all** command from the bookzone git repository directory. Once the daemon is running, the **make nc** command provides you a list of other make targets to be used to run through some tests of the module, as shown in Example 8-7.

EXAMPLE 8-7 Make Targets for Testing bookzone

```
$ make nc
Once ConfD is running,
you can use these make targets to make NETCONF requests:
make nc-hello            # YANG 1.0/1.1 capability and module discovery
make nc-get-config       # Get-config of all configuration data
make nc-get-auths-books  # Get-config with XPath and subtree filter
make nc-many-changes     # Edit-config with many changes (run once)
make nc-rollback-latest  # Rollback latest transaction
make nc-get-author       # Get the author of a single book
make nc-get-stock        # Get the stock qty of certain books

$ make nc-get-auths-books
# Get list of authors and books using XPath filter
netconf-console --get-config --xpath "/authors|books"
<?xml version="1.0" encoding="UTF-8"?>
<rpc-reply xmlns="urn:ietf:params:xml:ns:netconf:base:1.0" message-id="1">
```

```
  <data>
    <authors xmlns="http://example.com/ns/bookzone">
      <author>
        <name>Douglas Adams</name>
        <account-id>1010</account-id>
      </author>
      <author>
        <name>Malala Yousafzai</name>
        <account-id>1011</account-id>
      </author>
...
```

This Makefile serves as an excellent reference for applying ConfD to testing of any future module you create.

The yanglint tool can also be used to validate the module's structure as well as its instance data. Yanglint is one of the validators used by the YANG Validators website. If you provide yanglint with your module as well as a sample of instance data, you can confirm that the instance data conforms to your module's structure. As you develop automation code that uses your module or documentation code that includes sample usage of your module, it is a good idea to check the resulting instance data to ensure you're not introducing mistakes that could prevent critically timed configuration changes or be perpetuated to other consumers of your module. The following snippet shows yanglint validating the bookzone instance data from Example 8-6.

```
$ yanglint -f xml bookzone-example.yang bz.xml
err : Invalid value "978014038633" in "isbn" element. (/bookzone-example:books/
book[title='The Neverending Story']/format[isbn='978014038633']/isbn)
```

Sharing the Module Metadata

If you are building a module that isn't entirely private or proprietary, consider giving back to the community by uploading your module (and its metadata) for others to learn from. The YANG Catalog is able to provide the library of metadata it does because module authors (mainly vendors) contributed to it. Growing this library makes module development more consistent and easier. YANG Catalog is not limited to vendors only. Anyone should contribute who is writing a YANG module that can be generally used.

Instructions for uploading module metadata to YANG Catalog is found at https://yangcatalog.org/contribute.php#model_creator. The first step is to upload the module itself to a public GitHub repository. As of this writing, GitHub is the only supported location for modules from which YANG Catalog can read. YANG Catalog needs access to the module itself in order to obtain the *extractable* metadata. However, YANG Catalog does not serve your module for download. It only provides a link to the GitHub location.

NOTE

In the future, YANG Catalog may support additional source code repositories for accessing modules.

The next step is to request a YANG Catalog account. This account entitles you to add and modify modules for your organization. When an administrator creates your account, they request details for the namespace to which you want access. With the account created, upload the metadata by creating an HTTPS PUT request to https://yangcatalog.org/api/modules.

The body of the PUT request is defined in https://raw.githubusercontent.com/xorrkaz/netmod-yang-catalog/master/module-metadata.yang. This module's tree is shown in Example 8-8.

EXAMPLE 8-8 Module Metadata Tree

```
module: module-metadata
    +--rw modules
       +--rw module* [name revision organization]
          +--rw name                      yang:yang-identifier
          +--rw revision                  union
          +--rw generated-from?           enumeration
          +--rw maturity-level?           enumeration
          +--rw document-name?            string
          +--rw author-email?             yc:email-address
          +--rw reference?                inet:uri
          +--rw module-classification     enumeration
          +--rw organization              string
          +--rw ietf
          |  +--rw ietf-wg?   string
          +--rw source-file
             +--rw owner         string
             +--rw repository    string
             +--rw path          path
             +--rw branch?       string
```

For example, for contributing the metadata for the bookzone module (which is already in GitHub), Example 8-9 shows the body of the PUT request that pushes the metadata to YANG Catalog.

EXAMPLE 8-9 YANG Catalog Metadata Request for bookzone

```
{
  "modules": {
    "module": [{
      "name": "bookzone-example",
      "revision": "2018-01-05",
```

```
      "organization": "Book Zone",
      "author-email": "jlindbla@cisco.com",
      "module-classification": "not-applicable",
      "source-file": {
        "owner": "janlindblad",
        "repository": "bookzone",
        "path:": "bookzone-example.yang"
      }
    }]
  }
}
```

Once the metadata is submitted, a job ID is generated from YANG Catalog. You can poll this ID to get the job's status. When it completes, your module is now searchable within the catalog. Thanks for giving back!

Understanding Your Module's Impact

Another tool provided by the YANG Catalog is called "Impact Analysis." This tool provides you with a color-coded graph showing how one or more modules interrelate in terms of their dependencies and dependents. That is, Impact Analysis shows what modules depend on a given module, as well as what modules a given module depends on. Figure 8-2 provides an Impact Analysis graph showing both dependencies and dependents for ietf-routing.

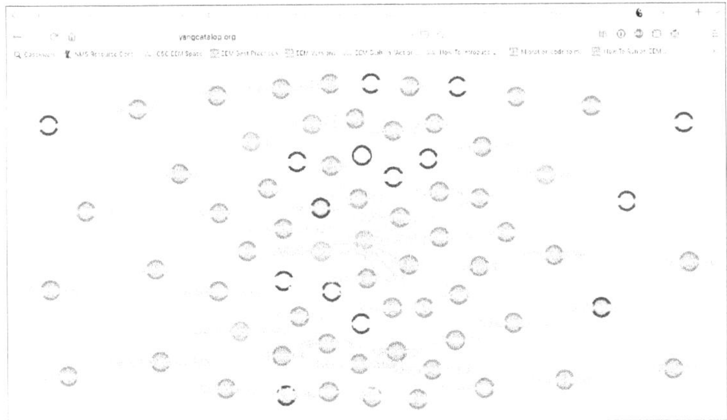

FIGURE 8-2 Impact Analysis for ietf-routing

The graph uses colors to depict the organization of the module nodes. The rings around each node depicts its maturity. In addition to maturity, a ring may also denote a *bottleneck module* (or blocking module), which is an unratified module holding up a number of modules from progressing. In other words, if you are working on a module for a standards body and it requires other modules to progress before yours can be ratified, the Impact Analysis tool provides you quick insight into where to focus additional work so that your module's development can continue.

Interview with the Expert

Q&A with William Lupton

William Lupton has been involved with the Broadband Forum (BBF) since 2003, representing a succession of member companies. He was a major contributor to the TR-069 family of CPE management standards, particularly to its (XML Schema–based) data modeling language, data models, and related tools. Since 2014, when BBF first adopted NETCONF and YANG for some of its projects, William has acted as a source of BBF YANG expertise, served as a founding co-chair of the BBF Common YANG Work Area, managed the publication of BBF YANG modules, given regular updates to IETF on BBF YANG status and plans, and contributed several fixes and enhancements to the pyang YANG processing tool. William has been BBF's Software Architect since 2015.

Question:

How many YANG modules has BBF published?

Answer:

As of December 2018, BBF has published 196 YANG files, of which 45 are modules and 151 are submodules. All of these are available in GitHub at https://github.com/BroadbandForum/yang and https://github.com/YangModels/yang, and are in the YANG Catalog.

Question:

Why are there so many submodules?

Answer:

The large number of submodules might be surprising. Some of the BBF YANG modules model quite complex underlying standards, and we decided to define submodules that correspond to the structure of the underlying standard. For example, the bbf-fast module models the ITU-T G.fast protocol. It has 13 submodules that correspond to high-level functions, and a further 22 submodules that correspond closely to the underlying ITU-T standards (G.9700, G.9701, and so on). This module and its submodules have a total of 10040 lines of code (including comments).

Question:

What is your process in developing YANG modules?

Answer:

All BBF YANG modules are associated with a BBF standard. For example, the bbf-fast module (just mentioned) is part of TR-355 (YANG Modules for FTTdp Management). The first step in generating new YANG modules is to propose and approve a new project (this might be a completely new project, or it might be an extension of an existing project). The YANG modules will then be developed in the context of this project. Each YANG project has its own git repository (a BBF Bitbucket repository), and YANG is contributed by creating a pull request. The project members discuss the pull request (using Bitbucket reviewing and commenting features) and then merge it. When a project is complete, it runs through the BBF's standard balloting processes. Finally, the BBF standard is published (as a PDF file) on the BBF website and the YANG is published and further distributed as described in the answer to the next question.

Question:

Can you give some more details about how you publish BBF YANG?

Answer:

I already mentioned that BBF YANG modules and submodules are published to GitHub and to the YANG Catalog. There are actually three steps:

STEP 1. The BBF YANG is tagged in the BBF Bitbucket repository and pushed to https://github.com/BroadbandForum/yang.

STEP 2. A pull request from https://github.com/BroadbandForum/yang to https://github.com/YangModels/yang is created.

STEP 3. The updated metadata for the files in https://github.com/BroadbandForum/yang is uploaded to the YANG Catalog (via its REST API).

Question:

What guidelines apply to BBF YANG modules?

Answer:

We require all BBF YANG modules to adhere to a set of BBF-specific guidelines that extend IETF's RFC 8407, "Guidelines for Authors and Reviewers of Documents Containing YANG Data Models." For example, we enforce IETF standards around YANG terms, YANG validation, module naming conventions, and so on.

Question:

How do you test your modules as you develop them?

Answer:

We ask that all YANG be run cleanly through the pyang and yanglint tools (using some standard BBF-specific "lint" options provided by the pyang "bbf" plug-in) before pull requests are created. We plan soon to enforce this by adding automatic testing that will prevent a pull request from being merged if its YANG contains errors.

Summary

This chapter explored a number of YANG-centric tools that aid you as a module author in writing and testing your modules. In addition to verifying module structure with ConfD, you saw how to test instance data as you build examples and production automation against your evolving module. Finally, your module's metadata is as valuable as the module itself. This chapter showed how to upload that metadata to the YANG Catalog to benefit the wider YANG community.

Endnotes

1. https://github.com/mbj4668/pyang
2. http://www.tail-f.com/confd-basic/
3. https://github.com/CESNET/libyang
4. https://github.com/xym-tool/xym
5. https://www.w3.org/TR/2004/REC-xmlschema-2-20041028/#regexs
6. https://yangcatalog.org/yangre/

Chapter 9

Automation Is as Good as the Data Models, Their Related Metadata, and the Tools: For the Application Developer

This chapter covers

- How to programmatically access YANG module metadata
- How to create customized views of YANG module data
- What libraries exist for programmatically communicating with devices using NETCONF and RESTCONF
- How to work with YANG data using object-oriented programming constructs

Introduction

This chapter explores interacting with YANG modules, metadata, and devices from an *application developer perspective*. It explains how to integrate YANG-based data and the protocols that use YANG data into your network configuration, monitoring applications, and workflows. At the end of this chapter, you will know what application program interfaces (APIs), libraries, and software development kits (SDKs) exist for processing YANG modules and their metadata, how to interact with devices, and how to use native language bindings based on YANG models. This chapter also introduces some examples you can use to start to write your own scripts and applications that make use of YANG model and instance data in programmatic ways.

Chapter 7, "Automation Is as Good as the Data Models, Their Related Metadata, and the Tools: For the Network Architect and Operator," and Chapter 8, "Automation Is as Good as the Data Models, Their

Related Metadata, and the Tools: For the Module Author," focused on tools for specific audiences to make working with YANG modules and protocols easier. Although some of these tools can either be incorporated into scripts or used as precursors to applications that drive automation, they are not libraries or APIs. In order to build more robust applications that automate configuration and service deployments, gather and correlate operational data, dynamically subscribe to telemetry publications and consume the streams, and so on, you as a developer want proper APIs and SDKs.

Working with YANG Modules

Tools such as yanglint, pyang, and YANG Catalog provide good ways to visualize the YANG module structure and describe the metadata surrounding YANG modules. While using the pre-built interfaces is good for direct human consumption, you may want to customize the view of YANG module schema data or fold YANG module metadata into your network management tools. You can use the APIs these tools provide in order to achieve customized and integrated results.

Integrating Metadata from YANG Catalog

If you are building a YANG model–based application to automate network device configuration or service deployment, it helps to have a holistic view of the YANG modules your application relies upon. Remember, your automation is only as good as the data models and their related metadata. Chapter 7 discussed the tools a network operator might use within the YANG Catalog that expose those metadata fields. In addition, YANG Catalog has a full set of APIs to perform searches and access the same metadata as the frontend tools.

How might you use YANG Catalog metadata within your automation application? Your network may have devices from different vendors or be running different versions of code, even from the same vendor. This means the devices could support different revisions of the same YANG modules. If your application encounters a revision of a module it doesn't yet recognize, it could invoke the YANG Catalog API to pull down that module's metadata and inspect its "derived-semantic-version" to see if the major version number changed between an already-known revision and this new one. If so, that indicates a non-backward-compatible change within the module. From there, inspect the module's tree diff to see the changes relevant to your application. That further inspection can be folded into your application's logic, or it can trigger a further manual audit from an engineer.

YANG Catalog provides a page[1] for developers who wish to contribute to it. This page describes a number of the REST APIs that it exposes. The APIs to publish metadata to YANG Catalog were already covered in Chapter 8, "Automation Is as Good as the Data Models, Their Related Metadata, and the Tools: For the Module Author" as part of tools for module design. In terms of metadata retrieval, YANG Catalog provides two main endpoints that accept Hypertext Transfer Protocol (HTTP) GET queries. The first, **/api/search/modules**, provides the means to retrieve all metadata for a specific module given its name, revision, and organization. This API endpoint uses commas to separate the multiple search keys. Example 9-1 shows a query for ietf-routing, revision 2018-03-13. Of course, the organization is the Internet Engineering Task Force (IETF).

EXAMPLE 9-1 Retrieving Metadata from YANG Catalog's REST API

```
 $ http https://yangcatalog.org/api/search/modules/ietf-routing,2018-03-13,ietf
{
    "module": [
        {
            "name": "ietf-routing",
            "namespace": "urn:ietf:params:xml:ns:yang:ietf-routing",
            "organization": "ietf",
            "prefix": "rt",
            "reference": "https://tools.ietf.org/html/rfc8349",
            "revision": "2018-03-13",
            "schema": "https://raw.githubusercontent.com/YangModels/yang/master/
standard/ietf/RFC/ietf-routing@2018-03-13.yang",
            "tree-type": "nmda-compatible",
            "yang-tree": "https://yangcatalog.org/api/services/tree/ietf-
routing@2018-03-13.yang",
            "yang-version": "1.1"
...
```

The other metadata retrieval endpoint allows you to search YANG Catalog for modules that include a specific metadata field value. This endpoint is **/api/search/{key}/{value}**. For example, you can retrieve all modules that use the Network Management Datastore Architecture (NMDA) schema tree type with a query to **/api/search/tree-type/nmda-compatible**. With both this API endpoint and the previous one, the results are every matching module and all their respective metadata fields. A variation exists, **/api/search-filter**, that uses the POST method and accepts parameters for the metadata values as well as the field to return. Using the same NMDA example, the request in Example 9-2 only returns the module name for those modules that are NMDA-compatible.

EXAMPLE 9-2 Retrieving Specific Metadata Fields from YANG Catalog

```
$ http POST https://yangcatalog.org/api/search-filter/name input:='{"tree-type":
"nmda-compatible"}'
{
    "output": {
        "name": [
            "ietf-msdp",
...
```

Other examples of YANG Catalog API calls are available from the contributor web page as a Postman collection.[2] Since all of YANG Catalog's APIs are RESTful, they are accessed using libraries and functions that deal with HTTP methods (for example, libcurl, Python's requests module, and so on). With the Postman collection, you can use Postman's code-generation capability to create an initial script for interacting with YANG Catalog.

Example 9-3 shows Python code that retrieves derived semantic version metadata from YANG Catalog for a particular revision of the ietf-routing module. This is compared to a previously known semantic version for the same module. If they are different, the YANG tree is retrieved from the catalog and stored for later comparison.

EXAMPLE 9-3 Python Script to Retrieve YANG Catalog Metadata

```
import requests

url = "https://yangcatalog.org/api/search-filter/derived-semantic-version"

KNOWN_SEMVER_MAJORS = [1, 2, 3]

payload = """
{
  "input": {
    "name": "ietf-routing",
    "revision": "2018-03-13"
  }
}
"""

headers = {
    'Content-Type': "application/json"
}

response = requests.request("POST", url, data=payload, headers=headers)

j = response.json()
semver_major = j['output']['derived-semantic-version'][0].split(".")[0]

if semver_major not in KNOWN_SEMVER_MAJORS:
    response = requests.request("GET", "https://yangcatalog.org/api/services/tree/
ietf-routing@2018-03-13.yang")
    fd = open("/models/trees/ietf-routing@2018-03-13_tree.txt", "w")
    fd.write(response.text)
    fd.close()
```

In addition to retrieving all module metadata for a module or set of modules, you can also search YANG Catalog for particular keywords by sending a POST to the **/api/index/search** endpoint. The search API, similar to the web frontend, allows you to specify keywords, search fields and other options, as well as filter the results so that only certain fields are returned. Example 9-4 shows Python code that searches for "route-distinguisher" typedefs and retrieves only the module name, node name, and node path fields in the result set.

EXAMPLE 9-4 Using the YANG Catalog Search API

```
import requests

url = "https://yangcatalog.org/api/index/search"

payload = """
{
  "search": "route-distinguisher",
  "type": "keyword",
  "case-sensitive": false,
  "include-mibs": false,
  "latest-revisions": true,
  "search-fields": ["module", "argument", "description"],
  "yang-versions": ["1.0", "1.1"],
  "schema-types": ["typedef"],
  "filter": {
      "node": ["name", "path"],
      "module": ["name"]
  }
}
"""

headers = {
    'Content-Type': "application/json",
}

response = requests.request("POST", url, data=payload, headers=headers)

print(response.text)
```

This example shows all the fields currently supported within the payload. The only mandatory field is "search." If the other fields are omitted, the values shown in the code (except for filter) are used as the defaults. There is no default filter, so all module and node metadata is returned if a filter is omitted.

Fields such as search-fields, yang-versions, schema-types, and node and module filters support a list of options. All supported values are shown for yang-versions and search-fields. The schema-types field supports values of *typedef*, *grouping*, *feature*, *identity*, *extension*, *rpc*, *action*, *container*, *list*, *leaf-list*, *list*, and *notification*. The filter fields enable you to control the result set. The allowed node filter values are *name*, *path*, *description*, and *type*. The module filter supports all of the metadata fields returned for a given module. Additionally, besides a "keyword" search, the type field accepts a value of *regex* to perform a regular expression search.

Embedding Pyang

In addition to executing pyang as a command, you can embedded pyang's backend into other Python applications to provide a YANG parser and easy access to the YANG module structures and schema. Why might you want to do this versus calling pyang from a shell or command script? In some cases, it might be easier to add a formatting plug-in to pyang to control its output and then call it from another script. However, as you work with large repositories of modules, and if you need to call pyang a number of times over that set of modules, the time it takes to instantiate pyang's internal context adds a lot of time to your application's execution.

Embedding pyang's backend libraries into your application means that you only need to build the internal context once and then use it (or manipulate it) from within your Python code directly. This includes accessing formatting plug-ins and validating module veracity.

To get started, create one or more **pyang.FileRepository** objects to hold your YANG modules and then instantiate a **pyang.Context** object. Once that **pyang.Context** object is instantiated, call the **add_module()** method to parse and add module objects to that context or call the **search_module()** method to find a module by name (and optionally revision) from the repositories. Once all your modules are added, the context object provides the entry point into the pyang internals. Example 9-5 shows Python code that creates a pyang context and searches it for an "ietf-routing" module. If found, the module's structure is pretty-printed using the **pprint()** method.

EXAMPLE 9-5 Creating a Pyang Context

```
#!/usr/local/bin/python2

from pyang import Context, FileRepository
import sys
import optparse

YANG_ROOT = '/models/src/git/yang/'

optparser = optparse.OptionParser()
(o, args) = optparser.parse_args()

repo = FileRepository(YANG_ROOT)
ctx = Context(repo)
ctx.opts = o

mod_obj = ctx.search_module(None, 'ietf-routing')
if mod_obj:
    mod_obj.pprint()
```

The **mod_obj** returned by **search_module()** is of type Statement, defined in the statement.py module included with pyang. The **__init__.py** file within the root of the pyang distribution includes the definition for the **Context** class, which shows additional methods available to contexts.

To give you an idea of the performance boost you may gain by embedding pyang into your application versus invoking it externally, consider Examples 9-6 and 9-7. Example 9-6 is a shell script that invokes pyang to print the name and revision of three YANG modules. This script points pyang to the YangModels GitHub repository discussed in Chapter 7. On a given platform, this script takes about 9 seconds to run. Most of that time is spent rebuilding the pyang internals each time it launches.

EXAMPLE 9-6 Shell Script That Calls Pyang Externally

```
#!/bin/sh

YANG_REPO="/models/src/git/yang"
RFC_ROOT="${YANG_REPO}/standard/ietf/RFC"

modules="ietf-i2rs-rib@2018-09-13.yang ietf-l3vpn-svc.yang ietf-ipv6-unicast-
routing.yang"

for m in ${modules}; do
  pyang -p ${YANG_REPO} -f name –name-print-revision "${RFC_ROOT}/${m}"
done
```

Example 9-7 provides the same functionality, only with pyang embedded into a Python script. The name plug-in is then invoked using the pyang context for all three modules at once. Since the context only needs to be built once instead of for each module, this script only takes 3 seconds to run. While 3 seconds versus 9 doesn't seem like a long time, notice how extrapolating this out for a larger number of pyang invocations makes for a compelling reason to embed it instead of execute it externally.

EXAMPLE 9-7 Python Script Embedding Pyang to Print Module Names

```
#!/usr/local/bin/python2

from pyang import Context, FileRepository
from pyang.plugins.name import emit_name
import sys
import optparse

YANG_ROOT = '/models/src/git/yang'
RFC_ROOT = YANG_ROOT + '/standard/ietf/RFC'

optparser = optparse.OptionParser()
(o, args) = optparser.parse_args()
```

```
repo = FileRepository(YANG_ROOT)
ctx = Context(repo)
ctx.opts = o

ctx.opts.print_revision = True

mods = ['ietf-i2rs-rib@2018-09-13.yang', 'ietf-l3vpn-svc.yang',
        'ietf-ipv6-unicast-routing.yang']
mod_objs = []

for m in mods:
    with open(RFC_ROOT + '/' + m, 'r') as fd:
        mod = ctx.add_module(m, fd.read())
        mod_objs.append(mod)

emit_name(ctx, mod_objs, sys.stdout)
```

Pyang Plug-Ins

When you run pyang with the **-f tree** argument to see a tree structure of a YANG module's schema, that tree format is implemented as a plug-in. Pyang allows for creating plug-ins to extend how it displays output (format plug-ins) as well as to alter module parsing behavior (backend plug-ins). Typically, if you are developing your own YANG modules, you may have a need to define new extensions. In that case, creating custom pyang backend plug-ins to properly validate those extensions (for example, within CI pipeline's test phase) is extremely useful. Likewise, formatting plug-ins can be quite powerful. As an example, the YANG Catalog suite created formatting plug-ins to generate the index data[3] that drives the Catalog search, as well as the YANG module tree interface[4] seen at https://yangcatalog.org/yang-search/yang_tree/ietf-routing.

In addition to the tree display plug-in, pyang comes bundled with a number of other plug-ins, one of which is yang-data, which instructs pyang how to parse elements that are defined using RFC 8040's yang-data extension. All of pyang's plug-ins are found in the location of its library's installation under the **plugins** subdirectory. For example, on Linux systems, this is typically **/usr/lib/python2.7/site-packages/pyang/plugins**.

Both types of pyang plug-ins declare a **pyang_plugin_init**() function and a class definition for the plug-in itself. Format plug-ins must register the formats they will provide as well as how to display the formatted output. The backend plug-ins vary depending on the YANG parsing behavior they are controlling. For example, they may register additional statement and grammar rules (as is the case for the restconf.py plug-in that parses yang-data).

Example 9-8 show the structure of the name.py pyang plug-in. This plug-in provides a "name" format that display a module's name and any main module to which it belongs (in the case of a submodule). This plug-in also takes an optional parameter to display the revision in addition to the name. A sample of this plug-in's output is shown in the snippet that follows Example 9-8.

EXAMPLE 9-8 Pyang's name.py Plug-In

```
"""Name output plugin

"""

import optparse

from pyang import plugin

def pyang_plugin_init():
    plugin.register_plugin(NamePlugin())

class NamePlugin(plugin.PyangPlugin):
    def add_output_format(self, fmts):
        self.multiple_modules = True
        fmts['name'] = self

    def add_opts(self, optparser):
        optlist = [
            optparse.make_option("--name-print-revision",
                                 dest="print_revision",
                                 action="store_true",
                                 help="Print the name and revision in" +
                                      "name@revision format"),
            ]
        g = optparser.add_option_group("Name output specific options")
        g.add_options(optlist)

    def setup_fmt(self, ctx):
        ctx.implicit_errors = False

    def emit(self, ctx, modules, fd):
        emit_name(ctx, modules, fd)

def emit_name(ctx, modules, fd):
    for module in modules:
        bstr = ""
        rstr = ""
        if ctx.opts.print_revision:
            rs = module.i_latest_revision
```

```
39                  if rs is None:
40                      r = module.search_one('revision')
41                      if r is not None:
42                          rs = r.arg
43                  if rs is not None:
44                      rstr = '@%s' % rs
45              b = module.search_one('belongs-to')
46              if b is not None:
47                  bstr = " (belongs-to %s)" % b.arg
48              fd.write("%s%s%s\n" % (module.arg, rstr, bstr))
```

The plug-in can be invoked on a YANG module with the following command. Note that, in this case, because the **--name-print-revision** argument was specified, the module name *and* its revision are printed.

```
$ pyang -f name --name-print-revision ietf-routing.yang
ietf-routing@2018-03-13
```

In the code shown in Example 9-7, lines 9 and 10 initialize the plug-in and register its class with the pyang framework. Because this is a format plug-in, **the add_output_format**() method is defined at line 13. This plug-in provides one output, called "name."

Optional arguments (like the --**name-print-revision** parameter in this plug-in) are added via the **add_opts**() method. The value of any optional parameters can be retrieved later in the plug-in via the **ctx.opts** object (as shown at line 37). If your plug-in doesn't require any optional parameters, omit declaring this method.

The critical method for displaying the results of the formatting is **emit**(), on line 30. In the case of the name plug-in, that is done via a static **emit_name**() function. The **emit**() method is invoked by pyang with a context object, the set of modules on which pyang was called, and an output file descriptor. The context object provides access to internal pyang structures as well as optional parameter values. Write the formatting output to the output file descriptor, as shown in line 48. Calling **print**() is not desirable because the output may be tied to a file (that is, when the pyang --**output option** is specified).

Example 9-9 shows the elided contents of the restconf.py backend plug-in. This plug-in does not provide any new output formats, but it does provide pyang the necessary knowledge to support RFC 8040–defined yang-data constructs.

EXAMPLE 9-9 Pyang's restconf.py Plug-In

```
restconf_module_name = 'ietf-restconf'

class RESTCONFPlugin(plugin.PyangPlugin):
    def __init__(self):
        plugin.PyangPlugin.__init__(self, 'restconf')

```

```
7   def pyang_plugin_init():
8       plugin.register_plugin(RESTCONFPlugin())
9
10      grammar.register_extension_module(restconf_module_name)
11
12      yd = (restconf_module_name, 'yang-data')
13      statements.add_data_keyword(yd)
14      statements.add_keyword_with_children(yd)
15      statements.add_keywords_with_no_explicit_config(yd)
16
17      for (stmt, occurance, (arg, rules), add_to_stmts) in restconf_stmts:
18          grammar.add_stmt((restconf_module_name, stmt), (arg, rules))
19          grammar.add_to_stmts_rules(add_to_stmts,
20                                     [((restconf_module_name, stmt), occurance)])
21
22      statements.add_validation_fun('expand_2',
23                                    [yd],
24                                    v_yang_data)
25
26      error.add_error_code('RESTCONF_YANG_DATA_CHILD', 1,
27                           "the 'yang-data' extension must have exactly one " +
28                           "child that is a container")
29
30  restconf_stmts = [
31      ('yang-data', '*',
32       ('identifier', grammar.data_def_stmts),
33       ['module', 'submodule']),
34
35  ]
36
37  def v_yang_data(ctx, stmt):
38      if (len(stmt.i_children) != 1 or
39          stmt.i_children[0].keyword != 'container'):
40          err_add(ctx.errors, stmt.pos, 'RESTCONF_YANG_DATA_CHILD', ())
```

Lines 12 through 15 add a new YANG statement for the **ietf-restconf:yang-data** extension. This allows pyang to recognize yang-data as a keyword in YANG modules, as well as to do further validation of the children of that keyword. That is, in the case of RFC 8040 yang-data, there is a rule that the **yang-data** extension must have exactly one (and only one) child that is a container. Lines 22 through 28 and the **v_yang_data**() function add this knowledge to pyang. Therefore, when pyang sees a module that contains yang-data, it applies the proper syntax checking to ensure the module is valid.

YANG Parsing with Libyang

Embedding pyang into your applications works very well if you are developing in Python. But what if you need YANG parsing support with other language bindings? Yes, you can fork and execute pyang as an external program, but as you saw, that can have performance implications. It will also require you to parse the textual output that comes back from it. This may require use of regular expressions or other "hacky" screen-scraping methods, which will add additional complexity to your code. Libyang[5] is a C library that provides YANG parsing and validation functions and is used in a number of open source projects like Free Range Routing,[6] Netopeer2,[7] and sysrepo.[8] It is also used to power the yanglint validator discussed in Chapter 8. Libyang is quick to adopt new YANG features and extensions and currently includes support for YANG 1.0 and 1.1, JSON and XML encoded data, default values in instance data (RFC 6243), and YANG metadata (RFC 7952). Because of C's embeddable nature, libyang also includes Simplified Wrapper and Interface Generator (SWIG) bindings for JavaScript, which enables libyang to be used within Node.js applications.

Like pyang, libyang supports printing module data in various formats, including a tree structure based on RFC 8340. Example 9-10 shows a simple libyang program that parses the ietf-routing module and prints its tree output.

EXAMPLE 9-10 Libyang Program That Prints ietf-routing's Tree Structure

```
#include <stdio.h>
#include <libyang/libyang.h>
#include <glib.h>

#define YANG_ROOT "/models/src/git/yang"
#define RFC_ROOT YANG_ROOT "/standard/ietf/RFC"

int
main(int argc, char **argv) {
  struct ly_ctx *ctx = NULL;
  char *routing_mod = NULL;
  const struct lys_module *mod;

  ctx = ly_ctx_new(NULL);
  ly_ctx_set_searchdir(ctx, YANG_ROOT);

  routing_mod = g_strdup_printf("%s/ietf-routing@2018-03-13.yang", RFC_ROOT);

  mod = lys_parse_path(ctx, routing_mod, LYS_IN_YANG);

  lys_print_file(stdout, mod, LYS_OUT_TREE, NULL);

  g_free(routing_mod);
  ly_ctx_destroy(ctx, NULL);

}
```

A libyang application needs to include **libyang/libyang.h** and link with **-lyang** to build and run properly. The full set of documentation is built with the libyang package and is found online at https://netopeer.liberouter.org/doc/libyang/master/, where it is built regularly.

The principal author of libyang (and the Netopeer project), Radek Krejčí, is interviewed at the end of this chapter, where he shares his perspective on enabling developers to harness the power of model-driven management and automation.

Interacting with the Network

Chapter 7 explored tools that allow you to interact with YANG-based servers using NETCONF and RESTCONF protocols. As an application developer, you want to embed clients for YANG-based protocols so that you can perform the same interactions within your applications. Additionally, you also may want to embed server capabilities into your applications. That is, you may have use cases where your application needs to be a NETCONF server (for example, if you are creating a NETCONF-based appliance). This section explores some libraries that enable you to satisfy both the client and server aspects of application development using YANG-based protocols.

NETCONF with Ncclient

The Python ncclient package is one of the most popular libraries available for building NETCONF clients. Ncclient is the underlying library that provides NETCONF support to the netconf-console (or ncc) utility covered in Chapter 7, and it also provides the NETCONF support for the scripts that YANG Suite generates, which was also explored in Chapter 7.

Ncclient is available in the PyPi repository and installed with the following command:

```
$ pip install ncclient
```

A primary goal of ncclient is to simplify operations between client applications and NETCONF servers by offering a straightforward, "Pythonic" interface. Ncclient supports the standard **<get>**, **<get-config>**, and **<edit-config>** operations, as well as supporting notifications and an extensible mechanism for handling custom remote procedure calls (RPCs). Although NETCONF should be standard across vendor platforms, at times there are subtle differences, and ncclient comes built with knowledge of some of these nuances. Of course, because it is open source, you can add other vendor handlers or capabilities you require. A sample script showing ncclient performing a **<get-config>** operation is shown in Example 9-11.

EXAMPLE 9-11 Ncclient Performing a **<get-config>**

```
import lxml.etree as ET
from argparse import ArgumentParser
from ncclient import manager
from ncclient.operations import RPCError

if __name__ == '__main__':

    parser = ArgumentParser(description='Usage:')

    # script arguments
    parser.add_argument('-a', '--host', type=str, required=True,
                        help="Device IP address or Hostname")
    parser.add_argument('-u', '--username', type=str, required=True,
                        help="Device Username (netconf agent username)")
    parser.add_argument('-p', '--password', type=str, required=True,
                        help="Device Password (netconf agent password)")
    parser.add_argument('--port', type=int, default=830,
                        help="Netconf agent port")
    args = parser.parse_args()

    # connect to netconf agent
    with manager.connect(host=args.host,
                         port=args.port,
                         username=args.username,
                         password=args.password,
                         timeout=90,
                         hostkey_verify=False,
                         device_params={'name': 'csr'}) as m:

        # execute netconf operation
        try:
            response = m.get_config(source='running').xml
            data = ET.fromstring(response)
        except RPCError as e:
            data = e._raw

        # beautify output
        print(ET.tostring(data, pretty_print=True))
```

In general, all ncclient code is wrapped within a **manager** object, which handles the underlying Secure Shell (SSH) connection to the device and provides a channel for sending RPCs and receiving responses. The script in Example 9-11 gets the entire running config and prints out the resulting eXtensible Markup Language (XML) text. It also demonstrates how to specify a device profile ("csr" in this case) to properly handle differences with specific vendor platforms. You may find that when interacting with different vendors, you have to specify the device parameters for a particular vendor's operating system in order to get the desired behavior.

Instead of retrieving the entire running config, fetch portions using either subtree or XPath-based filters. For example, if you just need to request only the OpenConfig **/network-instances** path, change the **get_config()** call to what is shown in the following snippet:

```
response = m.get_config(source='running', filter=('xpath', '/network-instances')).xml
```

Within the ncclient **manager** object, you can send custom RPCs to the device just as you perform standard requests. Example 9-12 demonstrates invoking an RPC called "default" that resets an interface to its default configuration.

EXAMPLE 9-12 Invoke a Custom RPC with Ncclient

```
import lxml.etree as ET
from argparse import ArgumentParser
from ncclient import manager
from ncclient.xml_ import qualify
from ncclient.operations import RPCError

if __name__ == '__main__':

    parser = ArgumentParser(description='Usage:')

    # script arguments
    parser.add_argument('-a', '--host', type=str, required=True,
                        help="Device IP address or Hostname")
    parser.add_argument('-u', '--username', type=str, required=True,
                        help="Device Username (netconf agent username)")
    parser.add_argument('-p', '--password', type=str, required=True,
                        help="Device Password (netconf agent password)")
    parser.add_argument('--port', type=int, default=830,
                        help="Netconf agent port")
    args = parser.parse_args()

    # connect to netconf agent
    with manager.connect(host=args.host,
                         port=args.port,
                         username=args.username,
                         password=args.password,
                         timeout=90,
                         hostkey_verify=False,
                         device_params={'name': 'csr'}) as m:
```

```
        # execute netconf operation
        try:
            default_rpc = ET.Element(qualify('default', 'http://cisco.com/ns/yang/
Cisco-IOS-XE-rpc'))
            ET.SubElement(default_rpc, qualify('interface', 'http://cisco.com/ns/
yang/Cisco-IOS-XE-rpc')).text = 'GigabitEthernet3'
            response = m.dispatch(default_rpc)
            print('RPC invoked successfully!')
        except RPCError as e:
            data = e._raw
```

What about telemetry support with ncclient? Although it does NETCONF notifications, it does not yet have support for telemetry technologies like the IETF YANG Push. However, there are forks of ncclient's code available that support this. Einar Nilsen-Nygaard, who shared his thoughts on tooling in Chapter 7, created one of these forks that offers YANG Push support. This ncclient fork[9] supports all the other operations that the stock ncclient supports, plus adds additional capabilities for streaming telemetry. Since YANG Push is, as of this writing, still in development at the IETF, Einar's modifications have not yet made it into the upstream. Einar also tracks the upstream ncclient distribution in his fork, so his can be used as a drop-in replacement for ncclient in the meantime; then, when YANG Push is ratified, the upstream distribution will have the same support. Example 9-13 subscribes to streaming telemetry memory stats from a device and prints the results it receives. The stream refreshes every second. A sample of the results are shown in Example 9-14.

EXAMPLE 9-13 Receive Telemetry with Ncclient

```
import lxml.etree as ET
from argparse import ArgumentParser
from ncclient import manager
from ncclient.operations import RPCError
import time

def yp_cb(notif):
    data = ET.fromstring(notif.xml)
    print(ET.tostring(data, pretty_print=True))

def err_cb(e):
    print(e)

if __name__ == '__main__':

    parser = ArgumentParser(description='Usage:')

    # script arguments
    parser.add_argument('-a', '--host', type=str, required=True,
                        help="Device IP address or Hostname")
```

```
    parser.add_argument('-u', '--username', type=str, required=True,
                        help="Device Username (netconf agent username)")
    parser.add_argument('-p', '--password', type=str, required=True,
                        help="Device Password (netconf agent password)")
    parser.add_argument('--port', type=int, default=830,
                        help="Netconf agent port")
    args = parser.parse_args()

    # connect to netconf agent
    with manager.connect(host=args.host,
                         port=args.port,
                         username=args.username,
                         password=args.password,
                         timeout=90,
                         hostkey_verify=False,
                         device_params={'name': 'csr'}) as m:

        # execute netconf operation
        try:
            response = m.establish_subscription(yp_cb, err_cb, '/memory-statistics',
              1000).xml
            data = ET.fromstring(response)
        except RPCError as e:
            data = e._raw

        # beautify output
        print(ET.tostring(data, pretty_print=True))
        while True:
            time.sleep(1)
```

EXAMPLE 9-14 Memory Statistics Subscription Results


```
<notification xmlns="urn:ietf:params:xml:ns:netconf:notification:1.0">
  <eventTime>2018-12-20T14:09:12.74Z</eventTime>
  <push-update xmlns="urn:ietf:params:xml:ns:yang:ietf-yang-push">
    <subscription-id>2147483653</subscription-id>
    <datastore-contents-xml>
      <memory-statistics xmlns="http://cisco.com/ns/yang/Cisco-IOS-XE-memory-oper">
        <memory-statistic>
          <name>Processor</name>
          <total-memory>2450272320</total-memory>
          <used-memory>337016136</used-memory>
          <free-memory>2113256184</free-memory>
          <lowest-usage>2111832096</lowest-usage>
          <highest-usage>1474310140</highest-usage>
```

```
      </memory-statistic>
      <memory-statistic>
        <name>lsmpi_io</name>
        <total-memory>3149400</total-memory>
        <used-memory>3148576</used-memory>
        <free-memory>824</free-memory>
        <lowest-usage>824</lowest-usage>
        <highest-usage>412</highest-usage>
      </memory-statistic>
    </memory-statistics>
  </datastore-contents-xml>
 </push-update>
</notification>
```

NETCONF Clients and Servers with Libnetconf2

Libnetconf2[10] is a C library alternative to ncclient that provides embedded NETCONF capabilities for your applications. Besides the language, another major difference between ncclient and libnetconf2 is that libnetconf2 provides support for adding both NETCONF client *and* server capabilities. That means you can use libnetconf2 like you did ncclient to connect to devices that run NETCONF servers and be able to perform **<edit-config>**, **<get-config>**, and **<get>** RPCs, for example. You can also use libnetconf2 to develop your own embedded NETCONF servers. Example 9-15 is a short libnetconf2 program that prints the XML contents of the OpenConfig **/network-instances** path from a device via a **<get>** RPC.

EXAMPLE 9-15 Performing a **<get>** RPC with Libnetconf2

```
#include <nc_client.h>
#include <libyang/libyang.h>
#include <stdio.h>

int
main(int argc, char **argv) {
  struct nc_session *session;
  uint64_t msgid;
  struct nc_rpc *rpc;
  struct nc_reply *reply;
  struct nc_reply_data *data_rpl;

  nc_client_ssh_set_username("netop");
  session = nc_connect_ssh("192.168.10.48", 830, NULL);
  rpc = nc_rpc_get("/network-instances", 0, NC_PARAMTYPE_CONST);

  nc_send_rpc(session, rpc, 1000, &msgid);
```

```
  nc_recv_reply(session, rpc, msgid, 20000, LYD_OPT_DESTRUCT | LYD_OPT_NOSIBLINGS,
&reply);

  data_rpl = (struct nc_reply_data *)reply;

  lyd_print_file(stdout, data_rpl->data, LYD_XML, LYP_WITHSIBLINGS);

  return 0;
}
```

In fact, the Netopeer2 suite, discussed previously, uses libnetconf2 to provide its NETCONF server capabilities. The Netopeer2 suite is designed to act as both a framework for building NETCONF tools and as a management system for local Linux devices. Through libnetconf2, Netopeer2 uses libyang for YANG loading, parsing, and validation. For its data store implementation, it relies on sysrepo, a YANG-native data store package.

In addition to base NETCONF over SSH, libnetconf2 supports NETCONF over Transport Layer Security (TLS) with Domain Name Security (DNS SEC) SSH key fingerprints. It also supports the fairly recent NETCONF Call Home spec, as well as does NETCONF event notifications. Its client API is designed to be very simple for performing basic RPCs, and it also provides an extensible framework to add in additional RPCs. Because it is a C library, it can be combined with frameworks such as SWIG[11] or various foreign function interfaces (FFIs) to provide bindings for other languages. Currently, a native Python binding is in the works as part of the libnetconf2 distribution.

Interacting with RESTCONF Servers

A compelling attribute of RESTCONF is that it behaves similarly to other HTTP-based RESTful APIs. Therefore, the libraries you use to interact with those APIs or those HTTP-based services also work for RESTCONF. Just about all modern languages have some mechanism to interact with HTTP-based services, and those same mechanisms work with REST-based APIs and RESTCONF. Some of these frameworks and libraries are shown in Table 9-1.

TABLE 9-1 REST Packages for Various Languages

Language	Framework/Library	URL
Python	requests	http://docs.python-requests.org/en/master/
C/C++	cURL	https://curl.haxx.se/
Ruby	Rest-client	https://github.com/rest-client/rest-client
Perl	REST::Client	https://metacpan.org/pod/REST::Client
Golang	Sling	https://github.com/dghubble/sling

Making YANG Language Native

At its core, YANG is an API. It represents a contract between two parties, such as a NETCONF client and a NETCONF server. The YANG module stipulates what that server will support, what that client can query, or what configuration that client can set. Figure 9-1 shows the layering of YANG-based protocols and where the API layer fits into this scheme.

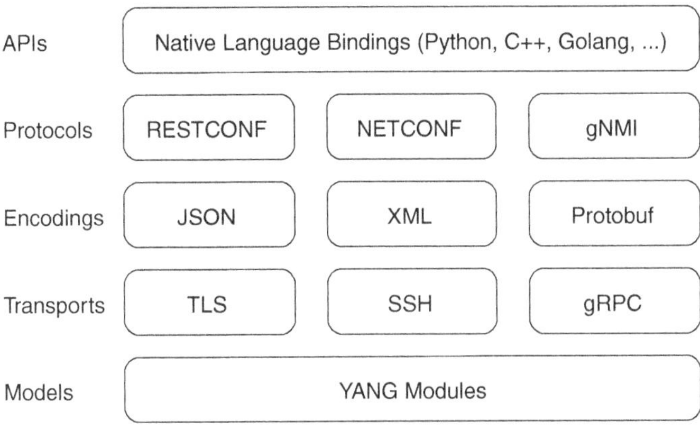

FIGURE 9-1 YANG-Based Protocol Stack

Up until this point, the tools and libraries already covered operate between the client and the server at the Protocols and Encodings layers, meaning they look at the raw payloads and the protocol semantics to transport them. However, you likely want to write applications that sit on that API layer such that those encoding and protocol semantics are abstracted away from your application. In other words, you want to interact with a NETCONF server using something that feels more native to the programming language you're working in. For example, you might want to use object-oriented constructs to edit or change configuration data or gather operational data from the device. This section covers how to make YANG-based protocols first-class citizens within your applications.

YDK

YDK, or the YANG Development Kit,[12] enables your applications to interact with YANG data models in a more application-native way. YDK is an open source project that allows you to take YANG modules and convert them into language-native packages so you can load them into your programs and applications just like you would any other library or module.

Currently, YDK supports Python, C++, and Golang package generation. YDK works by taking the YANG modules, parsing them, and converting them into per-language code packages. Those code packages become loadable modules or libraries within your applications (for example, for Python, you import the resulting modules; for C++, the code is compiled to libraries to which you link, and so on). So, whereas before you were creating an XML-encoded blob in order to perform an **<edit-config>**

operation on the device, now you load, for example, a Python module that has an object-oriented representation of that configuration that you want to change. Example 9-16 shows the XML needed to create a new interface using the openconfig-interfaces.yang module. Example 9-17 shows the same thing, but using the YDK-generated openconfig_interfaces module.

EXAMPLE 9-16 XML to Create a New Interface Using OpenConfig

```
<interfaces xmlns="http://openconfig.net/yang/interfaces">
  <interface>
    <name>Loopback0</name>
    <config>
      <name>Loopback0</name>
      <type xmlns:ianaift="urn:ietf:params:xml:ns:yang:iana-if-
type">ianaift:softwareLoopback</type>
    </config>
  </interface>
</interfaces>
```

EXAMPLE 9-17 YDK-Generated Python Code for a New OpenConfig Interface

```
intf = ydk.models.openconfig.openconfig_interfaces.Interfaces.Interface()
intf.name = 'Loopback0'
intf.config.name = intf.name
intf.config.type = ydk.models.ietf.iana_if_type.SoftwareLoopback()
```

Shorter, yes—and more Pythonic!

As shown in Example 9-17, once you instantiate an object representing the class of entity on which you want to operate, you then set properties on that object. When you're ready to interact with the device, YDK provides an abstraction layer for transmitting the object and receiving the results. This abstraction layer is flexible so that it can abstract multiple transport protocols and encodings. This includes NETCONF, gRPC Network Management Interface (gNMI), and RESTCONF protocols as well as XML, JavaScript Object Notation (JSON), and protobuf encodings. Replies from the device are also handled by this abstraction layer and converted from the raw encoding back into object instantiations. Therefore, in the case of a **<get>**, **<get-config>**, or telemetry publication where the device responds with data to the application, YDK presents this data as an object following the YANG-modeled API. Example 9-18 shows a complete YDK script that configures an interface with an IP address and then reads and prints statistics from this interface.

EXAMPLE 9-18 YDK Script to Configure and Gather Data from a Device

```
#!/usr/bin/env python

from ydk.services import CRUDService
```

```
from ydk.providers import NetconfServiceProvider

from ydk.models.openconfig.openconfig_interfaces import Interfaces
from ydk.errors import YError


def print_stats(**kwargs):
    if_filter = Interfaces()
    interfaces = kwargs['service'].read(kwargs['provider'], if_filter)
    for interface in interfaces.interface:
        if interface.name == kwargs['intf']:
            if interface.state.counters is not None:
                print('Stats for interface {}:'.format(kwargs['intf']))
                print('        in_unicast_pkts : {}'.format(
                    interface.state.counters.in_unicast_pkts))
                print('        in_octets : {}'.format(
                    interface.state.counters.in_octets))
                print('        out_unicast_pkts : {}'.format(
                    interface.state.counters.out_unicast_pkts))
                print('        out_octets : {}'.format(
                    interface.state.counters.out_octets))
                print('        in_multicast_pkts : {}'.format(
                    interface.state.counters.in_multicast_pkts))
                print('        in_broadcast_pkts : {}'.format(
                    interface.state.counters.in_broadcast_pkts))
                print('        out_multicast_pkts : {}'.format(
                    interface.state.counters.out_multicast_pkts))
                print('        out_broadcast_pkts : {}'.format(
                    interface.state.counters.out_broadcast_pkts))
                print('        out_discards : {}'.format(
                    interface.state.counters.out_discards))
                print('        in_discards : {}'.format(
                    interface.state.counters.in_discards))
                print('        in_unknown_protos : {}'.format(
                    interface.state.counters.in_unknown_protos))
                print('        in_errors : {}'.format(
                    interface.state.counters.in_errors))
                print('        out_errors : {}'.format(
                    interface.state.counters.out_errors))


def add_ip_to_intf(**kwargs):

    interface = Interfaces.Interface()
    interface.name = kwargs['intf']
```

```
49        subinterface = Interfaces.Interface.Subinterfaces.Subinterface()
50        subinterface.index = 0
51        addr = \
            Interfaces.Interface.Subinterfaces.Subinterface.Ipv4.Addresses.Address()
52        addr.ip = kwargs['ip']
53        addr.config.ip = kwargs['ip']
54        addr.config.prefix_length = kwargs['prefixlen']
55        subinterface.ipv4.addresses.address.append(addr)
56        interface.subinterfaces.subinterface.append(subinterface)
57
58        try:
59            kwargs['service'].update(kwargs['provider'], interface)
60        except YError as ye:
61            print('An error occurred adding the IP to the interface: {}'.
format(ye))
62
63
64    if __name__ == '__main__':
65
66        provider = NetconfServiceProvider(
67            address='192.168.10.48', port=830, protocol='ssh',
              username='netops', password='netops')
68        cruds = CRUDService()
69        add_ip_to_intf(ip='192.168.20.48', prefixlen=24,
70                       intf='GigabitEthernet2', service=cruds, provider=provider)
71        print_stats(intf='GigabitEthernet2', service=cruds, provider=provider)
```

This example demonstrates the object-oriented approach to programming with YANG as well as the abstraction YDK provides. The abstraction is seen in lines 12 and 59. Here, the **CRUDService** (Create, Read, Update, Delete) handles sending the necessary RPC details to the device via the **NetconfServiceProvider**. As part of the initial session establishment process, YDK learns the network element's capabilities and determines how to perform the CRUD operations. That is, if the device supports a writeable running configuration, YDK build the **<edit-config>** RPC at line 59 with the correct "running" target.

Lines 47 through 56 show how the openconfig-interafce.yang and openconfig-if-ip.yang modules translate to their API equivalents. The values set in these properties are checked by YDK *before* being sent to the network element since YDK understands the models' structures and constraints. YDK reports any errors caused by illegal values via Python exceptions. The following snippet shows the **YModelError** that is thrown if you accidentally use a string instead of an integer for **prefix_length** in line 54:

```
ydk.errors.YModelError: Invalid value ass for 'prefix_length'. Got type: 'str'.
Expected types: 'int'
```

YDK includes a number of prebuilt packages or bundles of models—that is, modules that are already converted from their YANG counterparts into Python, C++, or Golang libraries. These include an IETF bundle, an OpenConfig bundle, and a Cisco IOS XE and IOS XR bundle. You can choose to install only the bundles you need. The IETF bundle is required at a minimum.

These bundles may not be sufficient for the application you are building, however. If there are native modules for a particular vendor's platform that you are using—or if you've created your own service models—and you want to compile them into language-native packages, YDK offers a tool called the ydk-gen[13] (or YDK Generator) that allows you to take any module or any set of modules and convert them into the same native language bindings that are included with the YDK distribution. Ydk-gen is a Python application and comes either standalone or as a Docker container, so it is easy to use, even if you don't need it too often. API bundles are formally defined by creating JSON files that specify the bundle name (this is the model package or namespace to load), metadata about the bundle, and the module or modules to convert. Modules come from the local file system or from specific git repositories. Example 9-19 shows a sample bundle definition file that converts a single local YANG module. The definition for the IETF bundle is found at https://github.com/CiscoDevNet/ydk-gen/blob/master/profiles/bundles/ietf_0_1_1.json.

EXAMPLE 9-19 Sample YDK-Gen Bundle Definition File

```
{
    "name":"yangcatalog",
    "version": "0.1.0",
    "ydk_version": "0.8.0",
    "author": "YangCatalog.org",
    "copyright": "YangCatalog.org",
    "description": "YANG Catalog API model",
    "models": {
        "file": [
            "/models/yc.o/yangcatalog.yang"
        ]
    }
}
```

Once the bundle definitions are created, the **generate.py** command turns them into a package for the desired language. Taking the yangcatalog.json file shown in Example 9-18, Python bindings are generated and installed with the commands shown in the following snippet:

```
$ generate.py --python --bundle /bundles/yangcatalog.json
$ pip install gen-api/python/yangcatalog-bundle/dist/ydk*.tar.gz
```

Now you can begin using your YANG-modeled APIs in your application. In order to build more familiarity with the flow of developing with generated APIs, it helps to have good examples. The YDK distribution includes a number of samples that span different model bundles. You can typically find an example to use to see how to work with various data types and abstraction services. If you need more help, there is an active YDK community[14] where other network developers will help you out.

Pyangbind

Pyangbind[15] is another framework that generates native language bindings directly from YANG modules. Pyangbind is a pyang display plug-in that takes a YANG module or set of YANG modules and outputs a Python library file that represents those YANG module definitions. Functionally, pyangbind is like the "tree" display plug-in for pyang, except instead of generating an ASCII tree structure from the YANG module, it generates Python code.

Whereas YDK includes support for the Python, C++, and Golang languages, plus the abstraction layer for interacting with devices, pyangbind only produces Python bindings for the YANG modules, and it does not include the encoding/decoding and transport abstraction layers. While you still don't need to interact with the XML or JSON-encoded data, you still require a package (such as ncclient) in order to provide the device interaction piece. This means that pyangbind is a lighter-weight framework for working with object-oriented YANG within your applications. If you're only writing Python applications, pyangbind might be the right fit for your object-oriented YANG API solution.

Before using pyangbind in your applications, you must first run it against the YANG module or modules you want to convert to their Python equivalents. This is similar to how you use any other pyang display plug-in, except that pyangbind does not, by default, install itself into the pyang plugins subdirectory. The following snippet shows how to execute pyangbind against the openconfig-interfaces.yang and openconfig-if-ip.yang modules:

```
$ pyang --plugindir /local/lib/pyangbind -f pyangbind -o oc_if.py
/modules/oc/openconfig-interfaces.yang /modules/oc/openconfig-if-ip.yang
```

This creates an oc_if.py file that contains all the binding definitions for openconfig-interfaces.yang and openconfig-if-ip.yang. This module can then be used to build the payload for various NETCONF or RESTCONF operations. Those payloads can be used by ncclient or the requests module for sending the data directly to the device. Example 9-20 shows how to build an RPC payload using pyangbind and then using ncclient to add an IP address to an interface.

EXAMPLE 9-20 Building and Executing an RPC with Pyangbind and Ncclient

```
#!/usr/bin/env python

from oc_if import openconfig_interfaces
from pyangbind.lib.serialise import pybindIETFXMLEncoder
from ncclient import manager

```

```
7    def send_to_device(**kwargs):
8        rpc_body = '<config>' +
                 pybindIETFXMLEncoder.serialise(kwargs['py_obj']) + '</config>'
9        with manager.connect_ssh(host=kwargs['dev'], port=830,
              username=kwargs['user'],
              password=kwargs['password'], hostkey_verify=False) as m:

10           try:
11               m.edit_config(target='running', config=rpc_body)
12               print('Successfully configured IP on {}'.format(kwargs['dev']))
13           except Exception as e:
14               print('Failed to configure interface: {}'.format(e))
15
16   if __name__ == '__main__':
17
18       ocif = openconfig_interfaces()
19       intfs = ocif.interfaces
20
21       intfs.interface.add('GigabitEthernet2')
22       intf = intfs.interface['GigabitEthernet2']
23       intf.subinterfaces.subinterface.add(0)
24       sintf = intf.subinterfaces.subinterface[0]
25       sintf.ipv4.addresses.address.add('192.168.20.48')
26       ip = sintf.ipv4.addresses.address['192.168.20.48']
27       ip.config.ip = '192.168.20.48'
28       ip.config.prefix_length = 24
29
30       send_to_device(dev='192.168.10.48', user='netops',
                     password='netops', py_obj=intfs)
```

Lines 18 through 28 create an object representing the target interface to which the IPv4 address is added. Pyangbind includes serialization methods to turn those objects into XML or JSON-encoded data. Line 8 turns the interface object into XML using IETF rules and wraps it in a **<config>** element to use with ncclient.

In addition to serialization, pyangbind takes JSON or XML data from the device and deserializes that back into a Python object. Example 9-21 uses requests to gather interface stats as a JSON object, passes that object to pyangbind's JSON deserializer, and then prints various fields. All this happens without needing to interact with any JSON data directly.

EXAMPLE 9-21 Deserialize JSON Data with Pyangbind

```
1     import requests
2     from pyangbind.lib import pybindJSON
3     import oc_if
4
5
6     def print_stats(response):
7         py_obj = pybindJSON.load_ietf(
8             response.text, oc_if, 'openconfig_interfaces')
9         for index, intf in py_obj.interfaces.interface.iteritems():
10            if intf.name == 'GigabitEthernet2':
11                print('Bytes out : {}'.format(intf.state.counters.out_octets))
12                print('Bytes in  : {}'.format(intf.state.counters.in_octets))
13
14
15    if __name__ == '__main__':
16
17        url = 'https://192.168.10.48/restconf/data/openconfig-
interfaces:interfaces'
18
19        headers = {
20            'Accept': 'application/yang-data+json',
21            'Authorization': 'Basic bmV0b3BzOm51dG9wcw=='
22        }
23
24        response = requests.request('GET', url, headers=headers, verify=False)
25
26        print_stats(response)
```

Line 7 takes the raw response text as JSON and converts it into an instance of the **openconfig_interfaces** class. This object can be printed, manipulated, and sent back to the device, all without you needing to deal with the raw encoded data.

Interview with the Expert

Q&A with Radek Krejčí

Radek Krejčí is a researcher at CESNET, operator of the Czech national e-infrastructure for science, research, and education. He is an experienced developer and architect of various tools for network security monitoring, but mainly for network configuration. He is the author of the Netopeer project's open source NETCONF protocol implementation, which started as his bachelor's thesis and evolved into a toolset providing generic YANG and NETCONF libraries, a (YANG-based) validated data store, as well as complete NETCONF server and client applications.

Question:

What do you see is most needed in terms of YANG libraries and SDKs when it comes to making it easy to realize the full value of the abstraction data model–driven management that YANG promises?

Answer:

As for any library or SDK, it is the combination of a fine API and documentation that makes it successful. It must provide developers an easy and straightforward way to do exactly what they want or need. And because of YANG's complexity, there are many use cases, so it is quite a challenging task. The API must hide the complexity of YANG while still enabling even rare use cases.

Question:

What advice would you give to application developers who want to integrate YANG-modeled data into their Operations Support Systems (OSS) applications?

Answer:

Just do not reinvent the wheel, and try to use libraries and frameworks such as libyang and libnetconf2. YANG is very friendly to module authors, but less friendly to the tool developers. You already did the most important step, but just the first step, when you decided to use YANG to describe your data. Now, you are supposed to decide how much work it will be for you.

Summary

While YANG has been around for a while, it is very much trending in the network space now. As such, availability of YANG-based tools is growing. As Radek said, the right tools and libraries can jumpstart your development and allow you to focus on the value YANG brings to your application rather than you spending time reinventing functions and abstractions that have already been created. This chapter explored some of the APIs, libraries, and language binding tools that exist and are popular today that help streamline the application development process. As you put your applications together, remember to consider not just the model and its instance data you're using. Think, too, about the metadata that surrounds the modules you're using so that you can pre-validate instance data, confirm module support in your network elements, and check for potential non-backward-compatible changes that could have been introduced between versions. Chapter 10, "Using NETCONF and YANG," stitches together the business use case with the YANG model and abstractions generated by Network Services Orchestrator (NSO) to craft a workflow that shows the power and value of enabling your applications with YANG-modeled data.

Endnotes

1. https://yangcatalog.org/contribute.html
2. https://yangcatalog.org/downloadables/yangcatalog.postman_collection.json
3. https://github.com/YangCatalog/search/blob/master/scripts/pyang_plugin/yang_catalog_index.py
4. https://github.com/YangCatalog/search/blob/master/scripts/pyang_plugin/json_tree.py
5. https://github.com/CESNET/libyang
6. https://frrouting.org/
7. https://github.com/CESNET/Netopeer2
8. https://github.com/sysrepo/sysrepo
9. https://github.com/einarnn/ncclient
10. https://github.com/CESNET/libnetconf2
11. http://www.swig.org/
12. http://ydk.io
13. https://github.com/CiscoDevNet/ydk-gen
14. https://community.cisco.com/t5/yang-development-kit-ydk/bd-p/5475j-disc-dev-net-ydk
15. https://github.com/robshakir/pyangbind

Chapter 10

Using NETCONF and YANG

This chapter covers

- The example business case background for this chapter
- How to get started, a top-down service model approach
- Building from the bottom up with device templates
- How to connect the service YANG model to the device YANG models
- Setting up NETCONF on a couple of different devices
- Discovering what your devices can do for you
- Play around with creating, updating, and rolling back services
- Checking that the orchestrator is synchronized with its devices
- Seeing the NETCONF network-wide transactions in action

Introduction

The purpose of this chapter is to show a full story, starting with a business need and taking it all the way to verifying that it works correctly in the network. This chapter builds a somewhat real software-defined wide area network (SDWAN) service using the Network Services Orchestrator (NSO) product as the orchestrator. The first step is to design a YANG service model, map it to the device models, write a little bit of code to assist in that mapping, and then plug in some devices, configure them for NETCONF management, and try out the service with some service creation, modifications, and rollback. This chapter also examines how the service gets deployed from an orchestrator point of view as well as the NETCONF messages flying around between the orchestrator and devices. The project is available as a hands-on project you can clone from GitHub and then build, run, and play with as you please. Instructions for how to obtain the necessary free tools are found within the project README file at https://github.com/janlindblad/bookzone.

So the Story Goes

BookZone is a fictitious bookstore franchise. They already implemented a NETCONF/YANG-based solution to manage each of their store locations (see Chapter 3, "YANG Explained"). This interface is used by BookZone central management to add and remove authors and titles from individual store databases, and to monitor inventory counts.

BookZone naturally has many publishing houses as suppliers. Some of the best suppliers sell so many books with BookZone that it makes sense that the publishers have a direct connection to stores, to restock without involvement from the central office. This service is called "BookZone Store Connect."

Now, with each store offering a NETCONF/YANG interface, it is time to manage the Store Connect service using an orchestrated network service. In order to understand how the service is implemented in the BookZone enterprise network, have a look at the network diagram shown in Figure 10-1.

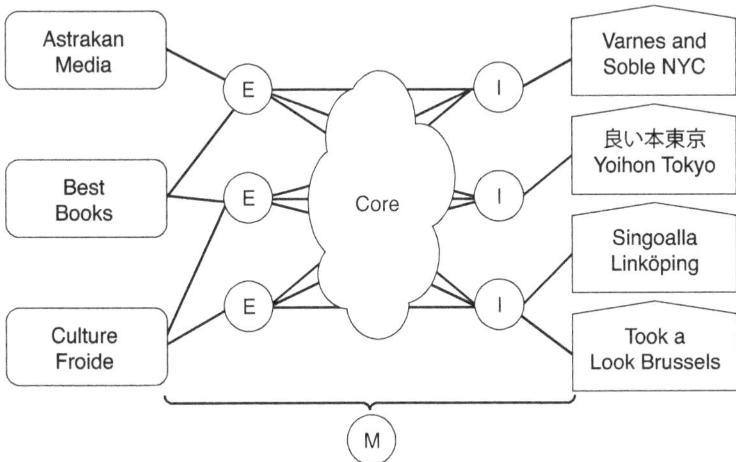

FIGURE 10-1 Network Diagram of the Store Connect Service

The device symbols marked "E" are externally facing routers, while the ones marked "I" are internally facing routers. The system marked "M" is the monitoring system. It may consist of a multitude of nodes and measurement devices, but from the point of view of the orchestration system, this is one device with a single application programming interface (API). This idea is often referred to as a "single system view."

This chapter uses a device-naming convention. The first letter of a device name indicates whether it's an externally or internally facing device. The second letter indicates the brand of the device, where "c" indicates a Cisco IOS XE device and "j" refers to a Juniper JunOS device. There is also a number at the end to distinguish multiple devices of the same role and brand. The seven devices in Figure 10-1 are called ej0, ej1, ec0, ij0, ic0, ic1, and m0. The YANG module developed in this chapter also refers to devices with names starting with "ei". The "i" refers to the Internet Engineering Task Force (IETF), meaning a device of any brand that uses the standard IETF interface YANG module.

Whenever a new publisher qualifies and signs up for the BookZone Store Connect service, the BookZone networking staff has to perform the following tasks:

- Allocate a virtual local area network identity (VLAN ID) for this publisher.
- Open up the firewall on relevant E routers to allow external connections from a specified set of IP addresses for each site of the publisher.
- Configure the E routers to place traffic for the publisher run over the allocated VLAN.
- Configure the I routers to terminate the traffic for the publisher run over the allocated VLAN.
- Configure the monitoring system to continuously monitor the connectivity/quality of the setup.

The core network does not need any configuration changes just because a new publisher joins. Nor are there any changes on the configuration of the stores in this scenario.

The networking department decided on the following rules for the service:

- The traffic of each publisher must run on a separate VLAN.
- Each publisher may have one or more sites.
- Each publisher site is connected to one E router.
- Each publisher site has a single range of allowed IPv4 addresses.
- Each store is connected to one I router.
- Each store has one management IPv4 address.
- The monitoring system must monitor all connections from the publisher site to the stores created.

With this background, the following sections are a closer look at what the BookZone network team came up with for their automation solution. They decided to implement their use cases based on the NSO platform. Note that several other controllers/orchestrators could have been used instead, such as OpenDaylight and CloudOpera, that also leverage YANG and NETCONF.

Top-Down Service Model

Generally, a "service" is developed either top down or bottom up. Which approach is the better one can be debated. To a high degree, what is better depends on the engineer doing the modeling. Network engineers often start bottom up, because then they are starting with known concepts and can abstract from there. Software engineers might start with the outward facing interface instead (that is, the service YANG model) and then drill down to figure out how that maps to the underlying infrastructure.

Let's go with the top-down approach, starting with designing the YANG service interface as the first step toward automating the Store Connect service. A service YANG model doesn't describe the interface of a device; instead, it describes how an operator wants to interact with the service at a high level.

The service models need to contain enough information to be used to configure all the low-level details required to configure the service on all the types of devices involved, as shown in Example 10-1. This does not mean that all low-level information must be present in the service model. Far from it. Many low-level configuration options may be hard-coded to a given value for a specific type of service, and many configuration settings may be computed or fetched from other systems by service code, so that the operator doesn't need to figure out a suitable value.

EXAMPLE 10-1 Store Connect Service YANG Module, Imports, Description, and Revision

```
module storeconnect {
  yang-version 1.1;
  namespace "http://example.com/storeconnect";
  prefix storeconnect;

  import ietf-inet-types {
    prefix inet;
  }
  import tailf-common {
    prefix tailf;
  }
  import tailf-ncs {
    prefix ncs;
  }
  import junos-conf-root {
    prefix jc;
  }
  import junos-conf-interfaces {
    prefix jc-interfaces;
  }
  import Cisco-IOS-XE-native {
    prefix ios;
  }
  import ietf-interfaces {
    prefix if;
  }

  description
    "Bla bla...";

  revision 2018-02-01 {
    description
      "Initial revision.";
  }
```

Example 10-1 shows bit of boilerplate YANG, which gives the service a name, description, and revision. It imports a number of YANG modules you're going to reference.

The next bit in Example 10-2 declares a list of stores. Each store has a network address and is connected to an I router, which must be among the devices NSO is managing. The configuration points out a specific interface to which the store is connected. The interface name is left as a free-form string. This modeling choice is debated later.

Finally, a leaf-list of tags is given for each store, as shown in Example 10-2. This set of tags on each store is meant to reflect general attributes of the store, such as its location, which languages it carries, how large the store is, and any specialties (such as focusing on fantasy and science fiction literature). This helps publishers know which stores they should target.

EXAMPLE 10-2 Store Connect Service YANG Module: The List of Stores

```
container stores {
  list store {
    key name;
    leaf name {
      type string;
    }
    container network {
      leaf address {
        type inet:ipv4-address;
      }
      leaf i-router {
        type leafref {
          path "/ncs:devices/ncs:device/ncs:name";
        }
      }
      leaf interface {
        type string;
      }
    }
    leaf-list tags {
      type string;
    }
  }
}
```

The next part, shown in Example 10-3, declares a list of publishers. Note that this is just the initial content of the publisher list. Soon, there will be more elements added to this list. Each publisher has a simple string name. The statements beginning with `tailf:` and `ncs:` are extension keywords (that is, they are declared using the `extension` keyword in YANG). Their meaning is proprietary to whoever declares them, but since the syntax for `extension` keyword is standardized, any YANG-compliant parser can read this module and get past the extensions without tripping over them. Many other languages do similar things using comments with special character sequences.

The `ncs:servicepoint` extension keyword tells the orchestrator that this list is a service. This means that service code registered with the name *storeconnect-servicepoint* will be invoked as changes are made to this part of the configuration. The service point is usually located in a list so that an operator can configure many instances of the service. This is illustrated by Example 10-3.

EXAMPLE 10-3 Store Connect Service YANG Module: The List of Publishers, Core Part

```
container publishers {
  list publisher {
    description "Storeconnect service for BookZone publishers";

    key name;
    leaf name {
      tailf:info "Name of publisher connecting";
      tailf:cli-allow-range;
      type string;
    }

    uses ncs:service-data;
    ncs:servicepoint storeconnect-servicepoint;
```

Example 10-4 shows container *network*, which contains a list of publisher sites. Each *site* has a *name* and an IPv4 *address* range.

EXAMPLE 10-4 Store Connect Service YANG Module: The List of Publishers, Network Part

```
      container network {
        list site {
          key name;
          leaf name {
            type string;
          }
          leaf address {
            type inet:ipv4-address;
          }
          leaf mask-len {
            type uint32 {
              range "0..32";
            }
            default 32;
}
```

Each publisher has a number of sites. Each site has a name and an IPv4 address range that is allowed to connect with BookZone. No matter which device type happens to sit at the location to which this site is connected, the address and mask are expressed as a dotted quad and an integer. Some devices use other formats in their management interfaces, as you shall soon see.

Each site is attached to a specific E router as well as a specific interface on that E router. This is modeled as a leafref, pointing to any device in the NSO managed device list. Here, you only want to let the operator select devices with the E router role. This is accomplished with a `must` statement that only allows selection of devices that have names starting with *ej*, *ec*, or *ei*.

There are some advantages and disadvantages with making models depend on naming conventions. Naming conventions are a weak form of architecture. On the other hand, if this sort of simple statement can prevent mistakes and make the operators' lives easier, why not? It's as easy to change the YANG as changing any other code. You need to decide for yourself in which situations you want to consider this a good or bad thing.

Then there is the interface reference. In the store model shown in Example 10-2, the interface reference was modeled as a simple string. The advantage is dead simple YANG as well as total decoupling between service-level YANG and device YANG. The disadvantage is that the operator gets no help at all in figuring out what valid values are. With a leafref, everyone sees what YANG list and leaf has the values to go here. A good client application displays the options in a drop-down menu or as tab-completion options.

Since this service supports devices of several different kinds, and not all device types support the IETF interface's YANG module, this service lists a number of different options it allows. This is the price to pay for being specific and helping the operator understand what the options are. Each interface reference has a `when` statement to only make it available with the right device type. Next, the leafref path follows the *e-router* leaf to the device it points to, and then goes into that device's configuration tree and down into the interface list (of the right kind, depending on device type).

The `require-instance false` statement is important to discuss. It allows the leafref reference to be broken so that devices can be removed without tearing down the services that depend on them. If you feel the operator should not be allowed to remove a device if a service depends on it, simply remove the `require-instance false` statement.

The device and interface selection configuration for both externally and internally facing routers is shown in Example 10-5.

EXAMPLE 10-5 Store Connect Service YANG Module: The List of Publishers, Interface Part

```
leaf e-router {
  must "starts-with(current(), 'ej') or "+
       "starts-with(current(), 'ec') or "+
       "starts-with(current(), 'ei')";
  type leafref {
    path "/ncs:devices/ncs:device/ncs:name";
  }
}
```

```
          choice interface-type {
            leaf junos-interface {
              when "starts-with(../e-router, 'ej')";
              type leafref {
                path "/ncs:devices/ncs:device[ncs:name=current()/../e-router]/"+
                     "ncs:config/jc:configuration/jc-interfaces:interfaces/"+
                     "jc-interfaces:interface/jc-interfaces:name";
                // The path above expressed using deref():
                // path "deref(../e-router)/../ncs:config/jc:configuration/"+
                //      "jc-interfaces:interfaces/jc-interfaces:interface/"+
                //      "jc-interfaces:name";
                require-instance false;
              }
            }
            leaf ios-ge-interface {
              when "starts-with(../e-router, 'ec')";
              type leafref {
                path "/ncs:devices/ncs:device[ncs:name=current()/../e-router]/"+
                     "ncs:config/ios:native/ios:interface/ios:GigabitEthernet/"+
                     "ios:name";
                // The path above expressed using deref():
                // path "deref(../e-router)/../ncs:config/"+
                //      "ios:native/ios:interface/ios:GigabitEthernet/ios:name";
                require-instance false;
              }
            }
            leaf ietf-interface {
              when "starts-with(../e-router, 'ei')";
              type leafref {
                path "/ncs:devices/ncs:device[ncs:name=current()/../e-router]/"+
                     "ncs:config/if:interfaces/if:interface/if:name";
                // The path above expressed using deref():
                // path "deref(../e-router)/../ncs:config/"+
                //      "if:interfaces/if:interface/if:name";
                require-instance false;
              }
            }
          }
        }
        leaf allocated-vlan {
          config false;
          type uint32 {
            range "1..4094";
          }
        }
}
```

The last leaf in Example 10-5, *allocated-vlan*, is a `config false` operational state element. The operator is not asked to enter a VLAN ID for this publisher. Instead, the service code allocates a free VLAN. The operator might still be interested to know what allocation was done, if only for debugging purposes. That allocation is given back to the operator through this leaf by the service code.

The last part of the publisher list is about which publishers should be connected to which stores. A simple policy could of course be that all publishers are connected to all stores. BookZone's policy is based on stores and publishers both listing tag keywords. If they have any tag keyword in common, they are connected. A tag keyword could be a specialty, like *science*, *manga*, or *cooking*. Or it could be mainstream books in a given language, like *English*, *French*, or *Mandarin*.

In order to make it easier to understand the model and for operators to fill in values that are in use, the tag is modeled as a leafref to any tag value in use by any store, with `require-instance false`. This means a particular keyword, such as *cd-rom*, can be dropped by the last store without the configuration becoming invalid even if there are some publishers that still want to connect with stores that market something that has gone out of fashion (such as *cd-rom*). The *number-of-stores* leaf is a read-only count of how many stores that carry the given tag filled in by the system, as a guide to publishers.

Example 10-6 shows the YANG model for configuring the mapping between stores and publishers.

EXAMPLE 10-6 Store Connect Service YANG Module: The list of Publishers, target-stores Part

```
      container target-stores {
        list tag {
          key tag;

          leaf tag {
            type leafref {
              path "/stores/store/tags";
              require-instance false;
            }
          }
          leaf number-of-stores {
            config false;
            type uint32;
          }
        }
      }
    }
  }
}
```

Bottom-Up Device Templates

In the end, the service needs to push configuration changes to the devices. In NSO, this part is often described using device templates. A device template pushes Extensible Markup Language (XML) data structures to devices with a mix of hard-coded values and expressions in curly brackets, as shown in Example 10-7. The expressions may draw input data directly from the service YANG and service code using XPath pointers. The expression `{/name}` picks up the value of leaf *name* directly from the service YANG. The expressions may also refer to variables computed and published by the service code. For example, `{$VLAN_ID}`.

EXAMPLE 10-7 Store Connect Service Template: Cisco IOS-XE Part

```
<config-template xmlns="http://tail-f.com/ns/config/1.0">
  <devices xmlns="http://tail-f.com/ns/ncs">
    <device>
      <name>{$DEVICE}</name>
      <config>

        <!-- CISCO XE1671 -->
        <native xmlns="http://cisco.com/ns/yang/Cisco-IOS-XE-native">
          <vrf>
            <definition tags="merge">
              <name>{/name}</name>
              <rd>300:{$VLAN_ID}</rd>
...
          <interface tags="nocreate">
            <GigabitEthernet>
              <name>{$INTERFACE}</name>
              <description tags="merge">connection to {/name}</description>
              <ip tags="merge">
                <address>
                  <primary>
                    <address>{$ADDRESS}</address>
                    <mask>{$MASK}</mask>
```

Further down in the same device template file is the mapping to a JunOS device, as shown in Example 10-8. The orchestrator automatically picks the right namespace(s) for the given device.

EXAMPLE 10-8 Store Connect Service Template: Juniper JunOS Part

```
        <!-- Juniper Junos18 -->
        <configuration xmlns="http://yang.juniper.net/junos/conf/root">
          <interfaces xmlns="http://yang.juniper.net/junos/conf/interfaces">
            <interface tags="nocreate">
              <name>{$INTERFACE}</name>
              <unit tags="merge">
                <name>{$VLAN_ID}</name>
                <description>connection to {/name}</description>
                <vlan-id>{$VLAN_ID}</vlan-id>
                <family>
                  <inet>
```

```
                <address>
                  <name>{$ADDRESS}/{$MASK_LEN}</name>
...
        <routing-instances
            xmlns="http://yang.juniper.net/junos/conf/routing-instances">
          <instance>
            <name>{/name}</name>
            <instance-type>vrf</instance-type>
            <interface>
              <name>{$INTERFACE}.{$VLAN_ID}</name>
            </interface>
            <route-distinguisher>
              <rd-type>300:{$VLAN_ID}</rd-type>
            </route-distinguisher>
            <vrf-import>{/name}-IMP</vrf-import>
            <vrf-export>{/name}-EXP</vrf-export>
```

The service also needs a device template for the monitoring system, but that is not shown here.

The service could equally well configure other services rather than devices this way, or a mix of lower-level services and devices. Some of the "devices" might be lower-level NSO systems in their own right.

Service Logic Connecting the Dots

A simple service might not need any service logic code at all, simply relying on the control logic available in the device templates. Most services need some sort of more complex calculations, assignments, or communications, however. This requires some code to compute good values to use in the templates.

This service was implemented in Python. If this isn't your forte, keep reading anyway. The gist of the code is explained at every step.

The first part, shown in Example 10-9, registers this class as responsible for the *storeconnect-servicepoint* declared in the YANG earlier. This is how the system knows which code to invoke when a particular service moves.

> **NOTE**
>
> The NSO product was called NCS before it was acquired by Cisco. Cisco already had several products called NCS, so decided to rename it. The programming APIs still reflect the old name.

EXAMPLE 10-9 Store Connect Service Code: Service Registration Part

```
# -*- mode: python; python-indent: 4 -*-
import ncs
from ncs.application import Service
```

```
# ------------------------------------------
# COMPONENT THREAD THAT WILL BE STARTED BY NCS.
# ------------------------------------------
class Main(ncs.application.Application):
    def setup(self):
        self.log.info('Main RUNNING')
        self.register_service('storeconnect-servicepoint', ServiceCallbacks)
    def teardown(self):
        self.log.info('Main FINISHED')
```

The next thing to do is to implement the `create()` method of the service. This method is called whenever a service is created or modified. It is supposed to take the input parameters from the service YANG, and possibly other inputs such as topology or server load situation, and configure devices or lower-level services. The interface towards the devices and lower-level services is always given by their YANG models. The service remains unaware of which protocol is actually used to convey this information, and whether it is a local or remote entity. The service data and resulting device changes live in the same transaction, so they either succeed or fail together. This means there is no need for error detection or recovery code in the service.

The top-level `create()` method, shown in Example 10-10, allocates a VLAN ID and updates the *allocated-vlan* operational data element from the YANG model, to reflect the assignment to the operator. Then it calls a method to configure the E routers, the I routers, and the monitoring system.

EXAMPLE 10-10 Store Connect Service Code: The **create()** Callback

```
# -----------------------
# SERVICE CALLBACK EXAMPLE
# -----------------------
class ServiceCallbacks(Service):

    # The create() callback is invoked inside NCS FASTMAP and
    # must always exist.
    @Service.create
    def cb_create(self, tctx, root, publisher, proplist):
        self.log.info('Service create(publisher=', publisher._path, ')')

        vlan_id = self.allocate_vlan(publisher)
        publisher.network.allocated_vlan = vlan_id
        mon  = self.config_e_routers(publisher, vlan_id)
        mon += self.config_i_routers(publisher, vlan_id, root)
        self.config_monitoring(publisher, mon)

        self.log.info('Service creation done')
```

The VLAN ID allocation could be done using a resource management component, but in order to keep things really simple, here it's just computed as a hash on the publisher's name. The code is found in Example 10-11.

EXAMPLE 10-11 Store Connect Service Code: The **allocate_vlan()** Method

```
def allocate_vlan(self, publisher):
    # Let's make this as simple as possible for now:
    # Just return a hash on the name (1000..2999)
    return 1000 + hash(publisher.name) % 2000
```

To configure the E routers, loop over the configured sites in the publisher's network. For each site, fetch the name of the interface that was configured and then check that a router device, an interface, and an address was given. If not, this site is simply skipped. Alternatively, an error could have been thrown, or these values could have been made mandatory or given default values in the YANG.

Next, a bag of template variables is created, and named variables are assigned suitable values. Near the end, the `e-router-template` is applied with the bag of variables. All this does is to update the ongoing transaction, which is pushed to the network at a later stage. Finally, the *name* of the leg is created, and the *address* and *vlan_id* are saved as input to the monitoring system. This is shown in Example 10-12.

EXAMPLE 10-12 Store Connect Service Code: The **config_e_routers()** Method

```
def config_e_routers(self, publisher, vlan_id):
    mon = []
    for site in publisher.network.site:
        site_interface = self.get_interface(site)
        if bool(site_interface) and bool(site.e_router) and bool(site.address):
            # e-router, address and interface are not mandatory in YANG
            # (they could have been => we would not have needed this)
            # Unless all three are set, we will simply skip this site
            vars = ncs.template.Variables()
            vars.add('DEVICE', site.e_router)
            vars.add('INTERFACE', site_interface)
            vars.add('ADDRESS', site.address)
            vars.add('MASK_LEN', site.mask_len)
            vars.add('MASK', self.ip_size_to_mask[site.mask_len])
            vars.add('VLAN_ID', vlan_id)
            template = ncs.template.Template(publisher)
            template.apply('e-router-template', vars)
            mon += [("%s-%s-int"%(publisher.name, site.name),
                    site.address, vlan_id)]
    return mon
```

Since you modeled the E router interface as a choice with one of many possible cases, getting the interface name actually requires a few lines on the code side. Since it was modeled as a `choice`, only one alternative can have a value. Example 10-13 shows the code that looks up which value is configured by the operator.

EXAMPLE 10-13 Store Connect Service Code: The **get_interface()** Method

```
def get_interface(self,site):
    if bool(site.junos_interface):
        return site.junos_interface
    if bool(site.ios_ge_interface):
        return "GigabitEthernet"+site.ios_ge_interface
    return site.ietf_interface
```

The `config_i_routers()` method, shown in Example 10-14, is similar to the `config_e_routers()` method from Example 10-12 in many ways. Only here, the code needs to first figure out between which publisher sites there should be a connection to a store. This is done by looping over all stores and checking if the publisher has any interest tags in common with the store in question. If so, they are connected. Every time a store is connected, that is recorded as a connection to monitor.

At the end is a loop to count the number of stores that carry each of the publisher's interest tags and then update the operational data to reflect this. The purpose is to detect any misspellings, or see how these numbers change, so that the publisher can change the interest tags over time.

EXAMPLE 10-14 Store Connect Service Code: The **config_i_routers()** Method

```
def config_i_routers(self, publisher, vlan_id, root):
    mon = []
    for store in root.storeconnect__stores.store:
        connect = False # Assume no connection to this store
        for tag in [x.tag for x in publisher.target_store.tags]:
            if tag in store.tags:
                # This publisher targets a tag that is
                # carried by this store. Let's connect!
                connect = True
                break
        if connect:
            self.log.info('connecting store ', store.name, ' to publisher ',
                          publisher.name)
            vars = ncs.template.Variables()
            vars.add('DEVICE', store.network.i_router)
            vars.add('INTERFACE', store.network.interface)
            vars.add('ADDRESS', store.network.address)
            vars.add('VLAN_ID', vlan_id)
            template = ncs.template.Template(publisher)
```

```
            template.apply('i-router-template', vars)
            mon += [("%s-%s-ext"%(publisher.name, store.name),
                     store.network.address, vlan_id)]
    for tag in [x.tag for x in publisher.target_store.tags]:
        publisher.target_store.tags[tag].number_of_stores_with_tag = len(
            [store for store in root.stores.store if tag in store.tags])
    return mon
```

Finally, the monitoring system needs to know about all the connections configured for E and I routers so that they are properly monitored for connectivity, quality of service, and asserting security policies. Example 10-15 shows the code that applies the template, once for each device configured by this service instance, so that everything configured is also monitored.

EXAMPLE 10-15 Store Connect Service Code: The **config_monitoring()** Method

```
def config_monitoring(self, publisher, mon):
    self.log.info('setup monitoring for ', publisher.name, ': ', len(mon), ' legs')
    vars = ncs.template.Variables()
    template = ncs.template.Template(publisher)
    vars.add('DEVICE', 'm0')
    for (mon_name, address, vlan_id) in mon:
        vars.add('MON_NAME', mon_name)
        vars.add('ADDRESS', address)
        vars.add('VLAN_ID', vlan_id)
        template.apply('monitoring-template', vars)
```

Setting Up NETCONF on a Device

When a NETCONF-capable device is powered on, generally the NETCONF subsystem is not ready for use. It first needs to be configured. How this is done obviously varies with each vendor and device family, and it might change over time. Let's take a brief look at a couple of different systems here to provide a general idea. Google is typically a good source for additional information of this kind.

On a JunOS device, after you install the necessary software and create a user with sufficient privileges, you need to create a crypto key pair. In a Linux environment, this could be accomplished as shown in Example 10-16.

EXAMPLE 10-16 Creating an RSA Crypto Key Pair for Setting Up SSH Communications

```
$ ssh-keygen -t rsa -b 2048 -f mykey
Generating public/private rsa key pair.
Enter passphrase (empty for no passphrase):
Enter same passphrase again:
```

```
Your identification has been saved in mykey.
Your public key has been saved in mykey.pub.
The key fingerprint is:
SHA256:zQuqZpBsFydGdRoVBrUhKRrHBEGQ7Nmg7oINJII3eUw jlindbla@JLINDBLA-M-W0J2
The key's randomart image is:
+---[RSA 2048]----+
|o++=..==B.       |
|.o. E .* o       |
|+ +0 ...         |
|=+=.* .  o       |
|=o = +  S o      |
|..= .   . . .    |
|o+ o  .   .      |
|o.. o.           |
|.  o.            |
+----[SHA256]-----+
$ ls mykey*
mykey          mykey.pub
$
```

Once the key is created, log in to the device, install the private key on the device, and enable NETCONF, as shown in Example 10-17.

EXAMPLE 10-17 Installing the Crypto Key Pair and Enabling NETCONF on JunOS

```
edit system login user username authentication
set load-key-file sftp://.../mykey
commit
edit system services
set netconf ssh
commit
```

On a Cisco IOS-XE device, the procedure is similar. First, a crypto key pair needs to be generated, Secure Shell (SSH) enabled, and the NETCONF-YANG subsystem started, as shown in Example 10-18.

EXAMPLE 10-18 Installing the Crypto Key Pair and Enabling NETCONF on IOS-XE

```
crypto key generate rsa modulus 2048
ip ssh version 2
netconf ssh
netconf-yang
```

It is certainly also possible to configure the system to use a key generated using `ssh-keygen`; just paste it under

```
ip ssh pubkey-chain, username username, key-string …
```

Once the device is configured, it is easy to do a quick check to verify that the NETCONF subsystem is operational. The standard port for NETCONF, as assigned by IANA, is port 830. Some implementations also allow connecting to the NETCONF subsystem on port 22, the IANA assigned port for SSH. Use an `ssh` client to connect, as shown in the following snippet:

```
ssh username@device -p 830 -s netconf
```

The device should respond with a hello message, which might look something like Example 10-19.

EXAMPLE 10-19 Hello Message Indicating the NETCONF Subsystem Is Operational

```
<?xml version="1.0" encoding="UTF-8"?>
<hello xmlns="urn:ietf:params:xml:ns:netconf:base:1.0">
<capabilities>
<capability>urn:ietf:params:netconf:base:1.0</capability>
<capability>urn:ietf:params:netconf:base:1.1</capability>
...
</capabilities>
<session-id>13</session-id></hello>]]>]]>
```

If this is what you see, close the SSH connection (Ctrl+D) and start playing with the device over NETCONF.

Discovering What's on a Device

Once you have a working connection to a NETCONF server, you can figure out what this system can do. There are three main mechanisms that NETCONF servers use to declare which YANG models they implement, which is the way NETCONF servers communicate what they do for a living.

The hello message lists all the device NETCONF capabilities, as well as all the YANG 1.0 modules that it supports, along with version and features for each module. Example 10-20 shows a short example listing some of the modules announced by a device. These module listings are often hundreds of lines long.

EXAMPLE 10-20 Hello Message Listing Some YANG 1.0 Modules

```
<capability>http://yang.juniper.net/junos/conf/fabric?module=junos-conf-fabric&
revision=2018-01-01</capability>
<capability>http://yang.juniper.net/junos/conf/firewall?module=junos-conf-firewall&
revision=2018-01-01</capability>
<capability>http://yang.juniper.net/junos/conf/forwarding-options?module=junos-conf-
forwarding-options&revision=2018-01-01</capability>
```

```
<capability>http://yang.juniper.net/junos/conf/interfaces?module=junos-conf-interfaces&
revision=2018-01-01</capability>
<capability>http://yang.juniper.net/junos/conf/logical-systems?module=junos-conf-
logical-systems&revision=2018-01-01</capability>
```

If one of the modules listed in hello is the ietf-netconf-monitoring module, as shown in the following snippet, additional information about the server may be retrieved:

```
<capability>urn:ietf:params:xml:ns:yang:ietf-netconf-monitoring?module=ietf-netconf-
monitoring&revision=2010-10-04</capability>
```

If supported, this module can tell you about the server capabilities, datastores, schemas (that is, modules), sessions, statistics, and available streams. Retrieve this information as shown in the following snippet; just add arguments for `--host`, `--port`, `--user`, and so on:

```
$ netconf-console --get --xpath /netconf-state
```

Example 10-21 shows what it could look like.

EXAMPLE 10-21 NETCONF Server Information Reply (Abridged)

```
<rpc-reply xmlns="urn:ietf:params:xml:ns:netconf:base:1.0" message-id="1">
  <data>
    <netconf-state xmlns="urn:ietf:params:xml:ns:yang:ietf-netconf-monitoring">
      <capabilities>
        <capability>urn:ietf:params:netconf:base:1.0</capability>
        <capability>urn:ietf:params:netconf:base:1.1</capability>
...
      </capabilities>
      <datastores>
        <datastore>
          <name>running</name>
          <transaction-id xmlns="http://tail-f.com/yang/netconf-monitoring">
1541-58483-523787</transaction-id>
        </datastore>
      </datastores>
      <schemas>
        <schema>
          <identifier>audiozone-example</identifier>
          <version>2018-01-09</version>
          <format>yang</format>
          <namespace>http://example.com/ns/audiozone</namespace>
          <location>NETCONF</location>
        </schema>
        <schema>
          <identifier>bookzone-example</identifier>
          <version>2018-01-05</version>
```

```
        <format>yang</format>
        <namespace>http://example.com/ns/bookzone</namespace>
        <location>NETCONF</location>
      </schema>
...
    </schemas>
    <sessions>
      <session>
        <session-id>15</session-id>
        <transport>netconf-ssh</transport>
        <username>admin</username>
        <source-host>127.0.0.1</source-host>
        <login-time>2018-11-01T08:59:15+01:00</login-time>
        <in-rpcs>1</in-rpcs>
        <in-bad-rpcs>0</in-bad-rpcs>
        <out-rpc-errors>0</out-rpc-errors>
        <out-notifications>0</out-notifications>
      </session>
    </sessions>
    <statistics>
      <netconf-start-time>2018-11-01T08:48:41+01:00</netconf-start-time>
      <in-bad-hellos>0</in-bad-hellos>
      <in-sessions>3</in-sessions>
      <dropped-sessions>0</dropped-sessions>
      <in-rpcs>4</in-rpcs>
      <in-bad-rpcs>0</in-bad-rpcs>
      <out-rpc-errors>0</out-rpc-errors>
      <out-notifications>0</out-notifications>
    </statistics>
    <streams xmlns="http://tail-f.com/yang/netconf-monitoring">
      <stream>
        <name>NETCONF</name>
        <description>default NETCONF event stream</description>
        <replay-support>false</replay-support>
      </stream>
      <stream>
        <name>Trader</name>
        <description>BookZone trading and delivery events</description>
        <replay-support>true</replay-support>
      </stream>
    </streams>
  </netconf-state>
 </data>
</rpc-reply>
```

Another interesting aspect of the schema (module) list is the RPC to download the actual YANG source for the module, as discussed in Chapter 7, "Automation Is as Good as the Data Models, Their Related Metadata, and the Tools: For the Network Architect and Operator." This is an optional feature, so your device may or may not support this operation, and even if it does, it may not apply to every possible YANG file.

Downloading the YANG from the device is a nice way for a NETCONF client to understand exactly what the interface is like. YANG files are often downloaded from public Git sites, but by downloading directly from the device, you don't have to go looking, so you'll be sure you found the right version for this particular device.

Because the hello message is getting so long on many devices, YANG 1.1 (RFC 7950) prescribes a different hello behavior for YANG 1.1 modules. Instead of listing all the YANG 1.1 modules as capabilities in hello together with the YANG 1.0 modules, only a single capability is listed in lieu of all YANG 1.1 modules:

```
<capability>urn:ietf:params:netconf:capability:yang-library:1.0?revision=2016-06-21&
module-set-id=2c6ee52de6f4e3db52497342fb3cc282</capability>
```

When this module is present in the hello message, the system may have some YANG 1.1 modules. Note the `module-set-id` attribute in the snippet just mentioned. By tracking the `module-set-id` in the hello message, the NETCONF client can tell whether or not reading the yang-module-library is required. If the `module-set-id` hasn't changed, the set of modules hasn't changed either. Use the following command to query the ietf-yang-library module list (add `--user`, and so on):

```
$ netconf-console --get --xpath /modules-state
```

The reply might look like Example 10-22. The `conformance-type` in the following reply is either `implement` or `import`, where `implement` means the module is really implemented on the server, while `import` means the module isn't implemented. The module is still included on the system because some groupings or types were imported from that module, so it isn't possible to compile the YANG modules without it.

EXAMPLE 10-22 List of Modules Supported by the Server Taken from ietf-yang-library

```
<rpc-reply xmlns="urn:ietf:params:xml:ns:netconf:base:1.0" message-id="1">
  <data>
    <modules-state xmlns="urn:ietf:params:xml:ns:yang:ietf-yang-library">
      <module-set-id>7aec0b1b1d4e5783ff4d305475e6e92c</module-set-id>
      <module>
        <name>audiozone-example</name>
        <revision>2018-01-09</revision>
        <namespace>http://example.com/ns/audiozone</namespace>
        <conformance-type>implement</conformance-type>
      </module>
      <module>
```

```
      <name>bookzone-example</name>
      <revision>2018-01-05</revision>
      <namespace>http://example.com/ns/bookzone</namespace>
      <conformance-type>implement</conformance-type>
    </module>
    <module>
      <name>iana-crypt-hash</name>
      <revision>2014-08-06</revision>
      <namespace>urn:ietf:params:xml:ns:yang:iana-crypt-hash</namespace>
      <feature>crypt-hash-md5</feature>
      <feature>crypt-hash-sha-256</feature>
      <feature>crypt-hash-sha-512</feature>
      <conformance-type>import</conformance-type>
    </module>
```

Another important thing a NETCONF manager often needs to know is whether someone else changed the configuration since the last time the manager was connected. Of course, one way to find out is to issue a full `get-config` and compare it with a saved result from earlier. Some devices support leaner mechanisms, such as a transaction ID or a timestamp of the last change. By simply reading the transaction ID or timestamp and comparing it with the latest known value, the manager can quickly discover if any out-of-band (OOB) changes took place.

There are several proprietary mechanisms for this. One of the more common ones is shown in Example 10-23 for reference. The manager sends a `get` request for the *transaction-id* leaf, augmented into the *datastore* list in the ietf-netconf-monitoring module, and looks at the `running` datastore.

EXAMPLE 10-23 Manager Checks the Latest **transaction-id** on a Device

```
<rpc xmlns="urn:ietf:params:xml:ns:netconf:base:1.0"
     message-id="3">
  <get xmlns:nc="urn:ietf:params:xml:ns:netconf:base:1.0">
    <filter>
      <netconf-state xmlns="urn:ietf:params:xml:ns:yang:ietf-netconf-monitoring">
        <datastores>
          <datastore>
            <name>running</name>
            <transaction-id xmlns="http://tail-f.com/yang/netconf-monitoring"/>
          </datastore>
        </datastores>
      </netconf-state>
    </filter>
  </get>
</rpc>
```

A device that supports this augmented leaf might reply as shown in Example 10-24.

EXAMPLE 10-24 Device Returns Latest **transaction-id**

```
<rpc-reply xmlns="urn:ietf:params:xml:ns:netconf:base:1.0"
           message-id="3">
  <data>
    <netconf-state xmlns="urn:ietf:params:xml:ns:yang:ietf-netconf-monitoring">
      <datastores>
        <datastore>
          <name xmlns:nc="urn:ietf:params:xml:ns:netconf:base:1.0">running</name>
          <transaction-id xmlns="http://tail-f.com/yang/netconf-monitoring">
1540-997164-482246</transaction-id>
        </datastore>
      </datastores>
    </netconf-state>
  </data>
</rpc-reply>
```

With this, you're ready to start your automation journey. To spark your imagination, the next section looks at what a small automation solution looks like, and how it behaves on the network.

Managing Services

How to set up an orchestration environment that allows YANG-based service configuration is beyond the scope of this book, but seeing how services are used and what they look like on a NETCONF level is central to the mission of this book.

Let's say you have the network setup described in the beginning of this chapter up and running. That is, you have three E routers (ej0, ej1, ec0), three I routers (ic0, ic1, ij0), a monitoring system (m0), a core network (ignored here), three publishers, four stores, and an NSO-based system orchestrating it all. On top of the NSO platform, you are running the Store Connect service application shown earlier in this chapter. This application contains a service YANG module, templates, and service code. It's now time to actually use this service.

As your tour begins, note that the NSO orchestrator was already installed and configured with operator logins and device YANG modules as well as loaded with the Store Connect service package. All the devices already mentioned were added to the device list and synchronized. This means that NSO has a full copy of the configuration of every managed device in memory. NSO only manages devices that are configured in the NSO device list.

As you are logging in to the NSO command-line interface (CLI), there are initially no stores or publishers configured. A quick way to fix that is to load some configuration data from a file that someone else prepared. To see what's about to change by way of the loaded file, the `show c` command, short for `show configuration`, displays the uncommitted configuration changes. Example 10-25 shows the initial data loading in a CLI interaction toward the NSO orchestrator.

EXAMPLE 10-25 Loading Stores' Configuration Data

```
admin connected from 127.0.0.1 using console on JLINDBLA-M-W0J2
admin@ncs# show running-config stores
% No entries found.
admin@ncs# show running-config publishers
% No entries found.
admin@ncs# con
Entering configuration mode terminal
admin@ncs(config)# load merge store
Possible completions:
  <filename>  storedstate  stores-init.xml
admin@ncs(config)# load merge stores-init.xml
Loading.
1.38 KiB parsed in 0.01 sec (77.27 KiB/sec)
admin@ncs(config)# show c
stores store Singoalla
 network address 10.0.0.3
 network i-router ij0
 network interface ge-0/0/1
 tags [ english french nobel small sweden ]
!
stores store Took-Look
 network address 10.0.0.4
 network i-router ij0
 network interface ge-0/0/0
 tags [ belgium english large ]
!
stores store Varnes-Soble
 network address 10.0.0.1
 network i-router ic0
 network interface GigabitEthernet0/0/2
 tags [ crime english large science usa ]
!
stores store Yoihon
 network address 10.0.0.2
 network i-router ic1
 network interface GigabitEthernet0/1/1
 tags [ english japan japanese manga nobel science ]
!
```

Next, you need to load some initial publisher configs into the same transaction. Each publisher is a separate service instance the way you modeled this. You are about to create three new service instances in a single transaction. To save some space, we'll only look at one of them here. The other two are similar. Example 10-26 shows the CLI interaction toward the central orchestrator.

EXAMPLE 10-26 Loading Publishers' Configuration Data

```
admin@ncs(config)# load merge publishers-init.xml
Loading.
2.02 KiB parsed in 0.04 sec (44.81 KiB/sec)
admin@ncs(config)# show full-configuration publishers publisher
Possible completions:
  Astrakan-Media   Name of publisher connecting
  Best-Books       Name of publisher connecting
  Culture-Froide   Name of publisher connecting
  <cr>
Possible match completions:
  network  target-store
admin@ncs(config)# show full-configuration publishers publisher Astrakan-Media
publishers publisher Astrakan-Media
 network site 1
  address          172.20.1.1
  mask-len         24
  e-router         ej0
  junos-interface ge-0/0/1
 !
 target-store tags belgium
 !
 target-store tags english
 !
 target-store tags french
 !
!
```

With all these changes loaded into the current transaction, it's time to commit them. Before you do, check what the system would do if these changes are committed. The command to show that is called `commit dry-run`. Plus signs indicate additions; minus signs indicate removals. Note that these changes are going to many different devices of different brands, YANG models and roles.

Since the full output is about 350 lines long, Example 10-27 just shows a sampling to give you a taste of what it looks like. Seven devices are touched by this network-wide transaction.

EXAMPLE 10-27 A **commit dry-run** to Inspect the Service Footprint on Devices (Abridged)

```
admin@ncs(config)# commit dry-run
cli {
    local-node {
        data  devices {
                  device ec0 {
                      config {
                          ios:native {
```

```
                           vrf {
+                              definition Culture-Froide {
+                                  rd 300:2620;
...
+                                  route-target {
+                                      export 300:2620;
+                                      import 300:2620;
+                                  }
...
                 device ej0 {
                     config {
                         jc:configuration {
                             routing-instances {
+                                instance Astrakan-Media {
+                                    instance-type vrf;
+                                    interface ge-0/0/1.2246;
+                                    route-distinguisher {
+                                        rd-type 300:2246;
+                                    }
+                                    vrf-import [ Astrakan-Media-IMP ];
+                                    vrf-export [ Astrakan-Media-EXP ];
...
                 device ij0 {
                     config {
                         jc:configuration {
                             routing-instances {
+                                instance Astrakan-Media {
+                                    instance-type vrf;
+                                    interface ge-0/0/0.2246;
+                                    interface ge-0/0/1.2246;
+                                    route-distinguisher {
+                                        rd-type 300:2246;
...
                 device m0 {
                     config {
                         netrounds-ncc:accounts {
+                            account bookzone {
+                                monitors {
+                                    monitor Astrakan-Media {
+                                       description "connectivity with standard qos";
+                                        template connectivity-std-qos;
...
+                               twamp-reflectors {
+                                   twamp-reflector Astrakan-Media-1-int {
+                                       address 172.20.1.1;
```

```
+                              port 6789;
+                          }
+                          twamp-reflector Astrakan-Media-Singoalla-ext {
+                              address 10.0.0.3;
+                              port 6789;
+                          }
```

This looks good, so let's commit it. Now at commit time, the managed devices hear about the change for the first time:

```
admin@ncs(config)# commit
Commit complete.
admin@ncs(config)#
```

During the commit, the service-level configuration change was computed to include the device-level changes; then the result was validated, written to the database, and finally communicated to all participating devices in a network-wide transaction.

We'll inspect the NETCONF messages between the client (orchestrator) and servers (all the devices) involved in network-wide transaction in the next section. If any device has an issue with the configuration change, the entire transaction is aborted. No device activated any part of the change at that point, so there should be zero service interruptions.

Another reason the orchestrator might abort the transaction is if it finds that a device configuration changed since last being synchronized, usually because of OOB changes (for example, by manual intervention by an operator on the device console or by action from another automation system). Many strategies for handling multiple managers in an automated process are possible. Generally speaking, automation gets easier the fewer managers (unaware of each other) that are involved—much like with your own work situation.

Since you committed a change, at this point it might be interesting to have a look at your running services from an operational point of view. Look at Example 10-28 and notice which devices are being touched by one particular service instance. Also notice the service's operational data (that is, the allocated-vlan and the list of store tags that this publisher targets) and how many stores each *tag* connects to.

EXAMPLE 10-28 Showing a Service Instance with Operational State

```
admin@ncs(config)# do show publishers
publishers publisher Astrakan-Media
 modified devices [ ej0 ic0 ic1 ij0 m0 ]
 directly-modified devices [ ej0 ic0 ic1 ij0 m0 ]
 device-list [ ej0 ic0 ic1 ij0 m0 ]
```

```
 network allocated-vlan 2246
        NUMBER
        OF
        STORES
        WITH
TAG     TAG
-----------------
belgium  1
english  4
french   1
...
```

At a later time, it might be interesting to go back and see exactly which device-level changes a particular service instance has incurred. The command `publishers publisher Astrakan-Media get-modifications` shows just that, but the output looks just like the dry-run output shown in Example 10-27, so it is not repeated here.

Now the services are up and running on the seven managed devices. What next? Let's see what happens if the publisher wants to modify the service. Say one of the publishers wants to drop the very generic store tag `english`. The tag is removed with a simple `no` command.

The orchestrator knows just what the service created last time on the devices (and any lower-layer services). When the `create()` method runs again now, the orchestrator notices that the method no longer creates some of the connection objects it created on the previous run. The orchestrator updates the transaction to remove exactly that diff. A `commit dry-run` shows what will happen, as shown in Example 10-29. The change affects three devices: ic0, ic1, and m0.

EXAMPLE 10-29 Showing What Would Happen if a Particular Store Tag Was Removed

```
admin@ncs(config)# no publishers publisher Astrakan-Media target-store tags english
admin@ncs(config)# commit dry-run
cli {
    local-node {
        data  devices {
                  device ic0 {
                      config {
                          ios:native {
                              vrf {
              -                   definition Astrakan-Media {
              -                       rd 300:2246;
...
              -                       route-target {
              -                           export 300:2246;
              -                           import 300:2246;
...
                  device ic1 {
```

```
                    config {
                        ios:native {
                            vrf {
-                               definition Astrakan-Media {
-                                   rd 300:2246;
...
-                                   route-target {
-                                       export 300:2246;
-                                       import 300:2246;
-                                   }
...
                device m0 {
                    config {
                        netrounds-ncc:accounts {
                            account bookzone {
                                twamp-reflectors {
-                                   twamp-reflector Astrakan-Media-Varnes-Soble-ext {
-                                       address 10.0.0.1;
-                                       port 6789;
-                                   }
-                                   twamp-reflector Astrakan-Media-Yoihon-ext {
-                                       address 10.0.0.2;
-                                       port 6789;
-                                   }
                                }
                            }
                        }
                    }
                }
            }
            publishers {
                publisher Astrakan-Media {
                    target-store {
-                       tags english {
-                       }
                    }
                }
            }
    }
}
```

This matches the publisher's expectations, so you can commit. Now look at the service's operational state in Example 10-30. The five devices touched by this service instance are now down to three. All configuration from this service instance on ic0 and ic1 is gone, so they are no longer part of the modified devices list for this service instance. The m0 device still has some configuration, so it is still listed.

EXAMPLE 10-30 Showing a Service Instance with Operational State after a Particular Store Tag Was Removed

```
admin@ncs(config)# commit
Commit complete.
admin@ncs(config)# do show publishers publisher Astrakan-Media
publishers publisher Astrakan-Media
 modified devices [ ej0 ij0 m0 ]
 directly-modified devices [ ej0 ij0 m0 ]
 device-list [ ej0 ij0 m0 ]
 network allocated-vlan 2246
         NUMBER
         OF
         STORES
         WITH
TAG      TAG
-----------------
belgium  1
french   1
```

Great. This was a productive morning. But after a change like this, a not entirely unlikely event is a phone call from someone who thinks the latest change wasn't such a good idea after all (sometimes expressed quite differently). In order to restore the service, either the latest transaction, all transactions back to a given point in time, or some specific set of transactions must be undone. The `rollback` command does that. The `rollback configuration` command creates a new transaction with content that undoes the previous transaction. A `commit dry-run` shows all the details, but in the interest of time, let's skip this. There is nothing special about a rollback transaction. It's simply yet another transaction that happens to make the configuration the same as (or similar to, in case of cherry-picked transactions to roll back) an earlier provisioned configuration. The `rollback` command sequence is shown in Example 10-31.

EXAMPLE 10-31 Rolling Back a Configuration Change

```
admin@ncs(config)# rollback configuration
admin@ncs(config)# show c
publishers publisher Astrakan-Media
 target-store tags english
 !
!
admin@ncs(config)# comm
Commit complete.
```

Manager Synchronization with Devices

Having observed the service-level management flow from the operator's perspective, it's now time to drop down to the underlying foundations and observe the same flow from a protocol perspective. Here, assume all devices involved communicate over NETCONF. In the real world, there is often a mix of different protocols and even among NETCONF devices, capabilities vary.

When the operator configures the orchestrator (NSO) with the devices to be managed, it connects to them to find out what kind of devices they are and to synchronize with them. The orchestrator starts by sending a hello message to each of the seven devices in its device list, as shown in Example 10-32.

EXAMPLE 10-32 Manager Sends Hello Message

```
<hello xmlns="urn:ietf:params:xml:ns:netconf:base:1.0">
  <capabilities>
    <capability>urn:ietf:params:netconf:base:1.0</capability>
    <capability>urn:ietf:params:netconf:base:1.1</capability>
  </capabilities>
</hello>
```

Each device responds to the hello message; the response from device m0 is shown in Example 10-33.

EXAMPLE 10-33 Manager Receives Hello Messages (Abridged)

```
<hello xmlns="urn:ietf:params:xml:ns:netconf:base:1.0">
  <capabilities>
    <capability>urn:ietf:params:netconf:base:1.0</capability>
    <capability>urn:ietf:params:netconf:base:1.1</capability>
    <capability>urn:ietf:params:netconf:capability:candidate:1.0</capability>
    <capability>urn:ietf:params:netconf:capability:confirmed-commit:1.0</capability>
    <capability>urn:ietf:params:netconf:capability:confirmed-commit:1.1</capability>
    <capability>urn:ietf:params:netconf:capability:validate:1.0</capability>
    <capability>urn:ietf:params:netconf:capability:validate:1.1</capability>
    <capability>urn:ietf:params:netconf:capability:rollback-on-error:1.0</capability>
...
    <capability>urn:ietf:params:xml:ns:yang:ietf-yang-library?module=ietf-yang-library&
revision=2016-06-21</capability>
```

Fairly similar responses from ej0, ej1, ec0, ic0, ic1, and ij0 were omitted. The manager takes note of the capabilities of each device. Here, all devices support the NETCONF base protocol, the candidate datastore, configuration validation (separate from activation), and `rollback-on-error` (that is, transactions). That's nice, because all of those are all required for a device to be able to participate in a network-wide transaction. All devices also support `confirmed-commit`, which allows you to use the most powerful form of network-wide transactions.

If one or a few devices are missing one or several of these capabilities, the manager can still go ahead with the devices that have the required support and handle those that don't in a best-effort kind of way at the end of the PREPARE phase of the transaction. This is not a full network-wide transaction, but it's significantly more reliable than a pure best-effort, scripted solution.

Looking at the hello response from the devices, the orchestrator notes that some devices announce the ietf-yang-library module capability. For those devices, the manager reads the list of modules on the device via a `get` operation on the *modules-state* list in the ietf-yang-library. Example 10-34 shows the request toward the m0 device.

EXAMPLE 10-34 Manager Reads ietf-yang-library modules-state

```
<rpc xmlns="urn:ietf:params:xml:ns:netconf:base:1.0"
     message-id="1">
  <get>
    <filter>
      <modules-state xmlns="urn:ietf:params:xml:ns:yang:ietf-yang-library"/>
    </filter>
  </get>
</rpc>
```

Similar requests are sent to the other devices supporting the ietf-yang-library. Example 10-35 shows the response from device m0.

EXAMPLE 10-35 Device Responding with Supported Modules by Listing modules-state (Abridged)

```
<rpc-reply xmlns="urn:ietf:params:xml:ns:netconf:base:1.0"
           message-id="1">
  <data>
    <modules-state xmlns="urn:ietf:params:xml:ns:yang:ietf-yang-library">
      <module-set-id>61e5be5ab84c9d7b2db0bef3aca036b7</module-set-id>
      <module>
        <name>iana-crypt-hash</name>
        <revision>2014-08-06</revision>
```

A similar response arrives from all other devices that support the ietf-yang-library (omitted here).

Next, the manager needs to synchronize the configuration data from each device to its own database. Example 10-36 is the request sent to device m0. Someone configured the manager so that it only cares about a single namespace on m0, so the manager issues a `get-config` to retrieve only that one YANG namespace to save time and memory.

EXAMPLE 10-36 Manager Synchronizing the Configuration from One Device

```
<rpc xmlns="urn:ietf:params:xml:ns:netconf:base:1.0"
     message-id="2">
  <get-config>
    <source>
      <running/>
    </source>
    <filter>
      <accounts xmlns="http://com/netrounds/ncc"/>
    </filter>
  </get-config>
</rpc>
```

Toward one of the other devices, the manager is configured to handle a few more YANG namespaces. Example 10-37 is the request toward ec0.

EXAMPLE 10-37 Manager Synchronizing the Configuration from Another Device

```
<rpc xmlns="urn:ietf:params:xml:ns:netconf:base:1.0"
     message-id="2">
  <get-config>
    <source>
      <running/>
    </source>
    <filter>
      <mdt-subscriptions xmlns="http://cisco.com/ns/yang/Cisco-IOS-XE-mdt-cfg"/>
      <mpls-ldp xmlns="http://cisco.com/ns/yang/Cisco-IOS-XE-mpls-ldp"/>
      <native xmlns="http://cisco.com/ns/yang/Cisco-IOS-XE-native"/>
      <netconf-yang xmlns="http://cisco.com/yang/cisco-self-mgmt"/>
      <pseudowire-config xmlns="urn:cisco:params:xml:ns:yang:pw"/>
      <mpls-static xmlns="urn:ietf:params:xml:ns:yang:common-mpls-static"/>
      <classifiers xmlns="urn:ietf:params:xml:ns:yang:ietf-diffserv-classifier"/>
      <policies xmlns="urn:ietf:params:xml:ns:yang:ietf-diffserv-policy"/>
      <filters xmlns="urn:ietf:params:xml:ns:yang:ietf-event-notifications"/>
      <subscription-config xmlns="urn:ietf:params:xml:ns:yang:ietf-event-
notifications"/>
      <interfaces xmlns="urn:ietf:params:xml:ns:yang:ietf-interfaces"/>
      <key-chains xmlns="urn:ietf:params:xml:ns:yang:ietf-key-chain"/>
      <routing xmlns="urn:ietf:params:xml:ns:yang:ietf-routing"/>
      <nvo-instances xmlns="urn:ietf:params:xml:ns:yang:nvo"/>
    </filter>
  </get-config>
</rpc>
```

A similar request goes to all other devices (omitted here). Each device responds with its configuration (also omitted here).

On devices that support this, the manager reads and stores the transaction ID that is current on that device, to make it possible to later quickly check if the configuration of the device was altered. The request for the `transaction-id` is shown in Example 10-38.

EXAMPLE 10-38 Manager Requesting **transaction-id** from a Device

```
<rpc xmlns="urn:ietf:params:xml:ns:netconf:base:1.0"
     message-id="3">
  <get xmlns:nc="urn:ietf:params:xml:ns:netconf:base:1.0">
    <filter>
      <netconf-state xmlns="urn:ietf:params:xml:ns:yang:ietf-netconf-monitoring">
        <datastores>
          <datastore>
            <name>running</name>
            <transaction-id xmlns="http://tail-f.com/yang/netconf-monitoring"/>
          </datastore>
        </datastores>
      </netconf-state>
    </filter>
  </get>
</rpc>
```

The devices that are asked respond. The previous request was sent to m0, which responds like Example 10-39. (The other device responses have been omitted.)

EXAMPLE 10-39 Device Responding with **transaction-id**

```
<rpc-reply xmlns="urn:ietf:params:xml:ns:netconf:base:1.0"
           message-id="3">
  <data>
    <netconf-state xmlns="urn:ietf:params:xml:ns:yang:ietf-netconf-monitoring">
      <datastores>
        <datastore>
          <name xmlns:nc="urn:ietf:params:xml:ns:netconf:base:1.0">running</name>
          <transaction-id xmlns="http://tail-f.com/yang/netconf-monitoring">
1540-997218-679912</transaction-id>
        </datastore>
      </datastores>
    </netconf-state>
  </data>
</rpc-reply>
```

At this point, the manager has retrieved the basic information it needs about the devices and has no pending work for them, so it closes the connection to each device. It would work fine to simply close the connection, but sending a polite `close-session` message, as shown in Example 10-40, makes everybody understand that the disconnection was intentional.

EXAMPLE 10-40 Manager Closing the Connection to All Devices

```
<rpc xmlns="urn:ietf:params:xml:ns:netconf:base:1.0"
     message-id="4">
  <close-session/>
</rpc>
```

Network-Wide Transactions

Let's look at the NETCONF exchange that takes place when the operator commits one of the transactions discussed earlier in this chapter.

First, the manager opens up the connection to all relevant devices and sends out a hello message. The hello response is compared with what the manager already knows about each device. If nothing changed, the manager proceeds to send out the configuration changes computed for each device in a few steps.

Example 10-41 shows the messages sent to device m0. These requests are sent in rapid succession, without waiting for a reply in between. These messages ask the device to clear the candidate datastore, lock it to prevent others from using it, and get a readout of the latest `transaction-id`. Similar messages are sent to all the other devices involved in this transaction in parallel.

EXAMPLE 10-41 Manager Preparing a Device for a Configuration Change

```
<rpc xmlns="urn:ietf:params:xml:ns:netconf:base:1.0"
     message-id="1">
  <discard-changes/>
</rpc>
...
<rpc xmlns="urn:ietf:params:xml:ns:netconf:base:1.0"
     message-id="2">
  <lock>
    <target>
      <candidate/>
    </target>
  </lock>
</rpc>
...
```

```
<rpc xmlns="urn:ietf:params:xml:ns:netconf:base:1.0"
     message-id="3">
  <get xmlns:nc="urn:ietf:params:xml:ns:netconf:base:1.0">
    <filter>
      <netconf-state xmlns="urn:ietf:params:xml:ns:yang:ietf-netconf-monitoring">
        <datastores>
          <datastore>
            <name>running</name>
            <transaction-id xmlns="http://tail-f.com/yang/netconf-monitoring"/>
          </datastore>
        </datastores>
      </netconf-state>
    </filter>
  </get>
</rpc>
```

The m0 device responds as shown in Example 10-42.

EXAMPLE 10-42 Device Responds with **ok** and the Latest **transaction-id**

```
<rpc-reply xmlns="urn:ietf:params:xml:ns:netconf:base:1.0"
           message-id="1">
  <ok/>
</rpc-reply>
...
<rpc-reply xmlns="urn:ietf:params:xml:ns:netconf:base:1.0"
           message-id="2">
  <ok/>
</rpc-reply>
...
<rpc-reply xmlns="urn:ietf:params:xml:ns:netconf:base:1.0"
           message-id="3">
  <data>
    <netconf-state xmlns="urn:ietf:params:xml:ns:yang:ietf-netconf-monitoring">
      <datastores>
        <datastore>
          <name xmlns:nc="urn:ietf:params:xml:ns:netconf:base:1.0">running</name>
          <transaction-id xmlns="http://tail-f.com/yang/netconf-monitoring">
1540-997218-679912</transaction-id>
        </datastore>
      </datastores>
    </netconf-state>
  </data>
</rpc-reply>
```

A similar exchange happens for all other devices (omitted here).

Since all devices responded positively, it's now time for the manager to send out the `edit-config` messages to each device with the respective actual configuration changes. The `edit-config` toward the candidate (shown in Example 10-43) is sent toward the m0 device.

EXAMPLE 10-43 Manager Sends an **edit-config** Toward One Device (Abridged)

```
<rpc xmlns="urn:ietf:params:xml:ns:netconf:base:1.0"
     message-id="4">
  <edit-config xmlns:nc="urn:ietf:params:xml:ns:netconf:base:1.0">
    <target>
      <candidate/>
    </target>
    <test-option>test-then-set</test-option>
    <error-option>rollback-on-error</error-option>
    <config>
      <accounts xmlns="http://com/netrounds/ncc">
        <account>
          <name>bookzone</name>
          <twamp-reflectors>
            <twamp-reflector>
              <name>Astrakan-Media-1-int</name>
              <port>6789</port>
              <address>172.20.1.1</address>
            </twamp-reflector>
```

In parallel, an `edit-config` is sent toward device ec0, as shown in Example 10-44.

EXAMPLE 10-44 Manager Sends an **edit-config** Toward Another Device (Abridged)

```
<rpc xmlns="urn:ietf:params:xml:ns:netconf:base:1.0"
     message-id="5">
  <edit-config xmlns:nc="urn:ietf:params:xml:ns:netconf:base:1.0">
    <target>
      <candidate/>
    </target>
    <test-option>test-then-set</test-option>
    <error-option>rollback-on-error</error-option>
    <config>
      <native xmlns="http://cisco.com/ns/yang/Cisco-IOS-XE-native">
        <vrf>
          <definition>
            <name>Culture-Froide</name>
            <address-family>
              <ipv4/>
```

```
          </address-family>
          <route-target>
            <import>
              <asn-ip>300:2620</asn-ip>
            </import>
            <export>
              <asn-ip>300:2620</asn-ip>
            </export>
          </route-target>
          <rd>300:2620</rd>
```

In parallel, another `edit-config` is sent towards device ij0, as shown in Example 10-45.

EXAMPLE 10-45 Manager Sends an **edit-config** Toward Yet Another Device (Abridged)

```
<rpc xmlns="urn:ietf:params:xml:ns:netconf:base:1.0"
     message-id="4">
  <edit-config xmlns:nc="urn:ietf:params:xml:ns:netconf:base:1.0">
    <target>
      <candidate/>
    </target>
    <test-option>test-then-set</test-option>
    <error-option>rollback-on-error</error-option>
    <config>
      <configuration xmlns="http://yang.juniper.net/junos/conf/root">
        <routing-instances xmlns="http://yang.juniper.net/junos/conf/routing-instances">
          <instance>
            <name>Astrakan-Media</name>
            <vrf-export>Astrakan-Media-EXP</vrf-export>
            <interface>
              <name>ge-0/0/0.2246</name>
            </interface>
            <interface>
              <name>ge-0/0/1.2246</name>
            </interface>
            <vrf-table-label/>
            <vrf-import>Astrakan-Media-IMP</vrf-import>
            <instance-type>vrf</instance-type>
            <route-distinguisher>
              <rd-type>300:2246</rd-type>
```

A similar exchange happens for all other devices involved in this transaction (omitted here).

The manager immediately also sends a validate request to each device involved. Example 10-46 shows the message sent toward m0.

EXAMPLE 10-46 Manager Requests Validation of the Candidate Datastore on a Device

```
<rpc xmlns="urn:ietf:params:xml:ns:netconf:base:1.0"
     message-id="5">
  <validate>
    <source>
      <candidate/>
    </source>
  </validate>
</rpc>
```

A similar exchange happens for all other devices involved in this transaction (omitted here).

In this case, notice that the device m0 responds with `ok` to the `edit-config` and to the `validate`, as shown in Example 10-47.

EXAMPLE 10-47 Manager Receives Positive Response to the **edit-config** and **validate** Requests on the Candidate Datastore on a Device

```
<rpc-reply xmlns="urn:ietf:params:xml:ns:netconf:base:1.0"
           message-id="4">
  <ok/>
</rpc-reply>
...
<rpc-reply xmlns="urn:ietf:params:xml:ns:netconf:base:1.0"
           message-id="5">
  <ok/>
</rpc-reply>
```

You have now completed the PREPARE phase in the transaction. If all devices reach this state with all happy `ok` messages, the manager goes ahead with the COMMIT phase.

If anything bad happens, such as a lost connection to a device or a negative validation response, the manager proceeds with the ABORT phase. Initiating the ABORT sequence is very simple in NETCONF—simply drop the connection. To be clear, a lost connection is the abort command. That way, any device that loses the connection to the manager in the middle of a transaction always aborts.

Since the transaction was only ever targeting the candidate datastore, no harm is done. The device operations, as guided by the running datastore, continue unaffected as before. There is nothing on the device that must be undone.

Assuming all devices responded well to the `edit-config` and `validate`, the manager decides to cross the transaction's *point of no return*. After this point, the transaction "happened" (is persisted), and a new transaction must be created to revert it, should the manager feel the desire to have the action undone. The manager commits by writing the transaction to stable storage (that is, disk) and telling all devices to go ahead with the transaction.

The manager tells a device to go ahead by sending a `commit` message to each participating device. In this case, the manager chose to also set the `confirmed` flag, indicating that a three-phase transaction (PREPARE, COMMIT, CONFIRM) will be used, as shown in Example 10-48.

EXAMPLE 10-48 Manager Sends a Confirmed **commit** Message to a Device

```
<rpc xmlns="urn:ietf:params:xml:ns:netconf:base:1.0"
     message-id="6">
  <commit>
    <confirmed/>
  </commit>
</rpc>
```

All devices participating in the transaction are now busy transferring the changes from the candidate datastore to their running datastore and implementing the new configuration. When done, each device returns an `ok` message. Example 10-49 shows the message from m0.

EXAMPLE 10-49 Device Sends a Confirmed **commit ok** Message

```
<rpc-reply xmlns="urn:ietf:params:xml:ns:netconf:base:1.0"
           message-id="6">
  <ok/>
</rpc-reply>
```

It is of course possible that a `commit` operation fails. It's not nice for a device to promise that the configuration is fine by responding `ok` to the validation and then fail when the actual `commit` arrives, but things can always go wrong regardless of promises.

The best way to deal with an over-promising device is to treat it the same whether the failure happens 2 milliseconds, 2 minutes, or 2 months after the transaction's point of no return. Hopefully, there is a supervision and recovery mechanism that deals with devices that fail because of connectivity, power, software bugs, attacks, or whatever. One recovery option might be to roll back the transaction from the manager.

When all devices have committed the change and returned `ok`, that's the end of the COMMIT phase. If this was a basic two-phase transaction, the connection could have been closed now, releasing locks and so on. In this case, as noted earlier, the manager requested a three-phase transaction with a CONFIRM phase. That is the phase that starts now.

During the CONFIRM phase, the manager determines whether or not the proposed new configuration, which is already running, is desirable. Is the service level agreement (SLA) met? Is the connectivity in place? Is the resource utilization still in the safe zone?

By default, the manager has at most 2 minutes to reach a decision about how to proceed. A shorter or longer timeframe may be specified by the manager, and the running timer extended, if desired. If the manager doesn't send a confirming `commit` message to a device within the timeout period, the device rolls back the configuration change. Similarly, if the connection to the manager is lost, the device rolls back, unless the manager asked the device to allow disconnects during the CONFIRM phase.

This scheme protects against accidentally cutting of the management network and then having to involve a red-faced human making a call to someone at the other end with specific recovery instructions.

When the manager has measured, evaluated, and finally determined the desirability of the change, it communicates the verdict to all participating devices by dropping the connection (or sending an abort message) for rolling back or by sending a `commit` message for keeping the change. Example 10-50 shows the `commit`, `transaction-id`, and `unlock` messages the manager sends to m0 for keeping the new configuration.

EXAMPLE 10-50 Manager Sends a Confirming **commit,** Reads **transaction-id** and Sends **unlock** to Devices

```
<rpc xmlns="urn:ietf:params:xml:ns:netconf:base:1.0"
     message-id="7">
  <commit/>
</rpc>
...
<rpc xmlns="urn:ietf:params:xml:ns:netconf:base:1.0"
     message-id="8">
  <get xmlns:nc="urn:ietf:params:xml:ns:netconf:base:1.0">
    <filter>
      <netconf-state xmlns="urn:ietf:params:xml:ns:yang:ietf-netconf-monitoring">
        <datastores>
          <datastore>
            <name>running</name>
            <transaction-id xmlns="http://tail-f.com/yang/netconf-monitoring"/>
          </datastore>
        </datastores>
      </netconf-state>
    </filter>
  </get>
</rpc>
...
<rpc xmlns="urn:ietf:params:xml:ns:netconf:base:1.0"
     message-id="9">
  <unlock>
```

```
    <target>
      <candidate/>
    </target>
  </unlock>
</rpc>
```

A similar exchange happens for all other devices involved in this transaction (omitted here). Example 10-51 shows the response from m0.

EXAMPLE 10-51 Device's Response to **commit**, **transaction-id**, and **unlock**

```
<rpc-reply xmlns="urn:ietf:params:xml:ns:netconf:base:1.0"
           message-id="7">
  <ok/>
</rpc-reply>
...
<rpc-reply xmlns="urn:ietf:params:xml:ns:netconf:base:1.0"
           message-id="8">
  <data>
    <netconf-state xmlns="urn:ietf:params:xml:ns:yang:ietf-netconf-monitoring">
      <datastores>
        <datastore>
          <name xmlns:nc="urn:ietf:params:xml:ns:netconf:base:1.0">running</name>
          <transaction-id xmlns="http://tail-f.com/yang/netconf-monitoring">
1541-83740-854414</transaction-id>
        </datastore>
      </datastores>
    </netconf-state>
  </data>
</rpc-reply>
...
<rpc-reply xmlns="urn:ietf:params:xml:ns:netconf:base:1.0"
           message-id="9">
  <ok/>
</rpc-reply>
```

When all devices have responded, the transaction is complete, and unless there are more transactions pending for a given device, the connection may be closed. Example 10-52 shows the message sent to m0.

EXAMPLE 10-52 The Manager's Goodbye to the Device. The Device Closes the Connection.

```
<rpc xmlns="urn:ietf:params:xml:ns:netconf:base:1.0"
     message-id="10">
  <close-session/>
</rpc>
```

Interview with the Experts

Q&A with Kristian Larsson

Kristian Larsson had an early interest in computer networks, acquiring his first Cisco router in his teens. Hardly surprising, his career was quickly absorbed by nascent ISP and mobile carriers, premier among them Tele2, for nearly a decade—first operating large IP networks, then designing and automating them. When Deutsche Telekom started a clean-slate networking project called TeraStream, headed by disruptive innovation industry leader Axel Clauberg and designed by Internet legend Peter Löthberg, it was only natural for Kristian to join. Kristian's DevOps profile with deep network design and programming skills are a perfect match for this all-new network design.

Question:

What's the new insight behind TeraStream?

Answer:

I think it's a refocus on the core tenets that made the Internet work well. You keep the network design simple. That leads to reliability, scalability, and enables you to automate its operation. Being simple, it is also much more cost efficient than the currently installed network. We run all services on top of this infrastructure, from residential Internet through business services and telephony to mobile. In a connected world, society runs on top of this network. It just has to work. If you run this network with software, then the software just has to work, too.

Traditionally automation is mostly about cost savings. We take a fundamentally different approach with a focus on reliability.

Question:

Deutsche Telekom (DT) is a major operator with lots of networks. How come DT came up with the idea to start from scratch? There are plenty of large and small operators around the world that didn't.

Answer:

That's a good question. Someone at DT realized a fresh start was needed to stay competitive. It's so much easier to build a simple solution when starting from scratch. Any established organization suffers from silo behavior, leading to piecemeal fixes. You're simply not going to get the same answer if you go to an existing organization and ask, how much smarter can you do what you do? It will never result in a globally optimal solution.

TeraStream is an excellent example where the whole is greater than the sum of its parts. When you can simplify some areas of your network, which allows you to automate it, it can in turn unlock completely new possibilities. Having a holistic view of the network and the software to manage it allows us to deliver a very efficient solution.

Question:

How did you get into the picture?

Answer:

I started my career operating networks and transitioned into more of design and architectural work, where I realized that automation was key. You can't run a network comprising thousands of routers without automation. I had always been scripting, one liners in bash, Perl, or similar, and used this for many years to do things at scale. I don't have a formal programming background but learned out of necessity. At one point I wrote my own configuration templating language. Looking back it wasn't the best of choices but it certainly was educational, and it did solve some domain-specific problems that would have taken a lot more boilerplate in other languages.

With the TeraStream project, my focus turned entirely to writing software, not just some helpful automation scripts, but a software system able to handle all aspects of building and operating an optical and IP network.

Question:

You said the network just has to work. What is it then that you do that just makes it work?

Answer:

(Laughter) Right. I guess it's first and foremost a way of working. We take Quality Assurance (QA) through Continuous Integration and Deployment (CI/CD) dead seriously. If you get into our development environment (we use GitLab) and open a merge request, the code will always be tested automatically in a virtual network before you are allowed to merge it.

Every merge request needs to have test coverage that proves the code works as intended. Same thing for documentation being up to date, and we encourage self-review. Good code and testing is important to us, in particular CI testing, where code is tested before deployment. Operating critical network infrastructure is different from doing daily deployments of a web app. Failure can be catastrophic, and rolling back might mean rolling a truck.

Much of this CI/CD infrastructure also doubles as development environment. We launch virtual routers for testing the same way as for a development environment. When you want to develop a new feature, you start a virtual network and work toward those routers. You can pick one or multiple router vendors to work with. Similarly, for testing, we use our software to configure a virtual network and then observe that network, making sure it conforms to our expectations. When someone asks, "Did you provision anything with this code?", the answer is "Yes, we've used the code to provision tens of virtual networks every day, day in and day out. We're very happy about the way this works." Repeatability is key in both testing and development. The ability to bring up a clean, virtual network easily and quickly is essential for good results.

Question:

What made you choose NETCONF and YANG for your network?

Answer:

Since the dawn of the Internet, operating IP networks has pretty much been about the command-line interface (CLI). I think it's clear to anyone who's tried to parse or generate CLI configuration that it's an interface primarily meant for human consumption. We needed something better to programmatically interface with our network devices. NETCONF/YANG was moving in the IETF, and we thought it was a good choice. Being purpose written, it is a protocol stack that is uniquely suited for the task. There are no other protocols that feature three phase commits, which NETCONF has, nor any modeling languages that can express network configuration and operational state as naturally as YANG can.

YANG in particular has struck a perfect balance of pragmatism and elegance. It, together with the meta-model behind it with declarative configuration, is applicable far outside the world of IP networks.

When you standardize on these protocols, you get rid of a whole swath of problems. It's somewhat ironic that we are still interfacing many routers over CLI even today. I have worked with vendors for many years, helping to improve their NETCONF/YANG implementations. Sadly, it takes a very long time. In many cases, the assumptions and behavior of the CLI permeate the design so that the device can't handle transactions properly. Transaction support is not something you can simply bolt on top of a legacy solution and get a good result. A proper implementation needs transactions at the core.

Our time is spent with a rather even split between development, testing, and integration toward legacy interfaces such as the CLI. As soon as a device has proper NETCONF/YANG support, that integration piece simply goes away. You don't need to spend time on it. It's a major time thief.

We're working toward NETCONF/YANG everywhere. If you place NETCONF/YANG alongside other protocols out there, there's no question that NETCONF/YANG is uniquely qualified for the task. It's really good for us.

Question:

Have your expectations on NETCONF/YANG come true?

Answer:

They have, yes. Not only when compared to a world of CLI scraping but also when compared to a lot of the RESTful APIs out there, you find that NETCONF/YANG typically provides a better experience.

Question:

You have come far in the automation journey. What's your next step?

Answer:

Our focus so far has almost entirely been on what I think of as the lowest layer of services, often called resource-facing services (RFS), that interface directly with devices. We're keeping feature parity across four different vendor platforms, so it requires a fair bit of work. The RFS layer exposes a device- and vendor-neutral interface on top of which other services can be built. Really cool things start to emerge when you get up a level or two. You can quickly leave the realm of classic network configuration; imagine predictive capacity planning with the network telling you what hardware to order, or even doing it for you, instead of the other way around—or root cause analysis across all network layers.

A new and interesting development is the application of formal verification on networks. There are some exciting new systems that can reason and prove correctness of your network. Some are focusing on the forwarding plane, like how packets are sent. Others are focusing on the policy layer, which is how your routing policies will work. It's a good complement to our existing CI testing.

Question:

Do you have any advice for folks who would like to get to where you are?

Answer:

First and foremost, it's about putting the right people together. Seeing how it's hard to find people with experience both in networking and software development, an alternative can be to team up in pairs; put the networking guy next to the programmer and let them work together. Another essential piece is to provide a development environment that is both true to reality and cheap and simple to set up. I think virtual routers play a crucial role there.

Question:

Do you have any advice for folks who would like to sell you some devices?

Answer:

NETCONF, please! *(Laughter)* Well, that's pretty much it. We have a plethora of hardware requirements, but from a network management perspective, it's all about proper NETCONF/YANG—and software deliveries in parity for physical and virtual routers so it can be easily tested!

Summary

This chapter started out describing a business automation idea for the fictitious enterprise BookZone, then discussed how the BookZone staff created a high-level service YANG module, capturing the user interface for the service. Next, it examined how this service could be implemented in an orchestrator using a little templates and code.

The next phase was about plugging actual or simulated devices into the orchestrator, configuring them for NETCONF, and checking that their capabilities match the expectations. With service and devices in place, it was time to create some service instances and observe how NETCONF messages play out on the network. Finally, services were modified, changes rolled back in a transactional manner, and observed on the wire.

At the end there was an interview with Kristian Larsson, automation engineer in the famous TeraStream project, about working toward complete automation.

Chapter 11

YANG Model Design

This chapter covers

- How to Get into the Right Mindset for YANG Modeling
- Specific, Detailed Advice for Your YANG Modeling Tasks
- Descriptions of Common Pitfalls to Avoid in Your YANG Modeling
- Discussion Around YANG Backward Compatibility

Introduction

RFC 8407, "Guidelines for Authors and Reviewers of Documents Containing YANG Data Models," contains a wealth of both high-level and very specific recommendations. This is the document guiding IETF YANG model reviews and discussions around modeling style. Although some of the recommendations may apply specifically to the Internet Engineering Task Force (IETF), and less to your situation, and although the document contains recommendations rather than hard rules, it's a very good read. This chapter provides additional content in the same spirit. Nonbinding recommendations, the occasional explanation of various rules in YANG, a list of common modeling mistakes to avoid and a discussion around backward compatibility.

Modeling Strategy

Before jumping into the specifics of modeling, let's have a look at the bigger picture, to get into the right mindset.

Getting Started

Suppose someone has asked you to write a YANG model, and you're wondering how to get started.

A YANG model is a contract between a server and client. The contract serves to set the interface and expectations between the two. In most cases, it's the server-side team that gets to write the YANG model (for example, vendors and many standards-defining organizations [SDOs]). Occasionally, it's more of a client-side effort (for example, OpenConfig and some strong buyers). In an ideal world, both parties should be present when the YANG contract is written (with a bit of a stretch, maybe IETF could be argued to be such a place, with some representation from both sides).

Regardless of which side you're on, it makes good sense to start with thinking about the client-side use cases. What will the client want to observe, configure, and be informed about? What level of abstraction is appropriate? What implementation details are unimportant? Next, start modeling the configuration and state information and then add notifications and actions.

Another common approach is to start from the bottom. Build your YANG model from what you have and what you know. Many vendors build their YANG models this way, to resemble their existing command-line interface (CLI) structure. This makes current users and implementers immediately feel at home, which is very important and efficient. It may not be the most strategic way of developing the management infrastructure long term, though, and it tends to cement old habits and promote a CLI-centric view.

Perhaps the best way to start is to look for existing models. No matter what you are up to, others have modeled similar things in the past. If you can import constructs from other modules, or augment your model into the context of a standard module, that may be a fast (and possibly even best) way forward. If you're talking about a well-known module, there is likely already client-side software using this module. Talk about getting ahead quickly! If importing is not an option, just shopping for inspiration and patterns is a great way to buy maturity in a short amount of time.

When you have a version of a YANG module ready, try it out! Get the tools to compile and validate it. Running `pyang -f lint` on the module is a good start, but it's not enough. Play with it. Be your own customer. You will quickly get a feel for what works and how users will like, or trip over, your constructs. This is also a great way to build test cases, document examples, and give demonstrations to stakeholders. Remember the age-old startup rule: Demo or die! Plenty of great tools for everything you need are available for free.

Collect feedback from users and implementers and look for alternative ways of modeling where things aren't perfect. Read up on particular relevant YANG topics. If you are struggling with some part of your model, maybe even connecting with one of the IETF YANG Doctors (the top YANG experts at IETF) might be an option—or participating in the various forums provided by vendors.

Before you declare victory and release the first version of your YANG model, especially if you are working in an SDO, have a YANG expert review your module or module set.

You, the Four-Star General

Looking out from your command post at the hill, you see thousands upon thousands of independent units, all lined up in clusters and arrays. All prepared to do your bidding, to the extent of their abilities and until the hour when their last signal electron or color photon has ebbed out. All intently waiting for your orders.

How can you make them conquer the world, and not trip over each other while attempting to do so?

Whether you manage a network, a corporation, a production plant, or an army, to be "in control" means the same thing. You need to control the flow of orders, delegate, and constantly receive streaming sensory input as well as alerts to unusual or dangerous situations.

The first thing you need to ensure is obedience. Whenever you issue an order, it should be treated with precision. If there is a problem with the order (for example, the order is incomprehensible to the receiving unit or does not fit the role of the unit), you want to know immediately so you can issue a revised order.

In order to keep clarity, an order issued should be accepted and applied in its entirety, or if rejected, not at all. Until the receiving unit acknowledges an order, the unit makes no changes in behavior. If you ask a unit what its orders are, it reports them back with nothing added and nothing removed. The exact same words are used. In no case will such a recitation of an order be mixed with other types of information, such as a status report or a list autonomous decisions made. Orders must be kept separate from operational information.

If a unit discovers a problem while executing the order, you want to know as soon as possible. Until you decide to take further action, you expect the unit to carry on as far as it is able, as long as it's not breaking or changing the initial order. If things are really bad, it may be better that the unit shuts down completely and calls for help.

Clearly, the receiving unit must have some autonomy—more for some units, less for others, depending on role, unit competence, and the sensitivity of the task. Even the most high-ranking autonomous units are not allowed to change orders they have received, or pretend that an autonomous decision was an order received.

Some of the units under control are supervisors, who delegate orders to units that they control. Every unit should normally be managed by exactly one supervisor. More than one supervisor works, if the scope of what is being managed by each supervisor is clearly delineated and not overlapping.

If an order contains multiple instructions, it is up to the unit to figure out how to accomplish the goals stated in the order. If you want to control the exact sequence that a unit carries out some instructions, issue multiple orders in a sequence that are acknowledged individually.

YANG Modeling Tips

Let's go through some of the situations you (and every other modeler) will find yourself in as you diligently work toward a finished module.

Naming a Module

If two YANG modules in the world are given the same name, they cannot coexist within the same RESTCONF server, since the module names are used as module identifiers.

In order to avoid unnecessary issues, the easy way out here is to ensure the module names are world unique. A good approach is to prefix the module name with the name of your organization. Example 11-1 provides some real-world module names relating to interfaces.

EXAMPLE 11-1 Collection of Good YANG Module Names

```
ietf-interfaces.yang
openconfig-interfaces.yang
xran-interfaces.yang
junos-conf-interfaces.yang
Cisco-IOS-XE-interfaces.yang
Cisco-IOS-XR-ifmgr-cfg.yang
```

The module name is not the only thing that needs to be unique. According to the specifications, the module namespace string must be world unique. To make unique namespace names without requiring a central registry, the official recommendation is to pick a namespace that starts with the organization URL and then append characters that might reflect the organizational structure within the organization, or any other intra-organization disambiguation mechanism, typically followed by the module name. Example 11-2 shows some real-world namespaces. SDOs often register their namespaces with the Internet Assigned Numbers Authority (IANA). Such namespace strings look quite different and generally start with `urn:`.

EXAMPLE 11-2 Collection of Good YANG Namespace Strings, Vendor Private Namespaces (Unregistered with IANA), and IANA Registered Namespaces

```
// Private namespaces
namespace "http://openconfig.net/yang/interfaces";
namespace "http://yang.juniper.net/junos/conf/interfaces";
namespace "http://cisco.com/ns/yang/Cisco-IOS-XE-native";
namespace "http://cisco.com/ns/yang/Cisco-IOS-XR-ifmgr-cfg";

// IANA-registered namespaces
namespace "urn:ietf:params:xml:ns:yang:ietf-yang-library";
namespace "urn:mef:yang:mef-topology";
namespace "urn:xran:interfaces:1.0";
```

It's not a good idea to use `urn:`-based namespaces unless you first register them with IANA. Or, as Internet pioneer Warren Kumari puts it: "It's a really, really bad idea (and poor form)."

Finally, since namespace names tend to be long and complicated, a shorter prefix string needs to be selected. Technically, according to the specifications, they don't need to be unique. In practice, however, users tend to understand the module references (which use the prefixes) a lot better if they, too, are unique. If you have a good module name, choosing that same string as the prefix might actually be an easy and great way to stay interoperable.

Publishing a Module

A YANG module is considered published when it reaches the hands of someone who might be upset if you go and change its contents. As soon as your YANG module is published, you should start thinking about backward-compatibility rules.

What backward compatibility means for YANG modules is defined in Section 10 of YANG 1.0, RFC 6020, and Section 11 in YANG 1.1, RFC 7950. This topic is also discussed later in this chapter. Basically, the rules say that a YANG module is backward compatible if anything a client could legally do toward this server with the old version of the YANG module is still possible to do now that the server uses the new YANG module.

The correct process to release a non-backward-compatible module is to give it a new namespace and filename. To make things easier for everyone, a new prefix is probably also in order. This makes it clear for everyone in the world that this is a new and not completely backward-compatible module.

In theory, module authors could make it easy for themselves by simply giving their modules new names and prefixes all the time. This is bad for the consumers of the model, however, as they will need to deal with a high number of different versions. To be attractive on the YANG interface market, it's wise not to release incompatible versions too often.

Sometimes it happens that a YANG module is published, and within a relatively short time, some weeks or months perhaps, some rather deep flaw is found by the wider community trying to consume the module. Once the flaw is fixed, typically in a non-backward-compatible way, the question comes up of whether the module name, namespace, and prefix must change. Formally, the answer is yes, but if the module with the flaw is deemed "un-implementable" (that is, the module can't currently be in any serious use), the damage to the user community might be greater if the name, namespace, and prefix are changed.

Regardless of what arguments for and against change are used to navigate in this name/namespace/prefix dimension, there are no reasonable arguments for publishing updated YANG modules without adding a revision statement in the module. The YANG specifications are quite clear: Always add a revision statement when anything is changed.

Choosing YANG Identifiers

The importance of names is often debated in computer science circles. "A name is just a name" is one way of looking at it. The computers don't care what the name is, as long as it is referenced at the right time and spelled correctly. A different perspective is that the names are the most important things of all, since they convey the semantic meaning of what is being manipulated. Structure and logic are just implementation details around them.

Be that as it may, all agree that good names are quite important when it comes to reaching a common understanding in interfaces such as YANG modules. An important principle to avoid human error is the principle of least surprise. Consistency, good order, and cleanliness are primary ways to keep the surprise factor down.

For this purpose, the YANG community decreed some rules for how identifiers in YANG modules should be formed. Many are quite arbitrary, but that is beside the point. A good interface should stick to these rules unless there is a (sufficiently) strong reason not to.

All YANG identifiers should be lowercase. This saves operators and programmers from reaching for the Shift key. There may be the occasional abbreviation that is so ingrained in people's minds that an uppercase symbol feels like the only option, but this conflicts with the all-lowercase expectation in YANG, so lowercase is generally recommended anyway.

Identifiers that consist of more than one word should use a dash (hyphen) to connect them. Programmers are used to using the underscore character, but network operations people are used to the dash. What's more, the dash character does not require using the Shift key in most locales.

Generally, be careful with using abbreviations. You, as module designer, obviously know them all. Many module users do not. The abbreviations you decide to use should be used consistently everywhere in your module.

Do not repeat the parent's name in child names. For example, the key leaf in list *interfaces* might be *name*. Don't call it *interface-name*.

Accepting a Blank Configuration

Since you're modeling the new cool feature that everyone want to use, it may be hard to imagine that it may be included in systems where the user might not be interested in your module—at least not right now.

It is therefore wise to ensure that an empty configuration is meaningful and is allowed. Even if Border Gateway Protocol (BGP) can't possibly work unless an Autonomous System (AS) number is configured, make sure that the AS number is only required if BGP is used at all.

A common way to do this is to place the entire module's contents in a presence container, as shown in Example 11-3. This allows a user to enable and disable the entire function and to only require any mandatory elements if the function is in use.

EXAMPLE 11-3 Mandatory Leaf Placed Inside a Presence Container to Allow a Blank Configuration

```
container bgp {
  presence "Enable BGP";
  leaf as-number {
    type uint32;
    mandatory true;
  }
```

The same consideration applies equally to the entire system. Your YANG may well be used in scenarios you did not initially think about (for example, in a controller environment far outside your own system or with only a day-zero configuration in a booting virtual machine).

Using Leafrefs

A YANG model's readability and value increase measurably every time a `leafref` is used to refer to something, rather than a plain string or integer. The leafref explains that a value not only has to conform to a basic type, but it points out a particular instance in a list. This makes a tremendous difference in how this information is displayed or entered into a system.

It may be possible for smart human users to infer the relationship even without the leafref modeling, but if automation is to be allowed, semantic hints like this must be given to the poor machines that lack our human intelligence. Fight for the rights of machines, make your design explicit!

A leafref that is part of the configuration requires that the instance it points at exists and that the target is a configurable element, too, as shown in Example 11-4. A transaction fails if the target element was deleted and the leafref pointer wasn't changed. Sometimes this is not what you want—for example, if you want some configuration to point to a piece of hardware that could in theory be removed at any time. In such cases, add the statement `require-instance false` to the leafref (requires YANG 1.1). This makes clear that the leafref target may or may not exist.

EXAMPLE 11-4 A **config true** Leafref to **config false** Data Allowed Through the **require-instance false** Statement

```
list sensor {
  config false;
  key  position;
  leaf position {
    type string;
  }
  ...
}
...
list threshold {
  key position;
  leaf position {
```

```
    type leafref {
      path /sensor/position;
      require-instance false;
    }
  }
  leaf max-temp {
    ...
```

Minding That XPath Feature

XPath expressions are essential in YANG—in a limited form in `leafref` paths, and in the full form in `when` and `must` expressions. Keep in mind that in YANG, it's explicitly XPath 1.0 that must be used. Any nifty functions you googled from XPath 2 or XPath 3 are not welcome here. This is because many features in the higher-level XPath standards require much more memory and are therefore not suitable for the embedded environments where YANG modules are often implemented.

Also, don't use any of the XPath axes—the things with double colons (`::`). Several of them are undefined in YANG (for example `preceding-sibling::`). The rest are just not very interoperable and are inefficient in many implementations (for example `ancestor::`). If you are keen that your YANG module is successful out there, stay away from the XPath axes.

It's very easy to accidentally write a seemingly simple XPath expression that requires implementations to wade through enormous amounts of data. Have someone with a computer science background think through how an implementation might evaluate your constraint. Modules containing constraints that prevent efficient implementations are not tolerated by the module consumers in the end. One particular example is using the XPath double slash (`//`) search operator. Don't use it.

Enumerating and More

In many cases, you will need to enumerate a number of different options. There are many ways to do that in YANG.

If you have a fixed collection of features that could be on or off, the `bits` type may be a compact way of bunching them all together. In case you ever want to extend the set of bits, you can do so by releasing a new version of your module in a backward-compatible way. You can never remove any of the bit definitions you published, however—at least not in a backward-compatible way.

Enumerations are probably the most common way to give a module user a number of different alternatives to choose from. Enumerations make good sense in a wide array of use cases. In case you ever want to extend the set of `enumeration` values, do so by releasing a new version of your module. This is backward-compatible. Like with bits, you can never remove published enumeration values, or at least it would break backward-compatibility if you removed any of them.

If you have bits or enumeration values that don't make sense on all implementations, use `if-feature` to mark them as not available on some systems. You can also leverage this mechanism if you have a hunch that some value(s) will not be relevant in the future. In that case, model such values with the statement `if-feature` legacy-feature. Newer systems can then choose not to support this *legacy-feature*, making those enumeration values or bits irrelevant. The YANG text still has to mention those *legacy-feature* values, though. Basically forever.

If you need maximum flexibility around what values are valid on a system, use `identity`. YANG identities are much like enumerations, but they allow the possible values to be defined in any YANG module, not only in the one that defines the type. This way, new values can be added over time by adding more identities belonging to the same category. They are added in the same module, in a new standard module, or in a proprietary module. They can also be removed. Just make sure your system doesn't support the YANG module that defines some identities, and they will no longer be available as options on that system. By making use of identities, you can create a very flexible set of values, controlled by which YANG modules are supported by a system.

Furthermore, identities are not necessarily just plain lists of possible values. Identities can have kind-of relations, as in X is a kind of Y. This makes identities ideal for modeling sets where there are large and ever-growing numbers of diverse types and subtypes of things. Network interface types come to mind, but sensor types or traditional object-oriented examples like vehicle types and geometric shapes are good examples as well. For example, a *GigabitEthernet* interface is a kind of *Ethernet* interface, which is a kind of *Interface*. A Generic Routing Encapsulation tunnel (*GRE-tunnel*) interface is a kind of *Tunnel* interface, which is a kind of *Interface*. So the *GRE-tunnel* is a kind of *Interface*, but not a kind of *Ethernet* interface.

When you're modeling things as identities with subclassifications, it's easy to create YANG models that trigger on a hardware component being, say, a sensor, a temperature sensor, or an over-temperature sensor for fire-alarm purposes.

In order to reap the benefits of future extensibility and subcategorization of identity values, remember you need to use the `derived-from()` and `derived-from-or-self()` XPath functions when comparing identity values in YANG, as shown in Example 11-5. If you use direct XPath equality tests, you will miss out on this future extensibility.

EXAMPLE 11-5 Proper Way of Comparing Identity Values

```
leaf sensor-type {
  type identity {
    base sensors:sensor-idty;
  }
}
container temp-thresholds {
// DON'T write   when "../sensor-type = 'sensors:temperature';
// since this will not allow for future sub-types of temperature sensors
  when "derived-from-or-self(../sensor-type, 'sensors:temperature');
  ...
}
```

Choosing Keys

When one is modeling lists, usually the most important modeling design question is what to pick as the list key(s). It should be the information piece(s) that uniquely identify which list entry someone is talking about. Sometimes what to choose for the key is obvious, sometimes not. Sometimes the obvious choice isn't a good one.

In YANG, the tradition is to pick so-called natural keys. That is, keys that make immediate sense to a user. The key for an interface list? The interface name. The key for a list of enterprise customers? The enterprise name. The key for a list of sensors? The sensor path.

The alternative to natural keys is so-called synthetic keys. That is, keys that have little or no intrinsic meaning, other than to identify the list entry. This could be an interface number (hello SNMP), a customer number, or sensor Universally Unique Identifier (UUID)—essentially a very large random number.

The advantage with natural keys is that they don't introduce lots of meaningless data into the system or indirections for operators or programmers to look up and cross-reference. This potentially reduces the number of mistakes operators and programmers make. The advantage with synthetic keys is that objects can be renamed easily without affecting the data structure. YANG in itself allows the modeler to use either approach, but natural keys are preferred.

Sometimes the obvious key isn't a good choice. Generally, access control lists (ACLs) have been keyed by rule numbers since they were invented, many decades ago, in command-line interfaces from most vendors. That legacy made it a very natural choice to pick rule numbers as the key to ACLs when these were modeled in IETF.

There is a problem with rule numbers, however. Not only are they in themselves meaningless to the operator (an ACL called "110" doesn't tell you anything about what it does). If the same ACL was called "Block Netflix," you'd have an immediate basic understanding. Worse is that rule numbers serve dual purposes: They are used for identification but also to sort list entries in the natural, numerically ascending order.

Initially, the user may create an ACL called "100," then another called "110." As time goes by and new rules are inserted, there is a (very real) possibility that more than nine ACLs must be inserted between the two. What then? Vendors came up with a palette of solutions to this problem (for example, a "renumber" command). This does not work well for a manager that won't know which rule is which after some operator invoked "renumber." The approach finally selected by IETF for this was instead to add a name leaf to all ACLs and to make the list `ordered-by user`.

NOTE

If you are used to networks with all Juniper devices, you might be smiling at this point—and rightfully so.

This means each ACL can be given a meaningful name, and the set of rules are not sorted by the name. Instead, ACLs are inserted "after" or "before" another, named ACL, or "first" or "last." From an industry automation perspective, this seemingly trivial shift of keys is actually one giant leap for mankind.

Another possibility when it comes to keys in a list is to have no keys. This is only allowed for operational (`config false`) lists, because there is otherwise no way to convey which list entry you are talking about. If you wanted to edit one of them, that would be a major problem. That keyless lists are allowed under some circumstances doesn't mean it's a good idea in all those circumstances.

Keyless lists are good if, for example, you have a notification or action defined that returns a list of 50 temperature readings. The readings themselves are not necessarily unique, so they can't be used as keys. You could introduce a synthetic key (for example, 1, 2, 3, …) to enumerate the readings, but that wouldn't add a lot of value, so a keyless list makes sense here.

Keyless lists are not good if, for example, you have an operational list with 50,000 log messages. It probably makes sense to use the timestamp as a key for those. The problem with keyless lists is that it's not possible to read the list in any other way than reading it all. There is no way to express where you'd like to start or stop reading from when there are no keys, so it's all or nothing. For operational lists that are potentially long, this is a terrible (no, horrible) idea from a management perspective. Imagine an operator waiting for the web portal to load all those 50,000 log messages, and the unnecessary load on the device, just to display the first page.

Types Empty and Boolean

The YANG type `empty` is very similar to type `boolean` in that it is often used to flag a certain condition (for example that something is enabled). A type `empty` leaf can exist or not exist, but cannot have any real value beyond that. A type `boolean` leaf can have the value `true` or `false`, or may not exist.

Type `empty` cannot be used as a list key in YANG 1.0. It is allowed in YANG 1.1, but is still rather awkward, as the absent value is represented as an empty string. This may not be the most obvious value to enter if you ask nonprogrammers. Type `empty` also cannot have a default value. Or perhaps better said another way, a type `empty` leaf always defaults to not existing.

When in doubt, it may be safer to use a type `boolean` leaf, since it has fewer restrictions on how it might be used in the future. On the other hand, if you use a `boolean` leaf, be sure to describe what it means if the leaf doesn't exist (for example, by giving it a default).

Reusing Groupings

In order to make a piece of YANG reusable in many modules, it needs to be a typedef or go in a grouping. Putting a piece of YANG into a submodule, to be included by multiple modules, is a tactic that doesn't work in YANG. A submodule must declare which main module it belongs to, and therefore (intentionally) only belongs to one main module.

In order to be reusable in multiple locations in multiple modules, groupings typically have to use relative paths in any `leafref`, `when`, or `must` expressions. If a grouping doesn't contain any `config false` statement, it may also be reusable in both `config true` and `false` contexts.

The reusability aspect of groupings makes it attractive to model pretty much everything as groupings. Some modelers have actually done this. The downside with this approach is that the models themselves often get harder to read, when much of the module consists of `uses` statements. Tools such as `pyang -f tree` certainly help to get an overview in this situation.

Deviating from a Standard YANG Module

There is only one thing worse than claiming to implement a standard YANG module, but then not doing it properly. That is to stay silent about any such deviations or omissions. Therefore, there is a YANG statement called `deviate` that allows implementers to officially declare in what ways an implementation differs from the standard. The existence of this keyword, however, does not imply in any way that clients will be able to deal with the declared deviation. In short, deviations are very poor substitutes for not implementing a standard.

A deviation is somewhat akin to an "out of order" sign hanging off a coffee machine or a conference room projector. It signals a non-ideal condition, but at least the user is made aware, doesn't waste her time figuring out the problem, and is less likely to send reports about the issue.

Deviations come in different grades. Light deviations are those cases where a device declares restrictions on what it can support. If a configuration that conforms to the deviated model is still valid when seen in the undeviated model, things can work out reasonably well. You can't claim to conform to the standard in this case, but it's reasonably close.

An infinitely better way for a device to declare that a certain feature isn't supported is to ensure the particular feature lives in a YANG file of its own, and the device simply doesn't announce it—or that the feature has a YANG `feature` statement attached, which the device doesn't publish.

From a programmability point of view, dark deviations are poison pills—as are of course any deviations from the published YANG models that are not declared. Dark deviations are cases where the device allows/requires configurations that standards-conforming devices do not understand (for example, new enumeration values, a changed structure, or changed types).

In between the two you have the "twilight zone." Deviated YANG `default` values go here. Sometimes they may be almost okay, but at other times they are very destructive.

A particular concern for any modeler that considers himself part of a standards-defining organization is this: It does not make sense for an SDO to have deviations in their models (for example, for deviating the work of some other SDO). This is like permanently building an "out of order" sign into the standard. Also, it deprives any implementer of your YANG module of their last resort. The implementer could not deviate from the SDO's deviation since deviations cannot be deviated.

Transient Configuration and Other Dependencies

One of the cornerstones in the YANG world is that it must be possible to tell whether a particular configuration is valid just by looking at the configuration itself and the YANG model that pertains to the configuration. Specifically, neither the current device state nor the phase of the moon must play any part in whether a given configuration is valid or not. This allows managers to predict the behavior of devices, execute network wide transactions, and so on.

From this follows that constraints on the configuration, usually in the form of `must` statements, must never refer to `config false` data. If they did, the validity of the configuration depends on the operational state, which isn't acceptable for automation scenarios.

This is a hard-and-fast rule in YANG, but some YANG compiler implementations aren't smart enough to understand what some complex `must` expressions in the modules actually refer to, and may let some violations of this rule sneak through. Be wary of such behavior, and make sure there are no dependencies on operational state in your YANG module. Even if the compiler you happen to use accepts it, it is still broken YANG. It won't be interoperable, and it is not a good idea from an architectural point of view.

One particular variant of dependency on operational state known in the SNMP world is called "transient configuration." In SNMP, it is possible to model a read-only object (for example, a loopback-interface) with read-write attributes (for example, the maximum transfer unit [MTU]). This situation roughly translates into YANG as a `config false` list with `config true` leafs. This is specifically outlawed in YANG, and probably all compilers would flag this as an error. A deeper discussion about how to properly mix `config true` and `config false` data is found in the "Network Management Datastore Architecture (NMDA)" section of Chapter 3, "YANG Explained."

Augmenting YANG Models

One of the true strengths of the YANG modeling language is that it allows one module to `augment` (that is, extend the contents of) any other module in a backward-compatible way. This makes it possible for SDOs to define basic, common structures that many vendors agree on and use, and for vendors to add their proprietary extensions into, within the same context.

One thing to remember when augmenting a model is that any user of the model being augmented may not be aware of the augmentation and must have the right to completely ignore it. This means that any configuration that is valid without the augmentation must remain so even when the augmentation is in effect. It is therefore generally not possible to augment in mandatory elements, or add new constraints, such as `must` or `when` expressions, restricting the data in the original module.

Types Anyxml and Anydata

The YANG types `anyxml` and `anydata` are primarily meant to be used when modeling the foundational RPC operations in NETCONF, RESTCONF, and so on. For example, when modeling the input to `edit-config` or output from the `get` operation, there is just no way to describe the valid data in any other way than to say it's any data encoded in Extensible Markup Language (XML) or JavaScript Object Notation (JSON).

These types are certainly available for use anywhere in a YANG model. Note, however, that since this data is opaque from a YANG perspective, any use of these types requires hard-coded functionality in clients. This reduces the value coming from the model-driven nature of YANG. Also, interoperability suffers unless the allowed data is described with minute precision.

Common YANG Mistakes

Besides the warm feeling of being involved in all the cool new standards under development, one good reason to sign up as an IETF YANG Doctor is to learn not only from your own mistakes, but also from those of others. Here follows a discussion around some of the most commonly occurring and/or most problematic issues found in reviews at IETF, other SDOs, and the industry at large.

Unclear Optional Leafs

One of the most common problems in YANG is when authors fail to describe what it means when an optional leaf does not exist. Remember, in YANG, a leaf that does not have a `mandatory true` statement or any `default` statement might well not exist at all. In fact, "no value" is typically the initial state of an optional leaf if it lacks a default.

It's quite clear what it means if a Boolean leaf *enable* is either `true` or `false` (the object it relates to is either in use or not), but what if leaf *enable* doesn't exist at all? The interpretation is clear as mud. Or what about a leaf with a range that does not include zero, or some other value that might be obvious if left unset? This is illustrated in Example 11-6.

EXAMPLE 11-6 Leafs with Unclear Meaning When Not Present

```
leaf enable {
   type boolean;
}
...
leaf mtu {
  type uint32 {
    range "68..65535";
  }
}
```

The best way to resolve this ambiguity is often to add a `default` statement (for example, `default true` or `default 1500`). After that, the leaf always has a value—ambiguity removed. If there is no reasonable default, another option is to make it `mandatory true` (that is, force the operator/programmer to fill in a value). This removes the ambiguity, but also gives the operator or programmer an additional, mandatory task to complete. The last option is to write in a `description` statement on the leaf concerning how a configuration with no value for this leaf should be interpreted. To leave this situation undefined is to beg for future interoperability issues.

Missing Ranges

While it makes good sense to start the modeling effort without going into details about the exact type, range, and restrictions for each leaf, a too common problem is that the module is published while these details were not yet worked out. This is illustrated in Example 11-7.

EXAMPLE 11-7 Underspecified Leafs, Lacking Ranges or other Format Declarations

```
leaf prefix-length {
  type uint8;
}
...
leaf mtu {
  type uint32;
}
...
leaf isbn {
  type string;
}
```

Interoperability is all about common understanding. Spelling out what the valid values are is therefore key.

Overusing Strings

In a YANG module, any type could theoretically be replaced by type `string` while still keeping the data unchanged.* This is obvious if you consider that all types have a textual representation that can be shown in the device's CLI or web interface. A lazy modeler could very well model every leaf as a string. Fortunately, this does not happen, since a lot of information is conveyed with the type information.

***NOTE**

Such a change is not backward compatible, however, since the wire representation might change. YANG-driven databases and such might be impacted.

Strings are good for modeling names of various kinds, where there should be no restriction on what the value might be. When referring to another YANG object, `leafref` is usually the right type, rather than `string`.

The most common case where modelers are overusing plain strings is when models from other modeling languages or APIs are translated to YANG. In any such translation effort, stay vigilant with the type information so that the lack of details in the original won't also afflict the new YANG module.

Bad String Patterns

Using the YANG `pattern` statement, a string leaf can be forced to conform to a regular expression. This is most useful for quickly and easily describing valid values. There are a couple of mistakes that happen rather frequently, however.

The first problem is that regular expressions come in several flavors. They are all similar enough to be dangerously confusing. The two dominating variants are the so-called perl-regex (a.k.a. python-regex) and the W3C-regex. The former is mostly used in scripting, while the latter comes from the Web and XML world. The YANG RFCs specifically state that the YANG `pattern` statements must use W3C-regex.

The two flavors are similar enough to make it impossible to always know for certain which flavor the author of an expression had in mind. In practice, however, there are a couple of indicators that reveal most invalid perl-regex expressions in YANG. A W3C-regex is always anchored at both ends, meaning the regex must match the entire value, from the first to last character. Since matching the entire value is by far the most common intent of pattern authors, a perl-regex usually contains anchor symbols at the head and tail. This means that if you see a pattern statement in YANG that begins with the caret symbol (^) and/or ends with the dollar sign ($), a perl-regex most likely invaded your YANG module. There are many other subtle differences as well, so simply removing the anchors is sometimes not enough to translate the expression to W3C-regex syntax.

Another problem that sometimes shows up in conjunction with regex patterns imported from other sources is that they may be very long. A pattern that is not readable by humans is not a good pattern to include in a YANG pattern statement. This is a contract, after all, that all parties must understand for good interoperability.

In this case, it may be better to describe the constraint in a description statement and leave it up to implementers to enforce the validity however they like. Massive regex patterns may also require large amounts of CPU time or memory to validate, and may therefore make a YANG model less applicable to constrained device types.

Example 11-8 is an authentic example of a YANG `pattern` statement that is unreadable, too long to be efficiently validated, and also uses the invalid (in YANG context) perl-regex syntax.

EXAMPLE 11-8 Invalid, Unreadable, and Inefficient Regex in a **pattern** Statement

```
pattern "^(([0-9]|[1-9][0-9]|1[0-9]{2}|2[0-4][0-9]|25[0-5])\.){3}([0-9]|[1-9][0-9]|1[
0-9]{2}|2[0-4][0-9]|25[0-5])$|^(([a-zA-Z]|[a-zA-Z][a-zA-Z0-9\-]*[a-zA-Z0-9])\.)*([A-Z
a-z]|[A-Za-z][A-Za-z0-9\-]*[A-Za-z0-9])$|^(?:(?:(?:(?:(?:(?:(?:[0-9a-fA-F]{1,4})):){6
})(?:(?:(?:(?:(?:[0-9a-fA-F]{1,4})):(?:(?:[0-9a-fA-F]{1,4})))|(?:(?:(?:(?:(?:25[0-5]|
(?:[1-9]|1[0-9]|2[0-4])?[0-9]))\.){3}(?:(?:25[0-5]|(?:[1-9]|1[0-9]|2[0-4])?[0-9])))))
))|(?:(?:::(?:(?:(?:[0-9a-fA-F]{1,4})):){5})(?:(?:(?:(?:(?:[0-9a-fA-F]{1,4})):(?:(?:[
0-9a-fA-F]{1,4})))|(?:(?:(?:(?:(?:25[0-5]|(?:[1-9]|1[0-9]|2[0-4])?[0-9]))\.){3}(?:(?:
25[0-5]|(?:[1-9]|1[0-9]|2[0-4])?[0-9])))))))|(?:(?:(?:(?:(?:[0-9a-fA-F]{1,4})))?::(?:
(?:(?:[0-9a-fA-F]{1,4})):){4})(?:(?:(?:(?:(?:[0-9a-fA-F]{1,4})):(?:(?:[0-9a-fA-F]{1,4
```

```
})))|(?:(?:(?:(?:(?:25[0-5]|(?:[1-9]|1[0-9]|2[0-4])?[0-9]))\.){3}(?:(?:25[0-5]|(?:[1-
9]|1[0-9]|2[0-4])?[0-9]))))))))|(?:(?:(?:(?:(?:(?:[0-9a-fA-F]{1,4})):){0,1}(?:(?:[0-9a
-fA-F]{1,4})))?::(?:(?:(?:[0-9a-fA-F]{1,4})):){3})(?:(?:(?:(?:(?:[0-9a-fA-F]{1,4})):(
?:(?:[0-9a-fA-F]{1,4})))|(?:(?:(?:(?:(?:25[0-5]|(?:[1-9]|1[0-9]|2[0-4])?[0-9]))\.){3}
(?:(?:25[0-5]|(?:[1-9]|1[0-9]|2[0-4])?[0-9]))))))))|(?:(?:(?:(?:(?:(?:[0-9a-fA-F]{1,4}
)):){0,2}(?:(?:[0-9a-fA-F]{1,4})))?::(?:(?:(?:[0-9a-fA-F]{1,4})):){2})(?:(?:(?:(?:(?:
[0-9a-fA-F]{1,4})):(?:(?:[0-9a-fA-F]{1,4})))|(?:(?:(?:(?:(?:25[0-5]|(?:[1-9]|1[0-9]|2
[0-4])?[0-9]))\.){3}(?:(?:25[0-5]|(?:[1-9]|1[0-9]|2[0-4])?[0-9]))))))))|(?:(?:(?:(?:(?
:(?:[0-9a-fA-F]{1,4})):){0,3}(?:(?:[0-9a-fA-F]{1,4})))?::(?:(?:[0-9a-fA-F]{1,4})):)(?
:(?:(?:(?:(?:[0-9a-fA-F]{1,4})):(?:(?:[0-9a-fA-F]{1,4})))|(?:(?:(?:(?:(?:25[0-5]|(?:[
1-9]|1[0-9]|2[0-4])?[0-9]))\.){3}(?:(?:25[0-5]|(?:[1-9]|1[0-9]|2[0-4])?[0-9]))))))))|(
?:(?:(?:(?:(?:(?:[0-9a-fA-F]{1,4})):){0,4}(?:(?:[0-9a-fA-F]{1,4})))?::)(?:(?:(?:(?:(?
:[0-9a-fA-F]{1,4})):(?:(?:[0-9a-fA-F]{1,4})))|(?:(?:(?:(?:(?:25[0-5]|(?:[1-9]|1[0-9]|
2[0-4])?[0-9]))\.){3}(?:(?:25[0-5]|(?:[1-9]|1[0-9]|2[0-4])?[0-9]))))))))|(?:(?:(?:(?:(
?:(?:[0-9a-fA-F]{1,4})):){0,5}(?:(?:[0-9a-fA-F]{1,4})))?::)(?:(?:[0-9a-fA-F]{1,4}))))|
(?:(?:(?:(?:(?:(?:[0-9a-fA-F]{1,4})):){0,6}(?:(?:[0-9a-fA-F]{1,4})))?::)))))$";
```

A YANG `pattern` feature that is little known and therefore underutilized is the `invert-match` substatement, shown in Example 11-9. This allows the modeler to easily exclude values that are illegal in a very precise and compact way. To describe the following rules without `invert-match` makes the pattern very long and complicated.

EXAMPLE 11-9 Good Use of Modifier **invert-match** to Rule Out Invalid Patterns

```
leaf hostname {
  type string {
    pattern '[a-zA-Z0-9]+[a-zA-Z0-9-]*';
    pattern '.*-' {
      modifier invert-match;
    }
    pattern localhost {
      modifier invert-match;
    }
  }
  description
    "The hostname must be at least one character long,
     start with a letter or number, and may contain dash (-) symbols,
     except first and last. The hostname must not be 'localhost'.";
}
```

Blank Configuration Made Invalid

Another rather common beginner's mistake often results when trying to resolve the issue with optional leafs, as discussed earlier. Some leaf is made mandatory, but in such a way that there is a chain of always-existing elements from the leaf all the way to the root. This makes the leaf mandatory in every configuration where the YANG module is present, as shown in Example 11-10.

EXAMPLE 11-10 Missing **presence** Statement on Container Makes Leaf as-number Globally Mandatory

```
module bgp {
...
  container bgp {
    leaf as-number {
      mandatory true;
      type uint32;
```

Even if the leaf you are modeling is crucial for the correct operation of the function you are modeling, it is wise to build a model where this functionality may be left completely unconfigured. A mandatory leaf that sits in a container that always exists must have a value in every conceivable configuration (for example, even in a day-zero, initial configuration).

This is rarely a good idea, and there are several ways to fix this. One is to give the leaf a default value. Another is to make one of the parent containers optional (that is, make it a `presence` container), among other solutions.

Misunderstanding When a Constraint Applies

The first common issue with `must` statements is to understand when they apply. The constraint of a `must` statement applies when the object it sits on exists (that is, is configured or has a default value). Containers are considered to always exist in YANG (unless they are `presence` containers), so a `must` statement on a container applies as soon as the parent of the container exists. If this is the module's top level (or another container that always exists, and so on), the `must` condition always applies. The following real-life exhibit (with the identifiers changed for anonymity) shown in Example 11-11 demonstrates the problem in several ways.

EXAMPLE 11-11 A **must** Statement That Always Applies

```
container top {
  must the-list {
    error-message "The-list must not be empty once initialized";
  }
  list the-list {
```

Here, the modeler fails to realize that the `must` statement applies from the start, and thus makes the initial, blank configuration invalid. To make a blank configuration valid, the container has to be a `presence` container, as shown in Example 11-12.

EXAMPLE 11-12 A **must** Statement That Applies When and Only When **top** Has Been Configured

```
container top {
  presence "Enables the top functionality";
  must the-list {
    error-message "The-list must not be empty once initialized";
  }
  list the-list {
```

At this point, the initial configuration is valid since the `must` statement only applies once the *top* `presence` container is created. On the other hand, the user can delete the *top* container at any time, thereby making the constraint not apply anymore.

The modeler's intent to make something mandatory once it has been set is not possible to express in YANG (even if a device could still implement this rogue behavior). This is highly intentional. In YANG, the validity of a future configuration must not depend on the current configuration. Basically, it should always be possible to go back to a configuration you had in the past—in other words, no "crappy little rules" (CLRs) that prevent automation flows or an operator from reinstating a backup.

Missing the Simple Constraints

Many modelers who strive to write good, tight models frequently use `must` and `when` statements in YANG when there are much simpler constructs available. The simpler constructs are both easier to read and understand, as well as easier for the system to validate at low computational cost, as shown in Example 11-13.

EXAMPLE 11-13 Constraints Built Using Complex and Slow **must** Expressions

```
// Uniqueness constraint
list tunnel {
  key "host port";
  leaf host { … }
  leaf port { … }
  leaf local-port { … }
  must "count(../tunnel[local-port=current()]) = 1";
…
// At least two instances constraint
must "count(name-server) >= 2";
list name-server {
…
```

```
// One or the other constraint
leaf ipv4-address {
  when "not(../ipv6-address)";
  ...
}
leaf ipv6-address {
  when "not(../ipv4-address)";
  ...
}
```

Using simpler YANG constructs such as `unique`, `min-elements`, `max-elements`, and `choice`, the modeler could write the mentioned constraints as shown in Example 11-14. This make them easier to read and easier for servers to implement correctly. Remember, YANG modules are contracts. The better they are understood by all, the more effective they are.

EXAMPLE 11-14 Constraints Built Using Simple and Fast YANG Mechanisms

```
// Uniqueness constraint
list tunnel {
  key "host port";
  unique local-port;
  leaf host { … }
  leaf port { … }
  leaf local-port { … }
...
// At least two instances constraint
list name-server {
  min-elements 2;
...
// One or the other constraint
choice ipv4-or-ipv6 {
  leaf ipv4-address { … }
  leaf ipv6-address { … }
```

Getting the Path Wrong

Anyone who has tried to teach someone the YANG rules for XPath navigation has to admit that this isn't anywhere near as simple as the file system metaphor seems to imply. Many of the YANG validation and authoring tools out there used to do little to help out, other than to give their users a false sense of security. Many tools didn't even look at the XPath expressions. No wonder then that a lot of YANG paths have gone astray over the years.

The tools situation has improved radically in recent years. Even if a malformed path has infected a module, bad tooling is no excuse for not fixing it ASAP when someone points out the problem.

Primarily two kinds of path problems are common. The first relates to the difference between schema tree paths and data tree paths. In Example 11-15, the paths traverse nodes that are part of the schema tree and must be disregarded when counting the number of ".." to use in the path.

EXAMPLE 11-15 **when** Expressions with Paths That Many Find Surprising

```
container top {
  leaf selector {
    type enumeration {
      enum first;
      enum second;
    }
  }
...
  choice first-or-second {
    case first {
      leaf f-value {
        when "../selector = 'first'";
        // "case" and "choice" don't count in the path
        type uint32;
...
  action doit {
    input {
      leaf doit-first-flavor {
        when "../../selector = 'first'";
        // "input" doesn't count in the path
        type string;
```

A look at the instance data tree usually helps quickly. To understand what the instance data tree looks like, observe what it looks like on an XML or JSON level. That is, run a `get-config` to see what the data tree looks like to ensure the paths are right. Check the preceding paths against this instance data, returned from `get-config`, for example. The `choice` and `case` nodes are not visible in the `get-config` reply.

```
<top>
  <selector>first</selector>
  <f-value>123</f-value>
```

The other common path problem in YANG relates to the XPath dot (.) expression. In XPath, the dot refers to the "context item." This is not necessarily the same as the YANG element the XPath expression sits on, although sometimes it is, which makes the dot a false friend. It generally takes an XPath expert to always know what the context item is.

If the current YANG node is what the modeler has in mind, it's much better to use the `current()` XPath function, which invariably refers to the YANG element the expression sits on. In the following expression in Example 11-16, the dot expression refers to the entire setting list. Clearly, this is not going to work as intended.

EXAMPLE 11-16 Incorrect Usage of the XPath Dot Expression

```
list setting {
  key name;
  ...
  leaf value {
    type int32;
  }
}
leaf max {
  type int32;
  must "not(../setting[value > .])" {    // Broken expression
    description
      "There must not be any setting with a value greater than max.";
  }
}
```

The modeler needs to express their intent that no *value* may be greater than *max*, as shown in Example 11-17.

EXAMPLE 11-17 Correct Usage of the XPath **current()** Function

```
leaf max {
  type int32;
  must "not(../setting[value > current()])" {
    description
      "There must not be any setting with a value greater than max.";
  }
}
```

Disconnected Multikey Leafrefs

Many YANG lists have more than one key leaf. When referring to list entries in such lists, the reference requires as many leafref elements as there are keys—one for each key. That is not quite enough, however.

As an example, take the sample model of a list of file servers in Example 11-18. The servers are keyed by data center, server number, and port number.

EXAMPLE 11-18 Multikey List to Be Referenced in Upcoming Examples

```
list file-servers {
  key "data-center server-num port";
  leaf data-center {
    type string;
  }
  leaf server-num {
    type unit8;
  }
  leaf port {
    type uint16;
  }
...
}
```

Now, in order to allow the operator to pick one to connect to, there need to be three leafrefs, each one pointing to one of the keys. A fairly common beginner's mistake is to model them as separate leafrefs, as shown in Example 11-19.

EXAMPLE 11-19 Disconnected References to Key Leafs in Multikey List

```
container connect-to {
  leaf dc {
    type leafref {
      path /file-servers/data-center;
    }
  }
  leaf num {
    type leafref {
      path /file-servers/server-num;
    }
  }
  leaf port {
    type leafref {
      path /file-servers/port;
    }
  }
}
```

This does allow leaf *dc* to point to any of the file server *data-center* values, *num* to point to any *server-num*, and *port* to point to any file server *port*. The problem here is that each of the leafrefs could be pointing at completely different list entries. Let's say we have the list of file servers shown in Example 11-20.

EXAMPLE 11-20 Sample Data in a Multikey List

```
Data-center  Server-num  Port
===========  ==========  =====
beijing      2           36002
beijing      2           36005
rio          1           38922
kiev         6           37222
kiev         7           37222
```

If someone configures the *dc* to be beijing, then *num* must be 2, and the valid values for *port* are 36002 or 36005. If *dc* is set to kiev and *num* to 7, the only valid *port* value is 37222. With the model shown in Example 11-19, it is possible to configure *dc* as beijing, *num* as 1, and *port* as 37222, which makes no sense at all. A better model is needed, as shown in Example 11-21.

EXAMPLE 11-21 Properly Connected References to Key Leafs in Multikey List Using **deref()**

```
container connect-to {
  leaf dc {
    type leafref {
      path /file-servers/data-center;
    }
  }
  leaf num {
    type leafref {
      path deref(../dc)/../server-num;
    }
  }
  leaf port {
    type leafref {
      path deref(../num)/../port;
    }
  }
}
```

By binding the leafrefs together like this, only valid combinations are configurable.

While `deref()` is a very handy XPath function, especially when connecting several key leafs in leafref paths, the YANG specification actually does not allow this. The `deref()` function is allowed in `must` and `when` expressions, but not in leafref paths, as shown in Example 11-21. Many YANG tools, servers, and clients accept `deref()` in leafref paths, however, and most people think the path is easier to read, write, and understand this way. Therefore, you should not be surprised if you encounter a `deref()` call in a `path` statement.

If you do encounter such an expression while using tools that do not allow the use of `deref()` in leafref paths, you should know any `deref()`-based expression can always be translated into a longer, universally valid expression containing the XPath `current()` function. In computer science circles, a guarantee that it is always possible to replace one kind of simple construct with another more complicated one is referred to as "syntactic sugar." The `deref()` function is syntactic sugar for one or more XPath predicates based on the `current()` function. Example 11-22 shows how the `path` statements from Example 11-21 are translated.

EXAMPLE 11-22 Properly Connected References to Key Leafs in Multikey List Without **deref()** in the Leafref Path

```
container connect-to {
  leaf dc {
    type leafref {
      path /file-servers/data-center;
    }
  }
  leaf num {
    type leafref {
      path /file-servers[data-center=current()/../dc]/server-num;
    }
  }
  leaf port {
    type leafref {
      path /file-servers[data-cetner=current()/../dc][server-num=current()/../num]/port;
    }
  }
}
```

You need to use this longer form based on `current()` in leafref paths whenever you publish a module that needs to have maximum interoperability.

Mixing Up For One, For Any, and For All

Most XPath YANG constraints impose some rule on one particular element, on all elements in a list, or require that at least one element in a list fulfills the requirement. Many YANG authors are mixing up these three forms of constraints and walk away with a syntactically correct XPath expression, but one with a different meaning than intended. Example 11-23 shows a YANG list that the next example will reference in several ways, to demonstrate the different meanings.

EXAMPLE 11-23 List to Be Referenced in the Next Example

```
list interface {
  key name;
  leaf name {
    type string;
  }
  leaf enabled {
    type boolean;
    default true;
  }
}
```

Four different references with constraints on the list in Example 11-23 are shown in Example 11-24. The first, leaf *one*, has a requirement that the particular list instance it points to must have *enabled* set to `true`. The second, leaf *one-without-deref*, does exactly the same thing, just without using the `deref()` XPath function. The third, container *any*, only exists if at least one of the interfaces has enabled set to `true`.

Finally, container *all* exists only if all the interfaces have enabled set to `true`. This is done by checking that there are no interfaces with enabled set to `false`.

Sometimes it may be tempting to use the XPath inequality operator (`!=`). In this particular case, exchanging = for `!=` and removing the `not()` would have worked fine. Many people find the meaning of `!=` in XPath highly nonintuitive, however, so to stay away from surprises, don't use it unless you are completely sure you know how to use it properly in XPath.

EXAMPLE 11-24 Condition Relating to One Specific List Instance (in Two Ways), to at Least One List Instance, and to Every List Instance

```
leaf one {
  type leafref {
    path /interface/name;
  }
  must "deref(current())/../enabled = 'true'";
}

leaf one-without-deref {
  type leafref {
    path /interface/name;
  }
  must "/interface[name=current()]/enabled = 'true'";
}
```

```
container any {
  when "/interface/enabled = 'true'";
…
}

container all {
  when "not(/interface/enabled = 'false')";
…
}
```

Performance of XPath Expressions

XPath is a very sharp tool. A good modeler expresses clearly defined constraints with just a few characters. It is essentially up to the server implementer to make sure the intent of the constraint is implemented in the server in an efficient way, but many servers use XPath evaluation engines to do the validation, and apply various degrees of optimization of the queries before they run. As a modeler, assume that the implementation is rather naive when it comes to evaluating the expression.

Example 11-25 demonstrates what a mess a few characters of XPath can cause.

EXAMPLE 11-25 XPath Expression That Might Be Slow to Validate, if Applied to a Large List

```
list tunnel {
  key "host port";
  leaf host { … }
  leaf port { … }
  leaf local-port {
    must "count(../../tunnel[local-port=current()]) = 1";
```

A simple server implementation that runs an XPath evaluation engine with the given expression for each entry in the list might work in the first tests but will cause problems as the data grows larger. The expression has quadratic complexity in the size of the list, so with 10 entries in the list, the server uses 100 fetch and compare operations. With 1,000 entries, it uses 1,000,000 fetch and compare operations. This is starting to be a nuisance. With a million entries in the list, a trillion fetch and compare operations are needed. The server management interface would essentially come to a halt, or possibly run out of memory.

As a modeler, it's worth considering how the data is being validated for those lists that may have large amounts of data.

In the case just discussed, using a `unique` statement (see the following snippet) instead of a `must` statement might turn this into a constant time operation. A really smart, optimizing server might be able to figure out that the XPath expression is really a uniqueness constraint and then implement it efficiently. Just don't count on it.

```
list tunnel {
  key "host port";
  unique local-port;
```

Backward Compatibility

People often ask whether YANG modules always have to be backward compatible, and, if so, how to determine whether or not a particular set of changes is considered backward compatible.

The simple answer is that RFC 7950 Section 11 (and RFC 6020 Section 10) has a set of rules that should be followed in order to make YANG modules backward compatible. Modules should always be backward compatible, as long as they use the same namespace identifier as an earlier version.

The longer answer is somewhat more complex. Why is it important to be backward compatible? The answer is that this depends. If you have full control over both client and server side of the YANG interface, you might be able to estimate the cost of being backward compatible vs. the cost of not being backward compatible. In this situation, if you find that the cost of being backward compatible is higher, then by all means implement any changes you need however you want. It's your business, after all.

IETF has bound itself to always stick with the backward compatibility rules in the RFCs for the standard modules published by the organization. This is reasonable, given that IETF has very little insight into the costs all around the industry for not being backward compatible. It also has a reputation for stable and useful YANG models to live up to. Breaking this mark of quality too often would not be strategic for IETF.

If you're not IETF, but still have a less than perfect understanding of the damage a non-backward compatible change will inflict on customers, partners and other stakeholders in the industry, it may be wise to stay on the conservative side with any changes. Better to be safe than sorry.

If you still change a YANG module in a non-backward-compatible way, what is the worst that could happen? Could your company get sued over marketing support for NETCONF and YANG (for example RFC 6241, 7950, and so on), then breaking the rules in section 11? Legal advice is not in scope for this book, but having said that and speaking from a layman's perspective, this possibility could probably not be ruled out completely, but sounds rather far-fetched. A much more real problem would be the risks of disappointing customers and, for SDOs, their target audience. Give your customers too much trouble, and you'll soon find them with a competitor, or possibly on their own.

The Rules Versus Staying Relevant

The backward-compatibility rules for configuration in the RFCs are fairly detailed and quite easy to understand. The gist of the whole section can actually be summarized in a sentence or two: All configurations valid in an earlier version of a module must remain valid in all newer versions of a module. The meaning of every valid configuration value must remain the same across the versions.

This means all lists and leafs have to remain in the model (with unchanged names), but you can add optional (nonmandatory) new ones. All enumeration values and all ranges have to stay the same, or can be expanded to allow new values. No new constraints (for example, `must`, `max-elements`, `mandatory`) on previously existing data can be added, but constraints can be removed. A `default` statement on a leaf may be added if there isn't one. The default value of a leaf that already had a `default` statement cannot be changed, however. Descriptions can be updated, but not in a way that changes how readers reasonably interpret the meaning of the text. The full set of specific rules is found in RFC 7950, Section 11. There is no point repeating them all here.

Despite all the restrictions on YANG model changes given, it can hardly be guaranteed that all clients that work fine with an earlier version of a model will also work fine with a later one. A properly programmed client would disregard any leafs it doesn't know about when reading the configuration from a server. But it may not be perfectly prepared for all kind of changes, and it is hard to tell beforehand if it is "perfectly prepared" or not. Also, what if the newer YANG module version changed an enumeration allowing an *interface* to be in *duplex* mode from `true|false` to `true|false|auto`? The client, using the original YANG module version, only knows about true and false, so would only set those. Which is fine. But what if it reads the config for some *interface* and expects true or false, but gets auto? How would it display this state to the user? This situation may not end entirely well.

From a client perspective, it's possible but far from trivial, to deal with changing YANG modules even when the Section 11 rules are followed.

In reality, however, it is the server implementations that tend to have the hardest time living up to the backward-compatibility requirements. Device vendors (and SDOs too, occasionally) find issues in released modules that need fixing, and there may be no way to keep the new YANG backward compatible if the problem is to be fixed. Sometimes vendors accidentally introduce non-backward-compatible changes without realizing it. Or an incompatible change may be consciously introduced to allow a cool new feature quickly and elegantly, disregarding any backward-compatibility issues. Vendors have to stay relevant, after all.

It is not uncommon therefore that device vendors release new versions of YANG modules that don't stick to all the backward compatibility rules in the RFCs.

The proper way for device vendors to handle any strong need to change a module in a non-backward-compatible way, according to the RFCs, is to create a new module (that is, a rather similar module but with a different namespace string). This tells all clients that they need to use and understand the new YANG module to manage that aspect of the server.

In principle, servers could support two or more YANG modules for the same functionality at once. It is then up to the client implementor to pick one or the other. In practice, however, this is often rather hard and expensive for server vendors to implement, test, document, and maintain over a product lifecycle, so this technique is not used much.

As mentioned earlier, YANG leafs, lists, containers, typedefs, and so on can never be removed in newer versions of a module. That would break clients that have not been updated for the newer version of the YANG module. In order to warn readers of the module that a particular leaf, list, or container is no longer considered the best way of interfacing with the server, the statement `status deprecated` or `status obsolete` can be applied to the YANG elements in a newer versions of a module, as shown in Example 11-26.

EXAMPLE 11-26 YANG File with Older Deprecated Leaf and Newer Replacement Leaf

```
module vendor-bgp-config {
...
  revision 2018-06-15 {
    description "Added support for 32-bit AS-numbers.";
  }
  revision 2018-01-01 {
    description "Original version.";
  }
...
    leaf as {
      type uint16;
      status deprecated;
      description
        "AS-number for BGP router. Deprecation note: use long-as instead.";
    }
    leaf long-as {
      type union {
        type uint32;
        type dotted-quad;
      }
      description
        "32-bit AS-number for BGP router in decimal or dotted quad form.";
    }
```

Status `deprecated` means that YANG element is no longer the preferred way to interface with the server, but the functionality is still there. Status `obsolete` means that while the YANG element is still part of the model, it may not have the full original functionality, or may even have no functionality at all. This clearly runs the risk of breaking clients that use it. Since a client using an obsoleted leaf in itself proves that the client has not been updated with the latest module changes, it also means it is unaware of the change and expects the full functionality.

Tooling

Many of the rules set forth in Section 11 of RFC 7950 can be tested algorithmically. In fact, the `pyang` tool, discussed in Chapter 7, "Automation is as Good as the Data Models, Their Related Metadata and the Tools: For the Network Architect and Operator," has a feature that will test two revisions of the same YANG module to see whether or not they are backward compatible. This algorithmic approach is not guaranteed, though. There are non-backward-compatible changes that could occur that are not easily detectable with tooling, and they are not checked today with pyang. In other words, the *semantics* of a node may change without any visible schema change. For example, in an early revision of a module a node's description said that the node represents an interface's bandwidth in bits per second, but in the next revision of the same module, the description is changed to say that the node represents bandwidth in kilobits per second. That changes the semantics or meaning of the node. But unless there is an associated `units` change or some other schema hint, it is very difficult to algorithmically detect this without applying some natural language processing. These types of changes are therefore not allowed by Section 11 of RFC 7950.

Maintaining backward compatibility in YANG modules is a noble goal that does help with adoption, as client and server development may not move at the same pace.

However, it is not without its problems. The strict rules for backward compatibility mean that a module needs to be near perfection from the time it is first released. While additional nodes can be added, nothing can simply be removed, and very few things can be changed while still maintaining backward compatibility. This is especially difficult for network equipment vendors that are moving to support model-based management. As they work to describe their existing architectures and features in YANG, they may have to iterate a number of times to get it right.

Native modules that are automatically generated from source code further compound this problem. As the underlying code and features change, subsequent YANG module revisions inherently pick up non-backward-compatible changes. It is not just vendors that are affected by this. People designing service modules face the same challenge in describing the service layer correctly the first time or else be faced with having to do deviations or if-feature additions to correct issues that arise when the module starts to be implemented.

Fortunately, the industry recognized that this is a problem that needs to be addressed. The OpenConfig group introduced the concept of *semantic versioning* for their YANG modules and bundles. This version follows the guidelines from semver.org and does allow for non-backward-compatible changes provided the major version component of the semantic version is incremented. Within the NETMOD working group in the IETF, a similar semantic version scheme is under discussion, as are guidelines for how non-backward-compatible changes can be made, and clarifying the ramifications of doing so. This notion of aiding in the identification of module compatibility issues directly led to the incorporation of the sematic-version and derived-semantic-version metadata fields in the YANG Catalog—which was covered in Chapters 7, 8, and 9—as well as the tooling to show those compatibility differences.

Interview with the Experts

Q&A with Andy Bierman

Andy Bierman is a co-founder of YumaWorks, Inc., which develops YANG automation tools. He has worked on network management standards since 1989, from RMONMIB to RESTCONF, and designed and developed many distributed network management servers for embedded systems.

He co-authored many IETF RFCs. In the world of YANG automation, he specified the NETCONF protocol (RFCs 6241, 6243, and 6470), the RESTCONF protocol (RFCs 8040 and 8072), the YANG Module Library (RFC 7895), and the Network Configuration Access Control Model (RFC 8341). He also standardized multiple YANG modules, including "A YANG Data Model for Hardware Management" (RFC 8348) and "A YANG Data Model for System Management" (RFC 7317).

Based on his YANG experience, he became one of the first YANG Doctors. Also, he created "Guidelines for Authors and Reviewers of Documents Containing YANG Data Models," specified by the IETF (RFC 8407).

Question:

Andy, you're one of the founding fathers of YANG. Ten years later, did your vision with YANG come true?

Answer:

The vision began with the XMLCONF design team in 2003. That led to the NETCONF WG and NETCONF protocol (RFC 4741) in 2006. But NETCONF did not really go anywhere until YANG came along. Now YANG is being used for many things, not just NETCONF.

Lots of standards-defining organizations, open source projects, and vendors are developing YANG modules. In my opinion, there are three factors to the success of YANG data modeling:

- **Ease of use**: It is fairly easy to get started because most of YANG is very intuitive, and it is not difficult to learn the basics without reading any documentation. There are no complex statements that are mandatory to use. The statements can appear in any order, and the structure of all statements is simple and consistent.
- **Automation tools**: YANG has become sophisticated source code for automation tools. Client and server code generation, transaction management, and many other complex tasks are driven by YANG data models.
- **Advanced features**: YANG has powerful validation and deployment features that are important for real-world platforms. It is easy to extend YANG, allowing new tools to be created all the time.

Question:

You have designed many YANG modules and help people as a YANG Doctor. What are the most common issues you have faced?

Answer:

Some issues have not changed much since I joined MIB Doctors around 1990. These are the biggest mistakes YANG developers make:

- **Not enough reuse**: It has always been difficult to know what data types and other constructs should be reused from existing modules, and which should be created in the new module. However, this is an important step to improving consistency. Designers should always check the standard data types modules first before creating a typedef or grouping.
- **No plan for exports**: Consider how other modules will extend or reuse the new module. This might lead to the use of YANG features or perhaps refactoring a large module into smaller modules. This is an important step to get right the first time, to improve stability.
- **Terse descriptions**: Authors often assume the readers of the YANG module will know as much about the subject matter as they know. This is almost never the case. Good description

statements can really help independent developers create correct implementations. Add detailed reference statements instead of copying normative text from another document.

- **Incorrect XPath**: It is not an error to use nonexistent nodes in XPath or compare a container to a leaf. Often designers do not use tools to validate the XPath in YANG modules. Since YANG is used as source code, these often result in bugs in the implementation. Check the compiler warnings! They are probably correct and your YANG is probably wrong!

Question:

What advice would you give to someone starting with YANG?

Answer:

I suggest learn by doing. Pick a real YANG module you want to understand. Use RFC 7950 as a reference and a learning tool. The examples are really good, so you can find a statement in the real module and easily learn about it from the RFC examples.

Learn to use YANG tools like pyang. Sometimes the "raw YANG" can be difficult to read because there are so many groupings used. Print out the YANG tree diagram and use that to help find your way around the module.

Learn by copying existing modules. Do not just cut-and-paste. Learn what the statements are for that you copy. Learn the design patterns these module use, especially the use of leafrefs to link data structures.

Summary

This chapter started off by going through the module creation process at a high level and explained how a modeler should look at the world: as a four-star general in charge of a battalion.

Next followed a selection of useful tips or discussions on all sorts of practical modeling topics. How do you choose a good module name? What happens once you publish a module? Why is it good to allow a blank configuration? How do you choose good keys for your list? When is it okay to declare a deviation, and what does that imply?

Then there was another list of the most common modeling mistakes to avoid. Many relate to leaving the module ambiguous or imprecise due to missing constraints. Another class of common errors relates to incorrect use of XPath expressions.

Next there was a section about backward compatibility—certainly a subject that can be discussed endlessly and is often seen to provoke heated debates. From a systems, evolvability, and customer retention perspective, finding the right backward-compatibility balance is key, just like being able to communicate clearly around this topic. This is how you build trust. Automation and YANG are all about clear interfaces, and what is a programming interface worth if it cannot be trusted?

Finally, there was an interview with Andy Bierman, one of the YANG founding fathers. Andy is also the editor of RFC 8407, "Guidelines for Authors and Reviewers of Documents Containing YANG Data Models," the document that IETF itself uses as a checklist when reviewing and maintaining the IETF standard modules.

References in This Chapter

As this chapter and book are coming to a close, remember that the aim of this project has always been to serve as the natural starting point, the map, the hands-on lab partner, and the place to return to for finding relevant pointers into deeper material.

Table 11-1 contains the references to external resources discussed in this chapter.

TABLE 11-1 YANG-Modeling Related Documents for Further Reading

Topic	Content
YANG review guidelines	https://tools.ietf.org/html/rfc8407 RFC 8407, "Guidelines for Authors and Reviewers of Documents Containing YANG Data Models."
IETF YANG Doctors	https://datatracker.ietf.org/group/yangdoctors/about/ The team of YANG experts who are assigned to review IETF's YANG modules before publication.
XPath 1.0 specification	https://www.w3.org/TR/1999/REC-xpath-19991116/ The XML Path Language (XPath) Version 1.0 specification. This is the kind of XPath used in YANG.
UUID Description	(search on Wikipedia) Article explaining the nature of a Universally Unique Identifier.
IETF ACL model	https://datatracker.ietf.org/doc/draft-ietf-netmod-acl-model/ IETF's access control list module in the NETMOD work group.
Pyang home page	https://github.com/mbj4668/pyang The home page of the Pyang compiler and tools collection.
W3C regex specification	https://www.w3.org/TR/2004/REC-xmlschema-2-20041028/#regexs Specification of W3C regular expressions.
YANG W3C Regex Expression Validator	https://yangcatalog.org/yangre/ Regular expression validator for YANG pattern statements.
YANG backward-compatibility rules	https://tools.ietf.org/html/rfc7950#section-11 Section 11 of RFC 7950 (for YANG 1.1) and Section 10 of RFC 6020 (for YANG 1.0) list all the YANG backward-compatibility rules.
Semver.org	https://semver.org/ Organization defining a standard for naming and interpreting three-part version numbers. The current version of the Semantic Versioning specification is 2.0.0.

Index

Symbols

^ (caret symbol), 445

$ (dollar sign), 445

// search operator (XPath), 437

!= operator, 455

Numbers

3GPP (3rd Generation Partnership Project), 267

A

AAA (Authorization, Authentication and Accounting), RADIUS, 46

ABORT phase (network-wide transactions), 421

aborted transactions (NETCONF configurations), reasons for, 409

accounting, FCAPS model, 3

ACID tests, 79

actions, 113–116

- input/output parameters, 113
- NETCONF, 184–185
- RESTCONF, 210–211

allocate_vlan() method, service logic, 396

Amazon EC2 (Elastic Compute Cloud), 17

ancestor:: axes (XPath), 437

anchor symbols, 445

Andreessen, Mark, 23

Ansible, 317–319

ANX (Advanced NETCONF Explorer), 328–329

anydata type, model design, 442–443

anyxml type, model design, 442

APIs (Application Programming Interfaces), 85

- applying to complex environments, 19
- benefits of, 18–19
- CLI as an API, 24–26, 57–58
- contract languages, YANG as, 61
- data model-driven management, 70
- NSO, 394–395
- REST APIs and YANG Catalog, 355–356
- YANG as native (primary) language, 373
  - pyangbind, 373
  - YDK, 373–378
- YANG Catalog
  - API calls, 355–358
  - REST APIs, 355–356
  - search API, 357–358

application development

- metadata
  - integrating from Yang Catalog, 355–358
  - keyword searches, 357–358
  - retrieving from Yang Catalog, 355–358
- NETCONF
  - libnetconf2, 371–372
  - ncclient, 366–371
- parsers
  - libyang, 365–366
  - pyang tool, 359–361

pyang tool
embedding, 359–361
plug-ins, 361–364
RESTCONF servers, 372
YANG as native (primary) language, 373
pyangbind, 373
YDK, 373–378
YANG Catalog
API calls, 355–358
integrating metadata, 355–358
keyword metadata searches, 357–358
REST APIs, 355–356
retrieving metadata, 355–358
search API, 357–358
architectures (telemetry), 236–238
assurance, services, 5
asynchronous notifications, NETCONF, 82
AudioZone YANG module, 142–146
augment statements, 142–146, 442
automation, 61
CLI and automation (networking trends), 7–9
DevOPS, networking trends, 11–13
hardware commoditization and disaggregation (networking trends), 7–9
reduced deployment times (networking trends), 6–7
services, 4
axes (XPath), 437

B

backward compatibility, modules, 434, 437, 457
native modules, 460
pyang tool, 459–460
rules versus relevancy, 457–459
bad string patterns, 445–446
base (identities), 107
BBF (Broadband Forum), 265
BGP-LS (BGP Link State) distribution, 15
Bierman, Andy, YANG model design, 460–462
bits type, model design, grouping features, 437
Bjorklund, Martin, 154–156
blank configurations
invalid blank configurations, 447
model design, 435–436
BookZone example. *See also* Store Connect service example
AudioZone YANG module, 142–146
bookzone-example module, 144–145
categorizing data, 106–112
configuration/operational data, separating, 117–122
containers, 98
identifiers, case-sensitivity, 104
isbn mandatory value, 98, 99
languages, 103–104
leafs
leafrefs, 103
mandatory values, 98
true values, 98
lists, 98, 101–102, 103
schemas, representing data in, 97–98
strings, 103–105
tables, representing data in, 97
title mandatory value, 98, 99
tree representations, 102–103
type definitions, 104–105
YANG modules, first example of, 99–100
boolean types, model design, 440
bottleneck modules, 349
bottom-up device templates, service development, 392–394
business telemetry, 231–232

C

:candidate datastores, 152
capabilities, NETCONF, 81–82, 153
CapabilityRequest operations (gNMI), 215–216
CapEx (Capital Expenditures), 16–17
caret symbol (^), 445
case nodes, 115, 130
case-sensitivity (identifiers), 104
categorizing data, BookZone example, 106–112
CBOR (Concise Binary Object Representation), 76
chaining services, 4–5
choice constraints, 449
choice nodes, 115, 130
Claise, Benoit
  CLI and automation, 6
  network management, 59–60
  Python, 12
  SNMP, 32
Clemm, Alex, 249–252
CLI (Command-Line Interface), 24–25
  as API, 24–26, 57–58
  automation and CLI (networking trends), 7–9
  data-model driven management, CLI scripts, 19–20
  Expect scripts, 8–9
  limitations of, 25
  network management, 8–9
  NSO interaction, 405–407
  show commands, 8
  VRF, examples of, 25
clients, NETCONF, 159, 160, 161–162
cloning repositories (modules), 283
close-session messages, NETCONF, 189
clouds
  elastic clouds
    Amazon EC2, 17
    networking trends, 16–18
  managing
    service management, 18
    system-level management, 17–18
collections, RESTCONF, 202
collectors (telemetry), 237
CoMI (CoAP Management Interface), 84
commit messages, NETCONF, 189
COMMIT phase (network-wide transactions), 421, 422
commit-dry-run, service management, 407–409
commits, service management, 407–409
commoditization (hardware), 9–11
common mistakes/problems, 443
  constraints
    applying, 447–448
    expression performance, 456–457
    mixing up constraints, 454–456
    simple constraints, 448–449
  invalid blank configurations, 447
  missing ranges, 444
  multikey leafrefs, 451–454
  strings
    bad string patterns, 445–446
    overusing strings, 444
  unclear optional leafs, 443
  XPath navigation, 449–451
compact mode (Protobufs), 242–243
compiling modules, 339–340
conditional content, 127–128
conditional telemetry, 236
ConfD, testing modules, 340–347
config_e_routers() method, service logic, 396
config_i_routers() method, service logic, 397–398
config_monitoring() method, service logic, 398
configuration datastores, NETCONF, 80

configurations
- blank configurations, model design, 435–436
- configuration/operational data, separating, 117–122
- FCAPS model, 3
- NETCONF configurations
  - aborted transactions, reasons for, 409
  - crypto key pairs, 398–400
  - hello messages, 400–404
  - listing device capabilities, 400–403
  - OOB changes, 404–405, 409
  - replying to hello messages, 403–404
  - verifying operation, 400
- preconfiguration, 149
- publisher configurations and NSO, 406–407
- RESTCONF configurations, creating/updating, 201–202
  - DELETE operations, 206
  - PATCH operations, 205–206
  - POST operations, 202–203, 210–211
  - PUT operations, 203–204
  - YANG-PATCH operations, 207–210
- SNMP, monitoring versus configuration, 57–58
- transient configurations, model design, 442

configured subscriptions (telemetry), 246

CONFIRM phase (network-wide transactions), 422–424

constraints, 122, 123, 125
- choice constraints, 449
- common mistakes/problems
  - applying, 447–448
  - mixing up constraints, 454–456
  - simple constraints, 448–449
- deref function (), 124
- mandatory true constraints, 122–123
- max-element constraints, 449
- min-elements constraints, 449
- must statements, 123–124, 126–127
- unique constraints, 449
- unique statements, 125–126

containers, 98, 127–128, 447

controllers, management architecture, 69–70

coordination (industry), YANG development, 270–274

copy-config messages, NETCONF, 189

create() method, service logic, 395

CRUDX operations, 82

crypto key pairs, NETCONF configurations, 398–400

cURL (client URL), 319–321

curl command, RESTCONF, 194, 207–208, 213

current() function, 126–127, 454

customer experience, services, 4

D

dark deviations, 441

data model-driven management, 59
- advantages of, 19
- APIs, 70
  - applying to complex environments, 19
  - benefits of, 18–19
- CLI scripts, 19–20
- components of, 70–74
- datastores (server architectures), 77–78, 80
- gNMI, protocol comparison table, 78
- NETCONF, protocol comparison table, 78
- networking trends, 18–20
- NMS, 70–71
- orchestrators, 71
- RESTCONF, 63–64, 78
- Schonwalder, Jurgen, 91–92

data model-driven telemetry, 86, 231, 325
- ANX, 328–329
- architectures, 236–238
- collectors, 237
- conditional telemetry, 236
- defined, 21, 230, 231

dial-in/dial-out modes, 241–243
encodings (protocol binding/serialization), 238
events
monitoring versus, 239
NETCONF event notifications, 243–244
YANG event notifications, 245–247
exporting data models, 21–22
feedback loops, 236
hardware-based telemetry versus, 21–22
mapping data models, 22
mechanisms, 242–243
monitoring events versus, 239
need for, 21–22
networking trends, 20–22
OpenConfig telemetry
OpenConfig streaming telemetry, 248–249
YANG Push and Friends versus, 247–248
Pipeline, 326–327
publishers, 237
reasons for using, 21–22
routers
destination groups, 241
sensor groups, 241
subscriptions, 241
sensor paths, 238
SNMP
data model-driven telemetry versus, 21–22
transitioning to telemetry, 232–235
streaming telemetry, 238 248–249
subscriptions
configured subscriptions, 246
creating, 241
dynamic subscriptions, 246–247
IETF YANG subscriptions, 244–245
on-change subscriptions, 239–241
periodic subscriptions, 239–241
requests, 238
transport protocols, 238, 239
use cases, 235–236
YANG Push and Friends, 244–245, 247–248
data models, 48
information models versus, 39–41, 64
managing networks with different data models, 41–48
properties of, 66–67
UML, 40
data nodes, 130
data tree paths, 450
datastores (server architectures), 77–78
:candidate datastores, 152
:intended datastores, 153–154
NETCONF, 80
NMDA, 152–154
:operational datastores, 153–154
pub/sub services, 244
:running datastores, 152
:startup datastores, 152
default and mandatory data, 126–127
default origins (NMDA), 190
default statements, 122–123, 441, 443
DELETE operations, creating/updating RESTCONF configurations, 206
delete-config messages, NETCONF, 189
delivering services, 4
dependencies, YANG modules, 260–262
deployments, reduced deployment times (networking trends), 6–7
deref() function, 124, 453–454, 455
dereferences, 129
derived-from() function, 128
designing modules, 336
compiling modules, 339–340
learning from others, 337–339
sharing metadata, 347–349
testing modules
ConfD, 340–347
yanglit tool, 347

validation, 339–340
YANG Catalog and, 337–339
destination groups (routers/telemetry), 241
deviation statements, 148–149
dark deviations, 441
light deviations, 441
model design, 441
device synchronization, 413–417
DevOPS
defined, 12–13
networking trends, 11–13
dial-in/dial-out modes (telemetry), 241–243
directories (modules), 283
disaggregation of software from hardware, 9–11
disconnected multikey leafrefs, 451–454
DMTF (Distributed Management Task Force), 266
documentation, OpenDaylight MD-SAL, 264
dollar sign ($), 445
double slash (//) search operator, 437
downloading pyang tool, 284
DSL (Domain-Specific Languages), 66
dynamic subscriptions (telemetry), 246–247

E

EANTC (European Advanced Networking Test Center), interoperability testing, 273
edit-config messages, NETCONF, 176–181
edit-data operations, NMDA, 189, 190
elastic clouds
Amazon EC2, 17
networking trends, 16–18
embedding pyang tool, 359–361
empty leafs, 116
empty types, model design, 440
encodings (protocol binding/serialization), 74
CBOR, 76
JSON, 75–76
Protobufs, 76
telemetry and, 238
XML, 75
enumeration, model design, 437–438
error-message statements, 127
ETSI (European Telecommunication Standards Institute), YANG development, 267
events
actions, 113–116
NETCONF, 243
event notifications, 243
stream notifications, 244
subscription notifications, 243, 244
notifications, 113, 116–117
RPCs, 113–116
telemetry monitoring versus events, 239
YANG event notifications, subscribing to, 245–247
Expect scripts, CLI (Command-Line Interface), 8–9
expenditures
CapEx, 16–17
OpEx, 16–17, 24
expressions (XPath)
performance, 456–457
quadratic complexity, 456
extension keywords, 146–148
extractable/non-extractable metadata, 289

F

FCAPS model, 3
accounting, 3
automation, 4
benefits of, 3
configurations, 3
faults, 3
performance, 3
security, 3, 4

FCAPS+E (Energy Management), 4
FD.io, 267
feature statements, 441
feedback loops
network management, 89–90
telemetry as, 236
finding modules, 283
grep command, 288
by metadata, 288–290
YANG Catalog, 287, 288–290
flow records, NetFlow and IPFIX
basic model, 34–35
development of, 33–34
example of flow records, 35–36
Forces (FORwarding and Control Element Separation), 15
framing messages, NETCONF, 169–171

G

get messages, NETCONF, 181–184
get_interface() method, service logic, 397
GetBulk operations, SNMP (Simple Network Management Protocol), 232, 233
get-config messages, NETCONF, 174–176
get-data operations, NMDA (Network Management Datastore Architecture), 189–190
GetNext operation, SNMP (Simple Network Management Protocol), 232, 233
GetRequest operations (gNMI), 216–219
get-schema messages, NETCONF, 189
gNMI (gRPC Network Management Interface), 19, 83–84, 214, 225, 270
CapabilityRequest operations, 215–216
GetRequest operations, 216–219
gRPC, 214–215
Protobufs, 76
protocol comparison table, 78
SetRequest operations, 219–224
SubscribeRequest operations, telemetry, 224–225
Google Protobufs. *See* Protobufs
Goyang, 85
grep command (UNIX), 288
grouping
data, 119
nodes, 130
reusing groupings, 440–441
gRPC, 214–215

H

hardware
commoditization, 9–11
data-model driven telemetry versus, 21–22
disaggregation, 9–11
HATEOAS (Hypermedia As The Engine Of Application State), 191, 195
hello messages
NETCONF, 161, 171–174
conformance type, 403–404
listing device capabilities, 400–403
module-set-id attributes, 403
replying to hello messages, 403–404
NSO, device synchronization, 413–417
HTTPie, 302–303

I

identifiers
case-sensitivity, 104
choosing, 435
identity, 107, 108
base, 107
identityref, 108–109
kind-of relations, 438
model design, 438
object-oriented identities, 438

IEEE (Institute of Electrical and Electronics Engineers), 266

IESG (Internet Engineering Steering Group), MIB modules (writable), 33

IETF (Internet Engineering Steering Group), 430

key data model-driven RFCs, 256–257

YANG development

dependencies, 260–262

ietf-routing YANG module, 260

key data model-driven RFCs, 256–257

models, 260

module and submodule RFCs, 257–259

modules and submodules extracted from IETF drafts, 259–260

YANG Push and Friends, 246, 247–248

YANG subscriptions and telemetry, 244–245

ietf-interfaces.yang module, 150–151, 152

ietf-routing YANG module, 260

ietf-routing@2018-03-13.yang module, 283–284

if-feature statements, model design, 437–438

ifIndex, defined, 41

impact analysis, 349

implement conformance type, NETCONF hello messages, 403–404

import conformance type, NETCONF hello messages, 403–404

import statements, 143–144

industry coordination, YANG development, 270–272

inequality operator (!=), 455

information models, 48

data models versus, 39–41, 64

UML information models, turning into data models, 64

input nodes, 130, 132–133

input/output parameters, actions, 113

installing

Netconf-console, 302–303

pyang tool, 284

YANG Suite tool (YANG Catalog), 299

instance data, 63, 97

:intended datastores, 153–154

intended origins (NMDA), 190

intent-based networking, networking trends, 22–23

interoperability testing, YANG development, 272–274

invalid blank configurations, 447

IP SLA, performance monitoring/reporting, 8

IPFIX (IP Flow Information Export)

basic model, 34–35

development of, 33–34

flow records, 35–36

limitations of, 36–37

NetFlow and, 45–46

isbn mandatory value (BookZone example), 98, 99

ITU-T (ITU Telecommunication) Standardization Sector, YANG development, 267

J

jq command, 302–322

JSON (JavaScript Object Notation), 75–76

RESTCONF and, 75–76

services, delivery, 4

K

key data model-driven RFCs, IETF and YANG development, 256–257

key statements, mulitple keys in, 119

key title statements, 98

keyless lists, 119, 440

keys

crypto key pairs, NETCONF configurations, 398–400

keys, 439

model design, choosing keys, 439–440

natural keys, 439

UUID, 439

keyword metadata searches in YANG Catalog, 357–358
kill-session messages, NETCONF, 189
kind-of relations (identities), 438
Krejci, Radek, 380–381
Kuarsing, Victor, 48–50

L

language native (primary), YANG as
pyangbind, 373
YDK, 373–378
languages
BookZone example, 103–104
YANG, 103–104
Larsson, Kristian, 425–428
leaf-list, 145
leafref, 103, 128–130
model design, 436–437
multikey leafrefs, 451–454
require instance false statements, 436–437
schema nodes, 130–142
leafs
default statements, 122–123
empty leafs, 116
leafrefs, 103, 128–130
multikey leafrefs, 451–454
schema nodes, 130–142
mandatory leafs, 447
mandatory values, 98
optional leafs, 443
true values, 98
type statements, 98
unclear optional leafs, 443
learned origins (NMDA), 190
libnetconf2, 371–372
libyang, parsers, 365–366
light deviations, 441
lists, 98
BookZone example, 101–102
key statements, mulitple keys in, 119
keyless lists, 119, 440
leaf-list, 145
leafref, 103
max keyword, 101–102
NETCONF device capabilities, 400–403
ordered-by users lists, 439
lock messages, NETCONF, 189
logic (services), 394
allocate_vlan() method, 396
config_e_routers() method, 396
config_i_routers() method, 397–398
config_monitoring() method, 398
create() method, 395
get_interface() method, 397
template variables, 396
loops (feedback)
network management, 89–90
telemetry as, 236
Lupton, William, 350–351

M

managing
clouds
service management, 18
system-level management, 17–18
services
aborted transactions, reasons for, 409
commit-dry-run, 407–409
commit, 409
modifying services, 410–412
NSO/CLI interaction, 405–407
operational state, 409–410
restoring services, 412
management architecture
controllers, 69–70

operators, 70
orchestrators, 70
RBAC, 70
YANG modules, 70
mandatory leafs, 447
mandatory true constraints, 122–123
mandatory true statements, 443
mandatory values, 98, 123–124, 126–127
mapping
YANG objects from MIB modules, 68–69
YANG-to-RESTCONF mapping, 75–76
max keyword, lists, 101–102
max-element constraints, 449
MEF Forum, YANG development, 265, 266
messages
framing, NETCONF, 169–171
NETCONF, 160, 189
close-session messages, 189
commit messages, 189
copy-config messages, 189
delete-config messages, 189
edit-config messages, 176–181
get messages, 181–184
get-config messages, 174–176
get-schema messages, 189
hello messages, 161, 171–174
kill-session messages, 189
lock messages, 189
message framing, 169–171
overview of, 171
partial-lock messages, 189
validate messages, 189
metadata
extractable/non-extractable metadata, 289
non-extractable/extractable metadata, 289
searching for modules by, by metadata, 288–290
sharing, 347–349
YANG Catalog
integrating metadata, 355–358
keyword searches, 357–358
retrieving metadata, 355–358
MIB modules
SNMP, 30
writable MIB modules, 33
YANG objects, mapping from MIB modules, 68–69
min-elements constraints, 449
missing ranges, 444
mistakes/problems, 443
constraints
applying, 447–448
expression performance, 456–457
mixing up constraints, 454–456
simple constraints, 448–449
invalid blank configurations, 447
missing ranges, 444
multikey leafrefs, 451–454
overusing strings, 444
strings, bad string patterns, 445–446
unclear optional leafs, 443
XPath navigation, 449–451
Moberg, Carl, 275–278
model-driven telemetry, 86, 231
models
designing, 431–432
anydata type, 442–443
anyxml type, 442–443
augment statements, 442
bits type, grouping features, 437
blank configurations, 435–436
boolean types, 440
choosing keys, 439–440
choosing YAG identifiers, 435
deviation statements, 441
empty types, 440
enumeration, 437–438
identities, 438

if-feature statements, 437–438
leafrefs, 436–437
naming modules, 433–434
publishing modules, 434
reusing groupings, 440–441
transient configurations, 442
XPath, 437
modularity, 146
multiple models, implementing for specific functionality, 274–275
YANG models, 61
service YANG models, 70
updating, 260

modifying services, 410–412

modularity in YANG models, 146

module

backward compatibility, 434, 437, 457
native modules, 460
pyang tool, 459–460
rules versus relevancy, 457–459
BookZone example, first example of, 99–100
bottleneck modules, 349
choosing, 283
compiling, 339–340
complexity of, 284
designing, 336
compiling modules, 339–340
learning from others, 337–339
sharing metadata, 347–349
testing modules, 340–347
validation, 339–340
YANG Catalog and, 337–339
deviation statements, 441
directories, 283
finding, 283
grep command, 288
by metadata, 288–290
YANG Catalog, 287, 288–290
ietf-routing@2018–03–13.yang module, 283–284
impact analysis, 349
metadata
integrating from Yang Catalog, 355–358
retrieving metadata from Yang Catalog, 355–358
sharing, 347–349
namespace strings, 433
naming, 100–101, 433–434
prefix strings, 434
publishing, 434
pyang tool
downloading/installing, 284
embedding, 359–361
printing modules in output formats, 285–287
viewing modules in tree output, 285–287, 305–310, 312–314
repositories
cloning, 283
creating with YANG Suite tool (YANG Catalog), 301
revision statements, 101
semantic versioning, 460
submodules, 440
testing
ConfD, 340–347
yanglit tool, 347
validation, 339–340
viewing details via YANG Catalog, 291–294
YANG
models, network element YANG modules, 69
namespace statements, 100
tree representations, 102–103
YANG Catalog
tree output view, 290–291
viewing module details, 291–294
YANG Suite tool, 294–298, 301–302

YANG modules, 61, 70
dependencies, 260–262
ietf-routing YANG module, 260
module and submodule RFCs, 257–259
module sets, 301
modules and submodules extracted from IETF drafts, 259–260
service delivery YANG modules, 70
types of, 67–68
module-set-id attributes, NETCONF hello messages, 403
monitoring
SNMP, monitoring versus configuration, 57–58
telemetry, events versus monitoring, 239
mulitple keys in key statements, 119
multikey leafrefs, 451–454
multiple models, implementing for specific functionality, 274–275
must statements, 123–124, 126–127, 447–448

N

namespace statements
prefixes, 100–101
YANG modules, 100
namespace strings, 433
naming, 460–462
device naming conventions, 385
modules, 100–101, 433–434
native modules, backward compatibility, 460
natural keys, 439
ncclient, 366–371
NCS. *See* NSO
NETCONF, 78–80, 158–159
ACID tests, 79, 81–82
actions, 184–185
Ansible, 317–319
ANX, 328–329
asynchronous notifications, 82
capabilities, 81–82, 153
clients, 159, 160, 161–162
client/server interaction, 77–78
configuration datastores, 80
defined, 58–59, 79
development of, 58–59
device configuration
aborted transactions, reasons for, 409
crypto key pairs, 398–400
hello messages, 400–404
listing device capabilities, 400–403
OOB changes, 404–405, 409
replying to hello messages, 403–404
verifying operation, 400
device synchronization, 413–417
event notifications, 243
event notifications, 243
stream notifications, 244
subscription notifications, 243, 244
fundamentals of, 159–162
hello messages
conformance type, 403–404
listing device capabilities, 400–403
module-set-id attributes, 403
replying to hello messages, 403–404
interoperability testing, 273
libnetconf2, 371–372
messages, 160, 189
close-session messages, 189
commit messages, 189
copy-config messages, 189
delete-config messages, 189
edit-config messages, 176–181
framing, 169–171
get messages, 181–184
get-config messages, 174–176
get-schema messages, 189
hello messages, 161, 171–174
kill-session messages, 189

lock messages, 189
overview of, 171
partial-lock messages, 189
validate messages, 189
ncclient, 366–371
netconf-console, 317
adding static routes, 314–315
determining support for devices, 303–310
displaying operational data, 315–317
gathering configured routing data, 310–312
installing, 302–303
passing modules to pyang tree view, 312–314
network management, 86–91
network managers, 159–160
network-wide transactions
ABORT phase, 421
COMMIT phase, 421, 422
CONFIRM phase, 422–424
point of no return, 422
PREPARE phase, 417–421
:notification capabilities, 186
notifications, 185–188
operations, 80–81
pre-provisioning, 149
preconfiguration, 149
protocol comparison table, 78
RESTCONF and, 82–83, 192–193
:rollback-on-error capability, 302–322
RPCs, 160, 166–169, 184–185
SDN, 15
security, 82
servers, 159, 160, 161, 186
SSH, 160–161
subsystems, 161
transactions, 78
ACID tests, 79, 81–82
three-phase transactions, 81–82
XML, 75, 160
attributes, 163
namespaces, 163–165
processing instructions, 166
tags, 162
YANG and, 5
YANG Suite tool (YANG Catalog), 299–302

netconf subsystem, 161

netconf-console, 317
configured routing data, gathering, 310–312
installing, 302–303
operational data, displaying, 315–317
pyang tree view, passing modules to, 312–314
static routes, adding, 314–315
support for devices, determining, 303–310

NetFlow and IPFIX, 45–46
basic model, 34–35
development of, 33–34
flow records, 35–36
limitations of, 36–37

network diagram, Store Connect service example, 385

network element YANG modules, 69

network management
feedback loops, 89–90
NETCONF, 86–91
transitioning from network operators to operations engineers, 60–61

network managers, NETCONF, 159–160

networking trends
CLI and automation, 7–9
data-model driven management, 18–20
data-model driven telemetry, 20–22
DevOPS, 11–13
elastic clouds (networking trends), 16–18
hardware commoditization and disaggregation, 9–11
intent-based networking, 22–23
NFV, 15–16
reduced deployment times, 6–7
SDN, 13–15
"software is eating the world," 23–24

NFV (Network Function Virtualization), 5
- cloud management, 18
- networking trends, 15–16

Nilsen-Nygaard, Einar, 331–334

NMDA (Network Management Datastore Architecture), 152–154, 171
- edit-data operations, 189, 190
- get-data operations, 189–190
- origins, 190

NMS (Network Management Systems)
- data model-driven management, 70–71
- data models, 48
- information models, 48
- IPFIX and, 45–46
- NetFlow and, 45–46
- RADIUS, 46, 48
- screen-scraping, 44–45
- SNMP, 28, 44, 45
- TACACS+, 47–48

non-extractable/extractable metadata, 289

not() function, 128

:notification capabilities, NETCONF, 186

notifications
- event notifications, 113, 116–117, 243–244
- NETCONF, 185–188, 243–244
- RESTCONF, 212–213
- SNMP, 232
- YANG, event notifications, 245–247

NSO (Network Services Orchestrator), 330, 405
- aborted transactions, reasons for, 409
- CLI interaction, 405–407
- commit-dry-run, 407–409
- commits, 409
- device synchronization, 413–417
- hello messages, device synchronization, 413–417
- modifying services, 410–412
- NCS and, 394–395
- network-wide transactions
  - ABORT phase, 421
  - COMMIT phase, 421, 422
  - CONFIRM phase, 422–424
  - point of no return, 422
  - PREPARE phase, 417–421
- publisher configurations, 406–407
- restoring services, 412
- services, operational state, 409–410

O

object-oriented identities, 438

on-change subscriptions (telemetry), 239–241

OOB (Out-Of-Band) changes, NETCONF configurations, 404–405, 409

Open ROADM MSA, 267

open source projects, YANG development, 267–268

Open Source Sysrepo project, 267

OpenConfig
- gNMI, 83–84, 214
- OpenConfig Consortium, 214
- streaming telemetry, 86
- telemetry
  - OpenConfig streaming telemetry, 248–249
  - YANG Push and Friends versus, 247–248
- YANG model, 268–270

OpenDaylight Project, The, 14
- OpenDaylight MD-SAL documentation, 264
- YANG development, 263–264

OpenFlow, 14

:operational datastore, 153–154

operational state, services, 409–410

operational telemetry, 231, 232

operations
- CRUDX operations, 82
- NETCONF, 80–81
- separating configuration/operational data, 117–122

operators, management architecture, 70
OpEx (Operating Expenditures), 16–17, 24
optional leafs, 443
orchestrators
data model-driven management, 71
management architecture, 70
ordered-by user lists, 439
origins, NMDA (Network Management Datastore Architecture), 190
output nodes, 130
overusing strings, 444
OVSDB (Open vSwitch Database) management protocol, 14

P

parsers, building with
libyang, 365–366
pyang tool, 359–361
partial-lock messages, NETCONF, 189
PATCH operations, creating/updating RESTCONF configurations, 205–206
pattern statements, 445–446
PCEP (Path Computation Element Communication), 14
performance
FCAPS model, 3
IP SLA, 8
SNMP, 30
periodic subscriptions (telemetry), 239–241
perl-regex, 445
ping operations, 184
Pipeline, 326–327
plug-ins, pyang tool, 361–364
point of no return (transactions), 422
pointers, 128–131
polling (SNMP), 232–234
POST operations, creating/updating RESTCONF configurations, 202–203, 210–211
Postman, 322–325
pre-provisioning, 149
preceeding-sibling:: axes (XPath), 437
preconfigurations, 149
predictates, 129
prefix strings, 434
prefixes, namespace statements, 100–101
PREPARE phase (network-wide transactions), 417–421
primary language, YANG as, 373
pyangbind, 373
YDK, 373–378
printing modules in output formats, pyang tool, 285–287
problems/mistakes, 443
constraints
applying, 447–448
expression performance, 456–457
mixing up constraints, 454–456
simple constraints, 448–449
invalid blank configurations, 447
missing ranges, 444
multikey leafrefs, 451–454
overusing strings, 444
strings, bad string patterns, 445–446
unclear optional leafs, 443
XPath navigation, 449–451
Pronghorn, 330–331
Protobufs, 76
compact mode, 242–243
self-describing mode, 242–243
protocols
binding. *See* encodings
gNMI, protocol comparison table, 78
NETCONF, protocol comparison table, 78
RESTCONF, protocol comparison table, 78
provisioning, 149
pub/sub services, 244
publishers (telemetry), 237
publishing modules, 434

purchase operations, 184–185

PUT operations, creating/updating RESTCONF configurations, 203–204

pyang tool

backward compatibility, 459–460

downloading/installing, 284

embedding, 359–361

plug-ins, 361–364

printing modules in output formats, 285–287

tree output, viewing modules in, 285–287, 305–310, 312–314

pyangbind, 85, 373

Python, 11–12

ncclient, 366–371

Netconf-console, 317

configured routing data, gathering, 310–312

installing, 302–303

operational data, displaying, 315–317

pyang tree view, passing modules to, 312–314

static routes, adding, 314–315

support for devices, determining, 303–310

pyang tool

embedding, 360–361

parsers, 359–361

YANG Catalog, retrieving metadata, 357

python-regex, 445

Q

quadratic complexity (expressions), 456

R

RADIUS (Remote Authentication Dial-In User Service), 46, 48

ranges (missing), 444

RBAC (Role-Based Access Control), 70

reduced deployment times (networking trends), 6–7

regex patterns, 445

repositories (modules)

cloning, 283

creating, YANG Suite tool (YANG Catalog), 301

require instance false statements, 390, 436–437

REST APIs and YANG Catalog, 355–356

RESTCONF, 82–83, 190, 319

actions, 210–211

calls

as transactions, 83

validation, 83

collections, 202

configurations, creating/updating, 201–202

DELETE operations, 206

PATCH operations, 205–206

POST operations, 202–203, 210–211

PUT operations, 203–204

YANG-PATCH operations, 207–210

cURL, 319–321

curl command, 194, 207–208, 213

data-model driven management, 63–64

HTTPie, 302–303

jq command, 302–322

JSON and, 75–76

NETCONF and, 82–83, 192–193

notifications, 212–213

operations, CRUDX operations, 82

Postman, 322–325

principles of, 191–192

protocol comparison table, 78

resources, reading/navigating, 194–201

servers, 193–194, 372

YANG-to-RESTCONF mapping, 75–76

restoring services, 412

reusing, groupings, 440–441

revision statements, 101, 109–112, 116–117

RFCs (Remote Function Calls)

key data model-driven RFCs, 256–257

RFC 3444, 64

RFC 3535, 56–58, 65, 90–91, 159, 222
RFC 5277, 243–244, 245–246, 247
RFC 6020, 63
RFC 6241, 68–69, 79, 159
RFC 6242, 159
RFC 6244, 65
RFC 6643, 69
RFC 7047, 14
RFC 7049, 76
RFC 7159, 75–76
RFC 7223, 69, 150–151
RFC 7252, 84
RFC 7650, 63
RFC 7923, 244, 245–246
RFC 8040, 76, 83
RFC 8259, 75
RFC 8340, 103
RFC 8341, 70
RFC 8342, 152, 153
RFC 8343, 152
RFC 8407, 430
YANG module and submodule RFCs, 257–259

ROADM, Open ROADM MSA and YANG development, 267

:rollback-on-error capability, NETCONF, 302–322

routers, telemetry
destination groups, 241
sensor groups, 241
subscriptions, 241

RPCs (Remote Procedure Calls), 113–116
gRPC, 214–215
NETCONF, 160, 166–169, 184–185
ping operations, 184
purchase operations, 184–185
setup-interface operations, 184
YANG Suite tool (YANG Catalog), 294–298

:running datastore, 152

S

schemas, 63
defined, 63
get-schema messages, NETCONF, 189
instance data and, 97
nodes, 115, 130–142
representing data in, 97–98
tree paths, 450
XSD, 75

Schonwalder, Jurgen, 91–92

screen-scraping, 44–45

scripts, YANG Suite tool (YANG Catalog), 294–298

SDN (Software-Defined Networking), 4–5, 15
BGP-LS distribution, 15
as control plane separation paradigm, 15
Forces, 15
NETCONF/YANG, 15
networking trends, 13–15
OpenFlow, 14
PCEP, 14

SDOs, YANG development, 267–268

search API, YANG Catalog, 357–358

searching
// search operator (XPath), 437
modules
grep command, 288
by metadata, 288–290
YANG Catalog, YANG Search feature, 288–290
YANG Catalog, keyword metadata searches, 357–358

security
FCAPS model, 3, 4
NETCONF, 82

self-describing mode (Protobufs), 242–243

semantic versioning, 460

sensor groups (routers/telemetry), 241

sensor paths, telemetry architectures, 238

serialization. *See* encodings
servers
architectures (datastores), 77–78
:candidate datastore, 152
:intended datastore, 153–154
:operational datastore, 153–154
:running datastore, 152
:startup datastore, 152
NETCONF, 80
NMDA, 152–154
pub/sub services, 244
NETCONF, 159, 160, 161, 186
RESTCONF servers, 193–194, 372
SSH, 161–162
service delivery YANG modules, 70
service YANG models, 70
services
assembling, 4–5
assurance, 5
automation, 4
bottom-up device templates, service development, 392–394
chaining, 4–5
cloud management, 18
customer experience, 4
delivery, 4
deploying, reduced deployment times (networking trends), 7
device synchronization, 413–417
logic, 394
allocate_vlan() method, 396
config_e_routers() method, 396
config_i_routers() method, 397–398
config_monitoring() method, 398
create() method, 395
get_interface() method, 397
template variables, 396
managing
aborted transactions, reasons for, 409
commit dry-run, 407–409
commits, 409
modifying services, 410–412
NSO/CLI interaction, 405–407
operational state, 409–410
restoring services, 412
network-wide transactions
ABORT phase, 421
COMMIT phase, 421, 422
CONFIRM phase, 422–424
point of no return, 422
PREPARE phase, 417–421
NSO, 330
Pronghorn, 330–331
pub/sub services, 244
SFC, 4–5
Store Connect service example, 385
bottom-up device templates, 392–394
device naming conventions, 385
network diagram, 385
networking staff tasks, 386
service logic, 394–398
service management, 405–412
top-down service development, 386–392
top-down service development, 386–392
SetRequest operations (gNMI), 219–224
setup-interface operations, 184
SFC (Service Function Chaining), 4–5
sftp subsystems, 161
sharing module metadata, 347–349
show commands
CLI, 8
show interface command, 44
SNMP (Simple Network Management Protocol), 27, 32, 158–159
basic model, 28
correlating with syslog messages, 45
GetBulk operations, 232, 233
GetNext operation, 232, 233

interface table, 233
limitations of, 29, 30–32, 44
MIB modules, 30, 33
monitoring versus configuration, 57–58
notifications, 232
performance, 30
polling, 232–234
requirements for, 30
SNMP Agents, 28–29
SNMP Manager, 28–29
SNMPsec, 27
SNMPv1, 27, 29
SNMPv2c, 27
SNMPv2p, 27
SNMPv2u, 27
SNMPv3, 27–28, 29
telemetry
data-model driven telemetry versus SNMP, 21–22
transitioning to, 232–235
UDP and, 233–234
uses of, 29

software
Andreessen, Mark, 23
disaggregation, 9–11
SDN, 13–14, 15
BGP-LS distribution, 15
as control plane separation paradigm, 15
Forces, 15
NETCONF/YANG, 15
OpenFlow, 14
PCEP, 14
"software is eating the world" (networking trends), 23–24

splitting functionality, 146

SSH (Secure Shell)
ncclient, 367–368
NETCONF, 160–161
servers, 161–162
subsystems, sftp, 161

:startup datastore, 152

status deprecated statements, 458–459

status obsolete statements, 458–459

Store Connect service example, 385. *See also* BookZone example
device naming conventions, 385
device synchronization, 413–417
network diagram, 385
networking staff tasks, 386
network-wide transactions
ABORT phase, 421
COMMIT phase, 421, 422
CONFIRM phase, 422–424
point of no return, 422
PREPARE phase, 417–421
service development
bottom-up device templates, 392–394
top-down development, 386–392
service logic, 394–398
service management
aborted transactions, reasons for, 409
commit dry-run, 407–409
commits, 409
modifying services, 410–412
NSO/CLI interaction, 405–407
operational state, 409–410
restoring services, 412

stream notifications (NETCONF), 244

streaming telemetry, 238, 248–249

strings, 101, 103–104
bad string patterns, 445–446
defining type of, 104–105
overusing strings, 444

subclassing, 107

submodules, 440
RFCs, 257–259
submodules extracted from IETF drafts, 259–260

SubscribeRequest operations (gNMI), telemetry, 224–225

subscription notifications (NETCONF), 243, 244

subscriptions (telemetry)

- configured subscriptions, 246
- creating, 241
- dynamic subscriptions, 246–247
- IETF YANG subscriptions, 244–245
- on-change subscriptions, 239–241
- periodic subscriptions, 239–241
- requests, 238

subsystems

- NETCONF, 161
- SSH, sftp, 161

synchronization (devices), 413–417

"syntactic sugar," 454

synthetic keys, 439

Syslog, 37–38

- basic model, 38
- defined, 38
- limitations of, 39
- messages, correlating SNMP with, 45

Sysrepo, YANG development, 267

system origins (NMDA), 190

T

tables

- categorizing data, 106
- representing data in, 97

TACACS+ (Terminal Access Controller Access-Control System Plus), 47–48

telemetry, 86, 231, 325

- ANX, 328–329
- architectures, 236–238
- business telemetry, 231–232
- Clemm, Alex, 249–252
- collectors, 237
- conditional telemetry, 236
- data-model driven telemetry
  - defined, 21
  - exporting data models, 21–22
  - hardware-based telemetry versus, 21–22
  - mapping data models, 22
  - need for, 21–22
  - networking trends, 20–22
  - reasons for using, 21–22
  - SNMP versus, 21–22
- defined, 230, 231
- dial-in/dial-out modes, 241–243
- encodings (protocol binding/serialization), 238
- events
  - monitoring versus, 239
  - NETCONF event notifications, 243–244
  - YANG event notifications, 245–247
- feedback loops, 236
- hardware-based telemetry versus data-model driven telemetry, 21–22
- mechanisms, 242–243
- model-driven telemetry, 86, 231
- monitoring, events versus, 239
- OpenConfig telemetry
  - OpenConfig streaming telemetry, 86, 248–249
  - YANG Push and Friends versus, 247–248
- operational telemetry, 231, 232
- Pipeline, 326–327
- publishers, 237
- routers
  - destination groups, 241
  - sensor groups, 241
  - subscriptions, 241
- sensor paths, 238
- SNMP, transitioning to telemetry, 232–235
- streaming telemetry, 238, 248–249
- SubscribeRequest operations (gNMI), 224–225
- subscriptions
  - on-change subscriptions, 239–241
  - configured subscriptions, 246
  - creating, 241

dynamic subscriptions, 246–247
IETF YANG subscriptions, 244–245
periodic subscriptions, 239–241
requests, 238
transport protocols, 238, 239
use cases, 235–236
YANG Push and Friends, 244–245, 247–248

templates
bottom-up device templates, service development, 392–394
services, variables, 396

testing
interoperability testing, 272–274
modules
ConfD, 340–347
yanglit tool, 347

title mandatory value (BookZone example), 98, 99
top-down service development, 386–392
transactions (NETCONF), 78
ACID tests, 79, 81–82
three-phase transactions, 81–82

transient configurations, model design, 442
transport protocols, 238, 239
tree diagrams, with XPath navigation, 124–125
tree output view
pyang tool, 303–310, 312–314
YANG Catalog, 290–291

tree representations, 102–103, 150–151
true values, 98
type definitions, 104–105
type statements, 98
typedef, reusing groupings, 440

U

UDP (User Datagram Protocol), SNMP and, 233–234
UML (Unified Modeling Language), 40, 64
unclear optional leafs, 443
union YANG construct, type definitions, 105
unique constraints, 449
unique statements, 125–126, 456–457
unknown origins (NMDA), 190
updating YANG models, 260
URL (Uniform Resource Locators)
cURL (client URL), 319–321
server URL finding in RESTCONF, 193–194

uses nodes, 130
uses statements, 119, 441
UUID (Universally Unique Identifiers), 439

V

validation
modules, 339–340
RESTCONF calls, 83
validate messages, NETCONF, 189
YANG Validator, 339–340
YANGRE, 340

versioning, 146
virtualization
NFV, 5, 15–16
VNF, 5

VRF (Virtual Routing and Forwarding) and CLI, 25

W

W3C-regex, 445
Ward, David, 15
Watsen, Kent, 225–226
when statements, 127
White, Russ, 50–52
writable MIB modules, 33

X

XML (Extensible Markup Language), 75
ncclient, 367–368
NETCONF, 79–80, 160

attributes, 163
namespaces, 163–165
processing instructions, 166
tags, 162
XSD, 75

XPath, 98–99
// search operator, 437
axes, 437
common mistakes/problems
mixing up constraints, 454–456
path navigation, 449–451
current() function, 126–127, 454
data tree paths, 450
deref() function, 124, 453–454, 455
derived-from() function, 128
expressions
performance, 456–457
quadratic complexity, 456
inequality operator (!=), 455
model design, 437
navigation, 449–451
not() function, 128
predictates, 129
schema tree paths, 450
tree diagrams, 124–125

XPath 1.0, 437

xRAN, 267

XSD (XML Schema Description), 75

Y - Z

YANG, 63
3GPP and YANG development, 267
actions, 113–116
as API contract language, 61
augment statements, 142–146
bases (identities), 107
basic model, 61
BBF and YANG development, 265
case nodes, 115
choice nodes, 115
constraints, 122, 123, 125
mandatory true constraints, 122–123
must statements, 123–124, 126–127
unique statements, 125–126
containers, 98, 127–128
defined, 61, 63
development of, 154–156, 265
3GPP and, 267
BBF and, 265
DMTF and, 266
ETSI and, 267
FD.io and, 267
IEEE and, 266
IETF and, 256–262
industry coordination, 270–272
interoperability testing, 272–274
ITU-T Standardization Sector, 267
MEF Forum and, 265, 266
Open ROADM MSA and, 267
open source projects, 267–268
OpenDaylight Project, The, 263–264
SDOs and, 267–268
Sysrepo and, 267
xRAN and, 267
deviation statements, 148–149
DMTF and YANG development, 266
ETSI and YANG development, 267
events
actions, 113–116
notifications, 113, 116–117, 245–247
RPC, 113–116
extension keywords, 146–148
FD.io and YANG development, 267
functions of, 62
grouping data, 119
identifiers, case-sensitivity, 104

identities, 107, 108
  bases, 107
  identityref, 108–109
IEEE and YANG development, 266
IETF and YANG development
  dependencies, 260–262
  ietf-routing YANG module, 260
  key data model-driven RFCs, 256–257
  models, 260
  module and submodule RFCs, 257–259
  modules and submodules extracted from IETF drafts, 259–260
industry coordination, 270–272
interoperability testing, 272–274
ITU-T and YANG development, 267
key title statements, 98
language native (primary), making, 373
  pyangbind, 378–380
  YDK, 373–378
languages, 103–104
leafrefs, 103
leafs, 98
  default statements, 122–123
  empty leafs, 116
  leafrefs, 103, 128–142
  mandatory values, 98
  true values, 98
  type statements, 98
lists, 98, 103
MEF Forum and YANG development, 265, 266
models, 61
  modularity, 146
  service YANG models, 70
  updating, 260
modules, 61, 70
  BookZone example, 99–100
  dependencies, 260–262
  designing, 336–349
  ietf-routing YANG module, 260
  module and submodule RFCs, 257–259
  modules and submodules extracted from IETF drafts, 259–260
  namespace statements, 100
  naming, 100–101
  network element YANG modules, 69
  revision statements, 101
  service delivery YANG modules, 70
  tree representations, 102–103
  types of, 67–68
must statements, 123–124, 126–127
NETCONF and, 5, 15
notifications (event), 113, 116–117, 245–247
objects, mapping from MIB modules, 68–69
Open ROADM MSA and YANG development, 267
open source projects and YANG development, 267–268
OpenDaylight Project and Yang development, 263–264
operators requirements, 65
parsers, building with pyang tool, 359–361
pointers, 128–131
RESTCONF, YANG-to-RESTCONF mapping, 75–76
revision statements, 109–112, 116–117
RPCs, 113–116
schema nodes, 115, 130–142
SDOs and YANG development, 267–268
strings, 101, 103–105
subclassing, 107
Sysrepo and YANG development, 267
tree diagrams, with XPath navigation, 124–125
tree representations, 102–103
type definitions, 104–105
union YANG construct, 105
unique statements, 125–126
uses statements, 119

xRAN and YANG development, 267
YANG-PATCH operations (RESTCONF), 207–210
YANG 1.0, 63, 75
YANG 1.1, 63, 100
YANG Catalog, 272
API calls, 355–358
development of, 287–288
finding modules, 287
impact analysis, 349
metadata
integrating metadata, 355–358
keyword searches, 357–358
retrieving metadata, 355–358
modules
designing, 337–339, 347–349
impact analysis, 349
integrating metadata, 355–358
retrieving metadata from Yang Catalog, 355–358
sharing metadata, 347–349
REST APIs, 355–356
search API, 357–358
tree output view, 290–291
viewing module details, 291–294
YANG Push and Friends, 244–245, 247–248
YANG Search feature (YANG Catalog)
extractable/non-extractable metadata, 289
searching modules by metadata, 288–290
YANG Suite tool (YANG Catalog), 294–298, 299, 302
device profiles, 300–301
distributions, 299
installing, 299
repositories (modules), creating, 301
YANG module sets, 301
YANG Validator, 339–340
yanglit tool, testing modules, 347
YANG-PATCH operations, creating/updating RESTCONF configurations, 207–210
YANGRE, YANG module validation, 340
YDK (YANG Development Kit), 85
goal of, 71
YANG as native (primary) language, 373–378
ydk-gen (YDK Generator), 377–378
Ygot (YANG go tool), 85

www.ingramcontent.com/pod-product-compliance
Lightning Source LLC
Jackson TN
JSHW062355041125
93610JS00005B/15

* 9 7 8 0 1 3 5 1 8 0 3 9 6 *